Publications of the Federal Institute for Culture and History of the Germans in Eastern Europe
Volume 74

In collaboration with the European Network Remembrance and Solidarity

Central and Eastern Europe after the First World War

Edited by Burkhard Olschowsky, Piotr Juszkiewicz, Jan Rydel

Translated by Sarah Patey et al.

De Gruyter
Oldenbourg

Bibliographic information published by the Deutsche Nationalbibliothek.

The Deutsche Nationalbibliothek lists this publication in the Deutsche Nationalbibliographie; Detailed bibliographic data are available online at **http://dnb.ddb.de**

Library of Congress Cataloging-in-Publication Data

A CIP catalog record for this book has been applied for at the Library of Congress.

© 2021 Bundesinstitut für Kultur und Geschichte der Deutschen im östlichen Europa, Oldenburg (BKGE)

© 2021 European Network Remembrance and Solidarity, Warsaw (ENRS)

Published by De Gruyter/Oldenbourg, Berlin/Boston

Cover image: Destruction of the Polish town Kalisz in 1918 with stamps, design: Martina Nitschke-Richter

Cover layout: NRD Design AGD, Oldenburg

Typesetting: Sylvia Ullrich, Isensee Verlag, Oldenburg

Printed and bound by Druckerei Hubert, Göttingen

ISBN: 978-3-11-059715-8

Contents

History of Memory

Appendices

Foreword

This book arose out of the conference 'Central and Eastern Europe After the First World War', held between 31 January and 2 February 2018 in the Embassy of the Slovak Republic in Berlin. We are especially grateful for the hospitality and support provided by Ambassador Dr Peter Lizák and Dr Viera Polakovičová, Embassy counsellor and Director of the Slovak Institute, both before and during the conference. The conference organisers were the Institute of European Network Remembrance and Solidarity, Warsaw, and the Federal Institute for Culture and History of the Germans in Eastern Europe, Oldenburg, in partnership with the University of Leipzig – Centre for Area Studies; the Jagiellonian University of Cracow, Department of Historical Anthropology; the Pavol Jozef Šafárik University in Košice, Department of History; the Hungarian Academy of Science, Institute for Humanities, Research Center for History; the Babeş-Bolyai University of Cluj-Napoca; and the Slovak Institute in Berlin.

Funding was provided by the Federal Government Commissioner for Culture and the Media (Germany), and the Ministry of Culture and National Heritage of the Republic of Poland as part of the multi-annual programme 'Niepodległa' 2017-2021.

The present volume has been prepared in collaboration with the open-air exhibition designed by European Network Remembrance and Solidarity, 'After the Great War. A New Europe 1918-1923', which has already visited a number of European cities and is continuing its tour.

The purpose of the European Network is to enable multilateral collaboration in the analysis and presentation of the history of the 20th century. The network has become a forum for international discussion of historical facts, and of historical images and the cultures of memory. A key aspect of its work is the acknowledgement of the perspective of the 'other', shaped by each individual's own specific historical experiences. These experiences include the First World War, which did not end in 1918 in Eastern Europe, where political and social conflicts, some of them violent, persisted until 1923. The introductory historical overview and the specific case studies in this volume present the origins, actors and events of these five turbulent years.

We are grateful to the authors for preparing their contributions to this book. We owe particular thanks to Dr Tobias Weger for his extensive support in compiling the introduction, and in the editing of individual chapters.

We would also like to thank Sarah Patey for much help both with translation and with language editing. The English version would not have happened without the help of the other persons in the translation team: Edward Assarabowski, Ruth Chester and Darren Chastney. Our gratitude goes also to Anna Clart for proofreading and to Sylvia Ullrich of the publishing house Isensee in Oldenburg for designing and laying out the text.

Finally, we owe thanks to Dr Winson Chu, Dr Simon Smith, and Agnes Fellner for reading through the texts and providing expert advice, to Benjamin Sasse for advice on content and presentation, and to Martina Nitschke-Richter and Lennart Hoes for the cover design.

Editors, in March 2021

Introduction

Burkhard Olschowsky, Piotr Juszkiewicz, Jan Rydel

This book addresses selected aspects of political, social, cultural and economic life in the years following the First World War in Eastern Europe. The division between 'Western Europe' and 'Eastern Europe' should not be understood as mapping onto the distinction most familiar to us, since it long pre-dates the East-West Cold War conflict after 1945. The historiography of the First World War and its consequences was long dominated by Anglo-Saxon, French and German interpretation and literature, in which events in Western Europe played a far larger part than events on the Eastern Front or the establishment of the new European order following 1918. In this part of Europe, military action and violent conflict continued well beyond the Armistice of 11 November 1918, the discussions between the warring parties at the Paris Peace Conference, and the peace treaties signed with the governments of the Central Powers. For about five years after the cease-fire agreement, violence and armed confrontation, both within and between states, continued to be the lived experience in many European regions, in spite of the efforts not only of new supranational institutions such as the League of Nations, but also within civil society, to find peaceful solutions to the various conflicts.[1]

This book's aim is not to suggest that 'Eastern Europe' was a homogeneous area, but rather to help shine a light onto a neglected part of Europe. The various contributors deal with issues not only within but also between nations, and adopt a comparative approach where appropriate. In most cases, they address these issues by foregrounding specific examples rather than adopting the approach of overarching analyses.

The editors have collaborated to provide in this introduction a description of the relevant historical structures and developments, in order to help the reader appreciate the context for the case studies in the subsequent chapters. The first section focuses on two debates within historical research. First, how should one define an appropriate periodisation for the First World War and its consequences? And second, how has it come about that global historiography has paid so much more attention to the Western Front than to the ways in which the First World War affected Eastern Europe? The second section recalls the significant factors affecting the time period covered in the book: the pervading presence of violence, successes and failures in establishing new states, the fate of prisoners of war following 1918, the 'Spanish flu' pandemic, and the high expectations East Europeans vested in France and the United Kingdom. The third section presents some of the key historical concepts of the period: postcolonial history, the relationship between social democracy and communism, pacifism, revisionism and modernisation. The fourth section then focuses on the bearers of memory in the years after 1917: what image did emigrants and refugees from Eastern Europe carry with them, and what role did veterans of the front play in defining the collective memory?

Throughout, the volume editors have been very conscious that they have necessarily had to be selective in their choice of topics, the chronology they present to provide context and the list of events between 1917 and 1923, and that they can make no claim to be comprehensive.

First Section

Periodisation

The conventional dating of the First World War encompasses the period between the 'July Crisis' and

Fig. 1: The former German Tannenberg National Monument in East Prussia. Contemporary Postcard.

the declaration of war at the start of August 1914 and the cease-fire on 11 November 1918. This period fits with the events of the war on the Western Front and the influential war narratives of the Entente nations and of Germany. An examination of the Eastern theatre of war would suggest a different periodisation. Jay Winter identifies an initial phase (1914-1917), characterised by an internal social consensus in favour of mobilisation against an external enemy, driven by the prevailing wartime conditions.

By 1917, it became clear to those involved that the nature of the war had changed. Once a confrontation between imperial powers, it had mutated into an internal revolutionary conflict in the wake of the Russian October Revolution, further exacerbated by the peoples' protests over inflation and the unfair burden of war. Winter argues that the second phase (1917-1923), 'the Second Great War', was characterised by fear, internal divisions and ethnic and religious violence, and affected not only the newly cre-

ated states and the regions of Central, Eastern and Southern Europe, but also Ireland[2] in Western Europe.[3] In many places in Eastern Europe, this coincided during the years after 1917 with revolutionary movements and efforts to achieve independence, and these in turn gave rise to tensions and acts of violence, especially by paramilitary groups. This turbulent period, Winter explains, lasted until 1923, when the Treaty of Lausanne established the territory of the new Turkish Republic and marked an end to Greek territorial ambitions in Asia Minor – resulting in the largest forced migration of peoples prior to the Second World War.[4]

Why was the war in the East forgotten?

This new historiographical insight – that fighting and violence continued beyond the autumn of 1918 in Eastern Europe – calls into question why any European assessment of the First World War persistently pays more attention to the fighting in Belgium, France and Italy between 1914 and 1918 than it does to the Eastern Front, or indeed to the subsequent far-reaching effects of the continued unrest during 1918-1923. This perceptual problem is clearly not because the First World War was less dramatic on the Eastern Front than on the Western Front. This introduction cannot hope to do more than allude to the various reasons for this collective mental blindness. It is often pointed out that history is written by the victors, and in this case the United Kingdom, France and the USA led the international narrative on the war. In the East, the Russian Empire had ceased to exist with the 1917 October Revolution, which was followed by a bloody civil war between the Red and White armies; the USSR was officially established on 30 December 1922, and its priorities did not include memorialising the soldiers of the former Tsarist Empire and their fight against the armies of Imperial Germany and the imperial and royal monarchy of Austria-Hungary. When 'the East' featured in the international discourse between the wars, it was mainly in debates over the state order in Central and South-Eastern Europe. Assessments of the military causes that led to the First World War overshadowed any consideration of its consequences. Both German and British historians ascribed the creation of the new European order to Polish, Czech and Romanian nationalism, rather than seeing it as the expression of emancipation by peoples who had previously lived under the domination of imperial powers. This one-sided interpretation exerted considerable influence on historiography. In Britain, the stereotypical images of 'Balkanised Europe' were widespread, and they were echoed in Germany by the common conception of Eastern European 'seasonal states'; these tropes shifted the perception of the realities on the ground in the region.

This context lends significance to the cultural discourse on the First World War during the interwar years. Images of the topographical memorials on the former Western Front have gained worldwide recognition. The battles and the trench warfare on the Austrian–Italian front are commemorated in the monumental war cemeteries of Sacrario di Redipuglia/Sredipolje (1938)[5] and Sacrario militare di Fagaré della Battaglia (1933-1935) in the Piave river valley,[6] and at the battle sites in the High Dolomites. Between

the wars, thousands of images sent far and wide on postcards and shown in cinema newsreels depicted the ossuary at Douaumont (1927-1932) near Verdun and the associated military cemetery, the memorial at Notre-Dame-de-Lorette (1920-1925) near Ablain-Saint-Nazaire, the memorial at Hartmannswillerkopf (1918-1921) in Alsace, and the memorials at Langemarck (1930-1932) and Ypres (1927) in Flanders. The only memorial in the East to gain recognition at a comparable level to its western counterparts was the Tannenberg Memorial. It was dedicated to the memory of the German victory in the Masurian region in the summer of 1914, setting up a link in political memory between the Battle of Tannenberg-Grunwald (a confrontation on 15 July 1410 between the Teutonic Knights and the Polish-Lithuanian army) and General Paul von Hindenburg (1847-1934), who later served as *Reichspräsident*. Built near the town of Hohenstein in East Prussia/Olsztynek between 1924 and 1927 in the expressionist architectural style, the Tannenberg Memorial evoked prehistoric sites and the Hohenstaufen Castel del Monte.[7]

The collective blindness to the fate of the East may also be explained by the fact that former battle sites were not as much revered as they were in the West. The Paris government believed that battle sites in eastern France not only commemorated lost lives but also served as a warning to neighbouring Germany, should it ever attempt an act of aggression towards France. The military cemeteries in the region of the town of Gorlice in Lesser Poland, however, easily match the French memorials in terms of their size and aesthetic appeal. They commemorate the confrontations between Austrian and Russian forces in the Tarnów-Gorlice area of Western Galicia between 1914 and 1918.[8] The fighting between the three powers that had partitioned Poland had taken the lives of Poles fighting on both sides, and in newly established country, the commemoration of losses was neither confrontational nor triumphalist. So it is perhaps not surprising that it was not until 2011 that the 'Line of the Eastern Front in the First World War in Lesser Poland' (Szlak Wschodniego Frontu I Wojny Świa-towej w Małopolsce) was laid out and opened to tourists in the voivodeship of Lesser Poland, with explanatory displays at the different sites along the route.[9] In Poland, a dense network of memorial sites and monuments commemorates the Second World

Fig. 2: The Galician town of Gorlice, which was heavily destroyed during the long and fierce fighting between the German-Austrian and the Russian armies in the summer of 1915.

War and its catastrophic consequences for the land and its inhabitants, which are far more prominent in the national conscience than memories of the First World War.[10]

Romania has a number of imposing memorial sites: the Triumphal Arch (Arcul de Triumf) in Bucarest, built between 1921 and 1936 to a design by the architect Petre Antonescu (1873-1965); the Mausoleum of Heroes (Mausoleul Eroilor, 1923-1938) in Mărăşeşti in Moldavia; and the Cross of Heroes (Crucea Eroilor) on Mount Caraiman in the Southern Carpathian mountains. Yet these too were less prominent than other memorials on the international stage. One of the most artistically significant memorials anywhere to the fallen of the First World War is the group of sculptures at Târgu Jiu in Walachia – although only a few well-informed historians of art in Western Europe have paid them the attention they properly deserve. It was created by the Romanian sculptor Constantin Brâncuşi (1876-1957), who was living and working in Paris. He abandoned the conventions and symbols of classical war memorials in order to create an intellectually evocative group that focused on inviting meditation on war and death rather than glorifying battle. The group consists of the 'Gate of the Kiss' (Poarta Sărutului), the 'Table of Silence' (Masa Tăcerii) and the 'Endless Column' (Coloana Infinitului).[11]

Artists also used literature and cinematography to memorialise the First World War. Film producers in Eastern Europe, however, were only very rarely able to dub their films or to produce subtitles in widely spoken languages in order to make them accessible to international cinema audiences. Examples include the film *Ponad śnieg* (Whiter than Snow), produced by Konstanty Meglicki (1890-1955) and inspired by a work of the famous novelist Stefan Żeromski (1864-1925), and the two films *Szaleńcy* (The Daredevil)

Fig. 3: The Heroes' Monument at Mărășești, Romania. The Romanian inscription of the Mausoleum bears the motto 'Întru slava eroilor neamului' (To the Glory of the Nation's Heroes) and indicates the names of famous World War I battlefields: 'Jiu – Olt – Sibiu – Coșna – Cireșoaia – Robănești – Neajlov – Dragoslavele – Predeal – C. Lung – Panciu – Răzoare – Brașov – Porumbacu – Mărășești – Mărăști – Oituz – Doaga – Muncel – Arabagi – Bărcuț – Amzacea – Prunaru – Cerna – Cașin – Valea Uzului – Sticlărie'.

(1928) and *Florian* (1938) by the director Leonard Buczkowski (1900-1967); all three films portrayed fictional events during the First World War, and remained unknown outside Poland. The renaissance of the First World War in Polish cinema eventually came in the 1980s, with the broadcasting of Bohdan Poręba's TV series *Polonia Restituta*, the 1983 drama *Austeria* (The Tavern) by Jerzy Kawalerowicz (1922-2007) and the 1986 comedy *C. K. Dezerterzy* (The Imperial and Royal Deserters) by Janusz Majewski (b. 1931). When these films were released, the political relations of the Polish People's Republic were not likely to favour the popularisation of Polish cinema in the Western world. The cinema-going public, therefore, mainly gained their perception of the war from films produced in France, Britain, the United States and Germany, which generally presented stories from the Western Front. Films produced in Russia, Poland, Hungary and Romania portrayed events on the Eastern Front, but their distribution remained largely confined to audiences within their respective countries. The film *Redl ezredes/Oberst Redl* (1985) by Hungarian director István Szábo (b. 1938) did achieve an Oscar nomination, albeit unsuccessful, by dint of being a German-Austrian-Hungarian co-production, which opened it up to much wider distribution than would have been available to a purely Hungarian film.

The East was largely invisible not only in film, but also in international literature. Literature from Eastern Europe rarely made much headway in the international market. There were a few notable examples,

Where the Fighting Still Goes On

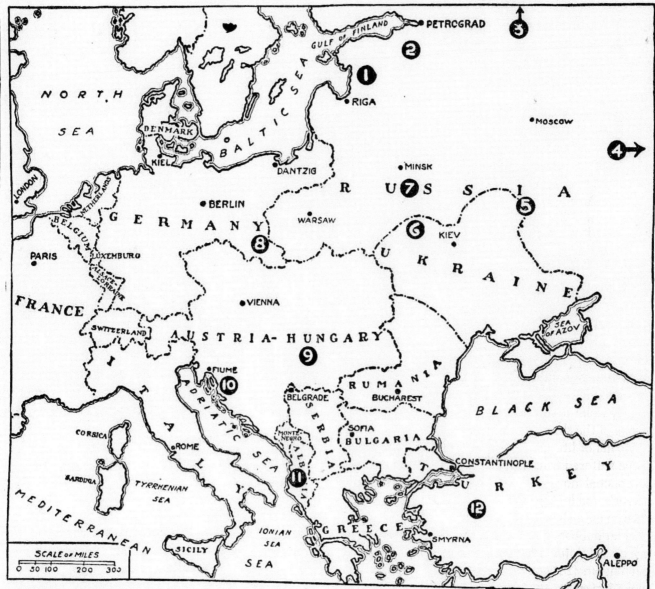

The first anniversary of the armistice sees fighting still going on in at least a dozen places in Europe and the Near East. The above map shows these twelve storm centers as follows:

1. In the Baltic region there is a four-cornered struggle between the Lett and Esth nationalist troops, the German-Russian monarchist force of Colonel Bermondt, and the Bolsheviki.

2. South of Petrograd the alleged anti-German forces of General Yudenitch are in contact with the "red" armies.

3. On the North Russian front the troops of the anti-Bolshevik Archangel government are still "sticking it out" in spite of the withdrawal of the British expeditionary force.

4. In Eastern Russia Kolchak's army is suffering one defeat after another at the hands of the "reds."

5. In Southern Russia there is the volunteer army of General Denikin making war on the "reds" and the Ukrainians.

6. In Volhynia and Podolia the troops of the Ukrainian directorate, under General Petlura, are facing the Bolsheviki on one side, the Poles on the other.

7. Along the Dvina the Polish-Bolshevik war continues.

8. In Silesia there is no actual fighting, but, something very much like a truce between the Poles and Germans.

9. Hungary, what with the Rumanian occupation and the White Terror, with its pogroms and wholesale executions, is very much in the state of war.

10. On the Adriatic fighting may start any moment between the Italians and Jugo-Slavs, with d'Annunzio's volunteers still holding "conquered" Fiume.

11. In Albania promiscuous fighting is going on, with Italians, French, Greeks, Serbians and Albanians participating.

12. In Asia Minor the Turkish nationalist forces of Mustappa Kemal Pasha are defying the Allies.

Fig. 4: Map of Europe, 'Where the Fighting Still Goes On'. *The New York Tribune*, 9 November 1919.

works that portrayed the war in all its grim reality from the point of view of the common soldier: the plays *The Last Days of Mankind* (Die letzten Tage der Menschheit, 1915-1922) by Karl Kraus (1874-1936), and *Drums in the Night* (Trommeln in der Nacht, 1919) by Bertolt Brecht (1898-1956); and the anti-war novels *All Quiet on the Western Front* (Im Westen nichts Neues, 1929) by Erich Maria Remarque (1898-1970) and *Higher Command* (Heeresbericht, 1930) by Edlef Köppen (1896-1939). A further exception was the comedic novel *The Adventures of the Good Soldier Švejk* (Osudy dobrého vojáka Švejka za světové války), by the Czech author Jaroslav Hašek (1883-1923), which has been translated into 58 languages, rewritten as a stage play, and produced as a film several times. The author, who tended towards political anarchism, wrote it as a Dadaist response to the absurdity of war. The novel was widely misunderstood in the West, where the figure of Švejk became seen as a stereotypical representation of what was assumed to be the Czech national characteristic of 'Švejkism'. Western readers seem to have missed the parody of a Czech soldier forced to serve against his will in the imperial and royal army and taking every sabotage opportunity available to him; and yet this novel reflects particularly well the situation of the small nations under the rule of the three great imperial powers.

Two major literary works about the war in Eastern Europe suffered from unfortunate publication dates. The epochal novel of Joseph Roth (1894-1939), *The Emperor's Tomb* (Kapuzinergruft), was distributed in 1938 by a publisher in exile in the Netherlands who in 1937 had published the German translation of a key work by a childhood friend of Roth, the Polish author Józef Wittlin (1896-1976). Wittlin had published his novel *Sól ziemi* in 1935, and the German translation *Das Salz der Erde* (The Salt of the Earth) had appeared in 1937. Roth's work gained posthumous international recognition as a masterly portrait of the dying days of the Habsburg Monarchy; Wittlin's, meanwhile, took much longer to gain the attention of a wider public.

Second section

Violence

Violence remained a widespread feature of daily political and social life in Eastern Europe during the years following the First World War, a reality that escaped the notice of selective western observers. This violence was rooted in many causes, and it was expressed in a variety of ways. It could be due to material want; it could be expressed through attacks on unpopular groups, or on those of different ethnicity or political persuasion. It was sometimes perpetrated by paramilitary groups, and sometimes escalated into civil war.

George L. Mosse (1918-1999) has suggested that war experiences brutalised those taking part and encouraged further violent acts, and this has been borne out in all the nations concerned. The myth of 'war experience' resonated in every nation that had taken part in the war; the losers, and especially the Germans, were particularly susceptible to this phenomenon. The trauma of the 1918 defeat made it difficult for them to engage rationally with the war and where its roots had lain.[12] Mosse and others have correctly emphasised that the experience of the First World War altered the attitude of the combatants to the use of violence. The vast majority of soldiers who had survived the war unhurt, however, returned to civil life in November 1918. As we shall see below, some became convinced pacifists, while others created patriotic mythologies from their experience in the trenches. The myth acquired a dangerously explosive political force in the defeated and the newly created nations, where conservative and nationalistic parties espoused it for their own purposes, and could instrumentalise it to promote paramilitary acts of violence.

There was a disparity, after 1918, in the potential of different nations to carry out acts of violence; the defeated nations' ability to mobilise for war was hobbled, while the victorious nations experienced a wave of pacifism.[13]

The Eastern European 'shatter zones' that had emerged from the downfall of the dynastic empires (Russia, Austria-Hungary, Germany, Turkey) were particularly vulnerable to outbreaks of violence; many were affected by disputed borders and the lack of a clearly defined new national order.[14]

Thanks to the First World War, the small local pre-1914 rivalries over territorial disputes and unfulfilled national aspirations had been transformed by 1918 into a generalised European struggle focused principally on ethnic and ideological differences. The war had served as a catalyst; as a result, revolutions had

Fig. 5: The town of Sokolniki, near Lvov. Jewish population in front of destroyed buildings likely done by Ukrainian forces in 1919.

broken out and then been carried through.[15] The stimulus was not only the USA's entry into the war on the Western Front in the spring of 1917 and the collapse of the Russian front six months later, but also the concept of the right to self-determination, propagated by Vladimir Ilyich Lenin (1870-1924) and Woodrow Wilson (1856-1924), who each promoted the concept according to their own specific national and international interpretation. Both presented the concept as a challenge to the empires of Central and Eastern Europe.[16]

The differences between these two politicians are telling. Wilson stated that the Allies' war objective should be the victory of democratic nationalism in Europe. The League of Nations was to bring peace and maintain the new post-war order. Lenin advocated an armistice at any price, and promoted national/ethnic independence that rested on the workers and farmers who rose up against dynastic empires. According to Lenin, the underclass's emancipation would lead to an international class revolution that would legitimate the use of violence. The Bolshevik view therefore encompassed the peoples of the whole world, making no difference between domestic and external politics.[17]

As Robert Gerwarth and John Horne have stated, the years following 1917/18 were marked by the emergence and triumph of diametrically opposed ideologies – principally fascism and communism – whose advocates had seized power in states such as the Soviet Union and Italy by 1923.[18] Both these ideologies spoke mainly to societies' lower classes, who had particularly suffered from harshness of the First World War: in Russia the farmers, in Italy the workers and the upper working class. Italy, one of the victorious nations in 1918, had suffered a high death toll during the war. The nationalists' suggestion that Italy had been betrayed by the high price they had paid for victory resonated with many Italians. Benito Mussolini (1883-1945) and his fascist movement held out the promise that violence within Italy and colonial expansion could together rectify the national sense of humiliation and restore a sense of Italy's greatness.[19]

The history of violence in the various forms it adopted following the First World War is only partly explained in the context of the larger developments such as revolutions, the breakdown of empires and new ideologies such as fascism and communism. Other factors include, for example, the ethnic conflicts that arose as new nation states and their borders were established, not only in Central and Eastern Europe but also in Western Europe. There are parallels between Poland (Upper Silesia) and (Northern) Ireland in terms of ethnic differentiation, the focus on 'kin states' – here, Germany and the United Kingdom respectively – and a readiness to engage in conflict, which in the case of Ireland additionally involved a strong confessional connotation.[20]

In many places, violence found fertile soil after 1918; the outcome differed, however, according to how diverse local political cultures had either held back or sharpened the experience of violence during war. Tradition and local structures, it emerged, had a greater effect than did war and revolution.[21]

Four principal factors influenced the way that violence spilled over from the Russian civil war into neighbouring countries: the lack of the state structures that would have provided a set of legal sanctions, the dissolving of the line that had divided the war front from the home front, the virulence of old social and ethnic tensions, and finally the motivational intensity of the new ideology.[22]

From 'Fighting Man' to Civilian

The Continuation of the War in Eastern Europe After 1918

In Eastern Europe, the First World War did not end in the autumn of 1918: it lingered on until 1923 in various armed conflicts, some of which resulted from the collapse of the Habsburg Monarchy, the Tsarist Russian Empire and the German Empire. The populations concerned suffered social upheavals to everyday life, but were also involved in struggles for emancipation and aspirations towards national statehood.

In the events that unfolded on the western and southern borders of Russia, it is not helpful to distinguish between military victors and losers. The First World War accelerated the end of the Tsarist Empire and opened up to its populations the possibility of national independence.[23] Western European actors – those involved in the peace negotiations and political observers more generally – often failed to fully appreciate the region's developments, which were complex and sometimes even contradictory.

The violent confrontations in Eastern Europe were often somewhat asymmetrical. Those involved were clearly not simply 'armed nations', i.e. ethni-

Fig. 6: Polish-German Fighting in Upper Silesia in May 1921.

cally homogeneous armies. In the 1919-1921 Polish–Soviet Russian war, the Polish General Lucjan Żeligowski (1865-1947) commanded, among other troops, Russian Uhlans, while the Russian side included Polish gunmen.[24] In some places, national confrontations also became intertwined with the Russian civil war, making the situation even more confusing. Wars of different intensities broke out between states, to establish states or to settle border disputes, as did civil wars, armed insurrections, uprisings and local conflicts arising out of established economic, ethnic and religious differences. The nature of a number of these armed conflicts changed over time. As Christoph Mick has shown, a conflict could manifest in a number of different forms.[25] The French intervention forces in southern Russia, for example, were faced with unclear frontlines and demotivated soldiers in their own and in Allied troops, and after a few months they withdrew from the theatre of war via Crimea in April 1919.

Fig. 7: Heimkehrer. 'The Grateful Homeland'. Austrian soldiers in front of a civilian clothing shop. The sign says: 'For Homecomers'. One soldier says to his comrade: 'It's really amazing how the new government takes care of us!'. Caricature, *Muskete*, Vienna, 16 January 1919.

The need for a new territorial order also emerged in the second area of post-imperial collapse: the regions of the former Habsburg Monarchy, including Poland and Romania. National states had emerged in these regions by the end of 1918, but there were persistent doubts about where the new national borders should run, given the multi-ethnic populations. In some regions, the state of uncertainty arising from conflicting territorial claims continued until 1923.

The Soldiers' Homecoming and the Experience of Reintegration

Millions of soldiers were demobilised at the end of 1918 and during 1919, and the transition from war to peace was made more difficult when they returned home and found that their world was much changed. As part of peace, they were hoping for normality and security. In fact, their post-war experiences varied widely. On the one hand, war veterans were publicly honoured and invited to contribute to the establishment of new states and the new order; at the other extreme, communities and societies that had experienced fundamental changes were discovering new forms of insecurity. These ranged from financial difficulties to continuing violence, exile and the loss of homeland.[26]

All former soldiers felt the difficulty of becoming accustomed to normal civilian life. Sometimes, demobilised soldiers experienced the new and unfamiliar relationships they returned to as a disconcerting lack of order. They could view these changes as either a stroke of luck or a threat. Some felt lucky to be able to help build a new state, and to help secure it from within as well as from the outside world. Many former 'fighters', however, sensed that their status was not securely established, in a context where no one was clearly enforcing national order. This threatening situation was aggravated if their war service was poorly recognised, and if they were offered few means, either material or emotional, of reintegrating into post-war society – as was especially true in the defeated nations.

There were millions of returning soldiers; to reintegrate them in such economically uncertain times was problematic, both politically and emotionally. Veterans from the large multi-ethnic empires faced not only the challenge of gaining national public recognition, but also the question, for each individual, of which of the new states was now his homeland.[27] For any soldier who had fought on the 'wrong' side, or whose country had suffered especially heavily in the defeat, his return was likely to be marked by caution, or possibly not celebrated at all. Those deeply affected by the war also experienced disillusionment and personal shame, especially those who, instead of returning as heroes, returned sick or disabled by the war. Those whose mental health had been damaged became a visible problem; both in and beyond medical circles this was soon labelled as 'shell-shock syndrome'.[28]

Demobilised soldiers returning from the front turned to the administrative authorities in their country for support in finding work and for medical care.

In many German cities, soldiers were afforded honour on their return. The years of economic hardship and the collapse of political order, however, stifled any sense of joyful celebration. Although people recognised the military achievements and patriotic deeds of the war, many were also crushed by grief at the senseless sacrifice of so many lives for the sake of the doomed German Empire. Friedrich Ebert, leader of the SPD and subsequently *Reichspräsident*, gave expression to this sense of ambivalence. On 10 December 1918, speaking to returning troops in Berlin, he gave credence to the myth that the German army had not been defeated in battle: 'It was not an enemy who conquered you.' Acknowledging the superior strength of the Allies, he said it was a patriotic 'duty' not to require any more 'pointless victims'.[29]

The myth of the 'stab in the back' had rapidly spread and been accepted in conservative and nationalist circles, but few war veterans believed it in the years immediately following the war. Hundreds of thousands of former soldiers had experienced first-hand the horror of the front and the inescapable truth of defeat.[30]

The consensus shared by veterans and the government was that swift social and political measures were needed on behalf of the 2.7 million disabled by the war.[31] Nevertheless, the narrative of the undefeated army, however, did not disappear, and it became fertile soil for the marginalisation of alleged traitors both in the medium and the long term.[32]

Western Europe's economic hardship and the psychological undermining of men's self-respect were magnified, both politically and psychologically, in East-Central Europe. Most Polish, Czech and Slovak soldiers had fought during the war in the uniform of a country other than the one they now hoped would support them. Disabled war veterans felt all the more aggrieved by their misfortune in that they had not willingly enlisted in the imperial army in which they had served.[33]

The new Polish state established in November 1918 was a country severely damaged by the war, and

Fig. 8: 'For the Country, My Eyes! For Peace, Your Money' (Per la Patria i miei occhi! Per la Pace il vosto denaro). Poster designed by Alfredo Ortelli in 1918.

faced with a set of political, economic, social and military challenges. The vast majority of the returning soldiers had enlisted as subjects of the German, Austrian and Russian Empires, each of which had imposed its own military training. They were now seeking their relatives and looking for work, or even simply for food.[34] The newly established state had inherited three different administrative systems, but it had no established welfare system. During the early post-war years, the institutions responsible for these functions had first to be set up, and the parameters of the required welfare policy had then to be defined, in particular for the war disabled.[35]

The Polish army was swiftly constituted, but the traditions resulting from over a century of partition had clearly left their mark. The personnel had inher-

Fig. 9: A former Austro-Hungarian soldier. Medical mechanical devices for the elbow joint in the Red Cross Hospital after the First World War at Villach, Carinthia.

ited varying patterns of military training, and the units exhibited a wide range of standards in terms of cultural, linguistic and educational achievement and even of literacy, especially among soldiers from the eastern regions of Poland. These differences were exacerbated by the animosity between the leading military figures Józef Piłsudski, Józef Haller and Józef Dowbor-Muśnicki. General Haller, a conservative nationalist, had established his own army in France in 1917, and was an opponent of Piłsudski. General Dowbor-Muśnicki had built his career in the Tsarist army and had then been promoted to commander of the forces of Greater Poland in Poznań. As such, in the name of the regional Supreme People's Council (Naczelna Rada Ludowa) he refused to commit 'his' soldiers to defend the Warsaw government.[36] The army thus had a conflicting heritage and internal political differences, and had experienced military con-

frontations with many neighbouring states; it also had a highly significant role to play in the establishment of the country whose integrity it guaranteed. Only in 1921, however, was it realistic to describe the Polish army as a unified and coherent conscript army.[37]

Society in the newly formed Czechoslovakia also bore unmistakable signs of the war's effects. Loyalty to Vienna had weakened in wartime, and indeed there had been few signs that the war with Russia was popular among the Czech population.[38] The foundational declaration of Czechoslovakia on 28 October 1918 indicated that the Czech Legion was to be the cornerstone of the future army which, in spite of ill-defined borders and potential future conflict, would guarantee sovereignty and provide defensive power. The Czech Legion had been constituted during the war, bringing under the command of its own officers Czech prisoners of war and deserting Czech soldiers. It included around 11,000 men in France, over 23,000 in Italy and around 75,000 in Russia.[39]

As the Austro-Hungarian Monarchy collapsed in the autumn of 1918 and different nations were established in its wake, an urgent question arose: should soldiers in the royal and imperial army be demobilised or should they carry on serving? On the one hand, the catastrophically poor supply lines and the exhaustion from the long war had led to increasing levels of desertion, and on the other hand there were growing demands for the remains of the large Habsburg army to be divided into unified national regiments.[40] The relationship between the soldiers of the former royal and imperial army and those of the much mythologised and idolised Czech Legion, who returned in November 1920, proved difficult. It was therefore crucial to establish a clear military hierarchy that would prove reliable should any of the threatened conflicts with neighbouring states break out.[41]

Notwithstanding the pacifist outlook of the elites in Plzeň and Košice, the newly established states such as Poland and Czechoslovakia made swift moves to build up their national defence forces.[42] Their principal concern was to secure or even extend their territories in any conflict with neighbours to the east. This engendered long-lasting bitterness in their relationships with these states (Hungary, Lithuania, Soviet Russia) and regions (western Ukraine, Carpatho-Ukraine). In January 1919, a Polish advance provoked

Fig. 10: Austro-Hungarian 'Homecomers' from Russian captivity, 1917.

a border conflict with Czechoslovakian troops over the duchy of Cieszyn, which was unusual in that both countries had sent official political representatives to the Versailles peace negotiations as victor nations. An energetic intervention by the French government helped to establish a delicate line of demarcation between the two countries.[43]

The situation in Hungary in 1918 was especially difficult. The territorial status quo was under threat, and there were both economic and social crises; behind all of these lay structural problems that would be neither simple nor quick to resolve. The multi-ethnic structure of the country was reflected, amongst other things, in the discrimination towards non-Magyar population groups. In the autumn of 1918, Slovaks, Croats, Serbs and Romanians had the opportunity to free themselves from Magyar imperialism by attaching themselves to the newly established neighbouring states, who in turn sought to extend their respective territories at Hungary's expense.[44]

The Habsburg Monarchy's symptoms of crisis echoed the situation of the Hungarian soldiers, who were dissatisfied with the supply situation for both the army and their relatives back home. The precarious position of the Austro-Hungarian prisoners of war held in Russia proved another destabilising factor. The cold and the lack of food, together with the carefully guarded status differences, soured relations between the Hungarian officers and the rank-and-file soldiers. As a result, thousands of prisoners of war became receptive to socialist ideas following the Bolsheviks' seizure of power. In March 1918, the Treaty of Brest-Litovsk between the Central Powers and the Soviet Russians enabled the return of the first prisoners of war to Hungary. Home at last, many of the returnees were suspected of being Bolsheviks and interned or even sent straight back to the front. When the news of their comrades' woeful welcome reached the hundreds of thousands still in Russia, sympathy for their own government began to wane.[45]

Because of the displacement practice of the royal and imperial army,[46] the Hungarian troops were fighting as one section among others at the Piave front. From the summer of 1918, the increasingly poor quality of the equipment and supplies significantly undermined army morale. In late October, the Hungarian government under Count István Tisza (1861-1918) embarked on a programme towards more independence, in order to reach a separate peace agreement with the Entente and to secure the Hungarian territory to the south and east. This gave rise to insistent calls for Hungarian soldiers to return home. Many obliged, not least in order to escape the heavy battle casualties of northern Italy, yet unaware that new military confrontations awaited them at home.[47]

In Austria, the heartland of the Habsburg Monarchy, the political, territorial and social changes of 1918 deeply unsettled the soldiers and the population as a whole. In early summer that year, most political personalities in Vienna, Budapest and other major localities believed that a reformed version of the Austria-Hungary would somehow survive. On 16 October 1918, Emperor Karl published his so-called 'People's Manifesto', calling for a league of independent nations, but by then matters had developed beyond his control, and the lands of the Crown of St Stephen had already fragmented irretrievably. Austrian soldiers in the imperial and royal army had experienced the centrifugal forces that would destroy the monarchy: worsening supplies in rural areas, strikes, mutinies and desertions, and finally the breaking up of their military units. In November, they returned to an altered homeland; instead of normality and security, they found uncertainty, social want, revolutionary tensions and riots.[48]

Their encounters with the prisoners of war returning from Russia gave an indication of how deep the sense of insecurity ran. The army high command and the War Surveillance Office considered that the POWs had come into such contact with Bolshevism that they were to be seen as a security threat. The returning prisoners were confined in a so-called 're-turnee' camp', subjected to medical examinations and a 'disciplinary re-education', and equipped to return to the front. The returning soldiers, poorly provisioned and humiliated, reacted with resentment and mutinied. The threat of Bolshevism was far greater in the popular imagination than in reality, especially since the Russian Revolution had gained few adherents among the Austrian soldiers.[49]

The months between November 1918 and June 1919 were marked by uncertainty, hunger and attempted uprisings organised by determined left-wing socialists. Austria was looking increasingly like a shrinking small nation heading towards failure. Clever domestic policy under the aegis of social democratic, Austro-Marxist leadership successfully averted disaster. In Vienna, the workers' and soldiers' councils, together with workers in industry, managed to introduce a series of social and political measures securing the newly established republic; some approved the associated image of 'red Vienna', while others were repelled by it.[50]

At the end of the war, Romania gained large territories that had previously belonged to the Habsburgs and to Russia. This was perhaps an unexpected development, after they had joined the war in 1916 on the side of the Entente and suffered several defeats in 1917. The establishment and consolidation of Greater Romania happened across cleavages that had divided not only Romanians from the minority populations – especially Hungarians, Germans, Jews, Ukrainians, and Russians – but also the centralisers of the former empire (Walachia, Moldavia, Dobruja) from the Romanian politicians of Transylvania, Banat, Bukovina and Bessarabia.[51]

Crucially, as the Russian and Austro-Hungarian Empires collapsed, Romania had at its disposal armed forces ready to fill the power vacuum. As Schmitt has stated: 'The integration – which some might describe as an annexation – of the new territories went somewhat less smoothly than the Romanian master narrative might suggest, and encountered rather more opposition.'[52] The Banat Swabians found integrating into the new state challenging, while the large majority of the Hungarian population rejected them.[53]

The Entente nations valued Romania as an ordered state providing a bulwark against both Bolshevism and the threat of revolution coming from Hungary. In the summer of 1919, Romanian forces, including many Transylvanian Saxons, defeated the Hungarian Soviet Republic and marched into Budapest. It was an act of revenge for the Central Powers' earlier cruel occupation policy, and they relished their triumph over the most significant of

Fig. 11: Freikorps poster calling for the Fights against Bolshevists, Poles, and famine. Hamburg, 1919.

their ethnic and political opponents.[54] It was not until the Western powers voiced a strong warning that the Romanian forces, after some looting, withdrew from Hungary in the autumn of 1919.[55] Following this military defeat, a major overhaul was needed to deal with the territorial gains and the resulting need for integration. The 335,000 war dead were generally commemorated along ethnic lines, and they were raised to the status of heroes.[56]

Paramilitary Groups and the Continuing War

Many conflicts broke out during the years shortly following the war, 1918 to 1923, between military and paramilitary groups; among both the victorious and the defeated nations of Central and Eastern Europe. These arose from local and regional disputes but shared some common features. First, few borders of

Fig. 12: Austrian propaganda poster in Slovenian language: 'Mother, don't vote for Yugoslavia, otherwise I'll have to go to war for King Peter!' (Mama, ne štimajte za Jugoslavijo, kar moram ajnrukat za kralja Petra!) 1 January 1920.

the new states were clearly defined or marked at the start of 1919. Second, the imperial powers' collapse created a power vacuum that not only exacerbated awareness of the ethnic distinctions between population groups, but also opened up opportunities for nationalist groups and individual governments. Third, the states of many regions no longer exercised a monopoly on power, and others had not yet claimed it; this gave rise to increased paramilitary activity and made the prospect of warlike conflicts inviting. Fourth, once the Russian Revolution and the subsequent civil war had unleashed violence, it gained validation as a political instrument, and this encouraged a spiralling of further violence between political groups and national or ethnic opponents, and called into question the legitimacy of state and regional authority.[57]

Dissatisfaction with the political and social situation as well as loss of status and of social respect combined to trigger different reactions: on the one hand, guilt was externalised, projected onto the 'other' – including Jews and/or Bolsheviks – and on the other hand there were calls for a strong hand to keep order, for authority that was not dependent on parties and democratic rules.

There were apparent advantages for both sides to using experienced fighting forces organised in paramilitary units: the men could avoid the difficult process of reintegration into civilian life, and indeed gain lucrative pay or even loot, while at the same time retaining their group solidarity and enhanced social respect. It was moreover in every state's political interest to keep the troops in uniform, since the defeated nations needed them to defend their territory, and the victorious nations needed them for defence as well as any attempts at territorial expansion. If necessary, they could also call on the paramilitary units, but the authorities were under no obligation to supply them with pay or any other favours. There was however a risk that the units could set themselves up as warlords and collaborate with their government's enemies to destabilise the state.

In Germany, Austria and Hungary, it was principally former officers and career soldiers who chose to join paramilitary groups, while ordinary soldiers were happier to return to civilian life. In those three countries, it was mainly men from the junior officer ranks, lieutenants and captains, who helped to develop and took command of the paramilitary groups.[58] In Germany and Austria, volunteer corps (*Freikorps*) emerged at the end of 1918 for the defence of homes and residents; their aim was to defend their homeland from the perceived threat of revolutionary soldiers' councils and from takeover by Bolshevik forces.[59]

In the first half of 1919, the German *Freikorps* became radicalised from their involvement in the government-sanctioned conflicts along the new border with Poland and in the Baltic region. They especially attracted young people, cadets and students, who were all too young to have been affected by the shock of the war of attrition during the First World War.[60] The Reich government also deployed the *Freikorps* in Germany to combat real or alleged revolutionary movements, such as the Munich Soviet Republic of 1919 and the Ruhr Red Army. The German Ministry of the Interior was turning a blind eye to many acts of antirepublican terror and even murder of persons who were suspected as 'left-wing radicals'.[61] Officially, the *Freikorps* were demobilised following the failed Kapp Putsch that they mounted in 1920; thereafter, they constituted themselves as an ultra-right-wing, strictly anti-democratic movement that subsequently contributed to the development of the NSDAP.[62]

In Austria, the People's Defence (*Volkswehr*) were the official armed forces instituted by the social democrats; their high command was faced with the emergence of the right-wing Home Guard (*Heimwehr*), who conducted a guerrilla war against Serb and Slovenian units in Carinthia and Styria in the winter and spring of 1919. The subsequently influential home-defence movement was rooted in this desire to defend the homeland from occupation by foreign troops.[63] The fact that many Slovenes lived in Carinthia was ignored and denied. This gave rise to the persistent myth of a defensive struggle, fed by organisations that were strongly anti-socialist and unashamedly anti-Semitic, and rejected parliamentary democracy. Their worldview was remarkably similar to the *Führer* ideology.[64]

After the declaration of the Soviet Republic in March 1919 in Hungary, paramilitary force played a significant role. The Hungarian government recognised the importance of mobilising effective forces under the command of former royal and imperial

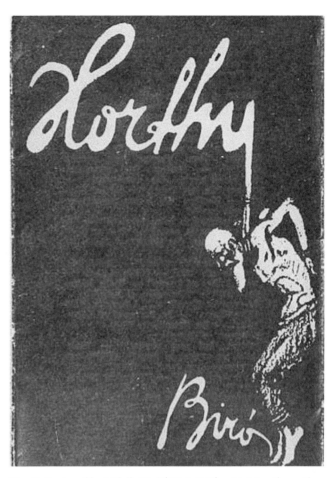

Fig. 13: Postcard by Mihály Biró (1886-1948) criticising the authoritarian right wing government of Miklós Horthy, Vienna 1920.

officers and occasionally making successful advances against the Czechoslovak army.[65] In Hungary, many high-ranking officers and officials with aristocratic backgrounds were imprisoned, taken as hostages and even murdered – between 350 and 1,000 people during the four months of the Soviet Republic. Romanian and Czechoslovak troops, sanctioned by the outcome of the Paris Peace Conference, marched into Hungary in the summer of 1919 and enforced an end to the short-lived experiment of the Hungarian Soviet Republic. Many soviet functionaries escaped to Austria and Soviet Russia, but the newly established Hungarian national army of the regent Miklós Horthy, aided by militias, overran the country between August 1920 and the end of 1921 in a wave of anti-Semitic-inspired terror, killing between 1,500 and 5,000 people and imprisoning 75,000 more.[66] Horthy was in sympathy with the militias. Hungary subsequently became a place of refuge for counter-revolutionaries

Fig. 14: Allegory of the Polish Victory in 1920. 'Forward Warsaw!' Painted by Zdzisław Jasiński.

in Europe, and offered those conducting uprisings in Bavaria and Austria somewhere to prepare and retreat to.[67]

In terms of paramilitary violence and the building of a nation, Poland offers a particular case study. The collapse of the Habsburg Monarchy, the Russian civil war and the defeat of Germany dramatically damaged the economic situation and gave rise to both internal and external conflicts; this also, however, presented an opportunity to unify the country and to extend the territory beyond seemingly linguistic borderlines. The Polish government adopted the federation plans of its leader Józef Piłsudski, and was prepared

to reckon with the risk that confrontations would emerge between a restored Poland and all its neighbours except Latvia and Romania.[68]

The most significant conflict – and one that threatened the very existence of the Polish state – was in 1919-1921 between Soviet Russia and an alliance of the forces of Poland and Ukrainian units under the command of Symon Petliura (1879-1926). The Polish army was at the time a rather heterogeneous collection of formations, and the fighting ran a chequered course, but the Poles were eventually victorious and gained significant territories to the east.[69] The victory over the Red Army at the 'Miracle on the Vistula' in August 1920 was thereafter promoted by the state, gaining influential mythical status, and was closely linked to Marshal Piłsudski. His political opponents, on the other hand, promoted the site as a religious lieu de mémoire.[70]

In 1919, Poland was engaged in military conflict with Lithuania and the West Ukrainian People's Republic, mainly over the towns of Vilnius and Lvov, and was finding it difficult to bring the fighting to a satisfactory conclusion.[71] These conflicts could be justified on defensive grounds, but neither state was a real threat to the Warsaw government, whereas Soviet Russia was. Following these border conflicts, the Second Polish Republic was marked by a tendency to latent antagonism, and to having a high opinion of its own strength.[72]

Prisoners of War After 1918

The popular images of the history of the First World War and its consequences in Eastern Europe often omit, among other things, any mention of prisoners of war; in reality, millions of soldiers endured war captivity. In the absence of accurate figures, early 21st-century historians estimate that roughly one in ten soldiers mobilised in the First World War ended up as a prisoner of war, so that the total number of men affected must have been between 6.6 million and 8 million.[73] Their treatment depended on the nation holding them and its usual practices, but was also very much at the mercy of how well its supply lines functioned. The binding text establishing the human rights principles regulating the treatment of prisoners of war was the Hague Convention of 18 October 1907.[74] Articles 4-20 of the Annex to the convention

Fig. 15: Romanian war-wounded soldiers in a Hungarian prisoners of war camp, 1918.

regulated the treatment of prisoners of war: it was to be humane. The state holding the prisoners was permitted to use their labour for civilian purposes – on the land, in trade, in industry or in public service – but not for any activities related to military operations. Food supplied to prisoners of war should be of the same quality as that supplied to the nation's own armed forces. It was not permitted to remove private possessions from prisoners of war. Officers were exempt from the requirement to supply labour, and were to be housed separately.

From 1914 onwards, the warring nations all largely disregarded these provisions. Prisoners of war were not only forced to work in defence industries, but also on front line fortifications, digging trenches and other similar duties.[75]

The International Red Cross was charged with overseeing the treatment of prisoners. Every day, it dispatched some 30,000 letters and packages from and to prisoners of war.[76] When the war came to a provisional end with the cease-fire negotiations in November 1918, it was estimated that the British were holding over 300,000 prisoners from opposing armies,

the French were holding 350,000, the Austro-Hungarians 900,000, the Russians 2.25 million and the Germans 2.4 million. Among those held in Germany, the highest number were soldiers of the former Russian Empire, followed by the French.

Article 20 of the annex to the Hague Convention specified that '[a]fter the conclusion of peace, the repatriation of prisoners of war shall be carried out as quickly as possible'. In reality, discussions at the Paris peace negotiations lasted for months before they concluded a peace settlement with the former Central Powers: Germany signed the Peace of Versailles on 28 June 1919, Austria the Peace of Saint-Germain-en-Laye on 10 September 1919, Bulgaria the Peace of Neuilly-sur-Seine on 27 November 1919, Hungary the Peace of Trianon on 4 June 1920 and Turkey the Peace of Sèvres on 10 August 1920. Each of these agreements came into force some time later, so that, for example, France did not release its German prisoners of war until January 1920, the effective date of the Peace of Versailles.[77] The French authorities in particular had made the conscious decision to use the labour of German prisoners of

Fig. 16: Stamp of the Czechoslovak Legions in Russia, 1919.

war during the months following the end of hostilities to rebuild the areas and towns destroyed during the fighting.[78]

The changed political realities and relationships in Eastern Europe presented particular challenges for the repatriation of Russian prisoners of war from Germany and Austria, and conversely of German and Austrian prisoners from the former Russian Empire. The last of the Russian prisoners of war did not return to their homes until 1922, and met with insecurity and violence when they did.[79] The Russians had taken German Bohemian folklorist Gustav Jungbauer (1886-1942) prisoner in 1915, though he had later managed to escape. Between 1919 and 1921, the

Czechoslovak Red Cross sent him to various prisoner-of-war camps and he worked to free those still held there whose homeland was now in the newly created Czechoslovak Republic.[80]

The great majority of these were German-speaking men: many Czechs and Slovaks who had ended up in prisoner-of-war camps after 1914 had abandoned their loyalty to Austria-Hungary and established their own army to fight with the Tsarist Russian troops against the Central Powers. Even before the founding of the joint Czech and Slovak state, they described themselves as the Czechoslovak Legion.[81] Similar units were established in France and Italy. In the civil war between Red and White Russian units in Russia, the Czechoslovak Legion fought on the side of the Whites during 1917/18. Following their initial success, from the summer of 1918 they were forced further and further east, especially once internal conflicts broke out within the White Russian side. Although Czechoslovakia was not yet a state, the USA acknowledged the Czechoslovak Legion as a fighting power; from September 1918, the Legion withdrew to Siberia. At the start of 1919, three divisions reached Irkutsk, and from there they continued their exodus to Vladivostok. From the port of Vladivostok, Allied ships helped to rescue 67,738 legionnaires between January and September 1920, who were then able to continue their journey and return to Czechoslovakia. From their very beginning, the Czechoslovak Legions were differentiated from the Polish Legions, who had been established as auxiliaries to the royal and imperial army and were later transferred to other military groups.[82] The fact that it had an armed fighting force was a significant factor when an independent Poland was established in 1918.

Although interwar Czechoslovakia and Poland treated the former legionnaires as heroes, in most other cases the situation of former prisoners of war was not an easy one in the societies into which they were repatriated.[83] They were not always included in the national discourse when soldiers were described as patriots ready to sacrifice their lives, nor did they share in the hero status of the war dead and the former fighters at the front; in many cases, they were treated with mistrust and suspicion.[84] Occasionally, however – in Poland, for example – war prisoners were depicted as a particular type of freedom fighter, which gave them a distinct status.[85]

Fig. 17: Russian prisoners of war in Austro-Hungarian captivity at the distribution of food, August 1917

Many prisoners of war had used their incarceration time to extend their skills, for example by learning a new language. The Polish poet Kazimierz Wierzyński (1894-1969), born in Eastern Galicia and a member of the imperial and royal army on the Eastern Front before being made prisoner by Russia in 1915, learnt Russian and made extensive studies in Russian literature. The outbreak of the revolution in the Russian Empire, however, complicated the repatriation of prisoners of war held in Russia, even after the Treaty of Brest-Litovsk.[86]

Founding States – Successes and Failures

The First World War and the October Revolution led to the collapse of the Russian Empire. This was driven in no small part by the nationalist movements within non-Russian populations who had at last, after the revolution in February 1917, gained the rights of association and of free speech; those living at the empire's periphery made especially effective use of these new rights. Previously ill-defined and uncoordinated national aspirations began to take shape as political programmes that met with varying degrees of success.[87] Differences between the various regions became sharper and somewhat altered after 1917. A number of factors influenced the 'national awakening' in these border areas: national traditions; the size of the nation's territory; the territory's proximity to other powers with expansive foreign policies; the population's ethnic and social-class configuration; and the links to Russia itself in terms of culture, language and religion.[88]

In many cases, the national movements enabled in February 1917 presented both nationalist and social demands; this was especially true of the peasants in

Fig. 18: Political poster, painted by Mikhail Sergeevich Kalmanson, after 1917. Out of the shadows of tsarism into the light of freedom. (lower right section)

Part 1: Rays of light are dawning on the country, stifled by tsarism.

Part 2: The violence of the depraved; The violence of the perpetrators;

The violence of those who bribe their way out of punishment.

Part 3: Son of the black chamber.

Part 4: Arises the people great, free, and powerful!

the non-Russian population groups – by far the largest social group numerically – for whom land ownership was crucial, as Andreas Kappeler has shown.[89] A number of conflicts were provoked when the lower classes of one ethnic group made claims on the territory of another ethnic group. The movements among populations in the western part of the empire that were largely composed of peasants often targeted their demands not at Russian but at Baltic German or Polish elites; Azeri peasants, meanwhile, crossed swords with the Armenian bourgeoisie.

The war was a key factor in the nationalist revolutions on the Russian periphery, even more than in the heart of Russia. The lack of supplies both on the land and at the front combined with general war-weariness to bolster mistrust of central government, and this led to the establishment of a series of nationalist army units.[90] In 1917, the western and southern border regions were moreover current theatres of war but with relatively stable fronts. As before, the Central Powers were leading Poles, Lithuanians, some White Russians, Ukrainians, Latvians and Baltic Germans; German troops' invasion of Riga at the end of August 1917 further increased the number of non-Russian ethnic groups living under German occupation.[91]

The two meetings of the Congress of the Peoples of Russia, held at the end of May in Petrograd and the end of September 1917 in Kiev, expressed growing confidence in opposing the centre. Poles and Finns were not involved. Their ambitions were already aiming beyond the level of autonomy being demanded by those who took part in the Congress. Lenin had postulated the right of nations to self-determination, and this had given wings to the dawning self-awareness of regions at the periphery of the Russian Empire. The Bolsheviks had assumed that non-Russian populations, most of which had an insignificant proportion of proletarians, could only be won over to the revolution with slogans promoting national self-determination.[92]

Lenin had made a realistic assessment of the ethnic and social centrifugal forces that were seeking to destroy the empire, and he hoped to enlist them to promote his own political movement. The Declaration of the Rights of the Peoples of Russia, promulgated on 15 November 1917, strengthened emancipatory nationalism vis-à-vis the chauvinism of Greater Russia that still strongly influenced some leading Bolsheviks. Several non-Russian population groups made full use of their right to self-determination, including of their freedom to declare independence from Russia and establish their own state.

The Bolsheviks had a reservation vis-à-vis the right to self-determination, and one that turned out to be significant: they assumed that population groups engaging in a socialist revolution, far from embracing separatism, would instead choose to join forces with the socialist republic. When they acknowledged in 1917/18 that this had been an illusion, it had far-reaching consequences for the nationalities politics of Soviet Russia.[93]

Tsarist Russia lost any influence it had had in Poland when the military forces of the Central Powers compelled its army to retreat in late summer 1915. In November 1916, the two Central Powers emperors declared the reestablishment of the Polish kingdom, and this altered the situation. Poland's future immediately acquired much greater significance in the context of international diplomacy. The Polish hopes that national independence was now within their grasp were however quickly dashed by the realities of life under German occupation.[94] The provisional Russian government in power after the February Revolution introduced significant liberalisation to their nationalities policy and reinstated Poland's autonomy, but this had little practical effect. Józef Piłsudski (1867-1935) and other interested politicians worked together with the Entente nations and the USA in hope and expectation of achieving national independence. France and the US president Woodrow Wilson in particular spoke out in favour of Polish independence, which indeed became a reality immediately following the military collapse of the Central Powers at the start of November 1918.[95]

At this point, the Soviet Russian government did nothing to prevent Poland from gaining its independence. Indeed, the independence of Finland (which had been achieved in December 1917) and that of Poland can be seen as an early litmus test for the national right to self-determination that Lenin had vehemently defended in the face of the internationalist arguments advanced by Rosa Luxemburg (1871-1919) and other Poland left-wing socialists.[96] Polish independence was later threatened in other ways during the 1919-1921 war between Poland and Soviet Russia, when the Red Army reached the gates of War-

Fig. 19. Marshal Józef Piłsudski with Gabriel Narutowicz who was assassinated by right-wing oppositionist only five days after his election to the first president of the Second Polish Republic in 1922. Image from 10 December 1922.

saw in August 1920. In the changing fortunes of that war, national sentiment was strengthened on both sides: the Russian 'one and undivided' fatherland was defended when the Poles marched on Kiev, and a few months later the Polish fatherland was defended when the Soviet Russian army marched on Warsaw. The conflict played a significant part in bolstering national identities.[97]

Matters developed very differently from Poland in Ukraine, chiefly because of the population's social structure and ethnic composition. Of Ukraine's 17 million inhabitants, 6.5 million belonged to non-Ukrainian minority populations – mainly Russians, Jews and Poles – and only around 6% lived in towns and cities, with Jews and Russians making up a third of the urban population. The social class one would generally expect to constitute the nationalist movement in a nation was exceptionally small.[98]

Matters were further complicated by the three successive identities of the Ukrainian state: on 25 December 1917, the All-Ukrainian Congress of Soviets declared the 'Ukrainian People's Republic of the Soviets' in Kharkiv. On 22 January 1918 in Kiev, the Central Rada then proclaimed the Ukrainian National Republic, and on 1 November 1918, the Western Ukrainian National Republic was proclaimed in Lvov. This last emerged from the domestically liberal former Austria-Hungary and was the only one able to claim a significantly Ukrainian national movement in terms of both quality and quantity.[99] The Western Ukrainian National Republic was born into military conflict with newly founded Poland and survived only until July 1919, when it suffered military defeat.[100]

Under the Treaty of Brest-Litovsk ('peace for bread'), signed in March 1918, the Central Powers

Fig. 20: Invasion of German units into Kamianets-Podilskyi, Ukraine, spring 1918.

forced the Bolsheviks to abandon their claim over Ukraine. The German and Austro-Hungarian troops safeguarded a semi-functioning Ukrainian state under the authoritarian rule of the conservative Pavlo Skoropadsky (1873-1945), while using Ukraine as a 'breadbasket' for supplies for their own home populations. Western European states had a poor understanding of the complexities of a country with three different foundational declarations. Ukraine moreover lacked effective lobbyists among their exiles who might, for example at the Paris peace negotia-

tions, have explained how matters stood for their country.[101]

The following government of the Ukrainian National Republic, led by Symon Petliura during 1919/20, failed to pull the country's tangled structures together into an effective state that would stand by their Polish allies in the war against Soviet Russia. Most Ukrainian-speaking peasants were mistrustful of any ideas of a nation or a state, preferring to give their allegiance to local or regional warlords (Atamans) who promised to provide bread and at least some degree of security as the Russian civil war escalated. The Bolsheviks offered such support on a wider regional scale, and more reliably than other groups; for historical and cultural reasons, however, they considered Ukraine an integral part of Russia, and they were therefore less inclined to apply the principle of national right to self-determination, which they had initially proclaimed, to the Ukrainians than to other populations.[102] On 18 March 1921, Poland and Soviet Russia signed the Peace of Riga, and this in effect brought Ukrainian independence to an end.[103]

Belarus was under a German protectorate when the Belarusian People's Republic was proclaimed on 25 March 1918, albeit without the agreement of the occupying power. The only national party, the

Fig. 21: Symon Petliura in front of the diverse troops of the Ukrainian Army, Kiev, 1 May 1920 (on the left side in black uniform with a black hat).

Fig. 22: The Belarusian People's Republic Rada (parliament) building, in Minsk 19 February 1918.

Belarusian Socialist Hramada, had a large following among the peasants, who made up over 90% of the Belarusian population. Inspired by the Ukrainian movement, intellectuals and soldiers established the Rada, a Belarusian house of representatives. Belarusian was made the official language, schools were opened and newspapers were published. In general, however, this government was able to achieve little. The socialist parties of the majority Russian and Jewish urban populations were dictating the life of the nation, but they had little support in the rural areas.[104]

The German government was ambivalent towards the new state. Although Germany never officially granted recognition to Belarus, the Berlin delegation endorsed the separation of Belarusian territory from Soviet Russia at the peace negotiations for Brest-Litovsk, and supported the Belarusians' resistance to Poland's plans for territorial encroachment.[105] After the withdrawal of German troops in November 1918, the Belarusian Socialist Soviet Republic was declared on 1 January 1919 and reincorporated into Soviet Russia – a clear sign of the strong support the Bolsheviks enjoyed in Belarus. In the November 1917 elections to the Russian Constituent Assembly, the Bolsheviks gained 63% of the vote in Vitebsk and 51% in Minsk.[106]

The Bolsheviks gained good support among urban and rural workers and among the military in the Baltic states of Latvia and Estonia, with 40% and more of the vote. Most non-Russians, however, did not vote for Russian parties but rather for their own national parties, who were working towards independence from Soviet Russia.[107] This came about as Russia's disintegration continued throughout 1917. Germany made the most of the opportunity to occupy Ukraine and the Baltic provinces, until the treaty of Brest-Litovsk on 3 March 1918 forced the Central Powers to retreat from the areas over which they had taken control. Germany and the Ottoman Empire exploited Russia's weakness to mount a new offensive that among other things led to the occupation of Ukraine and the remaining parts of the Baltic provinces. This deprived the Russian state of a third of its population and a significant proportion of its mining and industrial capacity.[108]

Latvia, like Ukraine, saw three different governments set up on three different occasions when a new state was declared. The socialist government of Pēteris Stučka (1865-1932) was supported by Moscow at the start of 1918, and enjoyed some support among Latvians. The bourgeois government under Prime Minister Kārlis Ulmanis (1877-1942), who was to serve as Latvia's prime minister several times between the wars, relied principally on support from the Allied powers in the First World War, but from time to time enjoyed military support from Germany and Estonia against the 'Latvian Riflemen' and the

Fig. 23: Kārlis Ulmanis, the first Prime Minister of the new Latvian state spent two months floating on the waters near Liepāja; he returned to the harbour on 27 June 1919 after the failed German coup d'état in Latvia.

Red Army. Following the German Baltic minority's military putsch against Ulmanis, there was for a short time – from the end of April until the start of June 1919 – a third government under Andrievs Niedra (1871-1942) as prime minister, which relied on the support of the German military forces that were still present in Latvia.[109]

The bourgeois Latvian government faced many challenges in setting up their new state. For a long time, they had neither money nor the necessary instruments of government, so were forced to work with the German occupation forces and German Baltic associations. By the summer of 1919, however, the relationship had become one of enmity. Representatives of the Jewish, Baltic German and Russian national minorities did not recognise them, and they initially enjoyed little support even among the Latvian population. The landless and the workers who made up a large part of the population were looking to the Bolsheviks for land distribution and the rule of the proletariat. Latvia's independence was not secured until the summer of 1920, thanks to peace accords with the German Reich and Soviet Russia.[110]

The Estonian national state emerged in the face of even stronger involvement by various military forces: especially German paramilitaries, Baltic German units and the White Guards. The United Kingdom offered its support to the Estonian bourgeois government of Konstantin Päts (1874-1956) but was not willing to send its own forces to the Baltic region. According to Article 12 of the Armistice of Compiègne, defeated German troops were to be sent to defend the Estonian state. German forces therefore remained in Estonia and further *Freikorps* soldiers were recruited.[111]

The relationships between the Germans and the Estonians on the ground, and between the German *Freikorps* and the German democratic government of Friedrich Ebert (1871-1925), were at best ambivalent. The German forces in Estonia were on the one hand desperately needed to repel the Red Army and achieve national independence. The Germans, however, had tainted their reputation by behaving exploitatively and narrow-mindedly during their 1918 occupation, arousing unwelcome memories among Estonians of the former rule by the Baltic German aristocracy. During 1919/20, the German *Freikorps*, moreover, behaved more like thugs than soldiers in

Fig. 24: General Rüdiger von der Goltz (left), commander of German *Freikorps* troops, and Pavel Bermondt-Avalov, commander of the so-called West Russian Volunteer Army, before a military parade in 1919. They fought together temporarily against the Red Army, but also against the Latvian government of Kārlis Ulmanis.

the northern Baltic. Their anti-democratic ethos increasingly made them a diplomatic liability, and after their return to Germany they became a serious danger in the domestic politics of the Weimar Republic. The route to independence was finally opened up for Estonia on 2 February 1920 by the Treaty of Tartu with Soviet Russia.[112]

The territorially expansive attempts by *Ober Ost*[113] were instigated by the ambition to establish a constitutional monarchy in Lithuania under German patronage. This became a reality when on 16 February 1918, after more than a century under Russian sovereignty, Lithuania was declared an independent state. Duke Wilhelm von Urach (1864-1928) was to be regent, taking the name of the Lithuanian hero Mindaugas II, and he was elected to office by the Lithuanian national council in July 1918. The Württemberg duke, however, never formally assumed the crown.[114]

Fig. 25: Estonian 'fighting men' in the Estonian-Soviet Russian war, 1919.

In the meantime, the situation had changed. On 2 January 1919, Polish defence forces occupied Vilnius, forcing the Lithuanian government to flee. Shortly thereafter, the Red Army and the Lithuanian

Fig. 26: A delegation of the Council of Lithuania in Berlin after discussing the first appointment of the Cabinet of Ministers with the new German government of Prince Maximilian of Baden. From left sitting: Jonas Staugaitis, Antanas Smetona, Konstantinas Olšauskas, standing: Jokūbas, Šernas, Jurgis Šaulys, Juozas Purickis, Vilius Gaigalas, Martynas Yčas, Augustinas Voldemaras, October 1918.

communists took over the city and proclaimed the Lithuanian-Belarusian Soviet Socialist Republic. In the peace treaty between Lithuania and Russia on 12 July 1920, the Soviet government returned Vilnius to the Lithuanian government. On 9 October, the Polish general Lucjan Żeligowski (1865-1947), in a surprise coup during the Polish–Soviet Russian war and in contravention of the Suwałki[115] cease-fire agreement, reclaimed the city for Poland. This reignited the conflict between Poland and Lithuania and poisoned relations between the two countries for the interwar period.[116]

During 1919/20, Poland and Soviet Russia were not the only areas at war with each other – Lithuania, Belarus and Ukraine were also fighting to achieve independent statehood. Of the three neighbouring Baltic states on Russia's western border, only Lithuania was able to achieve independence.[117]

To the south of Russia and especially in Transcaucasia (Azerbaijan, Armenia and Georgia), the establishment of nation states followed different patterns. The Bolsheviks had very little cultural traction there during 1917/18, as the three major ethnic groups voted for their own parties: the Georgians for the

Fig. 27: Red Army soldiers in Baku, 1 January 1920.

Mensheviks, the Armenians for the Dashnaks and the Azerbaijanis for the Musavat Party and other Muslim groups.[118]

When it was defeated at the end of 1918, Germany was no longer one of the powers present in the area. The region was economically and strategically important as a gateway to Asia and Soviet Russia, Turkey and the United Kingdom continued to tussle for dominance in the area. Between 1918 and 1922, the three Caucasian nations did manage to achieve independence, principally thanks to their persistent political will, but also because the traditional regional powers, Russia and Turkey, were weakened in the immediate post-war period. In the medium term, the three small states remained independent; the territories of Armenia and Azerbaijan were ethnically fragmented, which gave rise to mutual claims and a consequent inability to establish cooperation.[119]

Azerbaijan was independent only briefly, from May 1918 to April 1920, but had no fewer than five different governments in that time. The instability was mainly due to ethnic conflicts, opposition to a failed attempt at land reform by the Armenian bourgeoisie and the oil crisis in Baku. This gave the Bolsheviks the opportunity to present themselves as supporters of the poor Muslim rural population and to appeal to the unemployed among the Muslim and Russian populations.[120]

In February 1920, 70,000 Red Army soldiers marched into Azerbaijan; thanks to the diplomatic agreement between Soviet Russia and Turkey, they met with no serious resistance. When British troops occupied Constantinople in March 1920, the nationalists under Kemal Atatürk (1881-1938) were prepared to agree to the Russians seizing power in the Caucasus in exchange for Moscow's support for their liber-

Fig. 28: Mustafa Kemal Atatürk, here in his position as the Turkish defence minister in 1918/19.

ation struggle against the United Kingdom. This enabled Russian armaments to be moved through the Caucasus and on into Turkey. The Red Army, moreover, were for a while able to count on considerable Turkish Muslim support in their invasion of Azerbaijan. The leaders of the Azerbaijani national movement were subsequently imprisoned by the Soviets, and many were executed; Soviet troops also crushed uprisings in Azerbaijan.[121]

The Armenians claimed their right to self-determination and on 28 May 1918 declared the Democratic Republic of Armenia. The Armenian nation, fought over and jeopardised by the 1915/16 genocide, based much of its national identity on its fear and hatred of Turkey. The fact that Soviet Russia was

gaining influence on the small country seemed like a lesser evil in comparison. The Dashnaks, the political leaders in Armenia, sought to build an alliance with the Entente powers and in particular with the United Kingdom, which had long been active in the region south and west of the Caspian Sea.[122] The Treaty of Sèvres ensured Armenia's independence, but it never came into force because it was not signed by the USA, where domestic rivals to Wilson were promoting increasing isolationism, and it had not been ratified by Kemal Atatürk's Turkey.

Inspired by nationalistic enthusiasm, Armenia overestimated its own strength and invaded eastern Anatolia at the end of September 1920; in response, the Turks advanced on Yerevan in November 1920. The hoped-for alliance with the United Kingdom came to nothing; first, because Britain preferred to do business with Azerbaijan and its oil wells and, second, because the British government's general policy was to withdraw from Transcaucasia.[123]

The Armenian leadership had laid itself open to an ultimatum from Soviet Russia to cede power to a revolutionary committee, and Red Army forces arrived from Azerbaijan soon after. On 29 November 1920, the Armenian Soviet Socialist Republic was declared. The Treaty of Kars, signed on 13 October 1921, divided Armenia between Turkey and Soviet Russia. The Dashnaks entered a coalition with the Bolsheviks, but their Russian 'allies' soon began to persecute them and force them into exile, together with many other Armenian nationalists and intellectuals.[124]

Of the three Caucasian nations, Georgia was most viable as an independent state. The Georgians were very conscious of their own national history and culture. They had a large indigenous educated class, and the Mensheviks provided genuine national leadership. On 26 May 1918, the national assembly declared the Democratic Republic of Georgia independent. During the first six months of independence, Georgia was under the protection first of the German Empire and then of the United Kingdom.[125]

The coalition government consisted of Menshevik social democrats, national democrats and socialist federalists, and was led by Noi Zhordania (1868-1953). It took inspiration from German social democracy, which valued statecraft above social revolution. The government's programme included not only agrarian reform and social legislation, but also took a firm stand against Bolshevik and separatist movements in Georgia. As a result, they gained strong support from the Georgian population, including in rural areas.[126] The socialist milieus of Western Europe were also supportive of the Georgian program of reform. Karl Kautsky (1854-1938) and Ramsay MacDonald (1866-1937) had visited Georgia in 1920 and had spoken approvingly of their form of government.[127]

The weak point in the Georgian state was the presence of ethnic minorities in the country. The Ossetians and Abkhazians demanded self-government, but the central government in Tbilisi not only turned a deaf ear but interpreted the demands as an arrogant request to be confronted. This provided the Soviet Russian leadership with an opportunity to advance on Noi Zhordania's government. In May 1920, the Bolsheviks in Tbilisi tried to orchestrate a putsch, but it was easily put down by the Georgian army. On 7 May 1920, the Soviet government signed a treaty with Georgia recognising its independence on the grounds of the right to self-determination.[128]

Fig. 29: Armenian volunteers receive blessings from the Catholicos of All Armenians, George V, on the eve of the battle with Ottoman troops, summer 1918.

This recognition did not, however, protect Georgia from invasion by the Red Army in February 1921, when two communist party functionaries leading the military forces were in fact both of Georgian origin: Sergo Konstantinovich Ordzhonikidze (1886-1937)

Fig. 30: Karl Kautsky with the Georgian Social Democrats, Tbilisi, 1920. In the first row: S. Devdariani, Noe Ramishvili, Noe Zhordania, Karl Kautsky and his wife Luise Kautsky, S. Jibladze, R. Arsenidze; in the second row: Kautsky's secretary Paul Olberg, V. Tevzaia, K. Gvarjaladze, K. Sabakhtarashvili, S. Tevzadze, Urushadze, R. Tsintsabadze.

Fig. 31: Georgian Prime Minister Noe Zhordania in 1919.

counter the centrifugal forces exerted by its many ethnic groups not so much by taking a linguistically and culturally federalist approach as through dominance, uniformity and the use of violence. Caught between cultural traditions, national aspirations and the need to match these with capacity and realpolitik, it was only possible for those nations that had a clear and established historic and cultural identity, and could count on political and/or military support from Central and Western Europe, to achieve national independence.

The aspiration, whether realistic or utopian, to establish states was not limited to nations within the territories of the former Russian Empire. There were a number of experimental attempts at state-building in the Danube-Carpathian region in the years following the First World War. Three examples of this were the 'State of Rijeka' (Fiume, November 1918-September 1919); plans to create the 'Hutsul Republic' (November 1918-summer 1919) in the border area

and Joseph Stalin (1878-1953), who was also the People's Commissar for Nationalities and Commander of the Red Army southern front. Lenin had approved the Red Army's incursion, but he criticised Stalin for his 'rough greater Russian violence', which he said was 'taken from Tsarist methods and only very slightly softened with Soviet oil'.[129]

This highlighted a conflict of objectives in Lenin's beliefs[130] and within the Bolshevik movement in terms of their long-vaunted policy of the right to self-determination. The assumption that the populations of Tsarist Russia would abandon their separatist inclinations and choose to join Russia's socialist republic after the revolution turned out to be a fallacy. It appeared impossible to substitute an internationalist proletarian alternative to the evolution of nation states. At the end of 1922, the territories delineated by their linguistic unity were to be defined and incorporated into a new supranational state, the Union of the Soviet Republics, which was to shaped according to federalist principles.[131]

In practice, the Soviet Union turned out to be a large, potent and yet fragile structure that sought to

Fig. 32: German caricature of 1921: Soviet Russia and the Socialist Republic of Georgia. The Bolsheviks: 'Halt, surrender, – we love you to bits!', *Der wahre Jakob*, 1921.

between Poland, Slovakia and Hungary; and plans to grant autonomy to the Szeklers within Greater Romania.[132] Some very small geographical areas also made attempts at gaining autonomy. Some of those belonging to the Frisian minority in Schleswig-Holstein, which faced a choice between joining Denmark or Germany, developed the notion of having their own Frisian nation. Until the development of National Socialism, however, this small group was not sufficiently numerous to constitute a majority within the ethnic Frisians.[133]

An Invisible Enemy: The Spanish Influenza

As if the horrors of war, the violence and the anguish of destruction, mutilation and death were not enough; in the final stages of the First World War and the years immediately afterwards a new, invisible, but no less dangerous enemy was added to the mix: the so-called 'Spanish flu'. As we are now aware, the ways the virus spread included via droplets and aerosols, propelled through the air when an infected person coughed, and were absorbed by others. Children, pregnant women, the chronically ill and those suffering from bronchitis were especially vulnerable. In the absence of reliable data from all nations around the world, the total number of those who died from the flu can only be roughly estimated as 'between 20 and 50 million'.[134]

It is now also clear that the Spanish flu did not originate in Spain but was probably brought to Europe by US soldiers coming to join the war in its closing stages. It spread first in France and then through other Western European countries. Countries involved in the war, however, were censuring on military grounds what could be said in the press, so the first news of the devastating outbreak came from neutral Spain. It was this that led to the misleading name of the pandemic, which has since been generally adopted and codified.

Germany suffered around 300,000 fatalities due to the Spanish flu, Austria around 25,000. In the summer of 1918, the pandemic reached the Bohemian states. The comparatively good Bohemian healthcare services reacted by administering pain management, cardiovascular treatments, serum therapy, homeopathy and anti-bacterial preparations. The disease's swift spread was thought to be due to hunger and to

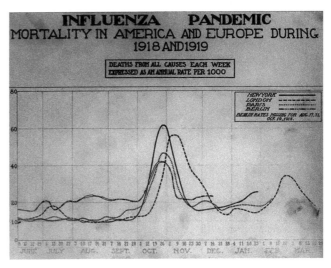

Fig. 33: 'The Spanish Influenza'. Chart showing mortality from the 1918 influenza pandemic in the US and Europe.

the lack of heating fuel in the cities. When the Czechoslovak Republic was proclaimed in the autumn of 1919, large numbers of citizens of the new state were suffering the consequences of the pandemic. The authorities ordered that all schools should be closed, and that everyone should wear coverings over the nose and mouth. Hospital conditions were nevertheless appalling, and the crematoria and burial grounds were overwhelmed by the numbers of dead bodies. Rumours and stories spread widely among the population, claiming that the new illness was a revived version of earlier plagues.[135] Hungary reached the peak infection point in October 1918, when around 100,000 people died as a result of the influenza.[136]

There were three waves of the epidemic in Poland. The peaks happened in December 1918 in the capital Warsaw, and again at the turn of 1919/20. Researchers estimate that Poland suffered between 200,000 and 300,000 deaths from the flu.[137]

The infection probably reached Russia in September 1918, when Allied troops came to the aid of the White Russians. The virus spread rapidly along the railway lines, especially in the west of the country, and cost the lives of more than 450,000 people.

The Spanish flu reached South-Eastern Europe from the north, arriving at the Vltava river and Bessarabia in July 1918. By September 1918, it had also wreaked havoc in the Kingdom of Romania, lead-

Fig. 34: 'Der Sarg der Schwester' (The Sister's Coffin). Two girls burying their sister, dead from the Spanish flu, while their father has still not returned from the front and their mother also suffers from the flu. Title page of the Austrian *Illustrierte Kronen-Zeitung*, 2 December 1918.

ing to severe cardiovascular and lung problems. Alexe Sulică (1884-1949), an epidemiologist working in the Transylvanian city of Brașov, provides contemporary observations on the causes, course and consequences of the Spanish flu. In late March 1920, he wrote an article for the *Gazeta Transilvaniei*, in which he explained:

> The miserable conditions that we have experienced for the last six years have naturally played a significant part in creating the particularly strong sensitivity to this illness. The epidemic penetrated a deeply afflicted population that was suffering from deprivations, insecurity and painful experiences of all kinds. Added to these were a lack of nu-

trition, stress, a lack of good sanitation, and disorientation, and these combined to facilitate the spread of the epidemic, while people were increasingly losing both physical and mental strength.[138]

It is estimated that around half a million inhabitants of South-Eastern Europe lost their lives to the flu. The epidemic's consequences were as severe in neighbouring Serbia as they had been in Romania.[139]

Prominent victims of Spanish flu in Central, East and South-Eastern Europe included the Hungarian writer Margit Kaffka (1880-1918); the artists Jan Autengruber (1887-1920), Gustav Klimt (1862-1918), Bohumil Kubišta (1884-1918) and Egon Schiele (1890-1918); the architect Otto Wagner (1841-1918); the opera singer Čeněk Klaus (1890-1918); the sociologist Max Weber (1864-1920); the Bolshevik Russian General Iakov M. Sverdlov (1885-1919) and the Romanian general Eremia Grigorescu (1863-1919); and Archduke Franz Karl of Austria-Tuscany (1893-1918). Others who suffered with the virus are known to have included Queen Maria of Romania (1875–1938), the writer Franz Kafka (1883-1924) and American President Woodrow Wilson (1856-1924), whose time at the Paris Peace Conference was overshadowed by a period of convalescence. Kafka and Wilson suffered from poor health and were therefore in the 'at-risk' group; when both died in 1924, it was most probably as a delayed consequence of the pandemic. Historians have woefully failed to give a balanced account of the epidemic's significance in terms of the number of deaths caused, but the total exceeded the number of lives lost on all the war fronts combined.

Expectations of France and Great Britain

After 1918, the nations of Eastern Europe had not only to redefine internal relationships within their country but also to find their place within the new world order. International relations were a way of promoting their own prestige and strengthening their own sense of security. The American president Woodrow Wilson served as a shining light for the citizens of many Central European states that had done well out of the Paris peace negotiations. In Czechoslovakia, for example, postcards were sold featuring his portrait alongside that of the first president, Tomáš G. Masaryk (1850-1937). The main station in Prague,

Fig. 35. The unveiling of the Wilson Statue in front of Prague's main railway station on 4 June 1928, commemorating the 10th anniversary of the Czechoslovak Republic.

which had borne the name of Emperor Franz-Joseph [Nádraží císaře Františka Josefa], was renamed 'Wilson Station' [Wilsonovo nádraží] in honour of the American statesman. There were great expectations bound up in these symbolic political acts, but they obscured the fact that although Wilson had been a significant player in reshaping Central Europe at the Paris Peace Conference, he had not been doing so with the explicit political support of the US Congress.

What expectations were there among the Central and South-East European states of the other two great powers among the Allies, the United Kingdom and France?

The relationship between Central Europe and Britain was very one-sided. Masaryk was a great ad-

mirer of the traditions of freedom in the history of Britain. He was well acquainted with English literature and culture.[140] Central Europe, however, was for the most part well beyond the mental horizon of large sections of British society. Rather than focus their attention on the nations of East-Central and Eastern Europe, the British preferred the USA or France. There were moreover widespread preconceptions in the Anglo-Saxon world, long predating the First World War, of the 'East' as a cultural backwater, which led to an assumption that Poles, Czechs, Slovaks and Yugoslavs were unlikely to be successful in running their own countries.[141] The book *Balka-*

Fig. 36: While many East European nations saw England and France as their allies and models of modern statehood, many Germans blamed these countries as the destroyers of Central Europe, as in the caricature 'Der Gipfel der Zivilisation' (The Summit of Civilisation) by Arthur Krüger, published on the front page of the German satirical magazine *Der wahre Jacob*, 25 February 1921.

Fig. 37: Fernand Vix as commander of the Allied Military Mission to Budapest in 1919.

nized Europe. A Study in Political Analysis and Reconstruction by the European correspondent of the *Chicago Daily News*, Paul Scott Mowrer (1887-1971), was published in 1921 and enjoyed great popularity. Not long after the end of the war, major disagreements had surfaced between France and Great Britain. They became apparent at the Washington Conference of 1921-1922, where the matter of reparations was discussed, and the United Kingdom was prepared to make certain concessions to the Central Powers. The British and French also diverged significantly in their opinion of the German–Soviet Treaty of Rapallo and its possible effects on Eastern Europe; where there were far stronger misgivings about the treaty in Paris than in London. In addition, neither Britain nor the USA offered assistance when French and Belgian troops occupied the Ruhr on 11 January 1923 in order forcibly to claim the reparations due to them.[142]

Since the 18th century, France had served as a cultural point of reference for the elites of Eastern Europe. The upper classes of Polish, Hungarian, Czech and Romanian society very much favoured the use of French as the language of the educated. In the 19th century, when Romania was experiencing emancipation, the nation had placed special value on its 'Roman' character, and the linguistic relationship with Italy and France was seen as building a cultural bridge to related peoples. Many Poles and Czechs had come to France during difficult periods of their history seeking political refuge; Romanians, on the other hand, often came to France of their own free will to study and work there. France was one of the victorious Allied nations after the First World War. However, having been one of the main theatres of war it was economically much weakened immediately thereafter because of the extensive destruction in the country's north and east. There were also internal tensions within the Third Republic. These had broken out again after the war's end, limiting the country's capacity to become involved in wider foreign political matters. France had been a strong defender of the interests of Central and South-East European nations at the Paris Peace Conference; in reality, however, its ability to provide effective protection was limited.[143]

Some nations treated certain of the diplomatic measures carried out by the French government with suspicion. Hungary especially disapproved of the sympathy France showed for Czechoslovakia, Romania and the alliance of the Little Entente, and of the sanctioning of the Peace Treaty of Trianon. Budapest, in fact, had been experiencing disillusion since soon after the end of the war: French Lieutenant-Colonel Fernand Vix (1876-1941) led the Entente's military mission in Budapest, and on 20 March 1919 he conveyed in what was later called the 'Vix-note' the decision reached at the Paris Peace Conference on 26 February that Hungary was to withdraw all military forces from its Eastern territories, up to and including Debrecen and Szeged. The measure had originally been intended to obstruct any further incursions by the communists. However, since Romanian troops were then due to advance into the vacated regions, which included Transylvania, there was a not-unreasonable suspicion in Budapest that the move was intended to forestall any future territorial surrender by Romania. Prime Minister Dénes Berikey (1871-1944) and President Mihály Károlyi (1875-1955)

Fig. 38: 'The Polish Victory' (La Victoire Polonaise). The cover portrays a fictional scene which suggests that a large proportion of French officers participated in the Polish forces' victory over the Red Army. General Maxime Weygand, who acted as a French military consultant in Poland in 1920, pointed out that this was inaccurate. *Le Petit Journal*, September 1920.

resigned their positions in protest at the Vix-note, and this opened the way for a provisional seizure of power by the communist Béla Kun (1886-1938) and his social democratic allies. The fact that Romanian troops had marched right into the capital Budapest to bring down the dictatorship left a deep mark on the Hungary's self-confidence; many Hungarians were offended at the partisanship shown by France, especially given the nationality of the Entente officers.[144]

In order to fully understand how things stood between France and Eastern Europe during the interwar period, it is essential not to overlook the economic and financial aspects of their relations. Large French companies made big investments, especially in Poland, Czechoslovakia and Romania. During the early 1920s, these major capital injections contributed to a measure of economic recovery in the countries concerned. These had previously been weakened due to earlier monetary reforms, inflation and alignment problems between countries that had formerly belonged to different states and had therefore operated under different economic systems.[145]

The expectations of France created internal contradictions within individual countries in Central and Eastern Europe. In the Polish army, General Józef Haller (1873-1960) held a very pro-French position, whereas his opponent Józef Piłsudski (1867-1935) was far more reticent on the matter. In fact, French officers provided military training during the key phase of the establishment the new state of Poland. One such officer was Captain (later General) Charles de Gaulle (1890-1970), who was in Poland from April 1919 to May 1920 and then again from June 1920 to January 1921.

Third section

Postcolonial History

The First World War was not only European in character, nor even simply a war between 'whites'. The sociologist William E. B. Du Bois (1868-1963), a scholar and human rights activist who himself had Afro-American roots, made this observation as early as 1915.[147] He was referring principally to the involvement of soldiers from their respective colonies in the armies of various countries, but also to the conflicts occurring on the continent of Africa, especially in Germany's colonial territories.

Colonial troops were a part of the armies of the Allied nations not only during the First World War but also in various conflicts during the following years in Eastern Europe. In its attempts to force the Ottoman Empire to open the Dardanelles Passage during 1915, the British Empire used units from the Australian and New Zealand Army Corps (ANZAC), who suffered especially heavy losses in the fighting at Gallipoli. The day the troops landed, 25 April 1915, has been a national day of commemoration in Australia and New Zealand (ANZAC day) since 1920.[148] The sense that they had fought to defend the interests of the British Empire fuelled a desire for independence in both countries. Although both nations are still nominally members of the Commonwealth, Australia and New Zealand share the memory of Gallipoli, a battle in the extreme south-east of Europe, as a foundation myth for the building of their respective nations.

France, Great Britain and Belgium all enrolled soldiers from their overseas colonies to take part in regional conflicts that happened after 1918. In the case of the 1923 occupation, France and Belgium temporarily stationed some 20,000 soldiers, mainly from Africa, in the Ruhr, and this was not an isolated example. French soldiers from sub-Saharan Africa were also stationed in the plebiscite regions of Upper Silesia; they were tasked with maintaining order and security during the 'plebiscite battles' between Germans and Poles. Many people projected their own preconceived racial stereotypes onto these soldiers. Their reservations about the 'other' then began to influence their view of the populations of the new states in Eastern Europe. Dr Wilhelm Raab (1895-1969), a doctor born in Vienna who also worked as a caricaturist, drew an image of a Czech legionnaire with a hand grenade and a Black African soldier in French uniform with a bloody knife captioned 'Brutalité, bestialité, égalité'. Under this savage cartoon was printed the following derogatory text: 'One is from Senegal, the other is called Dolezal. In the Rhine region, the Black man is stealing, in Prague and Cheb it's the Czech. Each is promoting the praise, honour and glory of France in his own way.'[149] The image was very widely used and was circulated as a postcard. In a kind of strangely inverted colonialism, the citizens of the newly established Czechoslovakia, together with the German-speaking populations living in the Bohemian states, were represented as being a 'foreign occupation' comparable to the French soldiers temporarily occupying the Ruhr.

Both before and after 1918 it was not only the presence of colonial people, but also the ideas of colonialism itself, that were never far away during the conflicts in Eastern Europe. German intellectuals, politicians and officials had discussed notions of superiority and ideas related to colonialism during the German Empire from 1871 onwards, in some cases even earlier.[150] These played a large part in defining the German occupation policies in the conquered regions of Eastern Europe between 1914 and 1918.[151] Following the end of the war, many German soldiers who had served in the former colonies were unable to find a place in the much-reduced military forces of the Weimar Republic, and instead fought with the German *Freikorps* and with other paramilitary fighting units.[152] It is not difficult to imagine that they brought their self-image as a dominant colonial force to the conflicts in which they were involved in Eastern Europe together with their sense of power and superiority over the local Slav and Baltic populations.

From a postcolonial perspective, the national movements towards emancipation following 1918 that drove the reconstitution of old states, the founding of new states and the regional changes among other states can be regarded as anti-colonial. The three empires that had defined Central, Eastern and South-Eastern Europe – Germany, Russia and Austria-Hungary – had included within their borders countless people who felt that their linguistic, cultural and political identity was under-valued in a multi-ethnic state. The Czech sociologist Tomáš Garrigue Masaryk, who later served as president of Czechoslovakia, described in his book *Nová Evropa. Stanovisko slovanské (The New Europe. A Slavic Standpoint)* the imperial German drive for domination in large parts of Europe:

Pan-Germanism aims at a German, German-led Central Europe, the substance of which is formed by Prussian Germany with Austria-Hungary; this latter empire played in the pan-German scheme only the role of a German colony, a bridge to Asia. Austria-Hungary is the vanguard of pan-Germanism in the Balkans and on toward Turkey. Through Turkey Berlin aims at Asia and Africa. In the West the pan-Germans endeavor to control some neighboring lands, such as Holland, Belgium, the Scandi-

Fig. 39: Caricature 'Brutalité, bestialité, égalité' (Brutality, Bestiality, Egality) by Wilhelm Raab (1895-1969). Contemporary postcard, which was reproduced in non-German newspapers to demonstrate German racism, for instance in *Videňské noviny* no. 16, 1921.

navian countries, and parts of France and Italy; but the principal concern of pan-Germanism is to keep the control of Austria-Hungary and, through it, of Turkey and of the Balkans.[153]

Masaryk described the emancipation of the 'little people' from imperial domination as the righting of a historical wrong. Furthermore he believed that the creation of the new Central European order after 1918 could also be described as a continental era of decolonialisation. In some of the states emerging from the former empires, the political discourse showed signs of colonial tendencies and aspirations. The moves by the new Polish Republic towards the east from 1918 onwards could, for example, arguably be described as a form of continental colonialism, echoing former early modern Jagellonian policies.[154] There were clear colonial aspects to the Liga Morska i Rzeczna (LMiR) (Maritime and River League), created in 1924, renamed the Liga Morska i Kolonialna (LMK) (Maritime and Colonial League) in 1930: it sought to dispatch Polish ships across the world's oceans and establish Polish settlements overseas.

In the case of Soviet Russia it soon became clear that in spite of the declared support for national self-determination, the communist system's expansion was driven by an impetus of not only political and quasi-missionary, but also inspired by the desire to recreate the imperial structures of the Tsarist Empire. This drive, as it affected the peoples of Central

Dyon naszych torpedowców na morzu.   Fot. W. Filanowicz.

Fig. 40: Front page of the first number of *Morze* (The Sea), the journal of the Polska Liga Morska i Rzeczna (Polish Sea and River League).

Asia and the neighbouring White Russians and Ukrainians, was clearly colonial in character. However after an initial phase in which indigenous peoples were promoted during the 1920s under the policy named 'korenizatsiya' (promoting indigenisation), and again briefly promoted under a new designation a decade later, they were finally overpowered by the domination of the Russian language over other languages, even though the multilingual character of the developing Soviet Union was given politically symbolic prominence.

Another example of continental colonial practice was the annexation of 'German Western Hungary', formerly part of the transleithanian part of Austria-Hungary. The annexation was negotiated by the Austrian delegation in the Treaty of Saint-Germain and confirmed by the Treaty of Trianon and, at the end of 1921, the region became known as federal Burgenland. A further example is Carpatho-Ukraine (Podkarpatská Rus), a region populated by a majority of Ruthenians that had also been part of the Hungarian Empire but had been allocated to the Czechoslovak Republic after the First World War. The officials controlling this region were Czech, and therefore not indigenous or from the Slovak territories that bordered it on the west; in spite of the long distance from Prague, the area thus used Czech as its official language. This measure was justified on the grounds that the many local variants of the Ruthenian language comprised none that was universally recognised as official.[155] Had the Ukrainian language been chosen, it could have given rise to the neighbouring Ukrainian Soviet Republic wishing to take over the region.

Historians have until now failed to acknowledge the full significance of the part played by colonial and postcolonial ideas and actions in the post-war years following 1918. This presents future researchers with a major opportunity, and it will involve letting go of some stereotypes and opinions that have held sway for many years.

Social Democracy – Communism

Public discourse after 1918 was marked not only by the political ideas of liberalism, conservatism, monarchism and fascism, but also and especially by the political spectrum's left-leaning tendencies – which were themselves highly heterogeneous. The

· LABOUR'S · MAY · DAY ·
DEDICATED · TO · THE · WORKERS · OF · THE · WORLD ·

Fig. 41: At the founding congress of the Second Socialist International in 1889, May 1st was proclaimed the 'day of struggle of the workers' movement'.

Second [Socialist] International was founded in 1889, on the occasion of the centenary of the French Revolution. It included representatives from socialist parties with differing traditions and characters, whose shared cause was the improvement of the social conditions of workers and labourers and who aimed at political participation in their respective countries. Almost without exception, they claimed to be guided in their activities by Karl Marx's (1818-1883) analysis of social economics and social theory.[156]

This association, which encompassed so many countries, took a stand at the start of the 20th century against the spread of nationalism and the militarisation of European states, and in favour of strengthening the workers' movement. Meanwhile, socialist parties in Western European countries were gradually gaining a foothold in the decision-making

Fig. 42: Reaction to the Russian Revolution in *Vorwärts*, the leading newspaper of German Social Democrats, 9 November 1917.

processes of their respective countries. They gained seats in parliaments and in France played a part in government.[157] In Germany, the SPD was represented in the Reichstag, becoming a force to be reckoned with in industrial conurbations. Most regions and countries in East-Central Europe now had socialist or social democratic parties, though they were relatively small in places lacking a major industrial base. In Austria-Hungary, they played a growing part in political life, but remained relatively insignificant. In Tsarist Russia, workers' parties were officially persecuted, so the majority of the activists of the Russian Social Democratic Labour Party emigrated to Central and Western Europe.[158]

The beginning of the First World War in the summer of 1914 presented the socialist parties of Europe with a choice between international socialist pacifism and the nationalism of their respective homelands. Even before the outbreak of war, varying national traditions and the differences in social or-

ganisation and political participation in individual countries had made it difficult for the Second International to present a united front. When the war began the strong call to ultimate self-sacrifice, exclusive love for one's country and the rejection of the 'other' made it difficult for more than a small number of socialists to give up their emotional ties to their own nation.[159]

The decision on whether to approve war credits split German social democrats between the Majority Social Democratic Party (Mehrheitssozialdemokratie, MSPD) and the Independent Social Democratic Party (Unabhängige Sozialdemokratische Partei Deutschlands, USPD), as it was called from April 1917. Socialists in France were facing a similar situation in that they resolved to set aside their internal differences and joined forces with the 'bourgeois' in what they called the Sacred Union (Union Sacrée).[160] In 1914, opinion in the United Kingdom's Labour Party was divided on the question of the war, with the paci-

Fig. 43: More exulting reaction to the Russian Revolution in *l'Humanité*, the leading newspaper of French Socialists, 9 November 1917.

fist wing led by Ramsay MacDonald (1866-1937) on the one hand and the patriotic wing by Arthur Henderson (1863-1935) on the other. The party did not officially split, however, thanks to its federal nature: in spite of their differences, the various groups worked together in the War Emergency Workers' National Committee.[161]

Representatives from several socialist parties who were opposed to the war met in conference in September 1915 in Zimmerwald and in April 1916 in Kiental, and voiced their dissatisfaction with the policy of 'party truce' that most socialist parties had adopted. In one resolution, they condemned the war credits, and in another they swore total solidarity with the victims of the war. Representatives at the Kiental Conference formulated their determination

to engage in revolutionary class warfare. This split in the workers' movement between revolutionaries and reformists was to become a split between communists and social democrats just a few years later.[162]

Reactions to the October Revolution

The Bolshevik seizure of power on 6 and 7 November 1917[163] called into radical question all conventions on traditional policy in both internal and external matters. On the very next day, in an unprecedented move, the 'Decree on Peace' called for Russia's withdrawal from the war with immediate effect, and the country was handed over to the peasants a few days later. Outside Russia, these revolutionary actions were greeted with sympathy and admiration in left-

Fig. 44: V.I. Lenin in the box of the Tauride Palace in Petrograd during the session of the Constituent Assembly, 18 January 1918.

leaning circles, and with astonishment and horror among right-wing politicians and soon also among liberals. The Entente governments encouraged these reactions because they were seriously concerned at the loss of Russia's involvement as their ally on the Eastern Front. They were no less surprised when the Bolsheviks managed to hold on to power for longer than a couple of weeks or even months – even the majority of Bolsheviks themselves had hardly expected it.[164]

War-weary members and adherents of socialist parties welcomed the news from the banks of the Neva. This was especially true of the German social democrats, where both wings of the party viewed the Bolsheviks positively. This favourable perception was helped by the earlier enmity with the previous Russian government. In the view of Philipp Scheidemann (1865-1939), an important supporter of the MSPD, the revolution was a step towards freedom; the USPD spokesman Hugo Haase (1863-1919) expressed similar views.[165]

Red October offered a particular challenge to the socialist workers' parties in France, the United Kingdom and Italy in their self-perception and their traditions, as they had supported the International until 1914.[166] In France, both the left and the bourgeois right wing referenced the October Revolution, but events in Russia had less influence in the United Kingdom. The Labour Party, since its inception, had wanted to be a popular party under a social democratic banner. Unlike their French and Italian comrades, they avoided ideologically driven debates and on the whole were happy to follow the pragmatic Russia policies of the government under David Lloyd George (1863-1945).[167]

Socialists in France had undertaken to support the national war effort at the start of the war but had rescinded this support by early September 1917, and the October Revolution and its consequences polarised their numbers. It seemed possible that Russia and the Central Powers might sign a peace treaty that could lead to a prolongation of the war on the Western Front – an appalling prospect for the majority of French workers. However, they were unwilling to support the nationalist and anti-Bolshevik policies of Clemenceau and his new cabinet.[168]

The news from Petrograd divided opinions among members of the Italian Socialist Party (PSI). To most delegates and union representatives, the revolutionary fervour was a red rag to a bull, but they were concerned that the radical Bolshevik drive to achieve peace might bring Austro-Hungarian divisions to the hard-fought Italian front. Revolutionary PSI members, however, saw the Bolsheviks as harbingers of pacifism and of revived Marxism. The theoretician Antonio Gramsci (1891-1937) wrote that Lenin had liberated Marxism from its positivistic and naturalistic 'incrustations'.[169]

The Dissolution of the Constituent Assembly:
A Litmus Test

When the Bolsheviks violently dissolved the constituent assembly as a constitutional body on 19 January 1918, because they had lost control of the majority, this was experienced as an ideological caesura for the international workers' movement. The dividing line between democracy and dictatorship had been crossed, giving rise to an international problem of deep and immediate significance.[170]

In the eyes of German social democracy, for both the MSPD and the USPD, socialism and democracy were inextricably linked. Majority socialists such as Otto Braun (1872-1955) accused the Bolsheviks of 'putschism' and anarchy.[171] The independents, who counted the theorists Karl Kautsky and Rosa Luxemburg among their number, made different arguments. Kautsky maintained that socialism could only win through democracy, not against it. The proletarian revolution, he asserted, could in the long term only be the revolution of the vast majority if it was in the interests of that majority, not as an armed dictatorship of a minority over the majority. This assertion was in direct contradiction to Marx and led directly to the civil war.[172]

Rosa Luxemburg was keenly aware of the Bolsheviks' delicate position vis-à-vis the peace negotiations for Brest-Litovsk, issues of nationality, and other difficulties, but she was nevertheless critical of their use of force. It is against this background that

Die
Russische Revolution
Eine kritische Würdigung

Aus dem Nachlass von
Rosa Luxemburg

Herausgegeben und eingeleitet
von
Paul Levi

Verlag Gesellschaft und Erziehung G. m. b. H.
I 9 2 2

Fig. 45: German edition of Rosa Luxemburg's book *Russian Revolution*, published as a book after her death by Paul Levi in 1922.

we can understand her most famous utterance as a left-wing socialist in criticising a self-declared dictatorship by the proletariat: 'Freedom only for the members of the government, only for the members of the party – though they are quite numerous – is no freedom at all. Freedom is always the freedom of the one who thinks differently.'[173]

In April 1919, the French Section of the Workers' International (SFIO) made an explicit and positive statement on the consequences of the October Revolution, though they included a 'pragmatic' proviso that revolution should not be confused with violence.[174] Among French socialists 1917 revived the idea of revolution, which they closely linked to the storming of the Bastille in 1789 and the Paris Commune of 1871.[175] From 1920 onwards, they faced a strong communist wing within the movement, which two years later would give rise to the French Commu-

Fig. 46: A stamp of the Austro-Marxist Otto Bauer on the 100th anniversary of his birth in 1981.

nist Party (PCF), but unlike many other left-wing parties in Europe the SFIO remained true to traditional Marxism.[176]

In Eastern Europe, the Czech Social Democratic Party became a state-supported party in 1918, fully and unconditionally supportive of the independence of the new Czechoslovakia, but not in favour of revolutionary experiments on the Russian model. When the Communist Party was set up in 1921 as an offshoot of the social democrats, it was inspired by original left-wing socialist ideas rather than the Bolshevik guidelines that aimed to spark off revolution in Central and Western Europe.[177]

The Polish Communist Workers' Party (KPRP) was set up in 1918 and opposed Polish independence. In the war between Poland and Soviet Russia (1919-1921), it took the side of Soviet Russia, thus ensuring its own marginalisation within Polish society. Coversely, the Polish Socialist Party (PPS), on the other hand, pragmatically adopted a position in support of the national state and of Józef Piłsudski during the post-war years, and was thus able to rely on its very broad intellectual base among the nation's cultural milieus.[178]

Developments in the lands of the former Habsburg Monarchy took a different course from their neighbours. The social democrats in Austria developed their own specific 'Austro-Marxist' policies: republican, anti-Habsburg, revolutionary and consistent with the constitution. This complex mix prevented the development of a communist party in Austria where it was the forlorn hope of Otto Bauer (1881-1938), the founder of Austro-Marxism, that his integral form of socialism would provide a basis for the reunification of the two competing Internationals.[179]

It was a significantly different story in Hungary. The Károlyi government resigned in November 1918 in response to the incursion of Czechoslovak, Romanian and Serb troops into Hungarian territory. In the face of dissatisfaction among the wider population and among the returning soldiers, the social democratic and communist parties joined forces in March 1919 to become the Hungarian Socialist Party and declared the Soviet Republic; given their decisive response to the territorial claims of neighbouring countries, this was initially well received even in bourgeois circles.[180] Contrary to the widely circulated 'legally vindicated' claims of the counter-revolutionary government of Miklós Horthy (1868-1957) that subsequently overturned the Soviet Republic,[181] it was not being directed from Moscow.[182]

The Establishment of Communist Parties in 1919 and of the Third International

Under Lenin's leadership, the Third International (the Comintern) was set up in March 1919 in Moscow. The prevailing optimistic mood that followed the October Revolution produced a favourable blend of pacifism, revolution and modern democracy, and provided apparent links to scholarship influenced by Marxism. The new association offered an inviting, unencumbered alternative to the spirit of compromise of the Second International's ideology, as well as to the war policies approved by many of the social democratic parties that had led to the social and psychological destruction suffered by many European countries. Following the years of national narrow-

Fig. 47: Delegates to the Comintern's second congress at the Uritsky Palace in Petrograd, 19 July 1920. Those identifiable are: Lev Karakhan (second from left), Karl Radek (third, smoking), Nikolai Bukharin (fifth), Mikhail Lashevich (seventh, in uniform), Maxim Peshkov (Maxim Gorky's son, behind the column), Maxim Gorky (ninth, shaved), Vladimir Lenin (tenth, hands in pockets), Sergey Zorin (eleventh, with hat), Grigory Zinoviev (thirteenth, hands behind his back), Charles Francis Phillips (pseudonym Jesús Ramírez) (white shirt and tie), Manabendra Nath Roy (jacket and tie), Maria Ulyanova (nineteenth, white blouse), Nicola Bombacci (with beard) and Abram Belenky (with light hat).

mindedness and 'patriotic' demands, many socialists found the prospect of freedom for the working classes under the banner of a worldwide revolution attractive, especially since the revolutionaries in Soviet Russia were inspired by both Marx and Engels.[183]

In those socialist parties where the majority opted to remain in the Second International, polemical disputes about ideology often led to splits and then to the creation of communist parties.

For Moscow, Germany and its sophisticated social democracy was of key importance: Comintern officials widely understood that the world revolution they were expecting and loudly proclaiming could only succeed if it started with Germany, a central European country where the workers' movement had

such a strong tradition. The Bolsheviks consequently promoted the independent German social democrats (USPD), especially since the more recently established KPD in its early years followed Rosa Luxemburg in opposing statements emanating from Moscow, and refused to join the Comintern.[184]

A split among the social democrat/socialist groups between those who supported the Third International and those who rejected it was not only an inescapable evil, but was actively encouraged in the case of the USPD and other parties. As Karl Radek (1885-1939) said at the Second Comintern Congress in the spring of 1920, it was right to hound those of timid and weak revolutionary spirit out of the party with a red-hot iron.[185] Those wishing to join the Third

Fig. 48: Bertha von Suttner, portrayed in 1906 by Carl Pietzner.

and this – among other factors – undermined the democratic basis of the Weimar Republic and paved the way for the rise of the National Socialists. It did not take long for the antagonism between social democracy and communism to become so fundamental that their common roots, and the danger from the rising force of National Socialism, were both disastrously disregarded.[188]

The Role of Pacifism

Since long before the First World War, a group of intellectuals in various countries had been supporting a philosophy that opposed military confrontations on principle and campaigned for peaceful solutions to disagreements. They held this ethical position on the grounds of humanistic, religious or political conviction, and those whose position was political ranging from bourgeois to left-wing revolutionaries and anarchists. Those described as pacifists thus expressed a huge variety of opinions.

People such as the Austrian peace activist Bertha von Suttner (1843-1914), who had written the novel *Lay Down Your Arms (Die Waffen nieder!)*; fellow Austrian and writer Alfred Hermann Fried (1864-1921); the Russian novelist Lev N. Tolstoy (1828-1910); the Alsatian theologian and doctor Albert Schweitzer (1875-1965); the left-wing German writer Kurt Tucholsky (1890-1935); the Scottish Labour politician Ramsay MacDonald (1866-1937); the French socialist Édouard Herriot (1872-1957) – these all held very varied social and world views, but were united in their strongly held principle of peace.

The experience of world war served as a catalyst to those who held both nationalist and pacifist convictions. The veteran organisations the Fédération interalliée des anciens combattants (FIDAC, Interallied Federation of War Veterans) and the Conférence Internationale des associations de mutilés de guerre et anciens combattants (CIAMAC, International conference of associations of war disabled and veterans) had considerable influence on the issues of military and moral disarmament among former soldiers. Among campaigning veterans in Eastern Europe, memories of suffering and deprivation sustained the pacifist cause; pacifists distanced themselves from militarism and expressed their support for international cooperation, for example under the aegis of

International had to fulfil 21 conditions, some of them restrictive, and the USPD's resulting break-up was exactly what the Comintern had been intending. Moscow expected that the pure socialists who were fit and ready for revolution would join their cause, but this cost them dear: many European socialists – such as Paul Levi (1883-1930), Boris Souvarine (1895-1984) and Charles Rappoport (1865-1941) – became disillusioned.[186] These and other independent intellectual minds became prominent critics of Soviet Russian communism, yet managed to avoid becoming tainted by the anti-Bolshevik thinking that circulated widely in bourgeois and conservative circles and had quickly developed in the early 1920s into a form of integral nationalist ideology laced with blatant anti-Semitism.[187]

The critics mentioned above were discredited as renegades and pursued. Within a few years the Comintern was disparaging those social democrats who stuck by the Second International as 'social fascists',

Fig. 49: Anti-war demonstration of SPD and USPD on the Schlossplatz in Berlin, 31 July 1921.

the League of Nations, as part of a proactive peace movement.[189]

In May 1920, the International Congress of War Wounded met in Tours; participants attended from France, Germany, the United Kingdom, Italy, Austria and Belgium. There were no veterans present from Poland, Czechoslovakia, the Baltic states or Soviet Russia. These countries were involved in wars over disputed borders and to establish new states, and moreover they set little store by matters to do with wellbeing and pensions. From the mid-1920s, however, veterans from these East-Central European countries began to take an active part in the pacifist work of the FIDAC, the CIAMAC and the International Congress of War Wounded. The Poles were reluctant to reject violence fully; aware of Germany's widespread revisionism of borders, and of the need to ensure that their country could defend itself, they promoted a defensive pacifism.

In the nations of Eastern Europe, the political implications of developing pacifism were very different from those in Western Europe. Those who expressed their pacifist views in public were to a large extent adherents of various Christian confessions. They were even isolated within their churches, of which many were more or less official state churches and therefore supportive of the military policies of the country concerned. Pacifism also enjoyed a significantly lower level of support among the intellectual elite in Eastern Europe than it did, for example, in Germany or in France.[191] The Polish writer Józef Wittlin, mentioned above, had experienced the First World War as a young man; he expressed his criticism of war in numerous essays and poems, and especially in his novel *Sól ziemi* 1935 (published in English translation as *The Salt of the Earth* in 1939). It was surely no coincidence that the historian Stanisław Estreicher (1869-1939) wrote about the love of peace in Poland

Fig. 50: French pacifist film 'J'accuse', directed by Abel Gance, France 1919.

in early modern times, but in his contemporary context of the military cult of the year 1930.[192]

Even in Czechoslovakia, where the leading politicians engaged conceptually with the idea of the new peace order in Europe that was an essential safeguard for their country, realistic expectations predominated in day-to-day decisions. The foreign minister Edvard Beneš (1884-1948) worked together with the League of Nations to design a security system that relied on arbitration and support agreements.[193] In Romania, the concept of pacifism was associated only with well-known individuals. One of these was the artist Octav Băncilă (1872-1944), who worked at the Academy in Iași. His socialist views influenced his choice of artistic subjects: the war, social injustice and the anti-Semitism that was endemic to Romanian society. Generally speaking, pacifism in Eastern Europe was found only among marginal groups and those who espoused left-wing politics, and it never gained the status of a mass movement.

In the immediate post-war years, there was a widespread sense of war-weariness in Germany, including among intellectual circles. It did not, however, evolve into a larger political movement. The journalist Carl von Ossietzky (1889-1938), who described himself as a pacifist, complained about this and wrote in a disenchanted essay on 4 October 1924 that German pacifism was 'always illusory, raving, obsessed by attitude, suspicious of the means used in politics, and suspicious of leaders who made use of these means'.[194] It was, he wrote, 'a world view, a religion, a dogma', and was therefore significantly different from the pacifism practiced in other countries.

In countries such as Poland, Czechoslovakia, Austria, Hungary and Romania, and indeed in the early USSR, it became especially popular to learn and speak Esperanto, a language devised by the Polish Jewish doctor Ludwik Lazar Zamenhof (1859-1917) in the year 1887.[195] Zamenhof, inspired by a utopian vision in which all peoples understood each other, had created Esperanto to serve as an international language that would serve to create and preserve peace. Esperanto was most widely spoken during the 1920s, yet even then, Esperantists were unable to promote their language sufficiently as a serious competitor to French and English, which were spoken across the world. The Esperantist conference in Prague in 1921 and the setting up of an Esperanto museum in the Vienna Hofburg in 1927 were also unable to raise the language's profile as much as they had hoped.

Revisionism

One of the greatest threats to peace in Eastern Europe arose from a particular form of political revisionism that consisted in querying the provisions of the Paris Peace Conference and calling them into question. The term 'revisionism' is used here to describe a tendency to interrogate a particular situation and to seek to re-examine it. Patterns of thought and interpretation can, for example, be reinvestigated in terms of philosophy, historiography or sociology. In the context of the history of Eastern, East-Central and South-Eastern Europe in the years immediately following the First World War, revisionism was a political endeavour to invalidate established agreements (treaty revisionism) and/or to reverse territorial losses (territorial revisionism). The countries most concerned in such practices during the interwar years were the former Central Powers: Germany, Austria, Hungary and Bulgaria.

The Entente nations stipulated that the German Empire should cede territory to Poland (the Poznań region, West Prussia, Eastern Upper Silesia and some smaller portions of Lower Silesia), Czechoslovakia (Hlučín), France (Alsace-Lorraine), Belgium (Eupen and Malmédy) and Denmark (Northern Schleswig). The Treaty of Saint-Germain forced Austria to cede South Tirol and the Val Canale to Italy; and Lower Styria, the Mieß (Meža) river valley south of the Karawanks mountain range to the kingdom of the

Die Zerstückelung Deutschlands.

Vom Reiche sollen in Ost und West 5½ Millionen Deutsche getrennt werden!

Fig. 51: 'Die Zerstückelung Deutschlands' (Germany's Amputation), a map published by the Gea Verlag in Berlin in 1919 during the Paris Peace Conference, showing Germany's territorial and economic losses.

Serbs, Croats and Slovenes. Politicians during the Italian Risorgimento had already tried, in the second half of the 19th century, to incorporate into the Italian kingdom territory as far north as the Brenner. As one of the victor nations in the First World War, Italy succeeded in forcing Austria to make the concession at the Paris Peace Conference. The territorial cession to Italy included the parts of Tyrol south of the main alpine ridges, including Bolzano, Bressanone and Merano. The description 'South Tyrol' has only been in general use since that time. The other description of the area was 'Oberetsch', the equivalent to the Italian 'Alto Adige', itself derived from the French 'Département du Haut-Adige' that had existed between 1810 and 1813. Austria retained its claim over South Tyrol, arguing that the majority of the area's population spoke German as their mother tongue.[196]

The Entente powers were especially hard on Hungary, as part of the Habsburg Empire, for its participation in the war on the side of the Central Powers. In military confrontations with Serb, Croat, Czechoslovakian and Romanian units during 1918/19, Hungary

61

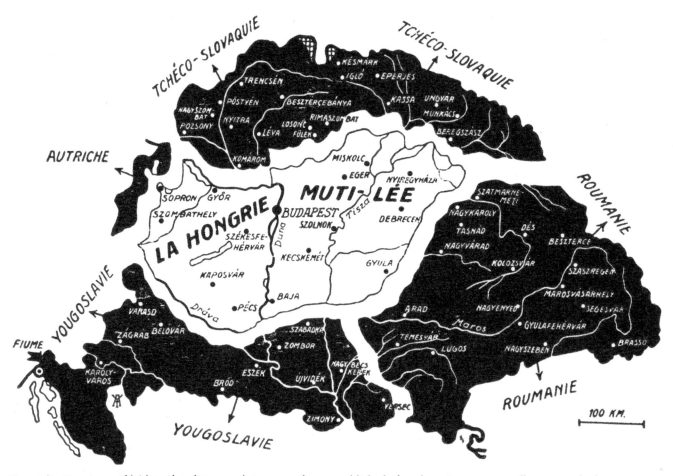

Fig. 52: 'La Hongie mutilée' (Mutilated Hungary), Propaganda map published after the Trianon Treaty, illustrating the lost Hungarian territories.

had already de facto lost more than two-thirds of its original territory. The peace agreements at Trianon on 4 June 1920 in effect confirmed the status quo, with the exception of Burgenland, which was to be ceded to the Republic of Austria in 1921.

Bulgaria was required by the Treaty of Neuilly-sur-Seine to cede Northern Thrace to the Entente (and subsequently to Greece) and the regions around Caribrod, Bosilegrad and Strumica to the Kingdom of the Serbs, Croats and Slovenes; the treaty also confirmed that Southern Dobruja was to be returned to Romania.[197]

These territorial changes all had long-term demographic, human and psychological implications, and this in turn provoked attempts at revisionism. The methods used to underpin these revisionist efforts ranged from diplomatic negotiations through to persuasive propaganda, territorial claims, paramilitary

action and military threats. A country making such claims often had to start by convincing its own population of the need to make the claim. Private individuals and national figures alike used media such as political speeches, books, leaflets, postcards, films and large display maps to convince those both in the country and abroad of their cause. Following 1918, the government used local folklore associations and scholarly institutes in the German Reich as significant political tools, as their actions would not be seen as officially representing the state, even though they might receive governmental support. Two such organisations were the German Foreign Institute (Deutsches Ausland-Institut, DAI), founded in Stuttgart in 1917, and the newly created Stiftung für deutsche Volks- und Kulturbodenforschung (a foundation for research into German folklore and cultural lands) in Leipzig; the Association for Germanness

Abroad (Verein für das Deutschtum im Ausland, VDA) and the Deutscher Schutzbund für das Grenz- und Auslanddeutschtum (a German defence league for Germans moved from borderlands and other nations, DSB) encouraged revisionist aims among many population groups. In 1925, the geographer Albrecht Penck (1858-1945) developed a map of 'German settlement and cultural lands', in which he identified many areas that had never belonged to Germany even before the provisions of the Treaty of Versailles. The map, and the intention behind it, revealed the desire for an outright revision and was the harbinger of future expansionist aims.[198]

In Austria, the League of Sudeten Germans (Sudetendeutscher Heimatbund, SHB) and the Southern March Association (Verein Südmark) were influential as ethnic community groups. Both maintained close links with similar organisations in Germany. The idea of reuniting 'German Austria' with Germany had been broached in 1918, but it was rejected by the Allies as well as Prussian German politicians and wide sections of Austrian society, who feared that they would be diminished as an appendix of the German Reich.

In Hungary, the government declared territorial revisionism a key principle of official policy. Magyar flags stood at half-mast until 1938, and school children had to pray daily before the start of lessons for their nation's rebirth. The geographer Pál Teleki (1879-1941), the acting prime minister, referred to a suggestive ethnic map – the 'carte rouge' – in which the bright red colour used to indicate the distribution of Hungarians in the Danube and Carpathian region made them far more prominent than members of other ethnic groups in the area.[199] Any revisionist claims Hungary made, however, stayed within the bounds of the areas that had belonged to the Kingdom of Hungary before 1918.

The Bulgarians found it hard to get over the loss of Southern Dobruja, which included the two districts of Durostor and Kaliakra and the Black Sea coast near Kap Kaliakra and Balčik so beloved by artists. Bulgarian authorities engaged in lively propaganda activity in support of the allegedly 'ancient' Bulgarian claim to the region. Paramilitary units were active in Southern Dobruja in the 1920s, mainly terrorising Romanian residents and offices in the area, and these caused particular concern.

The political rhetoric in the affected areas was infused with a range of nostalgic, historical and economic arguments as the situation required, drawing on biological and medical imagery of 'mutilation', 'amputation' and 'viability' to support them. From the 1920s onwards, English Labour politicians such as David Lloyd George (1863–1945) were increasingly inclined to support the claims for revision, whereas France was one of the least inclined nations to do so. Revisionism ultimately paved the way for the violent reordering of Europe during the 1930s: the return of the Saar in 1935, the occupation of the demilitarised Rhineland in 1936, the Austrian Anschluss, the Munich Agreement and the First Vienna Award in 1938, the occupation of the Memel region and of the remaining parts of Czechoslovakia in 1939 – and, as a consequence, the outbreak of the Second World War.

Modernisation

What people understand by 'modernisation' is inconsistent, fluid and at times contradictory due to the number of, often divergent, attempts to define the essential nature of the process of 'modernising' societies. They have thus far produced a great deal of literature, which cannot be adequately cited at this point due to the diversity of formulated research proposals. Max Weber's classic proposition, which often serves as a reference point for ruminations on modernity, is inherently complex. It simultaneously emphasises the primacy of the rationalisation of the human place in the world, crucial for European modernity and the way in which human activities are undertaken within it, and also the specificity of the Protestant ethic.[200] The way in which modernisation is defined is also influenced by differing assessments of its impact. Some envision modernity as an era in which human societies aim to democratically organise the framework in which they function, where technical and scientific progress removes the obstacles to development. Others, however, emphasise the dark side of modernisation – a break with traditional values, the loss of sources of identity, the excessive influence of technology and the dehumanising effect of rationalisation on the lives of individuals and human communities. Regardless of these differences, as Charles Taylor, a key theorist of modernity, has pointed out, it is still vital to distinguish between see-

63

Fig. 53: Painting 'Iron and Coal' by William Bell Scott, 1855-1860.

acting phenomena: industrialisation, technical progress, social mobility (migration for work, development of public transport), the development of communication systems (post, radio, telegraph), the development of soft economic infrastructure (technology and the logistics of financial transactions), growth of urbanisation, transformation of the family and the roles of its members, as well as social emancipation, which now casts social contrasts and tensions in a different light. In the cultural realm, on the other hand, the dynamic relationship between science and religion shaped modernisation's main front, bringing about clear progress in secularisation, but also a seemingly paradoxical intensification of theological debate and the search for ways of satisfying spiritual needs as an alternative to traditional religions.[202]

Economic and political liberalism, usually considered a manifestation of modernisation, did not always coincide in political theory and practice, and the relationship between them varied among European countries. This obviously increased tensions between traditional power structures and the economic activity of individuals and social groups. At the same time, it entailed a reshuffling of the social structure, especially given the rapid development of the bourgeoisie and its importance to the power structure. Intellectual perspectives of these reshuffles were, in turn, formed by the simultaneous development of various conflicting and interrelated political ideologies: conservatism, nationalism and socialism.

Describing the modernisation process in such general terms makes it possible to investigate the nature of the changes that determined its shape during the war and in the post-war period. As for the progress of political and economic modernisation in post-war Europe, the expected democratic revolution, as Norman Davies put it, proved to be an illusion, and technological and economic acceleration was severely hampered by the economic crisis at the end of the 1920s.[203] As Davies recalls, although the number of European republics increased from three before 1914 to sixteen after the end of the war, most of them soon repealed or abolished democratic principles in various ways.[204] The war was obviously an important impulse for the development of military technology. For example, the first tank was constructed in 1916, the first liquid fuel rocket in 1926 and an aircraft turbojet engine in 1930. However, there was also technologi-

ing modernisation as a process that in effect creates different civilisations with their own specific cultures: from regarding it as a process of change which, in any culture is always characterised by increasing secularisation of the prevailing worldview, by domination of instrumental reason and by an increase in scientific awareness.[201] In the former case, one thinks of the pluralism of various forms of human civilisation, among which European modernity is only one of many, with a specific culture understood as a regulatory system. In the latter, the focus is on the cultural neutrality of the modernisation process leading to a modern model, regardless of the cultural specificity of the community subject to modern development.

The main purpose of this publication is to describe the reality of Europe after the First World War, so we will omit here more detailed deliberations on the nature of modernisation, its sources and the impulses that trigger and sustain it. The transformation of a traditional agricultural society into an urban society experiencing industrialisation is complex. In determining the way of life of individuals and communities, we are therefore assuming that post-war modernisation was a continuation of the complex modernisation process of the 19th century. It consisted of an entire range of interconnected and intercal progress in many other areas after the war: the electric refrigerator appeared in 1917, the wristwatch in 1919, BBC radio in 1922, the small format camera (the 35 mm Leica, for example) in 1925, experimental television in 1926, the use of penicillin in 1928, and in 1931 the electron microscope enabled people to see previously unknown aspects of reality.

Europe's industrialisation nevertheless followed an irregular course, with a growing chasm in post-war years between industrialised and rural areas throughout the entire continent, and particularly in some specific countries. At times, the divisions deepened: Italy, for example, had an economically developed modern north and poor south. Moreover, the post-war recession caused high unemployment, which vitally affected the newly formed post-war republics that had an agricultural rather than an industrial profile, and faced tension between retained elements of an economic structure inherited from the past and the dynamic conferred by a new geography and the global economy. For example, the loss of the Russian market due to the revolution and the appearance of a border between independent Poland and Russia led to a 75% loss of production at the thriving textile centre in Łódź which, before the war, had been within the former Russian partition.[205]

However, the most important feature of post-war modernisation – in the widest sense, including political, social, economic and cultural phenomena – was the culmination in the years between the start of the war and the mid-1930s of criticism of the course of modernisation and its effects, which had been increasing over several decades. Modernisation processes had come to be perceived and described in terms of demise and degeneration in all its aspects: physical, social and spiritual. As Roger Griffin states, calls were made within the broad discourse at that time not only to reverse the negative consequences of modernisation, but also to shed its Enlightenment roots that degraded the environment of the individual, depleting him of vital strength and depriving him of physical and spiritual health.[206] There was a simultaneous proliferation of projects and ideological, political and social movements whose main motto was to regenerate degraded reality and fallen humanity.

The term 'regeneration' itself can, in some sense, be considered a key word to define this specific mod-

Fig. 54: Leica Model Ia, produced 1925-1936.

ernisation formula, which Griffin termed modernism, and covering a very diverse and broad front of regenerative projects and activities, including artistic ones. Their main goal, however, was not historical regression or rejection of modernity in general with its technological progress, scientific development and egalitarian tendencies in transforming society. On the contrary, as probably the most characteristic feature of Griffin's concept, those who advocated regeneration on many fronts sought to create a new version of modernity devoid of the flaws of its initial post-Enlightenment wave: to create a modernised world that was healthier, fairer and more rational. Perhaps, above all, they attempted to create a 'New Man', a more perfect embodiment, both intellectually and spiritually, who was both subject and object of an efficient social organisation. The time of the First World War particularly increased the sense that a re-generational cure for the world was needed, because this was a liminal and transitional time. It was experienced as a period of spiritual chaos that should be overcome in a new way, because religion was being called into question as the world's foundation.

Negative assessment of the first wave of modernity and its effects produced another consequence crucial to understanding the dynamics of modernism, namely the regenerators' specific attitude toward time and tradition. Contrary to popular belief, modernisers of the world and in art did not reject the past as such, but rather focused on what was to come. Criticism, in its most intense form, was levelled at the most recent past (even if it meant the Renaissance

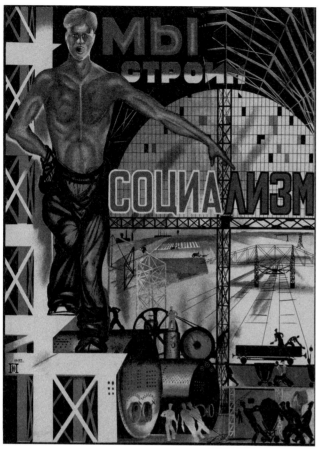

Fig. 55: A futuristic poster: 'We are building socialism', painted by Yuri Ivanovich Pimenov, 1927.

era). In fact, regeneration-oriented reformers directed their attentions toward a distant past in which they sought sources of regenerative energy in the form of forgotten patterns, principles and values that they intended to discover, extract and, very significantly, adapt and build a better version of the modern world. Accordingly, modernists considered the past to be crucial for building the future. This aspect of modernist thought thus makes it possible to understand the role (and importance) that the reformers' understanding of primeval [primordial] societies, the imaginary worlds of primitive and folk culture, as well as assumptions on the nature of childish creativity played in their projects.

In the sphere of art, the nature, scope and degree of radicalisation that artists undertook in response to the multifaceted call for regeneration can adequately be called 'modernism'.[207] Such an understanding of modernism would, naturally be diverse given the variety of regenerative ideologies, political orientations

and social initiatives that artists chose to associate themselves with, and the intensity of this association: the various forms of poetry and the styles they chose; what aspects of tradition they accepted or negated; and how they expressed and attained their artistic objectives. However, artists were always concerned with the need, conceived in re-generational categories – to renew society, people and their environment. Artistic modernism, in this sense, is thus an element of a broader re-generational front of countless renewal initiatives, a collection of social movements focusing on various forms of art interspersed with other non-artistic social initiatives. Obviously, the multifaceted European reform movement comprised of a vast number of reform campaigns is not the same as modernism according to Griffin. However, there is no doubt that this movement increasingly stridently referred to the positive and negative effects of civilisational development over time in the post-war period, and began to be influenced by various progressive political ideologies, national ideas, and achievements in many areas of contemporary science. The latter frequently assumed orderly organisational forms; these were then often institutionalised by state agendas and implemented via systemic social reconstruction instruments such as cooperatives.

Griffin's interpretative perspective also allows us to see variants of modernisation arising from the incredibly radical intensity of many of its intertwined aspects: rejection of a metaphysical basis, logistic rationalisation, conviction of the need for a regenerative mission, and utopian projects organising social reality within a properly ordered space prepared to welcome a 'New Man'. From this standpoint, the most radical experiments of planned modernisation in history were the revolutionary Soviet political and social reconstruction of the country as well as the Nazi and fascist revolt: both, in some aspects, equally as radical as each other.

Russian communists sought to destroy the existing social structure and create a new one, in its essence regenerative, because the classless society of Marxist ideology in some ways echoed the simplicity of prehistoric societies. A 'New Man' was to be created through a revolutionary process as a member of the new society: physically and spiritually superior, while intellectually comparable to Aristotle (384-322 BC),

Johann Wolfgang von Goethe (1749-1832) and Karl Marx – as envisioned by Leon Trotsky (1879-1940).[208] The Soviet modernisation plan covered all areas of life, eliminating private ownership, destroying family structure, collectivising agriculture and emphasising heavy industry such as machine manufacturing and chemical processing. The state pursued a forced growth rate without regard for social costs, whereas militarisation and widespread terror became the tools for radical modernisation. The symbol of this Faustian modernisation was the network of Soviet labour camps, the Gulag, whose prisoners worked on large construction projects (the White Sea Canal, the reconstruction of Moscow). In the 1930s, they made up 10% of the entire Soviet population, thus rendering the Gulag the largest employer in Europe in 1939.[209]

Nazism can also be characterised as the outcome of a similarly radical modernist project of total change, especially addressing culture in its broadest sense as a tool for forging a 'New Man' with the help of state power. In many European countries, modern artists and supporters of their art were linked with this general idea.

In June 1933, for example, the German National Socialist Students Association began a campaign to grant official recognition to German modernists such as Emil Nolde (1867-1956), Ernst Barlach (1870-1938), Erich Heckel (1883-1970) and Karl Schmidt-Rottluff (1884-1976) as an embodiment of the culture-forming mission of National Socialism, wholeheartedly supported by Joseph Goebbels – a proponent of artistic modernism at the time.[210] Hitler, who indulged in a modernised academism and did not share Goebbels's modernist aesthetic preferences, swiftly quashed these modernist impulses. However, it was not Goebbels' aesthetic preferences that characterised him as a modernist but, as Griffin writes, his deep conviction that the institutional and organisational might of a modern state could be employed to create a new national culture and a new historic era.

Germany's rebirth was to be unified by a total culture not only expressing the race's genius, but also embodying a new 'nomos' while also and laying the foundations of an organic community mandating solutions to problems created by the modern world. A central element of Goebbels' vision was the power of the latest mass communication technology at the

Fig. 56: Barbara and Stanisław Brukalski, Warsaw Housing Cooperative, unit no VII, house B, 1932-1937 in Warsaw.

time, which proved to be an ideal tool for bringing the new culture to life.[211] Its novelty was its paradoxical nature, because it stemmed from the alleged need to restore the previously functioning world order – now depraved by Christianity, the Enlightenment and industrialisation – which, as we have seen, had to be rejected and tamed to regain the original state of culture.[212]

In this perspective, Nazism, like modernism in general in the sense proposed by Griffin, proved to be a product of Europe's spiritual crisis. It was caused, people thought, by materialism and rationalism, which, in the face of the collapse of confidence in traditional religions, led to the expansion of theosophy, alternative medicine, neo-paganism, and yoga; as well as various aspects of life reform such as in the areas of body culture, changes in sexuality and social hygiene.

Italian fascism was perhaps less radical in terms of reconstructing society. However, here as well, as Giovanni Gentile (1875-1944) clearly states, was the idea of the state imposing an ethic of regeneration that was to overcome the atomisation and egoism that had emerged during the first phase of modernity in a

Fig. 57: Russian refugees walk on a rural road in November 1915.

liberal society.[213] From this standpoint fascist doctrine was to be a new secular theology, whose task was to spiritually form the 'New Man' – the main goal of its civilisational mission.[214] Evident in all of these three cases – Russian communism, German Nazism and Italian fascism – are local manifestations of pan-European modernism that in the wake of the First World War proved to be an ideological charge leading to another catastrophic conflict.

Fourth Section

Flight and Emigration to the West

Those who fled and emigrated from Eastern Europe, bringing with them their memories of home, were both numerically and socially significant. A particular aspect of the violence experienced during the First World War was that within a few weeks, hundreds of thousands of civilians who had been living in the theatres of war lost their homes and had to flee. At the start of the war, large numbers of expulsions and deportations stemmed particularly from Russia. The Tsarist authorities suspected not only Germans but also Jews in the Western provinces of being disloyal. By the end of 1915, they had either deported or forced 2.7 million people into inland Russia; by July 1917, the number had grown to at least 7 million refugees and evacuees.[215]

The resettlements, deportations and expulsions that occurred in Eastern Europe after the First World War were largely due to nationalist ideas fuelled by the concept of homogeneity and a strong need for security; few people felt comfortable with the idea of living with those who were ethnically or politically 'other'. Other major factors were increased poverty and the danger of illness in the years following the war. For millions of Jews, Armenians and other similar groups disadvantaged by their ethnic or religious affiliations, emigration seemed the only way out of their difficulties, especially when they did not have the option of moving back to a kin state.[216]

Many who had been uprooted from home were seeking to flee Russia and move to Western Europe or the USA. This conflict dynamic also encompassed regions in Eastern Europe where those related not only to minority but also to majority ethnic groups wished to escape from the violence caused by political and ethno-nationalist differences; they moved either to their kin state or to a state where they thought they would find better economic opportunities and political security.[217]

The territorial changes resulting from the Paris Peace Treaties, and from the establishment of new states in East-Central Europe, meant that hundreds of thousands of people lived in states where the titular nationality did not correspond to their own ethnic origins. The countries where this was the case were the particular targets of revisionist claims. The Minorities Treaties, which the Entente nations energetically promoted, obliged Poland, Czechoslovakia, Greece, Yugoslavia and Romania to ensure that minority ethnic groups were given basic human rights protection. There were, nevertheless, also large migration movements by the ethnic minority groups concerned about being unable to carry out their chosen profession – for example in public service if they were not sufficiently fluent in the state language – or their children could not be educated in their mother tongue.[218]

Fig. 58: Jewish refugees in Rowne, Poland, 1921.

In the early 1920s, for example, over 600,000 Germans left the Polish region that had formerly been part of Prussia. At least 100,000 migrated into the German Reich from Eastern Upper Silesia which, in 1922, was awarded to Poland. Around 150,000 Bulgarian refugees from the surrounding nations sought safety in the reduced state of Bulgaria.[219]

Fig. 59: Crowd of emigrants in the shipping office of the Red Star-American Line, Warsaw, 1921.

Fig. 60: Nansen passport of a Russian refugee, 1922.

In Hungary, however, political upheavals following 1918 caused much less migration. After the signing of the Trianon Treaty in June 1920, 425,000 Hungarians migrated from Slovakia, Romania, Serbia and Croatia into the part of the region that was still Hungary.[220] After the Hungarian Soviet Republic came to a violent end, however, several tens of thousands fled for fear of the 'white terror'. These political refugees, which included bourgeois intellectuals, often had to leave the country via adventurous routes and using false documents. Most were heading for Austria, althoug many also went to Czechoslovakia, and some to Romania and Yugoslavia, especially if they had been born in those places and could still claim citizenship.[221]

Furthermore, it was not only from Hungary that people 're-migrated'. Miners who had moved from Upper Silesia to the Ruhr then moved back in their thousands after 1918. They were inspired not only by the expectation of a boom in the coal-mining industry in their 'old home', but also by the establishment of the new Polish state.[222]

The collapse of the Tsarist Empire and the subsequent revolution and devastating civil war gave rise to the largest-ever movement of refugees and emigrants in European history. By 1922, around two million Russian civilians had left their home country, and about six million war refugees and evacuees moved to a different region within Soviet Russia.[223] In the confusion of the revolution, more than a million Poles fled from house and home in Russia.

The Russian Revolution was a social revolution, but it was also a call to egalitarianism – to creating a widespread homogenisation within the former Russian Empire. The vision of a 'new' society induced a levelling of living conditions and life ambitions. Here people felt compelled to adapt to new expectations in order to avoid being identified as a 'class enemy'.[224] This led to serious social, political and cultural consequences across the country. A large number of the most competent and independent minds had emigrated; this loss of much cultural wealth, combined with the political backwardness so long attributed to Russia, hindered any chance it might have had to develop an alternative democratic identity.

Russian emigrants principally settled in the capital cities of Germany, France, Yugoslavia and Bulgaria, and in Harbin in China. They were mainly from the upper classes of former Russian society, and in Soviet Russia had been under threat of repression: dispossession, imprisonment or even the death penalty. The first wave of emigrants as a result were from the nobility, a large number of the administrative and cultural elites, as well as senior military officers. They had fought on the side of the White Russians in the civil war and had been almost as deeply involved as the Red Russians in pogroms, mass shootings and other acts of extreme violence. The emigrants also included First World War Russian prisoners of war, ethnic Germans and many others who emigrated to escape extreme poverty.[225]

There were disproportionately high numbers of Eastern European Jews among the emigrants, fleeing

Fig. 61: Russian Balalajka Orchestra in Berlin, 1920s.

poverty, want and pogroms. Countries next to Russia were unwilling to receive them and instead treated them with hostility and moved many on to other countries.[226] Hundreds of thousands of Jews were helped by Jewish charitable organisations, and many were helped to emigrate to the United States.[227] A full spectrum of political views from Tsarist Russia was to be found among the Russian émigrés: representatives of the left and of liberal democracy, and many monarchists, but no Bolsheviks. The émigré communities were held together by little more than their shared rejection of Bolshevism, which barely concealed the social and political differences among them.[228]

These new arrivals, especially when they did not speak the local language (well), were more severely affected than the local populations by the worldwide economic and employment crisis in the years following 1918. Their status became even more fragile when in December 1921 the All-Russian Central Executive Committee and the Council of People's Commissars deprived exiles of their Russian citizenship, making them stateless overnight. Given this situation, in 1922 the League of Nations created a high commission for refugees, led by the highly respected former polar explorer, diplomat and Nobel Peace prize-winner, Fridtjof Nansen (1861-1930), who introduced the famous 'Nansen passport' for stateless refugees. The passport was recognised by 32 governments until 1923, and it offered considerable help to those who were granted one.[229]

Russian emigration and its consequences cannot, however, be adequately described only in terms of their deficiency and difficulties. In Paris, Berlin and Prague especially, but also elsewhere, cultural and intellectual life between the wars was tremendously enriched by Russian artists, academics, writers and musicians, and an authentic interest in Russia was kept alive in these places. Groups of émigrés also maintained political activity in the vague hope that they might one day be able to return to Russia. Their conspicuous anti-Bolshevism attracted some attention and support, especially in conservative circles in Central and Western Europe, and among the *Freikorps*, whose anti-Bolshevism was tainted with anti-Semitism and inspired by an ideology of integration that targeted both internal and external enemies.[230]

71

Endnotes

1. For a changing perception, see for instance Robert Gerwarth, *The Vanquished. Why the First World War failed to end, 1917-1923* (London: Allen Lane, 2016); translated version into German, Die Besiegten. *Das blutige Erbe des Ersten Weltkriegs* (München: Siedler, 2017).

2. After the 1916 Easter Rising in Dublin, which British authorities violently suppressed, the supporters of Irish independence gained the upper hand in Irish politics. The opposition of pro-British, mostly Protestant forces in Ulster and mostly Catholic independentists led to the Irish War of Independence (1919-1921), followed by the civil war (1922-1923) between forces of the Provisional Government and the Irish Republican Army (IRA). The government won this conflict, which led to the emergence of the Free State of Ireland – and the ongoing split of (British) Northern Ireland and the republican South. For further reading, see for instance Tim Pat Coogan, 1916: *One Hundred Years of Irish Independence: From the Easter Rising to the Present* (New York: Thomas Dunne Books, 2016).

3. Jay Winter's keynote at the conference 'Central and Eastern Europe after the First World War,' 31 January-2 February 2018 in Berlin.

4. Robert Gerwarth and John Horne, 'Paramilitarismus in Europa nach dem Ersten Weltkrieg. Eine Einleitung,' in *Krieg im Frieden: Paramilitärische Gewalt in Europa nach dem Ersten Weltkrieg*, eds. Robert Gerwarth, John Horne (Göttingen: Wallstein, 2013), 13; see Jochen Böhler, Włodzimierz Borodziej and Joachim von Puttkamer, 'Introduction,' in *Legacies of Violence: Eastern Europe's First World War*, eds. Jochen Böhler, Włodzimierz Borodziej and Joachim von Puttkamer (München: DeGruyter Oldenbourg, 2014), 1-9, here 1.

5. Marko Simić, *Auf den Spuren der Isonzofront* (Klagenfurt et al.: Mohorjeva Hermagoras, 2004).

6. Antonio Melis, *Il Piave sulle tracce della Grande Guerra* (Treviso: Editoriale Programma, 2014).

7. Frithjof Benjamin Schenk, 'Tannenberg/Grunwald,' in *Deutsche Erinnerungsorte* vol. 1, eds. Étienne François and Hagen Schulze (München: C.H. Beck 2001), 438-453.

8. Paweł Kutaś, *Cmentarze z I wojny światowej w powiecie gorlickim. Przewodnik* (Zakrzów: Wydawnictwo PROMO, 2015). See also Isabel Röskau-Rydel, 'Die Wahrnehmung des galizischen Kriegsschauplatzes in Kriegsberichten, Tagebuchaufzeichnungen und Erinnerungen von Deutschen und Österreichern,' in *Mutter: Land – Vater: Staat. Loyalitätskonflikte, politische Neuorientierung und der Erste Weltkrieg im österreichisch-russländischen Grenzraum*, eds. Florian Kührer-Wielach and Markus Winkler (Regensburg: Verlag Friedrich Pustet, 2017), 19-40.

9. This tourist route has been extended to other parts of Poland's national territory.

10. Cf. Jörn Leonhard, 'Legacies of Violence: Eastern Europe`s First World War – A Commentary from a Comparative Perspective,' in *Legacies of Violence*, 319-326, here 323.

11. Ernest Beck, *Brancusi's Endless Column Ensemble, Târgu Jiu, Romania* (New York: Scala, 2007).

12. George L. Mosse, *Fallen Soldiers. Reshaping the Memory of the World Wars (New York, Oxford: Oxford University Press 1990)*; see Liulevicius, Kriegsland im Osten; Piotr J. Wróbel, 'The Seeds of Violence. The Brutalization of an East European Region, 1917-1921,' *Journal of Modern European History* 1 (2003), 125-149.

13. Wolfgang Schivelbusch, *Die Kultur der Niederlage: Der amerikanische Süden 1865/ Frankreich 1871/ Deutschland 1918* (Berlin: Alexander Fest Verlag, 2001).

14. Aviel Roshwald, *Ethnic Nationalism and the Fall of Empires: Central Europe, the Middle East and Russia, 1914-23* (New York-London: Routledge, 2001); Alexander V. Prusin, *The lands between: Conflict in the East European borderlands, 1870-1992* (Oxford: Oxford University Press, 2010), 87-89.

15. Gerwarth, Horne, 'Paramilitarismus in Europa,' 14.

16. See Burkhard Olschowsky's article in this volume.

17. Dan Diner, *Das Jahrhundert verstehen: Eine universalhistorische Deutung* (München: Luchterhand, 1999), 85; Christoph Mick, 'Vielerlei Kriege: Osteuropa 1918-1921,' in *Formen des Krieges: Von der Antike bis zur Gegenwart*, eds. Dietrich Beyrau, Michael Hochgeschwender and Dieter Langewiesche (Paderborn: Schöningh Verlag, 2007), 311-326.

18. Gerwarth, Horne, 'Paramilitarismus in Europa', 13.

19. Wolfgang Schieder, *Faschistische Diktaturen: Studien zu Italien und Deutschland* (Göttingen: Wallstein, 2008), 99-102.

20. T. K. Wilson. *Frontiers of Violence: Conflict and Identity in Ulster and Upper Silesia 1918-1922* (Oxford: Oxford University Press, 2011); Jochen Böhler, *Civil War in Central Europe, 1918-1921* (Oxford: Oxford University Press, 2018), 175-177.

21. Dirk Schumann, *Europa, der Erste Weltkrieg*, 25.

22. Dirk Schumann, 'Europa, der Erste Weltkrieg und die Nachkriegszeit eine Kontinuität der Gewalt?' in Journal of Modern European History, 2003, 1, 24-43, here 32; see Dietrich Beyrau, *Krieg und Revolution. Russische Erfahrungen* (Paderborn: Schöningh, 2017), 209-212.

23. Richard Pipes, *The Formation of the Soviet Union: Communism and Nationalism, 1917-1923*, rev. ed. (Cambridge, MA: Harvard University Press, 1997), 155-241.

24. Norman Davies, *White Eagle, Red Star: The Polish–Soviet War, 1919-1920* (London: Macdonald & Co, 1972), 41-42.

25. Mick, Vielerlei Kriege,' 324-319; Böhler, *Civil War in Central Europe*, 157-166; Peter Holquist, 'Violent Russia, Deadly Marxism? Russia in the Epoch of Violence, 1905-1921,' Kritika 4, 3 (2003), 627-652.

26. Leonhard, *Der überforderte Frieden*, 551

27. Ibidem, 566.

28. See Joanna Urbanek's article in this volume.

29. Leonhard, *Der überforderte Frieden*, 556; Benjamin Ziemann, *Veteranen der Republik. Kriegserinnerung und demokratische Politik 1918-1933* (Bonn: Dietz, 2014), 65.

30. Ziemann, *Veteranen der Republik*, 66-67.

31. Sabine Kienitz, *Beschädigte Helden. Kriegsinvalidität und Körperbilder 1914-1923* (Paderborn: Schöningh, 2008), 151-237.

32. Leonhard, *Der überforderte Frieden*, 563

33. Eichenberg, *Kämpfen für Frieden*, 39-40.

34. Stephan Lehnstaedt, *Der vergessene Sieg. Der Polnisch-Sowjetische Krieg 1919-1921 und die Entstehung des modernen Osteuropa* (München: C.H. Beck, 2019), 14; Leonhard, *Der überforderte Frieden*, 566.

35. Eichenberg, *Kämpfen für Frieden*, 40.

36. Christhardt Henschel, 'Brüchige Einheit. Die polnischen Streitkräfte 1918-1921,' in *Fragmentierte Republik? Das politische Erbe der Teilungszeit in Polen 1918-1939*, eds. Michael G. Müller and Kai Struve (Göttingen: Wallstein, 2017) 39-67, here 59; Böhler, *Civil War in Central Europe*, 142; Andrzej Garlicki, *Józef Piłsudski 1867-1935* (Warszawa: Czytelnik, 1989), 207, 215-216, 255.

37. Of the nearly 3,000 Polish staff officers in 1921, 42% were drawn from the Habsburg army, 33% from the Tsarist army, 16% from the Polish legions, 6% from the German army and 3% from the so-called Haller Army, formed in France at the end of the war. Jan Rydel, 'Die Entstehung des polnischen Heeres in den Jahren 1918-1921,' *Österreichische Osthefte* 34 (1992), 383-395, here 391-392; Henschel, 'Brüchige Einheit,' 50; Julia Eichenberg, 'Von Soldaten zu Zivilisten, von Zivilisten zu Soldaten. Polen und Irland nach dem Ersten Weltkrieg,' in *Krieg im Frieden. Paramilitärische Gewalt in Europa nach dem Ersten Weltkrieg*, eds. Gerwarth and Horne, 276-297, here 279-280.

38. Leonhard, *Der überforderte Frieden*, 495

39. Ibidem, 497.

40. Martin Zückert, *Zwischen Nationsidee und staatlicher Realität. Die tschechoslowakische Armee und ihre Nationalitätenpolitik 1918-1938* (München: Oldenbourg, 2006), 34-35; Georg Plaschka, Horst Haselsteiner and Arnold Suppan, *Innere Front. Militärassistenz, Widerstand und Umsturz in der Donaumonarchie 1918*, vol. 2, Umsturz (München: Oldenbourg, 1974), 63, 101.

41. Natali Stegmann, *Kriegsdeutungen-Staatsgründungen-Sozialpolitik*, 68-69, 77-79; Zückert, *Zwischen Nationsidee und staatlicher Realität*, 44-45; Oswald Kostrba-Skalicky, 'Bewaffnete Ohnmacht. Die tschechoslowakische Armee 1918-1928,' in *Die Erste Tschechoslowakische Republik als multinationaler Parteienstaat*, ed. Karl Bosl (München: Oldenbourg, 1979), 439-528, here 457-459; Marcin Jarząbek, Legioniści i inni, 223-226.

42. Kostrba-Skalicky, 'Bewaffnete Ohnmacht,' 452-454.

43. Benjamin Conrad, *Umkämpfte Grenzen, umkämpfte Bevölkerung. Die Entstehung der Staatsgrenzen der Zweiten Polnischen Republik 1918-1923* (Stuttgart: Franz Steiner, 2014), 183-190; Wlodzimierz Borodziej, Maciej Górny, *Der vergessene Weltkrieg. Nationen 1917-1923* (Darmstadt: WBG Theiss, 2018) 160-161.

44. Leonhard, *Der überforderte Frieden*, 875.

45. Julia Richers, 'Revolution oder Gegenrevolution. Die ungarische Räterepublik als Echoraum des Roten Oktober,' in *Verheißung und Bedrohung. Die Oktoberrevolution als globales Ereignis*, ed. Ganzenmüller (Köln et al.: Böhlau, 2019), 189-212, here 196; Richard Lein, 'Between Acceptance and Refusal – Soldiers' Attitudes Towards War (Austria-Hungary),' in <https://encyclopedia.1914-1918-online.net/regions/Hungary> (accessed 15 April 2020).

46. The practice of displacement by the Austro-Hungarian army meant that soldiers generally fought far away from their home regions during the First World War.

47. Manfried Rauchensteiner, *The First World War and the End of the Habsburg Monarchy, 1914-1918* (Köln et al.: Böhlau, 2014), 999; Zückert, Zwischen Nationsidee und staatlicher Realität, 35.

48. Pieter M. Judson, *Habsburg: Geschichte eines Imperiums* (München: C.H. Beck, 2017), 544, 552-554.

49. Wurzer, *Die Kriegsgefangenen der Mittelmächte in Russland*, 494-495; 521; Judson, *Habsburg*, 543-544.

50. Ernst Hanisch, *Der große Illusionist: Otto Bauer 1881-1938* (Göttingen: Vandenhoeck & Ruprecht 2011), 166-181; see Manfred Rauchensteiner, *Unter Beobachtung. Österreich seit 1918* (Köln et al.: Böhlau, 2017), 83-88; *Das Rote Wien. 1919-1934. Ideen, Debatten, Praxis* (Wien: Wien Museum, 2019).

51. Jens Oliver Schmitt, 'Hundert Jahre Einsamkeit. Grundzüge der Geschichte Rumäniens,' Osteuropa vol. 69, no. 6-8 (2019), 7-36, here 16-17; Florian Kührer-Wielach, *Siebenbürgen ohne Siebenbürger? Zentralstaatliche Integration und politischer Regionalismus nach dem Ersten Weltkrieg* (München: DeGruyter, 2014), 335-350; Maria Hausleitner, *Die Rumänisierung der Bukowina. Die Durchsetzung des nationalstaatlichen Anspruchs Grossrumäniens 1918-1944* (München: Oldenbourg, 2001), 83-214.

52. Schmitt, 'Hundert Jahre Einsamkeit,' 17.

53. Harald Heppner, Rudolf Gräf, 'Romania,' Chapter: Romania at the End of the War (1918-1920), in <https://encyclopedia.1914-1918-online.net/article/romania> (accessed 15 March 2020).

54. Schmitt, 'Hundert Jahre Einsamkeit,' 18.

55. Magda Ádám, *The Versailles System and Central Europe* (Aldershot: Ashgate, 2004), 34-36.

56. Danilo Šarenac, 'Commemoration, Cult of the Fallen (South East Europe),' in <https://encyclopedia.1914-1918-online.net/article/commemoration_cult_of_the_fallen_south_east_europe> (accessed 15 March 2020).

57. Boris Barth, *Europa nach dem Großen Krieg: Die Krise der Demokratie in der Zwischenkriegszeit 1918-1938* (Frankfurt/Main-New York: Campus, 2016), 37-38; Maciej Górny, 'Post-War Societies (East Central Europe),' in <https://encyclopedia.1914-1918-online.net/article/post-war_societies_east_central_europe> (accessed 10 May 2020).

58. Bernhard Sauer, 'Freikorps und Antisemitismus in der Frühzeit der Weimarer Republik,' in *Zeitschrift für Geschichtswissenschaft* vol. 56, 1 (2008), 1-25; Robert Gerwarth, 'Im "Spinnennetz". Gegenrevolutionäre Gewalt in den besiegten Staaten Mitteleuropas,' in *Krieg im Frieden. Paramilitärische Gewalt in Europa nach dem Ersten Weltkrieg*, eds. Gerwarth and Horne, 108-133, here 109-110.

59. Gerwarth, 'Im "Spinnennetz",' 112-113; Rauchensteiner, *Unter Beobachtung. Österreich seit 1918*, 80-81.

60. Vejas Gabriel Liulevicius, *Kriegsland im Osten. Eroberung, Kolonialisierung und Militärherrschaft im Ersten Weltkrieg* (Hamburg: Hamburger Edition, 2002), 279; See Josef Bischoff, Die letzte Front 1919 – *Geschichte der Eisernen Division im Baltikum 1919* (Berlin: Schützen-Verlag, 1935), 11-14.

61. See Klaus Gietinger, *Der Konterrevolutionär. Waldemar Pabst – eine deutsche Karriere* (Hamburg: Edition Nautilus, 2009), 120-127, 143-156; Wolfram Wette, *Gustav Noske. Eine politische Biografie*, (Düsseldorf: Droste, 1987), 316-317.

62. Bernhard Sauer, 'Vom "Mythos eines ewigen Soldatentums". Der Feldzug deutscher Freikorps im Baltikum im Jahre 1919,' *Zeitschrift für Geschichtswissenschaft* vol. 43, 10 (1995), 869-902, here 876-878; Hagen Schulze, *Freikorps und*

73

Republik 1918-1920 (Boppard: Harald Boldt Verlag, 1969), 22-35, 90-102, 125-131, 288-325; Barth, *Europa nach dem Großen Krieg*, 54-55; Ernst Rüdiger Starhemberg, *Die Erinnerungen* (Wien-München: Amalthea, 1991), 58-66.

63. Arnold Suppan, *Jugoslawien und Österreich 1918-1938. Bilaterale Aussenpolitik im europäischen Umfeld* (Wien: Verlag für Geschichte und Politik, München: Oldenbourg, 1996), 567-602, 925-929, 941-948; Rauchensteiner, *Unter Beobachtung*, 80-82; Hannsjoachim W. Koch, *Der deutsche Bürgerkrieg. Eine Geschichte der deutschen und österreichischen Freikorps 1918-1923* (Berlin: Ullstein, 1978), 279-299.

64. Barth, *Europa nach dem Großen Krieg*, 49-50.

65. Béla Bodó, 'Actio und Reactio. Roter und Weißer Terror in Ungarn 1919-1921,' in *Die ungarische Räterepublik 1919. Innenansichten – Außenperspektiven – Folgewirkungen*, eds. Christian Koller and Matthias Marschik (Wien: Promedia, 2018), 69-82, here 72; György Borsányi, *The Life of a Communist Revolutionary, Béla Kun* (Boulder: Social Science Monographs, 1993), 156, 175-176.

66. Tamás Révész, 'Post-War Turmoil and Violence (Hungary)' in <https://encyclopedia.1914-1918-online.net/article/post-war_turmoil_and_violence_hungary> (accessed 10 April 2020); Béla Bodó, 'The White Terror in Hungary, 1919-1921: The Social Worlds of Paramilitary Groups,' *Austrian History Yearbook* vol. 42 (2011), 133-163, here 138-143, 152-157; Gerwarth, 'Im "Spinnennetz",' 121; Baron Albert von Kaas and Fedor von Lazarovics, *Der Bolschewismus in Ungarn* (München: Südost-Verlag Adolf Dresler, 1930), 251-252.

67. Lajos Kerekes: Von *St. Germain bis Genf. Österreich und seine Nachbarn, 1918-1922* (Köln et al.: Böhlau 1979), 195; Barth, *Europa nach dem Großen Krieg*, 51-52.

68. Włodzimierz Borodziej, *Geschichte Polens im 20. Jahrhundert* (München: C.H. Beck, 2010), 97-103.

69. Andrzej Friszke, *Państwo czy rewolucja. Polscy komuniści a odbudowanie państwa polskiego 1892-1920* (Warszawa: Wydawnictwo Krytyki Politycznej, 2020), 510-512.

70. Heidi Hein, *Der Piłsudski-Kult und seine Bedeutung für den polnischen Staat 1926-1939* (Marburg: Verlag Herder-Institut, 2002), 140-142, 223-226; Józef Maria Bartnik and Ewa J. P. Storożyńska, *Matka Boża Łaskawa a Cud nad Wisłą* (Warszawa: Wydawnictwo Sióstr Loretanek, 2011).

71. Christoph Mick, *Kriegserfahrungen in einer multiethnischen Stadt: Lemberg 1914-1947* (Wiesbaden, Harrasowitz, 2010), 212-232; Piotr Łossowski, *Konflikt polsko-litewski 1918-1920* (Warszawa: Książka i Wiedza, 1996); Lech Wyszczelski, *Wilno 1919-1920* (Warszawa: Bellona, 2008); Garlicki, *Józef Piłsudski*, 212-219.

72. Andrzej Garlicki, *Siedem mitów Drugiej Rzeczypospolitej* (Warszawa: Czytelnik, 2013), 218-238; Hans Henning Hahn, 'Internationales Staatensystem und Staatsbildung um 1918. Die Urkatastrophe des 20. Jahrhunderts als innere und äußere Ordnungsbildung,' in *Historie* vol. 12 (2018/2019), 119-130, here 128; Barth, *Europa nach dem Großen Krieg*, 46.

73. Arnulf Scriba, 'Erster Weltkrieg. Kriegsverlauf. Kriegsgefangenschaft,' in *Lebendiges Museum Online*, <https://www.dhm.de/lemo/kapitel/erster-weltkrieg/kriegsverlauf/kriegsgefangenschaft.html> (accessed 13 June 2020).

74. 'Übereinkommen vom 18. Oktober 1907, betreffend die Gesetze und Gebräuche des Landkrieges (IV. Übereinkommen der II. Haager Friedenskonferenz),' in *Reichsgesetzblatt für die im Reichsrat vertretenen Königreiche und Länder* (Wien: 1913), 587-616.

75. Andrzej Chwalba, *Samobójstwo Europy. Wielka Wojna 1914-1918* (Kraków: Wydawnictwo Literackie, 2014), 459.

76. Laurent Marti and Jean-Pierre Gaume, *Objets du silence. Œuvres et objets des camps et des prisonniers 1900-1992* (Genève: Musée international de la Croix-Rouge et du Croissant-Rouge, 1992), 138.

77. Heather Jones, Violence against Prisoners of *War in the First World War. Britain, France and Germany*, 1914-1920 (Cambridge et al.: Cambridge University Press, 2011), 296-300.

78. Scriba, 'Erster Weltkrieg. Kriegsverlauf. Kriegsgefangenschaft,' in *Lebendiges Museum Online*.

79. Georg Wurzer, *Die Kriegsgefangenen der Mittelmächte in Russland im Ersten Weltkrieg* (Göttingen: Vandenhoeck & Ruprecht, 2005).

80. Gustav Jungbauer, *Kriegsgefangen* (Budweis: Moldavia, 1921).

81. David Bullock, *The Czech Legion 1914-20* (Oxford: Osprey Publishers, 2008).

82. Marcin Jarząbek, *Legioniści i inni. Pamięć zbiorowa weteranów I wojny światowej w Polsce i Czechosłowacji okresu międzywojennego* (Kraków: Wydawnictwo Universitas, 2017); Jarosław Centek, 'Polish Legions,' *International Encyclopedia of the First World War*, <https://encyclopedia.1914-1918-online.net/article/polish_legions> (accessed 13 June 2020).

83. *Kriegsgefangene im Europa des Ersten Weltkriegs*, ed. Jochen Oltmer (Paderborn: Schöningh, 2006); Natali Stegmann, *Kriegsdeutungen, Staatsgründungen, Sozialpolitik. Der Helden- und Opferdiskurs in der Tschechoslowakei 1918-1948* (München: Oldenbourg, 2010).

84. Hannes Leidinger and Verena Moritz, 'Der Sinn der Erfahrung. Gedanken über den Umgang mit Selbstzeugnissen ehemaliger Kriegsgefangener des Ersten Weltkriegs,' in *In russischer Gefangenschaft. Erlebnisse österreichischer Soldaten im Ersten Weltkrieg*, ibid. eds. (Köln et al.: Böhlau, 2008), 7-36.

85. Julia Eichenberg, *Kämpfen für Frieden und Fürsorge. Polnische Veteranen des Ersten Weltkriegs und ihre internationalen Kontakte, 1918-1939* (München: Oldenbourg, 2011), 63-66.

86. Reinhard Nachtigal, 'Die Repatriierung der Mittelmächte-Kriegsgefangenen aus dem revolutionären Rußland. Heimkehr zwischen Agitation, Bürgerkrieg und Intervention 1918-1933', in *Kriegsgefangene*, ed. Jochen Oltmer, 239-266.

87. Gerhard Simon, *Nationalismus und Nationalitätenpolitik in der Sowjetunion: Von der totalitären Diktatur zur nachstalinschen Gesellschaft* (Baden-Baden: Nomos Verlagsgesellschaft, 1986), 34.

88. Joshua Sanborn, *Imperial Apocalypse: The Great War and the Destruction of the Russian Empire* (Oxford: Oxford University Press, 2014); Maureen Healy, *Vienna and the Fall of the Habsburg Empire: Total War and Everyday Life in World War I* (Cambridge: Cambridge University Press, 2004); Michael A. Reynolds, *Shattering Empires: The Clash and Collapse of the Ottoman and Russian Empires, 1908-1918* (Cambridge et al.: Cambridge University Press, 2011).

89. Andreas Kappeler, *Rußland als Vielvölkerreich: Entstehung – Geschichte – Zerfall* (München: C.H.Beck, 2020), 289.

90. Jörn Happel, 'Die Revolution an der Peripherie,' in *Die Russische Revolution 1917*, ed. Heiko Haumann (Köln et al.: Böhlau, 2016), 91-104, here 93-94

91. Heiko Haumann, 'Das Jahr 1917 in den Metropolen und in den Dörfern,' in *Die Russische Revolution 1917*, ed. Heiko Haumann, 73-90, here 77-79; Kappeler, *Rußland als Vielvölkerreich*, 290.

92. Jörn Happel, 'Die Revolution an der Peripherie,' 91-104, here 91-92; Simon, *Nationalismus und Nationalitätenpolitik*, 34.

93. Simon, *Nationalismus und Nationalitätenpolitik*, 35.

94. Arkadius Stempin, *Das vergessene Generalgouvernement. Die Deutsche Besatzungspolitik in Kongresspolen 1914-1918* (Paderborn; Schöningh, 2020), 177-181, 500-501; Borodziej, *Geschichte Polens im 20. Jahrhundert*, 84-87.

95. Borodziej, *Geschichte Polens im 20. Jahrhundert*, 88-89.

96. See the article by Burkhard Olschowsky in this volume; Rosa Luxemburg, *Nationalitätenfrage und Autonomie*, edited and translated by Holger Politt (Berlin: Karl Dietz Verlag, 2012).

97. Wolfgang Templin, *Der Kampf um Polen. Die abenteuerliche Geschichte der Zweiten Polnischen Republik 1918-1939* (Paderborn: Schöningh, 2018), 106-117.

98. Henry Abramson, *A Prayer for the Government: Ukrainians and Jews in Revolutionary Times, 1917-1920* (Cambridge, MA: Harvard University, 1999), 9-10.

99. Felix Schnell, 'Historische Hintergründe ukrainisch-russischer Konflikte,' in *Aus Politik und Zeitgeschichte* vol. 47-48 (2014), 9-16, here 12.

100. Torsten Wehrhahn, *Die Westukrainische Volksrepublik zu den polnisch-ukrainischen Beziehungen und dem Problem der ukrainischen Staatlichkeit* (Berlin: Weißensee Verlag, 2004), 127-157, 223-228.

101. Borodziej, Górny, *Der vergessene Weltkrieg*, 162; Caroline Milow, *Die ukrainische Frage 1917-1923 im Spannungsfeld der europäischen Diplomatie* (Wiesbaden: Harrassowitz, 2002), 440-445.

102. Serhy Yekelchyk, 'Bands of Nation Builders? Insurgency and Ideology in the Ukrainian Civil War in *War in Peace: Paramilitary Violence in Europe after the Great War*, eds. Robert Gerwarth and John Horne (Oxford: Oxford University Press, 2012), 107-125; Jurij V. Kotljar, 'Bauernrepubliken in der Südukraine: Der Kampf um Macht und Staatlichkeit,' in *Loyalität, Legitimität, Legalität. Zerfalls-, Separations- und Souveränisierungsprozesse in Ostmittel- und Osteuropa 1914-1921*, eds. Alfred Eisfeld and Konrad Maier (Wiesbaden: Harrassowitz, 2014), 9-22, here 9-14.

103. Some Ukrainians saw the Peace of Riga as a renewed partition of the country. Piotr S. Wandycz, *Soviet-Polish Relations, 1917-1921* (Cambridge, MA: Harvard University Press, 2013), 284; Michael Palij, *The Ukrainian-Polish Defensive Alliance, 1919-1921* (Edmonton: Canadian Institute of Ukrainian Studies Press, 1995), 171-183; Conrad, *Umkämpfte Grenzen*, 240, 245, 249-251.

104. Steven L. Guthier, 'The Belorussians: National Identification and Assimilation, 1897-1970,' Part I: 1897-1939, *Soviet Studies* vol. 29, no.1 (1977), 37-61, 49-57; Kappeler, *Rußland als Vielvölkerreich*, 292.

105. Dimitri Romanowski, *Belarus und Weimar-Deutschland: wirtschaftliche, wissenschaftlich-technische und kulturelle Beziehungen* (Hamburg: disserta-Verlag, 2015), 54-56; *Węzeł polsko-białoruski 1918-1921. Dokumenty i materiały*, ed. Wojciech Materski (Warszawa: ISP PAN, 2018), 12, 15, 17, 430.

106. Kappeler, *Rußland als Vielvölkerreich*, 296.

107. Stephen Jones, 'The Non-Russian Nationalities,' in *Society and Politics in the Russian Revolution*, ed. Robert Service (London: Palgrave Macmillan, 1992), 35-63; Kappeler, *Rußland als Vielvölkerreich*, 296.

108. Templin, *Der Kampf um Polen*, 69; Kappeler, *Rußland als Vielvölkerreich*, 298; see the parliamentary debates on the peace treaties of Brest-Litovsk, Reichstagsprotokolle, 130th and 131th sittings on 20 and 22 February 1918, <https://www.reichstagsprotokolle.de/Blatt_k13_bsb00003407_00139.html> (accessed 17 October 2020).

109. Annemarie H. Sammartino, *The Impossible Border: Germany and the East, 1914-1922* (Ithaca: Cornell University Press, 2010), 55; The disciplined and powerful Latvian Riflemen were a core part of the Red Army. Andrew Ezergailis, *The Latvian Impact on The Bolshevik Revolution. The First Phase: September 1917 to April 1918* (New York: Columbia University Press, 1983); Heinrichs Strods, 'Drei Alternativen der Staatlichkeit Lettlands in den Jahren 1917-1920,' in *The Independence of the Baltic States: Origins, Causes, and Consequences: A Comparison of the Crucial Years 1918-1919 and 1990-1991*, eds. Eberhard Demm, Roger Noël and William L. Urban (Chicago: Lithuanian Research and Studies Center, 1996), 36-45; See Claus Grimm, *Jahre deutscher Entscheidung im Baltikum 1918/1919* (Essen: Essener Verlagsanstalt, 1939), 437-443.

110. Tomas Balkelis, *War, Revolution, and Nation-Making in Lithuania, 1914-1923* (Oxford Scholarship Online, 2018), 97-109.

111. Diner, *Das Jahrhundert verstehen*, 86-87; Georg von Rauch, *Geschichte der baltischen Staaten* (Hannover: Verlag Harro v. Hirschheydt, 1986), 62; Akten des Bundesarchivs zur Räumung des Baltikums im Herbst 1919, <https://www.bundesarchiv.de/aktenreichskanzlei/1919-1933/10a/bau/bau1p/kap1_1/para2_5.html;jsessionid=02E818F2B2BD6F367B9DF115C717D759?highlight=true&search=Bermondt%20F%EF%BF%BDrst%20Awaloff&stemming=false&pnd=&start=&end=&field=all> (accessed 15 April 2020).

112. Borodziej, Górny, *Der vergessene Weltkrieg*, 453-454.

113. Ober Ost: the Supreme Commander of All German Forces in the East.

114. Liulevicius, *Kriegsland im Osten*, 268-271; Eberhard Demm, 'Anschluss, Autonomie oder Unabhängigkeit? Die deutsche Litauenpolitik im Ersten Weltkrieg und das Selbstbestimmungsrecht der Völker,' in *The Independence of the Baltic States*, eds. Demm, Noël and Urban, 193-199.

115. The Suwałki cease-fire on 7 October 1920 was supposed to bring an end to the border confrontations between Poland and Lithuania.

116. Martin Hellmann, *Daten der polnischen Geschichte* (München: dtv, 1985), 179-185; Piotr Lossowski, *Konflikt polsko-litewski 1918-1920* (Warszawa: Książka i Wiedza, 1996); Conrad, *Umkämpfte Grenzen*, 266-274; Isabel Röskau-Rydel, 'Historische Hintergründe ukrainisch-russischer Konflikte. Pol-

nisch-litauische Beziehungen zwischen 1918 und 1939,' *Jahrbücher für Geschichte Osteuropas* vol. 35, 4 (1987), 556-581.

117. Martin Aust, *Die russische Revolution. Vom Zarenreich zum Sowjetimperium* (München: C.H. Beck, 2017), 180.

118. Werner Zürrer, *Kaukasien 1918-1921: Der Kampf der Grossmächte um die Landbrücke zwischen Schwarzem und Kaspischem Meer* (Düsseldorf: Droste, 1978), 18-41; Kappeler, *Rußland als Vielvölkerreich*, 296.

119. Orlando Figes, *Die Tragödie eines Volkes: Die Epoche der russischen Revolution 1891 bis 1924* (Berlin: Berlin Verlag, 2014) 751-752.

120. Tadeusz Świętochowski, *Russian Azerbaijan 1905-1920: The Shaping of a National Identity in a Muslim Community* (Cambridge, MA: Cambridge University Press, 1988), 147-152.

121. Audrey L. Altstadt, *The Politics of Culture in Soviet Azerbaijan, 1920-40* (London-New York: Roudledge, 2016), 25-33; Figes, *Die Tragödie eines Volkes*, 752.

122. Richard G. Hovannisian, *The Republic of Armenia, Vol. 2: From Versailles to London, 1919-1920* (Berkeley et al.: University of California Press, 1982), 249-252.

123. Figes, *Die Tragödie eines Volkes*, 753.

124. Terry Stavridis, 'The Armenian Question 1918-20,' in <https://www.researchgate.net/publication/279556219> (accessed 15 July 2020), 1-51, here 41-43; Figes, *Die Tragödie eines Volkes*, 754.

125. Ronald Grigor Suny, *The Making of the Georgian Nation* (Indiana: Indiana University Press, 1988), 192-199.

126. Suny, *The Making of the Georgian Nation*, 205-206.

127. Eric Lee, *The Experiment: Georgia's Forgotten Revolution, 1918-1921* (London: Zed Books, 2017), 186-189; Karl Kautsky, *Georgien. Eine sozialdemokratische Bauernrepublik. Eindrücke und Beobachtungen* (Wien: Wiener Volksbuchhandlung, 1921).

128. Leonard Shapiro, *Soviet Treaty Series, vol. 1, 1917-1928* (Washington: Georgetown University Press, 1950), 45. Significantly, however, the peace treaty between the RSFSR and Georgia was not included in the ten-volume collection of documents kept by the Soviet Foreign Ministry Vnesnaja Politika SSSR; Arsène Saparov, 'From Conflict to Autonomy: The Making of the South Ossetian Autonomous Region 1918-1922,' *Europe-Asia Studies* vol. 62, no. 1 (2010), 99-123, here 101-110.

129. Wladimir Iljitsch Lenin, *Studienausgabe, vol. 2* (Frankfurt/Main: Fischer, 1970), 275-277; Figes, Die Tragödie eines Volkes, 756.

130. See Burkhard Olschowsky's article in this volume.

131. Simon, *Nationalismus und Nationalitätenpolitik*, 35. Kappeler, *Rußland als Vielvölkerreich*, 302.

132. See *Blick ins Ungewisse. Visionen und Utopien im Donau-Karpaten-Raum 1917 und danach*, ed. Angela Ilić et al. (Regensburg: Verlag Friedrich Pustet, 2019); ibidem Ljubinka Toševa Karpowicz, 'The State of Rijeka of the Italian National Council [23 November 1918-12 September 1919],' 19-32; Nataliya Nachayeva-Yuriychuk, 'National Identity and its Role in State Building: the Example of the Hutsul Republic,' 33-50 and Nándor Bárdi and Csaba Záhorán, 'Utopia in the Shadow of Catastrophe: The Idea of Székely Self-Determination after the Collapse of Austria-Hungary,' 73-94.

133. Tobias Weger, *Großschlesisch? Großfriesisch? Großdeutsch! Ethnonationalismus in Schlesien und Friesland, 1918-1945* (München: Oldenbourg DeGruyter, 2017), 568-584.

134. 'Past Pandemics,' in <https://www.euro.who.int/en/ health-topics/communicable-diseases/influenza/pandemic-influenza/past-pandemics> (accessed 14 June 2020).

135. Harald Salfellner, *Pandemie španělské chřipky 1918/19 se zvláštním zřetelem na České země a středoevropské poměry*. PhD Thesis, Praha (1. Lékařská fakulta Univerzity Karlové v Praze) 2017.

136. K. David Patterson and Gerald F. Pyle, 'The Geography and Mortality of the 1918 Influenza Pandemic', *Bulletin of the History of Medicine* vol. 65 (1991), 4-21, here 13.

137. Marek L. Grabowski, Bożena Kosińska, Józef P. Knap and Lidia B. Brydak, 'The Lethal Spanish Influenza Pandemic in Poland,' *Medical Science Monitor* vol. 23 (2017), 4880-4884.

138. Alexe Sulica, 'Considerațiuni asupra epidemiei actuale de gripa,' *Gazeta Transilvaniei*, 83th year, no. 58, 29th March 1920, 1.

139. Milorad Radusin, 'The Spanish Flu. Part II: The Second and the Third Wave', *Vojnosanitetski Pregled* vol. 69 (2012), 917-927.

140. Margaret Macmillan, *Paris 1919. Six Months that Changed the World* (New York: Random House, 2001), 229-242.

141. For an analysis of the German and British perception of Czechoslovakia, see: Eva Hahnová, *Dlouhé stíny předsudků. Německé a anglické stereotypy o Češích v dějinách 20. století* (Praha: Academia, 2015).

142. Paul Scott Mowrer, *Balkanized Europe. A Study in Political Analysis and Reconstruction* (New York: E. P. Dutton & Company, 1921).

143. Pierre Bonnefous, *Histoire politique de la Troisième République. L'après-guerre* (Paris: Presses universitaires de France, 1968), 248.

144. For this information, the editors would like to thank Dr. habil. Ibolya Murber of ELTE, Budapest. See also Peter Pastor, 'Franco-Rumanian Intervention in Russia and the Vix Ultimatum: Background to Hungary's Loss of Transylvania,' in *The Canadian-American Review of Hungarian Studies* 1 (1974), 12-27.

145. Bernard Michel, 'La présence française en Tchécoslovaquie et en Pologne de l'entre-deux-guerres à la prise du pouvoir des communists,' in *Le rayonnement français en Europe centrale du XVIIe siècle à nos jours*, eds. Olivier Chaline, Jaroslaw Dumanowski and Michel Figeac (Pessac: Maison des sciences de l'homme d'Aquitaine, 2009), 93-109, here 100-102.

146. Frédéric Guelton, 'Le capitaine de Gaulle et la Pologne (1919-1921),' in *Les relations entre la France et la Pologne au XXe siècle*, eds. Bernard Michel and Józef Laptos (Kraków: Eventus, 2002), 113-127.

147. Julian Go, *Postcolonial Thought and Social Theory* (Oxford: Oxford University Press, 2016), 28.

148. For detailed information, see Frank Bongiorno, 'Rembering Anzac', in *History, Memory and Public Life. The Past in the Present*, eds. Anna Maerker, Simon Sleight and Adam Sutcliffe (London: Routledge, 2018), 183-207.

149. Willi Raab, *Und neues Leben blüht aus den Ruinen. Stationen meines Lebens 1895-1939*, eds. Ernst Holthaus and Ernst Piper (München: Allitera, 2009), 132-133. 'Der eine ist aus Senegal, der andere heißt Dolezal. // Im Rheinland stiehlt der Neger, der Tschech' in Prag und Eger. // Ein jeder sorgt auf seine Weis' für Frankreichs Ehre, Ruhm und Preis.'

150. For a postcolonial reading of Gustav Freytag's novel *Soll und Haben*, see Kristin Kopp, *Germany's Wild East. Constructing Poland as Colonial Space* (Ann Arbor: The University of Michigan Press, 2012), 29-56.

151. Christoph Kienemann, *Der koloniale Blick gen Osten. Osteuropa im Diskurs des Deutschen Kaiserreiches von 1871* (Paderborn: Schöningh, 2018), 243-257.

152. Susanne Kuss, *Deutsches Militär auf kolonialen Kriegsschauplätzen. Eskalation von Gewalt zu Beginn des 20. Jahrhunderts* (Berlin: Ch. Links, 2010), 414.

153. Tomáš Garrigue Masaryk, *Nová Evropa. Stanovisko slovanské* (Praha: Gustav Dubský, 1920), 206.

154. Borodziej, Górny, *Der vergessene Weltkrieg*, 479-480.

155. Jan Rychlík and Magdaléna Rychlíková, *Podkarpatská Rus v dějinách Československa* (Praha: Nakladatelství Vyšehrad: 2016), passim.

156. Horst Lademacher, *Die Illusion vom Frieden. Die zweite Internationale wider den Krieg 1889-1919* (Münster: Waxmann, 2018).

157. Hermann Walther von der Dunk, *Kulturgeschichte des 20. Jahrhunderts*, vol. 1 (München: Deutsche Verlags-Anstalt, 2004), 126.

158. Ralf Hoffrogge, *Sozialismus und Arbeiterbewegung in Deutschland und Österreich. Von den Anfängen bis 1914* (Stuttgart: Schmetterling Verlag, 2017).

159. von der Dunk, *Kulturgeschichte des 20. Jahrhunderts*, 261.

160. André Keil, 'Zwischen Kooperation und Opposition – Die britische Arbeiterbewegung und das "War Emergency Workers National Committee" während des Ersten Weltkrieges,' *Jahrbuch für Forschungen zur Geschichte der Arbeiterbewegung* no. 3 (2014), 7-26.

161. Anne Kriegel, *Aux origines du communisme français: 1914-1920 contribution à l'histoire du mouvement ouvrier*, vol. 2 (Paris: La Haye, 1964), 171-175.

162. Bernard Degen and Julia Richers eds., *Zimmerwald und Kiental. Weltgeschichte auf dem Dorfe* (Zürich: Chronos, 2015).

163. According to the Julian Calendar, on 24 and 25 November 1917.

164. See Burkhard Olschowsky's chapter in this volume. Gerd Koenen, 'Ein Zeitalter wird besichtigt, Kommunismus als Weltgeschichte, 1917-2017,' in *Verheißung und Bedrohung*, 25-43, here 29.

165. Detlef Lehnert, 'Die Oktoberrevolution in der Wahrnehmung der deutschen Sozialdemokratie,' *Jahrbuch für Historische Kommunismusforschung*, 2017 (Berlin: Metropol Verlag), 117-130, here 122-123.

166. Bruno Naarden, *Socialist Europe and Revolutionary Russia: Perception and Prejudice 1848-1923* (New York: Cambridge University Press, 1992).

167. Thomas Knoll, 'Die Resonanz der Oktoberrevolution in Frankreich und Großbritannien (1917-1921)', in *Verheißung und Bedrohung*, 149-171, here 165-167; Hannsjoachim W. Koch, 'Das britische Rußlandbild im Spiegel der britischen Propaganda 1914-1918,' *Zeitschrift für Politik* vol. 27, no. 1 (1980), 71-96, here 71-74.

168. Heinrich August Winkler, 'Demokratie oder Bürgerkrieg. Die russische Oktoberrevolution als Problem der deutschen Sozialdemokraten und der französischen Sozialisten,' *Vierteljahreshefte für Zeitgeschichte* vol. 47, 1 (1999), 1-24, here 2.

169. Citation from Hans Woller, 'Toxische Fernwirkungen. Die Resonanz der Oktoberrevolution in Italien,' in *Verheißung und Bedrohung*, 173-188, here 176-177; Gerwarth, *Die Besiegten*, 206.

170. Winkler, 'Demokratie oder Bürgerkrieg,' 3; See Alexander Stein, 'Für und wider die Konstituante,' in *Diktatur statt Sozialismus*, ed. Jörn Schütrumpf, 165-168.

171. 'Die Bolschewiki und wir,' *Vorwärts*, 15 February 1918.

172. Karl Kautsky, Die Diktatur des Proletariats, 2 ed. (Wien: Volksbuchhandlung, J. Brand, 1918), 15, 33-39; Karl Kautsky, 'Demokratie und Diktatur,' in *Diktatur statt Sozialismus. Die russische Revolution und die deutsche Linke 1917/18*, ed. Jörn Schütrumpf (Berlin: Karl Dietz Verlag, 2017), 142-148, here 142-143.

173. Rosa Luxemburg, 'Zur russischen Revolution (1918),' in Rosa Luxemburg, Gesammelte Werke, ed. Institut für Marxismus-Leninismus beim ZK der SED, vol. 4, (Berlin: Dietz Verlag, 1974), 359; Friszke, *Państwo czy rewolucja*, 212-214.

174. Winkler, 'Demokratie oder Bürgerkrieg,' 6.

175. François Furet, *Das Ende der Illusion*, 89; *Die Zweite Internationale 1918/19. Protokolle, Memoranden, Berichte und Korrespondenzen*, ed. Gerhard A. Ritter, vol.1 (Berlin: Dietz, 1980), 209.

176. Winkler, 'Demokratie oder Bürgerkrieg,' 14-15, 22; Tony Judt, 'The French Socialist Party 1920-1936,' in Tony Judt, *Marxism and the French Left. Studies in Labour and Politics in France, 1830-1981* (Oxford: Clarendon Press 1986), 115-168; Furet, *Das Ende der Illusion*, 87-90.

177. Josef Harna, 'The Building of a State,' in *History of the Czech Lands*, eds. Jaroslav Pánek and Oldřich Tůma (Prague: Karolinum Press, 2011), 395-432, here 395-402; H. Gordon Skilling, 'The Formation of a Communist Party in Czechoslovakia,' *The American Slavic and East European Review* vol. 14, no. 3 (1955), 346-358, here 346-347, 354-355.

178. Friszke, *Państwo czy rewolucja*, 536-537, 540; Georg W. Strobel, *Die Partei Rosa Luxemburgs, Lenin und die SPD: Der polnische 'europäische' Internationalismus in der russischen Sozialdemokratie* (Wiesbaden: Franz Steiner, 1974), 685-692; Templin, *Der Kampf um Polen*, 78, 134-138; Andrzej Garlicki, *Józef Piłsudski 1867-1935* (Warszawa: Czytelnik, 1988), 238, 243.

179. Uli Schöler, 'Bolschewismus und Sozialdemokratie. Die österreichischen Sozialdemokraten und Sowjetrussland,' in *Marxismus als Sozialwissenschaft. Rechts- und Staatsverständnisse im Austromarxismus*, eds. Andreas Fisahn, Thilo Scholle and Ridvan Ciftci (Baden-Baden: Nomos Verlagsgesellschaft, 2018), 177-191.

180. Julia Richers, 'Revolution oder Gegenrevolution. Die ungarische Räterepublik als Echoraum des Roten Oktober,' in *Verheißung und Bedrohung*, 189-212, here 200-202.

181. Dokument Nr. I: 'Haftbefehl des königlichen Strafgerichtshofes zu Budapest vom 26. Dezember 1919, Zahl 5736 gegen den Volksbeauftragten für Äußeres der ungarischen Räteregierung Béla Kun', in Aktenstücke aus dem Archiv Ungarischer Gerichtshöfe über die Prozesse einiger Kommunisten, 1919-1920 (Budapest: Königl. Ung. Staatsdruckerei, 1920), 11-25, here 21; Henry Charles Schmitt, *Die Rote Hölle in Ungarn: bolschewistische Momentbilder* (Bern: Verlag Ferd. Wyss, 1919).

182. W.I. Lenin, 'Mitteilung über ein Funkspruch mit *Béla Kun*,' in W.I. Lenin, *Werke*, vol. 29, March-August 1919 (Berlin: Dietz Verlag, 1984), 213.

183. Furet, *Das Ende der Illusion*, 89.

184. Berhard H. Bayerlein, 'Transnationalisierung und weltrevolutionäres Scheitern. Die Komintern und Revolutionsvorbereitungen deutscher Kommunisten in der Zwischenkriegszeit,' in *Verheißung und Bedrohung*, 47-74, here 53.

185. Der zweite Kongreß der Kommunistischen Internationale. Protokoll der Verhandlungen vom 19. Juli in Petrograd und vom 23. Juli bis 7. August in Moskau (Hamburg: Verlag der Kommunistischen Internationale, Carl Hoym, 1921), 260.

186. Peter Lösche, *Der Bolschewismus im Urteil der Deutschen Sozialdemokratie* (Berlin: Colloquium Verlag, 1967), 250-257, 269-276.

187. Paul Levi, *Zwischen Spartakus und Sozialdemokratie. Schriften, Aufsätze, Reden und Briefe* (Frankfurt/Main: Europäische Verlagsanstalt, 1969); Furet, *Das Ende der Illusion*, 151-163; Lenin, Studienausgabe, vol. 2, 369-371.

188. Josef Schleifstein, Die *'Sozialfaschismus'-These. Zu ihrem geschichtlichen Hintergrund* (Frankfurt/Main: Verlag Marxistische Blätter, 1980).

189. Julia Eichenberg, *Kämpfen für Frieden und Fürsorge*, 133-175; Wolfram Wette, 'Einleitung. Probleme des Pazifismus in der Zwischenkriegszeit,' in *Pazifismus in der Weimarer Republik. Beiträge zur historischen Friedensforschung*, eds. Karl Holl and Wolfram Wette (Paderborn: Schöningh, 1981), 9-25, here 13-15.

190. Eichenberg, *Kämpfen für Frieden*, 176-193; Bernd Weisbrod, 'Die Politik der Repräsentation. Das Erbe des Ersten Weltkrieges und der Formwandel der Politik in Europa,' in *Der Erste Weltkrieg und die europäische Nachkriegsordnung: sozialer Wandel und Formveränderung der Politik*, ed. Hans Mommsen (Köln et al.: Böhlau, 2000), 13-42, here 20-21.

191. In many societies, pacifists were branded defeatists who lacked a sense of patriotism and national pride.

192. Stanisław Estreicher, *Pacyfizm w Polsce XVI stulecia* (Poznań: Księgarnia swiętego Wojciecha 1930).

193. Daniel Jetel, *Eine zwiespältige Beziehung. Der Völkerbund und die Sicherheit der Ersten Tschechoslowakischen Republik 1919-1938* (Zürich: Ph.D. Thesis, 2017), 155-159.

194. Carl von Ossietzky, 'Die Pazifisten,' in *Das Tage-Buch*, eds. Stefan Großmann and Leopold Schwarzschild, 5. Jahrgang (Berlin: Tagebuch-Verlag, 1924), 1400-1403, here 1402.

195. Umberto Eco, *Die Suche nach der vollkommenen Sprache* (München: C.H. Beck, 1995), 329-336.

196. Rolf Steininger, *South Tyrol. A Minority Conflict of the Twentieth Century* (New Brunswick-London: Transaction Publishers, 2009), 5-63.

197. R. J. Crampton, *A Concise History of Bulgaria* (New York: Cambridge University Press, 2005), 144-152.

198. Tobias Weger, 'Vom "Alldeutschen Atlas" zu den "Erzwungenen Wegen". Der "Deutsche Osten" im Kartenbild 1905-2008,' in *Osteuropa kartiert – Mapping Eastern Europe*, eds. Jörn Happel and Christophe von Werdt (Berlin et al.: LIT, 2010), 241-264.

199. Róbert Keményfi, 'Die Rezeption deutscher Vorstellungen von Expansion und „ethnischer Landschaft" in der ungarischen Geographie der Zwischenkriegszeit,' in *Aufbruch und Krise. Das östliche Europa und die Deutschen nach dem Ersten Weltkrieg*, eds. Beate Störtkuhl, Jens Stüben and Tobias Weger (München: Oldenbourg, 2010), 447-468.

200. Max Weber, *Protestantische Ethik und der Geist des Kapitalismus* (Tübingen: Verlag von J.C.B Mohr, 1934).

201. Charles Taylor, 'Two Theories of Modernity,' *The International Scope! Review*, vol. 3, no. 5 (Summer 2001), 9, <https://pdfs.semanticscholar.org/6139/29a76b1448df8d5201017904 7555fb964338.pdf> (accessed 14 January 2020). See also Charles Taylor, *Sources of the Self: The Making of the Modern Identity* (Cambridge, MA: Cambridge University Press, 1996).

202. Recommended literature: Max Weber, *The Protestant Ethic and the Spirit of Capitalism*, transl. Peter Baehr and Gordon C. Wells (London: Penguin, 2002); Max Horkheimer, Theodor W. Adorno, *Dialectics of Enlightenment* (Stanford: Stanford University Press, 2007); Charles Taylor, *Sources of the Self. The Making of Modern Identity* (Cambridge MA: Harvard University Press, 1989); Antony Giddens, *Modernity and Self-Identity: Self and Society in the Late Modern Age* (Stanford: Stanford University Press, 1991); *Multiple Modernities*, ed. Shmuel N. Eisenstadt (New York: John Wiley & Sons, 2017); Niklas Luhman, *Observations on Modernity*, transl. William Whobrey (Stanford: Stanford University Press, 1998).

203. Norman Davies, *Europa. Rozprawa z historią* (Kraków: Znak, 2004), 1001.

204. Davies, *Europa*, 1001.

205. Davies, *Europa*, 1018.

206. Roger Griffin, *Modernism and Fascism. The Sense of the Beginning under Mussolini and Hitler* (New York: Palgrave MacMillan, 2007).

207. Piotr Juszkiewicz, *Cień modernizmu* (Poznań: Wydawnictwo Naukowe UAM, 2013). On artistic modernisation in Central and Eastern Europe, see Andrzej Szczerski, *Modernizacje. Sztuka i architektura w nowych państwa Europy Środkowo-Wschodniej. 1918-1939* (Łódź: Muzeum Sztuki w Łodzi, 2010).

208. Richard Pipes, *Rewolucja rosyjska* (Warszawa: Wydawnictwo Naukowe PWN, 1994), 109-110.

209. Davies, *Europa*, 1022. On Gulag see Anne Applebaum, *Gulag: A History of Soviet Camps* (London: Penguin Books, 2003).

210. Griffin, *Modernism*, 252.

211. Ibidem, 253.

212. Ibidem, 256.

213. Ibidem, 194.

214. Ibidem, 193.

215. Eric Lohr, *Nationalizing the Russian Empire: the campaign against enemy aliens during World War* I (Cambridge, MA: Harvard University Press, 2003); Jonathan Frankel, Crisis, *Revolution, and Russian Jews* (Cambridge et al.: Cambridge University Press, 2009); Peter Gatrell, *A Whole Empire Walking. Refugees in Russia during World War I* (Bloomington: Indiana University Press, 1999), 3-32; Piotr J. Wróbel, 'Foreshadowing the Holocaust: The Wars of 1914-1921 and Anti-Jewish Violence in Central and Eastern Europe,' in *Legacies of Violence*, 169-208, here 180-192.

216. The concept of 'kin state' could be misunderstood in the sense that all minority populations in Eastern Europe might have a 'kin state' they could claim as their own. For certain minorities in the interwar years, however, the idea of a 'kin

state' was an almost mythical idea, as it was for the Jews where the state of Israel was not yet in existence, and the British Palestinian Mandate was not a territory that Zionist sympathisers felt especially drawn to. Minorities with a nomadic way of life, such as the Tatars, Circassians and Roma, had no link to any specific state. Prior to the First World War, quite a few minority population groups had multiple identities and integrated day-to-day into the state where they lived. During and after the First World War, minorities were often required to commit to a national identity, or they were allocated a notional nationality that did not correspond to their ethnic reality.

217. Beyrau, *Krieg und Revolution*, 190-193.

218. Michael Mann, *The Dark Side of Democracy. Explaining Ethnic Cleansing* (New York: Cambridge University Press, 2012), 67; Diner, *Das Jahrhundert verstehen*, 61-62; Gerwarth, Die Besiegten, 274-275.

219. Joachim Rogall, *Die Deutschen im Posener Land und Mittelpolen* (Berlin: Langen/Müller, 1998), 130; Antoni Czubiński, *Wielkopolska w latach 1918-1939* (Poznań: Wydawnictwo Poznański, 2000), 80; *Lexikon der Vertreibungen. Deportation, Zwangsaussiedelung und ethnische Säuberung im Europa des 20. Jahrhunderts*, eds. Detlef Brandes, Holm Sundhaussen and Stefan Troebst (Köln et al.: Böhlau, 2010), 92-94.

220. István Mócsy, *The Effects of World War I: The Uprooted: Hungarian Refugees and Their Impact on Hungary's Domestic Politics, 1918-1921* (New York: Columbia University Press, 1983), 12.

221. Eszter P. Gantner, *Budapest - Berlin. Die Koordinaten einer Emigration 1919-1933* (Stuttgart: Franz Steiner, 2011), 159.

222. The numbers are estimated at over 150,000 between 1918 and 1939. David Skrabania, 'Arbeitsmigrationen und Mobilität zwischen Oberschlesien und dem Ruhrgebiet und Reichsinneren (1860er-1920er Jahre),' in *Migrationsgeschichte Oberschlesiens. Globale Mobilität in regionaler Perspektive*, ed. Claudia Kraft (to be published).

223. Michael R. Marrus, *Die Unerwünschten. Europäische Flüchtlinge im 20. Jahrhundert* (Berlin et al.: Schwarze Risse/Rote Strasse, 1999), 68-72.

224. Jochen Oltmer, 'Kleine Globalgeschichte der Flucht im 20. Jahrhundert,' in *Flucht historisch, Aus Politik und Zeitgeschichte* 26-27 (2016), 18-25, here 19.

225. Bettina Dodenhoeft, *Lasst mich nach Russland heim: russische Emigranten in Deutschland von 1918 bis 1945* (Frankfurt/Main: Peter Lang, 1993), 10-11; Irina Mchitarian, *Zum bildungspolitischen Umgang mit den pädagogischen Initiativen der russischen Emigranten in Deutschland, der Tschechoslowakei und Polen (1918-1939)* (Bad Heilbrunn: Klinkhardt, 2006), 37.

226. About Polish anti-Semitism see the conversation between the Polish politician Roman Dmowski and the co-founder of the 'American Jewish Committee', Louis Marshall (1856-1929), held in New York, 6 October 1918. in Collection Woodrow Wilson Papers: Series 5: Peace Conference Correspondence and Documents, 1914-1921; Subseries A: Policy Documents, 1914-1919, <https://www.loc.gov/resource/mss46029.mss46029-384_0018_1148/?sp=649&r=-0.975,-0.071,2.95,1.413,0> (access 15 May 2020).

227. Oleg Budnitskii, *Russian Jews Between the Reds and the Whites, 1917-1920* (Philadelphia: University of Pennsylvania Press, 2012), 243-248; Bruno Cabanes, *The Great War and the Origins of Humanitarianism, 1918-1924* (New York: Cambridge University Press, 2014), 143-154, 163-164; Philipp Ther, *The Dark Side of Nation-States: Ethnic Cleansing in Modern Europe* (Oxford: Berghahn, 2014), 66; Borodziej, Górny, *Der vergessene Weltkrieg*, 184-190.

228. Karl Schlögel, 'Einführung: Die Zentren der Emigration,' in *Der grosse Exodus. Die Russische Emigration und ihre Zentren 1917-1941*, ed. Karl Schlögel (München: C.H. Beck, 1994), 9-20, here 12-13.

229. Cabanes, *The Great War and Humanitarianism*, 135-139, 168-173.; Marrus, *Die Unerwünschten*, 99-104.

230. Fritz Mierau ed., *Russen in Berlin. Literatur Malerei Theater Film 1918-1933* (Leipzig: Reclam, 1991); Zdenek Sládek, 'Prag: Das "russische Oxford",' in *Der große Exodus*, 218-233; Robert Harold Johnson, 'Paris die Hauptstadt der russischen Diaspora,' in *loc. cit.*, 260-278.

The Second Great War, 1917-1923

Jay Winter

In this paper, I present a bifurcated interpretation of the history of the Great War, dividing it into two parts, the first lasting from 1914 to 1917, the second from 1917 to 1923. In this way, I want to take advantage of two major changes in historiography that have occurred in recent years: first, a shift of the geographical epicentre of the war from Paris to Warsaw, and secondly, a shift in the chronology of the war, one which recognises its failure to end in 1918. The interpretation I want to offer suggests that there was a crisis in 1917 that separates the first three years of the conflict from the years that followed, and which was largely the result of powerful economic and demographic pressures that destabilised all the combatants, though the Central powers more than the Allies. This crisis abated somewhat in the west in 1918 but continued in the east in an exacerbated form for the following five years. Hatred, hunger and class conflict were radicalising elements in the disorder of the post-Imperial world, set adrift by the collapse of the Romanoff, Hohenzollern, Habsburg and Ottoman empires. Post-imperial violence was endemic in these regions, merging civil war and ethnic and national conflicts that played out in what we might well call the Second Great War. My claim is that the passage from wartime crisis to post-imperial violence was seamless, and part of one complex but distinctive phase of European history, starting in 1917 and terminating more or less in 1923.

From One War to Another

The illusion that the Great War ended on 11 November 1918 grew out of a Western-front myopia about the war, which I for one shared for all too long. Thirty years ago, I argued that among the many reasons for war in 1914 was that Britain and Germany were pre-

pared to engage in armed conflict over control of northwestern Europe. Britain could not allow a German victory over France, which would place the German navy in occupation of the Channel ports, and thereby in control of British trade routes providing 75 percent of the British food supply in 1914. That war, won by France, Britain and their allies, ended in 1918, and the Peace Treaty of 1919 put a seal on the victory, lasted until Hitler's rewriting of 1918 in 1940 twenty-one years later.

But all the other theatres of the Great War were left in a state of chaos and uncertainty made all the more threatening by the potential spread of the Russian Revolution throughout Europe. Who can claim that the period 1919-1923 was one of peace? Various white armies, supported by a mismanaged military expedition of the victorious Allies, tried and failed to overthrow the Bolshevik regime. Civil war in Russia left only calamity in its wake, as did the Red thrust into Poland and its defeat not far from the gates of Warsaw. Italy lost the peace and her parliamentary regime collapsed, with a little help from Mussolini and King Victor Emmanuel. The states created out of the Austro-Hungarian Empire were riven by class and ethnic conflicts, which overlapped in ways that ensured the bloodshed would continue for a considerable period of time. And the collapse of the Ottoman Empire produced anything but peace. In the aftermath of the first peace treaty of Sèvres, elements of the defeated Ottoman army, reassembled and mobilised by Mustafa Kemal Atatürk, reconquered their own soil, against Greek, British, French and Italian forces that had occupied Anatolia after November 1918.

War bled into civil war, transforming the face of Central, Southern, and Eastern Europe. One inevitable result of this shift of emphasis in violence from inter-

Fig. 1: Smyrna in flames and the panicked escape of the Greek population, September 1922.

national to internecine was ethnic cleansing. One of the most terrifying instances of demographic displacement occurred in Turkey, where Christians by the millions moved west from Anatolia to Europe, and Muslims moved east into what became the Turkish Republic in 1923. When the Treaty of Sèvres was scrapped and replaced by the Treaty of Lausanne in 1923, the Turkification of the new nation was codified in international law. The process that began with the Armenian genocide of 1915 was completed on the shores of Smyrna, burned to the ground in 1922. Christian Smyrna vanished; Muslim Izmir rose in its place. The euphemism of 'population exchange' was coined to cover the naked reality of murder, rape, and pillage.

So my claim is, in fact, twofold. In addition to changing the chronological parameters of the war that began in 1914, we must also register a change in the character of collective violence over the subsequent decade; for I contend that there was a fundamental difference in the way war was waged in 1914-17 as compared to 1917-23.

What primarily separated these two phases was that prior to 1917, war mobilisation entailed the forced unification of social classes and ethnic groups behind a national or imperial war effort. To be sure, this effort succeeded in a muffling or masking of internal conflicts, as the combatants sought to provide their armies with the men and materiel needed for victory. After 1917, internal conflicts re-emerged, perhaps with added force because of their suppression during the previous three years, turning a culture of war mobilisation into a culture of war anxiety. The former aimed at unity, while the latter focused on internal divisions, hatreds and resentments, some long-standing, some newly invented or deployed in new ways.

In effect, in early 1917, after 30 months of war, all combatants faced the emergence of this different, second type of war culture. Alongside *l'Union sacrée* there emerged a host of fractures, with the suspicion, or worse, of one's fellow countrymen providing the basis for attacks – rhetorical or physical – that previously had focused on the enemy. By 1917, the enemy lived within the gates, posing a threat to the nation and the war effort. This was as true of Irishmen in-revolt against Britain in 1916 as it was of Jews in Imperial Germany, whose supposedly low levels of military participation became the subject of a botched army census that wound up proving the opposite. Jews were in fact disproportionately present at the front. The Jewish census was quickly shelved and the archives destroyed, but the sentiments behind it festered.

The war within took on a new form on the Ides of March 1917, the day that Tsar Nicholas II abdicated. Now, the old order on both sides faced a new menace: the prospect of social unrest leading to revolution and civil war. The spectre of trans-national class conflict intersecting with global military conflict justifies our sense of rupture in the midst of the Great War. That threat fed the new culture of war anxiety, which emerged as the material and human toll the conflict exacted spiralled to unprecedented levels. It is this upheaval, evident from the early months of 1917, which requires us to divide the war into two parts. Bitterness about domestic traitors grew and deepened ominously after the Armistice of November 1918. The politics of *domestic* division and hatred dominated political, economic, and social life for years thereafter.

Thus, by mid-1917 both sides of the conflict experienced a sea change in the way they understood the war. They moved away from a culture of war mobilisation, appropriate to what was essentially an imperial conflict, towards a culture of war anxiety informing the revolutionary and post-imperial conflicts in 1917-18 and after.

This difference between imperial and revolutionary perspectives was made blindingly explicit on 23 November 1917, when the new Bolshevik regime in Russia published verbatim in *Pravda* the contents of reports emanating from the Tsar's Foreign Ministry, producing undeniable evidence of the imperial future the Allies had in mind. These imperial ambitions became problematic when the United States entered the war in April 1917. President Wilson's commitment to open diplomacy and the principle of self-determination cut right across the imperial outlook and designs of the other belligerents. If tens of millions of men had suffered and died on both sides simply so that imperial power could change hands, then those leading these nations at war who claimed they were champions of democracy were liars and hypocrites.

Multiple social divisions re-emerged in a deepened form, in this, the opening phase of the Second Great

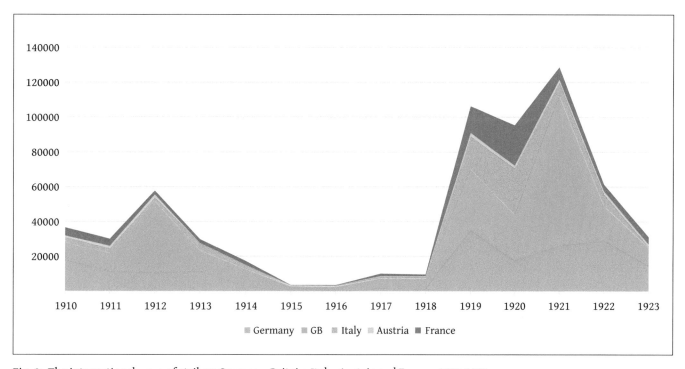

Fig. 2: The international wave of strikes: Germany, Britain, Italy, Austria and France, 1910-1923.

Month-Year	Specie in Reichsbank	Notes in Circulation
Sept-1914	1,787	4,491
Sept-1915	2,457	6,158
Sept-1916	2,503	7,370
Sept-1917	2,506	10,205
Sept-1918	2,563	15,334

Table 1 with Reichsbank gold holdings and paper notes in circulation, 1914-1918 (millions)[1].

War, and on both sides. Independently of the Russian revolution, domestic conflict broke out in industry. After three years of industrial mobilisation, the first stage of a series of massive strike-waves spread through Europe, lasting until roughly 1923.

The phenomenon was war-related in the way it reflected wartime inflation and inequality of sacrifice, but it also followed secular trends. Since the 1880s, moments of major trade union growth were often followed by strike activity. The year 1917 presented no exception; there had been a massive influx into trade unions in all combatant countries after 1914.

Furthermore, the intensity of the strikes in 1917 and after suggested that the postponement of workers' demands regarding wages and conditions of labour, which had occurred in all belligerent countries and some neutral ones since 1914, acted like the lid of a pressure cooker. Inflation fuelled the fire, and trade unions and other social groups, in particular women protesting shortages and outrageous food and fuel prices, took to the streets or laid down their tools. They did so despite understanding the desperate needs of the war machine.[2] Indeed, the March revolution in Russia was triggered by a women's protest over bread prices.

Wartime inflation was much worse among the Central powers than among the Allies. In part this was because Germany could not borrow on the international capital market in the way the Allies could. But it was also a political choice, a gamble by the German leadership that it could just print money and recover later by exploiting those countries they intended to crush. The critical moment when price inflation began its exponential leap was in late 1916, when the German high command came to power and ordered a second industrial mobilisation as the means to victory. In Table 1, we can see that in mid-1917, Germany printed four times as many Deutschmarks as it had in its reserves; a year later, the figure was six times the reserves, and then the floodgates opened.

In Table 2, we find confirmation that Germany ran its war effort differently than Britain did. Germany quadrupled the money in circulation; it paid for the war by inflation. Britain in contrast doubled the money supply; it paid for the war mostly by loans. Inflation destroyed savings, and created the conditions in which, despite or even because of price controls, a thriving black market operated. Inflation lined the pockets of the rich and made it necessary for everyone in Germany to break the law in order to feed their families. The way Germany waged the economic war ensured that class struggle would take on a new and more dangerous form in 1917; it pointed to the glaring gap between the profiteers and everyone else and between a corrupt elite and a cold and hungry population, worn out by three years of war.

Unsurprisingly, in 1917, the domestic political truce of the first half of the war came to an end. The German Social Democratic Party split in early 1917; those wanting an end to the war met at Gotha on 6 April and founded the USPD, the Independent Social Democratic Party. Once again, women's groups were prominent in this radicalisation of the political left. The British Liberal party also split, in part over personalities, in part over conscription and the suppression of the 1916 rising in Ireland. In France, Georges Clemenceau (1841-1929), who became prime minister in November, was a divisive leader. He had his Radical colleague Joseph Caillaux (1863-1944) arrested for advocating peace negotiations: Caillaux was convicted of treason in 1918.[3]

Wartime violence exposed violent internal conflicts within the combatant countries. In 1917, bloody race riots broke out in the United States in East St Louis, Illinois, and even more ominously in Houston, Texas, where 156 black soldiers mutinied. Sixteen civilians and four soldiers died during the riots. Subsequently, 19 soldiers were hanged and over 40 imprisoned for long terms.[5] In 1918, American socialist leader Eugene Debs (1855-1926) went to prison for violating the Espionage Act by urging men to resist the draft.[6] One opponent of the war, Robert Prager (1888-1918), a German national and trade unionist, was

	Monetary base				Money supply			
	Germany		Britain		Germany		Britain	
Date	Marks	% increase per annum	Pounds	% increase per annum	Marks	% increase per annum	Pounds	% increase per annum
31 Dec. 1913	7,22		259		17,233		1,154	
31 Dec. 1914	10,157	+ 41	367	+ 42	19,514	+ 13	1,329	+ 15
31 Dec. 1915	11,918	+ 17	359	- 2	23,175	+ 19	1,434	+ 8
31 Dec. 1916	15,912	+ 34	419	+ 17	29,202	+ 26	1,655	+ 15
31 Dec. 1917	24,789	+ 56	471	+ 12	43,801	+ 50	1,939	+ 17
31 Dec. 1918	43,608	+ 76	624	+ 32	66,359	+ 52	2,429	+ 25

Table 2 with changes (%) in the monetary base and money supply, Britain and Germany, 1913-1918[4].

lynched in Maryville, Illinois. His killers were acquitted.[7] The gloves were off in domestic as well as in global politics.

Polarisation marked the advent of the increasingly strident political right as well. When the German *Reichstag* issued its peace resolution in July 1917, disgruntled deputies and their supporters set up the *Vaterlandspartei* (Fatherland party), with the notable support of Admiral von Tirpitz (1849-1930) and the industrialist Alfred Hugenberg (1865-1951).[8] By then, the German war effort was almost entirely in the hands of a military-industrial group that gave the army whatever it needed, but at the price of creating massive bottlenecks and shortages on the home front. Social protest intensified just as economic difficulties multiplied.

For the French, the war crisis of early 1917 antedated the Chemin des Dames offensive and the mutinies which followed its failure. There is no evidence that social agitation on France's home front influenced these mutinous soldiers, who refused to continue the futile and bloody offensive launched by General Nivelle (1856-1924) on 16 April.[9] Instead, both the mutiny and the existence of widespread unrest on the home front reflected the exhaustion and anger felt by a substantial part of the French population To them, as to many around the world, the war appeared to be endless. The war of 1914-1917 had pro-

duced a massive stalemate. Neither side enjoyed an advantage sufficient to bring the warring parties to the conference table. In 30 months of war, the two sides had lost perhaps seven million men killed in action or dead of wounds, and another 15 million wounded or made prisoners of war. The giant campaigns of 1916, which we today call the battles of Verdun and the Somme, had not changed by one iota the strategic balance on the Western front. Fatigue, anger, suspicion and social friction were evident everywhere.

If only for this reason, I believe it makes sense to divide the Great War in two. The first Russian revolution may be taken to be a turning point, the moment that the political character of the war changed. I call it the 'climacteric' of 1917, both internationally and domestically.[10] The Russian revolution did not cause this crisis; it embodied a larger sea change in public attitudes to the war.

In France, the slow but palpable development in 1917 of a new set of representations of war was hardly surprising. After all, it was only 46 years earlier – that is, within living memory – that a communist revolution in Paris had followed a failed war. Earlier traditions of revolutionary warfare in the 1790s were also a mainstay of the history taught in French schools. In 1917, alongside older images of the determination of the French nation to fight on until victory, there appeared a new and striking set of representations of la *Grande Guerre* as an apocalypse, as the end of one world and the beginning of another. For example, the winner of the Prix Goncourt in 1916, Henri Barbusse (1873-1925), ended his novel *Le Feu* with a post-apocalyptic scene of soldiers on both sides emerging from the trenches with a vision of a new world to build. Barbusse had been severely wounded in combat. He was not a pacifist, but a man who spoke for a growing number of people who believed that the war had to transform the international order that had precipitated the catastrophe.

The strength of the 'imperial' war cultures of the 1914-1917 period was that they were dominated by compelling representations of war as a fight to preserve old and valued ways of life.[11] The new 'revolutionary' war cultures of the 1917-and-after period were marked by anger and a sense of domestic injustice, as well as more than a touch of what Nietzsche termed *ressentiment*.[12] But they also gestured towards positive transformations, in the hope that something good would come out of the conflict's immense suffering. The two antipodes – imperial war and revolutionary war – were both in play from 1917 on.

If I have persuaded you that the Great War fractured in 1917, it still remains for me to persuade you that the new culture of war anxiety, with its emphasis on the enemy within, informed the collective violence that continued in Europe, in particular in Central, Southern and Eastern Europe, until 1923. If so, it then follows that the Second Great War may be dated from 1917 to 1923.

Post-Imperial Violence against Civilians

The end of the war in 1918 signalled the beginning of a number of wars to determine the borders of post-imperial Eastern Europe. Much of this violence was directed against civilians. When the nascent Polish army defeated Ukrainians and captured the Galician

Fig. 3: Sacked Hasidic synagogue in Lvov, after November 1918 pogrom.

city of Lvov, there followed from 22 to 24 November an attack on Jews and Jewish property in the city. Approximately 150 Jews were killed and 500 shops destroyed.[13]

The Piłsudski-Paderewski government condemned the attacks, which they ascribed to bandits and others driven to violence by hardships and hunger. Hagen's study of the violence reveals the source of anger was the perceived difference between Jewish wealth and Polish poverty, configured in such a way that the Jews symbolically or materially 'owed' their Polish attackers the goods (and lives) they took. Here is evidence of the breakdown of law and order in the aftermath of the Armistice; the spill over of wartime hatreds into post-war violence directed against a Jewish minority whose 'neutrality' as between Ukrainians and Poles was seen as a smokescreen for betrayal. Violence, including murder, thus informed a kind of retributive justice in the eyes of the perpetrators.

There is substantial evidence of the unleashing of violence on ethnic, class or national enemies throughout Eastern Europe in the first months after the Armistice. One case is now known as the Finnish civil war. It started in February 1918, with an offensive by armed groups supported by the new Bolshevik regime. Aligned against them were conservative forces backed by the German army, whose military detachments were in Finland. Battles for Tampere and Helsinki were won by the White Guard and German force, and plans to establish a German-backed monarchy in Finland were dashed only by the November defeat of Germany. What made this encounter significant was the use of terror not only during the fighting, but in its aftermath as well. Perhaps 12,500 Red Guards died in captivity at the hands of the Whites. Here is one case among many to suggest that when national wars bled into civil wars, the limits on the maltreatment both of civilians and of those in uniform, whether prisoners or not, disappeared.[14]

The civil wars in the Baltic States showed the same resort to indiscriminate violence. On 1 December 1918, Latvian territory was invaded by Bolshevik forces. Riga fell to them on 3 January 1919. Thereafter, an unstable alliance of Latvian and Estonian forces, alongside elements of German para-military groups pushed back, first against the Bolsheviks, and then against each other. German forces captured Riga on 22 May, but then refused to leave. They had their own agenda: to create a German presence in the Baltic States. This mad idea – mad in the context of a lost war – vanished when they were expelled by their erstwhile allies, the combined Latvian and Estonian forces. Further fighting established Latvian independence, ratified by the Latvian-Soviet Treaty of 1920.[15]

What happened in the Baltic States was a microcosm of the civil war that waged across Soviet Russia from 1917 to 1922. My aim is not to give a full account of the dozens of civil wars going on within the greater struggle for mastery of post-imperial Russia;[16] it is merely to signal that from Helsinki to Yerevan and beyond that to Vladivostok, sporadic to intensive explosions of violence marked the conflicts over the future of what ultimately became the Union of Soviet Socialist Republics.[17]

My claim here is twofold. First, these internecine conflicts were exercises in butchery and pillage under conditions of hunger verging on famine. Second, the civil war was deformed by the presence, albeit in relatively small numbers, of Western troops who initially took Bolshevik Russia's withdrawal from the conflict as treachery, and who were determined to reassert Western interests in Russia by the overthrow of the Bolshevik regime itself. Their failure and that of their many allies in the White armies to do so was as decisive in ending the second Great War as the Bolshevik revolution was in ending the first Great War in 1917.

What was distinctive about the Russian civil war – alongside the Polish war of Independence and the Baltic civil wars – was the extent to which civilians were caught up in the cross-fire in ways that made the first Great War in most instances look relatively polite and orderly. A taste of the cruelties of these civil wars may be gained by a perusal of Anna Akhmatova's (1889-1966) poetry, Isaac Babel's (1894-1940) *Red Cavalry* or Pasternak's *Dr Zhivago*.

The exception to this distinction between pre- and post-1917 is the Armenian genocide. That crime provides the bridge between the first Great War and the second, since it announced a policy of war against a people not for what they were said to have done – supported the Russian war effort – but for who they were. Biopolitics, in the form of the murder of a people, became a weapon of war in 1915.

Here was a harbinger of terrible things to come, both in the Second Great War and after.[18] Similarly premonitory were the crimes associated with red and white terror, first in Berlin and Munich, and then in Budapest in 1919 and after. The violence of these civil wars left a legacy of bitterness that took generations to fade away.

Hunger and Famine

The Second Great War, stretching from 1917 to 1923, also resembles the first Great War with respect to hunger. Food shortages and the lack of basic necessities crippled the war effort of Germany and Austria-Hungary in 1917, just as they did in many parts of the Russian and Ottoman empires. Indeed, I have argued that these shortages were built into the way the war was waged within the Central powers. The Allies proved capable of distributing the goods and services needed by the armed forces without consigning their own peoples to hunger and disease. Here again, 1915 offered a foretaste of the problem of food shortages that spread throughout Eastern Europe from 1917 on.[19] Civilians in occupied Belgium and France – children in particular – were fed by the first foreign aid programme in history, the American relief effort. In the last two years of the war, hunger was a major factor in exposing the fundamental weakness in the Central Powers' way of waging war. The problem lay less in supply than in distribution. The Allies controlled prices and profits, while in Germany the worst price inflation in world history began in 1917 and abated only in 1923. Inflation destroyed savings, crippled markets and distribution networks, empowered a massive black market and exacerbated internecine hatreds.

Twenty years later, Hitler made sure that the German people would not once again go hungry in a world war. He displaced onto the shoulders of Jews and other *Untermenschen* the misery that the German leadership had forced on its own population from 1917 on.[20]

Worse was to come in the second Great War. Part of the reason was that Germany's military collapse left its forces deep within the old Russian Empire. Virtually all the grain-producing areas were sites of ongoing violence, and the power vacuum produced by the Armistice meant that 1919 was going to be a year

of hunger for the bulk of the population living in the east, including in the new Bolshevik Russia, assailed on all sides by counter-revolutionary bands and armies.

The Allies made things worse – in clear violation of international law – by continuing the blockade of German ports until the German delegation signed the Peace Treaty in June 1919. That meant hunger and soaring death rates in Vienna and Berlin, but also in the densely populated areas of the new Poland and adjacent territories. A demographic crisis followed, with outbreaks of typhus, dysentery, and cholera made worse by the appearance of the worst influenza pandemic in world history.

In 1919, the US Congress established the American Relief Administration. In the following four years, it provided food aid to 23 European countries, as well as to Turkey and the remains of the Ottoman Empire. One-fifth of this aid went to Poland, feeding Polish schoolchildren, and probably feeding Polish soldiers in the Polish-Soviet war. In 1921, famine of potentially catastrophic proportions impelled the Bolshevik government to work with the Hoover Food Aid program. It worked because Hoover realised that even though agricultural production was crippled by war and civil war, the real problem of avoiding famine was the need to provide transportation through a chaotic and strife-torn rural landscape. That he did, using his expertise as a civil engineer with knowledge of the Russian terrain. He was not alone. There were many other European and local agents who made a difference. Together, they were able to save the lives of a generation of children in Russia, Ukraine, and Belarus.[21]

No one has been able to provide a reliable accounting of the loss of life that took place during the Russian civil war and the Polish-Soviet War. Demographer Boris Urlanis (1906-1981) claimed that the figure of 300,000 was the most nearly accurate for those who died in combat in the Polish-Soviet war; of these deaths, perhaps 175,000 were suffered by the White armies and civilians, and 125,000 by the Red armies. But to account for those on both sides who died of disease he added a figure of 450,000. No one knows how many perished in the White and Red Terror in Russia, or in the countless skirmishes that marked the civil war as a whole. Caution suggests that we accept that the total number who died of disease, combat, or exe-

Fig. 4: Women thank the representatives of the American Aid Administration, Samara Province, 1922.

cution exceeded one million in what became the Soviet Union. These losses crippled the new regime, and according to Orlando Figes, the industrial working class, in whose name the Revolutions of 1917 were launched, had disappeared five years later. The Soviet state took the place of this vanished class, and we all know the devastating consequences of this series of catastrophes – Figes calls it 'a people's tragedy'[22] – when Stalin and his circle took over the Soviet state and waged war on his own people for nearly 30 years.

Conclusion

I am not one of those historians who believe in the concept of a Thirty Years War lasting from 1914 to 1945. Hitler changed the meaning of war first in 1939 in Poland and then again in 1941 when he invaded the Soviet Union and turned war as politics into war as racial extermination. All the same, one of the advantages of the notion that there were two Great Wars between 1914 and 1923 – not just one which ended in 1918 – is that it provides us with clues as to what led from the First World War to the Second. The politics of hatred, of hunger and of the maltreatment of civilians can be traced directly to what I call the first

Great War from 1914 to 1917, but these vectors of violence were profoundly deepened and radicalised during the second Great War from 1918 to 1923. Anti-Semitism was alive and well before these dates, but it grew by leaps and bounds in 1918 and after. The viciousness of the confused fighting among different armies representing different national factions and ethnic groups only worsened when these conflicts were fused (and confused) with the Russian civil war.[23]

It is in the period of 1918 to 1923 that we can find abundant evidence of the process historian George Mosse (1918-1999) terms 'brutalisation'. He used it in a different sense than I use it today. He believed that exposure to mass death in 1914-18 brutalised both the men who endured it and the societies for which they fought.[24] I believe he is mistaken on this point. The shocking effects of the great battles of Verdun and the Somme should never be underestimated, but the overwhelming majority of the men who fought them returned either to combat or to their homes as recognisable human beings, with their commitments and values more or less intact.[25] Mosse, I contend, is wrong on the dating but right on the essence of the story; for there exists abundant evidence that there was a far-reaching brutalisation of norms – much more damaging than the brutalisation of individuals – in the period 1918-23 and after. It was then that economic and demographic disasters hit societies in a state of disorder and weakness that simply did not exist on the eve of the First World War. 1913 was a good year; 1919 was a terrible one. After 1918, civil war was fought out against the backdrop of famine, class conflict and ethnic hatreds not unknown, certainly, before 1918, but not mixed together in the same witches' brew.

In a nutshell, the historiographic shift I propose in this keynote lecture is to limit the prevailing interpretation of total war to the years it best describes, namely, 1914 to 1917, and to apply the term 'post-imperial civil war' to the much more chaotic, vicious and costly configuration of violence that spread all over Eastern and Southern Europe in the period of the second Great War.

It is not in the first Great War of 1914-17 but in this second Great War that the seeds of the radical conflicts of the 1930s must be sought. The German army in 1914 to 1917 was in no sense a prototype of the Nazi armies under Hitler, but when Ludendorff and Hindenburg took over in late 1916, they started a transition that slowly but surely prepared the way for the dark future ahead. The same is true for the Soviet Union, where civil war turned a regime with many facets, including both liberal and authoritarian ones, into a monster. Without Italy's diplomatic failures in Paris in 1919 and the parallel intensification of class conflict in the immediate aftermath of the war, Mussolini would have had no chance of seizing power. Contingency matters. And the contingent processes that won out in the second Great War were hardly democratic. Despite a period of recovery in the later 1920s, the world economic crisis exposed the anti-democratic political tendencies feeding off the profound social and ethnic divisions that remained the ultimate legacy of the second Great War. The tragic dimension of the Great War was evident well before 1917, but until now historians have emphasised the theme of remobilisation, as marking the renewal in that year of the commitment of home populations to the even greater sacrifices required of them three years after the outbreak of the war.[26] The full story, however, is more complicated. It needs to acknowledge that after three years of war there was a

shift away from an emphasis on mobilisation of whole societies and a dangerous deepening of the social fissures within them. What I term the culture of war anxiety expressed an increasing sense of anger over injustice and privilege, which cut right across the *union sacrée* of the first part of the conflict. The emergence of this competing war culture, one of resentment rather than of rallying around the flag, constituted, I claim, a significant development in the cultural history of the Great War.

The culture of war anxiety remained in evidence long after the formal end of the conflict. At the level of family life, deep anxiety was inevitable in the case of widows, orphans and those caring for the millions of men wounded in the war. Divorce rates in many parts of Europe reached levels much higher than in pre-war years. Would the victors realise the peace for which they had paid so high a price? Would the vanquished ever be able to escape from the disaster of the war and of the peace following it?

Here, too, the concept of a different war culture emerging in the second half of the conflict and enduring after the armistice provides a way of avoiding the binary thinking that has long dominated the literature in the field. Instead of insisting on black and white choices – patriotism versus pacifism, consent versus coercion, mobilisation versus mutiny – we should recognise that the predominant colour of wartime was grey. Contradictory messages existed in vigorous incompatibility. The Great War was simply too big to be encompassed by one cultural code or by one war culture.

In 1917 and after, the culture of war anxiety did not so much displace the culture of war mobilisation as challenge and destabilise it. Most contemporaries still yearned for victory, but not at any price. This was the most disturbing message of the Bolshevik revolution, one which haunted all combatants in the last year of the war.

Focusing on the emergence of a culture of war anxiety in 1917 also helps us go beyond another binary division: that of cultural mobilisation during the war and cultural demobilisation thereafter. To be sure, there was a slow and painful disengagement of populations, social groups, and governments from wartime hatreds, but the lethal mixture of civil war and social revolution marked winners like Italy as much as it did losers like Germany, Austria, and Russia. The early post-war anti-imperial violence in Egypt, India, Korea and China touched on the global interests of Britain, France and Japan in direct and palpable ways. While (with the exception of Russia, Ireland, Poland and Turkey) the culture of war mobilisation ended when the troops came home in 1919, the culture of war anxiety mutated into what I would term a culture of post-war anxiety, accompanying various forms of economic instability and social and racial conflict that flowed directly from the war itself. America's Red Scare and paroxysms of racial violence form part of the same tapestry of violence and exclusion woven both during and after the war. The conventional dates arising from the peace treaties have only a surface utility. There had been too much bloodshed and too much bitterness to enable societies to close the door on the hatreds, antagonisms, and anxieties of wartime.

Why did this paroxysm of violence between 1917 and 1923 come to an end? One reason is sheer exhaustion. There was a limit to the capacity of these societies to endure endless violence. Furthermore, by 1924, the economic chaos of the immediate post-war years had died down, and most European countries in both the east and the west renewed their pre-war growth trajectories that had been interrupted by the war.[27] One other reason European life stabilised in the mid-1920s was the Western powers' recognition that the Soviet Union was here to stay. Similarly, the slow but steady reincorporation of Weimar Germany into the European community and the League of Nations reduced international tensions for a time. Of course, after 1929, none of the stability conditions that had made post-war European recovery possible survived the world economic crisis, but that is another story.

For these reasons, I urge a reconsideration of the terminal dates of the Great War. I stick to 1914 as its beginning, not because I underestimate the significance of the Balkan wars of 1912 and 1913, but because they did not trigger a global conflict. Neither did the Russo-Japanese war of 1904-1905, which could also be said to have set in motion forces that spanned the century. I do, however, propose the new ending date of 1923. The dividing point between my two Great Wars is 1917, when revolution and social conflict returned to the centre of the European stage and all societies had to confront significant social divisions. It was then that new representations of war, shot

through with anxiety, emerged alongside older representations of heroic solidarity. Those anxieties did not evaporate in 1918 but rather took on new and at times even more violent forms in the context of civil war and revolution. In the decade of the Great War, representations were not immutable: they changed over time as the war itself changed, giving to both the conflict and its aftermath the bitter taste they have never lost.

Endnotes

1. Source: Konrad Roesler, *Die Finanzpolitik des Deutschen Reiches im Ersten Weltkrieg* (Berlin: Duncker & Humblot 1967), Appendix Table 13.
2. Charles Tilly, *Strikes, Wars and Revolutions in an International Perspective* (Cambridge and Paris: Cambridge University Press and Éditions de la MSH, 1989); Leopold Haimson with Giulio Sapell (eds.), *Strikes, Social Conflict and the First World War. An International Perspective* (Milano: Feltrinelli, 1992).
3. Manuel Gomez-Brufal, Joseph Caillaux: *Traitre ou visionnaire* (Paris: Dualpha éditions, 2014).
4. Note: For Britain the money supply is M3 as defined by Cappie and Webber (Monetary history, pp. 13 ff., 241 ff.) to include all deposits with bank but excluding deposits at credit and mortgage banks and in postal giro accounts, but to exclude deposits at savings banks. Interbank deposits could not be deducted. Soures: (Germany) Carl-Ludwig Holtfrerich, *The German Inflation 1914-1923*, (Munich: DeGruyter, 1986), 50-51. (Britain) Forrest Cappie and Alan Webber, A Monetary history of United Kingdom, 1870-1982, (London: George Allen and Unwin, 1984), 57, 84.
5. Harper Barnes, *Never Been a Time: The 1917 Race Riot That Sparked the Civil Rights Movement* (New York: Walker & Company, 2008).
6. Ernest Freeberg, *Democracy's Prisoner: Eugene V. Debs, the Great War and the Right to Dissent* (Cambridge, MA:, Harvard University Press, 2008).
7. E.A. Schwartz, 'The Lynching of Robert Prager, the United Mine Workers, and the Problems of Patriotism in 1918,' *Journal of the Illinois State Historical Society* 95, no. 4 (Winter 2003), 414-437.
8. Richard Bessel, 'Mobilization and Demobilization in Germany, 1916-1919,' in State, *Society and Mobilization During the First World War*, edited by John Horne (Cambridge: Cambridge University Press, 2002), 50-67.
9. André Loez and Nicolas Mariot (eds.), *Obéir / Désobéir. Les mutineries de 1917 en perspective* (Paris: La Découverte, 2008).
10. On the use of the term 'climacteric' in economic history, see Donald N. McCloskey, 'The British Iron and Steel Industry, 1870-1914: A Study of the Climacteric in Productivity,' *Journal of Economic History* 29, No. 1, The Tasks of Economic History* (Mar., 1969), 173-175.

11. Stéphane Audoin Rouzeau and Annette Becker, 1914-1918 *Retrouver la guerre* (Paris: Gallimard, 2000).

12. Marc Ferro, *Ressentiment dans l'histoire: Comprendre notre temps* (Paris: Odile Jacob, 2007).

13. William W. Hagen, 'The Moral Economy of Ethnic Violence: The Pogrom in Lwow, November 1918,' *Geschichte und Gesellschaft* 31, no. 2 (Apr. - Jun., 2005), 203-226.

14. Sirkka Arosalo, 'Social Conditions for Political Violence: Red and White Terror in the Finnish Civil War of 1918,' *Journal of Peace Research* 35, no. 2 (1998), 147-166.

15. On Latvia, see Geoffrey Swain, 'The Disillusioning of the Revolution's Praetorian Guard: The Latvian Riflemen, Summer-Autumn 1918,' *Europe-Asia Studies* 51, no. 4 (1999), 667-86.

16. On which, see Timothy Snyder, *The Reconstruction of Nations: Poland, Ukraine, Lithuania, Belarus, 1569-1999* (New Haven: Yale University Press, 2004).

17. Figes, Orlando, 'The Red Army and Mass Mobilization during the Russian Civil War 1918-1920,' *Past & Present*, no. 129 (1990), 168-211.

18. Jay Winter, 'Under Cover of War: The Armenian Genocide in the Context of Total War', in Robert Gellately and Ben Kiernan (eds.), *The Specter of Genocide. Mass Murder in Historical Perspective* (Cambridge, Cambridge University Press, 2003), 189-214.

19. Jay Winter, 'Paris, London, Berlin: Capital cities at war,' in Jay Winter and Jean-Louis Robert (eds.), *Capital Cities at War: Paris, London, Berlin 1914-1919* (Cambridge: Cambridge University Press, 1997), 3-24.

20. Lothar Borchardt, 'The Impact of the War Economy on the Civilian Population,' in *The German Military in the Age of Total War*, ed. William Deist (Leamington Spa: Berg, 1985), 110-120.

21. Benjamin M. Weissmann, 'The Aftereffects of the American Relief Mission to Soviet Russia,' *The Russian Review 29*, no. 4 (1970), 411-21.

22. Orlando Figes, *A People's Tragedy 1891-1924* (London: Penguin, 1996).

23. On this and on many other points, I share the interpretation of Robert Gerwarth, *The Vanquished: Why the First World War Failed to End, 1917-1923* (London: Allen Lane, 2016). My interpretation does not separate the vanquished and the victors.

24. George Mosse, *Fallen Soldiers* (New York: Oxford University Press, 1990).

25. See Antoine Prost, 'Les limites de la brutalization. Tuer sur le front occidental, 1914-1918,' *Vingtième Siècle*, 81 (2004), 5-20.

26. John Horne has been at the forefront of this interpretation of cultural mobilisation and demobilisation. See his essay 'Demobilizing the Mind: France and the Legacy of the Great War 1919-1939', George Rudé lecture, <https://h-france.net/rude/wp-content/uploads/2017/08/vol2_Horne_Final_Version.pdf> (accessed 10 March 2018).

27. Stephen Broadberry and Alexander Klein, 'Aggregate and Per Capita GDP in Europe, 1870-2000: Continental, Regional and National Data with Changing Boundaries', <http://citeseerx.ist.psu.edu/viewdoc/download?doi=10.1.1.361.386&rep=rep1&type=pdf> (accessed 10 March 2018).

History of Conflicts

Destroyed church during the First World War in Wigry, North-Eastern Poland.

The Central European Civil War, 1918-1921*

Jochen Böhler

In Western Europe, the end of the Great War in November 1918 also marked the end of armed struggle. This was not the case in the areas further to the East, where the collapse of the Russian, Habsburg, Ottoman, and German Empires, the repercussions of the Bolshevik revolution, and struggles for national independence blocked the road to peace in the years after the armistices of 1918. It was the final stage of a worldwide conflict, which turned from a largely conventional war between these very empires into a civil war between their heirs.

Historiography has had difficulty dealing with this seemingly random agglomeration of armed conflicts. Christoph Mick has identified as many as eight different types of war in Central and Eastern Europe in the wake of the Great War: 'civil wars and state wars, state building wars and revolutionary wars, wars of conquest and of liberation, offensive and defensive wars'.[1] Jonathan D. Smele's new interpretation of the Russian civil war follows this line: He describes it as not one entity, but as a whole decade of intermingled several civil wars in Russia that comprised 'national wars, international wars, interethnic wars and conflicts, wars of national liberation, and local adjuncts of the ongoing world struggle'.[2] Stainley G. Paine therefore proposes plainly to do away with the term civil war and use 'the wars of the tsarist succession' instead.[3]

Revolution – National Conflicts – Civil War

There are, of course, good arguments for this kind of differentiation. But by splitting up embattled postwar Central and Eastern Europe into such a variety of taxonomic entities, one risks missing the forest for the trees. As Joachim von Puttkamer rightly assesses, 'the immediate post-war period in this region appears in general accounts as a nearly impenetrable jungle of overlapping revolutions and national conflicts that is better left to a handful of specialists'.[4] But with the keywords 'revolution' and 'national conflicts', one can pick one's way through this jungle, and Peter Gatrell has done so convincingly:

Two decisive shifts in geopolitics make sense of these conflicts. The first new element was the Bolshevik revolution in November 1917, which had repercussions far beyond Russia. A second, related element was the struggle for the legacy of the disintegrating empires of Austria-Hungary, Germany, Russia, and Ottoman Turkey, a process entailing the creation of new nation-states, often with the kind of friction such as border disputes, territorial claims, and population movements that encouraged armed conflict.[5]

The first element marks the constituent features of the Russian civil war, the second of the Central European civil war and of related, but not immediately connected, developments in Southeastern Europe.

The depiction of the Central European armed clashes between 1918 and 1921 as part of one ongoing civil war in which several nation states were formed challenges the prevailing interpretation of isolated bilateral conflicts between clearly defined nation states and their respective civilian and armed citizens: Poles against Lithuanians, Poles against Russians, Poles against Ukrainians, Poles against Germans, Poles against Czechs. It does so deliberately because we deprive ourselves of important insights as long as we ignore that these conflicts were not only often intermingled, but all had something essential in common: 'Thus after the Great War arises a new war of nations' (*hoc modo post magnum bellum mun-*

Fig 1: 'Head and Shoulders to the defense of Petrograd!' Russian propaganda poster against the Whites during the Russian civil war, Revolutionary Military Department of the Republic, 1918.

danum exorta nova bella nationum), the chronicler of the Jesuit college in the Galician town of Chyrów noted at the turn of 1918/19.[6] Clearly defined nations simply did not exist at the dawn of Central Europe's era of independence. Accordingly, nation states were rather the result of this encompassing civil war, even if they had officially been – with equal ostentation and haste – already declared at its outset. The Central European Civil War served as a catalyst to carve the future populations of the Central European post-war states out of the mass of imperial subjects they had represented only a few years before. Its outcome defined the boundaries between them and often led to their international recognition. As the strained relationships between these new states' titular nations and their respective minorities between the world wars show, these battles were not solely directed outwards, but inwards as well.

Following Gatrell's definition, it makes sense to treat this civil war theatre separately from the contemporaneous civil war in Russia, where the rise of national ambitions was superimposed by and intermingled with other powerful ideological currents. The main opposing powers – the Bolshevik ('Red') and the conservative ('White') movement – fought over the future of one country: Would Russia become a Soviet state, or would the old order return, even if in a moderated form? Peasant bands for their part fought for more autonomy and against interference and heteronomy from the capital, regardless of whether they were ruled by imperial elites or a Bolshevik nomenclature. Foreign intervention to the North, South and East, half-heartedly launched to contain the 'Bolshevik threat', further blurred the picture. Although the experience and forms of violence that strongly accompanied the Russian Civil

War resemble those of the Central European Civil War, its vast disarray of concurring and competing ideological agendas made it a genuinely different conflict. In Central Europe, many different national armies fought for one political vision – the nation state – to be realised in just as many different countries. The two conflicts overlapped in the Polish eastern borderlands (Kresy), where Lithuanian, Latvian, Estonian, Belarusian, Polish and Ukrainian nationalists would – sometimes united, sometimes apart – fight for their own state and in the meantime against a Bolshevik takeover.

What Makes a Civil War a Civil War?

Having delineated two different battle zones, I must still defend my notion of the Central European Civil War against the established definition of civil war. The Oxford English Dictionary calls it a 'war between the citizens or inhabitants of a single country, state, or community', and Payne adheres to this notion.[7] In my view, such definitions, though usually applied to the phenomenon, are too static, since they do not acknowledge the fact that countries, states, communities and identities undergo significant changes in the course of civil wars. Thus, civil wars by their very nature are transitional phases rather than periods of standstill. Historical examples where they marked the decline or rise of empires are legendary: the Peloponnesian War, the Roman Civil Wars, the French Revolutionary Wars, to name only the most prominent ones.

The case of Central Europe is unique, however, because here civil war set in immediately *after* imperial power – exerted by three different monarchs – was abolished in the course of conventional war and revolution. Thus, it was a post-colonial battle for a share of former imperial lands, which resulted in the establishment of a multitude of nation states. 'This is what the device of national self-determination logically suggests', writes Joshua Sanborn, 'not peace emerging from war, but the shift from an interstate war to an intrastate war.' With respect to its tendency to transgress pre-existing borders, he adds: 'These civil wars, especially those in periods of decolonization, are hardly parochial or limited', and 'great wars', on the other hand, 'are almost by definition conglomerations of multiple conflicts that proceeded simulta-

Fig. 2: 19th-century depiction of Sulla's troops entering Rome, 82 B.C.

neously'.[8] Other knowledgeable authors have characterised the region in our period of interest as 'a protean world of shifting allegiances, civil wars, refugees and bandit gangs, where the collapse of old empires had left law and order, trade and communications in shreds'[9], as the theatre of 'a more extended European civil war'[10] and as 'a series of interconnected [inchoate and deadly] wars and civil wars' such as modern Europe had only witnessed once before, namely during the Thirty Years War of the seventeenth century.[11] Those conducting the most recent discourse on civil war, who see it as a human constant stretching from the dawn of mankind to our modern world, agree that it does not necessarily respect existing or emerging frontiers: 'Yet how do we tell civil wars apart from other kinds of wars, when so many internal conflicts spill over their countries' borders or draw in combatants from outside [...]?', asks David Armitage. His answer is as simple as it is ingenious: 'Civil war is, first and foremost, a category of experience; the participants usually know they are in the midst of civil war long before international organizations declare it to be so.'[12]

The notion of a Central European Civil War follows that line by concentrating on the experience rather than on the taxonomy of civil war. Its two main characteristics – unrestrained violence and blurred boundaries between the protagonists – have been decipherable since the very outset of civilisation. In Thucydides' *History of the Peloponnesian War*, we learn:

The Corcyraeans were butchering those of their countrymen whom they thought hostile to them:

Fig. 3: Map of Poland and East Central Europe 1918-1921.

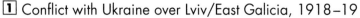

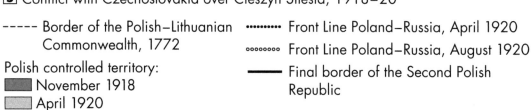

1 Conflict with Ukraine over Lviv/East Galicia, 1918–19
2 Conflict with Lithuania over the Vilnius area, 1919–20
3 Conflict with Germany over Poznan/Greater Poland, 1918–19
4 Conflict with Germany over Upper Silesia, 1919–21
5 Conflict with Czechoslovakia over Cieszyn Silesia, 1918–20

- - - - Border of the Polish–Lithuanian Commonwealth, 1772

Polish controlled territory:
■ November 1918
□ April 1920

·········· Front Line Poland–Russia, April 1920
∘∘∘∘∘∘∘∘ Front Line Poland–Russia, August 1920
——— Final border of the Second Polish Republic

bringing their accusations, indeed, against those only who were putting down the democracy; but some were slain for private enmity also, and others for money owed them by those who had borrowed it. Every mode of death was thus had recourse to; and whatever ordinarily happens in such a state of things, all happened then, and still more. For father murdered son, and they were dragged out of the sanctuaries, or slain in them; while in that of Bacchus some were walled up and perished.[13]

Julius Caesar was reading from the same page when he noted in his *Bellum Civile*:

The terror they had been thrown into by their generals, the severity shown in punishing, and the new oath they had been obliged to take [...] changed the soldier's minds, and reduced the war to its former state. [...] In a civil war[,] it was lawful for every soldier to choose what side he pleased; that the same legion, who a little before had fought on the side of the enemy, might, without scruple, return again to the same cause.[14]

Fig. 4: Soldiers and civilians in the streets of Lvov/Lviv, during the Polish-Ukrainian fight for the city in November 1918.

Civil War in Central Europe

Like in ancient Greece and Rome, the radicalisation and ambivalence of civil war led to considerable uncertainty, ubiquitous fear and arbitrary violence in post-imperial Central Europe, undergirding my argument for treating its population's experiences of war, paramilitary conflict, and violence during 1918-1921 as a coherent entity, a 'transnational zone of paramilitary violence'.[15] Geographically in the eye of the cy-

Fig. 5: Snapshot of an unknown Polish paramilitary unit in Upper Silesia in 1920.[21]

clone, late-1918 Poland harboured not only hope for a glorious future, but also the memory of a nightmarish past. Its independence materialised in shattered spaces. Before its moment of glory in November 1918, Poland suffered enormously under the effects of the war and witnessed some of the most fervent battles of the Eastern Front. The country was exploited, and the occupying Germans, Austrians, and Russians killed or deported hundreds of thousands of its inhabitants far to the East and West. Epidemics and famine plagued the rural and urban population in late 1918, and people were still dying in large numbers. With the retreat of the troops of the 'Supreme Command of All German Forces in the East' (Ober Ost), large parts of Eastern Poland lacked any form of effective state control for months or even years. The area turned into something that has recently been dubbed Poland's 'Wild East'.[16] The future US President Herbert Hoover (1874-1964), then heading the American Relief Ad-

ministration, correctly noted in 1919 that parts of Poland had witnessed seven invasions and retreats during the war, accompanied by mass destruction and hundreds of thousands of casualties.[17]

But this nightmare was far from over by 1919. Between late 1918 and early 1921, Poland was in a permanent state of declared or undeclared war on literally all frontiers except the Romanian. The emerging ethnic Polish nation state claimed territories that hosted minorities of almost all nations involved in the Central European Civil War. Not surprisingly, contemporaries living in Central Europe, especially in its borderlands, experienced the aftermath of the Great War as a time of fratricidal struggle, of neighbour fighting neighbour. Marceli Handelsman (1882-1945), a Polish-Jewish historian who earned international fame between the wars, noted in the summer of 1920:

> I will remember my conversation with a Lithuanian peasant in Ogrodniki. He told me that he lived there in Ogrodniki, while his brother-in-law was down in Bereźniki. Now, he said, this is Lithuania, and that's Poland. It used to be one, but now there's a border between Bereźniki and Ogrodniki; there's a war on. Is that how things should be? Don't we all go to the same church? Isn't it a disaster that brothers are divided and fighting?[18]

Michał Römer (1880-1945), a lawyer of Polish-Lithuanian origin, called this phenomenon – a little more sophisticatedly – a 'bellum omnium contra omnes'.[19] Letters, diaries and memoirs written between 1918 and 1921 in all languages of the region prove that their authors experienced the forceful disruption of a mixed population that had been living together more or less peacefully over centuries as a tragedy. They thus contradict the simplistic national narratives of united people fighting for a national independence that patronising empires had previously deprived them of, and which was contested by malevolent neighbours after 1918.

As mentioned above, the main theatres of the Central European civil war were situated in the borderlands of the emerging Second Republic of Poland. With the Habsburg Empire collapsing, Ukrainians and Poles both aimed to take over Galicia. The conflict over the cultural capital Lvov started in early November 1918, with the Poles proving victorious after three weeks of heavy street fighting, but the undeclared Polish-Ukrainian war lasted until the summer of the following year. Lithuania and Poland were at strife about the possession of Vilnius and the surrounding area, which Polish forces (allegedly without the consent of their military command) seized in October 1920. Between 1918 and 1921, Polish and German paramilitaries fought over the Poznań area and Upper Silesia, as did Polish and Czech paramilitaries over Cieszyn Silesia.[20]

Although they overlapped in time, at first glance we seem to be dealing here with isolated bilateral conflicts Poland fought with its neighbours to the East, North, West and South. In reality, the situation was much more complicated. Temporary, geographical and political lines blur in times of civil war, and that is exactly what happened in Central Europe after the end of 1918. The imperial armies' withdrawal from the battlefields of Central Europe left a vacuum, turning the area into a *tabula rasa* in which groups of various political, national or ethnic backgrounds tried to seize the moment. In late 1918, Poland had at least two political representations – the government in Warsaw headed by Józef Piłsudski (1867-1935), and the Polish National Committee in Paris under the leadership of Roman Dmowski (1864-1939). The two factions were divided over the territorial aspects of literally all of the ongoing border struggles, and so much at enmity that the newborn republic faced both a domestic civil and a territorial partition. The Polish peasants – who after all made up 80 percent of the population – largely ignored the call to the arms, since they needed every hand to rebuild their land and widely mistrusted the promises and feared the consequences of 'national independence'. In the meantime, two different Ukrainian state representations – the Ukrainian People's Republic and the West Ukrainian National Republic – partly sided with, partly fought against the Poles, while Lithuanians first fought against the Red Army, then sided with the Bolsheviks against the Poles. Except for a clash of arms between Poles and Czechs in January 1919, which lasted only a week, the struggles at Poland's southern and western borders were fought by paramilitary organisations that at least officially had no connection to their respective governments in Warsaw, Berlin or Prague.

Fig. 6: Polish-Czech war in Cieszyn, Silesia, late January 1919: According to Polish eye witnesses' reports, most of these twenty Polish soldiers were killed by Czech legionnaires from the 21 Czechoslovak Regiment after their surrender on 26 January 1919.

Paramilitary Violence as Encompassing Experience

As a matter of fact, in late 1918 none of the emerging nation states between Weimar Germany and Soviet Russia had a consistent and organised army at their disposal. On the contrary, they all had to be hastily built up initially from a core of a few thousand recruits who some months before had been fighting on different sides of the Great War's fronts. Equipment was insufficient, discipline was at its lowest ebb, desertion was a mass phenomenon and instead of protecting their own citizens, soldiers of these 'national armies' often pillaged the countryside or even engaged in anti-Jewish pogroms.[22]

The vengeance with which the battles following the world war were fought, and the paramilitary violence which accompanied them, differ dramatically from those of the First World War itself, a modern war by contrast, which though highly militarised was still largely fought according to the laws of war between 1914 and 1917.[23] The subsequent battles are more reminiscent of the fierce armed clashes in the Balkans in 1912/13, which *preceded* the First World War. The violent course events took after 1918, and the deliberate targeting of civilians, rooted in this conventional war's shift into a civil war. It now became a war of ethnically defined nations in which all sides regarded 'their' respective civil population as allies and 'other' civilians as enemies of their state-building project. This attitude corresponded with an awakening military and national enthusiasm within the belligerent societies: all of a sudden, independence no longer seemed merely a distant dream, but a reality within reach. 'As we stopped at a small country station', the young American lawyer Artur Lehman Goodhart (1891-1978) noted on his train ride through Czechoslovakia in the summer of 1919, 'we saw a troop of young boys about fourteen years old marching past in military step. Instead of real guns they carried small wooden imitation ones. "It does not seem as if these people believe that the world's last war has just been finished", said the Colonel [a fellow traveller]. "You will get very tired of this militarism before you are through with your trip. Chauvinism has become popular everywhere. As far as I can judge, every second day in these new Central European countries is a holiday to celebrate their sudden national independence."'[24]

Conclusion

The depiction of the post-war conflicts in Central Europe between 1918 and 1921 as one civil war is unusual, if not provocative and criticisable. It surely needs at least a more encompassing treatment than can be delivered on the pages of this short essay. I am not arguing that authors who dealt with these conflicts separately and underlined their differences were entirely wrong. I am saying that two elements were imminent to all of those conflicts: they were fought by nations in the making that were not united and clearly defined at the outset, but whose members (excepting Ukrainians and Belarusians) built their respective nation states in the course of these very events; and they all featured a level of paramilitary violence which – together with their notion as fratricidal struggles – made them more of a tragic than a heroic experience for the population living in the contested borderlands.

Endnotes

* This contribution is a shortened and revised version of the chapter 'The Central European Civil War' in Jochen Böhler, Civil War in Central Poland, 1918-1921. The Resurrection of Poland (Oxford: Oxford University Press, 2018).

1. Christoph Mick, 'Vielerlei Kriege: Osteuropa 1918-1921', in Formen des Krieges: Von der Antike bis zur Gegenwart, eds. Dietrich Beyrau, Michael Hochgeschwender and Dieter Langewiesche (Paderborn: Schöningh, 2007), 311-326, here 311.

2. Jonathan D. Smele, The 'Russian' Civil Wars 1916-1926: Ten Years that Shook the World (Oxford: Oxford University Press, 2015), 36.

3. Stanley G. Payne, Civil War in Europe, 1905-1949 (New York: Cambridge University Press, 2011), 33.

4. Joachim von Puttkamer, 'Collapse and Restoration: Politics and the Strains of War in Eastern Europe,' in Legacies of Violence: Eastern Europe's First World War, eds. Jochen Böhler, Włodzimierz Borodziej and Joachim von Puttkamer (München: Oldenbourg, 2014), 9-23, here 10.

5. Peter Gatrell, 'War After the War: Conflicts, 1919-1923', in A Companion to World War I, ed. John Horne (Chichester, Malden: Wiley-Blackwell, 2010), 558-575, here 558.

6. Cited after 'Fragment kroniki klasztoru i konwiktu oo. Jezuitów w Chyrowie za lata 1918-1919,' in Kościół rzymskokatolicki i Polacy w Małopolsce Wschodniej podczas wojny ukraińsko-polskiej 1918-1919: Źródła, ed. Józef Wołczański (Kraków: Wydawnictwo Naukowe Uniwersytetu Papieskiego Jana Pawła II, 2012), vol. 2, 27-79, here 28. Thanks to Maciej Górny for this quote.

7. Entry 'civil war, n.', in: Oxford English Dictionary: online, eds. Michael Proffitt, Philip Durkin and Edmund Weiner <www.oed.com> (accessed 14 June 2018).

8. Joshua A. Sanborn, Imperial Apocalypse: The Great War and the Destruction of the Russian Empire (Oxford: Oxford University Press, 2014), 237, 4.

9. Margaret MacMillan, Paris 1919: Six Months that Changed the World (New York: Random House, 2003), 207.

10. Peter Holquist, 'Violent Russia, Deadly Marxism? Russia in the Epoch of Violence, 1905-1921,' Kritika: Explorations in Russian and Eurasian History 4, no. 3 (2003), 627-652, here 644-645: 'The violence of the Russian Civil War appears not as something perversely [sic] Russian or uniquely Bolshevik, but as the most intense case of a more extended European civil war, extending through the Great War and stretching several years after its formal conclusion.'

11. Robert Gerwarth, The Vanquished: Why the First World War Failed to End, 1917-1923 London: Allen Lane, 2016), 7.

12. David Armitage, Civil Wars: A History in Ideas (New York: Alfred A. Knopf, 2017), 15, 238-239.

13. Thucydides, The History of the Peloponnesian War, ed. Henry Dale (New York: Harper & Brothers, 1891), 207.

14. Caius J. Caesar, The Commentaries of Caesar, Translated into English: To Which is Prefixed a Discourse Concerning the Roman Art of War, ed. William Duncan (St. Louis: Edwards & Bushnell, 1856), 233, 246. Thanks to Matthew Trundle for point-

ing out these and other relevant publications on the classical period.

15. Robert Gerwarth, 'The Central European Counter-Revolution: Paramilitary Violence in Germany, Austria and Hungary after the Great War,' *Past and Present* no. 200 (2008), 175-209, here 177.

16. Kathryn C. Ciancia, 'Poland's Wild East: Imagined Landscapes and Everyday Life in the Volhynian Borderlands, 1918-1939' (PhD thesis, Stanford University, 2011).

17. Włodzimierz Borodziej, *Geschichte Polens im 20. Jahrhundert* (München: Beck, 2010), 97.

18. Marceli Handelsman, *W piątym pułku Legjonów: Dwa miesiące ofensywy litewsko-białoruskiej* (Zamość: Zygmunt Pomarański & Spółka, 1921), 25-26.

19. Michał Römer, *Dzienniki, 1916-1919*, ed. Agnieszka Knyt (Warszawa: Karta, 2018), 689 (entry of 1 April 1919).

20. For a comparative overview of these conflicts, see Benjamin Conrad, *Umkämpfte Grenzen, umkämpfte Bevölkerung. Die Entstehung der Staatsgrenzen der Zweiten Polnischen Republik 1918-1923* (Stuttgart: Steiner, 2014); Jochen Böhler, Civil War in Central Europe, 1918-1921. The Resurrection of Poland (Oxford: Oxford University Press, 2018).

21. The image was probably taken by Captain James A. Stader of the US Army, who was engaged in the exchange of German and Polish prisoners of war. For reasons unknown, he noted on the reverse side "Polish irregulars for the plebiscite. In reality the Murder Squad". Polish and German paramilitaries both committed acts of terror against each other and the civilian population during the Polish-German conflict over Upper Silesia.

22. Piotr Wróbel, 'The Seeds of Violence: The Brutalization of an Eastern European Region, 1917-1921,' *Journal of Modern European History 1*, no. 1 (2003), 125-149; Alexander Victor Prusin, *Nationalizing a Borderland: War, Ethnicity, and Anti-Jewish Violence in East Galicia, 1914-1920* (Tuscaloosa: University of Alabama Press, 2005); Piotr Wróbel, 'The Revival of Poland and Paramilitary Violence, 1918-1920', in *Spießer, Patrioten, Revolutionäre. Militärische Mobilisierung und gesellschaftliche Ordnung in der Neuzeit*, eds. Rüdiger Bergien and Ralf Pröve (Göttingen: Vandenhoeck & Ruprecht, 2010), 281-303; William W. Hagen, *Anti-Jewish Violence in Poland, 1914-1920* (New York: Cambridge University Press, 2018).

23. Włodzimierz Borodziej and Maciej Górny, *Imperia*, vol. 1 of *Nasza wojna* (Warsaw: Foksal, 2014).

24. Artur L. Goodhart, *Poland and the Minority Races* (London: Allen & Unwin, 1920), 13-14.

How the Habsburg Monarchy, Austria and Hungary Were Drawn into the Russian October Revolution between 1917 and 1919*

Ibolya Murber

In the years preceding World War One, a political, economic and social crisis had been developing in the Austrian-Hungarian Monarchy, caused principally by structural changes arising from the mutation from an agrarian to an industrial state[1] and the complications of multiethnicity; this was exacerbated by the First World War.[2] In the summer of 1914, the Monarchy set out ambitious aims for the war, but in fact suffered defeats on several fronts. It was able to achieve some temporary territorial successes, but these were mainly due to financial and military support from its German ally, which in turn caused a power imbalance in the German–Austrian alliance. The profound changes in Russia during 1917 led on the one hand to the fall of the Tsarist regime, and on the other to a power grab by the Bolsheviks in November; as a result, Russia pulled out of the war and the situation deteriorated into an extremely bloody and violent struggle as Communist power took hold, and to a civil war that lasted until 1922. These internal Russian events created waves both internationally and transnationally, sending pulses around the world,[3] with long-term consequences that echoed through much of the 20th century.

The fallout from both the February and November Russian revolutions contributed to exposing the internal weaknesses of the Habsburg Empire and plunged the Dual Monarchy into ever more complex difficulties; it eventually disintegrated in November 1918. Once Russia had ceased to be a military opponent – de facto after the October Revolution in 1917 and de jure after the Brest-Litovsk Peace Treaty in March 1918 – the Habsburg Monarchy was no longer required to play a balancing role among European powers. A new political power landscape developed, in which the victor nations began to take note of the demands of different national groups within the former multi-ethnic states. The Entente forces relied on the internal collapse of the Dual Monarchy, and during the final year of the war gave overt support to national separatist movements. This undermining of the Habsburg Empire gave rise to various ideas and claims aimed at creating new territorial outlines in Central Europe. Although the example set by Russia was not the immediate cause of the disintegration, it served to accelerate it and exerted a powerful symbolic force.[4] It was not only the continuing internal crisis that led to the collapse of the Habsburg Empire, but also its military defeat, and the political decisions made by the victorious Allies granting self-determination, at the expense of the Habsburg Monarchy, to the nations of East-Central and South-Eastern Europe.

1917–1918: Crisis and Developments Within Social Democracy

In military terms, the Eastern Front facing Russia was highly significant to the Habsburg Monarchy. In Vienna, the collapse of the Tsarist regime in the spring of 1917 seemed a favourable development. There, as in Berlin, it seemed to offer the prospect of a swift victory on the Eastern Front. This would not only have facilitated military progress on the Western Front, but also helped to allay difficulties in keeping supplies flowing.[5] In the event, neither happened. The rulers in Vienna and Budapest perceived the internal changes within Russia, and especially the forced abdication of the Tsar and the establishment of a Bolshevik leadership, as a threat to the survival of monarchy.[6]

In the first two years of the war, the Habsburg Monarchy pursued 'party truce' politics (*Burgfriedenspolitik*). The disappointment caused by unfulfilled war objectives, however, exacerbated the internal political tensions and the gulf between the Austrian and Hungarian halves of the Empire. The Austrian Social Democrats were the principal beneficiaries as the war years dragged on, since the Hungarian Left were not able to establish sufficient prominence. A decisive factor was the need for a mediator between the state and the working classes in the face of the increasing social and economic tensions produced by war.

The Social Democrats were important to the state in several ways. The union structures, which extended onto the shop floor, enabled them to exercise particular forms of social and political influence. The Austrian Social Democrats were therefore a more attractive option than the equivalent party in Hungary, a disparity due to numerous reasons. The Austrian Hereditary lands were more heavily industrialised, so that the population had a higher proportion of industrial workers. From 1907, all men had the right to equal suffrage and a secret ballot, which enabled the development of workers' political parties; in the 1911 Reich elections, the parties of the Left gained 82 seats and became the strongest faction in the parliament.[7]

Fig. 1: Karl Renner, Social Democrat and Austrian Chancellor of the First Republic 1918-1920, President of the Second Republic 1945-1950.

Although industrialisation had begun in the 1880s in the Hungarian part of the Empire, Austria-Hungary had remained a mostly agricultural country, with a smaller proportion of industrial workers among the general population. The limited census suffrage allowed neither the emergence of a workers' party nor any representation for the workers in parliament. After 1918, politicians acknowledged that state social care required a fundamentally new approach, and this led to the involvement of the Social Democrats in Austrian political power after 1918. The Austrian government, under the Social Democrat Chancellor Karl Renner (1870-1950) in alliance with the Christian Socialist Party and the Greater German People's Party (Großdeutsche Volkspartei), conducted consensus politics with collective responsibility. The government hoped that the development of social services would strengthen the links between the working class and the state that cared for them, and ensure their increasing integration into Austrian society.[8]

Even before the end of the war, the older political elite had granted concessions to the social democratic leadership. The Social Democrat Karl Renner, for example, was appointed to a post on the directorate of the Ministry for Food.[9] Never before had a Social Democrat been given an official appointment. In the summer of 1917, Renner was even offered a post in government, but the Social Democrats turned

Fig. 2: Allegory of deprivation, a woman searches for scraps of coal, Vienna, in March 1919.

Fig. 3: 'March of the Workers' Councils', Jännerstreik, Vienna 1919.

the offer down.[10] This implied that the Social Democrats had a shared responsibility for government policy. Unlike in Austria, Hungary suffered no food shortages in 1918, so the Hungarian government had less need to ally themselves with the Social Democrats in order to appease a restive working class. Instead, the major landowning elite carried out very restrictive policies right through to the end of the war. State initiatives to improve conditions for factory workers and other employees focused on specific business and economic issues; on a national level, they generally failed to yield either improvements in care and working conditions or higher wages.

The increase in support offered by the Left during the war resulted in better recruitment among the unions. The Austrian and Hungarian social democratic parties only supported the strikes as long as this was to their advantage. When this was no longer

the case, they made every effort to calm the situation and prevent riots.[11] This was characteristic of the ambivalent attitude of Austromarxists: they were radical in what they said, but moderate in what they did. The Hungarian Left too tended to act in this way, until the proclamation of the Soviet of Councils (*Räterepublik*) in March 1919.

The Russian February Revolution took the capital cities of the West by surprise. In the late autumn of 1917, very few political observers outside Russia reckoned on further, even wider-reaching political upheavals there.[12] The events of February 1917 had met with a comparatively positive reaction, but the governments of Europe were far more critical of the Bolshevik revolution in the following November. In both internal and external politics, the Bolsheviks overturned many features of regulated democratic order. Their impulse towards radical change was per-

Fig. 4: 'For the Republic', the fall of the monarchy with Jacobean symbolism, Hungarian poster painted by Mihály Biró, November 1918.

ceived among other things as a threat to Western civilisation. In 1917, Emperor Karl I (1887-1922) proposed a policy of measured reform and social consensus for Austria, to be drawn up in collaboration with the Social Democrats. From the late autumn of 1917, the Hungarian parliament also had to make social policy concessions, and it adopted legal measures to establish social security. Unlike their Austrian party colleagues, however, the Hungarian Social Democrats were unable to exert influence on these measures, as they had no parliamentary mandate.

By the start of 1918, Austrian food supplies had become critically low. On 14 January 1918, the government halved food rations per head. This set off a wave of strikes in Vienna New Town (Wiener Neustadt), organised by left-wing proletarian groups; these affected industrialised cities initially, but gradually spread across the entire Monarchy. Austrian and Hungarian Social Democrats made strenuous efforts to control the strikes and bring them to an end. How-

ever, they died down of their own accord, as the leadership were insufficiently well organised.[13] Their experience of the 1918 'January strike' (Jännerstreik) led the governments of Austria and Hungary to react with increasing severity to any public protest gathering.[14]

Vladimir Ilyich Lenin had nurtured high hopes that the Jännerstreik would spark a revolution in Austria, or at the very least inspire an outcome more favourable to Russia at the peace negotiations in Brest-Litovsk.[15] However, his hopes were to be dashed. For the Austrian and Hungarian Social Democrats, the lesson from the spate of strikes was that radical demands such as those made in Russia had found an echo in the Monarchy and led to the splintering of the Left, but that social democracy itself had little influence on these developments.

Late Autumn 1918 to Spring 1919: The Dominance of Social Democracy in the Shaping of the New State

During 1918/19, immediately following WWI, the major impact of revolutionary ideas emanating from Soviet Russia increased throughout Central Europe; this encouraged an appetite for world revolution, which was widely perceived as an existential requirement for the acceptance of a new social order. In the successor states to the former Habsburg Monarchy, there was strong reaction to reports from Russian emigrants and to attempts to establish the new social order by setting up left-wing proletarian councils. The right-wing bourgeoisie saw the 'spectre of Communism' as a virulent threat, and attached the label not only to radical left-wing groups but also, by implication, to the more politically moderate Social Democrats who, they maintained, were deriving advantage from post-monarchical conditions and would open the country up to Bolshevik influence. After 1918, there was widespread fear throughout society of a Communist expansion under the banner of proletarian internationalism; between the wars, right-wing parties and organisations across Central Europe countered this by calling for law and order, and appealing to what they hoped was a sense of national community.

The end of the monarchy shared by the two countries, and the new start in both Austria and Hungary, led to widespread political and social lambasting. In

1918, German Austria and Hungary had both lost significant proportions of the territories they had held under the Habsburg Dual Monarchy. Both national economies were affected, most clearly in terms of the supply situation. These profound changes gave rise to war weariness among the people and undermined any feeling of national community. Each of the two now diminished states was uncertain of its political future, and suffered from a lack of focus and a dwindling sense of social cohesion. In response, the population mobilised to mount strikes, demonstrations and riots. The new governments of Austria and Hungary, now both strongly Social Democrat, had to address these challenges.[16] Both governments were largely composed of new politicians who had scant experience of being in government. After 1918, both states included not only a traditional centre of power but also, in parallel, new democratically established power structures such as worker and soldier councils, although these had no major influence on the shaping of the new state. The new political leaderships in Vienna and Budapest were acting along similar lines, which promised to yield a democratic and more socially aware political system.

On 21 October 1918, the Provisional National Assembly for German Austria, consisting of all German-speaking Reich Assembly deputies, met in Vienna and agreed on the establishment of an independent Austrian State, designated 'German Austria'. The Great Coalition of Social Democrats, Christian Socialists and Greater Germans was jointly established by the parties represented in the Reich Assembly at the end

Fig. 6: Béla Kun, leader of the Hungarian Soviet Republic, March-August 1919.

of October 1918,[17] and they agreed on a common crisis management agenda. Moderate left-wing, liberal and conservative parties established a broad consensus that conferred both legitimacy and a sense of stability on this political rebirth.

Austrian social democracy was strong and significant enough among the parties to be able to impose certain demands, such as their participation ratio in the government.[18] The other participants in the coalition were well aware that the social democracy was in a strong position at the time. Being unable themselves to produce a viable solution to the current crisis, they agreed to the plan drawn up by the 'Austro-marxists'. Carlo Moos has suggested that this pragmatic approach to a consensus-led solution was a result of the Habsburg political heritage.[19] Thanks to the wider political consensus and the cohesive influence of social democracy, and in spite of the considerable efforts of the radical Left in the spring of 1919, the birth of the young Republic in Austria took place in a relatively peaceful atmosphere. There was general relief at this apparent success, which in reality cast a temporary mask over the very real and widely divergent visions of the future nurtured by the right-wing and left-wing popular parties.

The Hungarian National Council was made up of three parties. On the one hand, the Independence Party led by the Liberal Democrat Count Mihály Károlyi (1875-1955) was in the parliament. On the other hand, the Radical Democrats – the party of urban intelligentsia – and the Social Democrats were opposition parties without parliamentary representation. Hungary's new beginning was thus not based

Fig. 5: Declaration of the Hungarian Republic on 16 November 1918 by Prime Minister Count Mihály Károlyi (right) and János Hock (1859-1936), President of the National Council.

Fig. 7: 'Proletarians of all countries unite!', Expressionist Hungarian poster, 1919.

on an agreement between political parties. Political life was focused on the person of Mihály Károlyi. He dominated the affairs of state not only because of his key central position among the departments of state, but also because of the political parties' weakness. There were many common features between the political programmes of the Austrian Social Democrats and the one adopted on 8 October 1918 by the Hungarian Social Democrats. The Hungarian Social Democrats, in common with all other Hungarian parties, insisted on the inviolability of Hungarian sovereignty. The new Hungarian government, in spite of its defeat in the war and the growing armies of its new neighbour states, held firmly to the idea of a 'Great Hungary', an idea they had neither the military nor the political means to bring about. The government's failure in March 1919 led to the resignation of Mihály Károlyi and to the proclamation of the Hungarian Soviet Republic (Räterepublik) under the leadership of Béla Kun (1886-1936).

The victor nations saw Hungary's claim to its prewar territories as endangering the new international 'collective security' order in Central and Eastern Europe, which principally favoured the successor states of the Habsburg Monarchy and the German Empire, while carving up the territories of the defeated nations and burdening them with reparation debts. The lack of international recognition was hard on Hungary, which nevertheless pursued pro-Western, Entente-friendly policies similar to Austria's. Lack of foreign policy success and a failure to manage either the domestic crisis or the economic challenges had all contributed to the collapse of Károlyi's ruling coalition of bourgeois radicals and Social Democrats, so the calls from some parts of Hungarian society for radical political solutions were welcomed.

There were some differences between the Communist parties of Austria and Hungary. The Communist Party of German Austria, the first Communist Party of Central and Western Europe, was set up on 3 November 1918 by a small group of intellectuals living in Austria. The lack of strong leadership among the Austrian Communists seriously compromised the party's effectiveness. Franz Koritschoner (1892-1941), who had known Lenin in exile in Switzerland, and the Social Democrat Friedrich Adler (1879-1960) both turned down the party leadership positions offered them by Moscow.[20]

The Hungarian Communist Party was created by Béla Kun on 24 November 1918. He had been taken prisoner of war in Russia in 1916, and while there he had become a follower of the Russian Bolsheviks. A practical and highly charismatic politician, as a student in Klausenburg/Kolozsvár[21] he had had a lively relationship with the Social Democratic Party. Because of his organisational abilities and his relationship with the Bolshevik leadership, Lenin had tasked him not only with setting up the Communist Party in Hungary but also with mounting a coup.[22] The new party was well received not only by returning prisoners of war but also by the war-wounded and the unemployed. Béla Kun's emphatic criticism of Hungarian social democracy, which until the establishment of the Räterepublik had followed an Austromarxist policy, focused on discrediting the moderate leftwing government parties and creating division among them. The attacks by protagonists of the Hun-

Fig. 8: Call for a general strike in support of the Bolsheviks in Russia and the Hungarian Soviet Republic by the Communist Party of German Austria, July 1919.

garian *Räterepublik*, added to what was in any case a complex political landscape, made it very difficult for the Social Democrats to push through the consensus-driven, pragmatic political programme they had adopted, or to effectively utilise their low-key revolutionary rhetoric modelled on Austria's.

March – August 1919: The Hungarian Räterepublik

The proclamation of the Hungarian Räterepublik on 21 March 1919 alarmed the decision-makers at the Paris Peace Conference. In order to contain any further spread of Communism beyond Hungary, they aimed to isolate Hungary from its neighbouring states, and especially from Austria. As far as Austria was concerned, the containment strategy rested on the one hand on concessions such as lifting the economic blockade and extending an invitation to the Paris Peace talks, and on the other hand on threatening to stop supplies from the Allies if a Soviet-style experiment were to take place. In order to prevent a 'domino effect', the Entente countries granted Austria a significant level of trade credit in March 1919.[23]

The Social Democrats felt threatened by the example of Russia and by the establishment of Communist parties in both Austria and Hungary. Austromarxism was founded on emphatically democratic parliamentarism, and it found the *Räterepublik* unsympathetic. Otto Bauer (1881-1938), a founder of Austromarxism who served as Austrian Foreign Minister from November 1918 to July 1919, argued that if the proletariat were to exercise dictatorship over the urban bourgeois and rural farming communities, this would

Fig. 9: Otto Bauer, Austrian politician and founder of Austromarxism.

undermine the unity and consensus within Austrian society, and it should not be allowed.[24] He was typical of the Janus-faced ambivalence of Austromarxism: an emphasis on revolutionary objectives and a simultaneous instinct for moderation and sophisticated realpolitik. In response to pleas from Béla Kun that Austria should align itself to the soviet movement and the world revolution, Bauer and others warned that establishing an Austrian *Räterepublik* would lead not only to civil war but also to the immediate cessation of supplies from the Entente nations, causing a catastrophic shortage of food in the country.[25]

The Russian October Revolution and Bolshevik upheavals served as a model for the Hungarian *Räterepublik*. Kun hoped for a revolution that would spread in a similar way to the one in Russia; he made the mistake of relying on a collaboration in the summer of 1919 between the Hungarian army and the Soviet Red Army.[26] And indeed, the fate of the Hungarian *Räterepublik* depended on other factors as well. Kun's increasingly violent *Räterepublik* fell not only because of a conservative nationalist counterrevolution or because of insufficient support among the Hungarian public, but also because of its isolation from outside nations. It had not received political or diplomatic recognition from the Western nations, and the anticipated military assistance from Soviet Russia had failed to materialise, since the Red Army was tied up with the civil war in Russia.

The Russian example had a different impact on social democracy in Austria than in Hungary. When the Hungarian *Räterepublik* was set up, the Austrian Social Democrats raised the alarm about social experiments, and this temporarily strengthened their position. They were delicately balanced between support given by liberal democrats sympathetic to the Left, while setting themselves clearly apart from the Communist experiment and the associated violent social upheavals. The Hungarian Social Democrats, on the other hand, were unable to resist being drawn in by Bolshevism. The political position of the Hungarian Social Democrats was distinctly weaker, and their lack of a vision of society either before or during WWI meant that the national democratic republic proclaimed in the late autumn of 1918 was not clearly social democratic in character. Hungarian social democracy was therefore not in a position to counter the populist arguments of the *Räterepublik*, nor especially to offer their own reform ideas to counter either the confiscation of large landholdings or land reform. The Hungarian Social Democrats lacked leaders capable of standing up to a seizure of power by the Communists.

From 1920 onwards, political power gradually organised itself into left-wing and right-wing groupings. The Austrian collaboration between Social Democrats and Christian Socialists had arisen out of necessity; it now began to crumble, and the governing coalition resigned in 1920. Once the Romanian army had forced the Hungarian *Räterepublik* out of office, the political and military situation gradually settled down, and from March 1920 a coalition of National Conservatives and the Party of Small Landowners took over the government. This shift to the right, in both countries, went hand in hand with an increasingly strong and persistent sense of threat from internal enemies, not only left-wing sympathisers but also Jews, both of whom were suspected of having Bolshevik sympathies. Hungary and Austria both suffered military defeat, both failed to acknowledge fault, both suffered from territorial 'amputation' and a damaged national self-image, and these proved to be a heavy burden to bear throughout the interwar years. As a result, both countries were vulnerable in the 1930s and early 1940s to falling under the influence of dictatorships ruled by nationalist, egalitarian and ethnically purist worldviews.

*This article was written in 2017-2018, during my fellowship at the Alfred Krupp Wissenschaftskolleg in Greifswald.

Endnotes

1. Gerhard Botz, 'Gewaltenkonjunkturen, Arbeitslosigkeit und gesellschaftliche Krisen. Formen politischer Gewalt und Gewaltstrategien in der Ersten Republik,' in *Das Werden der Ersten Republik. Der Rest ist Österreich, vol I.*, eds. Helmut Konrad and Wolfgang Maderthaner (Wien: Carl Gerold's Sohn, 2008), 339-362, 360.

2. Peter Krüger, Ostmitteleuropa und das Staatensystem nach dem Ersten Weltkrieg. *Im Spannungsfeld von Zentren, Peripherien, Grenzen und Regionen, in Mentalitäten – Nationen – Spannungsfelder. Studien zu Mittel- und Osteuropa im 19. und 20. Jahrhundert. Beiträge eines Kolloqims zum 65. Geburtstag von Hans Lemberg*, ed. Eduard Mühle (Marburg: Verlag Herder Institut 2001), 53-68.

3. Julia Richter, 'Die Resonanz der Revolution in globaler Perspektive,' in *Die russische Revolution 1917*, ed. Heiko Haumann (Wien-Köln-Weimar: Böhlau Verlag, 2016), 105-117.

4. Verena Moritz, *1917. Österreichische Stimmen zur Russischen Revolution* (Wien: Residenz Verlag, 2017), 34.

5. Wolfram Dornik, 'Verwaltung des Mangels. Die österreichisch(-ungarisch)en Kriegszentralen 1914-1918,' in *Wirtschaft. Macht. Geschichte. Brüche und Kontinuitäten im 20. Jahrhundert*, Festschrift für Stefan Karner, Veröffentlichungen des Ludwig-Boltzmann-Institutes für Kriegsfolgen-Forschung, eds. Gerhard Schöpfer and Barbara Stelzl-Marx (Graz-Wien-Raabs: Leykam Verlag, 2012), 264.

6. Hans Hautmann, *Die verlorene Räterepublik. Am Beispiel der Kommunistischen Partei Deutschösterreichs* (Wien: Europa-Verlag, 1971) 230.

7. Peter Berger, *Kurze Geschichte Österreichs im 20. Jahrhundert* (Wien: Universitätsverlag der Hochschülerschaft an der Universität, 2008), 17.

8. Monika Senghaas, *Die Territorialisierung sozialer Sicherung. Raum, Identität und Sozialpolitik in der Habsburgermonarchie* (Berlin: Springer Verlag, 2013), 247.

9. Hans Loewenfeld-Russ, *Im Kampf gegen den Hunger. Aus den Erinnerungen des Staatssekretärs für Volksernährung 1918-1920* (Wien: Verlag für Geschichte und Politik, 1986), 67.

10. Siegfried Nasko, *Karl Renner. Zu Unrecht umstritten? Eine Wahrheitssuche* (Wien-Salzburg: Residenz Verlag, 2016), 191-193.

11. Tamara Scheer, 'Die Kriegswirtschaft am Übergang von der liberalen-privaten zur staatlich-regulierten Arbeitswelt,' in *Die Habsburgermonarchie und der Erste Weltkrieg, Die Habsburgermonarchie 1848-1918*, vol. XI., ed. Helmut Rumpler (Wien: Verlag der Österreichischen Akademie der Wissenschaften, 2016), 480.

12. Moritz, *Österreichische Stimmen*, 30-31.

13. Moritz, *Österreichische Stimmen*, 36.

14. Lajos Varga, *Háború, forradalom, szociáldemokrácia Magyarországon 1914. július-1919. Március* (Budapest: Napvilág Kiadó, 2010), 171.

15. Moritz, *Österreichische Stimmen*, 38.

16. Ibolya Murber, 'Die ungarischen und österreichischen Sozialdemokraten und die russischen Revolutionen 1917,' in *Russische Revolutionen 1917. Presseanalysen aus Vorarlberg und internationale Aspekte*, ed. Rheticus-Gesellschaft, Schriftenreihe der Rheticus-Gesellschaft 73 (November 2017), 165-181.

17. Following the National Assembly elections in February 1919, the coalition established between Social Democrats and Christian Socialists held power until June 1920.

18. The three conditions laid down by the Social Democrats are in the minutes in the Österreichisches Staatsarchiv (henceforth ÖStA), Archiv der Republik (henceforth AdR), Neues Politisches Archiv (henceforth NPA), Staatsratsprotokolle (henceforth StRP) Karton 1. Staatsratssitzung am 30 October 1918.

19. Carlo Moos, *Habsburg post mortem. Betrachtungen zum Weiterleben der Habsburgermonarchie* (Wien-Köln-Weimar: Böhlau Verlag, 2016), 77.

20. Hans Hautmann, *Die verlorene Räterepublik. Am Beispiel der Kommunistischen Partei Deutschösterreichs* (Wien-Zürich: Europaverlag, 1971), 79.

21. The city of Kolozsvár has been part of Romania since the Trianon Peace Agreement, and is now called Cluj-Napoca.

22. György Borsányi, *Kun Béla. Politikai életrajz* (Budapest: Kossuth Kiadó 1979), 77.

23. ÖStA, AdR, Bundeskanzleramt (henceforth BKA), Kabinettsratsprotokolle (henceforth KRP), 24 March 1919.

24. More on Otto Bauer and the roles of Bauer and Béla Kuns in Ibolya Murber, 'Die ungarischen und österreichischen Sozialdemokraten und die russischen Revolutionen 1917,' in *Russische Revolutionen 1917. Presseanalysen aus Vorarlberg und internationale Aspekte*, ed. Rheticus-Gesellschaft, Schriftenreihe der Rheticus-Gesellschaft 73 (November 2017): 165-181.

25. ÖStA, AdR, NPA, Nachlass Otto Bauer Dossier IX. Ungarn. PR. 1919-Z-2171. Wien, 16 June 1919.

26. Lajos Árokay, *Kun Béla* (Budapest: Zrínyi Kiadó 1986), 89.

'The Red Scare' in Yugoslavia: The Hungarian Soviet Republic and the Beginning of Yugoslav Anti-Communism 1919-1921

Rastko Lompar

Introduction

'Austria-Hungary also has become a nest of revolutionary infection', wrote Béla Kun (1886-1938) in April 1918.[1] He was right, of course. He and his fellow Bolsheviks had succeeded in bringing their 'infectious' ideas home. After the resignation of Mihály Károlyi's (1875-1955) government, the Hungarian Soviet Republic (HSR) was created. At the same time, a new state was being formed on its southern border: the Kingdom of Serbs, Croats and Slovenes (KSCS). Yugoslav/Serbian historiographers have by no means neglected the relations between the Yugoslav communists and the HSR,[2] the early history of the Communist Party of Yugoslavia (CPY)[3] or the relations between Yugoslavia and Hungary in this period.[4] However, they have placed little emphasis on the nature of Yugoslav anti-communism, its reasons and its language, since Marxist historians usually understood it as a foundation of 'bourgeois society' and took it for granted. Indeed, the Kingdom of Yugoslavia was fiercely anti-communist and refused to recognise the Soviet Union until 1940. However, that does not mean that it was always *equally* anti-communist, or that anti-communism was always expressed in the same way. In this paper, I aim to describe the influence of the HSR in the formation of the first phase of Yugoslav anti-communism (1919-1921), and to highlight what differentiated it from later phases.

The Hungarian Soviet Republic and the Communist Revolution in Yugoslavia

Although the Yugoslav and Hungarian communists had earlier established lasting connections,[5] the first concrete discussions were held in Budapest in February 1919. An agreement was reached for the Yugoslavs to support the communist takeover in Hungary, and in return for logistical and financial assistance in the future.[6] Soon after the talks, couriers carrying money began to cross the Drava River and enter Yugoslavia.[7] The most notable amongst the Yugoslav communists in Hungary, Ivan Matuzović (1886-1938), was responsible for the creation of the Yugoslav Communist Fraction (YCF) in Hungary, which was the main body of Yugoslavs in the HSR.[8]

Fig. 1: Emblem of the Communist Party of Yugoslavia, 1920-1952.

Fig. 2: Yugoslav communist revolutionary and politician Ivan Matuzović.

Although there is some dispute regarding the exact date of its creation, the YCF was most probably formed in late March 1919.[9] It was (generously) financed by the Hungarians, and governed by a Directorate of 12.[10] Initially consisting of 60 members, it later expanded. It published its own newspaper, *Crvena zastava* (The Red Flag). It was formed on the same principle as the Hungarian party, by the merging of social democrats and communists.[11] Despite the proclaimed unity, differences between the two fractions were still evident. The main point of dispute was whether the YCF should focus on the revolution in Yugoslavia (communists), or on organising and educating the Yugoslav minority in Hungary (social democrats). The Hungarian leadership correctly assessed that Yugoslavia was not set on attacking them, and decided on formally declaring peaceful intentions whilst covertly supporting the communist in-

surgency. The Hungarian 'comrades' therefore supported the communist point of view within the YCF.[12] The main aims of the YCF were the mobilisation of Yugoslavs (mostly ex-prisoners of war) for the Red Guard and propaganda towards the Yugoslav military and civilian populace. According to some sources, the YCF created around 50 different leaflets and 10 brochures during its existence.[13] Members were encouraged to accept the HSR as their own country and to support it wholeheartedly. 'We, Yugoslav socialists, will defend the Hungarian proletarian republic with our lives against any reaction, since in the triumph of the Hungarian proletariat we see the victory of the Yugoslav workers!', the first issue of *Crvena zastava* proclaimed.[14]

Yugoslavs were involved in the HSR's armed forces from its inception. After their number grew, however, they were organised in a special military unit.

Fig. 3: The notable Communist journal, *Plamen* [The Flame].

In May 1919, the First Yugoslav (Balkan) Red Battalion was formed and deployed on the Yugoslav border with hopes that their presence would demoralise the Yugoslav troops and hasten the impending revolution.[15] The battalion was also tasked with providing food to Budapest, and bypassing the trade embargo imposed on the HSR.[16] Soon after in July, another Yugoslav unit, the Second Yugoslav (Balkan) Red Battalion was created and deployed on the Romanian front. However, the unit was ill prepared and quickly decimated by advancing Romanians. After the initial clashes, it had lost 56% of its men. Communist historians attributed its failure to treason among the Hungarian officer cadre.[17]

In contrast to these military endeavours, propaganda efforts were proving to be very effective. Leaflets in Serbo-Croatian, which appeared as early as January 1919, were systematically disseminated across Yugoslavia. With the communist takeover, Hungarian airplanes began crossing the border and dropping them over Yugoslav cities.[18] The Hungarian press constantly produced sensational reports about class turmoil and revolution in Yugoslavia. Those reports, which were often reprinted in the foreign (mostly Italian) press, were damning to the international reputation of the young Yugoslav state.[19] Dozens of communist agitators poured over the border and successfully caused a stir amongst the tired and homesick troops. Some deserted and crossed over to the Red Guard. A special publication aimed at them, *Crveni vojnik* (The Red Soldier), was printed in Kaposvár.[20] However, convinced by the initial successes, the Hungarian government decided to support the impending revolution in Yugoslavia with force. Nationalists such as Gyula Hajdu (1886-1973) demanded a military campaign against Yugoslavia in order to retake lost 'Hungarian soil'.[21]

The orders for revolution were carried to Zagreb by Béla Kun's emissary, Alfred Diamantstein (1896-1941). Despite the fact that he was not completely trusted by local communists, he quickly established contact with Josip Metzger (1883-1945), an ex-Austro-Hungarian officer and a Croat separatist.[23] The two plotted to organise a coup within the army, and used the money Diamantstein had brought with him from Hungary to convince dissatisfied soldiers. The revolt was supposed to spread all across Croatia and Slovenia, and was planned for 21 July 1919. On that

Fig. 4: Delegates at the First Congress of the Socialist Labour Party Yugoslavia (of Communists), Belgrade, 20-23 April 1919.[22]

date, a nation-wide strike in solidarity with the HSR was scheduled. After the initial shots, the Hungarian Red Guard was supposed to cross the border and invade Yugoslavia.[24] A key role in the attack was given to the Yugoslav units of the Red Guard. They were ordered as follows: 'Keep on Serbian hats and coats during the attack to convince the Serbs that there is mutiny in their own army.'[25] The strike, promptly forbidden by the authorities, was indeed carried out, but the revolution amounted to no more than sporadic unrest. The authorities' efficient response quickly quelled the unrests in Ljubljana, Osijek and Zagreb, and after some bloodshed in Varaždin and Maribor. The Red Guard never came.[26]

The First Phase of Yugoslav Anti-Communism

In Yugoslavia, the HSR's proclamation was met without panic. The press reported on the communist takeover very casually, whilst the government remained convinced that little changes were happening in Hungary. The revolution was seen as a nationalist Hungarian revolt, caused by the territorial demands of the Entente, whose socialist nature was purely a facade.[27] The press reported with the same view: socialism was simply a tool to 'preserve Hungarian imperialism', claimed the Belgrade journal *Pravda*.[28] The Minister of Internal Affairs, Svetozar Pribićević (1875-1936), referred to the communist takeover as an 'operetta revolution'.[29]

The KSCS was not interested in the overthrow of the Hungarian government. It was well aware of the fragility of both the internal and the international situation, and had no intention of waging an unpopular war for the sake of others. The leader of the Yugoslav deputation at the Paris Peace Conference, Nikola Pašić (1845-1926), was clear in a report to Belgrade: 'We are more threatened by Bulgarians, Albanians and even Italy! and even Italy, than Hungarian Bolshevism!'[30] The KSCS therefore rejected French pressure to attack Hungary in April 1919.[31] The Hungarian-Yugoslav border remained peaceful, despite some small clashes, which were sporadically mentioned in the Yugoslav press as attacks by the HSR.[32] When the successes of the Romanian army became more and more apparent, the Yugoslavs became worried that a triumphant Romania would be rewarded with disputed land in the Banat. In July 1919, the Yugoslav government therefore became more interested in intervening against the HSR. However, Yugoslav documents reveal just how small a role the communist nature of Hungary played in decision-making. Out of the 17 key documents regarding the possible intervention, 16 make no mention of communism. The war is simply regarded as a war against Hungary.[33] The Yugoslavs made their involvement in the war conditional on an assurance of protection by the Great Powers from Italian aspirations, and promised only 8,000 troops for the intervention corps. The Entente was displeased with the Yugoslav demands, and ultimately the war was over before Yugoslavia had time to intervene.

Although the KSCS was not ready to intervene in Hungary, it was also not ready to idly watch the communist takeover. The Socialist Workers' Party of Yugoslavia (Communists) was formed in April 1919, and boasted a vast membership. Alongside their legal activities, communists were engaged in planning a revolution. The HSR's involvement is mentioned above. The illegal activities were the reason for a series of raids and imprisonments of the communists in April 1919.[34] Those were followed by the arrest of Kun's courier Diamantstein in July 1919, and the subsequent highly publicised trial.[35] The 'Diamantstein affair' was the first big anti-communist trial, which lasted for almost a year, and ended in April 1920 with Diamantstein's sentencing to three months in jail.[36] As early as July 1919, the police and the authorities were aware that the revolution was scheduled to coincide with the general strike. The press therefore called on the workers not to strike in support of the HSR. 'Although it is clear as day that we are still at war with *the Hungarians...* some of our workers, misinformed by their leaders, wish to join the strike.' Those 'treacherous' workers should leave for Hungary, the articles read, as they were so eager to support it.[37] Participation in the communist strike was framed as treason to the national interest in a time of war.

The leadership of the Communist Party denied any involvement in the planning of a revolution and proceeded to win around 198,000 votes in the 1920 elections. However, the government decided to stop tolerating the Communist Party of Yugoslavia's subversive actions and outlawed it in December 1920.[38] This prohibition was not done via legal means, but was simply proclaimed as a governmental decision without due process. The legal irregularities were presented as a necessity, due to the dire danger to the State. The document outlawing the CPY read: 'Many open and secret enemies of our state and people have cunningly joined the communist movement. Those defeated in war aim to take revenge on this country by instigating and supporting the unrest,'[39] Communists and many liberals, however, opposed the measure. Foreign diplomats noticed the explosive atmosphere in Belgrade as well. The German envoy in Belgrade notified his government that due to 'imminent communist attack', the Yugoslav authorities had outlawed the CPY. He mentioned the unusual nature of the ban, since it was done, as he put it, 'via poster'.[40] A bitter war broke out between the CPY and police and military authorities. Although the attempted assassination of Regent Alexander was unsuccessful, the war claimed the life of Minister of Internal Affairs Milorad Drašković (1873-1921), the politician responsible for outlawing the CPY, in July 1921. The fact that such a high-profile victim fell to the communists, as well as the brutal nature of his assassination (he was shot while playing with his children),[41] solicited a strong response. The events of early 1921 were the point of no return for the Kingdom of Yugoslavia and the Communist Party, and they mark the end of the first phase of Yugoslav anti-communism.

What defined the first phase of Yugoslav anti-communism was the depiction of communism as hostile

Fig. 5: Minister of Internal Affairs Milorad Drašković.

to Yugoslavia, not because it was a nation state, but because communism was against the Entente. It was not portrayed as hostile towards all nationalism, but rather as a vessel of some nationalism – in other words, as synonymous with revisionism. This does not mean that communism was not branded as a fundamentally mistaken ideology. It certainly was. However, the anti-communist discourse was quite vague; it lacked the damning accusations and colourful examples of a later time. Communism was labelled in 19th-century terms, such as nihilism, defeatism, anarchism and terrorism. The policies of the HSR were constantly described as 'cunning', 'deceitful' and 'twofaced', since it publicly advocated for peace, but actually strove for revolution and the renewal of Great Hungary.[42] The revolution was presented not so much as a triumph of evil, but of chaos.[43] There is a clear absence of the anti-Semitism[44] and vague no-

tions of conspiracy that became so prevalent later. The 'morally decadent' and 'sexually perverse' nature of communism was rarely highlighted. Another distinction between this and later stages of Yugoslav anti-communism is the fact that there was no mass anti-communist organisation capable or willing to fight the Communists in the streets. Whilst hundreds of thousands joined anti-communist paramilitaryorganisations in Germany, Hungary and Austria,[45] Yugoslavia did not have its 'Freikorps' or 'White Guard'. A first similar organisation, the Organisation of Yugoslav Nationalists, was created in March 1921, and it ignited its anti-communist activities, which involved violent clashes, after Drašković's assassination.[46]

The Evolving Image of the Hungarian Revolution and the Later Phases of Anti-Communism

During the following years, the image of the HSR and communism in general changed substantially in the Yugoslav public sphere. A great example of the new and changing stance towards the Hungarian revolution is the series of articles in the main pro-government journal *Vreme*, which commemorated the 10th anniversary of the Hungarian revolution. Despite stating the already established 'revisionist' and 'anti-Entente' attitude of the revolutionaries, and the German support for it, the writers presented the revolution more and more as 'international' and guided

Fig. 6: Members of the 'Red Justice' terrorist cell Alija Alijagić, which assassinated the minister Milorad Drašković in 1921: Nikola Petrović, Rodoljub Čolaković, Stevo Ivanović and Dinko Lopandić (from left to right).

Fig. 7: Hungarian communist revolutionary and politician Béla Kun, the de facto leader of the Hungarian Soviet Republic in 1919.

from Moscow. Therefore, they began to label Béla Kun as a Jew.[47] Revolutionaries were Hungarian nationalists no more, but puppets of Moscow. 'Budapest awoke on March 21 under the terrorist regime. Red flags were hung. Red stripes were spread across the streets, and busts of *Russian* Bolsheviks on top of red pedestals looked as if they had grown out of the soil overnight.'[48] A clear pattern can be seen here: the flags were not Hungarian but red, the leaders were not Hungarians but Russians, etc. The trend of focusing on the communist/foreign nature of the revolution is evident throughout the existence of the KSCS.[49] The defeat of the Bolsheviks was presented as a great victory, and the 'red regime' was further delegitimised by claims that it had stolen more than two billion kronas from the Budapest banks.[50] Simultaneously, Béla Kun was presented to the Yugoslav public as the main communist conspirator who might ignite a revolution at any moment. It was claimed that he was still connected with Yugoslav communists and still tasked with carrying out the revolution in the Balkans.[51] His fingerprints were seen in every communist plot, from Denmark to Brazil.[52] Attempts were made to discredit him as a 'madman', a 'morphine addict' and even as unpopular amongst his fellow communists.[53]

A great example for the new type of Yugoslav anti-communism in the 'non-government sphere' can be found in the most notable Yugoslav fascist politician, Dimitrije Ljotić (1891-1945). He had a personal connection with the HSR and the revolutionary turmoil rooted in 1919. While serving as a Serbian officer in northern Dalmatia, he was entrusted with safeguarding the railway from Delnice to Bakar. In his 1938 autobiography, he proudly recalled that he crushed the general strike by arresting 36 rebellious railway workers. He claimed that the 'strike was purely communist in nature', and intended to ignite a communist revolution – a clear distinction from the 1919 description of the strike as pro-Hungarian.[54] However, true to his radical notions of the complete rebirth of a nation, he was unsatisfied with the 'white' regime in Budapest, which he saw as insufficiently revolutionary, and nothing more than a triumph of the capitalists, who succeeded in defeating the communists but prolonged the 'dying order'.[55] A convinced anti-Semite, Ljotić continued to paint an image of the HSR as a plot of the internationalist 'Judeo Bolsheviks'. During the on-going Spanish civil war, his journal *Otadžbina* (Fatherland) sarcastically commented that Spain was defended by 'such Spaniards' as Béla Kun and Georgi Dimitrov (1882-1949), mimicking his depiction of the HSR.[56] Indeed, Kun's Jewish origin served as an additional argument for the new explanation of the Hungarian revolution. Ljotić warned the Yugoslav public: 'In every Jew lies the blood-thirsty Béla Kun.'[57]

Conclusion

In conclusion, the period between 1919 and 1921 ultimately decided the relations between the Communist Party and the governing elites of the Kingdom. The mutual decision that no coexistence was possible, and that only struggle would determine the winner, shaped the Yugoslav 20th century. It seems clear that the proclamation of the Hungarian Soviet Republic played a key role in this decision. Communism went from being an exotic and far-away enemy to an imminent danger to the state. Equally, it became interwoven with Hungarian nationalism and revisionist claims. The attempted revolution, the outlawing of the CPY and ultimately the assassination of a Minister of the Interior Milorad Drašković were key steps along the path of radicalisation. On the other hand, the anti-communist propaganda during that period was very different from the propaganda of the mid-1920s and especially 1930s. As underlined above, the anti-communist discourse of 1919-1921 was almost entirely devoid of anti-Semitism and notions of a world conspiracy. The depiction of communism as a vessel of revisionism quickly made way for a new and more potent description, which became normative.

Endnotes

1. Béla Kun, *Revolutionary Essays* (London: Carl Silenger, 1977), 5.
2. On the Yugoslav involvement in the HSR, see: Vujica Kovačev, *Na zajedničkom frontu revolucije* [On the Common Revolutionary Front] (Beograd: Institut za savremenu istoriju, 1987); Ivan Očak, *U borbi za ideje Oktobra* [Fighting for the Ideas of October] (Zagreb: Stvarnost, 1976); Toma Milenković, 'Međusobne veze i uticaj Mađarske Sovjetske Republike na radnički pokret u Vojvodini [Mutual connections and the influence of the HSR on the worker's movement in Vojvodina],' *Prilozi za istoriju socijalizma* 4 (1967): 1-57; Toma Milenković, 'Nekoliko dokumenata o delatnosti jugoslovenskih internacionalista u Mađarskoj Sovjetskoj Republici 1919. godine [Some Documents on the Activities of Yugoslav Internationalists in the HSR 1919]', *Prilozi za istoriju socijalizma*, 6 (1969) 331-355.
3. On the early history of the CPY, see: Vladimir Ćopić, *život i djelo* [Vladimir Ćopić, Life and Work] (Rijeka: CHRP, 1978); Zorica Stipetić, *Argumenti za revoluciju-August Cesarec* [Arguments for Revolution-August Cesarec], (Zagreb: CDD, 1982); Коста Николић, *Бољшевизација КПЈ 1919-1929* [Bolshevization of CPY 1919-1929], (Београд: Институт за савремену историју, 1994); Toma Milenković, 'Doprinos Filipa Filipovića stvaranju KPJ [Filip Filipović's Contribution to the Creation of the CPY],' *Socijalizam* 1 (1979) 155-178. On the police repressions against the communists during that period, see: Ljubomir Milin, *Beli teror* [White Terror] (Novi Sad: Progres, 1959); Горан Милорадовић, *Карантин за идеје* [Quarantine for Ideas] (Београд: Институт за савремену историју, 2004).
4. See: Vuk Vinaver, *Jugoslavija i Mađarska 1918-1933* [Yugoslavia and Hungary 1918-1933] (Beograd: Institut za savremenu istoriju, 1971); Andrej Mitrović, *Jugoslavija na konferenciji mira 1919-1920* [Yugoslavia at the Peace Conference 1919-1920] (Beograd: Zavod za izdavanje udžbenika SRS, 1969); Andrej Mitrović, *Razgraničenje Jugoslavije sa Mađarskom i Rumunijom 1919-1920* [Delimitation between Yugoslavia and Hungary and Romania 1919-1920] (Novi Sad: Institut za izučavanje istorije Vojvodine, 1975).
5. Kovačev, *Na zajedničkom*, 25-47; 57-70.
6. Stipetić, *Argumenti*, 110; Kovačev, *Na zajedničkom*, 90.
7. Milenković, *Doprinos*, 165.
8. A rival Slovene Communist Fraction, formed by some Slovene communists, was destroyed and integrated into the YCF, after an unsuccessful attempt to secede from the HSR and to form the 'Mur republic' (Kovačev, *Na zajedničkom*, 108-109).
9. See: Николић, *Бољшевизација*, 38; Danilo Kecić, 'Mađarska Sovjetska Republika i radništvo Vojvodine [HSR and the workers of Vojvodina]', *Polja* 243 (1979) 1.
10. Kovačev, *Na zajedničkom*, 139-142.
11. Milenković, *Nekoliko*, 332; Николић, *Бољшевизација*, 38; Kovačev, *Na zajedničkom*, 102-104.
12. Stipetić, *Argumenti*, 110-112; Kovačev, *Na zajedničkom*, 120-121. The relations between Hungarian and Yugoslav communists were not always as cordial. Yugoslavs complained that 'Hungarians trust no one. They use any opportunity to hinder other nations' (Milenković, *Nekoliko*, 346).
13. Kecić, *Mađarska*, 2. In addition, the HSR financially supported Yugoslav communist journals, the most notable being Plamen [The Flame], a Zagreb-based journal edited by two Croatian communist writers, August Cesarec and Miroslav Krleža. Although the editors denied the financial ties, the journal was committed to supporting the revolution and called 'to storm the modern European Bastille!' (Plamen, 2, 1919).
14. *Црвена застава*, 5.4.1919.
15. Milenković, *Nekoliko*, 333-334; Kovačev, *Na zajedničkom*, 198-199; 203-204.
16. Očak, *U borbi*, 273.
17. Kovačev, *Na zajedničkom*, 215-219.
18. *Време*, 31.7.1929; Vinaver, *Jugoslavija*, 58.
19. Vinaver, *Jugoslavija*, 59.
20. Milenković, *Nekoliko*, 347.
21. Očak, *U borbi*, 274; Kovačev, *Na zajedničkom*, 127.
22. On the 2nd party congress, held in June 1920 in Vukovar, the party changed its name to Communist Party of Yugoslavia.
23. This was the first but not the last case of cooperation between the CPY and various separatist movements. The communists championed both social and national liberation of 'oppressed' peoples within the KSCS. Therefore, they established contacts with Croat and Bulgarian separatists as well as with Montenegrin federalists. For a more detailed overview of the cooperation between communists and various separatist movements, see: Николић, *Бољшевизација*.
24. Kovačev, *Na zajedničkom*, 135-136, 146-147; Milenković, *Vladimir*, 112-113.
25. Milenković, *Nekoliko*, 342.
26. Milenković, *Vladimir*, 114; Kovačev, *Na zajedničkom*, 147-153; Stanislava Koprivica Oštrić, 'Vojnička pobuna u Varaždinu 23.7.1919 [Military Rebellion in Varaždin 23.7.1919],' *Povijesni prilozi* 1 (1983) 65-94.

27. Mitrović, *Jugoslavija*, 177-178; Mitrović. *Razgraničenje*, 158.
28. *Правда*, 4.4.1919.
29. Милорадовић, *Карантин*, 91.
30. Vinaver, *Jugoslavija*, 55.
31. Vinaver, *Jugoslavija*, 50; 56-57; 61.
32. *Правда*, 2.8.1919.
33. Mitrović, *Jugoslavija*, 181.
34. Kovačev, *Na zajedničkom*, 132-133.
35. Николић, *Бољшевизација*, 39.
36. See: Ivan Očak, *Afera Diamantstein: prvi antikomunistički proces u Kraljevstvu SHS* [Diamantstein Affair: the First Anti-Communist Trial in the Kingdom of SCS] (Zagreb: Naprijed, 1988).
37. *Правда*, 20.7.1919.
38. Николић, *Бољшевизација*, 88; Milin, *Beli*, 33-37.
39. Милорад Драшковић, *У одбрану отаџбине* [In Defense of the Fatherland] (Београд: Млада демократија, 1921), 2
40. Politisches Archiv des Auswärtiges Amtes, RAV Belgad, 45/1, Keller an AA 30.12.1920.
41. *Политика*, 22.7.1921.
42. *Novosti*, 27.4.1919; *Правда*, 6.7.1919; *Правда*, 11.7.1919; *Правда*, 13.7.1919.
43. *Ptujski list*, 27.7.1919.
44. I do not claim that no connection between Jews and communism was made during that time, but rather that it was not part of the anti-communist mainstream. During that phase, anti-Semitic undertones of anti-communism were most prevalent in ex-Austrian-Hungarian parts of KSCS. A high-ranking official from Bosnia and Herzegovina, Atanasije Šola, internally referred to communism as the 'poison of Jewish demagogy' (Милорадовић, *Карантин*, 131). Additionally, *Crvena Zastava* (9.4.1919) protested against the claims made in the Zagreb journal Novosti that the majority of leaders of HSR were Jewish, claiming that this was a lie and that even if it were not, communists did not recognize differences between nations' and that these accusations were insignificant.
45. See: Robert Gerwarth, 'The Central European Counter-Revolution: Paramilitary Violence in Germany, Austria and Hungary after the Great War,' *Past & Present* 200 (2008) 175-209; Bela Bodo, 'Paramilitary Violence in Hungary after the First World War,' *East European Quarterly* 28 no. 2, (2004) 129-172.
46. See: John Paul Newman, *Yugoslavia in the Shadow of War* (Cambridge: Cambridge University Press, 2015), 150-166.
47. *Време*, 21.3.1929.
48. *Време*, 1.4.1929.
49. See for example: *Правда*, 26.3.1937.
50. *Време*, 26.6.1929; *Време*, 12.8.1929.
51. *Време*, 4.9.1927; *Правда*, 29.4.1928; *Време*, 1.5.1928; *Време*, 6.2.1936.
52. *Правда*, 4.12.1934; *Време* 1.6.1936.
53. *Време*, 11.10.1927; *Правда*, 5.8.1928. On the other hand, Živojin Pavlović, a convinced Yugoslav anti-Stalinist who fled from the USSR, lamented his murder and claimed in 1940 that Kun had been the 'most popular personality'amongst the communist émigrés in Moscow, as well as a 'genius' organiser, who was always given the hardest tasks (Слободан Гавриловић, *Живојин Павловић и Биланс совјетског термидора* [Živojin Pavlović and the The Balance-Sheet of the Soviet Thermidor] (Београд: Evro-Giunti, 2011), 234.
54. ДимитријеЉотић, *Сабрана дела* 11 [Collected Works] (Београд: Задруга, 2001), 47-48.
55. Димитрије Љотић, *Сабрана дела* 2, 49.
56. *Отаџбина*, 11.12.1936.
57. Archives of Yugoslavia, Milan Stojadinović collection (37), 21-152, I tebi se obraćamo.

Internationalism or National Separatism. The Relationship Between Košice Social Democracy and Czechoslovakia 1918–1919*

Attila Simon

Power interests after the First World War and the altered aspirations of the Habsburg monarchy after self-determination fundamentally changed ethnic ratios in Central Europe, and thereby created a wholly new regional situation. Yet the establishment of new borders failed to resolve the region's ethnic problems, for although most of the newly emerged countries were defined as 'nation states', in reality these multi-ethnic countries had numerous problems. The ratio of national minorities was 28% in Romania, 31% in Poland, 26% in Yugoslavia and 35% in Czechoslovakia[1] – while the latter country's national unity was merely a fiction.

Various national scenarios came to light after the First World War ended, including the plan for German-Austria, Hungarian efforts to restore the pre-war status, and a Central European Federation plan dreamt up by the Hungarian minister of nationalities 1918-1919, Oszkár Jászi. The clear frontrunner, however, was the Czech project to restore the Czech state and enlarge its historical borders. In terms of Czech politics, this 'Czechoslovakia' was understood as a rebirth of the former Kingdom of Bohemia, but slightly larger, while the Czechoslovak Republic also included areas in particular with significant Hungarian and German population.

Hungarians who came to Czechoslovakia – and who maintained a strong sense of affiliation to the idea of Hungary – found it very hard to identify with the new situation. Since Czechoslovakia's foundational constitutional status had been considered a mere stop-gap. Hungarians initially felt rejection within Czechoslovakia, and this was reinforced by constant Hungarian revisionist propaganda and by the insensitive and dictatorial behaviour of the Czech state towards minorities. Hungarians gradually came to terms with the new reality after Czechoslovakia's final borders were

Fig. 1: The Honvéd memorial in Košice, reminiscent of the Hungarian revolution of 1848/49 against the domination of the Austrian Habsburgs. The memorial was built in 1906.

recognised, and as the Czechoslovak state gained economic and political resilience. This held true for the entire political spectrum within the Hungarian minority – including Hungarian social democrats.

While social democracy is generally considered an internationalist movement, within this left-wing movement – alongside the typical conflict between right and left wings – internationalism and nationalism were already at loggerheads in the early twentieth century.[2] This issue gained significance during the First World War, when most left-wing movements assumed the nationalist discourse and joined the pro-war faction. Such movements justified this position as being only a short-term measure, promising to return to business-as-usual proletariat internationalism after the war.[3] But it is now clear that this generally did not happen, and the post-war years in several countries – including Czechoslovakia – brought about a further strengthening of nationalist tendencies.

Although the Kingdom of Hungary that existed until 1918 was a multinational state in which national Hungarians represented approximately 50% of the population, the country's political elite consisted exclusively of Hungarians and of those willing to assimilate into Hungary. This was also true of the Social Democratic Party of Hungary, which until the war's end retained the idea of a united Hungarian state and only provided incomplete and unsatisfactory responses to demands from non-Hungarian workers.[4] Although the extraordinary party conference of 13 October 1918 approved a programme centred around the country's democratisation, representatives of the Slovak social democrats – grouped into the Slovak executive committee of social democrats – did not participate in the meeting. As they had already discussed

Fig. 2: The pedestal of the demolished Honvéd memorial on 17 March 1919 with Czechoslovak soldiers.

the issue of a common Czech-Slovak state with other Slovak political subjects, they strongly disagreed with the way in which the headquarters of the Budapest social democrats supported the integrity of Hungary.[5]

At end of the First World War, the area of present-day Slovakia was an organisationally unified yet nationally divided social democracy. The break-up of Hungary and the emergence of successor states continued apace, with each social democratic organisation responding to the new situation in accordance with its national affiliation: Slovak organisations supported the rise of Czechoslovakia, German and Hungarian organisations insisted they wanted to belong to Hungary. Within the social democratic framework – in territories from Hungary to Czechoslovakia – a fissure developed that turned these recent allies into adversaries.

In this study, I wish to present some points in this process through the example of Košice (Kassa, Kaschau) social democracy. I will primarily concentrate on how Košice social democracy responded to events in late 1918 and early 1919, and how such events influenced relations with the newly-established Czechoslovak Republic.

The history of Košice's social democracy is particularly interesting because this city has always been central to Hungarian-Slovak historical debates, which both parties wish to exploit for themselves. Discussions about Košice largely centre around the city's ethnic composition, often on the basis of contradictory censuses. Originally German, from the mid-nineteenth century to the mid-twentieth century this city witnessed oscillating ethnic majorities: Slovak in 1880, Hungarian in 1910, Slovak in 1930, and Hungarian once again in 1938.[6] Although conventional ethnic historiographies have failed to explain the contradictory results of individual censuses, we now know that the key is the Košice population's tendency to switch between ethno-identification codes. This multilingual-based ability enabled residents to select their declared nationality in accordance with the current political and economic situation, as well as social circumstances and interests.[7]

In terms of this current study, it is important to point out that although at the time of the state coup, i.e. late 1918/early 1919, numerous Slovaks lived in Košice. As the young Slovak historian Ondrej Ficeri points out, such Slovaks had not yet been involved in the ethnicisation of the Slovak-speaking population[8] and they did not comprise a municipal community with political goals or bodies. Hence not only Hungarian but also contemporary Slovak sources refer to Košice as a city with a Hungarian character, where the Hungarian language was predominantly spoken on the streets and whose population was emotionally associated with the concept of a Hungarian state.[9]

The city's character naturally had a significant impact on local social democracy, which as the Upper Hungarian Social Democratic Party functioned as a distinct regional organisation of the Social Democratic Party of Hungary. The Košice hinterland was more Slovak than Hungarian, yet the Upper Hungarian social democratic leadership was solely Hungarian. However (as Frank Henschel indicates), although Košice social democrats were strongly attached to the idea of a Hungarian state, they were also familiar with foreign ideas of internationalism as well as multilingualism.[10]

In the present study I will therefore address Košice social democracy as an ethnic Hungarian organisation, and through that example I will seek to present the resulting dilemmas for Košicean as well as generally Hungarian social democracy in Czechoslovakia. I shall focus only on how Košice social democracy responded to three key events: the war's end and the establishment of Czechoslovakia; the city's occupation by the Czechoslovak army and the consolidation of new power; and the declaration of the Hungarian Republic and the struggle between Hungarian Bolsheviks and Czechoslovakia.

On 27 October 1918, Gyula Andrássy (1860-1929) the Younger (the Austro-Hungarian monarchy's minister of foreign affairs) wrote to US President Woodrow Wilson (1856-1924) to request a separate peace for the monarchy and recognition of Yugoslavs' and Czechoslovaks' right of self-determination. Almost immediately, however, the situation in Central Europe changed dramatically. On 28 October, Czechoslovakia's independence was proclaimed in Prague, and two days later, in Turčiansky Svätý Martin, the Slovak political elite released the Declaration of the Slovak Nation, which stated a willingness to build a common state with the Czechs. In Budapest, the citizens' democratic revolution (the Aster Revo-

Fig. 3: The town hall of Košice 1918.

lution) won and the victors simultaneously declared the Hungarian People's Republic.

These revolutionary changes at the end of October and the beginning of November 1918 saw Slovak and Hungarian social democrats living in the area of today's Slovakia with quite distinct sentiments and mannerisms, because Slovak social democrats were already openly supporting the Czechoslovak project. This is additionally evidenced by the Martin Declaration signatories, including subsequent leaders of Slovak social democracy such as Emanuel Lehocký (1876-1930) and Ivan Dérer (1884-1973).[11] On 25 December 1918, this culminated in a meeting at which the Slovak social democrats unanimously signed up to the concept of a common state with the Czechs, and supported the establishment of a common Czechoslovak Social Democratic Party, which was formed on 30 December 1918.[12] This clear support for the Czechoslovak project stemmed from the fact that

Fig. 4: Miklós Molnár (1887-1946), the last Hungarian Government Commissioner of Kassa/Košice.

for the Slovak left wing, this period was both a democratic and a national revolution – hence, the Slovak social democrats led by Ivan Dérer remained faithful advocates of the common state throughout the period of the first Czechoslovak Republic.

For the left wing in Košice, however, this period had the opposite effect. Even though local newspapers had already reported on the meeting in Turčiansky Svätý Martin and the declaration of an 'independent Slovak country' on 31 October,[13] Košice inhabitants, including social democrats, paid such reports scant attention and did not associate them with their own futures. They instead focused on the Civic-Democratic revolution that won in Budapest on 31 October and subsequently in other Hungarian cities – in Košice the social democrats led the change and also gained strong positions in the Košice Hungarian National Council formed on the same day. Social democrat Miklós Molnár (1887-1946) became

president of the council and Budapest's appointed government commissioner. Since the establishment of the Hungarian People's Republic and the country's democratisation were victories for the Košice social democrats, the events of those weeks further strengthened their connection with the concept of a Hungarian state. This in turn created a strong psychological barrier to the adoption of new national borders as defined in Paris.

On the same day (25 December) that the Slovak social democrats agreed to join the Czechoslovak Social Democratic Party, their Košice comrades also held their congress – but with opposite outcomes: the Košice social democrats declared the unity of Hungary and Košice's place in the new democratic Hungarian state. However, they rejected a military defence of the city against the Czechoslovak army. One of their leaders, Lajos Surányi (1885-1969), described Prague politics as imperialist ('We're threatened from the east by communism and from the west by imperialism'[14]), and called on their Czech and Slovak comrades to support a plebiscite on disputed territories.[15]

The Czechoslovak occupation of Košice became a certainty following the *Pichonoca* – the first demarcation line between Czechoslovakia and Hungary on 21 December 1918. As this line extended south of Košice, the only question remaining was when the occupation would occur and what the local population's response would be. Košice's government commissioner, Miklós Molnár – who was meeting Czechoslovak government representative Milan Hodža (1878-1944) in Budapest – sought assurances that the occupation would not hinder the city's administration or political continuity, and that the Czechoslovak troops would acknowledge that the peace treaty with Košice also applied to Hungary.[16] Yet this idea was an illusion. After the city's occupation on 29 December, a new power – which Košice considered an integral part of the Czechoslovak Republic – immediately deposed the city's leadership, Mayor Béla Blanar (1866-1932) and Commissioner Molnár.

The occupation of the city and the first weeks of the new power brought about surprisingly few conflicts. This was due to the new authorities' benevolent and hesitant behaviour – they had not even initiated a peace conference and aimed to avoid escalating the conflict. So although they replaced the

KASSAI MUNKAS

A FELSÖMAGYARORSZÁGI SZOCIÁLDEMOKRATA PÁRT POLIȚIKAI HETILAPJA

ELŐFIZETÉSI ÁRAK

Egész évre 20 kor. Félévre 10 kor.
Negyedévre 5 kor.
Egyes szám ára 40 fillér.

Megjelenik minden szombaton.

SZERKESZTŐSÉG :
Mészáros-utca 39. szám. — Telefonszám 498.
KIADÓHIVATAL :
Drab Sándor könyvkereskedése, Kovács-
utca 22. — Telefonszám 607.

X. évfolyam. | **Kassa, 1919. január 25.** | **4. szám.**

Risposta al Signor Generale Piccione!

Signor Generale! Noi non abbiamo avuto l'onore di sentire dalla Sua bocca propria la risposta rivoltaci. Abbiamo però appreso, che il Signor Generale s' è espresso, di collaborar volentieri con ognuno, che coopera alla fondazione e al consolidamento delle relazioni normali. E noi con tutte le nostre forze lavoriamo a questo fine. Noi siamo stati quelli, che per commando sacrosanto - del governo ungarico popolare e della democra ia sociale-internazionale impedimmo lo spargimento dei sangue, soprappiù noi siamo stati quelli, che li 28. ottobre, 1917., quando, dopo 3 mesi di un periodo di posizione infernale, giungemmo sull'altura di San Martino e vedemmo, che la Sua patria dalla Punta Sdobba. fino alle Dolomiti stà in fiamme, vedendo la ter·ibile devastazione della Sua bella patria, ci vennero le lagrime agli occhi. E Lei pure ci punisce. Ci punisce perché ancora sempre non ci permette di poter ricevere i nostri giornali professionali e politici di lingua ungherese. Ci punisce, perché permette, che vengano congedate dal loro posto povere persone innocenti impiegate presso istituzioni pubbliche.

Signor Generale! Voglia gentilmente prendere a saputa, che noi lavoratori socialisti di lingua ungherese non ci indentifichiamo con quella oligarchia feudale di lingua ungherese, che da prima fece patir la fame e poi mandò il popolo al macello della guerra. Noi da decennii combattemmo contro questi boia. fino a che il 31. ottobre dell'anno passato li abbiamo distrutto completamente. E il vero giudice non può punire per i crimini dei boia i loro distruttori.

Anche in riguardo alla disoccupazione informarono male il Signor Generale! L' amore al lavoro del lavoratore ungherese è mondialmente conosciuto Prima dell' occupazione boemo-slovacca non ci fu a Kassa mancanza di lavoro. Mentre li 18. gennaio a. c. il numero dei disoccupati ammontò già a 1400 dirim petto a 108 impieghi. Ciò addimostra evidentemente, che non si può avere in orrore la disoccupazione dei lavoratori di Kassa, al contrar o è urgentemente necessario, che per mezzo dell' importo del carbone e del ferro anche in questo campo subentri un miglioramento. Alla consolidazione delle circostanze normali son quindi necessarie le occasioni del lavoro, buoni salarii, il godimento della cultura nella nostra madrelingua, la libertà e la dignità umana.

Kassa, li 24. gennaio 1919.

Con distinta stima :
il Partito sociale democratico di Kassa.

Magyarország kilátásai az angol világpolitika szempontjából.

A Pitt testvérek uralma óta világos, avagy burkolt formában az angol világpolitika meghatározott célokat követ, mely célok elérésében és kivivásában egyedül és kizárólag az ész politikája által vezérelteti magát, félretéve pillanatnyi érdekeket, sovinistikus hiuságot, sőt nem véve figyelembe barátot, szövetségest, avagy ellenséget.

E politikának veleje : miképpen lehet megvalósitani, hogy egy aránylag kis nép egy óriási világbirodalomnak ura és parancsolója legyen, azt nemzeti és világpolitikai érdekeinek szolgálatába állitja, szédítő kereskedelmének és ipari exportjának biztositására kiaknázza.

A külpolitikában ezen világhatalmi állás eléretett azáltal, hogy a tengerek korlátlan uralmát sikerült évszázados következetes politikával megvalósitani. Fokozatos munkával felőrölt minden ellenséget, mely e politika megvalósitásának utját állotta. A spanyol nagy armadának megsemmisítése, valamint a trafalgári ütközetben a legnagyobb számbavehető vetélytársnak, a franciának

legyőzetése utján megtudta valósitani és fentartani azt az elvet, hogy hajóhada mindig kétszer akkora legyen, mint az összes tengeri haderővel biró államok hadi-egységei.

Ezzel kapcsolatosan állandóan fejlesztette keres-kedelmi hajóhadá·, kihasználva e részben a szövetsé-gesek és a semleges kis államok elszigeteltségét.

A második lépcsőfok -volt a világrészeket és ten-gereket összekötő legfontosabb szorosoknak és tengeri átjáróknak biztositása és egymással való összeköttetésük.

A Földközi tengeren megszerezte magának a nyilt erőszak és a titkos diplomácia minden eszközével a spanyol Gibraltárt és vele szemben Tangert és Ceutát. Mindkettőt félelmesen megerősitve uralja a Földközi tenger és az Atlanti óceán kijáratát és bejáratát. Mint támaszpontokat félelmetes erősségé épitette ki Maltát és s syriai támaszpontokat.

Mikor Lesseps genialitása megteremt tte a Suezi csatornát és ez által 2000 km-rel megröviditette az Indiába·való átjutást, Anglia volt az, mely nagy titok-

Fig. 5: Title page of the newspaper *Kassai Munkás* (The Worker of Košice).

city's top governance level (the government commissioner, mayor, chief police captain, postmaster and railroad director) with their own appointees, they left lower-level posts in place for those not openly hostile to the new state. The city's police force is a good example: apart from the replacement of the police captain, it continued to operate as before, even though the police were unsympathetic to the Czechoslovak state, and as one Czechoslovak report stated, 'the police team had to be disarmed in more serious situations'.[17]

Yet this fragile peace was short-lived; from mid-February 1919 onwards, it was followed by a period of conflict and violence between the Košice population and the new power. During this time, social democrats played a crucial role by leading a functional city council, which – as the original city authorities were suspended and inoperable – was the key mouthpiece for the Košice population.

The conflict peaked in a city-wide general strike from 14 to 18 February 1919.[18] The workers' council declared the strike in response to increased frustration with high unemployment, low state-sector salaries, and poor food supply. The strike was widespread, involving blue collar workers, city officials, and rail workers, and included shuttered shops and restaurants. Critical work was performed by Czech employees and the army. Although the nine-point memorandum the workers' council sent to the government included economic and social demands, and residents of Slovak nationality also laid down their tools, most Košice inhabitants regarded the strike as a political act against Czechoslovakia and a 'quiet' demonstration for Hungarian statehood.

The Slovak political elite, including left-wing politicians, viewed the strike as an act of irredentism orchestrated from Budapest.[19] Ivan Dérer, the Slovak social democratic leader, expressed support for the

Fig. 6: Social democrats from Košice in the internment camp in Ilava. : 1. Lajos Surányi, editor of the newspaper Kassai Munkás; 2. Béla Stier, typographer; 3. Sándor Drab, typographer; 4. Béla Aranyosi, shop owner's assistant; 5. Jenő Stein, shop owner's assistant; 6. Géza Borovszky, water pipe installer; 7. György Banekovics, typographer; 8. Zoltán Kendi, lawyer; 9. József Bukovinszky, carpenter; 10. Lipót Feinsilber, painter; 15. Katalin Molnár, wife of government commissioner Miklós Molnár; 16. Jakub Bomba, baker.

government's tough approach to the strike as follows: 'There could be no other response to this Budapest-arranged political act than to sack all those who participated.'[20] Even though the strike had a political background, Košice social democracy did not need help from Budapest, for it had organised the strike itself.

The strike was further aggravated by the poor relationship between the Slovak and Hungarian social democrats. The Slovaks saw the Hungarians as irredentists, while the Hungarians regarded Slovak politicians as being in subjection to Czech nationalism and imperialism. Yet the strike representing only the beginning of open confrontation, which escalated when Czechoslovak soldiers shot at demonstrators, killing two women, less than a month later.

The Hungarian Republic was declared on 21 March 1919 in Budapest, which directly impacted Czechoslovakia's internal policy. The Prague government viewed the Hungarian Bolsheviks' attempt to involve neighbouring countries in the revolution as a threat – hence it imposed martial law in southern Slovakia, banned public gatherings, and interned workers' leaders, especially Hungarians and Germans.

On 22 March a report of the Bolshevik power grab in Hungary arrived in Košice. The next day, the chief police captain Josef Kohout (1875-1952) suspended the Social Democratic Party's activities, closed the Workers' House and forbade publication of the *Kassai Munkás* [Košice Workers] weekly newspaper. From 28 March, leading officials from Hungarian public life – including social democratic leaders – began to be interned at Ilava and Terezín prisons.[21] In April and May, the leadership of the social democratic movement for Slovakia was interned at Ilava camp. Newspapers reported that a congress of left-wing groups was organised in the camp, which proceeded in accordance with statutes (elected congress chairman

Fig. 7: The main street of Košice shortly before the invasion of the Hungarian Red Army in June 1919.

and minutes taken) and discussed post-internment steps.[22]

However, Prague perceived the Hungarian Republic as a threat but also an opportunity to further enlarge Slovakia's borders. Czechoslovak troops accordingly began to attack Hungary on 27 April, but success proved elusive in the first weeks of the war as the soldiers held the 'second demarcation line'. The Hungarian Red Army launched a counter-attack on 27 May, however, and in subsequent days occupied a significant part of Slovakia, including Košice, on 5 June.

This military conflict represented another critical point in the gradual alieneation of Košice social democracy from the Czechoslovak social democrats. While the Czechoslovak Social Democratic Party and its Slovak counterpart resolved to defend Slovak territory, Košice's population warmly welcomed the Red Army with Hungarian flags – although who they were

honouring only became apparent when the Bolsheviks demanded that the red-white-green tricolours be replaced by red flags[23] and when the new power inundated the city with countless decrees.

During the Hungarian Republic period, the gap widened between (Czecho)Slovak and Košice (Hungarian) social democrats. Already political opponents, they now also held opposite positions in the military conflict. The schism between former comrades was also demonstrated by the fact that while Slovak social democrats held positions in the Czechoslovak government, leaders of the Košice leftwingers found themselves interned at Czechoslovak prisons.

The decision of the Peace Conference's Supreme Allied Council on 12 June 1919 forced the Hungarian army to withdraw to its new national borders, which represented the beginning of a consolidation process in Slovakia. After the border's stabilisation, Košice

Fig. 8: French General Edmond Charles Adolphe Hennocque (1860-1933) with other officers in Košice 1919. From 1919 to 1922 General Hennocque ruled Subcarpathian Ruthenia as a military governor and also commanded the Czechoslovak units there. The French military mission built up the Czechoslovak army in those years.

social democrats had to come to terms with the finality of Hungary's break-up and prepare for life in Czechoslovakia.[24] Košice social democracy and Hungarian social democrats in Slovakia faced two alternatives: they could either create a separate and independent movement against Czechoslovak social democracy that defined a Hungarian – specifically Hungarian-German – Social Democratic party; or they could join Slovak and Czech comrades. While the social democratic tradition of internationalism supported the second option, the experience of the first months of 1919 told the opposite story. Czechoslovak social democracy chose to turn away from the social democratic path towards far-right politics and – even more gravely – nationalism. A Bratislava-based Hungarian left-wing weekly stated the following about the Czech Social Democrats: 'They are strong nationalists and chauvinists, and their policies are directed not against capitalism but towards other nationalities. They stand in the service of imperialism.'[25]

Despite their extreme position, leaders of the Hungarian social democrats were interested in cooperation and, in the long-term, in organisational union with the Czechoslovak party. Their vision was to create a party where all three nationalities (Czechoslovaks, Hungarians and Germans) would have equal rights and influence, as reflected in the proposed new party name (Internationalist Socialist Party of Czechoslovakia).[26] The vision was unrealistic in the circumstances, and Prague was not involved in the party's internationalisation.

Rapprochement between Hungarian and Czechoslovak socialists was complicated by the struggle between right and left. While Slovak social democrats mostly chose the Second International, Hungarian workers – dissatisfied with Prague's government policy – were largely drawn towards the Communist International (Comintern) vision. This development was also related to the failure of social democracy's internationalisation in Czechoslovakia and the emergence of the international left as the Communist Party of Czechoslovakia. But that's another story.

Endnotes

* This study was produced as part of the research project *Trianon 100 HAS-Momentum Research Group*.

1. In connection with the new post-Versailles Agreement situation in Central Europe, see Ignác Romsics, *Nemzet, nemzetiség és állam Kelet-Közép- és Délkelet-Európában a 19. és 20. században* (Budapest: Napvilág Kiadó, 1998).
2. Juraj Benko, 'The National Question in the Central European Socialist Movement and the Emergence of Czechoslovakia,' in *Slovenské dejiny v dejinách Európy: vybrané kapitoly*, ed. Dušan Kováč (Bratislava: Veda, 2015), 375.
3. Marián Hronský, 'Workers' Movement in Slovakia up to 1918,' in *Kapitoly z dejín sociálnej demokracie na Slovensku*, ed. Stanislav Sikora (Bratislava: Vydavateľstvo T.R.I.Médium, 1996) 43.
4. For an overview of Hungarian Social Democratic Party policy during the First World War, see Lajos Varga, *Háború, forradalom, szociáldemokrácia Magyarországon: 1914. július–1919. március* (Budapest: Napvilág, 2010).
5. It should be noted that several Hungarian social democracy leaders, in parallel with those supporting the integrity of Hungary, recognise the right of nations to self-determination. See Péter Sipos, 'A szociáldemokrácia és a nemzeti sorskérdések,' in *Útkeresések. A magyar szociáldemokrácia tegnap és ma*, ed. István Feitl, György Földes and László Hubai (Budapest: Napvilág, 2004), 326.
6. According to censuses from 1880, 1910, 1930 and 1938, the ratio of Hungarians and Slovaks in Košice was as follows: Hungarians: 38.3%, 75.4%, 16.4%, 76.6%, Slovaks: 39.5%, 14.8%, 60.2%, 16.3%. Forum Institute for Minority Research. Database of Hungarians in Slovakia. <http://telepulesek.adatbank.sk/telepules/kassa-kosice/> (accessed 11 December 2017).
7. For an overview of Košice inhabitants' ethnicity, see Ondrej Ficeri, *Etnické identity obyvateľov Košíc v medzivojnovom Československu*, dissertation thesis (Banská Bystrica: Matej Bel University, 2017).
8. Ficeri, *Etnické identity*, 59.
9. Of course, Slovak sources also recall that this is a Magyarised city, where the original Slovak city is hidden under the Hungarian surface. National Archives of the Czech Republic, Prague (NA CR), Fund Presidium of the Ministry of the Interior, AMV 225 (f. AMV-PMV 225), Box 1455, 225-1455-3b.
10. In 1896, on the occasion of 1000 years of statehood, Košice social democrats printed statements in Hungarian, German and Slovak. Frank Henschel, *'Das Fluidum der Stadt …': Urbane Lebenswelten in Kassa/Košice/Kaschau zwischen Sprachenvielfalt und Magyarisierung 1867-1918* (München: Collegium Carolinum, 2017), 236-237.
11. For a list of Assembly participants who received the Martin Declaration, see Xénia Šuchová, *Annex II – Political system in Slovensko v Československu (1918-1939)*, eds. Milan Zemko and Valerián Bystrický (Bratislava: Veda, 2004), 547.

12. For an overview of Slovak social democrats' activities, see Xénia Šuchová, 'Sociálna demokrácia na Slovensku v prvých rokoch Československa (1918-1920),' in *Kapitoly z dejín sociálnej demokracie na Slovensku,* ed. Stanislav Sikora (Bratislava: Vydavateľstvo T.R.I.Médium, 1996), 109-145.

13. *Felsőmagyarország,* 31 October 1918, 2.

14. Miklós Molnár, *Kassától Košicéig: Történelmi adatgyűjtemény az 1918-19 évi forradalom, vörösuralom és a csehszlovák köztársaság megalakulása idejéből. II.* (Kassa: 1942), 449.

15. *Kassai Hírlap,* 28 December 1918, 2-3.

16. Although Hodža had initially accepted Molnár's conditions, the agreement was ultimately not signed. Molnár, *Kassától II,* 401-405.

17. NA CR, f. AMV-PMV 225, kart. 1455, 225-1455-3b.

18. For an overview of the strike, see *Kassai Munkás,* 22 February 1919, 1–4.

19. Josef V. Kohout, the first Czechoslovak police captain of Košice, recalls the strike and the role of social democracy as follows: 'The Bolshevised Košice Social Democratic Party with its Hungarian-Jewish leadership played a dual role. The Košice Workers Council had the main role in calling and enforcing a general strike – doubters were forced to lay down their tools with threats. Hence, the Košice Social Democratic Party expressed its loyalty to the Hungarian government and continued working against the Czechoslovakian regime in Slovakia.' Jozef V. Kohout, 'Occupation of Košice by the Czechoslovak army on 29 December 1918 – Events in January & February 1919,' in *Slovenský prevrat. sv. IV.,* ed. Karol A. Medvecký (Bratislava: Komenský, vydavateľská a literárna spol. s r.o., 1931), 297, 288-299.

20. Šuchová, *Sociálna,* 117.

21. Although the issue of internment is yet to be fully explored, useful information is provided by Todd Huebner in 'The Internment Camp at Terezín, 1919,' *Austrian History Yearbook* XXVII (1996), 199-211. Tamás Gusztáv Filep writes about certain aspects of Hungarians' interment in *Főhatalomváltás Pozsonyban 1918-1920* (Pozsony: Kalligram, 2011), 91-109.

22. *Kassai Munkás,* 30 August 1919, 7.

23. Faragó, A szlovenszkói, 48.

24. The political situation in Hungary also played a role in the acceptance of the new situation, where the fall of Bolshevism was followed by white terror and a strict right-wing regime.

25. *Népszava,* 31 August 1919, 2.

26. *Kassai Munkás,* 17 March 1920, 3.

Charades at Versailles: Poland and the Ukraine at the Paris Peace Conferences

Wolfgang Templin

A conference can create a framework that usefully limits discussions that might otherwise range more widely. This chapter will address the relevant events leading up to the peace conferences; the positions of Poland and the Ukraine during the conference; and the treaties' and conventions' significance in the later history of the two countries.

A brief look at the immediate background to the negotiations will serve to explain the composition of the Polish delegation and its internal conflicts, and the situation of the Ukrainian representatives.

Preconditions and Background

Those sitting around the negotiating tables in Paris included an official delegation from the very newly established Republic of Poland. Also present were representatives of the various strands of the Ukrainian independence movement, all striving to win sovereignty for their country.[1]

The new states in East-Central Europe, set up as a result of negotiations and agreed treaties, feature in many accounts of the European situation following the end of WWI According to these accounts, the victorious Entente powers were the ones to decide and dictate these negotiations and treaties. This, however, presents only one side of the real story.

It is true that the Polish representatives, and to a greater extent the Ukrainians, exerted very limited influence on the course and outcomes of the Paris peace conferences. The victorious Entente powers – the USA, Great Britain and France – were far more influential. Together with Italy, which had aligned itself to the winning side, they constituted the negotiating side of the 'Big Four'.

In historiographical literature, the term 'Versailles' has come to designate a multiplicity of separate conferences, of meetings of committees and sub-committees, held in a variety of Parisian suburbs. The 'Versailles Treaty' itself was signed in June 1919 in the Palace of Versailles, and it was followed by a succession of subsidiary treaties and accords, which in the case of Poland and the Ukraine were not concluded until 1923. The politicians, advisers and specialists taking part in the various stages of conferences held in the Parisian suburbs took up various positions over the course of the negotiations, in part because the negotiators found the ethnic and territorial situation in Eastern Europe confusing. The talks' final outcomes reflect this confusion.

Poland's re-emergence as a state of considerable political and economic importance was in significant ways an act of self-liberation. The sovereign state of Poland was founded during November and December 1918, and the Entente powers subsequently largely accepted the propositions its representatives put forward.

Those campaigning for the Ukraine's independence were less successful. They were let down by their weak and divided front, and frustrated by the Entente policy to prioritise accommodation with Soviet Russia.

The Rebirth of Poland

The choice of France and Paris to host the conference held particular significance for Poland. France had become a popular destination for Polish emigrants during the more than 130 years following the Partition of Poland. As each insurrection in Poland against the Partition was in its turn put down, a new wave of emigrants flowed towards Western Europe and France. In 1917, a Polish National Committee was set up in Paris under Roman Dmowski (1864-1939) to

Fig.1: The Polish politician Roman Dmowski.

represent the interests of parties and groups of exiles with right-wing conservative and nationalist views. As Germany headed towards defeat and preparations for the Paris conferences were underway, Dmowski was working towards being acknowledged as Poland's official representative. He based his claim on significant support from various Polish Partition territories and an army established in France, which consisted of Polish prisoners of war and volunteers under the command of General Józef Haller (1873-1960). As the leader of the Polish National Democrats (ND),[2] he was recognised in many West European capitals, and he benefited from a multitude of international diplomatic and political contacts.[3]

His most important Polish adversary, Józef Piłsudski (1867-1935), derived his authority from having a leading member of the influential Socialist Party (PPS) for many years.[4] He had commanded the Polish legion, founded in August 1914, and from August 1917 to November 1918 he had been interned in Magdeburg Castle for refusing to take the oath to the German Emperor.

He returned to Warsaw on 10 November and became the most important politician and military leader at the time of the founding of the new Polish state.

The names of Roman Dmowski and Józef Piłsudski stood for the two camps fighting for Polish independence at the time of the founding and early development of the Second Polish Republic. Piłsudski and his adherents, who included Socialists, Liberals and Conservatives as well, campaigned for a sovereign, multinational and multiconfessional democratic Polish Republic. Their idea was for it to be allied with its eastern neighbours, independent Ukraine, Lithuania and Belarus, in a federation inspired by the tradition of the Polish-Lithuanian Aristocratic Republic. How the federation, confederation or alliance of independent states was to be shaped, and the territorial claims involved, was to be settled in a process of negotiation and conciliation. The same method was later used to decide on the borders. Piłsudski's very varied group of adherents and supporters shared a sense of patriotism that was free of chauvinism and xenophobia, and they were ready and willing to respect the political mentality of other nations. They were also open to shaping a partnership of equality with neighbouring nations that were not prepared to engage fully in a federation.[5]

Roman Dmowski represented a significant – albeit splintered – spectrum of right-wing conservative and nationalist groupings, and he aimed to create a fundamentally ethnic Polish, traditional and Catholic Poland, in which national and confessional minorities would be tolerated but not given equal rights. He questioned the existence of an independent Ukrainian nation, and considered the Ukrainians and Belarusians to be an ethnic group incapable of establishing their own state. He held similar views of the Lithuanians. And unlike Piłsudski, Dmowski was not opposed to an alliance with Russia to counterbalance Poland's ancient enemy, Germany.

In order to succeed in getting Polish demands met at the Paris conferences, Piłsudski and Dmowski had to find a compromise position. Before the two sides – the group in Warsaw and the representatives of the

Polish National Committee in Paris – were able to do this, events were set in motion in Berlin that would bring the founder of the Polish state to the capital of Poland.

The wave of revolution reached Berlin on 9 November 1918. Only a few weeks earlier, Max von Baden (1867-1929) had been appointed German Chancellor, announced the abdication of the Emperor and appointed the leader of the majority Social Democrats, Friedrich Ebert (1871-1925), as acting head of state. In the early afternoon, his fellow party member Philipp Scheidemann (1865-1939) announced the founding of the German Republic from a Reichstag balcony. Two hours later, from a balcony of the City Palace in Berlin, Karl Liebknecht (1871-1919) announced the birth of the Free Socialist Soviet Republic.

Emperor Wilhelm II (1859-1941) had been in his headquarters in Spa, Belgium, since the end of October 1918, nursing a variety of adventurous ambitions. On one day he would plan to hurry to the front in order to die a hero's death amidst his troops, and on the next, to march with steadfast and loyal regiments on Berlin in order to overcome the mutineers. In the end, it was only the earnest entreaties of his entourage, both military and civilian, that persuaded him to accept abdication and exile in the Netherlands.

In Warsaw and Poland, the German occupation soldiers, over 30,000 strong, had been affected by the unrest for several weeks. News from Germany and Russia was reaching the country from outside, and internally there were difficult relationships and uncertainties about supplies – combined, these lead to strikes, looting and attacks. General Hartwig von Beseler (1850-1921), commanding the German forces in Warsaw, was in frequent and anxious contact with Berlin and knew that he would not be able to control the situation for much longer. The three members of the Polish regency council, a German-led pseudo-government, kept encouraging him to summon to Warsaw the one man who could prevent a conflagration.

The Berlin authorities therefore resorted to calling upon the diplomat Count Harry Kessler (1868-1937), who had known Piłsudski when he commanded the legions on the Volhynian front. He was to fetch the commandant, with his adjutant and fellow prisoner Kazimierz Sosnkowski (1885-1969), out of prison

Fig. 2: The Polish statesman Józef Piłsudski, Chief of State 1918-1922, de facto leader of the Second Polish Republic as the Minister of Military Affairs 1926-1935.

and convey them to Warsaw as quickly as possible. Piłsudski was to serve as a member of the regency council to help stabilise the situation until the Berlin disturbances had subsided.

Piłsudski was of course keen to regain his freedom, but not to carry out the task for which he had been designated. Fully aware that the Germans were relying on him, he refused every call on his loyalty, both in Magdeburg and Berlin. Unlike Dmowski, he was prepared to compromise with Germany because he saw Russia as the principal threat to Poland. However, he was not prepared for Poland to continue as a mere satellite state.

Count Kessler returned to the Magdeburg prison on 8 November 1918 to fetch the commandant and Sosnkowski and take them on a lively car trip to Berlin.[6]

On the evening of 9 November, at the general headquarters in Spa, the Emperor's royal train was assembled, and Wilhelm II crossed the border into the Netherlands aboard it the next morning. A significantly smaller special train had been made ready in

Berlin, and it conveyed Piłsudski and Sosnkowski to Warsaw on the morning of 10 November.

The overnight journey gave Piłsudski the opportunity to reflect on his time in prison and on developments since July 1917. Magdeburg was not the first place he had visited during his brief eighteen-month imprisonment. The only accusation against him was his refusal to take the oath; he had therefore been given privileged treatment, being moved from prison to prison before his arrival in Magdeburg in August 1917. His conditions there were tolerable, but he lived in isolation and lodged in a special building on prison grounds, where the German press was his only source of information on the war's progress.

His post was censored and reached him several weeks late. He knew that time was on his side, so he waited out his months in Magdeburg stoically, read and wrote a lot and played many games of patience, one of his favourite activities. He celebrated his 50th birthday in Magdeburg on 5 December 1917 and – many weeks late – received news of the birth of his daughter Wanda in February 1918.

As the special train crossed the Polish border in the night and stopped briefly at a small station, music began to play on the platform. A blind violinist was playing a tune that immediately arrested the attention of the two travellers. The legionnaires' song 'Wir, die erste Brigade' ('We, the First Brigade') had become popular. It could not, however, have been a coincidence that they were hearing it just at that moment.

When the train arrived in Warsaw the commandant and his companion were welcomed by various groups waiting on the platform, though without any great celebrations or speeches. During the preceding evening and night, news of Piłsudski's arrival had reached key members among the circle of the military Secret Legion Organisation (POW),[7] the leaders of the Socialist Party and the members of the regency council. It was these people who were waiting on the platform. Piłsudski met each of the delegations during the course of 10 November to conduct initial discussions. They established the key elements necessary to the founding of the Polish state. These steps were vital preparation for the Polish negotiating position at the Paris conference table.

The members of the regency council, initially somewhat hesitant, were keen to include Piłsudski as a fourth member of the council, but he made it clear that he did not want such a role. He was not interested, he told them, in becoming a dictator, but he needed to have full executive military and civil power. If Poland was to have any hope of becoming a state and surviving as such, it was essential that an army be established in the shortest possible order.

The first steps were to proclaim the Polish Republic, to constitute a provisional government made up of representatives of the various parties and to take measures to ensure public order. In order to achieve this, Piłsudski could call on the POW forces and members of the administration established by the regency council, as well as on specialised personnel from the various Partition territories. The POW's influence extended into the soldiers' councils of the German garrison, which was to be disarmed and escorted back to Germany.[8]

Piłsudski exerted pressure on his socialist companions, who had already established a provisional government, to accept political compromises and a coalition government. The reborn Poland had no scope for extreme socialist demands. He announced that he stood for the whole nation, not just for a particular political camp. Conservatives and the right wing had never submitted to socialist dominance, and the left wing included Soviet socialist groups keen to join forces with Vladimir I. Lenin (1870-1924) and the Bolsheviks. Poland was not yet even fully reestablished and it was already under threat of being torn apart by civil war.

It was important to develop an initial political compromise so that public order could be secured, and preparations could be made for elections and a process to establish a constitution. This was the only way to ensure that the victor nations would accept the idea of a Polish Republic and recognise the authority of the Polish delegation at the forthcoming peace negotiations.

Incredibly, they managed it. The Germans, however, were forced to abandon any hope that their pseudo-state would survive, and not long afterwards they were engulfed in the political wrangling that led to the establishment of the Weimar Republic.

In order to save the republic, Friedrich Ebert and other Social Democrats joined forces with members of Imperial Army and were able to put down the Spartacist uprising in January 1919. All were keen to

Fig. 3: Józef Piłsudski, and Prime Minister Ignacy Paderewski arriving at the opening of the Polish Parliament, Warsaw, January 1919.

challenge the existence of the barely-created Polish state, which they denounced as a historic monstrosity and challenged in every way possible.

Lenin and the Bolsheviks were fighting to maintain the power they had but recently gained; they saw the Ukraine as an integral part of Russian sovereign territory, and were very anxious to see the establishment of a dependent Soviet Polish state. These plans, too, were frustrated.

Fighting broke out in early November 1918, threatening any potential conciliation between Poland and the Ukraine. In Lvov, military forces of the West Ukrainian People's Republic, proclaimed on 1 November, together with Ukrainian militias sought to gain control of the city and met with resistance. Those resisting were the city's inhabitants, university students and pupils, who took it on on themselves to represent the Polish claim to Lvov. The Polish military forces in Lvov had no unified command structure and represented a variety of political affiliations, and the rapid Ukrainian offensive took them

by surprise. Many Ukrainians wanted to rid themselves of the hated Polish dominance and hound all Poles out of public positions. The situation deteriorated, and there were attacks against civilians, looting and increasingly violent battles. Anyone on either side hoping to achieve a sensible compromise was fighting a losing battle, and all attempts at negotiation failed. The archbishops of Poland and Ukraine called for a ceasefire, which the troops eventually complied with. Socialist Poles advocating an independent Ukraine volunteered to join in fighting with the Polish side.[9]

Once the Polish troops had occupied Lvov, they inflicted a pogrom on the Jewish inhabitants. Parts of the Jewish defence militias had taken sides with the Ukrainians, and this inflamed antisemitic tendencies within the Polish population and fanned the pogrom's flames.

Roman Dmowski was following all these events from Paris and laying plans to take over the government with the help of the political majority he commanded in the country. In this, he would be assisted by the popularity of the world-famous pianist and composer Ignacy Paderewski (1860-1941), whom he sent from Paris to Poland in December 1918. Paderewski arrived in Poznań on 26 December to a storm of enthusiasm, accompanied by British liaison officers. The National Democrats were the predominant party in Poznań. An insurrection gave impetus to attempts to ensure a Polish takeover of the administration of the city and of the whole province, which had previously been progressing at a snail's pace.

Paderewski's arrival in Warsaw exposed which of the two rivals had the more realistic one Dmowski's hopes were dashed by the power of Paderewski's character. The pianist was not a political animal; he was keen to serve his homeland through his music and his committment to humanitarian causes. His appointment to the Paris Committee had not bound him to the ideological position of Dmowski and the National Democrats. In spite of the differences between the 'Lithuanian' and the cosmopolitan artist, Paderewski and Piłsudski soon developed a relationship of respect and indeed friendship.

At the start of January 1919, Warsaw officers sympathetic to the National Democrats planned a putsch to overthrow Piłsudski. Paderewski and, later, Dmowski would not be involved in any government affairs. The dilettante putsch attempt failed, and Piłsudski turned the tables on the conspirators. He exposed those who had initiated the so-called 'Theatre Putsch' as ridiculous, but did not impose draconian punishment. Only a new form of compromise would be able

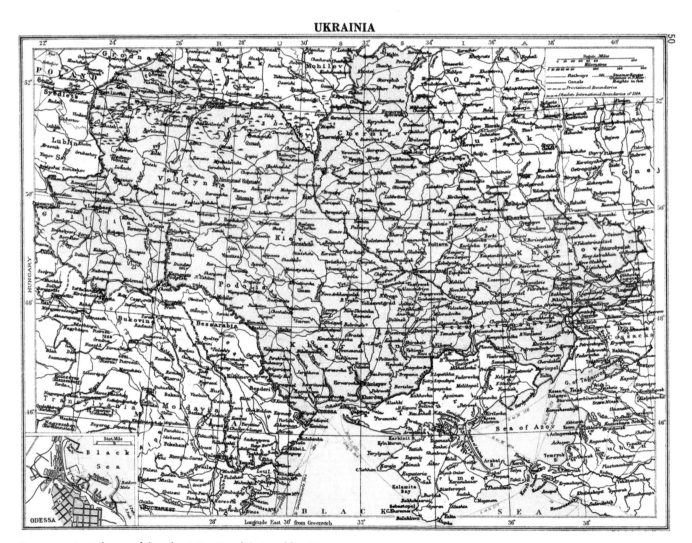

Fig. 4: Provisorial map of the Ukrainian People's Republic, 1919.

to save the increasingly weakened republic and rescue the Polish negotiating position in Paris, where the peace negotiations were about to open formally. Piłsudski persuaded Paderewski to take on the role of prime minister and to lead a coalition government that included Socialists, National Democrats, Conservatives and representatives of the various farmers' associations. Many government positions were allocated to independents. This meant that political extremists on either wing could be held in check.

Paderewski agreed to take on the position, shuttled between Paris and Warsaw and remained one of Poland's most important representatives in the Paris discussions. Dmowski, in Paris, was the official leader of the Polish negotiating delegation. Piłsudski did his best to ensure that his most highly trusted representatives were also present to check the influence of the National Democrats. In Warsaw, he was leading the establishment of the state; with his close advisers, he worked to set up an army that could resist the Soviet Russian threat, staging the 'Wonder of the Vistula' in August 1920. Painstaking work was required of the Polish representatives in Paris to resolve or overcome internal differences of opinion on the boundaries of Poland, on relations with neighbours to the east and on visions of a future Poland.

There was no lack of voices at the Paris negotiating tables casting doubts on Poland's right to exist and the Polish Republic's chances of survival. Speaking for France, Georges Clemenceau (1841-1929) expressed the highest respect for Poland and the hope that its restoration would make amends for one of the greatest crimes in history. President Woodrow Wilson (1856-1924) made a generous promise to Poland in his Fourteen Points. The British, however, and the assembled advisers and specialists thought very differently. It was possible to construe Wilson's call for a unified, independent and self-governing Poland in a variety of ways.

The British expert on Polish affairs, Lewis Namier (1888-1960), who was himself of Polish–Jewish extraction, called for a campaign against Dmowski and his adherents. He may well have had a point, given the antisemitic attitudes of many National Democrats and of Dmowski himself. Because of his fear of Polish antisemitism, he believed that Poland should exist only as a subsidiary state, but this was not a realistic position. He underestimated the strength of republi-

can feeling among socialist and Liberal forces in the reborn Poland. Nationalism, xenophobia and antisemitism were alien to these forces and to their leader, Piłsudski.

The Polish question became one of the most complicated issues tackled during the protracted negotiations, and it occupied committees and sub-committees until well beyond the summer of 1919.

The Failure of the Forces for Ukrainian Independence

The representatives of the Ukrainian independence movement sitting around the Paris negotiating tables were divided into various groups and strands, and they did not have the status of an official delegation. The proposal in the 1917 Treaty of Brest Litowsk for an independent Ukrainian state existed only on paper. It had arisen from the interests of Germany as a participant in the war, and from the negotiating skill of the Bolsheviks. When the first Bolshevik delegation refused to accept the German conditions for a ceasefire and peace, the German military machine was set in motion.

Under the name 'Operation Faustschlag', German troops occupied nearly all Ukrainian territories and other parts of the Baltic region. Lenin decided that he would, for the time being, put up with the presence of German troops on Ukrainian soil, and use the peace accord as a badly needed breathing space.

He assumed that the German Spring offensive to the West was doomed to failure, and that the war would end in Germany's defeat. His comrades were keen to begin a life-and-death struggle, but he persuaded them that the setback would only be temporary. He played for time, demonstrating yet again his tactical skill. In later trading negotiations, he made it clear to his comrades that he wanted to hang the capitalists with the rope they were selling him.

In Ukraine, the military independence forces of the Central Council were caught between Soviet Ukrainian military units, the armies of the White Generals and the German troops, and were wiped out. The Ukrainians in Paris were representing an entity that could barely be described as an actual state, and and they were ignored and dismissed to an even greater extent than were the Poles.[10]

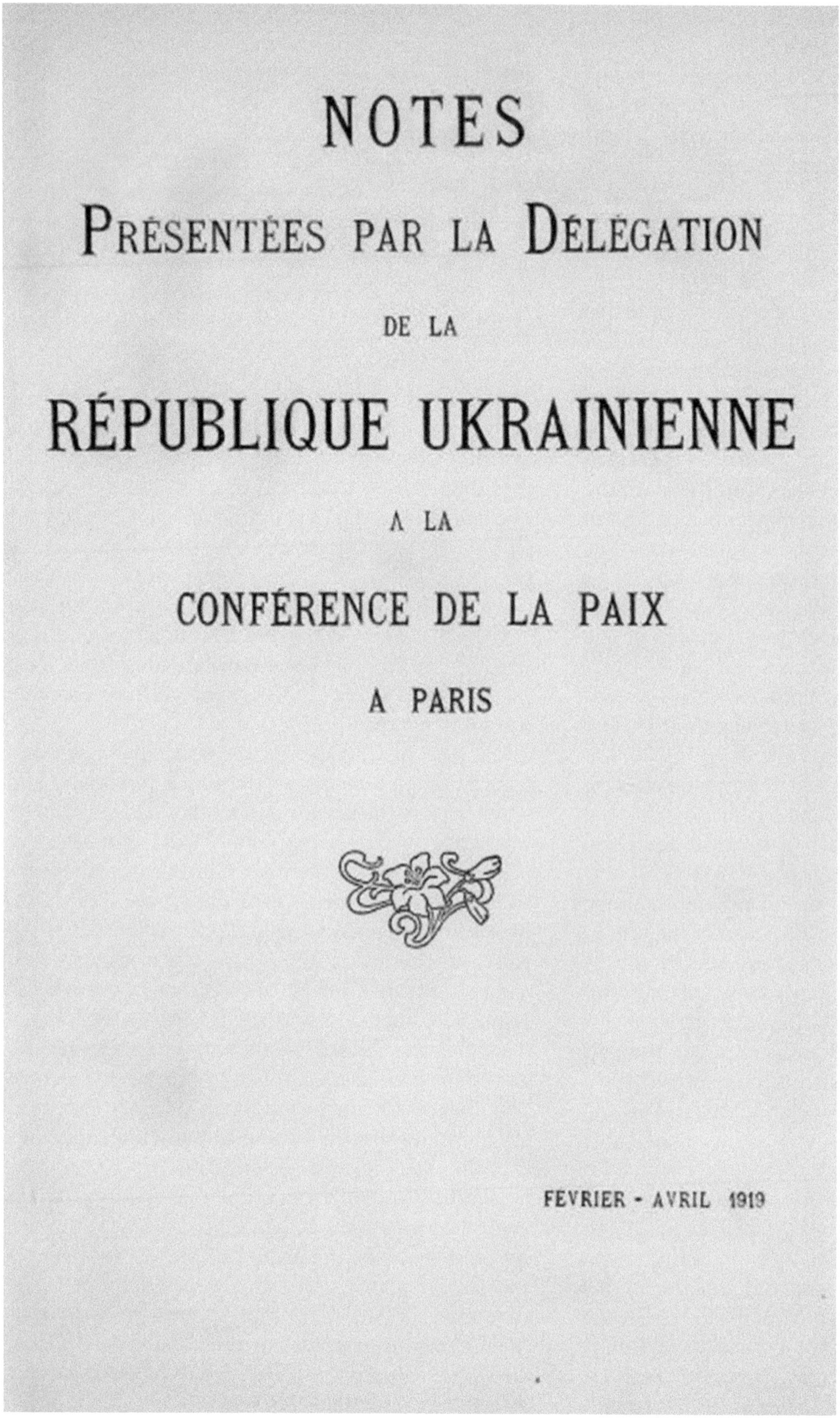

NOTES

Présentées par la Délégation

DE LA

RÉPUBLIQUE UKRAINIENNE

A LA

CONFÉRENCE DE LA PAIX

A PARIS

FÉVRIER - AVRIL 1919

Fig. 5: Diplomatic notes of the Ukrainian delegation to the Paris Peace Conference from February to April 1919.

When not in an official capacity, the British lead negotiator, Lloyd George, behaved with forthright brutality. He had only once, he asserted, met a Ukrainian, and he was not certain that he ever again wanted to meet another. The English prime minister's complete lack of knowledge of anything relating to East-Central Europe was clear for all to see.

It was Lloyd George also who repeatedly sought to frustrate attempts to build up a Polish army and strengthen Polish defences. He was sympathetic to the Bolshevik Soviet social experiment and hoped that if the West were accepting of it and keen to build trading relationships they would be able to foster liberalisation there.

In matters concerning the effective independence of Ukraine, the attitudes of the allies' leading representatives were based on ignorance, prejudice and a fixedly favourable view of the developments in Soviet Russia.

Independence movements had been operating in Ukraine's Russian and Habsburg-owned territories since the second half of the 19th century, striving for national autonomy and self-reliance and adopting a variety of social and political positions. Members of these movements made an initial attempt to create an autonomous state during and after the First World War, and the Ukraine's independence was declared in January 1918. Socialists, monarchists and conservatives struggled for dominance within the structures of the nascent Ukrainian state, and a state-building process in West Ukraine subsequently posed a constant threat to the central Ukrainian government.

Both German military forces and Russian Bolsheviks sought to instrumentalise the Ukrainian independence forces for their own ends. Lenin's promise of an independent Ukraine, which lasted only until the end of the civil war, served to consolidate his own efforts to gain power. His concept of a 'red' Greater Russia, created under his own leadership, would tolerate only a Soviet Ukraine and, as a satellite state, a territorially diminished Soviet Poland. Ultimately, the Paris negotiations settled the fate of Ukraine far less definitively than they did the future of the Polish Republic. This was due in part to the failure of the Polish–Ukrainian Federation plan, which was linked with the names of Piłsudski and Symon Petljura (1879-1926), and to an even greater extent to the

Fig. 6: The Ukrainian politician Symon Petljura, President of the Ukrainian People's Republic 1918-1921.

success of the Soviet experiment, which the Western Allies increasingly came to accept.[11]

As a result of the negotiations in Riga, which lasted until the spring of 1923, Ukraine was divided into two: a pseudo-state, Soviet Ukraine, and West Ukraine, which was incorporated into the Polish Republic. It was not until decades after the end of the Second World War that Ukraine would become a truly independent state. Moreover, its Russian neighbour continues to call its sovereignty into question to this day

Endnotes

1. Margaret Mac Millan, Die Friedensmacher: Wie der Versailler Vertrag die Welt veränderte (Berlin: Propyläen, 2015), 283ff.

2. ND – Narodowa Demokracja.

3. Andrzej Nowak, Polska i trzy Rosje, Studium polityki wschodniej Józefa Piłsudskiego (do kwietnia 1920 roku) (Kraków: Arcana, 2001), 421; Grzegorz Krzywiec, Szowinizm po polsku. Przypadek Romana Dmowskiego (1886-1905) (Warsaw: Neriton, 2009), 191.

4. PPS – Polska Partia Socjalistyczna.

5. Jan Józef Lipski, Dwie ojczyzny – dwa patriotyzmie. Uwagi o megalomanii narodowej i ksenophobii Polaków (Warsaw: cdn, 1982), 17ff.; Wolfgang Templin, Der Kampf um Polen. Die abenteuerliche Geschichte der Zweiten Polnischen Republik (Paderborn: Schöningh, 2018).

6. Harry Graf Kessler, Tagebücher 1918-1937 (Frankfurt/Main: Insel Taschenbuch, 1995).

7. POW – Polska Organizacja Wojskowa.

8. Andrzej Garlicki, Józef Piłsudski. 1867-1935 (Kraków: Wydawnictwo Znak, 2008); Bohdan Urbankowski, Józef Piłsudski. Marzyciel i Strateg (Warsaw: Wydawnictwo Sysk i S-ka, 2014), 164.

9. Best-known among the Polish socialists who dedicated their programmatic writings before 1918 and their political activities to campaigning for the Ukraine's independence and against the National Democrats' Ukraine policies were Tadeusz Hołówko, Henryk Józefski, Ignacy Daszynski and Leon Wasilewski. Mirosław Boruta, Wolni z wolnymi. Równi z równimi. Polska i Polacy o niepodległości wschodnich sąsiadów Rszeczpospolitej (Kraków: Arcana, 2002), 45.

10. Frank Golczewski, Deutsche und Ukrainer 1914-1939 (Paderborn: Schöningh, 2010).

11. Jan Pisuliński, Nie tylko Petljura, Kwestia ukraińska w polskiej w polskiej polityce zagranicznej w latach 1918-1923 (Toruń: Wydawnictwo naukowe UMK, 2013), 323.

History of Ideas

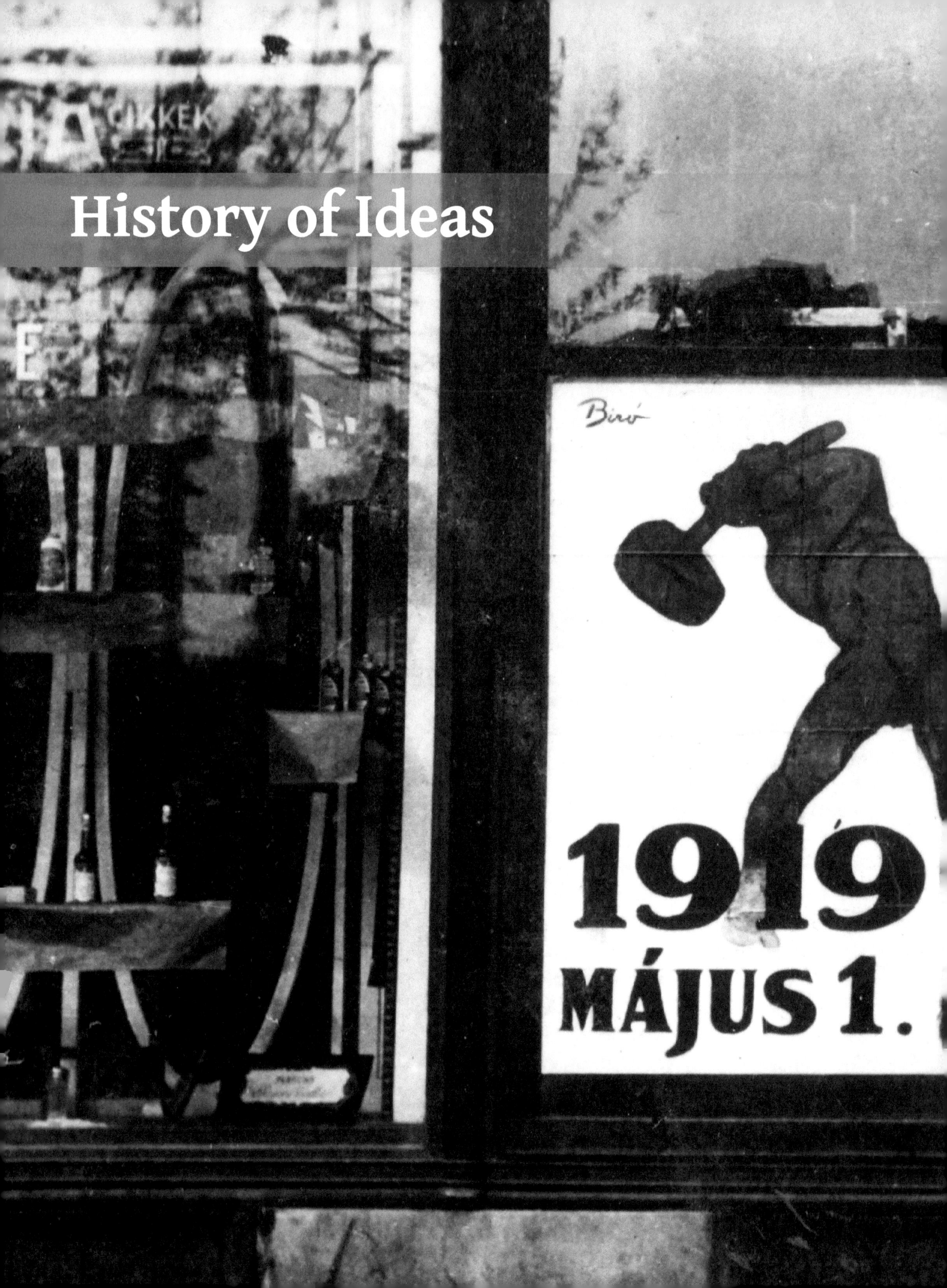

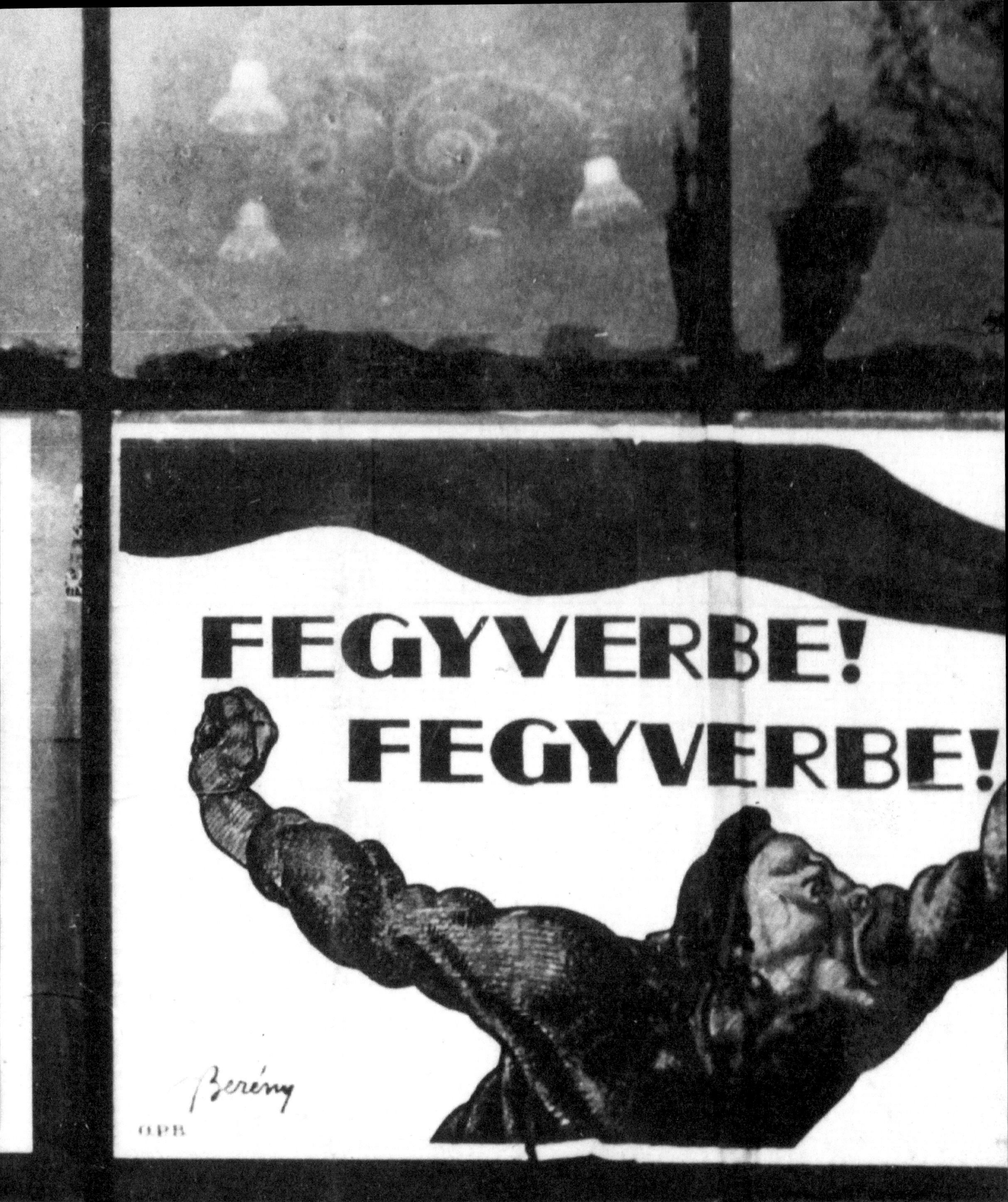
FEGYVERBE!
FEGYVERBE!
Berény
OPB

1 May-Decorations from Hungarian Soviet Republic, 1919.

Vladimir Ilyich Lenin and Woodrow Wilson on the Self-Determination of Nations

Burkhard Olschowsky

This article addresses the concept of the self-determination of nations, which was to become a visionary and assertive underlying principle for the political and legal emancipation of multi-ethnic societies. It focuses on two political representatives of their respective countries, the American president Woodrow Wilson (1856-1924) and the Russian revolutionary Vladimir Ilyich Lenin (1870-1924), and on the different ways these two statesmen understood national self-determination at the start of the 20th century, and then enforced it during and after the First World War. I will take account not only of the biographies of the two men but also of the histories of their two countries, and of the interplay between their views and the contrast between their respective historical contexts.

The intellectual and legal origins of the concept of the right to self-determination go back to the Ameri-

Fig. 1: Declaration of Independence of the United States presented by drafting committee to the 1776 Congress, painted by John Trumbull 1819.

Fig. 2: Ulyanov family in Simbirsk 1879: (standing left to right) Olga, Alexander and Anna; (sitting from left to right) mother Maria Alexandrovna, their younger daughter Maria, Dmitry, father Ilya Nikolayevich and Vladimir (front right).

The concept of self-determination remained prominent throughout the 20th and 21st centuries; indeed, it became one of the most successful political and legal slogans, not only undergirding nations' claim to equal rights but also providing the basis for an international order of self-governing nations, along the same lines as the United Nations.[3]

The Nation as Reference Point

The right to self-determination was defined with reference to a nation. Nations evolved along very different paths, but the idea of a nation held out the promise to anyone who was recognised as belonging to it that they would have a share in the collective achievements of a community defined by its language, its origins and its traditions. Lenin to some extent invoked the Austro-Marxists Otto Bauer (1881-1938) and Karl Renner (1870-1950), who had drawn on their experiences in the multi-ethnic Habsburg Empire to examine in detail the concept of the nation and the many ways in which it exerted its appeal. The idea of the nation could be weaponised under the slogan 'national self-rule', since the working classes generally placed a higher value on their national allegiance than on internationalism.[4]

Lenin was well aware of the significance of state independence, and it later became clear that he was equally conscious of the international dimension of the right to self-determination; Bauer and Renner, meanwhile, saw the right to self-determination above all as a national privilege.[5] There was an unparalleled attraction to seeing the nation as a shared resource, provided the nation also functioned as a state. All national movements wanted above all to have their own state.[6] A state defined who could and could not claim solidarity with the nation, providing a border that gathered together those who were members and excluded those who were not. It embodied the promise of something fundamentally new in the long history of statehood: an open society of basically equal citizens collaborating as one nation. This symbiosis between state and nation made the nation state seem a very attractive option.[7] In Eastern Europe especially, a vision of a future that was furthermore legitimated by the prospect of the right to self-determination exerted a particular appeal.

can Declaration of Independence (1776) and the French Revolution (1789). First and foremost, the right to self-determination emphasises that the people are sovereign, and that the government is answerable to the people. The concept was then taken up in the 19th century by nationalist revolutionaries such as Giuseppe Mazzini (1805-1872) and applied to ethnic national groups.[1]

The principle of national self-determination became a powerful political lightning rod in the multi-ethnic empires of Europe, where tensions desperately needed resolution. As the First World War and its many geopolitical and ideological upheavals drew to a close, the concept of the right to self-determination and of the principle of self-determination gained new prominence as a means of emancipation; key political leaders of the time, in particular Woodrow Wilson and the Russian party leader Vladimir Ilyich Lenin, were quick to see that it could serve their own political purposes.[2]

Lenin's Understanding of the Right to Self-Determination

Vladimir Ilyich Ulyanov, known by his alias Lenin, had been born in 1870 in Simbirsk (now Ulyanovsk), and had grown up in the multi-ethnic south of the tsarist empire. He was partly of Jewish extraction, but he had not suffered any ethnic discrimination during his youth. He was brought up at home to be a Russian European.[8]

During and after his law studies he became increasingly involved in the proletarian social democratic movement in Russia. His early travels to European countries such as Germany, France and Switzerland confirmed his international outlook. According to Boris Meissner, '[h]e detested any manifestation of what he called Great Russian chauvinism. His knowledge of ethnogeography and his privileged background meant that his view of the "national question" could differ from that of his Party comrades'[9] among the Russian-speaking revolutionaries: 'The young Lenin sought to find ways to address the "national question" in the light of the specific problems arising from the multi-ethnic character of the Russian empire.'[10] He was strongly influenced by the international debates on the right to self-determination and the anti-tsarist, early Socialist writings of Alexander Herzen (1812-1870), Michail Bakunin (1814-1876) and, especially, Georgi Plekhanov (1856-1918).[11]

Lenin understood the right to self-determination to mean the right of a nation with a clear territorial delineation to decide whether it wanted to become separate or to remain a part of its existing union – in other words, to assert its claim as an independent national state with territorial autonomy.[12] In 1903, Lenin evolved his understanding of the right to self-determination against the background of the debate among the large General Jewish Labour Bund and the Social Democracy of the Kingdom of Poland and Lithuania (SDKPiL). Both groups, however, resisted Lenin's efforts to create a centralised organisation for the Russian Social Democratic Labour Party (RSDLP), inspired by the cultural and organisational autonomy of the Austrian model. Subsequently, at the 2nd conference of the Russian Social Democratic Workers' Party, the Jewish Bund split away from the Party and the Polish Social Democrats ruled out any merger with their Russian sister party.[13]

In 1912, Lenin's thinking on the question of the right to self-determination once again became highly relevant when the question arose of keeping the 'Caucasian' Party members in the RSDLP and at the same time offering them the prospect of national independence.[14] Lenin's own party, the Russian Social Democrats, were very irritated by his commitment to the issue of nationalism. At the Second International he engaged in further lively debate on the matter with his party comrades and with other Russian intellectuals. Both before and after the 1915 conference in Zimmerwald he fiercely defended his conviction that the principles of the Second International encompassed the principle of self-determination for nations and thus also the freedom to declare independence from another state, and that it was therefore legitimate to mobilise the masses to resist national oppression.[15]

Lenin conducted a year-long discussion with Rosa Luxemburg (1871-1919), one of the leading theoreti-

Fig 3: The Polish-German politician and theoretician Rosa Luxemburg.

Fig. 4: After the First World War Wilson as a segregationist paid little attention to a couple of racist riots against African Americans in the United States while campaigning for democracy in Europe. Editorial cartoon by William Charles Morris in *New York Evening Mail* about the East St. Louis riot of 1917.

The Right to Self-Determination after the October Revolution

Following the October Revolution, which admittedly was more akin to a coup d'état against the provisional government, Lenin presented the 'Decree on Peace' on 26 October 1917 to the All-Russian Congress of Soviets. In it he demanded an immediate cease-fire and offered to all the warring nations and their governments an immediate start to negotiations to settle a just and democratic peace.[19]

It was an astonishing step to take, which following three years of war led to an immediate suspension of conflict, and it hugely boosted trust in the Bolsheviks among war-weary Russian farmers. The peace decree strengthened the right to self-determination among smaller nations especially, as they could now not be held against their will within the borders of a larger state. The theoretical musings of a revolutionary were now going to be measured against the reality of striving for political independence within multinational post-tsarist Russia.[20]

Lenin had addressed the issue of the right to self-determination for colonial nations as early as 1917, and in the following months he would renew his demands for the purposes of propaganda. Out of regard for the colonial powers of England and France, and his own support for racial segregation, Woodrow Wilson was not interested in supporting these demands.[21]

Following the October Revolution and Lenin's election as chair of the Council of People's Commissars in November 1917, the newly established Russian foreign policy was in some ways ambivalent. On the one hand, the Bolsheviks published the 'Declaration of the Rights of the People of Russia', which enshrined in law the principle of self-determination for all nations, enabling them to defect from the ill-defined nationality policies of the Provisional Government. On the other hand, the new leadership tried to stem the disintegration of the state as the power of the Bolsheviks was supposed to extend to the country's periphery.[22]

This new nationalities policy was assiduously monitored, especially in the regions close to Russia's western and southern borders. The Finnish parliament, which declared Finnish independence on 23 November 1917, was the first to gain recognition

cians of Polish and later German social democracy, whom he acknowledged to be a 'revolutionary Socialist', on the 'problem of the question of nationalism'.[16] She was convinced that achieving a Europe-wide revolution would necessitate collaboration between the Polish and Russian Labour movements, and she rejected the idea that Poland might become independent from Russia. Luxemburg obviously failed to recognise that national independence was the principal driving force behind Poles' political activity, right across the left-orientated parties.[17] The notion of emancipatory nationalism was the main reason for the support all parts of Polish society gave to Józef Piłsudski (1867-1935), and which enabled him to lead Poland to independence in 1918 at the end of the war.[18] In this respect Lenin and Piłsudski, who had known each other for decades, fully shared a realistic assessment of the ethnic and social centrifugal forces seeking to blow apart the tsarist empire.

Fig. 5: A Volhynian peasant with his children during First World War.

from Soviet Russia.[23] When further regions – Estonia, Latvia, Lithuania, Ukraine, Georgia, Armenia, Azerbadjan and Turkestan – all followed the Finnish example, the Bolsheviks began to fear that Soviet Russia would fall apart before it had consolidated its power in peripheral regions. As a result, they either simply did not recognise the independence declarations of these provinces and states, or only did so under international pressure. After the Bolshevik takeover, there was a fundamental change to how the 'national question' was addressed: the constitutional reforms, which would otherwise have been determined by the nationality principle, had diminished in importance in the face of the domestically conducted class struggle.[24]

Soviet Russia's nationalities policy was primarily aimed at solving domestic issues. It became a foreign policy issue where a national group made a claim for their own territory and declared independence. Poland's opportunity to claim the right to self-determination was more fruitful than that of Ukraine.

Western Europe recognised the partitioned Poland and territorial autonomy was granted at the time of the Provisional Government in Russia.[25] Poland's efforts to gain independence were strongly supported during the final year of the war by Woodrow Wilson and the Entente, whereas the Ukraine could only rely on brief selfish support from Germany and Austria-Hungary, who were principally serving their own best interests.[26]

In 1914 Lenin had made sketchy statements about Ukrainian independence. He abandoned any thoughts of it during the Russian civil war, favouring instead an alliance with Ukrainian farmers against the White Guards.[27] Unlike Joseph Stalin (1878-1953) and other Party functionaries, Lenin was trying hard to ensure that Ukraine, Armenia and other regions would have a fair deal in a 'Union of European and Asian Soviet Republics'.[28]

The Russian civil war, with its wide range of forces and competing interests, temporarily obscured the distinction between domestic and foreign policy. Eth-

Fig. 6: 'Russian peace' (La Pace Russa). In this poster, the Bolshevik Russia that assented to the Treaty of Brest-Litovsk is represented as a serf, bayonets in the back, forced to carry out death's terrible work, designed by Sergio Canevari, 1918.

nic, social and ideological lines of conflict overlapped, and class and independence struggles became confused.[29] Various states formerly within Russia had claimed self-determination and obtained independence, notably the Baltic states and Finland. The Bolshevik leadership, however, were not intending to destroy the Russian Empire, but rather to shore it up through revolution, first within Russia and then worldwide. Lenin saw more clearly than other Bolsheviks that in order to secure the solidarity and cooperation of the working class beyond Russia's boundaries, it was necessary first to abandon the tsarist policy of oppressing non-Russian national groups.[30]

The Bolsheviks and the West

The governments of the Entente nations displayed confused uncertainty on hearing about the seismic changes in Russia. The new leadership acted in a way incompatible with all received political wisdom: Lenin's Decree on Peace, which was immediately adopted, the publication of secret treaties and appeals to the workers in the 'West' gave rise to con-

Fig. 7: The signing of the ceasefire agreement between Germany and its allies and Soviet Russia on 15 December 1917 in Brest-Litovsk. From the front, left side: Hakkı Paşa (Ottoman Empire), Kajetan Mérey (Austria-Hungary), Prince Leopold of Bavaria, General Max Hoffmann, Colonel Peter Gawtschew (Bulgaria). From the front, right side: Lev Kamenev, Adolf Joffe, Anastassija Bizenko and Admiral Vasili Altfater.

sternation among the Entente nations, who shrank away from discussing their war aims between them. They were especially severely hit by the loss of Russia as a military ally; Russia was now engaging in peace negotiations with the German Empire and with Austria-Hungary at Brest-Litovsk in order to end a war that was overwhelmingly unpopular at home, and to ensure its own political survival. The allies had no consistent idea, let alone any strategic plan, about how to deal with the new Russian government, especially since they avoided direct contact with Lenin and other leading Bolsheviks, and Paris, London and Washington were reliant on the fragmentary impressions of the various emissaries present.[31]

The struggle for a solution in Brest-Litovsk became a test case for implementing the promises of peace and self-determination. The negotiations, moreover, thrust the participants onto a tense world stage from which none of the First-World-War participants could withdraw, because the opponents sitting opposite them had a radically different understanding of peace and had a new world order in view.[32]

Both sides instrumentalised the right to self-determination at the negotiating table to shore up their own position. The head of the Russian negotiating team, Adolf Abramowitsch Joffe (1883-1926), emphatically told the leader of the Austrian-Hungarian delegation, the foreign minister Ottokar Count Czernin (1872-1932), that nations' right to self-determination should be made available as widely as possible around the world, in order to enable mutual love between 'these liberated nations'. Czernin defended himself from this suggestion by referring to the sovereignty of the Habsburg monarchy, and the possibil-

Fig. 8: Woodrow Wilson's parents, Joseph Ruggles Wilson and Janet Woodrow Wilson.

ity that the talks might fall through. Joffe jovially retorted: 'But I hope we shall succeed in triggering a revolution in your country too.'[33]

The German delegation leader, Richard von Kühlmann (1873-1948), secretary of state in the foreign office, was hoping that from a position of military strength he could conclude a peace agreement that would establish a German protectorate over a bloc of independent east-central European states. The Supreme Army Command favoured annexation, and von Kühlmann sought to obtain this with reference to the right to self-determination of Ukraine, Estonia, Latvia and Lithuania. He presented this plan both in the German Reichstag and during the negotiations with Joffe, and later with Leon Trotsky (1879-1940), who took over leadership of the Russian negotiations from 8 January 1918.[34]

The Russian side rejected Kühlmann's suggestion, citing the right to self-determination, since the will of the people could clearly not be expressed so long as

foreign troops occupied the territories in question. Addressing Western European socialists, Trotsky furthermore demanded that they should grant the right to self-determination to their oppressed colonies.[35] The Supreme Army Command observer at the peace negotiations, General Max Hoffmann (1869-1927), rejected this appeal to the right to self-determination. The Russian government, he claimed, did not even grant the right within their own borders to Ukraine, while 'the nations in the occupied regions had clearly and unambiguously expressed their wish to become separate from Russia'.[36]

The Central Powers engineered a meeting between the Russian and the Ukrainian delegations, but the charged atmosphere eliminated any chance of reaching an understanding. The Ukrainians confidently pointed to their state's independence, and accused the Russians of being completely uninterested in the right to self-determination, for all that they claimed otherwise.[37]

The Russian negotiating team, for their part, referred to the fact that it was Bolshevik forces that had captured Kiev by the beginning of February 1918, and insisted that the principle of national self-determination required that the revolutionary masses should seize power. This process always and everywhere took precedence over the principle. In Brest-Litovsk, the Ukrainian Rada delegation cooperated with the Central Powers' dominant forces and concluded their own separate peace treaty, which in the eyes of the Bolsheviks meant that they had turned traitor to the revolution.[38]

Wilson's Understanding of the Right to Self-Determination

Woodrow Wilson had been raised in the southern states of the USA. His father was a pastor in the Presbyterian Church, and his mother also came from a clerical family. The young Wilson was shaped in his way of life and his understanding of the world by his Calvinist convictions. Later critics were wrong, however, in accusing him of constantly going around quoting the Bible. He was no fundamentalist, and did not see the Bible and science as being in contradiction.[39]

As a child, he had experienced the defeat of the Confederates in the American civil war between 1861 and 1865. As a young man, he treasured the memory of his childhood homeland, but he did not unduly lament the disappearance of the Old South or the Confederacy. He recognised that, had the southern states become independent, they would have fallen even further behind the northern states in economic terms, and would have been isolated in international terms.[40]

Wilson had enjoyed a remarkable academic career at the end of the 19th century. At the age of 32 he became a professor of history in Middletown, Connecticut, and two years later a professor of law in Princeton. By 1917, Lenin had already been taking an interest in the subject of nations' right to self-determination for several years; Woodrow Wilson was fourteen years Lenin's senior, but his origins and career had given him little acquaintance with the subject. Wilson had received a broad interdisciplinary academic education, but his own nation, the USA, remained the focus of his research and interests. As a moderate Southern segregationist and convinced statist, his background was completely different from that of Lenin, a professional international revolutionary. In 1893 Wilson published a history of the American civil war, which, given that it came from the pen of a Southerner, was remarkably thorough and unbiased.[41]

His view was that the total defeat of the South in the American civil war precluded the option of independence for the southern states, and required instead that the two sides become reconciled and equal, in order to become integrated as one nation in one state. As Jörg Fisch has argued, if one excludes the oppressed and permanently disadvantaged indigenous peoples, 'unlike the Russia and many European states, the USA was not a multi-ethnic state in the sense of having territories with different ancestral histories. From this point of view, the USA (apart from Mexico) had no difficulties with nationalities and so-called border nations. Against the background of the United American States, Wilson's concept of self-determination was in effect self-government, the government of the people by the people.'[42]

In the context of his academic work, Wilson made a comparative examination of constitutional law in Great Britain and the USA, and was greatly influenced by the writings of the economist Walter Bagehot (1827-1877) and above all the philosopher Edmund Burke (1729-1797). According to these two

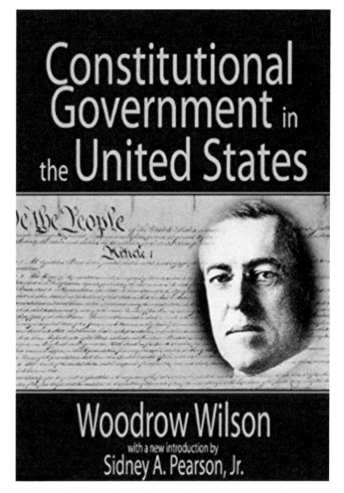

Fig. 9: Book cover of Woodrow Wilson's Constitutional Government.

authors, political life was not founded on abstract principles, but on historical experience and evolved tradition. In his book *Constitutional Government*, published in 1908, Wilson emphasised that the defence of freedom must form the core of any political constitution. He also asserted that a nation's constitution must be capable of evolving to remain relevant, but barring radical upheaval. Wilson was a professor but also nurtured political ambitions, and he maintained that any social change should be guided and controlled by a set of moral and religious values.[43] Wilson not only thought that the American nation – free from monarchy or commitment to colonies – was better equipped for this challenge than the states of Europe, but also that it was predestined to serve as a model democratic republic for other states.[44]

Fig. 10: Woodrow Wilson's speech to Congress with the request a declaration of war against Germany, 2 April 1917.

Moving on from academic publications, Wilson started on a successful political career: in 1910 he was voted in as Governor of New Jersey for the Democrats, and two years later elected as President of the United States. He was re-elected in 1916 thanks to the slogan 'He kept us out of the war'. In a speech to the League to Enforce Peace on 27 May 1916, he promised that the USA would collaborate in setting up an association of the nations. This established his claim to be an advocate for the security and integrity of smaller nations. He maintained that all nations should have the right to make sovereign decisions over their own fate.[45]

In pursuing this line of argument, the president was subtly preparing his fellow citizens for political and military participation in the First World War, even though – as he pointed out in his introduction – he had no interest in becoming involved in the competing European forces that had led to the war. Wilson offered a solution in his speech to the US Senate on 22 January 1917 entitled 'Peace without Victory', in which he outlined the new internationalism he had in mind. When he announced to the nation on 2 April that he intended to declare war, he added the famous slogan: 'The world must be made safe for democracy'. It was only through the establishment of democratic states that would work together, he asserted, that long-term peace could be secured. So it was that Wilson enthusiastically welcomed the fall of the tsar in the February Revolution, and proclaimed that the Russian people had a democratic soul.[46]

The United States and Russia

The USA and Soviet Russia were to exert an unprecedented influence on Europe's fate after 1918. Their politicians' actions and ideas on political order awoke both hopes and fears across Europe; the two states, having hitherto been peripheral, therefore increasingly took note of each other and developed their policies each with an eye on the other. The new superpower in the West was conscious of its economic and military strength, and was able to characterise its president, Woodrow Wilson, as the bringer of peace. In economic and military terms, post-tsarist Russia was a collapsed state, yet it embodied the political allure of peace and self-determination. With missionary zeal, Lenin was meanwhile calling on the working masses to rise up in revolution in their own countries. His rallying cry was politically powerful, and it aroused both positive and negative reactions among all those who had been involved in the war.[47]

On 6 April 1917 the USA entered the war on the side of the Entente and against the Imperial German Reich and its allies. Russia, an ally of the Entente, was no longer an autocracy but a democratic partner, and this lent weight to Wilson's call to fight for democracy in nations where the people had shown they wanted it, and gave him increased authority in persuading his fellow Americans of the need to join in the war. It was clearly right to deploy 'peace and justice' to counter an autocratic claim to power.[48]

Wilson's call for a liberal political order was immediately challenged by the October Revolution and the Bolshevik proclamations. Wilson's and Lenin's projects, however, did in fact display some similarities. Both were raising universal and global claims on the basis of a social interpretation of the social environment.[49] Wilson's 'peace without victory' and Lenin's 'peace without annexations or indemnities' shared some features, and there were further similarities: the appeal to the principle of self-determination, the critical view of the European imperial powers, the rejection of secret treaties and the commitment to a new internationalism. That the two perspectives presented by Wilson and Lenin each elicited widespread interest suggests that other peace solutions had exhausted their appeal.[50]

Lenin's concept of unconditional peace, published on 7 November 1917 as his Decree on Peace, was rapidly and widely circulated in the 'West' and caused consternation in the French and British governments. Paris and London (and indeed Washington) decided it was preferable simply not to acknowledge the Bolshevik government and to avoid any discussion of war aims. The governments of the Entente and the USA nevertheless felt under so much pressure from the Decree on Peace that they were then forced to explain their own aims for the peace.

Wilson and the Bolsheviks

Wilson presented his Fourteen Points, a peace programme for Europe, in his speech to Congress on 8 January 1918. It was no accident that this coincided with the negotiations leading to the Treaty of Brest-Litovsk. And Wilson managed to include some words of praise for the Bolsheviks. He acknowledged that they were conducting their negotiations 'very justly, very wisely [...] in the true spirit of modern demo-

Fig. 11: Wilson's kind intentions for Russia symbolized by a torn-away bear with the Jacobin hat, drawn by Arthur Johnson, published in *Kladderadatsch* 1917.

Fig. 12: Lincoln Colcord, US-American journalist and advocate of good American-Russian relations, early 1920s.

cracy'.[51] He stressed that Russia was entitled to obtain 'opportunity for the independent determination of her own political development and national policy' and to expect 'a sincere welcome into the society of free nations under institutions of her own choosing'.[52] Behind these warm words, however, was a careful calculation aimed at preventing any German peace conditions that would have undermined Russia.[53]

Wilson saw the Russian population as an important part of the international public he hoped to address through his speech. On 13 January 1918, the US embassy in Moscow sent a telegraph to say that Lenin agreed with Wilson's speech and thought it promoted peace. Wilson's careful choice of words hit a different tone from those of the Entente governments, who made no effort to hide their anti-Bolshevik feelings, and as a result his speech was well received in Russia and among the Bolsheviks.[54] Wilson viewed a military intervention in Soviet Russia with extreme scepti-

cism. From 1918 to 1920, he committed to no more than the defensive and ultimately aborted deployment of 5000 US soldiers in Arkhangelsk and 8000 in Vladivostok, to secure munitions for the Allies and help the Czechoslovakian Legion evacuate from Russia.[55]

By the start of 1918 Wilson had not yet reached a firm view on the Bolshevik coup; he had been consulting those around him, as he also did before the start of the Paris Peace Conference. One of these was Lincoln Colcord (1883-1947), who had made a name for himself as a young political columnist on the *Philadelphia Public Ledger*, and who had been recommended to the president's circle of associates by Edward Mandell (Colonel) House (1858-1938). Colcord argued that the new Russian government should be approached with an open mind, and rejected the image of Russian anarchy and chaos widely presented in the US press. He argued that the new Russian ruling party's efforts to achieve peace should be taken seriously, and that their government should be recognised.[56] Secretary of State Robert Lansing (1864-1928), however, opposed recognition of the new Russian government, as he judged that they had forced their way into power and were exerting class-based despotism. The US indeed did not grant Russia full recognition, but the administration made every effort to maintain channels of communication with Petrograd and Moscow.[57]

Notwithstanding the seizure of power by the 'Maximalists', as the Bolsheviks were named in liberal and conservative circles, at the start of 1918 Wilson expressed some sympathy for the large east European nation that only a few months earlier had cast off the tsarist yoke. With half an eye to the Central Powers, he insisted on 'the evacuation of all Russian territory and such a settlement of all questions affecting Russia as will secure the best and freest cooperation of the other nations', and that Russia's further development should be given every encouragement.[58]

Even when ideological differences came between Wilson and the Bolsheviks, he recognised that the Western powers did not have the means to force a sympathetic regime upon Russia, nor would it be legitimate for them to do so.[59] It was indeed far more likely that foreign intervention would provoke a wave of patriotic reaction in favour of the Bolsheviks,

Fig. 13: Wilson with his advisors, including ministerial and military personnel, at the Versailles Peace Conference; depicting Edward Colonel House, Secretary Robert Lansing, President Wilson, Henry White, General Tasker H. Bliss (from left to right).

as the French government discovered to their cost when they attempted to intervene in southern Russia at the end of 1918. Any intervention, moreover, would have contradicted – before the whole world – the undertaking in the Fourteen Points that Russia too was promised the ability to determine its own political development.[60] In the light of the October Revolution, Wilson indeed urged his Allied colleagues not to overlook the rights of the workers.[61]

Wilson's occasionally contradictory attitudes towards Soviet Russia were also reflected among his advisers and officials in the US Department of State. There could be major differences of opinion on a coherent foreign policy for the USA vis-à-vis the huge country lying to the east of Europe and the north of Asia. This was especially true of Wilson's close adviser Colonel House and Secretary of State Robert Lansing.[62]

Lenin and the Bolsheviks on Wilson

Lenin viewed the USA and Wilson with a certain amount of benevolence from his place of exile in Switzerland, as they had been far less involved than France and England in the First World War and were free of colonial baggage. After his return to Petrograd in the spring of 1917 and the USA's entry into the war, however, he changed his view. In his April Theses, he called for unity among all groups and factions established on the basis of internationalism and proposed a new concept of worldwide society in conflict with Wilson's perspective. Lenin unflinchingly described the struggle between democratic nations and autocratic governments, as Wilson saw it, as a 'predatory war by the ruling classes'.[63]

Behind Lenin's declamatory style, his political attitude vis-à-vis the USA was thoroughly consistent and pragmatic. He was keen to nurture wide-ranging working relationships with the government and with American society in order to foster beneficial economic contacts. He was not particularly interested in encouraging American workers to follow the Russian example of revolution, but rather in establishing effective relations between the two countries, in the short term in order to stave off any military intervention in Russia by the US administration, and in the medium term to build up preferential relations between the USA and Soviet Russia.[64]

On the occasion of the ratification of the Treaty of Brest-Litovsk on 11 March 1918, the president con-

Fig. 14: Georgy Vasilyevich Chicherin, People's Commissar for Foreign Affairs in the Soviet government 1918-1930.

firmed that he wanted to 'secure for Russia once more complete sovereignty and independence in her own affairs and full restoration to her great role in the life of Europe and the modern world'.[65] The Bolsheviks responded unambiguously on 14 March in a message addressed to 'nations bleeding to death and suffering from the imperialist war', announcing that the time was approaching 'when the working masses in all bourgeois nations would throw off the yoke of capitalism and establish a Socialist civic order that would be the only guarantee of a just and lasting peace'.[66] This admirably summarised the revolutionaries' proposed worldwide programme. It was no longer possible to overlook the ideological and social divide between Petrograd and Washington.

In the next few months of 1918 the Bolshevik representatives fluctuated in their interactions with the US administration between preaching the proletar-

ian revolution and appeals for freedom, justice and signs of increasing trust. This last request made explicit reference to Wilson's fundamental principles: the right to self-determination for nations and the 'New Diplomacy', which amongst other things excluded secret treaties.[67] The leading Bolsheviks understood foreign policy in a variety of ways, ranging from the 'revolutionary' foreign policy favoured by Leon Trotsky, Karl Radek (1885-1935) and the Comintern associates to a more pragmatic approach that satisfied Lenin and Foreign Commissar Georgy Vasilyevich Chicherin (1872-1936).[68]

When the Soviet Russian government were under pressure from the White Guard in the summer of 1918, they signalled to Washington and to the Entente governments their preparedness to repay their debts and to renege on their threat of world revolution. A few months later matters changed, however, once the Red Army had seen off the threat of the 'Whites'.[69]

Russia was an unseen presence at the Versailles Peace Conference. The developments in the former tsarist empire served as a constant reference during the conference; the delegations from Paris, London and Washington, however, were unable to agree on a shared position vis-à-vis the Bolsheviks.[70] The American diplomat William C. Bullitt (1891-1967) led a special mission that renewed efforts in February 1919 to revive earlier discussions, but these failed under pressure from the Republics of Councils set up at the time in Hungary, Bavaria and Bremen, and the strikes in central Germany and in the Ruhr. The Western allies found vindication for their scepticism, indeed their fear in the face of the growth of Bolshevism.[71]

Comparing Lenin's and Wilson's Understanding of the Right to Self-Determination

The US president sought to seize the initiative as the end of the First World War approached, and to develop a formula for lasting peace in Europe. The USA, as world leader in economic and soon also in military terms, now needed to create a correspondingly high political profile. In order to persuade his sceptical fellow Americans to join the war, Wilson had increasingly spoken about self-rule for nations, and about

Fig. 15: Woodrow Wilson 1919.

the fight against despotism and autocracy.[72] Democracy was necessary, he asserted, to underpin future world peace.[73]

If Wilson wanted to play a central role in the debates on peace in Europe, then he had no other option than to show an interest on Lenin and his ideas.[74] He adopted in part Lenin's format for defining the right to self-determination for nations, but not the content. On 11 February 1918 Wilson spoke in public for the first time about self-determination and the right to self-determination, but he did not intend this to imply that the wishes of the nations involved would determine peace-time territories.[75] He chose his explanatory words extremely cautiously and carefully avoided any explicit definition. In keeping with his times, the US president naturally only considered self-determination for white people, since his convictions held that non-whites lacked the fundamental education and moral and political requisites for self-rule.[76]

There was a certain irony here. The US president was reluctant to adopt the definition of right to self-

determination widely accepted in Europe, yet his listeners, and especially the east European nations, were expecting to hear about Lenin's understanding of right to self-determination rather than Wilson's. They wanted to hear it from Wilson rather than Lenin, however, and understandably so, given the political and military situation in 1918.[77]

Huge hope was invested in Wilson, who was seen as the most powerful man in the world, and also as a neutral external mediator. Lenin, on the other hand, was seen as a chancer who divided society into classes and used carefully targeted force. The bourgeoisie above all were appalled by him, since they were excluded from the left-wing proletariat and therefore were accorded little long-term prospect of success.[78]

An idea put forward by Lenin therefore carried less weight than one presented by Wilson. Nor were the two men on an equal footing. In 1918, Wilson became a key figure in world politics, one to whom many looked for peace and justice. Lenin, on the other hand, was a professional revolutionary, hardly known outside Russia before late 1917 except among socialist groupings and parties.[79]

Fig. 16: Vladimir I. Lenin 1920.

Fig. 17: Cartoon depicting Wilson with his vision of a League of Nations. His US opponents and other political observers often characterized him as an idealist and moralist, 1919.

Wilson's and Lenin's Dilemmas

Having led the USA into the war, Wilson had lost his earlier status as a mediator by 1918. He had cast his lot in with France and Great Britain, whose governments would not contemplate losing to the Central Powers. The ambition Wilson had voiced of a 'peace without victory' remained a chimera. In the United States there was growing opposition to the president's policies. His Republican opponents, who had fiercely rejected Wilson's internationalist reform policies, were gaining influence thanks to a surge of jingoistic enthusiasm for the war among Americans who saw imperial Germany as the root of all the evils of the world.[80]

It was Wilson who had introduced the key concept of self-determination and promoted the idea of a League of Nations; as Jörg Fisch has correctly pointed out, he was therefore inextricably involved in the challenge of establishing peace. Had his original message been received in the American sense he had intended – as an encouragement to establish self-rule and democratisation – then a clear and consistent plan of action might have evolved.[81]

By 1918, Wilson's self-determination was received as a principle granting legitimacy to nation states. As a result, this legal structure gained an intrinsic value, and it then gave shape to the negotiations in Paris and to the establishment of the League of Nations. It aroused huge expectations of the notion of national independence, undeliverable even by Wilson. Robert Lansing had warned at the end of 1918 of the risks inherent in the right to self-determination as it was described: 'The phrase is simply loaded with dynamite. It will raise hopes which can never be realised. It will, I fear, cost thousands of lives. In the end it is bound to be discredited, to be called the dream of an idealist who failed to realise the danger until too late to check those who attempt to put the principle into force. What a calamity that the phrase was ever uttered! What misery it will cause!'[82]

Things did not turn out quite so badly, but by twelve months after the end of the war it had become clear that any true implementation of Wilson's intentions would be dependent on a great many other factors. Wilson's Fourteen Points had raised great hopes among the German people, but they had been given an insipid peace agreement and felt betrayed; this sentiment was no doubt exacerbated by self-deception over the scale of their defeat and a collective denial of reality among the population of the new Weimar Republic.[83] Matters were not improved by Wilson's clumsy domestic policies. Republicans did not trust Wilson's far-reaching but poorly defined plans for a new peace order. At the turn of the year in 1919/1920, the US Congress refused to back the Versailles Treaty and entry into the League of Nations.[84]

The right to self-determination as promoted by Lenin until 1917, and which Wilson adapted a year later, gave rise to a number of serious questions that needed to be tackled by the international community. The post-war territorial arrangements discussed at the Versailles Peace Conference were influenced by factors that were beyond the victor nations' control. These included the fact that language statistics were to be a decisive factor in determining national borders, and that a plebiscite over territorial changes could favour one of the defeated nations. The representatives of the relevant victor nations – Georges Clemenceau (1841-1929), David Lloyd George (1863-1945) and Woodrow Wilson – had to choose between accepting these factors and the consequent weakening of their position, which affected their popularity both at home and among the newly established nations, or breaking their commitment to the defeated powers, which risked causing frustration and fanning political radicalisation.[85]

Lenin too had nourished unrealistic expectations and was forced to face reality. From 1917 onwards, up to 40 national entities with varying levels of stability emerged across the lands that had formerly constituted the Russian Empire. On 31 December 1917 the Bolsheviks recognised Finland's independence under the right to self-determination. But they were not prepared to do the same for Ukraine. Until 1920, they also resisted granting independence to the Baltic states. The Bolshevik party leadership had before then fiercely resisted the concept of federalism, but they finally adopted it in order to prevent any further Russian disintegration.[86]

Thanks to the Bolshevik seizure of power, the revolutionary solution of the national question prevailed over efforts at constitutional reform, and the territorial principle prevailed over the concept of the nation as an association of people. In the Russian civil war, however, the nationality principle lost ground to the concept of class struggle, and in the context of Bolshevik centralisation the Russian territorial principle led to the establishment of a union of national regional entities (the later Soviet Republics).[87]

Illusions?

Both Lenin and Wilson faced difficulties in the years following 1917/1918 in persuading their fellow citizens to accept the principle of the right to self-determination. Both encountered vigorous opposition from domestic political opponents. Each had a sense of superiority in terms of intellect and ideals, and made the mistake of resorting to ignoring them and indulging in patronising polemics. They displayed remarkable inertia vis-à-vis the clear reservations intimated by close political colleagues such as Nikolai Bucharin (1888-1938) and Joseph Stalin in the case of Lenin, and Secretary of State Robert Lansing and William C. Bullitt in the case of Wilson. And in each case, their now failing health impaired the ability of each man to assert his position.

Lenin's great illusion was the notion of world revolution. His fundamentalist belief was a conviction

Fig. 18: Lenin speaks at the inauguration of a monument for Karl Marx and Friedrich Engels, Moscow, 16 November 1918.

that history, as he understood the writings of Karl Marx (1818-1883), would follow a clearly defined path into the future. He himself worked with missionary zeal to ensure that these ideas became reality. And indeed the revolution did break out; however it was not, as the theory suggested, in one of the developed capitalist nations but in backward Russia, with serious consequences for that vast nation and for the development of political antagonism throughout the 20th century.[88]

In terms of both his actions and his words, Wilson was a complex and somewhat contradictory character. On the one hand he was a statist who believed in America's moral exceptionalism and her special mission in terms of historical progress, yet he also saw himself as an internationalist, believing passionately that the USA must take a leading role in promoting world peace. 'As president, he was convinced that he represented the true will of the peoples, one that he would be able to carry out through peaceful changes in the international order.'[89]

Fig. 19: Cartoon about the difficulty of reconciling the different ideas of self-determination and territorial claims in the cartography after the Paris Peace Conference, drawn by Clifford Berryman 1919.

Their own contemporaries already recognised that both Wilson and Lenin were 'do-gooders'. Wilson was 'the first to foresee that without a worldwide association of countries the nations would be unable to sustain their existence. A second attempt at improving the world through social and political means was carried out in Russia. [...] It is clear that mankind must choose between Lenin and Wilson.'[90]

With the benefit of a century's hindsight, it is clear that at first glance Lenin and Wilson each failed because of their far-reaching utopian ideas and the persistently severe social and national damages inflicted by the 'Great War'. On the one hand lay a worldwide classless society; on the other was an international peaceful order of sovereign and democratic nations.[91] Lenin's radical vision was lived out for decades in violent and dramatically inhumane form; in contrast, Wilson's efforts to establish worldwide standards promoting peace, and his principles that fostered beneficial co-existence among the nations, are still doing good one hundred years later.

Endnotes

1. Bernhard Fisch, *Das Selbstbestimmungsrecht der Völker. Die Domestizierung einer Illusion* (München: C.H. Beck, 2010), 80-82, 93-97, 121-122.
2. Cristian Cercel, 'Selbstbestimmungsrecht,' in *Online-Lexikon zur Kultur und Geschichte der Deutschen im östlichen Europa*, 2012. <http://ome-lexikon.uni-oldenburg.de/53890.html> (accessed 15 November 2019).
3. Fisch, *Selbstbestimmungsrecht*, 17-20.
4. Otto Bauer, 'Unser Nationalitätenprogramm und unsere Taktik,' ('Der Kampf', I, 1907/08) in Otto Bauer, *Werkausgabe*, vol. 8 (Wien: Europaverlag, 1980), 75, 78; Karl Renner, *Das Selbstbestimmungsrecht der Nationen in besonderer Anwendung auf Österreich* (Leipzig-Wien, Franz Deuticke, 1918); Heinrich August Winkler, 'Der Nationalismus und seine Funktionen,' in *Nationalismus*, ed. Heinrich August Winkler (Königstein/Ts.: Verlag Anton Hain, 1978), 5-48, here 11-12; Hans Mommsen, 'Die sozialistische Arbeiterbewegung und die nationale Frage in der Periode der I. und II. Internationale,' in ibid., 85-98, here 94-95.
5. Günter Decker, *Das Selbstbestimmungsrecht der Nationen* (Göttingen: Verlag Otto Schwartz, 1955), 154.
6. Theodor Schieder, 'Typologien und Erscheinungsformen des Nationalstaats,' in *Nationalismus*, ibid., 119-137.
7. Dieter Langewiesche, *Der gewaltsame Lehrer. Europas Kriege in der Moderne* (München: C.H. Beck, 2019), 264.
8. Robert Service, *Lenin. Eine Biographie* (München: C.H. Beck, 2000), 501.
9. Service, *Lenin*, 501.
10. Boris Meissner, 'Lenin und das Selbstbestimmungsrecht der Völker,' *Osteuropa*, 4 (1970), 245-261, here 245.
11. Dietrich Berndt, *Entwicklung und Konzeption des Selbstbestimmungsrechts der Völker bei Lenin*, Dissertation (Münster: 1972), 36-42; Service, *Lenin*, 85-87, 126-128, 131; Georgi W. Plechanow, *Sozialismus und politischer Kampf* (1883), (Berlin: Dietz Verlag, 1975).
12. Meissner, 'Lenin und das Selbstbestimmungsrecht,' 245.
13. Stanley W. Page, 'Lenin and Self-Determination,' in *The Slavonic and East European Review* vol. 28, no. 71 (1950), 342-358, here 344-346.
14. Page, 'Lenin and Self-Determination,' 350.
15. Robert Craig Nation, *War on War: Lenin, the Zimmerwald Left, and the Origins of Communist Internationalism* (Durham: Duke University Press, 1990), 97-168.
16. Wladimir Iljitsch Lenin, 'Die sozialistische Revolution und das Selbstbestimmungsrecht der Nationen,' in W.I. Lenin, *Werke*, vol. 22 (Berlin: Dietz Verlag, 1960), 144-159, here 156-159.
17. Rosa Luxemburg, 'Nationalitätenfrage und Autonomie,' in Rosa Luxemburg, Internationalismus und Klassenkampf (Neuwied–Berlin: Hermann Luchterhand Verlag, 1971), 220-278; Wladimir I. Lenin, 'Der "Praktizismus" in der nationalen Frage,' in Wladimir I. Lenin, *Zur nationalen Frage* (Berlin: Dietz Verlag, 1954), 91-100, here 96-97.
18. Klaus Zernack, *Polen und Russland. Zwei Wege in der europäischen Geschichte* (Berlin: Propyläen, 1994), 393.

19. Dekret über den Frieden, 8. November 1917, Aufrufe und erste Dekrete der Sowjetmacht, <http://www.trend.infopartisan.net/100JAHRE/100jahre-12-1.html> (accessed 10 January 2020).

20. The Declaration of the Rights of the People of Russia was proclaimed on 2 November 1917. Figes, *A People's Tragedy*, 503; Michail Prischwin, *Tagebücher. Band I 1917 bis 1920* (Berlin: Guggolz, 2019), 80, 85-86; Eckart Conze, *Die große Illusion: Versailles 1919 und die Neuordnung der Welt* (Berlin: Siedler, 2018), 101.

21. Report, Secretary of State, 31 December 1917, Image 130 of Woodrow Wilson Papers: Series 5: Peace Conference Correspondence and Documents, 1914-1921; Subseries A: Policy Documents, 1914-1919, 1 Nov. 1917 - 9 July, 1919; Lenin's draft of the theses on the national and colonial question for the Second Congress of the Communist International, 5 June 2020, <https://www.marxists.org/deutsch/archiv/lenin/1920/06/natfrag.htm> (accessed 10 January 2020); see also Erez Manela, *The Wilsonian Moment: Self Determination and the International Origins of Anticolonial Nationalism* (Oxford: Oxford University Press, 2007), 26-28, 34, 43, 52, 110, 195-196.

22. Richard K. Debo, *Revolution and Survival: The Foreign Policy of Soviet Russia, 1917-18* (Liverpool, Liverpool University Press), 16-21; Stanley W. Page, 'Lenin, the National Question and the Baltic States, 1917-19,' in *The American Slavic and East European Review* vol. 7, no. 1 (1948), 15-31.

23. Jörn Leonhard, *Der überforderte Frieden. Versailles und die Welt 1918-1923* (München: C.H. Beck, 2018), 76.

24. Cf. Josef Stalin, 'Der Oktoberumsturz und die nationale Frage,' in Josef Stalin, *Der Marxismus und die nationale und koloniale Frage* (Berlin: Dietz, 1952), 102-112, here 106-107.

25. Orlando Figes, *A People's Tragedy: The Russian Revolution* (New York: Viking, 1997), 174-175; Martin Aust, *Die russische Revolution. Vom Zarenreich zum Sowjetimperium* (München: C.H.Beck, 2017), 114.

26. Serhy Yekelchyk, 'Freischärler als Baumeister der Nation? Rebellion und Ideologie im ukrainischen Bürgerkrieg,' in *Krieg im Frieden. Paramilitärische Gewalt in Europa nach dem Ersten Weltkrieg*, eds. Robert Gerwarth and John Horne (Göttingen: Wallstein, 2013), 177-200, here 190-192.

27. Roman Szporluk, 'Lenin, "Great Russia", and Ukraine,' *Harvard Ukrainian Studies* vol. 28, no. 1-4 (2006), 611-626, here 618-619; See Georg von Rauch, 'Sowjetrußland zwischen West und Ost. Zur weltpolitischen Standortbestimmung des Kommunismus in den Jahren 1917 bis 1924,' in *Die Folgen von Versailles 1919-1924*, ed. Hellmuth Rößler (Göttingen–Zürich–Frankfurt/Main: Musterschmidt, 1969), 7-18, here 13.

28. Lenin, 'Der "Praktizismus" in der nationalen Frage,' 98-99.

29. Christoph Mick, 'Vielerlei Kriege: Osteuropa 1918-1921,' in *Formen des Krieges: Von der Antike bis zur Gegenwart. Krieg in der Geschichte*, eds. Dietrich Beyrau, Michael Hochgeschwender and Dieter Langewiesche (Paderborn: Schöningh, 2007), 311-326.

30. Fisch, *Selbstbestimmungsrecht*, 137.

31. Lloyd C. Gardner, Safe for Democracy: *The Anglo-American Response to Revolution, 1913-1923* (New York: Oxford University Press, 1984), 151-154.

32. Leo Trotzki, *Mein Leben. Versuch einer Autobiographie* (Frankfurt/Main: Fischer, 1987), 322-323.

33. Pieter M. Judson, *Habsburg. Geschichte eines Imperiums* (München: C.H. Beck, 2017), 558-560.

34. Richard von Kühlmann, *Erinnerungen* (Heidelberg: Lambert Schneider, 1948) 524-525; Trotzki, *Mein Leben*, 314, 324; Dülffer, 'Die Diskussion um das Selbstbestimmungsrecht,' 119.

35. Gardner, *Safe for Democracy*, 160.

36. Wolfdieter Bihl, *Österreich-Ungarn und die Friedensschlüsse von Brest-Litovsk* (Wien: Böhlau, 1970), 771-772.

37. Conze, *Die große Illusion*, 108-109.

38. Leonhard, Der überforderte Frieden, 114; Trotzki, *Mein Leben*, 325-327; Andreas Kappeler, *Kleine Geschichte der Ukraine* (München: C.H. Beck, 1994), 165-176.

39. Manfred Berg, Woodrow Wilson: *Amerika und die Neuordnung der Welt* (München: C.H. Beck, 2017), 19, 24-25; Allen Lynch, 'Woodrow Wilson and the Principle of "National Self-Determination": A Reconsideration,' *Review of International Studies* vol. 28, no. 2 (2002), 419-436, here 423.

40. Berg, *Woodrow Wilson*, 20-21; Woodrow Wilson, *Division and Reunion, 1829-1889* (New York-London: Longmans, Green & Co., I893), 90-93.

41. Frederic Bancroft, 'Review: Division and Reunion, 1829-1889 by Woodrow Wilson,' *Political Science Quarterly*, vol. 8, no. 3 (1893), 533-535; Woodrow Wilson, *A History of the American People* (New York–London: Harper and Brothers, 1902).

42. Fisch, *Selbstbestimmungsrecht*, 151-152.

43. Woodrow Wilson, 'Constitutional Government,' in *The Papers of Woodrow Wilson*, 1908-1909, vol. 18, ed. Arthur Stanley Link (Princeton: Princeton University Press, 1975), 69-272, here 71-72; Berg, *Woodrow Wilson*, 28, 58.

44. Leonhard, *Der überforderte Frieden*, 80-81.

45. Berg, *Woodrow Wilson*, 106-108.

46. Woodrow Wilson, 'To the Fourth All-Russia Congress of Soviets, 11 March 1918,' in *The Papers of Woodrow Wilson*, Digital Edition, vol. 46, 16 January - 12 March 1918 (Charlottesville: University of Virginia Press, Rotunda, 2017), <https://rotunda.upress.virginia.edu/founders/WILS-01-46-02-0642> (accessed 3 November 2019); Berg, Woodrow Wilson, 121.

47. Jost Dülffer, 'Die Diskussion um das Selbstbestimmungsrecht und die Friedensregelungen nach den Weltkriegen des 20. Jahrhunderts,' in *Die Verteilung der Welt. Selbstbestimmung und das Selbstbestimmungsrecht der Völker*, eds. Elisabeth Müller-Luckner and Jörg Fisch (München: De Gruyter Oldenbourg, 2011), 113-139, here 118; Report of David R. Francis (ambassador to Russia) to secretary of state R. Lansing concerning the diplomatic activities of the Bolshevik government, 31 Dec.1917, Image 128 of Woodrow Wilson Papers: Series 5: Peace Conference Correspondence and Documents, 1914-1921; Subseries A: Policy Documents, 1914-1919, 1 November 1917- 9 July 1919.

48. John Milton Cooper, *Woodrow Wilson: A Biography* (New York: Alfred A. Knopf, 2009), 6, 387; Dietrich Geyer, 'Wilson und Lenin: Ideologie und Friedenssicherung in Osteuropa 1917-1919,' *Jahrbücher für Geschichte Osteuropas* no. 3, 4 (1955), 430-441, here 431-432; Lynch, 'Woodrow Wilson and the Principle of "National Self-Determination",' 424.

49. Herman Kesser, 'Den weltpolitischen Defätisten!,' *Neue Zürcher Zeitung*, 27 October 1918; Leonhard, *Der überforderte Frieden*, 91.

50. Dan Diner, *Das Jahrhundert verstehen. Eine universalhistorische Deutung* (München: Luchterhand, 1999), 59.

51. Gardner, *Safe for Democracy*, 161; George Kennan, *Soviet-American Relations, 1917-1920*, vol. I: Russia Leaves the War (New Jersey: Princeton University Press, 1956), 264-267.

52. Geyer, 'Wilson und Lenin,' 435; Wilson's 'Fourteen Points' speech, in *Presidential Speeches, Woodrow Wilson Presidency, University of Virginia*, <https://millercenter.org/the-presidency/presidential-speeches/january-8-1918-wilsons-fourteen-points> (accessed 8 January 2020).

53. Derek Heater, *National Self-determination: Woodrow Wilson and his Legacy* (New York: St. Martin's Press, 1994), 36.

54. Arno J. Mayer, *Wilson vs. Lenin: Political Origins of the New Diplomacy 1917-1918* (Ohio: Meridian Books, 1959), 372-373; Gardner, *Safe for Democracy*, 162-163.

55. Ian C.D. Moffat, *The Allied Intervention in Russia, 1918-1920: The Diplomacy of Chaos* (Basingstoke: Palgrace Macmillan, 2015), 265-275.

56. Christopher Lasch, *The New Radicalism in America 1889-1963: The Intellectual as a Social Type* (New York–London: W.W. Norton & Co., 1965), 245-246; Lincoln Colcord to Woodrow Wilson, December 3, 1917, in *The Papers of Woodrow Wilson* vol. 45 (Princeton: Princeton University Press, 1984), 191-193.

57. Public statement by Robert Lansing, 4 December 1917, in *The Papers of Woodrow Wilson*, vol. 45, 205-207; Kennan, *Soviet-American Relations, 1917-1920*, 378-396; Letter by R. Lansing to W. Wilson about the using of unofficial channels to the Bolshevik government, 10 January 1918, in *Woodrow Wilson Papers: Series 5: Peace Conference Correspondence and Documents, 1914-1921*; Subseries A: Policy Documents, 1914-1919; 1 November 1917- 9 July 1919.

58. Message from President Wilson, 8 January 1918, in *Vier Kundgebungen des Präsidenten Wilson zur Friedensfrage* (Berlin: Verlag von Weimar Hobbing, 1918), 3-7, here 6; Wilson's 'Fourteen Points' speech, in Presidential Speeches, Woodrow Wilson Presidency.

59. David W. McFadden, *Alternative Paths: Soviets and Americans, 1917-1920* (New York: Oxford University Press, 1993), 33.

60. 'An Address to a Joint Session of Congress, 8 January 1918,' in *The Papers of Woodrow Wilson* vol. 45, 537; See Berg, *Woodrow Wilson*, 146; Włodzimierz Borodziej and Maciej Górny, *Der vergessene Weltkrieg. Nationen*, vol. 2 (Darmstadt: Theiss, 2018), 433-437; David Steigerwald, 'The Reclamation of Woodrow Wilson?' *Diplomatic History* vol. 23, no. 1 (Winter 1999), 79-99, here 88; McFadden, *Alternative Paths, 322-324*.

61. Quote MacMillan, *Die Friedensmacher*, 108-109.

62. McFadden, *Alternative Paths*, 34-44; Alexander L. George and Juliette L. George, *Woodrow Wilson and Colonel House: A Personality Study* (New York: Dover Publication, 1964), 157-176.

63. Quote Geyer, 'Wilson und Lenin,' 432-433.

64. McFadden, *Alternative Paths*, 15-32.

65. US State Archive, Telegram, Washington, 11 March 1918, Convey following message from President to the people of Russia through the Soviet Congress, The Acting Secretary of State to the Consul General at Moscow, File No. 861.00/1284a, <https://history.state.gov/historicaldocuments/frus1918Russiav01/d398> (accessed 15 January 2020), 395-396.

66. Quote Geyer, 'Wilson und Lenin,' 436-437.

67. *Offener Brief Tschitscherins an Woodrow Wilson, 24. Oktober 1918* (Berlin: A. Hoffmanns Verlag, 1918), 1-11, here 4-9.

68. Richard K. Debo, *George Chicherin: Soviet Russia's second Foreign Commissar*, PhD thesis (University of Nebraska, 1964), 100; McFadden, Alternative Paths, 21-24.

69. John M. Thompson, *Russia, Bolshevism, and the Versailles Peace* (München: De Gruyter, 2015), 90-91, 115-116; Margaret MacMillan, *Die Friedensmacher. Wie der Versailler Vertrag die Welt veränderte* (Berlin: Propyläen, 2015), 120.

70. Leonhard, *Der überforderte Frieden*, 719.

71. McFadden, *Alternative Paths*, 218-243; Gerhard Schulz, *Revolutionen und Friedensschlüsse 1917-1920* (München: dtv, 1967), 192-193; Leonhard, *Der überforderte Frieden*, 720.

72. Fisch, *Selbstbestimmungsrecht*, 152.

73. Arthur Herman, *Lenin, Wilson, and the Birth of the New World Disorder* (New York: Harpers Collins Publisher, 2017), 207-208, Berg, Wilson, 119.

74. Gardner, *Safe for Democracy*, 160; Fisch, *Selbstbestimmungsrecht*, 153.

75. Marc Frey, 'Selbstbestimmung und Zivilisationsdiskurs in der amerikanischen Außenpolitik 1917-1950,' in *Die Verteilung der Welt. Selbstbestimmung und das Selbstbestimmungsrecht der Völker*, eds. Elisabeth Müller-Luckner and Jörg Fisch (München: De Gruyter Oldenbourg, 2011), 157-174, here 160; Lynch, 'Woodrow Wilson and the Principle of 'National Self-Determination', 425.

76. Fisch, *Selbstbestimmungsrecht*, 153.

77. See Heater, *National Self-determination*, 44-46; 'Orędzie Wilsona,' *Kurier Warszawski*, 25 January 1918; Fisch, Selbstbestimmungsrecht, 155.

78. Fisch, *Selbstbestimmungsrecht*, 156; Tomáš Garrigue Masaryk, *Die Weltrevolution: Erinnerungen und Betrachtungen 1914-1918* (Berlin: Reiss, 1927), 190, 317; 'Terror maksimalistów,' *Kurier Warszawski*, 14 November 1917; Franz v. Liszt, 'Gewaltfrieden oder Völkerbund,' *Neue Zürcher Zeitung*, 27 October 1918; 'Rußland unter den Bolschewisten,' *Neue Zürcher Zeitung*, 31 October 1918; 'Russia's critical hour ,' *Times*, 9 November 1917; A. Grigorjanz, 'Diktatur des Proletariats,' *Vorwärts*, 9 November 1917; 'Die neuen Männer,' *ibid.*, 9 November 1917.

79. 'Lenin w Krakowie,' *Kurier Warszawski*, 15 November 1917; 'Kerenski und Lenin,' *Berliner Tageblatt*, 12 November 1917; 'Die Isvestija gegen den Vorwärts,' and 'Das neue russische Ministerium,' *Vorwärts*, 11 October 1917.

80. Fritz Klein, 'Schicksalsjahr 1917: Wilson oder Lenin. Weichenstellung der Weltgeschichte,' *UTOPIE kreativ* vol. 203 (September 2007), 836-850, here 844.

81. Fisch, *Selbstbestimmungsrecht*, 156-157.

82. Robert Lansing, *The Peace Negotiations. A Personal Narrative* (Boston: Houghton Mifflin Company, 1921), 97-98.

83. Klaus Schwabe, *Versailles: Das Wagnis eines demokratischen Friedens 1919-1923* (Paderborn: Schöningh, 2019), 65-67, 130-166.

84. Richard Striner, *Woodrow Wilson and World War I. A Burden Too Great to Bear* (Lanham: Rowman & Littlefield, 2014), 230-233; John Milton Cooper, *The Warrior and the Priest. Woodrow Wilson and Theodore Roosevelt* (Cambridge, Mass.: Belknap Press of Harvard University Press, 1983), 340-343.

85. Fisch, *Selbstbestimmungsrecht*, 157.

86. Boris Meissner, 'Lenin und das Selbstbestimmungsrecht der Völker,' *Osteuropa* no. 4 (1970), 245-261, here 255-256.

87. Meissner, 'Lenin und das Selbstbestimmungsrecht,' 255.

88. Fritz Klein, 'Schicksalsjahr 1917: Wilson oder Lenin. Weichenstellung der Weltgeschichte,' *UTOPIE kreativ* vol. 203 (September 2007), 836-850, here 844-845.

89. Berg, *Woodrow Wilson*, 12.

90. Herman Kesser, 'Den weltpolitischen Defätisten!,' *Neue Zürcher Zeitung*, 27 October 1918; Cf. Harry Graf Kessler, *Tagebücher 1918-1937* (Berlin: Insel Verlag, 2017), 121-122.

91. Cf. Robert Lansing, *Die Versailler Friedens-Verhandlungen. Persönliche Erinnerungen* (Berlin: Verlag von Reimar Hobbing, 1921), 75.

Between Nation and Empire: The Post-Habsburg Adriatic Question and the Fascist Idea of Europe 1919-1922

Marco Bresciani

The prevailing accounts of the 'origins' of Italian fascism from 1919 to 1922 position themselves within a long history of Italy, which begins at least in the 1860s with the formation of the new Kingdom of Italy and which is articulated by military defeats, political failures, and social upheavals. In this interpretative paradigm, the First World War constitutes an event of crucial but conflicting significance. On the one hand, the enormous war effort, which concluded with vic-

tory in 1918, accelerated and crowned the process of national construction that was moulded by the first great collective experience of a united Italy; on the other, the dissatisfaction with the territory gained and with the new international arrangement of the post-war period fed a state of crisis which substantiated the possibility of a turn to revolutionary socialism and ultimately opened the way to fascism and the collapse of Italy's liberal institutions. In this post-war

Fig. 1: The nationalist poet and politician Gabriele D'Annunzio, Fiume/Rijeka, 12 September 1919.

Fig. 2: The British economist John Maynard Keynes.

states which succeeded Austria-Hungary. In a passage of *The Economic Consequences of the Peace*, published in late 1919, John Maynard Keynes (1883-1946) – the former British Treasury bureaucrat involved in the Versailles Peace Conference – stated with acuteness: "If the European Civil War is to end with France and Italy abusing their momentary victorious power to destroy Germany and Austria-Hungary now prostrate, they invite their own destruction also, being so deeply and inextricably intertwined with their victims by hidden psychic and economic bonds".[3]

Applying Keynes' remark to post-1918 Italy, this chapter argues that the 'myth of the mutilated victory' crystallised the more profound and basic reality of a quite different 'mutilation' or 'destruction'. The disintegration of its historic enemy, the Austro-Hungarian Empire, transformed the geopolitical and economic structure of post-war Italy and had a destabilising effect on national public opinion. The Adriatic Question, or rather the problem of the political, economic and symbolic definition of the space onto which the history of Italy and of Central and Eastern Europe was superimposed and counterposed, constituted a crucial aspect of the post-war crisis.[4]

Fascism Against the Habsburg Legacy

The Italian army occupied the Upper Adriatic immediately after the signing of the armistice in Padua, in November 1918. However, the region was destabilised by the uncertainty of the long negotiations

Fig. 3: Advertising poster of *Avanti*, the newspaper of Italy's Socialist Party, 1919.

Italian crisis, scholars have long attributed a central function to the 'myth of the mutilated victory', a term coined by poet and politician Gabriele D'Annunzio (1863-1938), which they deem to have catalysed the darkest and most disturbed elements of national public opinion. Nevertheless, the pure and simple adoption of the 'myth of mutilated victory', an explanation that is completely internal to the nation, to interpret the collective psychology and the political conflict in post-war Italy appears to ascribe an excessive weight to the question of territorial acquisition *as such*.[1]

A recent collection of essays, edited by Mark Cornwall and John Paul Newman, has raised the issue of the legacy of a defeated and collapsed state such as the Habsburg Empire in the processing of the experience of the First World War within the successor states.[2] This approach, though focused in another direction, can contribute to a repositioning of the question of the origins of fascism within a European perspective, shifting, at least in part, the trajectory of the Kingdom of Italy after 1918 nearer to that of the and the ensuing animosities over the new border between the Kingdom of Italy and the Kingdom of Serbs, Croats and Slovenes, which was finally defined by the Treaty of Rapallo, signed in November 1920. In the summer of 1920, the fascist movement, founded by Benito Mussolini (1883-1945) in March 1919, organised itself into armed squadrons and went on the offensive, beginning from the plurinational area of the Upper Adriatic that Italy had gained at the end of the First World War.[5]

In fact, the socio-political conflicts in this border territory, fed by tensions between different nationalist groups (Italian, Slovenian, Croatian), were among the most violent, and the local section of the *Partito Socialista Italiano* (PSI; Italian Socialist Party) adopted a decidedly internationalist and revolutionary position and soon transferred en masse to the Communist Party. As a consequence, Mussolini's polemic towards the socialist press and especially towards *Il Lavoratore* [*The Worker*], the socialist daily newspaper of Trieste, was particularly harsh. His article on 6 August 1920,

'Bolscevismo imperiale' ['Imperial Bolshevism'], constituted a direct response against the direction of *Il Lavoratore*, which on 1 August, in the face of Soviet advances in Polish territory, had hastily concluded: 'Russia is no longer an Asiatic myth lost between two continents and dreamily between two eras, but is a European reality that has all the energy of an armed and uncontrollable phalanx.'[6] The defeat of the Red Army at the Battle of Warsaw, in the middle of August, quickly dissolved the hopes of exporting the Soviet revolution to Germany and from there to the rest of Europe. In those same weeks between July and September, Trieste and the new border territories on the Upper Adriatic became a real laboratory for the violent practices of the fascist squads, where aggression towards the socialists intertwined and often mixed with that towards the 'Slavs', and anti-socialism developed alongside anti-Slavism, a radically new version of nationalism. In a speech at Pola on 21 September 1920, Mussolini explained the imperial mission of fascism, rooted in the special position of the Upper

Fig. 4: Benito Mussolini on a seaplane in the Adriatic Sea, 1920s.

Adriatic region in the Mediterranean Sea and in Italy in Europe:

> The future of Italy is on the Mediterranean Sea. [...] Italy must be a bridge between East and West. The demographic factor pushes Italy towards expansion into the Mediterranean and towards the East. Nevertheless, it is necessary that the Adriatic Sea, one of our gulfs, should be in our hands in order to realise this Mediterranean dream. In the face of a race such as the Slavs, inferior and barbaric, we must not pursue a politics of the carrot but a politics of the stick.[7]

Fig. 5: Book cover of Pietro Gorgolini's *La Rivoluzione fascista*, edited in Torino 1922.

In this context, marked by extreme international instability and by a rapidly shifting redefinition of sovereignty and of the national borders of post-Habsburg Central Europe, the projects and aspirations of the Italian nationalists took on more concrete form with the hope of coming to fruition in the near future. At the same time the new order, which had emerged from the First World War and was centred on the ascending power of the United States, confronted the Italian nationalists with new problems, opportunities, and obstacles. It was Mussolini who brought together these contradictory aspects of the post-war period in an important public speech given at the Rossetti Theatre in Trieste on 6 February 1921:

> In the shift of the axis of civilisation from London to New York (which already has seven million inhabitants and which will soon be the largest human agglomeration on Earth) and from the Atlantic to the Pacific, there are those who foresee a gradual economic and spiritual decline of our old Europe, of our small and marvellous continent which has up to only yesterday been a guide and light for all peoples. Will we be party to this darkening and eclipsing of the 'role' of Europe in the history of the world? To this disturbing and troubling question we reply: it is possible. The 'life' of Europe, especially in the area of Central Europe, is at the mercy of the Americans. Moreover, Europe presents us with a tormented political and economic landscape, a thorny tangle of national questions and of social questions, and at times it happens that communism is the mask of nationalism and vice versa. A 'united' Europe does not seem a very close reality.[8]

These ideas were anything but exclusive to Mussolini and they circulated with particular frequency in the environment of early fascism. The same positioning emerged in a speech given by the fascist journalist Pietro Gorgolini (1891-1973), entitled 'Cos'è il bolscevismo?' ('What is Bolshevism?') and delivered at the University of Camerino in April 1919, but probably also given at other conferences. He recalled the anarchic character of Bolshevism, the 'extreme formulation of a socialist utopia': a generalised sense of 'ruin' and 'anarchy' offered the essential key for understanding Russian events. The revolutionary process had brought to light from 'under the previously solid and now miserably shattered skin of Europeanism, the barbarous and oriental foundation of a people who had remained enslaved and primitive'. The cycle of war and revolution had halted 'its process of Europeanisation', provoking 'a return to barbarism' which made 'the neighbouring peoples tremble at the idea of an invasion by the Trotskyist hordes'. According to Gorgolini, the link between the events in the post-war Upper Adriatic and the Bolshevik threat was evident and immediate:

> Whoever has been on the eastern Adriatic coast and has had contact with the Slavs at the beginning of our occupation, if they have good eyesight, has seen flash the grim spectre of the true and greatest enemy of the Latin people, Slavism; but behind Slavism is Bolshevik Russia. [...] Russian Bolshevism or Slavo-Balkan Bolshevism, which is the same thing with different expressions and different fortunes, is barbaric expansionist unrest that strives to free that gigantic populace from the chains of an old oriental recklessness, of a degenerate aristocracy and a vice-ridden bourgeoisie, in order to direct it, without scruples, towards the intellectual, social and perhaps even political invasion of the West, with the same ravenous appetites of old invasions but now without the restraint and without the respect which the great memory of the Roman Empire commanded.[9]

In this respect, the disrupting social, political, and cultural backlash of the Russian and Bolshevik Revolutions indirectly influenced early fascism and Mussolini, contributing to a radical widening of their political culture and imagery compared to those of the pre-1914 nationalists. In the fascist perceptions, what Adam Tooze has recently called the 'Eurasian crisis' involved Europe as a whole and threatened it from without, but its political consequences and implications were ambivalent.[10] On the one hand, this representation was based on the perception of the weakness, disintegration, and anarchic self-destruction of the 'Slavic world', summarised by the Russian Revolution; on the other hand, this representation was complemented by the sense of unity and strength of the 'Slavic world', embodied by the expansionist project of 'Pan-Slavism'. The fascists identified the

'Slavic world' with the 'Russian world', alternately understood as a European or as an un-European, Asiatic world. In Mussolini's vision, the Upper Adriatic region played a crucial role as an extreme offshoot of the 'Slavic world' and, through this, of 'Russian' influence. Therefore, whether the 'Reds' or the 'Whites' prevailed in the Russian civil war was entirely irrelevant. Both seemed to share 'an immense dream of imperialism', that is, 'the great empire from the Baltic to the Mediterranean, from the cold sea to the warm sea': this pan-Slavic project directly assailed Italy's borders insofar as it included 'pressing towards the Adriatic sea, the extreme and ravenous descendants of the Slavic world'.[11] It is not by chance, therefore, that Trieste became the venue for Mussolini's key speeches outlining European and global political vision, which were increasing imbued with anti-Slavism; it constituted a sort of outpost of an imaginary geopolitical space, which simultaneously defined both the enemy of fascism and its national and imperial mission.[12]

This vision was in fact largely indebted to the writings and speeches of the radical nationalists and fascists of the Upper Adriatic, such as Attilio Tamaro (1884-1956), amateur historian, Trieste journalist, and author of many historical works on the region, a nationalist who converted to fascism. Tamaro focused his writings on the political and economic crisis that had shattered post-1918 Trieste: he argued that the collapse of the former Austro-Hungarian hinterland, in spite of its political annexation to the Kingdom of Italy, had led to a sort of 'economic disannexation' of the entire northern Adriatic region.[13] As a solution to this crisis, Trieste and the Adriatic were to serve as a starting point for political, economic, and eventually military expansion in both directions. On the one hand, he argued that strategic control of the Adriatic sea, with the aim of eliminating the 'Slavic' threat in the region, represented the only way in which Italy could construct a new dominion over the Mediterranean and guarantee its liberty and independence in world politics. On the other hand, Tamaro reaffirmed the urgency of challenging (and changing) the post-war economic order in Central Europe, which was considered to be against Italian interests.[14]

Even before the war, some of the most brilliant and aggressive voices from the Italian nationalists

Fig. 6: The Italian nationalist and journalist Attilio Tamaro.

reorganising the European order. In his article 'Cinque anni dopo il crollo dell'Impero absburgico' ('Five Years after the Collapse of the Habsburg Empire'), published in *Il Secolo* (*The Age*) on 21 November 1923, Tamaro explained the background to his political position. Italy's complete lack of plans for the reconstruction of Central Europe after the unexpected disintegration of the Habsburg Empire was rooted in a profound misunderstanding of that empire itself. Tamaro developed a harsh criticism of the politics of nationality, which he believed to severely undervalue the unity of the imperial connections within the Habsburg territories. With the notable exception of the Italians, the peoples oppressed by the Austro-Hungarian Monarchy in fact oppressed each other through nationalist conflicts much more than they were oppressed by the central government in Vienna: they fought 'not to destroy the State or the

Fig. 7: Book cover of Attilio Tamaro`s Storia di Trieste, edited in Rome 1924.

under the Habsburg Monarchy, such as Ruggero Fauro (1892-1915) alias Timeus and Tamaro himself, had advocated positions of expansion and annexation eastwards, by claiming the need for a greater Italy extending its control over Central Europe, the Balkans, and the Near East. Nevertheless, none of them hoped, or even believed, that the annexation of Trieste and the whole Upper Adriatic would eventually imply the collapse of the Habsburg Empire; they did not even deem that possible.[15]

In consequence, Tamaro's criticism of the postwar European order changed rapidly into a claim for an active, revisionist position that offered a strong justification for fascism. Italy had to prepare its plans for the economic reconstruction of Central Europe after the fall of the Habsburg Empire, which had fragmented into a plurality of plurinational spaces. Tamaro toyed with the idea of a fascist alliance with Austria and Hungary against the 'Slavs', with the aim of confronting the post-imperial power vacuum and

Throne but to take over the government of the State itself'.[16] The 'oppressed peoples' shared a visceral hatred of the Italians; when the empire collapsed, the Italians were therefore, paradoxically, only able to form stable relationships with those condemned as 'oppressors': the Austrians and the Hungarians. Nevertheless, the reorganisation of the political and economic order of Central Europe, in which Italy could play an important role, was still to come. According to Tamaro, it was a widely held opinion in pre-1914 Italy that the Austro-Hungarian Monarchy was 'an artificial state dominated and held together against the will of the people by a tyrannical dynasty, by German bureaucracy, by a barbaric police force'. Tamaro maintained that 'the particular condition of the Italian territories that were subject to Austria' was projected onto the Habsburg Empire in its entirety; the empire was then interpreted as 'a plurinational, unnatural monstrosity'. However, the disintegration of Austria-Hungary brought to light 'the powerful economic and political ties that united its members to the centre and to each other'. He then explained:

> Now the character of the relationships that passed between government and peoples can be understood: the conflicts that agitate the successor states, as well as the systems adopted by the 'liberated' nations, demonstrate that the struggles which first battered the state were not between dominated populace and dominating government, but between peoples, each hoping to dominate their adversary within a specific border.

With penetrating analysis, which however led to a fascist revisionist position, Tamaro concluded: 'The self-same varied plurinationality of all the successor states is a posthumous justification of the plurinationality for which Austria-Hungary has been so violently blamed.'[17]

Not incidentally, Tamaro, like the other fascists, had internalised one of the major lessons of the First World War concerning the possibility of the disintegration of the modern states: since some states (notably the continental empires such as the Habsburg Empire) *did* fall apart, the successor states in East-Central Europe *might* fall apart again. This fascist conviction marked a deep difference from the pre-1914 nationalists, who did not consider the possibil-

ity of the disruption or destruction of the successor states; the fascists built their project of political power on that possibility.

The Destruction and Reconstruction of States

Fascism was born in 1919 as a movement avowedly aimed at overcoming the traditional political dichotomy between Right and Left; from 1920 onwards, however, Mussolini with increasing insistence claimed the political 'reactionary' space available on the 'Right'. He offered a justification for this turn in an article in February 1920, in which he described Lenin 'as the greatest amongst the living and the most alive amongst the greatest reactionaries of Europe' – 'the only one who had the courage to be reactionary in both the old-fashioned and the modern sense (in reaction, that is, to all the economic, political and moral disintegrations of social life)'.[18]

Mussolini was attracted by 'the vast, terrible experience of corpore vili' in revolutionary Russia in so far as it was an example of the destruction and reconstruction of a new state, an example through which fascism could be defined. The comparison with what was happening under the Bolshevik regime helped Mussolini to construct a model that could inspire the construction of his own regime, which faced up to and resolved the question of the 'crisis of authority' in post-war Italy. Post-war Italy was in fact struck by the 'western political chaos' that had turned the state into an 'elastic and intangible' notion: everywhere 'a continual collision between old and new authority', 'an interference or coexistence of contradictory powers' characterised the political landscape of post-war Europe. In the upside-down mirror of Lenin's Russia, a solution emerged: 'A state that has overcome the crisis of authority. A state in the most concrete expression of the word. A state, that is, a government, made up of men who exercise power, imposing iron discipline on individuals or groups, "repressing" when necessary.'[19]

Mussolini closely tied this reflection on the concept of "reaction" to the transformation of the fascist movement and to the definition of its violent project of the conquest of power in the course of the early 1920s. This was not so much inspired by an abstract or theoretical concept of the state but rather by the

Fig. 8: Book cover with Benito Mussolini of Attilio Tamaro's publication *Venti Anni di Storia*, published in Rome, 1952.

real and changeable relationship between chaos and the state, between the destruction and reconstruction of the state's authority, between the disintegration and reintegration of the post-war political and social order. If the Russian Revolution had demonstrated that 'failed' states could be dissolved, the experience of the Bolshevik regime revealed that states could re-emerge from anarchy. From Mussolini's point of view, the new Soviet State represented not so much a static model – he harboured doubts concerning its extreme statism – as a generator of energy to feed anti-state subversion in Italy and to work to grasp power for the fascists. More than the definition of a true and individual theory of state sovereignty, in fact, the fascists and their *duce* were interested in the comparison between the contingent European situation – 'western' – and that of Soviet Russia: from this they derived their demand for a new power, identified with the end of the rule of law, and their conception of the 'fascist state' as an oxymoron that

revealed the activism and the dynamism intrinsic to fascism. Instead of designating a political position, 'reaction' in Mussolini's discourse came to define a momentous turning point not only in the post-war period but in European history, with respect to which the 'reactionary' forces demonstrated a greater capacity for political adaptability.[20]

Mussolini disseminated this interpretation of post-war Europe in a key text, 'Dove va il mondo?' ('Where is the world going?'), published in *Gerarchia*, and in an abridged form in *Il Popolo d'Italia* in February 1922. The duce sketched a brief account of the post-war crisis and of its dominant political forces:

The day after the armistice, the pendulum swung violently to the Left in both the political and social fields. Two empires collapsed: the Hohenzollern and the Habsburg, while another, that of the Romanovs, had preceded them. [...] In 1919-20, all of Central and Eastern Europe was afflicted by the political crisis of stabilising the new regimes, aggravated and complicated by the crisis that we call socialist, that is, by the attempts to realise some of the postulates of socialist doctrine. [...] There is no doubt that the end of 1920 signalled the culmination of the social crisis of the Left in all of Europe. But in the fifteen months between then and now, the situation has changed. The pendulum has swung back to the Right. After the wave of revolution, we now have the wave of reaction; after the red period (the red hour), we now have the white hour. As always happens, the nation which swerved most violently to the Left is that which, for some time, has been walking more quickly to the Right: Russia. The Russian 'myth' has now faded.

Mussolini recognised a common historical destiny between the 'three nations' – Russia, Germany, and Italy – impelled by a 'social and spiritual movement' directed to the Right, which was attempting not so much the quashing of the 'extremist exaggerations of the immediate post-war' but 'a much more vast and radical revision of values'. He believed that, beyond the history of the post-war era, it was European history in its entirety from the French Revolution to the First World War that evidenced a radical and enduring change, which defined itself through the new 'leaning to the Right'. The two years 1919 and 1920 had represented the culmination of a long demo-

Fig. 9: Fascist propaganda poster concerning a congress of the Italian Fascists Living Abroad (Avanguardisti dei Fascie all' Estero).

cratic evolution and the starting point of its reversion, legitimising the transition to an era dominated by 'new aristocracies' in which the masses could not be 'protagonists', but were rather 'the instrument of history'. The year 1921 had marked the end of the nineteenth century – 'the century of revolutions' – and the beginning of the twentieth century – 'the century of restorations': 'Revolution is within this reaction. A revolution of salvation to spare Europe from the miserable end that awaited it if democracy had continued to rage unchecked.'[21]

Not by chance, Mussolini's reflection on the fascist state became increasingly intense with the deepening of the political crisis during the course of 1922 and with the fascists' consequent growing willingness to assume direct power. In particular, Mussolini addressed again the crucial question of whether fascism was 'a movement for the restoration of state authority or a subversion of that authority', clarifying it as a false dilemma: the true problem was *which* state in the context of the current political crisis. The state was defined as a 'system of hierarchies', but the vitality of these hierarchies was nourished by the 'spirit' of the 'most chosen parts' of society. To the extent to which the 'decline of hierarchies' was equivalent to the 'decline of states', only a revolution could substitute or renovate 'the declining or inadequate hierarchies'. 'Fascism does not deny the state; it affirms that a national or imperial civic society cannot be conceived except under the form of the state; it therefore does not go against the idea of the state, but it reserves the right to act freely with regard to that particular state which is the state of Italy.' Fascism, which considered itself 'the state in potential and to come', contrasted and subverted 'the state in act', that is to say, the liberal state. The fascist hostility towards the liberal state was motivated not only by the huge expansion of the state's economic role, which made it 'semi-socialist' and 'monopolist', but also and above all by the 'crisis of hierarchies' which were 'without spirit' and which provoked the 'crisis of the state'.[22]

Conclusion

To better grasp the links between the fascist search for a new political order and the crisis in the post-Habsburg Upper Adriatic, it is useful to return to the *Origins of Totalitarianism* and to the distinction that Hannah Arendt makes between 'continental imperialism' and 'overseas imperialism':

> While overseas imperialism, its antinational tendencies notwithstanding, succeeded in giving a new lease of life to the antiquated institutions of the nation-state, continental imperialism was and remained unequivocally hostile to all existing political bodies. Its general mood, therefore, was far more rebellious and its leaders far more adept at revolutionary rhetoric. While overseas imperialism had offered real enough panaceas for the residues of all classes, continental imperialism had nothing to offer except an ideology and a movement. Yet this was quite enough in a time which preferred a key to history to political action, when men in the midst of communal disintegration and social atomisation wanted to belong at any price. Similarly, the visible distinction of a white skin, whose advantages in a black or brown environment are easily understood, could be matched successfully by a purely imaginary distinction between an Eastern and a Western, or an Aryan and a non-Aryan soul. The point is that a rather complicated ideology and an organisation which furthered no immediate interest proved to be more attractive than tangible advantages and commonplace convictions.[23]

While Arendt identified 'continental imperialism' with the fundamental prerequisite of totalitarian movements like those of the Nazis or Communists, which aspired to expansion in Central and Eastern Europe (therefore excluding fascism), Italian fascism can be considered as a movement that combined elements from both 'continental imperialism' and 'overseas imperialism': on the one hand, contempt for the rule of law, rejection of the nineteenth-century model of the liberal nation-state and the modern capacity for mobilisation through ideology and organisation; on the other hand, the pursuit of a maritime empire following the collapse of the continen-

Polish-Czechoslovak Border at Jurgów, 1920s.

Cuius Regio Eius Natio.
Arguments to Legitimise Territorial Claims Against Austria

Arnold Suppan

The Great War may have begun as a clash of empires, a classic Great-Power war, but it ended as something far more morally and politically charged: a crusading victory of the Entente coalition that proclaimed itself the champion of a new world order. For a hundred years, World War I has occupied a fixed place in the collective memory of most European and many non-European countries – the 'Great War'. The war's sudden end proved a seminal turning point for Central and Eastern Europe. Austria-Hungary and the Ottoman Empire had disappeared, and Germany and Russia were on their knees. Almost all nationalities within the Russian, German, Austro-Hungarian and Ottoman empires agitated for 'national revolutions', demanding the right to self-determination, the sepa-

ration of nations from empires and the creation of independent nation states. Although Wilson had demanded in his 'Fourteen Principles' of 11 February 1918 that 'every territorial settlement involved in this war must be made in the interest and for the benefit of the populations concerned', the majority of the new so-called 'nation states' – Finland, Estonia, Latvia, Lithuania, Poland, Czechoslovakia, the enlarged Romania, Hungary, Austria, Yugoslavia, and Bulgaria Albania, the enlarged Greece and Turkey, as well as, temporarily, Ukraine – became so more *de iure* than *de facto*. Most contained any number of national and religious minorities, some 25 million people altogether: over six million Germans, over five million Ukrainians, five million Jews, over three million Magyars, almost two million Belarusians, one million Turks, 0.7 million Russians, 0.7 million South Slavs and 0.5 million Albanians remained as new national or religious minorities.[1]

The Paris Peace Conference

On 18 January 1919, the Peace Conference convened at the Quai d'Orsay in Paris. French Premier Georges Clemenceau (1841-1929), British Prime Minister David Lloyd George (1863-1945), US President Woodrow Wilson (1856-1924), and Italian Prime Minister Vittorio Orlando (1860-1952) presided over the drafting of the Treaties of Versailles, Saint-Germain, Trianon, Neuilly, and Sèvres. The Germans, German-Austrians, Hungarians, Bulgarians, and Turks were not invited to negotiate the terms of peace. At the peace negotiations, Clemenceau won only part of what France had been hoping for, but did gain the construction of a security system in East-Central and South-Eastern Europe. France and Great Britain seemed to be the masters of the European scene. Of

Fig. 1: 'The Paris Peace Conference Is Radically Changing the Map of Europe'. Cartoon by Clifford Berryman, *Washington Evening Sun*, 18 February 1919.

Fig. 2: The Austrian Peace Delegation Arriving at Saint-Germain, 14 May 1919.

course, they forgot that they owed American taxpayers billions of dollars – just as they forgot that the Americans were already running the railroads and controlling the coal and food supplies in East-Central Europe. Therefore, the Austrian Section Head Richard Schüller stated: 'During our initial most difficult time, Americans – the Hoover Mission and the Quakers – were our only friends and made a deep impression on the minds of our people.'[2]

While Lenin's and Wilson's ideas of national self-determination echoed through Central and Eastern Europe, and the British strategy supported democratisation of the political systems as the best way to ensure regional stability, all nationalities of the former Habsburg monarchy hoped that the Peace Conference in Paris would reach decisions in their favour. Comparing all these demands, only the core regions of the Polish, Bohemian, Austrian, Hungarian, Romanian, and South Slavic lands were undisputed; all 'borderlands' were up for discussion. Immediately after the war, however, latent nationalist tensions erupted into bitter disputes over contested borders and trade barriers. Social conflicts overlaid ethnic and territorial clashes 'to produce a boiling cauldron of violent animosity'.[3]

By September 1917, President Wilson had already ordered his personal adviser Colonel Edward M.

House (1858-1938) to begin preparations for a peace conference. House organised the so-called 'Inquiry' with 126 members in October 1918. By 21 January 2019, the renamed 'Division of Political and Territorial Intelligence' had prepared 'An Outline of Tentative Recommendations', proposing the independent countries Poland, Czechoslovakia, German-Austria, Hungary, and Yugoslavia. Because House and other US politicians recognised the increasing propagandistic information spread by the Entente, the Inquiry established 24 field missions. On 26 December 1918, Archibald C. Coolidge (1866-1924), US diplomat in St Petersburg, Paris, and Vienna, Professor of East European History since 1910 and Director of the university library at Harvard, was appointed as head of a field mission for Austria-Hungary, making Vienna his headquarters and establishing people in Prague, Budapest, and Zagreb.[4]

The Carinthian Question

At the turn of 1918/19, following regional battles in South-Eastern Carinthia and Lower Styria, the provincial governments of Carinthia and Styria requested that a field mission led by Professor Coolidge join the armistice talks in Graz. Coolidge sent two US officers who disobeyed their instructions and after a special field mission proposed formulating an 'administrative demarcation line'. Between 27 January and 6 February 1919, a four-person US mission toured via Marburg/Maribor[5] through Slovene-German mixed South-Eastern Carinthia. Lieutenant Colonel Sherman Miles (the head of the mission), together with two US officers, reported to Professor Coolidge in Vienna: '[T]here are many Slovenes who do not wish to join Yugoslavia [...] – we strongly recommend that the final frontier between Austria and Yugoslavia in the province of Carinthia be drawn along the watershed of the Karawanken mountains.' Yet Professor Robert J. Kerner advised: 'Thus the Drau-Mur-line would appear to answer the demands for a good boundary.' The Yugoslav delegation in Paris protested against the publication of the Coolidge report and on 18 February at the Council of Ten demanded a demarcation line including the German-Austrian cities of Klagenfurt and Villach. The French Foreign Minister Stéphane Pichon criticised

Fig. 3: The US diplomat and expert for Eastern Europe Archibald Cary Coolidge.

could change this decision. The Peace Conference fixed a plebiscite in two zones and ordered that they be cleared of all troops. Both sides – the Carinthian government (backed by Vienna) and the Slovene government (backed by Belgrade) – launched propaganda campaigns and tried to help the population with goods and money. While the German-Carinthian side focused on anti-Serbian, anti-Orthodox, and anti-militaristic slogans, and underlined the strong economic ties within Carinthia, the Slovene side – supported by most of the Roman Catholic parish priests – emphasised the ethnic and linguistic communal spirit. In July 1920, the Allied Plebiscite Commission under the leadership of the British Colonel Capel Peck (1871-1949) arrived in Klagenfurt and ordered that the Austro-Yugoslav demarcation line be opened. In the plebiscite on 10 October 1920 in Zone I, monitored by British, French and Italian officers, 59% of the population decided to remain in Austria; a

the 'actions of a certain Mister Coolidge', and Marshal Ferdinand Foch told the Yugoslavs: 'Whatever you have occupied shall remain in your possession.'[6]

Under the US advisers' influence, the *Commission des Affaires Roumaines et Yugoslaves* recommended to the Council of Four a plebiscite in South-Eastern Carinthia, and on 12 May, Clemenceau, Lloyd George, and Wilson took this advice. On 27 May, the US President, like a 'stern Protestant preacher' (Zara Steiner), stated in the Council of Four:

> The Slovene people in the southern part of the [Klagenfurt] basin were economically, intimately connected with the northern people. This question could not, therefore, be considered merely from a political and ethnical point of view.[7]

Neither the occupation of South-Eastern Carinthia by Yugoslav troops under the command of a Serbian general, nor the direct appeal to Wilson by the Bishop of Ljubljana Anton Bonaventura Jeglič (1850-1937), and the Slovene Governor Janko Brejc (1869-1934),

Fig. 4: Postage stamp of 'Deutschösterreich' for the Carinthian plebiscite, 1920.

plebiscite in Zone II (with Klagenfurt) was therefore dropped. Approximately 11,000 Germans and Slovenes each had voted for Austria, with only 15,000 Slovenes voting for Yugoslavia.[8]

Italy versus Yugoslavia and Austria

When the Peace Conference began, the Italian delegation paid little attention to the creation of the new principles in foreign relations and seemed interested only in gaining all the territories the secret Treaty of London (26 April 1915) had foreseen, with the addition of Fiume. Such an attitude met the opposition of President Wilson, who demanded Italy's borders fall 'along clearly recognizable lines of nationality'. Nevertheless, Italian troops had been entering Trieste,

Il nemico, il barbaro aguzzino è disfatto, e le terre fatte sacre da un anno di martirio tornano alla Patria. Il tricolore dei fratelli che aspettavano si leva fiero a baciare, nel fulgore della Vittoria, le lacere gloriose bandiere dell'Esercito liberatore. *(Disegno di A. Beltrame)*

Fig. 5: Visual emphasis on the Italian victory over the Habsburg Empire after the battle of Vittorio Veneto (24 October to 3 November 1918), magazine cover of *La Domenica del Corriere*, 10-17 November 1918.

Pola, Fiume, Zara/Zadar and Sebenico/Šibenik since November 1918. When the Italian delegation stubbornly refused a compromise solution, Wilson appealed directly to the Italian people, and the Italian delegates left the Peace Conference in order to reinforce their authority at home. With this political mistake, Italy's role became less influential. The Italians were to give up most of the Dalmatian mainland and accept a free state in Fiume. The occupation of the port by the nationalist poet and air force veteran Gabriele d'Annunzio (1863-1938) could not change this retreat. Soon after the Carinthian plebiscite, the Belgrade government had to negotiate an agreement with the new Italian government of Prime Minister Giovanni Giolitti (1842-1928) and Foreign Minister Count Carlo Sforza (1872-1952). In the Treaty of Rapallo, signed on 12 November 1920, Italy kept the whole of Littoral, Trieste, Istria, the islands of Cherso/Cres, Lussino/Lošinj and Unie/Unije, though in Dalmatia only the city of Zara and the islands of Lagosta/Lastovo and Pelagosa/Palagruža; Fiume/Rijeka was to become a buffer state between the two countries, but was divided between Italy and Yugoslavia in 1924. The 350,000 Slovenes and 150,000 Croats in Italy became new minorities without minority rights. Nevertheless, the myth of the 'mutilated victory' (*vittoria mutilata*) was born in Italy. Of course, the main reasons were Italy's passing over from the division of the former German colonies and some decision-making by the 'Big Three' in the former Ottoman Empire.[9]

Because the Entente had promised Italy a future border at the Brenner Pass in exchange for entering the war against Austria-Hungary, at the Peace Conference the Rome government demanded not only the Italian part of South Tyrol but also the district of Ampezzo populated by Ladinians and the whole of the German parts of South Tyrol, although 220,000 Germans, 19,000 Ladinians and only some 6,000 Italians lived north of the Salurner Klause. The German- and Italian-speaking districts were separated from each other by a very distinct natural barrier. The Tyrolese Government argued:

> Never in the course of history did the Brenner and the middle ridge of the Alps form the Italian frontier, and never were they a separating barrier between the nations. [...] For many centuries, Ger-

man has been the language of the law-courts, of the churches and of the schools in German South Tyrol. [...] The German Tyrolese, north and south of the Brenner, are not only of one and the same stock, but they have also the same culture, and their economic situation is also the same. But the German Tyrolese are quite different from their Italian neighbours in Italian Tyrol.

On 26 February 1919, the Tyrolese Government sent a petition to President Wilson, arguing that it was proven that the territories from Kufstein to the Salurner Klause

[...] are solely, and in a compact mass, inhabited by Germans; [...] The Germans as well as the Ladinians of Tyrol have repeatedly declared their earnest wish to remain united, and to decide their future for themselves. [...] The people of Tyrol [...] trust in the realization of the President's ideal political aims, as put down in the 14 points of his message.[10]

The Italian Prime Minister Vittorio Orlando talked dramatically about Austria being Italy's main enemy during the war; his deputies in Paris kept hold of the London Treaty and argued with strategic reasons and that the Poles, Czechs, Romanians, and Yugoslavs were breaking the principle of nationality as well. Other notes by the Austrian Government and the Tyrolean Diet to the Council of Ten followed, offering a military neutrality of German Tyrol. Even the threat of a Tyrolean *irredenta* or an *Anschluss* of North Tyrol to Germany did not help. In mid-April of 1919, the Council of Four decided in Italy's favour. Wilson himself would later admit that he conceded the territory based on 'insufficient study' and that he came to regret this 'ignorant' decision.[11]

In Vienna, the question of Austria's union with Germany, the *Anschluss*, stood foremost in the political discussion. Although some industrialists, bankers, employers and workers feared the German competition, and some Catholics feared Prussian Protestantism, by 12 November 1918, the German-Austrian National Assembly (consisting of Social Democratic, Christian Social and Pan-German deputies) had already unanimously voted for this union. Foreign Secretary Otto Bauer (1881-1938), the leader of the

leftist Social Democrats, declared himself particularly in favour of the union and began negotiations with Berlin. It soon became clear that the assembly had been mistaken, as France protested with great energy and Germany did not dare accept the Anschluss, fearing the loss of more territories to France and Poland if she tried to achieve a union with Austria. Nevertheless, before the delegation left to Paris, Bauer instructed them 'to take our stand on the principle of self-determination'.[12]

The Bohemian Lands Between Czechoslovakia and Austria

At the end of October and beginning of November 1918, the leaders of the Germans in Bohemia and Moravia had proclaimed four German-Austrian provinces: *Deutschböhmen* in North Bohemia with its centre at Reichenberg/Liberec, the *Sudetenland* in North Moravia and Austrian Silesia with Troppau/Opava as its capital, *Deutsch-Südmähren* with Znaim/Znojmo as its administrative centre and finally the *Böhmerwaldgau* with its capital in Prachatitz/Prachatice. After unsuccessful negotiation attempts between members of the Czech National Committee and the German Bohemian spokesmen, the provisional government of *Deutschböhmen* had sent a note of protest against the 'imperialistic encroachments of the Czech State' to President Wilson. But the French Foreign Minister Pichon rejected the plebiscite and arbitration proposed by the Austrian government: 'The Czecho-Slovak state has for its boundaries, at least until the decision of the Peace Conference is reached, the boundaries of the historic provinces of Bohemia, Moravia and of Austrian Silesia.' Although Foreign Minister Edvard Beneš (1884-1948) had warned the Prague government to 'avoid all struggles and bloody riots in the German parts of Bohemia', he initiated a policy of *faits accomplis* in order to secure the territories claimed by the new state. First, he proposed bringing a French military-political mission to Prague; he then mentioned the danger of Bolshevism in Vienna and Budapest and requested the subordination of the (small) Czechoslovak army (some troops from the garrisons at home and from the Italian front) to the supreme commander of the French forces, Marshal Ferdinand Foch (1851-1929). For a few weeks in November and December 1918,

Fig. 6: 'Sláva a pad provincie Deutschböhmen' (Glory and Fall of the Province German Bohemia), book title by František Cajthaml, Ústí nad Labem 1919.

Czech troops occupied the German-populated towns and villages in Bohemia, Moravia, and Silesia without major incident. The Germans' rather passive attitude was largely rooted in fear of social strife or even the sort of revolution that was already rocking neighbouring Germany. Meanwhile, the new Czechoslovak President Tomáš Garrigue Masaryk (1850-1937) had skillfully mobilised the pro-Czech lobby in Britain and the USA.[13]

When the Czechoslovak Finance Minister Alois Rašín (1867-1923) separated the Czechoslovak currency from the Austrian, effected on 25 February 1919, and started a strongly deflationary policy, a wave of German protests erupted against the overstamping of the banknotes. While many Germans had invested in war loans, which were now devalued, in the final analysis the Sudeten Germans also benefited because the Czechoslovak crown became a stable national currency. However, the monetary measure merged with the inaugural session of the newly elected Parliament of the Austrian Republic on 4 March 1919. As the Prague government had banned the holding of elections to that parliament in the Bohemian and Moravian border areas, the German Social Democratic Party organised a general strike. This time the Czechoslovak government did not hesitate to use armed force: 54 demonstrators were killed, 84 heavily wounded.[14]

Beneš and the Czechoslovak Prime Minister Karel Kramář (1860-1937) presented Czechoslovakia's case to the Council of Ten on 5 February 1919. At first, Beneš claimed Bohemia, Moravia, Austrian Silesia and Slovakia 'for ethnographical reasons'. He spoke of 'old historical causes that armed the Czech people against the Germanic masses', and that 'the Czechs had always felt that they had a special mission to resist the Teutonic flood'. While he reduced the number of the Germans in Bohemia from 2,467,724 to 1.5 million, he enlarged the number of the Czechs from 4,241,918 to 4.5 million. For the whole Republic, Beneš counted 10 million 'Czechoslovaks', while the Czechoslovak census of 1921 mentioned only 8,819,663.[15]

Beneš considered the 'best argument' for claiming the whole of Bohemia the fact that the 'Czecho-German parts of Bohemia contained nearly the whole of the industries in the country'. Therefore, Beneš concluded: 'Without the peripheral areas, Bohemia could not live.' When Lloyd George enquired what reasons might have led to the concentration of industries on the edges of the country, Beneš replied that the presence of water-power, coal, and minerals explained it. Explaining the ethnic composition of the population engaged in these industries, Beneš made the assertion 'that the majority was Czech', only 'the employers chiefly German'. When Lloyd George asked whether German deputies had represented the area in question in the *Reichsrat*, Beneš had to agree, explaining 'that the voting areas were so contrived as to give the Germans a majority'. The former Austrian deputy Kramář did not correct this false assertion, although he had approved the Cisleithanian voting reform in 1906. Now, Lloyd George 'enquired whether the inhabitants of these districts, if offered the choice would vote for exclusion from the Czecho-Slovak state or for inclusion. Beneš replied that they would vote for exclusion, chiefly through the influence of the Social Democratic Party, which thought that the Germans would henceforth have a Social Democratic regime.' This was another contradiction in Beneš' argumentation, claiming, on the one hand, that the majority of the (working) population in the industrial regions was Czech, while confirming on the other the strength of the German Social Democratic Party who represented the workers.[16]

When the Council of Four discussed the report of the Commission on Czechoslovak Affairs, the Sudeten German matter was settled quickly and almost casually. The head of the commission, Ambassador Jules Laroche (1872-1961), insisted: 'The inhabitants of these regions were accustomed to live in close connection with the rest of Bohemia, and did not desire separation.' In the end, the Council accepted Clemenceau's suggestion to opt for the simple solution of following the pre-war border between Germany and Bohemia and to include more than three million Germans in the new Czechoslovakia.[17]

In his famous *Mémoire III: Le problème des Allemands de Bohême*, Beneš presented further geographical, political, and historical assertions for the new borders of Czechoslovakia. Beneš concluded his *Mémoire III* with a typical perversion of the arguments: 'We respect the principle of nationality, but are of opinion that this principle should not be applied where it would imperial [sic!] the independence of another nation.'[18]

Fig. 7: 'Hands Off German Homeland Soil', postcard emitted in Vienna by the Hilfsverein für Deutschböhmen und das Sudetenland (Assistance Association for German Bohemia and the Sudetenland), 1919.

Austria Cannot Live

Upon receiving the first draft of the Peace Treaty, on 2 June 1919, at the castle of Saint-Germain, the Austrian delegates of State Chancellor Karl Renner (1870-1950) 'felt very sad, bitter and depressed when we realised that Austria had received harsher terms than Germany'. The Sudetenland was allotted to Czechoslovakia, South Tyrol to Italy and a greater part of Carinthia, including the capital Klagenfurt and Lower Styria with Marburg, to Yugoslavia. Reparations and other financial clauses were copied from the conditions imposed on Germany. But added to these conditions was the confiscation of all property held by Austrians in the territories of the former monarchy, now within the frontiers of Czechoslovakia, Poland, Yugoslavia, Romania, and Italy. Therefore, Schüller's note 'Austria cannot live' was the first to be transmitted to the Supreme Council, protesting with great energy the confiscation of property in the territories of former Austria-Hungary. Indeed, the confiscation of property belonging to Austrian citizens in the territories of former Austria-Hungary was replaced by the interdiction of such confiscation. However, the German districts of the Bohemian lands were lost, as were German South Tyrol and Marburg. Renner did not defend the last draft of the Treaty in the Austrian Parliament, but stressed that Austria had no choice but to accept it. Therefore, the Social Democrats and Christian Socials voted for the Treaty under protest, and Renner signed it at the castle of Saint-Germain on 10 September 1919.[19]

Since the French government especially wanted to create 'an eastern barrier' (*cordon sanitaire*) in East-Central Europe as a counterweight to Germany, the Allies tacitly tolerated the inclusion of the borderlands with clearly visible German and Magyar majorities into Poland, Czechoslovakia, and Romania. Even Clemenceau, the chief architect of the Paris peace treaties, had some doubts: 'Yes, this treaty will bring us burdens, troubles, miseries, difficulties, and that will continue for long years. I cannot say for how many years, perhaps I should say for how many centuries, the crisis which has begun will continue.'[20]

Endnotes

1. Paul Robert Magocsi, *Historical Atlas of East Central Europe. From the Early Fifth Century to the Present* (London: Thames & Hudson, 2 ed., 2002), maps 30, 32a, 33, 38; Arnold Suppan, *The Imperialist Peace Order in Central Europe: Saint-Germain and Trianon, 1919-1920* (Wien: Verlag der Österreichischen Akademie der Wissenschaften, 2019), maps 1 and 2. On the soil of the former Ottoman Empire, another ten nation-states were established.

2. Zara Steiner, *The Lights That Failed. European International History 1919-1933* (Oxford–New York: Oxford UP, 2005), 80-130; Adam Tooze, *The Deluge. The Great War, America and the Remaking of the Global Order, 1916-1931* (New York: Viking, 2014), 20-21, 125-154, 281-293; *Unterhändler des Vertrauens. Aus den nachgelassenen Schriften von Sektionschef Dr. Richard Schüller*, ed. Jürgen Nautz (Wien: Verlag für Geschichte und Politik; München: Oldenbourg, 1990), 223, 246, 254; Goodyear's Memoir, *Hoover Institution Archives (HIA), Stanford University*, Goodyear papers, box 2.

3. *Die Tschechoslowakischen Denkschriften für die Friedenskonferenz von Paris, 1919-1920*, ed. Hermann Raschhofer (Berlin: Heymann, 1937); *Außenpolitische Dokumente der Republik Österreich 1918-1938* (henceforth ADÖ), eds. Klaus Koch, Walter Rauscher and Arnold Suppan, 3 vols. (Wien: Verlag für Geschichte und Politik, 1993-1996); *Documents diplomatiques français sur l'histoire du bassin des Carpates 1918-1932*, eds. Magda Ádám, György Litván and Mária Ormos, 2 vols. (Budapest: Akadémiai kiadó, 1993-1995); *Československo na pařížské mírové konferenci 1918-1920* [Czechoslovakia at the Paris Peace Conference 1918-1920], eds. Jindřich Dejmek, František Kolář and Jan Němeček, 2 vols. (Praha: Ústav mezinárodních vztahů/Karolinum/Historický ústav Akademie věd ČR, 2001-2011); Josef Kalvoda, *The Genesis of Czechoslovakia* (Boulder, CO.-NY: East European Monographs, 1986), 437-465; *Edvard Beneš, Němci a Německo*, eds. Dagmar Hájková and Pavel Horák, vol. 1 (Praha: Masarykův ústav a Archiv AV ČR, 2014), 345-349; Kay Lundgren-Nielsen, *The Polish Problem at the Paris Peace Conference: A Study of the Policies of the Great Powers and the Poles, 1918-1919* (Odense: Odense UP, 1979); Ivo J. Lederer, *Yugoslavia at the Paris Peace Conference: A Study in Frontiermaking* (New Haven, CN: Yale UP, 1963); Arnold Suppan, *Jugoslawien und Österreich 1918-1938. Bilaterale Außenpolitik im europäischen Umfeld* (Wien: Verlag für Geschichte und Politik; München: Oldenbourg, 1996), 468-656; *Slovenci v očeh Imperija. Priročnik britanskih diplomatov na Pariški mirovni konferenci leta 1919. The Slovenes in the Eyes of the Empire. Handbooks of the British Diplomats Attending the Paris Peace Conference of 1919*, ed. Ernest Petrič (Ljubljana: CEP, 2007); Marina Cattaruzza, *L'Italia e il confine orientale 1866-2006* (Bologna: Il Mulino, 2007), 93-94, 124-134.

4. Lawrence Gelfand, *The Inquiry. American Preparations for Peace 1917-1919* (New Haven–London: Yale University Press, 1963); David Hunter Miller, *My Diary at the Peace Conference of Paris. With Documents*, 21 vols. (New York: Appeal Print, 1924–1928), here vol. 4, 243-245; *The Intimate Papers of Colonel*

House, ed. Charles Seymour, vol. 4 (Boston: Houghton Mifflin, 1926), 232-233.

5. Miles reported to Coolidge that – on 27 January 1919 in the town of Marburg – Yugoslav soldiers shot into a group of German-Austrian demonstrators, killing thirteen and wounding sixty, including children. See *Die Berichte der Coolidge-Mission im Jahre 1919. Die mitteleuropäischen Interessen der Vereinigten Staaten von Amerika nach dem Ersten Weltkrieg*, ed. Christine M. Gigler (Klagenfurt: Verlag des Kärntner Landesarchivs, 2001), 125-129.

6. Martin Wutte, *Kärntens Freiheitskampf 1918-1920* (Klagenfurt: Verlag des Geschichtsvereins für Kärnten, 3 ed., 1985), 146-160; *Zapisnici sa sednica Delegacije Kraljevine SHS na Mirovnoj Konferenciji u Parizu 1919-1920*, eds. Bogdan Krizman and Bogumil Hrabak (Beograd: Kultura, 1960), 30-53; Claudia Kromer, *Die Vereinigten Staaten von Amerika und die Frage Kärnten 1918-1920* (Klagenfurt: Verlag des Geschichtsvereins für Kärnten, 2 ed., 1996), 77-81; Andrej Mitrović, *Jugoslavija na konferenciji mira 1919-1920* (Beograd: Zavod za izdavanje udžbenika Socijalističke Republike Srbije, 1969); Suppan, *Jugoslawien*, 523-58 and map 4; *ADÖ*, vol. 1, doc. 69, 72, 83, 99, 100, 139, 144, 151, 162; Gigler, *Coolidge-Mission*, 68-125; Andrej Rahten, 'The Paris Peace Conference and the Slovenes', in Petrič, *Slovenci v očeh Imperija*, 296-303.

7. Hunter Miller, *My Diary*, vol. 16, 264-70; *The Treaty of Saint-Germain: A Documentary History of its Territorial and Political Clauses*, eds. Nina Almond and Ralph H. Lutz (Stanford–London–Oxford: Stanford UP, 1935), 364-81; Ádám, Litván and Ormos, *Documents diplomatiques français*, vol. 1, doc. 204, 227, 239, 323, 326; Steiner, *The Lights*, 35.

8. Sarah Wambaugh, *Plebiscites since the World War. With a Collection of Official Documents* (Washington: Carnegie Endowment for International Peace, 1933), vol. 2, 126-130; *Koroški plebiscit. Razprave in članki* [The Carinthian Plebiscite. Treatises and articles], eds. Janko Pleterski, Lojze Ude and Tone Zorn (Ljubljana: Slovenska matica, 1970); Suppan, *Jugoslawien*, 523-528; Tamara Griesser-Pečar, *Die Stellung der slowenischen Landesregierung zum Land Kärnten 1918-1920* (Klagenfurt/Celovec: Mohorjeva, 2010), 375-443; *The Land Between. A History of Slovenia*, ed. Oto Luthar (Frankfurt/Main: Peter Lang, 2008), 380-381.

9. Ivo Banac, *The National Question in Yugoslavia. Origins, History, Politics* (Ithaca, NY–London: Cornell UP, 1984), 264-270; Cattaruzza, *L'Italia*, 147-164; Memorandum of the Government of Tyrol, February 1919, *ADÖ*, vol. 1, doc. 170 A; Steiner, *The Lights*, 88-90; Tooze, *The Deluge*, 308-311. It is difficult to grasp why Wilson accepted the transfer of more than half a million Slovenes and Croats as well as 220,000 German-Austrians to Italian sovereignty but struggled with the port city of Fiume/Rijeka, containing 25,000 Italians and 15,000 South Slavs, in 1910. See Arnold Suppan, *Zwischen Adria und Karawanken*, Deutsche Geschichte im Osten Europas 7 (Berlin: Siedler, 2 ed., 2002), 244.

10. Memorandum Staatsamt für Äußeres, Vienna, January 1919, *ADÖ*, vol. 1, doc. 141 A; Memorandum Tiroler Landesregierung, Innsbruck, February 1919, *ADÖ*, vol. 1, doc. 170 A; Tiroler Landesregierung to President Wilson (Paris),

Innsbruck, 26 February 1919, *ADÖ*, vol. 1, doc. 170. Point 9 of the 14 points spoke of an adjustment of the Italian frontier on clearly recognisable national lines.

11. *Corriere della Sera* (Milan), 12 March 1919; Verfassungsausschuss der Tiroler Landesversammlung to the Council of Ten (Paris), Bern, 22 March 1919, *ADÖ*, vol. 2, doc. 200; State Secretary Bauer to the Peace Conference (via The Hague), Vienna, 28 March 1919, *ADÖ*, vol. 2, doc. 204; Staatsamt für Äußeres to foreign missions (without Italy), Vienna, 9 April 1919, *ADÖ*, vol. 2, doc. 209; Tiroler Landesregierung to President Wilson, Innsbruck, April 1919, *ADÖ*, vol. 2, doc. 221 A; Margaret MacMillan, *Paris 1919. Six Months That Changed the World* (New York: Random House, 2005), 247; Steiner, *The Lights*, 88; Michael Gehler, *Tirol im 20. Jahrhundert. Vom Kronland zur Europaregion* (Innsbruck–Wien: Tyrolia, 2 ed., 2009), 72-74.

12. Protocols of the Austrian-German negotiations, Berlin, 27 February-2 March 1919, *ADÖ*, vol. 1, doc. 171-173, 175-177; Instruction Staatsamt für Äußeres for the Delegation to the Paris Peace Conference, May 1919, *ADÖ*, vol. 2, doc. 232; Nautz, *Unterhändler des Vertrauens*, 231-32.

13. Note Adler to Tusar, Vienna, 9 November 1918; Protocol of the German/Austrian-Czechoslovak conference, Vienna, 16 November 1918; Note Bauer to Tusar, Vienna, 24 November 1918; Report Freissler to Renner, Troppau, 3 December 1918; Note Bauer to Tusar, Vienna, 7 December 1918; Note circulaire Bauer, Vienna, 8 December 1918; Note verbale Bauer, Vienna, 17 December 1918; Memorandum Bauer to all governments of the Entente and the United States, Vienna, 25 December 1918, *ADÖ*, vol. 1, doc. 13, 20, 33, 62, 74, 75, 96, 104; Kalvoda, *Genesis*, 435-448; Steiner, *The Lights*, 83; *Facing History: The Evolution of Czech-German Relations in the Czech Provinces, 1848-1948*, eds. Zdeněk Beneš and Václav Kural (Praha: gallery, 2002), 80-81. In the Znaim weekly *Deutscher Mahnruf*, 'a German peasant's son' protested on 1 February 1919: 'The Thaya flows to Austria and not to Bohemia. For centuries we have taken our goods from Vienna and brought our products to Vienna. Not one of our peasants has ever left for Prague, and we are German and always want to stay with our national comrades! We are a part of Lower Austria and never wanted to be separated from it!' See Tereza Pavlíčková, *Die Entwicklung des Nationalitätenkonflikts in der Znaimer deutschen Presse 1850-1938* (Olomouc: Universita Palackého v Olomoucí, 2013), 218.

14. The Austrian Government protested several times against the Czech occupation of *Deutschböhmen* and the *Sudetenland* as well as against the shootings on 4 March 1919. See Report Marek to Bauer, Prague, 10 January 1919; Note Bauer to Tusar, Vienna, 6 March 1919; Notes circulaires Bauer to all Missions of neutral States, Vienna, 7, 8 and 13 March 1919, *ADÖ*, vol. 1, doc. 126, 180, 182, 184, 186; Beneš and Kural, *Facing History*, 81.

15. The Czechoslovak census of 15 February 1921 summed up Bohemia by nationality as follows: 4,401,107 'Czechoslovaks', 2,230,213 Germans, 12,578 Jews, 6,135 Magyars, 3,365 Poles and 10,505 'Russians' (including Ukrainians and Carpathian Ruthenes). See *Volkszählung in der Čechoslo-*

vakischen Republik vom 15. Februar 1921, ed. Statistisches Staatsamt (Prag: Bursik & Kohout, 1924).

16. David Lloyd George, *Memoirs of the Peace Conference*, vol. 2 (New Haven: Yale UP, 1939), 608; Hájková and Horák, *Beneš*, 345-349; Steiner, *The Lights*, 53; Arnold Suppan, 'Die imperialistische Friedensordnung Mitteleuropas in den Verträgen von Saint-Germain und Trianon,' in *Die Habsburgermonarchie 1848-1918*, eds. Helmut Rumpler and Anatol Schmied-Kowarzik, vol. 11, part 1, 2 (Wien: Verlag der Österreichischen Akademie der Wissenschaften, 2016), 1257-1341, here 1272-1274.

17. Dagmar Perman, *The Shaping of the Czechoslovak State. A Diplomatic History of the Boundaries of Czechoslovakia 1914-1920* (Leiden: E. J. Brill, 1962), 172; *Bohemia and Moravia*, ed. Historical Section of the Foreign Office of Great Britain, Peace Handbooks 4 (London: H.M. Stationery Office, 1920). In a series of articles on the proposed borders of the new Czechoslovakia, Seton-Watson operated a double standard: While he stressed that 'the lands of the Crown of St. Wenceslas (Bohemia, Moravia) have formed a single unit since the Dark Ages', he did not recognise the same argument for the kingdom of St. Stephen. Moreover, he called the Austrian and Hungarian statistics not 'trustworthy'. Therefore, Seton-Watson repeated the Czech argument that there is 'less injustice in placing nine million Czecho-Slovaks – in this case the whole race – under alien rule, than in placing two, or even two-and-a-half million [sic!] out of seventy million Germans under Czech rule'. See Rubicon [Seton-Watson], 'Czecho-Slovak Claims', in *R. W. Seton-Watson and his Relations with the Czechs and Slovaks. Documents 1906-1951*, ed. Jan Rychlík et al., vol. 1 (Praha–Martin: Ústav T. G. Masaryk/Matica Slovenská, 1995), 278-292.

18. Kalvoda, Genesis, 435-442; cf. Mémoire I (*Les Tchécoslovaques. Leur histoire et civilisation. Leur lutte et leur travail. Leur rôle dans le monde*), II (*Les revendications territoriales de la république Tchécoslovaque*), IV (*Le problème de la Silésie de Teschen*), V (*La Slovaquie. Le territoire revendiqué de la Slovaquie*), VI (*Le problème des Ruthenes de Hongrie*), VII (*Les Serbes de Lusace*), VIII (*La Haute Silésie Tchèque. Région de Ratibor*), IX (*Le problème de la région de Glatz*), X (*Problèmes des rectifications des frontières Tchécoslovaques et Germano-Autrichiennes*), XI (*La république Tchécoslovaque et son droit à la réparation des dommages de guerre*); The memoranda of the German Bohemian Provincial Government, Vienna, 25 April 1919, *ADÖ*, vol. 2, doc. 226, 226 A, 226 B, 226 C, 226 D, 226 E, 226 F; cf. Raschhofer, Die Tschechoslowakischen Denkschriften.

19. Minute of the National Assembly, Vienna, 7 June 1919, *ADÖ*, vol. 2, doc. 268; Draft Riedl, Vienna, June 1919, in *ADÖ*, vol. 2, doc. 276; Draft Staatsamt für Heerwesen, Vienna, June 1919, *ADÖ*, vol. 2, doc. 280; Note Bauer to Allizé, Borghese, Cunningham and Halstead, Vienna, 17 July 1919, *ADÖ*, vol. 2, doc. 312; Peace Delegation to Staatsamt für Äußeres, Saint-Germain, 20 July 1919, *ADÖ*, vol. 2, doc. 316; Draft Eichhoff, Saint-Germain, July 1919, *ADÖ*, vol. 2, doc. 318; Minute of the National Assembly, Vienna, 26 July 1919, *ADÖ*, vol. 2, doc. 327; Note Renner to Clemenceau, Saint-Germain, 15 August 1919, *ADÖ*, vol. 2, doc. 336; Minute of the National Assembly, Vienna, 6 September 1919, in *ADÖ*, vol. 2, doc. 355; Nautz, *Unterhändler des Vertrauens*, 237-242. On 27 July 1919, Bauer resigned as State Secretary because of his failures in the South Tyrol and 'Anschluss' policies. See Bauer to Seitz, Vienna, 25 July 1919, *ADÖ*, vol. 2, doc. 324.

20. Cf. Georges Clemenceau, *Grandeur and Misery of Victory* (New York: Harcourt, Brace & Co., 1930).

The Options for a Negotiated Peace in the Danube Region: Hungary and Neighbouring Countries after the 1918 Aster Revolution

László Szarka

The Death Throes of the Habsburg Monarchy and the Collapse of Multinational Hungary

Count Ottokar Czernin (1872-1932), who served as imperial and royal foreign minister for the Habsburg monarchy from December 1916 to April 1918, wrote self-deprecatingly in his memoirs about the fall of the Austro-Hungarian Empire: 'It is of course not possible to say how the collapse of the monarchy would have played out if the war had been avoided [...]. We had to die. We were able to choose the manner of our death, and we chose the worst possible option.'[1]

The Hungarian prime minister Count István Tisza (1861-1918), who was a powerful and symbolic figure in Hungary during the war years, also devoted much thought to the causes of the fateful demise of the Dual Monarchy. In a letter to the Foreign Minister Stephan Burián von Rajecz (1851-1922) on 16 December 1917, he wrote a very critical assessment of what he had learnt of President Woodrow Wilson's (1856-1924) first message of peace: 'We have received official notification of the war of extermination; as long as our enemies insist that this is their purpose in this war, then our very existence is under threat and we must strain every sinew to defend ourselves. Our opponents must make big changes in their approach before we can agree to the kind of peace President Wilson is suggesting.'[2] A year later, on 18 October 1918, he acknowledged the defeat of the Monarchy in the Hungarian parliament and commented that its most important consequence would be the end of Austrian/ Hungarian dualism, giving way to a monarchy of personal union and the need for peace negotiations on the basis of President Wilson's principles.[3] In spite of deep divisions among the Hungarian political elites,

Fig. 1: Count István Tisza, Prime Minister of Hungary 1903-1905 and 1913-1917. He was assassinated during the Aster Revolution on 31 October 1918.

both the government and the opposition were equally convinced by the end of the war that the opposing parties would reach a peace compromise within the framework of the peace negotiations.[4]

Wilson's peace initiative, drafted between 1916 and 1917, included some extremely daring statements on national self-determination; the important point was, in Wilson's somewhat flowery language, an aspiration to a negotiated peace. Point 10 of his

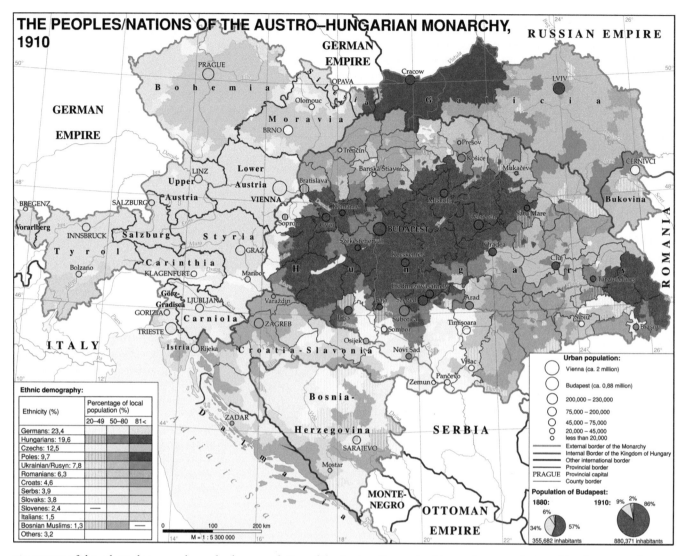

Fig. 2: Map of the ethnic demography and urban population of the Austro-Hungarian Monarchy, 1910, designed by the Research Institute of Ethnic and National Minorities, 2020.

first peace plan still gives rise to different interpretations. 'We wish to see the place that the peoples of Austria-Hungary hold among the nations protected and secured; they should be allowed the freest opportunity for autonomous development.'[5] There were repeated efforts in Hungary to interpret this statement literally. The opposition parties sympathetic to the Entente and those who supported the peace, and the Social Democrats – not represented in parliament – took it to mean that reform was needed that would lead to internal national autonomy. It is known, however, that Wilson and his Secretary of State Robert Lansing (1864-1928) were constantly altering their plans, until in June 1918 they decided that the solu-

tion to the monarchy question was the establishment of independent states.[6]

The political elites in Austria and Hungary did not fully appreciate this until October 1918. Rather than hastily engaging in negotiations with non-Hungarian national groups or trying to create an internal federation, Sándor Wekerle (1848-1924), the last Hungarian Prime Minister for the Dual Monarchy, rejected the federalistic declaration announced by the young king and Emperor Karl (1887-1922) in the manifesto he published on 18 October 1918.[7] In the last few decades, the established consensus has continued to be that there was a wide range of reasons for the demise of the multi-ethnic dynastic empires and the emergence of multi-ethnic national states in East and Central Europe, and that the momentum and trajectory of the crises were determined both by internal and external political reasons, as well as by social, regional and national factors.[8]

This essay addresses the late Hungarian approach to the ending of the war and the preparations for the negotiated peace; these were designed to consolidate the post-war situation in the hope of giving a positive impetus to inter-ethnic relations within the Hungarian multi-ethnic state. During the war's final stages, an alliance of opposition parties confronted the war policies of Count Tisza and the government of Sándor Wekerle in the Hungarian National Assembly. The king's appointment of János Hadik (1863-1933) as the new prime minister on 27 October did nothing to appease the dissatisfied and radicalised masses. Returning soldiers staged massive demonstrations, riots and strikes, and the so-called Chrysanthemum Revolution then broke out on 28 October. In the midst of the chaotic military and political situation at the end of the war, the Hungarian National Assembly had three principal objectives: an immediate end to the war; the democratic transformation of the country; and a new cooperation between the ethnic nationalities in an independent Hungary in order to achieve a just peace settlement at an international peace conference.[9]

At the end of October, following the collapse of the Austro-Hungarian Dual Monarchy, the Kingdom of Hungary's outlook was in many respects complicated, possibly even hopeless. The Hungarian coalition government, which lacked its own army and diplomatic corps and had no international profile on its own account, was facing an especially difficult task both domestically and internationally. The victorious nations made almost weekly territorial claims on the Hungarian People's Republic, established on 16 November.[10]

The Southern Slav nations declared their independence at the end of October and the beginning of November, closely followed by the Czecho-Slovaks and then the Romanians. In the course of preparing for the peace conference, the government of the Hungarian People's Republic suggested a provisional solution in order to prevent a descent into anarchy and possible civil war. The challenge presented by the regional nature of multi-ethnicity in Hungary threat-

Fig. 3: The Hungarian conservative politician Sándor Wekerle, Prime Minister of Hungary 1892-1895, 1906-1910, 1917-1918, portrait by Gyula Benczúr, 1911.

ened to cause national disintegration; establishing a federation and autonomy for ethnic groups might have offered a solution. Few politicians could see any other options; the social democrat minister in the Károlyi government, Zsigmond Kunfi (1879-1929), explained that one of the consequences of losing the war was the surrender of the country's non-Hungarian regions. Prime Minister Mihály Károlyi (1875-1955) and the majority of his government hoped that a radical transformation of the country into a kind of 'eastern Switzerland' would satisfy the non-Magyar ethnic groups.[11]

Hungary as an 'Eastern Switzerland'

In November 1918, the Hungarian Minister of Nationalities Oszkár Jászi (1875-1957), during negotiations with non-Magyar politicians, attempted to formulate a procedure to define a Swiss model for Hungary on the basis of a constitutional proposal. The Károlyi

Fig. 4: 'A Death Song of the Austro-Hungarian Monarchy' with reference to the Hungarian Soviet Republic in the form of a man with the Jacobean cap, 1919. The book written by Karl Kraus. The cover illustrated by Mihály Bíró.

government's new 'integrity concept' could, it seemed, be achieved as a federation of autonomous regions on the Swiss model. Jászi promoted this rather than Wilson's self-determination model, which would have led to a compromise granting Slovaks, Romanians, Serbs and Croats self-determination outside the state. Autonomy for the Hungarian nationality groups, the Károlyi government believed, could help consolidation and encourage dialogue with the national assemblies of the non-Magyar nations. Moreover, Jászi was keen to present the ideas as initial proposals to the negotiations at the international peace conference in Paris.

Meanwhile, the country's international position remained a source of tension, as the Entente had not yet recognised the Hungarian People's Republic. This meant, among other things, that '[u]ntil such time as the general peace conference gathers, we wish to establish any institutions and guarantees that will secure the peaceful co-existence of the nationalities of Hungary, without prejudicing future decisions on boundaries.'[12] As minister, Jászi was keenly aware of the national revolutions that had shaken the monarchy, and judged that national autonomy was the only remaining peaceful option to keep the country from disintegration. He saw this system of internal autonomous states as a kind of nationally agreed temporary measure, and made it the central feature of his policy as minister for 'Preparing for the Self-Determination of the Hungarian Nationalities' in the Károlyi government.[13]

In advance of the negotiations in Arad on 13 and 14 November 1918 with the Romanian National Assembly of Transylvania and of the east Hungarian Romanians, the concept of national autonomous nations within a federated state had become generally accepted among members of the Károlyi government and other Hungarian national leaders, regardless of other differences in their political positions, as the last possible option for maintaining internal state cohesion.[14]

The autonomous ethnic regions ('cantons') that Jászi wanted to establish in accordance with the ethnic majority principle in the disputed regions had earlier been considered the principal aim for nationalities within Hungary. By early December, given the country's deepening isolation and increasing military threats, no one on the Hungarian side expected to achieve more than the establishment of a clear

Fig. 5: The social scientist Oszkár Jászi, Hungarian Minister of Nationalities 1918/19.

alternative to the country's division. Alongside this, they also entertained fond hopes for the implications of the principle of national self-determination: 'The government of the Hungarian People's Republic accepts its responsibility as determined by such a decision to grant the right to Romanians, Serbs and Ruthenians living in this country to determine, by plebiscite, which region they wish to attach themselves to.'[15] It is important here to bear in mind the Hungarian preparations for peace at the Nationalities Ministry and the newly established Foreign Ministry in Budapest, which included, as a memo of 8 December makes clear, a proposal that national self-defence should be organised on the basis of individual ethnic regions only.[16]

Jászi's 'temporary measure policy', designed to last until the peace conference met and implemented its decisions, offered each ethnic nation living in Hungary an opportunity to establish appropriate differentiation, as confirmed by opposition parties in the various national regions. The governments in Prague and Bucharest were making every effort to shape the undertakings of the Entente nations to their own advantage before the peace conference even started; this could only be achieved by presenting a *fait accompli* – in other words, by effecting a military occupation.

Creating Cantons – Hungary as a 'Composite State'

The Károlyi government sought to find a peacefully negotiated solution to the military operations conducted by the Southern Slav, Romanian and Czechoslovakian forces. The troops were aiming to establish a so-called national delimitation by clearly identifying the borders of the regions with a Hungarian majority in Transylvania, and in Southern and Northern Hungary. The Romanian National Assembly in Arad published an ultimatum on 9 November demanding that 26 counties in Transylvania and Eastern Hun-

gary be immediately handed over to Romanian control. The ministry led by Jászi quickly developed its concept of an 'Eastern Switzerland' that would properly and accurately reflect the ethnic reality.

In the negotiations between Hungarians and Romanians on 13 and 14 November 1918, Jászi suggested instituting a temporary measure, valid until the peace conference, and the division of Transylvania into cantons. These measures were to be determined according to the statistics on the different national groups. The Romanian National Assembly in Hungary and Transylvania presented a memorandum to the Hungarian government on 9 November. '[A]ccording to the right to self-determination of national groups and in the interest of our nation (the Romanians in Hungary) and of the minorities who live in the same region to defend public order, their property and their personal safety', it gave the Hungarian government three days to provide an answer. The Romanian

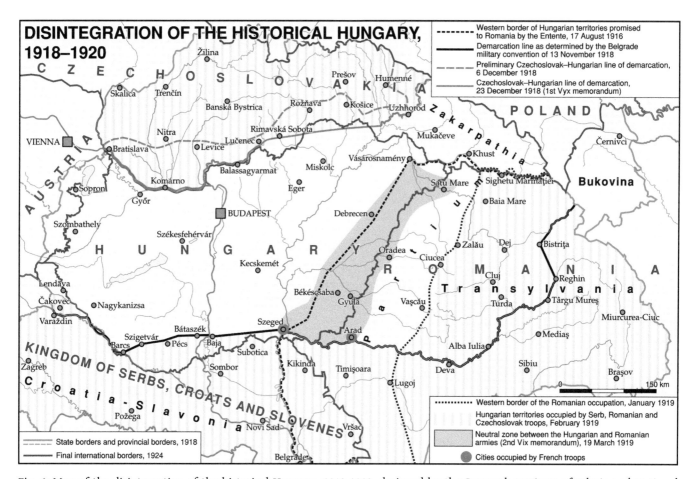

Fig. 6: Map of the disintegration of the historical Hungary, 1918-1920, designed by the Research Institute of Ethnic and National Minorities, 2020.

ultimatum demanded 'full powers of government' in the 26 Transylvanian and East Hungarian counties.[17] Following a decision by the Hungarian council of ministers on 10 November, Jászi traveled with a delegation to Arad in order to conduct negotiations with members of the Romanian National Assembly to explore solutions to the situation in the light of the ultimatum.[18]

The Hungarian delegation presented two different options in the Arad negotiations. On the first day, Jászi suggested that autonomous Romanian cantons should be established wherever there was a Romanian majority in the region that included the 26 counties claimed by the Romanian National Assembly, whilst also guaranteeing rights of autonomy to the smaller Hungarian-speaking areas. Jászi made a similar suggestion for the Transylvanian and East Hungarian counties that had Hungarian majorities.[19] On the second day of the negotiations, the Romanian delegation turned down the Hungarian suggestion on the grounds that establishing the cantons would be too complicated and would exacerbate the conflicts between national groups. Vasile Goldiş (1862-1934) announced that Jászi's proposal denied the rights of the Romanian people to independence.[20] Jászi maintained that until there was a decision from the peace conference, domestic peace should be secured by means of a temporary agreement. 'If we wish to have peace, then it is unthinkable that we should create a merely temporary situation that will bring harm to Hungarians, Germans, Serbs and Saxons [...].'[21]

Jászi then offered an 11-point statement for shared governance. It proposed that Transylvania and Eastern Hungary should be divided into districts and towns according to ethnic majority, to be under Romanian and Hungarian administration. A joint government commission was to establish the new system of administration.[22] Both Jászi's suggestions were turned down in the Romanian National Assembly. On the second day of the conference, Iuliu Maniu explained that the National Assembly had refused the Hungarian interpretation of the 'Wilsonian principles' because they would give to those in Hungarian enclaves within so-called closed Romanian districts, for example in Transylvania, rights that the Romanians thought appropriate only when given to whole nationality groups and closed national regions.

After the fiasco in Arad, Jászi gave a significantly

Fig. 7: The Czech politican Milan Hodža, Prime Minister of Czechoslovakia 1935-1938.

more realistic assessment of the resolution to the Slovakian question, taking account of the establishment of the Czechoslovakian state: 'As a result of the Czech efforts, it is clear that the Slovakian question too can only be settled at a national peace conference.'[23] At the negotiations in Budapest with Milan Hodža (1878-1944), the delegate of the Czecho-Slovak government, and the delegation from the Slovakian National Assembly, agreement was reached on the likely demarcation line, which would follow the language boundary between Hungarian and Slovak. Following vigorous discussions in the council of Hungarian ministers, Jászi established a plan for a so-called 'Slovak empire'. In essence, this encompassed the five northern counties with an almost exclusively Slovak population, and the majority Slovak districts of the other ten counties in Upper Hungary – 67 districts altogether – which would be placed under Slovakian administration.[24] On 1 December, the Prague government blocked the Budapest negotiations. Three

Fig. 8: Symbolical image about the territorial losses of Hungary after the treaty of Trianon, 4 June 1920, contemporary postcard.

Jászi's aims may not have met with success during the negotiations, but it is important to remember that the ministry had managed within less than a month to elaborate propositions that, had they been carried out in the decades before the outbreak of WWII, would have been acclaimed and declared a revolutionary new solution to Hungary's nationalities question.

Jászi maintained that the provisional Hungarian nationalities policy, which for a brief interim period was to be based on an agreement between national groups, would seek to satisfy three claims. In order to realise the generally respected right to self-determination as defined by Wilson, the offer of cultural and regional autonomy would undoubtedly, by late summer of 1918, have given rise to a revolutionary basis for negotiations. With a settlement that would ensure domestic peace, and a joint plan between then nationalities to ensure public provisioning, there was hope that cooperation between the autonomous elements might become a practical reality. The application of the 'Swiss' model to the state also laid the foundations for the creation of a national pattern of cantons. Enshrining these in law would have given the temporary measures some stability and could have led to the development of self-determination and maintaining the principle of territorial integrity until the peace conference had reached its final decisions. Without either support from the great powers or adoption by the Romanians, the Slovaks, the Serbs or the Transylvanian Saxons, the establishment of an 'eastern Switzerland', even if only for a short interim period, was simply a further example of historic ideas that came too late. The proposed reshaping of Hungary along the lines of a multi-faceted 'composite state' structure suggests that a settlement along ethnic and territorial lines might have been a possible outcome of two-way negotiations at the end of the war. With the advantage of hindsight, it seems that had a definition of borders according to ethnic majorities – the most challenging task in solving the conflicts between nationalities – been carried out in conjunction with 'Swiss autonomies' for minorities, this might have made just as significant a contribution to a negotiated peace as the much-disputed imposition of new borders following a plebiscite. At the end of the war, what counted in terms of politics was not primarily the quality of the recommendations but rather the way in which states, groups and indi-

agreements on nationalities were already – or nearly – completed and due to be enshrined in law: Ruthenian autonomy in Carpathian Ukraine, Slovenian autonomy of the region Prekmurje and the right of self-determination of the Hungarian Germans. However, given the hopeless political isolation of the Hungarian People's Republic, the prospect of these ever being realised were becoming increasingly dependent on the military situation in the country and the intentions of neighbouring countries.[25]

The Jászi ministry's main aim can be roughly defined as an attempt by Budapest to mitigate the policies of the Western great powers by means of agreements with neighbouring states. Yet Jászi was aware that his Swiss-inspired plan to create cantons would not promote homogeneous language groups or the establishment of an independent state, and that consequently it was unlikely to succeed.[26]

viduals were able to influence and gain trust at the Paris Peace Conference. As a defeated nation, and as a part of the much maligned Dual Monarchy, Hungary was not likely to benefit from much sympathy, let alone understanding, from either large or small victor nations of WWI.

Endnotes

1. Ottokar Czernin, *Im Weltkriege* (Berlin–Wien: Ullstein, 1919), 38.

2. Tisza István, *Összes Munkái*, vol. 6. (Budapest: Magyar Tudományos Akadémia, Franklin-Társulat, 1937), 114. On Tisza Gabor Vermes's war policies, see István Tisza, *The Liberal Vision and Conservative Statecraft of a Magyar Nationalist* (New York, Columbia University Press, 1985), 584-613.

3. Stenographic Protocols of the 824th session of the Hungarian House of Delegates, 17 October 1918, in *Országgyűlési Képviselőházi Napló*, vol. 1910, XLI., 398-406.

4. István Diószegi, 'Der Ungarische Nationalismus und der Zerfall der Monarchie,' in *Hungarians in the Ballhausplatz. Studies on the Austro-Hungarian Common Foreign Policy*, ed. Diószegi István (Budapest: Corvina, 1983), 320-345, here 338-342; Robert Gerwarth, *Die Besiegten. Das blutige Erbe des Ersten Weltkriegs*, (München: Siedler, 2017), 230-233.

5. Jörn Leonhard, *Die Büchse der Pandora. Geschichte des Ersten Weltkrieges* (München: C. H. Beck, 2014), 883-885; Leonard V. Smith, 'The Wilsonian Challenge to International Law,' *The Journal of the History of International Law*, 13 (2011), 179-208.

6. Quoted from Rolf-Peter Magen, *Staatsrecht. Eine Einführung*, seventh, rev. edn (Berlin–Heidelberg–New York–Toronto: Springer, 1985), 94-96, here 95.

7. Dániel Szabó, 'Die Agonie des historischen Ungarn. Die einheitliche und unteilbare ungarische Nation im Weltkrieg,' in *Die Habsburgermonarchie und der Erste Weltkrieg, vol. XI/1/2. Vom Vielvölkerstaat Österreich-Ungarn zum neuen Europa der Nationalstaaten*, ed. Helmuth Rumpler (Wien: Verlag der Österreichischen Akademie der Wissenschaften, 2016), 679-710, 706-707; Helmuth Rumpler, *Die Völkermanifest Kaisers Karls vom 16. Oktober 1918. Letzter Versuch zur Rettung des Habsburgerreiches* (Wien: Verlag für Geschichte und Politik, 1966).

8. Leonhard, *Die Büchse*, 386-396, 895-909; Peter Haslinger, 'Austria-Hungary,' in *Empires at War 1911-1923*, eds. Robert Gerwarth and Erez Manela (Oxford: Oxford University Press, 2014), 73-90.

9. Péter Hanák, 'Ungarn im Auflösungsprozeß der Österreichisch-Ungarischen Monarchie,' in *Grundlagen und Folgen, in Versailles – St. Germain – Trianon*, ed. Karl Bosl (München–Wien: R. Oldenbourg, 1971), 37-48, here 44-46; Salamon Konrád, *Az őszirózsás forradalomról és az első köztársaságról. Harag és elfogultság nélkül* (Budapest: Éghajlat Könyvkiadó, 2012), 33-34.

10. Gerwarth, *Die Besiegten*, 241-253.

11. Zsolt K. Lengyel, *Auf der Suche nach dem Kompromiß. Ursprünge und Gestalten des früheren Transsilvanismus 1918-1928* (München: Verlag Ungarisches Institut, 1993), 87-103.

12. Interview with Minister Jászi, *Világ*, 19 November 1918, 1-2.

13. Oskar Jászi, *Der Zusammenbruch des Dualismus und die Zukunft der Donaustaaten* (Wien: Manz'sche Verlags- und Universitätsbuchhandlung, 1918), 35-36; György Litván, *A Twentieth-Century Prophet: Oszkár Jászi, 1875-1957* (Budapest–New York: CEU Press, 2006), 137-156.

14. Protocols of the Hungarian council of ministers, 18 December 1918. National Archives of Hungary, Budapest, MNL OL K-27. Pál Schönwald, *A magyarországi 1918-1919-es polgáridemokratikus forradalom* (Budapest: Közgazdasági és Jogi Kiadó), 60; János Kende, *A Magyarországi Szociáldemokrata Párt nemzetiségi politikája 1903-1919* (Budapest: Akadémiai Kiadó, 1973), 102.

15. László Domokos, *Kis káté a Magyarországon élő nemzetek önrendelkezési jogáról* (Budapest: Lantos A. Könyvkereskedése, 1919), 13.

16. National Archives of Hungary – Budapest, MNL OL K-40, 1919-XX-100.

17. National Archives of Hungary – Budapest, MNL OL, K-40, 1918-IX-240.

18. Peter Haslinger, *Arad, November 1918. Oszkár Jászi und die Rumänen in Ungarn 1900-1918.* (Wien–Köln–Weimar: Böhlau, 1993), 122-140; Zsolt K. Lengyel, 'Niedergang, Wiederherstellung, Neugestaltung, Zusammenbruch. Ungarische Reform- und Zukunftsentwürfe für Siebenbürgen am Vorabend und während des Ersten Weltkrieges', in *Umbruch mit Schlachtenlärm. Siebenbürgen und der Erste Weltkrieg*, ed. Harald Heppner (Köln–Weimar–Wien: Böhlau, 2017), 53-113, here 98-107; Ernő Raffay, *Erdély 1918-1919-ben*, (Budapest: Magvető Kiadó, 1987), 66-69; László Szarka, 'Iratok az 1918. novemberi aradi magyar-román tárgyalások történetéhez', *Regio 5*, 3 (1994), 140-166.

19. Szarka, *Iratok*, 153.

20. Szarka, *Iratok*, 154.

21. Szarka, *Iratok*, 148-149

22. According to Point 1 of the new proposal, 'the Hungarian government would hand over the administration of all districts and cities having a Romanian majority to the Romanian National Assembly. In this region the administration would be carried out by the Romanian government'. Szarka Iratok, 163-164.

23. 'Cseh, román és szerb csapatok Magyarországon,' *Népszava* (1 November 1918), 1.

24. László Fogarassy, 'Hodža Milán és a Károlyi-kormány', *Palócföld 24* (May 1990), 72-88; *Slovenský rozchod s Maďarmi. Dokumentárny výklad o jednaniach dr. Milana Hodžu ako čsl. plnomocníka s Károlyiho vládou v listopade a prosinci 1918 o ústup maďarských vojsk zo Slovenska* (Bratislava: Slovenský denník, 1929), 27-71. The 'Slovak Empire' plan, published in the Budapest newspaper 'Nap' on 1 December 1918, 1-2; László Szarka, 'A méltányos nemzeti elhatárolódás lehetősége 1918 végén,' Regio 1 (January 1990), 60-62; The map of the 'Slovakian empire' is available in the Jászi ministry archive. National Archives of Hungary, Budapest, MNL OL K-40, 1918-II-353.

25. Pál Schönwald, *A magyarországi*, 122-138.

26. Domonkos, *Kis káté*, 35.

The Dynamic of Post-War Political Structures in Multi-Ethnic Regions: Transylvania at the End of 1918

Andreea Dăncilă

Even though we are now reaching the centenary of the events concluding the Great War, the historical narrative of how a 'borderline region'[1] such as Transylvania emerged from the uproar of 1914-1918 is not yet fully established. Particularly within the frame-work of Romanian historiography, the issue has remained somewhat overshadowed by the grander narrative of the events that enabled this formerly imperial province to unite with the Romanian Kingdom on 1 December 1918.[2]

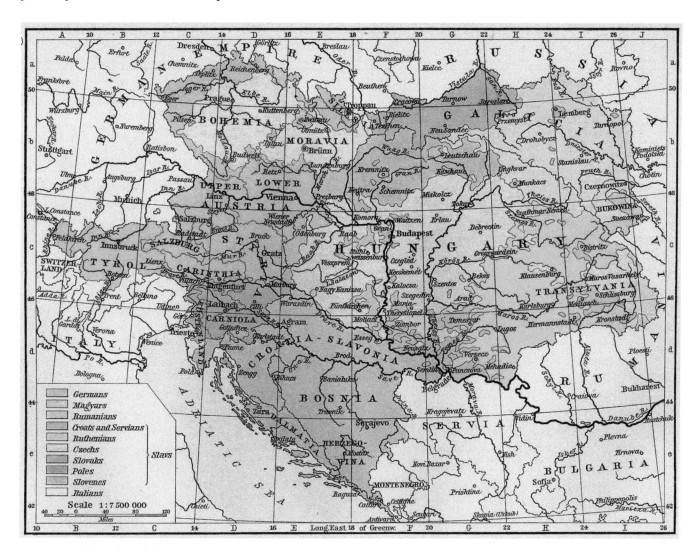

Fig. 1: Map of the ethnical distribution in Austria-Hungary, 1911.

Fig. 2: The Romanian politician Alexandru Vaida Voevod.

Transylvania with Romania, and it marked the start of a political pathway allowing for unitary coordination.

From Budapest to the Regional Hubs: The Symbolic Geography of the New Political Centres

After Hungary's political leaders publicly admitted that they had lost the war, the emblematic Romanian politician from Transylvania, Alexandru Vaida Voevod (1872-1950), spoke during the parliamentary meeting of 18 October 1918 in Budapest to argue that, according to the principle of self-determination, Romanians from Hungary no longer recognised the authority of the Hungarian Parliament. Only the executive committee of the Romanian National Party,[4] he claimed, now represented the current political interests of the Romanian nation. He added: 'We are no longer nationalities, but nations!'[5]

That October, most ethnic groups under the Austro-Hungarian monarchy constituted themselves into national councils, organs that could be considered as political patterns functioning across the empire by the end of 1918.[6] These structures represent intermediate forms of power management in the transition from imperial to national administration,[7] as well as signs that the central state institutions' authority was weakening. Budapest remained the acknowledged political centre of Transylvania after the war, hosting the headquarters of the Hungarian National Council, the Romanian National Council, and the Saxon Parliamentary Club from late October onwards; Hungary's German National Council would later also be established here.

Early November witnessed a movement of key bodies from the centre, including the Romanian National Council's transfer to Arad (the political centre of the Romanian National Party in Transylvania) and the establishment of a German-Saxon Executive Committee in Sibiu/Nagyszeben/Hermannstadt (the home of the Transylvanian Evangelical-Lutheran Church's episcopal residence and the historical Transylvanian Saxon political centre). The movement had an obvious symbolism: the capital, Budapest, no longer served as the political focus for non-Hungarian groups in Transylvania.

The run-up to December 1918 nevertheless featured a spectacular succession of highly politically effervescent events, wherein multiple scenarios were considered, and various competing national projects violently intersected. In a multi-ethnic region such as Transylvania,[3] these changes involved a series of inherent crises in terms of political positioning and re-positioning in a context that was still particularly unstable, both externally and internally.

Transylvania was an ethnic palette overlaid with a series of confessional adherences, which made it an ideological melting pot from the war's end onwards. It is therefore extremely challenging to analyse how national options crystallised against the backdrop of the unsettled atmosphere of the final months of 1918.

Starting from these premises, I will be studying what could be called Transylvania's first transfer of power, which occurred between 30 October and 1 December 1918. On 30 October the first novel power structures emerged in this region, and it was on 1 December that a national assembly decided to unite

Despite these shifts inside Transylvania, which aimed to establish better control of the area and to safeguard authority, a group of Saxons continued to be active in the heart of Hungarian politics until December 1918[8] – an understandable strategy, since this group was best equipped to negotiate a favourable minority status with all political partners.

Even the Hungarian National Council in Budapest operated a policy of regional centralisation through the establishment of a Transylvanian Committee drawn from its own ranks, and located in the central Transylvanian city of Cluj/Kolozsvár/Klausenburg, the same city in which the provincial parliament (diet) had voted in 1867 to unite Transylvania and Hungary. Thus, in early November, the majority of the politically representative structures for the most significant ethnic groups in Transylvania were transferred from Budapest to centres in this region.

Alongside the Romanian, Hungarian, and German Councils, which can be regarded as the truly political bodies in the area, various guard-like military organisations affiliated to these councils also emerged. Any power clusters outside this council-guard tandem were increasingly devoid of legitimacy, leading to a true inflation of authority structures, e.g. paramilitary guards, civil guards, and councils of students, soldiers, workers, etc in this period.

The existence of these hybrid structures is symptomatic of the crisis of the central authority and the consequent legitimacy problems. Despite this internal clustering of power structures in Transylvania, we should not overlook the role that the two competing political forces of the Hungarian government in Budapest and its Romanian counterpart in Iaşi[9] continued to play. Through official or less official channels, the two power poles tried to influence and coordinate the Transylvanian scenario playing out at the end of the war.

The location of the power centres in Transylvania at the end of 1918 not only illustrates the political options and developments available both to the Hungarian and non-Hungarian ethnic groups at this period, but also exemplifies the dilution of Hungarian authority in the regions and the emergence of political islands with national legitimacy.

Arad, Cluj/Kolozsvár/Klausenburg or Sibiu/Nagyszeben/Hermannstadt were not randomly chosen places for these new Transylvanian power structures, but rather sites of memory *(lieux de mémoire)* that were highly significant for the communities they represented. They were valuable strategic points on the Romanian, Hungarian, and German map of collective emotions, capable of reviving legacies of the past.

The Dialogue Between the Transylvanian Power Structures

Although the front's collapse fermented revolution among all ethnic groups within the Empire, the soldiers and of the former POWs returning from Russia became further radicalised when they encountered the shortcomings and trauma their families had experienced at home. The struggle for survival, while famine was everywhere, as well as the strong feeling that the war's costs had not been equitably distributed, pushed many unruly soldiers and other rebel elements to resort to thefts, violence, and destructiveness. This further illustrates the transition from state violence to paramilitary violence that was so intense within the ex-Austro-Hungarian Empire.[10]

The Romanian, Hungarian, and Saxon national councils operating in Romania were frightened by the violence of these movements, which had become unstoppable by late October or early November, and their main concern was restoring calm and soothing spirits. They issued documents that clearly reflect the spontaneous uncontrolled nature of these rebel movements, scattered throughout the area and reaching unexpected dimensions.[11]

In a highly flammable social context, these councils of various ethnicities settled on cooperation as the best solution. On 1 November 1918, the representatives of the Romanian National Council (Teodor Mihali, 1855-1934), the Hungarian National Council (János Hock, 1859-1936), and the Saxons (Wilhelm Melzer, 1858-1929) signed a common appeal, urging people to defend domestic law and join forces.[12]

From the end of the war, the Hungarian authorities were interested in creating in Transylvania structures similar to ethnically mixed councils and guards, organised according to supra-national criteria. Political and military organs of this nature thus emerged in early November – and even in the localities in which the Romanian, Hungarian, and German National Councils were already operating, a common

Fig. 3: Romanian troops marching in Cluj, Transylvania, 1918.

committee constituted by delegates from each military-political council was established. Within a few
days, however, Romanian-Hungarian relations
shifted from cooperation to segregation, and Romanian leaders abandoned the idea of ethnically mixed
control institutions. An increasing number of community leaders had reservations about the initial
plan; they requested an ethnic organisation and not
'hermaphrodite' solutions, as one leader of the Romanian National Council described these mixed committees.[13]

It should be noted that the first fault lines in these
joint organs appeared during discussions about
which authority should be the object of an oath of
loyalty.[14] The Romanians refused to recognise the
central Hungarian authorities' primacy. The matter
reveals the heated pitch the issue of ethnic and national identification had reached at the end of the

war. The multi-ethnic guards experiment involved a
process of ideological and political clarification
within the central leadership of the Romanian National Council. For the Hungarian authorities, the
consolidation of power structures based on ethnic
criteria represented a critical vulnerable point. Lajos
Varjassy (1852-1934), the government commissioner
for Arad, commented, 'Hungarian society viewed the
setting up of the Romanian guards with great disap-
proval as it was convinced that they served not only
the maintenance of law and order, but were secretly
preparing for the takeover of the empire.'[15]

In such a restless context, the Saxon element
found it more difficult to assume a public position. At
the end of the war, the leaders of this community had
three options: neutrality, supporting the Hungarian
revolution or joining the cause of the Transylvanian
Romanians, who would reportedly soon be incor-

porated within the borders of the Romanian Kingdom. The Saxon elite therefore chose to establish contacts with the two sides interested in its support, the Romanians and the Hungarians, both in Budapest, where the German National Council operated, and in Sibiu/Hermannstadt, through the German Saxon National Committee.[16]

Amid the disorganisation present in all levels of Transylvanian society, the power structures that emerged during this period took on political, military, economic, and administrative privileges. In order to formally take over the Romanian administration in Transylvania, the Romanian leaders initiated a series of negotiations with the representatives of the Hungarian government. The ultimatum tone of these negotiations and the maximalist agenda circulating at the time were relevant to the new authority status acquired by the Romanian National Council. The assurances of the Romanian state and the Romanian army located on the Transylvanian border, waiting for a sign from the Entente to intervene in the area, obviously heavily contributed to this position of strength and security. From mid-November, after negotiations between Romanian and Hungarian leaders had failed, the process of Transylvania breaking away from Hungary was accelerated, despite the promises made by the newly proclaimed People's Republic of Hungary. A propaganda war accompanied this power transfer from the Hungarian to the Romanian authorities, each side trying to internationalise their cause by stressing the destabilising Bolshevik threat. Political projects attempting to resist the transfer of power included the notion of a Transylvanian Szekely Republic, envisioned in December 1918.[17]

The Leadership of the Transylvanian Power Structures

The war, and especially its denouement, created a social space of contestation, which functioned as an incubator for political leaders. The Romanian middle class became politically active during October and November,[18] in a region in which, significantly, the Romanian National Party had been allowed to send only ten representatives to the Parliament in Budapest before the war, and where the typology of the politician in the modern sense of the term barely

Fig. 4: Romanian postcard 1918-1919 with the new territories, symbolic images and the Romanian King Ferdinand I (1865-1927), including the dedication 'In memory of the realization of the great ideal of unifying all Romanians'.

existed. Ever since the turn of the century, however, a Romanian intellectual elite had gained an increasingly significant profile in Transylvania and had become integrated into a broader framework of contestation against the empire.[19] The pre-war years familiarised Transylvania's Romanian public with a radicalised political discourse, used in a number of campaigns that the elite directed towards rural populations where the Romanian element density was also the highest. The capacity of the Romanian National Council in Arad to create command networks immediately after the war was indeed due to a remarkable mobilisation effort across the Romanian world. There were two notable types of elites within the structure of the new organs of power, the national councils and guards: a traditional elite, consisting on the one hand of priests and teachers (often a person was both), lawyers, and leaders of nationalist movement, and on the other hand of a new group of dynamic military men returned from the front and eager to use their military rank as political capital.

Many documents mention numerous delegates from the Central Romanian National Council, priests, students, intellectuals who travelled through Romanian villages and urban centres in order to establish local councils and guards. They transformed the socially motivated rebellions into a national revolution, with a national programme.

The Hungarian leadership registered a major failure at the end of the war when it attempted to induce

Fig. 5: Hungarian politician and zoologist István Apáty.

a novel concept of loyalty towards the Hungarian state among the elites of the national groups in Transleithania.[20] On 13 November 1918, minister Oszkár Jászi's proposed solution of a canton-organised Transylvania was no longer considered viable by Romanian elites, whose political expectations were directed towards complete separation from Budapest.

In the Hungarian case, although new leaders such as Mihály Károlyi (1875-1955) and Oszkár Jászi (1875-1957) rode in on a wave of revolutionary sympathy, they failed to impose their championed reforms on the old structures of a conservative elite keen on maintaining its status.[21] Although a regime change had occurred in Budapest, the Hungarian political elite who operated in the power structures of Transylvania was conservative, mired in the paradigm of the unitary Hungarian national state.

Precisely for these reasons, his Romanian counterparts refused to engage in discussion with István Apáty (1863-1922), the President of the Transylvanian Committee – part of the Hungarian National Council – and a former rector of the Ferenc József University in Cluj, as he was seen as a typical chauvinist intellectual of the Dualist Hungary era. Although the there were major changes in governmental staff following the October revolution, the entire state and county apparatus remained the same at the Transylvanian county level,[22] with few exceptions. The Hungarian leaders' image at this period was relevant for an elite lacking consensus, with an ever-contested legitimacy, fragmented by multiple political strategies. This explanation of the Hungarian political elite's vulnerability should not exclude the international context – the Great Powers' reaction to the issue of Hungary's territorial integrity, which strongly confused the entire Hungarian political class.[23]

While the Romanian political leadership's presented themselves as state builders, with a discourse heavily influenced by national messianism, the Hungarian elite posed as social reformers, following a script that reveals a desperate need to maintain the old state borders.[24]

In the case of the Saxons, the end of 1918 merely extended an older debate that had split their political elite into two camps: the representatives of the younger generation who were waiting for a new policy towards the Hungarian government (the so-called 'Greens') on the one hand, and those who favoured a policy of cooperation and appeasement with the Hungarian leaders ('the Blacks') on the other.

The period under analysis is one of profound debate among this community's elite, who, although apparently divided in terms of political strategies, managed to remain prudent and keep open communication channels with the Romanian and Hungarian sides alike, both interested in having Saxons involved in their projects.

To conclude, while the Romanian political leadership in Transylvania appeared to be a consensually united elite, the Hungarian leadership seems to have been out of tune with the contemporary circumstances, enmeshed in the legacy of its past and confused in its strategic thought. Caught between the Romanian and Hungarian national projects, the

Transylvanian Saxon political elite was questioning its future, faced with the need to analyse responsibly the competing offers of the Budapest government and the Romanian leaders from Transylvania and Romania. As it lacked the pressure of having its own national project, it was also the most open to negotiation.

Final Remarks

The period between October and December 1918 constituted an ex-lex interval for Transylvania, in which a series of 'multiple sovereignties'[25] functioned, constituting power structures that formulated coherent and simultaneously incompatible claims to either control the state or establish themselves in a state form. While confusion reigned in late October and early November about how they were supposed to organise themselves and operate in the field, the various councils functioning in Transylvania were clarified and strategically consolidated over time. The political structures therefore gained the capacity to grant a political-national sense to this entire transition. The national councils' authority also stemmed from the fact that these organs coordinated guard-like military structures, and therefore gained central control over violence in the region. By acting in accordance with the principle that authority belongs to those who impose change, and not to those who endure it,[26] the Romanian political elite in Transylvania acted as a proactive force, taking over the initiative to negotiate with the Hungarian authorities, setting the rhythm according to which events would unfold and compelling the Hungarian political leadership to assume a reactive stance.

The continuous change of Transylvanian political centres, difficult to follow by a historian unfamiliar with the realities of the area, was not a Brownian movement occasioned by the surrounding unrest, but a dynamic relevant for the way in which the

Fig. 6: The Great National Assembly that decided the Union of Transylvania with the Romanian Kingdom, Alba Julia, 1 December 1918.

national groups of a multi-ethnic region chose to politically position themselves at the end of World War I. Nevertheless, a forum in which the three major ethnic groups in Transylvania – Romanians, Hungarians, and Saxons – could voice their complaints was gradually built against this chaotic and unpredictable backdrop. Finally, the first stage of power transfer in Transylvania was a litmus test of national loyalty for all the ethnic groups living in the region.

Endnotes

1. For the particularities of these border regions in the context of World War I, see Mark Biondich's study 'Eastern Borderlands and Prospective Shatter Zones: Identity and Conflict in East Central and Southeastern Europe on the Eve of the First World War,' in *Legacies of Violence. Eastern Europe's First World War*, eds. Jochen Böhler, Włodzimierz Borodziej and Joachim von Puttkamer (München: Oldenbourg Verlag, 2014), 25-50.

2. For an overview of how Romanian historiography has analysed the Great War over the years, see Florin Ţurcanu's study 'Une guerre oubliée: la Première Guerre mondiale,' Cités, 29, no. 1 (2007), 157-160. <https://www.cairn.info/load_pdf.php?ID_ARTICLE=CITE_029_0157> (accessed 15 April 2019).

3. According to the last pre-war official census, that of 1910, Transylvania had the following ethnic structure: 909,003 Hungarians (34.20%), 231,403 Germans (8.71%), 1,464,211 Romanians (55.08%), 2341 Slovaks (0.09%), 51,201 others (1.93%), total: 2.658.159. M. Stat. Közlemények. Új sorozat Vol. 64 (Budapest, 1920); Magyar Országos Levéltár (Budapest), F 551 apud. Zoltán Szász, 'Economy and Society in the Era of Capitalist Transformation,' in *History of Transylvania*, III, ed. Béla Köpeczi (New York: Columbia University Press, 2002), 559.

4. For a detailed picture of this party activity, see Keith Hitchins, *A Nation Affirmed: The Romanian National Movement in Transylvania 1860/1914* (Bucharest: The Encyclopedic Publishing House, 1999).

5. This political mutation can be understood if we consider Oscar Jászi's definitions according to which nation means 'a fully mature nationality which has reached its complete independence as a state building organism', while nationality represents 'a struggling national entity which under the sway of a dominant nation has not yet reached its complete independence'. Oscar Jászi, *The Dissolution of the Habsburg Monarchy* (Chicago: The University of Chicago Press, 1929), 26; Vaida's speech in *1918 la români. Desăvârșirea unității național-statale a poporului român. Documente externe 1916-1918*, ed. Augustin Deac, et al., VII (București: Editura Ştiinţifică şi Enciclopedică, 1989), 40.

6. András Siklós, Revolution in *Hungary and the Dissolution of the Multinational State 1918* (Budapest: Akadémiai Kiadó, 1988), 10.

7. Nicolae Bocşan, *Marele Război în memoria bănăţeană 1914-1919* (Cluj-Napoca: Presa Universitară Clujeană, 2012), 81.

8. Vasile Ciobanu, *Germanii din România în anii 1918-1919* (Sibiu: Honterus, 2013), 22-48.

9. In the autumn of 1916, German and Austro-Hungarian troops occupied two thirds of Romania's territory, including the capital, Bucharest; the Romanian authorities were forced to retreat to the north of the country, in Iaşi.

10. Robert Gerwarth, John Horne, *War in Peace: Paramilitary Violence in Europe after the Great War* (Oxford Scholarship Online, 2013). <http://www.oxfordscholarship.com/view/10.1093/acprof:oso/9780199654918.001.0001/acprof-9780199654918> (accessed 15 April 2019).

11. For an inventory of all these revolutionary manifestations see the National Archives of Romania, Bucharest, *Fond Consiliul Dirigent* (Directory Council) and the National Archives of Cluj-Napoca, *Fond Gărzile Naţionale* (National Guards), 1918.

12. Siklós, *Revolution in Hungary*, 110.

13. 1918 la români..., vol. VII, 540.

14. Peter Weber, *De la Kolozsvár la Cluj. Ultimul episod al regimului ungar în „capitala" transilvană*, <http://altera.adatbank.transindex.ro/pdf/11/008.pdf> (accessed 15 April 2019).

15. Siklós, *Revolution in Hungary*, 143.

16. Paul Şeulean, *Comunitatea germană din Cluj, Sibiu şi Timişoara 1918-1939: abordare comparativă*, I (Cluj-Napoca: Argonaut, 2012), 65-66.

17. Ivan T. Berend, Gyorgy Ranki, 'The Economic Problems of the Danube Region After the Breakup of the Austro-Hungarian Monarchy,' in *War and Society in East Central Europe*, eds. Bela Kiraly, Peter Pastor and Ivan Sanders, VI (New York: Columbia University Press, 1982), 89-106.

18. Szász, *History of Transylvania*, 764.

19. Szele Áron, *Nationalism, National Movements and the Dissolution of the Austro-Hungarian Monarchy. Case-Study: the Activity and Discourse of the Romanian National Party of Transylvania 1900-1914* (Budapest: Central European University, 2008), 5.

20. István I. Mócsy, *The Effects of World War I. The Uprooted: Hungarian Refugees and their Impact on Hungary's Domestic Politics 1918-1921* (New York: Columbia University Press, 1983), 8.

21. William Batkay, 'Trianon: Cause or Effect-Hungarian Domestic Politics in the 1920's,' in *War and Society in East Central Europe*, eds. by Bela Kiraly, Peter Pastor, Ivan Sanders, VI (New York: Columbia University Press, 1982), 509-528.

22. Mócsy, *The Effects of World War I*, 8.

23. For a contextualization of the political and military commitments Hungary had to take at the end of 1918 and for the international dialogue with the Entente leaders see Peter Pastor, *Hungary Between Wilson and Lenin: The Hungarian Revolution of 1918-1919 and the Big Three* (New York: Columbia University Press, 1976), Mária Ormos, From Padua to the Trianon 1918-1920 (Budapest: Akadémiai Kiadó, 1990).

24. Mócsy, *The Effects of World War I*, 8.

25. Charles Tilly, *From Mobilization to Revolution* (New York: McGraw-Hill, 1978).

26. Alexander Kojève, *Noţiunea de autoritate* (The Notion of Authority) (Cluj-Napoca: Tact, 2012), 35.

New Beginnings in Romanian Political Life after the First World War

Marcela Sălăgean

At the beginning of the 20th century, the evolution of Romanian political life was influenced by several factors, the most important being the First World War, the Union of Transylvania, Bukovina and Bessarabia with the Romanian Kingdom, and the reforms adopted during and immediately following the war. These events all had important consequences for Romanian society, which had to face new challenges

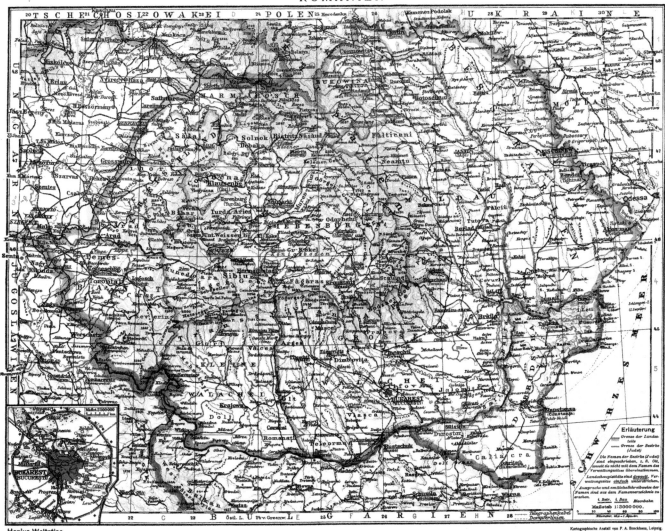

Fig. 1: Map of 'Greater Romania' with counties and historical regions, 1918.

that altered the old social and political structures, giving birth to a very different Romania from the one that had existed before the outbreak of the war.[1]

It is well known that 'Greater Romania' had already become a physical reality before the Peace Treaty was signed, and one of the priorities the authorities faced was integrating the new territories, a process that often proved difficult even for the most experienced leaders. In fact, the need for national unity had a much more realistic basis than the euphoria generated by the idea of a Greater Romania. And the complexity of the problems to be solved was evident to all those involved in the process of integrating the united provinces, even before the administrative and institutional consolidation of the new state, which was to be multi-ethnic and multi-confessional, with more complex economic, political, social, and cultural structures than those of the Old Romanian Kingdom.[2]

The integration's success was all the more important as the accomplishment or failure of that process would impact the country's status and evolution, both domestically and internationally. Even though, as a whole, the administrative and legislative unification extended further than was originally thought, ending only at the end of the Second World War, the process was complex, engaging politicians as well as academics, lawyers, economists, and civil servants in debates and projects.[3] They all agreed that Romania was starting to resemble Western Europe, but they could not decide on the paths that the country had to follow. Thus, several groups began to emerge, most significant among these being the Europeanists, the traditionalists, the agrarians, and the Marxists. For example, the Europeanists regarded Romania as a part of 'Europe', considering that the country had no choice but to follow the path of economic and social development taken by the urbanised and industri-

Fig. 2: Iuliu Hossu, Greek Catholic Bishop of Gherla, celebrates with dignitaries the declaration of unification of Transylvania, Bessarabia, and Bukovina with the Romanian Kingdom, Alba Iulia (Transylvania), 1 December 1918.

alised West. The promoters of this trend argued that the decisive role in Romania's development was played by the indigenous bourgeoisie. Europeanism's opponents were the traditionalists. Lacking receptivity to any Western influences, they were looking for patterns of development in local traditions, in the heritage of the rural Romanian world and the Orthodox religion, and even in various influences coming from the Orient. They rejected the city, which they considered too abstract, and modern industry, which they found too rational, too inappropriate for the Romanians, a contemplative people, not accustomed to capitalist discipline.[4]

In the end, the Europeanists' view triumphed: the country needed to develop and modernise following the model of developed European countries. Intense legislative activity therefore began in 1918, with reforms promulgated by the government in Bucharest extended automatically throughout Greater Romania, although the local realities of the united provinces had to be taken into account. Programmes were adopted which stipulated the need for a new constitution, administrative and legislative unification, economic stability, and fundamental rights and freedoms for the citizens. Policymakers therefore developed several laws to strengthen the democratic regime: laws regarding freedom of the press, and freedom of association and assembly; laws regarding agricultural reform, education reform, and economic and administrative reforms; laws regarding rights for workers and ethnic minorities, freedoms for all religions and confessional groups recognised by the state, and many others. These were modern provisions that, once enacted alongside the Constitution adopted in 1923, formed the basis for the country's development and modernisation.[5]

Nevertheless, legislative activity that would bring the country progress in as many fields as possible could not exist in Romania without a political system able to reflect and find itself in the realities of the country following 1918. The formation of Greater Romania inevitably reshaped the political scene, and it was clear, as early as the beginning of 1919, that political live would be quite different from what it had been in the country before the war. The Union gave rise to new political parties and traditions, and electoral reform opened participation in politics up to a much greater number of citizens than ever be-

Fig. 3: Alexandru Vaida Voevod, Prime Minister of Romania 1919-1920, 1932, and 1933.

fore.[6] Only then did the great mass of peasants and city workers, who became politically active with the right to vote, first come to the attention of political parties and leaders, forcing them to think of new provisions in their programmes, new strategies and political messages, in order to obtain the vote of the electoral body, of whom 80% were now peasants.

The first elections based on the universal vote in the history of Greater Romania took place in November 1919. No political party gained the majority. The National Liberal Party gained 103 representative the Peasant Party 61 representatives, the Romanian National Party of Transylvania won 169 representatives, the Peasant Party of Bessarabia 72 representatives, the Democratic Union Party of Bucovina 27 representatives and the Socialist Party 7 representatives. There were also 22 representatives of ethnic minorities.[7] Under these circumstances, a 'parliamentary bloc' was established, formed mainly from the political parties of the united provinces. The parliamentary bloc government was chaired by Alexandru Vaida Voevod (1872-1950), leader of the Transylvanian Romanians, appointed prime minister on 1 December 1919.

The elections in November 1919 represented a failure for the old politicians, and it became obvious that, after 1918, the political parties in the Old Romanian Kingdom had to change their entire political strategy.[8]

An analysis of Romania's interwar political life reveals a vital factor: although the parties established before the First World War continued to operate, new ones were beginning to gain power, some coming from the united provinces, some emerging as a result of new, post-war ideological currents and trends. First, the parties in the Old Romanian Kingdom had to win supporters in the united territories. In turn, if they wanted to be actors and decision-makers in the country's politics, regional parties also needed elec-

toral support across the country. There was a political expansion in both directions, from the Old Romanian Kingdom to the united territories and vice versa, and at least for a while they retained strong influence on their initial mass of voters. The latter phenomenon was most visible during the parliamentary elections in the autumn of 1919, especially in Transylvania where, in the years immediately following the Union, the Romanian National Party (Partidul Național Român) and especially its leading personalities continued to enjoy great popularity among their electorate, although the liberal presence was increasingly evident, mainly in urban settings. But, despite the fact that it continued to uphold the democratic principles then promoted at the European level, the Romanian National Party seems to have ended with Transylvania's Union with the Romanian Kingdom. Like the other parties, the Romanian National Party also faced a lack of popularity in other regions of the country. In order to gain votes across the country, the Transylvanians' party needed to fuse with a popular party from the Old Kingdom.[9] After several negotiations and a first short-lived fusion with the Romanian Nationalist Party (Partidul Naționalist-Democrat) headed by Nicolae Iorga (1871-1940), Iuliu Maniu (1873-1953) turned his attention to the Peasant Party (Partidul Țărănesc), a party that appeared on the political scene in the Old Romanian Kingdom in 1918, created by a group of teachers, priests and peasants led by Ion Mihalache (1882-1963), and which represented the interests of the rural elites and the small towns of South-Eastern Romania. The Romanian National Party and the Peasant Party merged in October 1926, resulting in the emergence of the country's second largest political party, the National Peasant Party (Partidul Național Țărănesc). This party's programme included guaranteeing citizens' rights and freedoms, administrative reform based on decentralisation and local autonomy, removing justice from political influences, granting loans to peasants, developing education, stabilising the monetary situation, recognising rights for workers, and accepting foreign capital.[10] At the same time, it was the party that, throughout the interwar period, was the most important opposition to the National Liberal Party (Partidul Național Liberal).

The National Liberal Party, meanwhile, represented Romania's greatest political power in the in-

Fig. 4: Iuliu Maniu, head of Transylvania's Directory Council from 2 December 1918.

terwar period and ruled the political scene in the first interwar decade. After a short period of organisation and expansion in the newly annexed territories, the liberals ruled between 1922 and 1927, a period that entered Romania's contemporary history as the era of the greatest liberal successes.[11] The dominant element within the National Liberal Party was the financial elite grouped around the Romanian Bank, headed by the Brătianu family. However, having to take into account the new realities created after 1918, the liberal leaders developed a political programme that required among other things the adoption of a new constitution, administrative and legislative unification, the stabilisation of the economy, and the equality of rights for all citizens. In order to expand its organisation into the united provinces, the National Liberal Party merged with the Peasant Party of Bessarabia (Partidul Țărănesc din Basarabia) and the Democratic Union Party of Bucovina (Partidul Democrat al Unirii).[12] In Transylvania, the liberals drew on the collaboration of Romanian, Hungarian and even German elites from the economic, and especially the banking, sector. It was already known that some Transylvanian banking institutions had merged with similar institutions run by elites of the National Liberal Party, and Romanian researchers are beginning to explore this phenomenon. The economic doctrine through which the National Liberal Party promoted its ideology was embodied in its 'by ourselves' politics – namely, the state had to intervene in the economy to protect the indigenous bourgeoisie. In fact, the party, through the political measures it had adopted, wanted to support and promote domestic capital.

Besides the National Liberal Party and the National Peasant Party, there were a number of other political parties in interwar Romania, representing both different political orientations and different ethnic minorities. Yet of the many parties during this time, except for the two major parties analysed above, only a few had come to power, such as the People's Party (Partidul Poporului) and the Nationalist Democratic Party.[13] For example, the success enjoyed by the People's Party, led by General Alexandru Averescu (1859-1938), was due to the 'Averescu myth',[14] which appeared on the grounds of dissatisfaction with the liberals who, in the early years of the interwar period, were blamed for all the difficulties the country was going through. Under these circum-

Fig. 5: Alexandru Averescu, army general and Prime Minister of Romania 1918, 1919-1921, and 1926-1927.

stances, a large part of the electorate, especially of the Old Romanian Kingdom, put their hopes in the political formation created by General Alexandru Averescu, whose popularity was growing very high. However, the People's Party was not in government for long, failing to cope with competition from the National Liberal Party and, later, the National Peasant Party. As for the other party mentioned, the Democratic Nationalist Party, whose political agenda focused primarily on the development of education, it found itself in the elite of the Romanian political scene, mainly due to the prestige of its leader, the historian Nicolae Iorga.

The political organisations of the ethnic minorities, including the Hungarian Union (Uniunea Maghiară/Magyar Szövetség), the Hungarian People's Party (Partidul Popular Maghiar/Magyar Néppárt), the Hungarian National Party (Partidul Național Maghiar/Magyar Nemzeti Párt)[15], the German National Party (Deutsche Nationalpartei), the German People's Party (Deutsche Volkspartei), the Union of Germans in Romania (Union der Deutschen in Rumänien), the Swabian People's Party (Schwä-

Fig. 6: Nicolae Iorga, historian, politician and poet, President of the Deputies' Assembly and Senate of Romania.

bische Volkspartei), the Romanian Jewish Union (Uniunea Evreilor Români), the Jewish Party (Partidul Evreiesc),[16] were also active in interwar political life with representatives in Parliament and local administrative structures in Romania and they contributed to the diversification of political life at that time. In fact, the history of the ethnic minorities' parties in interwar Romania was not just political, but also socio-economic and cultural.

At the same time, external influences brought left-wing (such as the Social Democratic Party/Partidul Social-Democrat) and extreme left-wing parties (such as the Romanian Communist Party/Partidul Comunist Român), as well as right-wing (such as the National Christian Party/Partidul Național Creștin) and extreme right-wing parties (such as the Legion of the Archangel Michael/Legiunea Arhanghelului Mihail, known after 1930 as the Iron Guard/Garda de fier), to the Romanian political scene, parties that

during the interwar period elections did not succeed in winning the necessary number of votes to accede to power.[17] Only the National Christian Party led by the Transylvanian Octavian Goga (1881-1938) came to power for a few weeks, thanks to King Carol II's (1893-1953) intervention, when no political party gained a majority in the elections of late 1937. But even in that case, it was not genuinely a National Christian government, because the key posts (Internal Affairs, Justice, Foreign Affairs) were entrusted to non-party individuals. The Goga government did not represent a party or coalition of parties, but was instead solely the expression of the royal will. By call-

Fig. 7: Book cover of *History of Romanians in Faces and Icons* (*Istoria Romînilor în Chipuri și Icoane*) by Nicolae Iorga, first published 1905.

ing Octavian Goga to power, King Carol II achieved several goals. First, he gave satisfaction to the right-wing current, thus avoiding the rule of the extreme right as represented by the Legionnaires. Secondly, he removed other political opponents, especially the National Peasants of Iuliu Maniu.

As far as the voters' options were concerned, they were extremely contradictory, because a large number of citizens lacked any political culture. They voted according to a certain state of mind, generated by the hopes of a providential man who would hold the perpetrators 'accountable'. Most often, citizens voted because the vote was mandatory and they wanted to avoid a possible fine. Sometimes, voters put their stamp on the front page – which always featured the list of the ruling party. This is why spectacular results have been recorded, none of which could be considered an expression of the electorate's political voice. For example, the National Liberal Party obtained 6.8% of the votes in 1920, then 60.3% in 1922, dropped to 7.3% in 1926 and climbed to 61.7% in 1927. The People's Party registered 42.4% in 1920, dropped to 6.5% in 1922, rose to 52% in 1926, then failed to reach the electoral threshold in 1927, as it only gained 1.9%. In turn, the National Peasant Party won 32.1% of the votes in 1927, climbed to 77.7% in 1923, to drop to 15% in 1931.[18]

On the whole, the interwar Romanian political system underwent a series of transformations, including: 1) the dissolution of the conservative parties; 2) the consolidation of the National Liberal Party; 3) the establishment of new parties and their imposition on political life; 4) the integration within the Romanian state of the regional parties that led the movements for the unification of Transylvania, Bucovina and Bessarabia with Romania; 5) the founding of the Peasant National Party; 6) the appearance and affirmation of parties belonging to ethnic minorities; 7) the emergence of extremist organisations. The dynamics of the political parties during the interwar period was as follows: a) between 1918 and 1921, there was a maximum proliferation of political parties; b) between 1922 and 1926, a fusion trend with a bipolar result: the National Liberal Party and the National Peasant Party; c) between 1927 and 1932, disagreements registered in almost all parties and primarily in the governing ones; d) between 1933 and 1937, the appearance of dissident groups inside

Fig. 8: Romanian King Carol II, regency 1930-1940.

the democratic parties; e) in 1938, the formation of a single party, the National Renaissance Front (only members of this party were able to hold leading positions in the central and in local administrations).[19]

An analysis of the political system and the interwar political dynamics reveals that eleven governments operated during the first decade of the interwar period. Meanwhile, the 1930s characterised by the alternation in power of National Liberals and National Peasants. Government changes were followed by the dissolution of the Parliament only when the new cabinet did not belong to the same party.

The European political evolution, and especially the coming to power of extremist regimes in the middle of the interwar period, could not spare Romanian domestic political life. Thus, despite the efforts made to consolidate the new-born state, the domestic political regime began to slip to the right in the second half of the 1930s, as in many other parts of Europe, and the Romanian inter-war democratic regime reached its end in the wake of the outbreak of the

Second World War. But despite the problems that arose during these twenty years, whether they came to power, or had representatives in Parliament and in the local structures, or fought for a longer or shorter period of time, all political parties in interwar Romania operated in a clearly defined legislative framework, guaranteed by the fundamental state law.

Although the political life of Greater Romania lasted for only two decades, and although it included both smaller and larger errors, it irreversibly put its mark on the administrative, economic, social, and cultural development not only of that period, but of the ones that followed. Progress made in adopting numerous legislative provisions for the modernisation and development of the country, as well as the names and reputations of some political parties and leaders, has remained in the collective memory of the Romanians, despite the regime and the political system that Romania experienced in following decades. Even today, different structures and components of Romanian society will appeal with some nostalgia to the interwar period's models and examples of success.

Endnotes

1. Vlad Georgescu, *Istoria românilor. De la origini pînă în zilele noastre* (București: Editura Humanitas, 1992), 204.

2. Stephen Fischer-Galati, *România în secolul al XX-lea* (Iași: Institutul European, 1998), 45.

3. Marcela Sălăgean, *Introducere în istoria contemporană a României* (Cluj-Napoca: Presa Universitară Clujeană, 2013), 10-21. See also Marcela Sălăgean, 'Romania between 1919 and 1947,' in *History of Romania. Compendium*, eds. Ioan Aurel Pop and Ioan Bolovan (Cluj-Napoca: Institutul Cultural Român, 2006), 583-615, here 586.,

4. For further details, see Keith Hitchins, *România 1866-1947* (București: Editura Humanitas, 1994), 319-359.

5. Sălăgean, *Introducere*, 10-20.

6. Hitchins, *România 1866-1947*, 409. See also: Zigu Ornea, *Tradiționalism și modernitate în deceniul al treilea*, (București: Editura Eminescu, 1980).

7. Aurel Constantin Soare, Ioan Scurtu and Daiana Fotescu, 'Dinamica structurilor politice,' in *Structuri politice în Europa Centrală și de Est (1918-2001)*, vol. I, ed. Ioan Scurtu (București: Editura Fundației Culturale Române, 2003), 49-88, here 79.

8. Ioan Scurtu and Gheorghe Buzatu, *Istoria Românilor în secolul XX (1918-1948)* (București: Editura Paideia, 1999), 122-123.

9. Marcela Sălăgean, 'De la România Mare la România Unită. Procesul integrării: teritorii, populație, infrastructură, economie,' in *Arhivele Totalitarismului*, Anul XXVI, no.100-101, 3-4 (2018), (București: Institutul Național pentru studiul totalitarismului, 2018), 62-77, here 72.

10. Ioan Scurtu, *Istoria contemporană a României 1918–2001* (București: Editura Fundației România de Mâine, 2002), 102.

11. Georgescu, *Istoria Românilor*, 205.

12. Sălăgean, *Introducere*, 22.

13. Georgescu, *Istoria Românilor*, 206.

14. For more details, see: Constantin Argetoianu, *Memorii. Pentru cei de mâine. Amintiri din vremea celor de ieri*, vol. 6, 1919-1922 (București: Editura Machiavelli, 1996).

15. For further details, see Tóth Szilárd, 'De la passivism la activism politic – înființarea Partidului Maghiar,' in *Multiculturalism în Transilvania după Conferința de Pace de la Paris*, coord. Marina Trufan, Marius Mureșan, (Cluj-Napoca: Editura Casa Cărții de Știință, 2019), 124-148,

16. Sălăgean, *Introducere*, 21-30.

17. Ibid.

18. Scurtu and Buzatu, *Istoria Românilor*, 108.

19. Ibid., 242-249.

The Vulnerability of a Small Post-Colonial State: Georgia's International Prospects in 1918

Beka Kobakidze

Just before the outbreak of the Great War, the idea of political independence was far from the mind of the Georgian political elite. In an era of Great Powers, international law left no room for self-determination and sovereignty for smaller nations. Moreover, the conquest of the weaker by the stronger was legal, and the practical protection provided by the United Nations (UN), the Organization for Security and Cooperation in Europe (OSCE) and other peacekeeping and monitoring missions did not yet exist. Located in the heart of the turbulent Caucasus region – wedged between the Ottoman and Russian Empires – Georgia could therefore hardly dream of independence. The Georgian political elites fluctuated between advocating for political autonomy and cultural self-governance in their nationalist claims.

The only way to secure long-lasting independence was to find a great power as a protector, but who would risk countering the Russians and the Ottomans in the distant region of the Caucasus? Unexpectedly, the Great War provided such an opportunity, as Germany aimed to stir up internal turmoil in Russia and force it to lay down arms. This would eventually allow Germany to concentrate its troops on its 'western frontier' against the Allies and drive their march all the way to India, thus menacing the British Orient. At the very beginning of the war, the German Foreign Office and the Supreme Army Command (*Oberste Heeresleitung*) sponsored national committees, such as those of the Baltic, Finnish, and Georgian people. These committees formed paramilitary groups, organised uprisings against the Russian Empire and recruited prisoners of war of Baltic, Finnish and Georgian origin. The German Empire was committed to granting Georgia independence after victory.[1] Nevertheless, the most popular Georgian Social Democratic Party stayed loyal to Russia and maintained a *defensist*

Fig. 1: German Military in Tiflis, Summer 1918.

position, hoping for a democratic transformation of Russia as well as the enhancement of national rights in the Caucasus. The pro-German Georgian Committee was comprised of Georgian rightists, who subsequently shaped the National Democratic Party. Yet the two parties made a deal that they would not go against each other and that in the end one of their sponsors was to be a victor; thus, they agreed that both were working in the national interest.[2]

The Russian Empire was unable to handle years of intense warfare. Following the abdication of Tsar Nicholas II (1868-1918) in February 1917, the German-sponsored Vladimir Lenin successfully overthrew of the provisional government in October 1917, and the Bolshevik party's dictatorship was subsequently inaugurated. The Soviets withdrew Russia from the war, abandoned the Caucasus frontier and – in accordance with the Brest-Litovsk Treaty of 3 March 1918 – handed the provinces of Batumi and Kars over to the Ottoman Empire.

The Bolsheviks' seizure of power triggered the political secession of Transcaucasia from Russia. Geor-

Fig. 2: Map of Georgia, March 1918.

gians, Armenians and Azerbaijanis did not recognise the Soviet Government and first declared the Transcaucasian Commissariat and then the Transcaucasian Federative Republic. Within the framework of the aforementioned stillborn entities, Georgians and Armenians went to war against the Ottomans in order to defend their territories from conquest. As the military power of the opposing sides was dramatically unequal, Transcaucasia was in danger not only of losing the provinces of Batumi and Kars, but also of being completely conquered by the Ottomans. It was at this point that the political connections with the Germans, established by the Georgian Committee, were activated.

During the Great War, Germany was allied with the Ottoman Empire and could not afford to ignore Turkish interests. The Ottomans were primarily targeting Armenian territories in order to realise pan-Turkish ambitions and pave a way to their Azerbaijani kinsmen. The Germans, on the other hand, were interested in Georgian manganese mines, the Baku-Batumi railway and the Baku oil industry. Conse-

Fig. 3: Coat of Arms of the Democratic Republic of Georgia 1918-1921.

238

Fig. 4: First Georgian Foreign Minister, Social Democrat Akaki Chkhenkeli (sitting in the centre). Summer of 1918, Berlin. All members of his delegation, surrounding him in this photograph, were members of the Georgian Committee or other rightist Georgian politicians. They had been establishing ties with Imperial Germany since 1914 and were now helping the ruling Social Democratic Party to protect Georgian national interests in Berlin.

quently, they were least interested in Armenia. The German military attaché in Constantinople – General Otto von Lossow (1868-1938), who was mediating between the Transcaucasians and the Ottomans – advised Georgians that they would have to declare independence if they wished to secure German protection,[3] as the German Empire was unable to protect all of Transcaucasia.

Georgia's Declaration of Independence

And so Georgian independence was declared on 26 May 1918. Two days later, Georgia and Germany signed an agreement in the Georgian seaport of Poti that served as a *de facto* recognition of Georgian independence.[4] The treaty with the Ottoman Empire was signed on 4 June in Batumi through German mediation. With the treaty, Ottoman Empire recognised Georgia's independence. Although the Ottomans continued to occupy the Batumi region and the districts of Akhaltsikhe and Akhalkalaki, the rest of the country was spared from invasion,[5] and a narrow strip of Armenian land was left around Erevan. In August 1918, Germany negotiated another treaty with Soviet Russia, whose Article 13 reads as follows: 'Russia agrees to Germany's recognising Georgia as an independent State.'[6]

Germany provided security guarantees to Georgia, protecting it from both of its potentially aggressive neighbours. Moreover, Germany deployed up to 20,000 troops to the Caucasus for security provisions, began investing in the Georgian economy and assisted in the state-building process. The Germans acted cautiously and planned everything step by step. First, they secured legal guarantees of Georgian independence from its neighbours; second, they deployed troops to ensure stability; and finally, they commenced negotiations with the Georgian delegation,

Fig. 5: Map of Georgia, June 1918.

headed by the foreign minister Akaki Chkhenkeli (1874-1959), on the protectorate agreement and *de jure* recognition.[7]

Georgia's carefully designed security architecture collapsed like a house of cards after the German defeat in November 1918. The fate of the newly born country now lay in the hands of the victors. In December 1917, after the Bolshevik coup, France and Britain had summoned a conference in Paris. They had to discuss how to fill the gaps created by the Russian abandonment of the Allied cause. On 23 December, they reached an agreement that the Caucasus would fall under British responsibility, while Ukraine, Crimea, and Bessarabia would go to France.[8]

During the war, the Allies were too busy fighting on other frontiers to implement the agreement, but after the Armistice of Mudros with the Ottomans and the Armistice of Compiègne with the Germans, in December 1918, the British deployed up to 20,000 troops to the Caucasus.[9] Great Britain was to some extent unprepared

and even unqualified for the mission, because the Caucasus had been an internal region of Russia just a year before – the British had never seen the need to formulate a policy or study the region. Discussions on policy-making commenced very hastily at the end of October.

By September 1918, the Georgians too had sensed that the Great War would end unfavourably. The diplomatic envoy Zurab Avalishvili (1876-1944) departed from Berlin to Norway in secrecy to meet with the Allied (English, French, Italian, US) ambassadors, behind the Germans' backs, and to hand over memoranda explaining that the pro-German foreign policy was not a Georgian choice, but rather a necessity for survival. In reality, the memoranda claimed, Georgia wished to have close and good relations with the Allies.[10] Moreover, after the end of the war, a pro-German foreign minister Akaki Chkhenkeli was dismissed and advised to keep a very low profile. All other pro-German diplomatic envoys were replaced simultaneously.[11]

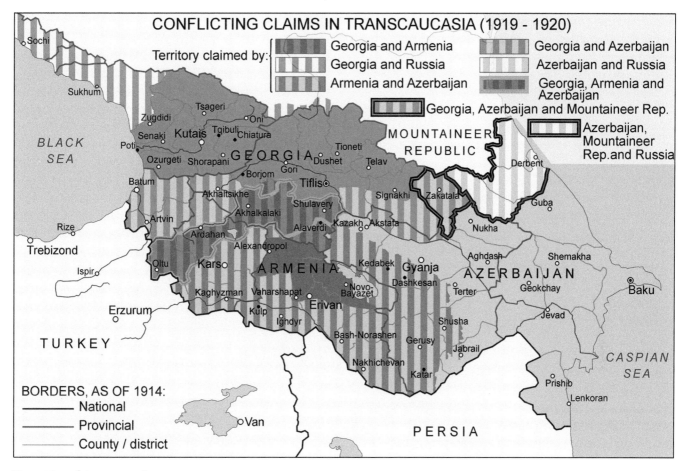

Fig. 6: Map of Transcaucasia 1919-1920.

Regional Challenges

Georgia faced not only external threats but also regional challenges. Before 1918, the Caucasus had been placed under the Tsarist administration and enjoyed a unified economy. If the local population suffered from the national suppression, that suppression stemmed from Russia. Since the Russian 'umbrella' was now gone, the Georgians, Armenians and Azerbaijanis had to share and divide the imperial economic legacy and political power as well as draw boundaries between the newly born states. These were extremely difficult tasks to deal with amicably. With the exception of the Kutaisi governorates (*guberniia*), Transcaucasia was all but devoid of ethnically homogenous territorial units. Moreover, the Armenian political, cultural and economic elites were coming from Tiflis and the city was now set to become the capital of an independent Georgia. Parts of

the Tiflis *guberniia* such as the districts of Akhalkalaki and Lori were overwhelmingly populated by Armenians, although administratively, economically and, as the Georgians claimed, historically they were indisputably a part of Georgia. In the spring of 1918, when Russia deserted the Caucasus and the Ottoman offensive was marching towards Erevan, Georgia seemed to be Armenia's only ally in opposing the foreign invasion. When the Germans threw a 'life belt' to Georgia, the latter seceded from the Transcaucasian Federation, thus upsetting the Armenians.

After the end of the Great War, bitter memories and claims between the two republics came to the surface. In November 1918, Armenia was no longer an unprotected martyr country, whose only hope was Georgia. In July, the French Prime Minister Georges Clemenceau (1841-1929) wrote to the head of Armenian delegation in Europe Boghos Nubar Pasha (1851-1930):

I am happy to confirm to you that the government of the Republic [of France], like that of Great Britain, has not ceased to place the Armenian nation among those peoples whose fate the Allies intend to settle according to the supreme laws of humanity and justice.[12]

The British Prime Minister, David Lloyd George (1863-1945), noted in his memoirs:

From the moment war was declared, there was not a British statesman of any party who did not have in mind that if we succeed in defeating this inhuman [Ottoman] Empire, one essential condition of the peace we should impose was the redemption of the Armenian valleys forever from the bloody misrule with which they have been stained by the infamies of the Turk.[13]

During the war, the Allies were too far away to implement their Armenophile plans, but at the end of 1918 they were in the Caucasus. In the United States, the Armenophile movement reached an extreme point: in December 1918, the Senate adopted a resolution supporting an Armenia stretching between three seas, the Mediterranean, Black, and Caspian Sea.[14]

Armenia thought it was time to join the Russian and Ottoman controlled territories of Armenia into a united independent country. Moreover, Armenians now considered Georgia a rival rather than an ally, and judged it the right time to take the territories of Lori and Akhalkalaki and exact revenge for the past 'misconduct'. These premature judgements spurred Armenia to initiate an ill-advised war against Georgia in December 1918. Its main goal was the occupation of Lori and Akhalkalaki, but some hot-headed nationalists also targeted Tiflis. The war did not produce a victor, as British troops quickly arrived in the Caucasus and demanded an armistice from both parties. This war left wounds that would remain unhealed for years to come in terms of disputed territories, undivided economic assets and so on.[15]

In a short interim period between the end of the First World War and the war with Armenia, on 21 November the Georgian government compiled instructions for its diplomats, advising Georgia to support the Armenian claims towards the Ottoman Empire to ensure that the bulk of the Armenian policy would be focused on the Turkish territories, thus relieving Georgia. Furthermore, it would have been much more beneficial for Georgia to be paired with Armenia than with Azerbaijan, as the former was on favourable terms with the Allies.[16] Nevertheless, the plan proved to be short-lived, and Georgia was forced to make a deal with Azerbaijan. This decision was instigated for a number of reasons. First, both countries had an immediate border with Russia, the main threat; Georgia and Azerbaijan were to be responsible for blocking the Russian drive over the Caucasus mountain range, while Armenia was menaced by Turkey. Second, the Baku-Batumi oil pipeline and the railway line made Georgia and Azerbaijan economically dependent on each other, making friendship the only choice. Neither Georgia nor Azerbaijan needed Armenia for transit purposes or other economic reasons. Third, both countries were former allies of the Allied enemies: Georgia had possessed a strategic partnership with defeated Germany and Azerbaijan with the defeated Ottoman Empire. The close ties between Georgia and Azerbaijan and their unification in the same political, economic, and security packages were no mere coincidence of circumstance, but an international standpoint. Great Britain's foreign secretary Lord George Curzon (1859-1925) was a champion of Caucasian independence and wrote the following in a memorandum to the Cabinet:

[Azerbaijan] has no more moral claim to independence than have the inhabitants of the Persian provinces of Ghilan and Azerbaijan. At the same time it is very difficult, if not impossible, to treat Georgia in one way and Azerbaijan in another. If the Russians are allowed to cross the Caucasus range and occupy Azerbaijan at one end of the Batoum-Baku railway, the liberties of Georgia can never be secure.[17]

The Allies succumbed to wishful thinking in their initial euphoria, viewing their victory as a kind of magic wand that would make all their commands and wishes easily come true across the world. When Lord Curzon told Prime Minister Lloyd George during a Cabinet meeting that Great Britain needed to pay some sort of price to get the Turks out of the Caucasus, the latter replied:

What it would be if we were so beaten that the German fleet was in the Thames, with garrisons at Greenwich and other parts of London; – the German Fleet in the 'pool' ready to bombard London. Would it then be worthwhile for us to bargain about distant colonies when the whole of our country was at Germany's mercy? If Admiral Calthrop[18] reached Constantinople, nothing else really mattered.[19]

The Allies and the Armenians alike were misled by this short-sighted perspective.

The Positions of Soviet Russia and Great Britain

The Bolsheviks were in power in Moscow and did not really care about the Allied plans. Even the 'White' General Anton Denikin (1872-1942), commander of the Volunteer Armies of South Russia and an Allied protégé, ignored the British ultimatum in the first half of 1919 while waging a civil war against the Bolsheviks. He first occupied the Black Sea towns of Sochi and Gagra, at that time administered by Georgia, and then moved to the North Caucasus and carried out his conquest of the mountainous Republic. Despite the fact that the Ottoman Sultan was in Allied captivity, in Eastern Anatolia Mustapha Kemal's insurgent movement was emerging and gaining success in the Turkish War of Independence. Both Mustapha Kemal and Lenin were leading anti-systemic wars, both were fighting to regain former imperial territories and were interested in expelling Allied troops from the Caucasus – and most importantly, both were heavily threatened and embargoed by the Allies. Therefore, probably for the first time in history, the rival states of Russia and Turkey were forced to unite in the face of the bigger threat posed by the Allied Powers and their protégés, the Transcaucasian Republics. Therefore, probably for the first time in history, the rival states of Russia and Turkey were forced to unite in the face of the bigger threat posed by the Allied Powers and their protégés, the Transcaucasian Republics.

As time passed, the victors of the Great War lost their illusions. They recognised that statements and moral encouragement did not suffice as security provisions for the Caucasian States; what was needed

Fig. 7: Second Georgian Foreign Minister Evgeni Gegechkori (1881-1954) (on the right) and British High Commissioner in Transcaucasia Oliver Wardrop (1864-1948), August 1919.

was substantial support with a long-lasting troop deployment, the supply of arms and munitions, and similar measures. The Allies were exhausted by four years of war, their economies and societies were in need of recovery – and the Caucasus was too peripheral an issue to warrant engaging in a distant war in a turbulent region. During the Eastern Committee meeting of 2 December 1918, the British foreign undersecretary Sir Robert Cecil stated:[20] 'I do not in the least contemplate that any European Power will be able to take possession of these Caucasus districts, nor do I think it at all desirable. They would be perfectly insane to do it. The Russians had 150,000 men there to hold it.'[21] Before their defeat, the Germans were interested in Baku oil and Georgian manganese, but the British owned 23% of the world's manganese supplies in India, and they obtained politically safer and cheaper Mesopotamian oilfields after the war. Gaining possession of the Caucasian natural resources would therefore hardly have been considered a cost-effective enterprise.

Once the German-designed security architecture had collapsed, it was clear that Georgia had to look for another great power as a protector, now among the victors. Although the British troops deployed on the ground seemed to be its best option, Britain was too busy in various quarters of the world, and liberal social reforms, electoral democracy, the Labour pacifist movement and most importantly four exhausting years of war had made the British coalition cabinet somewhat sceptical about the prospects of a new adventure. In addition, Georgia was a former ally of Germany and might have looked unreliable. To a certain extent, Georgia was lucky because it had two friends among the British policy makers. The first was a chairman of the Eastern Committee, foreign secretary from 1919 and a former viceroy of India, Lord George Curzon. He had travelled to Georgia several times during his youth and admired the Georgian people. As Lloyd George put it in his memoirs:

[Curzon] was mostly concerned about rescuing Georgia from the contamination of Bolshevism. He had a special affection for the Caucasus. He had paid a visit to that region some years before and had acquired great admiration for its gallant mountaineers. The thought of abandoning them to the despotism of Lenin and Trotsky filled him with horror, and he fought to the end for the retention of British forces in Georgia.[23]

Nevertheless, Curzon was guided by pragmatic policies: since he wanted to sign a protectorate agreement with Persia, he saw an independent Caucasus as the best buffer shield to a revived Russia.[24] The second man was Oliver Wardrop,[25] a former consul-general in Bolshevik Moscow who served as His Majesty's High Commissioner to Transcaucasia from 1919 to 1920; he was long connected to Georgia. A Georgian speaker, he admired Georgians and was an ardent supporter of their independence. In October 1918, Wardrop, then an employee of the Political Intelligence Department of the Foreign Office, drafted a favourable lengthy memorandum on Transcaucasia.[26] The Foreign Office elaborated several other documents on the basis of this document, and Lord Curzon finally submitted a fourteen-point draft resolution on Transcaucasia to the Eastern Committee. Curzon argued that '[of the Caucasian states] Georgia is the most advanced and has the strongest claims to early recognition'. The draft resolution treated Georgia's territorial claims favourably; most importantly, Curzon was asking for a British mandate over the Caucasus. This met with strong opposition from Arthur Balfour, Robert Cecil and Michael Montague, and Curzon's initiative failed as a result. The version

Fig. 8: Headquarters of British Military Intelligence in Tiflis, 1919.

of the memorandum that was finally adopted retained points favourable to Georgia, but the possibility of a mandate was dismissed.[27]

This resolution was transferred to the guidelines of the British Delegation to the Paris Peace Conference,[28] but could pretty words have an actual impact on policy without an effective mandate? Curzon therefore fought to retain the British troops in the Caucasus, clashing with the newly appointed war secretary Winston Churchill, who was an ardent supporter of a 'united and undivided Russia' with White Generals at its head.

The Paris Peace Conference of 1919-1920 brought together all great and minor political actors from various quarters of the world. It was the biggest diplomatic forum of history so far, in which a new world map and a new world order were to be drafted. Lloyd George, Balfour, Curzon, Churchill, Clemenceau, Stefan Pichon, President Woodrow Wilson, and the other leaders were making long-lasting decisions. Among many questions, they had to deal with one peripheral issue – the future of the Caucasus. The decision-makers considered their attitude towards Georgia in light of their policy dynamics towards Russia and the former Ottoman Empire.

The year 1918 was a turbulent and stressful one. Georgia had to clarify its relations with its regional neighbours Armenia and Azerbaijan without any involvement of the Russian Empire; it was forced to change three patrons and adjust its foreign vector three times, from Russia to Germany and from Germany to Great Britain. Nevertheless, at the start of the Paris Peace Conference everything was up in the air. Such was the vulnerability of a small post-colonial state.

Endnotes

1. See more details in: Wolfdieter Bihl, *Die Kaukasus-Politik der Mittelmächte*, vol. 1 (Wien–Köln–Graz: Böhlau, 1975); Lasha Bakradze, germanul-kartuli urtiertobebi pirveli msoflio omis dros (Tbilisi: Pegasi, 2010).

2. Noe Jordania, *chemi tsarsuli* (Tbilisi: Sarangi, 1990), 71-72; Revaz Gabashvili, *rats makhsovs* (What I remember) (Tbilisi: Gulani, 1992), 149-150.
   Jordania was a leader of the Georgian Social Democratic Party and prime minister of Georgia during the independence years (1918-1921). Gabashvili was one of the leaders of the National Democratic Party.

3. For more on this topic, see: *Dokumenti i materiali po vneshnei politiki zakavkazya i gruzii* (Tiflis: 1919); Baron Friedrich von Kressenstein, *chemi misia kavkasiashi* (Kutaisi: Motsameta, 2002). Von Kressenstein was a commander of the German troops in the Caucasus.

4. See the full text of the agreement in: Georgian National Historic Archives (GNHA) 1864/1/11.

5. See the full text of the treaty in: GNHA 1864/2/11 (in French); *dokumenti i materiali po vneshnei politiki zakavkazya i gruzii* (in Russian) (Tiflis: 1919), 343-366.

6. Papers Relating to the Foreign Relations of the United States (FRUS), *Russia 1918*, vol. 1, 602.

7. Werner Zurrer, *Kaukasien 1918-1921* (Düsseldorf: Droste Verlag, 1978), 79-110.

8. British Cabinet Papers (CAB) 28/3 I.C. 37, 23 December 1917.

9. For detailed maps of the British military deployment in the Caucasus, see: British War Office Papers (WO) 153/785 Persia and Caucasus, Situation Maps 1916-1920.

10. FRUS, Russia 1918, vol. 2, 639-642; Archives du Ministère des Affaires Étrangères de la France (AMAE), Europe, Russie, Caucase (Georgie) 1918-1919, vol. 10, 833 f.; GNHA 1864/2/71/1-23; Zurab Avalishvili, *sakartvelos damoukidebloba 1918-1921 tslebis saertashoriso politikashi* (Tbilisi: Mkhedari, 2011), 141-148; on this topic, see the report of the French ambassador Edmond Bapst to Foreign Minister Stefan Pichon in AMAE, Europe 1918-1940, URSS, Georgie 1918-1919, vol. 648, 4-5.

11. GNHA 1864/2/53/2-4; 1864/2/45/119.

12. *The Case of Armenia* (New York: 1919), 9.

13. David Lloyd George, *Memoirs of The Peace Conference*, vol. II, (New Haven: Yale University Press, 1939), 811-812.

14. Richard Hovannisian, *The Republic of Armenia*, vol. I (Los Angeles: University of California Press, 1971), 261.

15. See the Armenian and Georgian interpretations of this war in: Richard Hovannisian, *The Republic of Armenia*, vol. I (Los Angeles: 1971); Archil Chachkhiani, *dashnakta natsionalistur-ekspansionisturi ideologia da somkhet-sakartvelos omi 1918-1919 tslebshi* (Tbilisi: Aradani, 2007).

16. GCHA 1861/4/3/5-6.

17. CAB 24/95 CP 336.

18. Admiral Calthorp (1864-1937) – Commander of the British Mediterranean Forces, the British High Commissioner in Constantinople.

19. CAB 23/14 Minutes of the War Cabinet Meeting, 26 October 1918.

20. This was a consulting body to the Cabinet dealing with issues relating to the 'British Orient', i.e. from the eastern shores of the Mediterranean to India, including the Caucasus. The Eastern Committee was created on 10 March 1918, and dissolved in January 1919. Lord Curzon was the chairman, and the other members included the chief of the imperial general staff Sir Henry Wilson, foreign secretary Arthur Balfour and state secretary for India Sir Edwin Montague.

21. CAB 27/24 Eastern Committee 40th Meeting, 2 December 1918 (annex).

22. See Curzon's early accounts on Georgia in: George Nathaniel Curzon, *Russia in Central Asia* (London: Longmans, Green & Co., 1889), 28-29; George Nathaniel Curzon, *Persia and The Persian Question*, vol. 1 (London: Frank Cass & Co., 1966), 61-69.

23. David Lloyd George, *Memoirs of The Peace Conference*, vol. II (New Haven: Yale University Press, 1939), 213-214.

24. See more on this topic in: Donald Ewalt, 'The Fight for Oil: Britain in Persia, 1919,' *History Today* 31, no. 9 (1981); John Fisher, 'On the Glacis of India: Lord Curzon and British Policy in The Caucasus, 1919,' *Diplomacy and Statecraft* 8, no. 2 (1997), 50-82.

25. See more on him in: *Sir Oliver Wardrop 150*, ed. Beka Kobakhidze (Tbilisi: Irida, 2015).

26. CAB 24/68 GT 6176 Memorandum on the Political Situation in Transcaucasia.

27. CAB 27/24 Eastern Committee 42nd Meeting, 9 December 1918 (annex).

28. CAB 29/2 P-84 Peace Conference: Memorandum on Armenia and Transcaucasia.

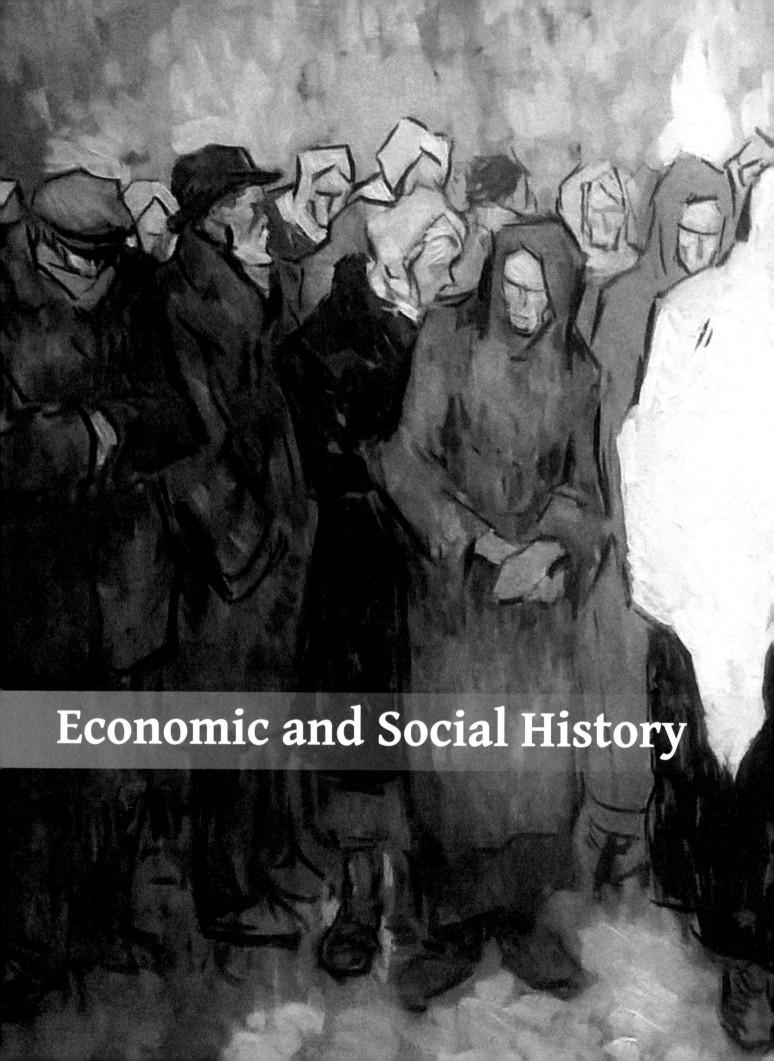

Economic and Social History

'Coada la pâine' (Queuing for Bread). Painted by Nicolae Tonitza, 1920.

East-Central Europe after the First World War: Fiscal and Monetary Policies in a Time of Economic Transformation

Maciej Górny, Włodzimierz Borodziej †

One of the most pressing problems facing emerging countries in East-Central Europe at the end of the First World War was control over the economic situation. Poverty, although in itself capable of destroying social ties, had a dangerous accomplice at the time: chaos in all spheres of economic life ranging from industrial production to monetary policy. In observing the challenge of a return to stable development, it is not difficult to see analogies between the problems facing the young countries of East-Central Europe and the much later reconstruction of the socio-economic foundations of order in this part of the world. In 1918, as in 1989, a process of systemic transformation took place.[1]

There is no equilibrium between the quantity of academic literature on these two 20th-century transformations: 1989 has attained its own subject sections in specialised bookstores and its 'successes' and 'pathologies' still remain a current subject of public debate, while 1918 revives every so often, mainly in discussions among economists searching for a historical verification of subsequent theories explaining interdependencies between such events as inflation, unemployment, or state intervention.[2] The quantitative differences are also reflected in the breadth of view. Work dedicated to economic transformations after 1918 is most frequently based on dry economic jargon and is limited to an analysis of numerical data. Literature on the transformation after 1989 addresses an entire range of social and cultural phenomena related to the systemic change, which are, significantly, still present in the memory of adult Europeans in the early 21st century.

A comparison of these two radical turns in the history of the continent has only recently appeared in historiography. Florian Kührer-Wielach and Sarah Lemmen, who contributed to it, propose that the transformation process be treated not as a single breakthrough, but rather as a complicated process of irreversible change encompassing all spheres of life: politics, culture, economics and social relations.[3] East-Central Europe, as they note, is the best region of the continent for such comparisons, because the events of 1989, as in 1918, impacted it to the fullest extent possible. Nearly everything changed almost overnight: authority, state borders, currency, and social hierarchy. Both of these transformations had their winners and losers, produced scandals and ideological disputes. In both cases galloping inflation and empty shelves also played a prominent role.

Four years of a wartime economy sharply intensified a traditional problem of East-Central Europe: chronic lack of capital. Each new country (as well as broken up Bulgaria and expanded Romania) had to face not only social disturbances, a meltdown of state revenues, but also a lack of trust in its own currency. It was not always easy to state which currency was official. There were many, particularly after the November 1918 breakthrough. Juliusz Zdanowski (1874-1937), economist and right-wing politician, gave the following assessment at the end of November 1918 of the state of the financial market in Lublin, several weeks earlier still the capital of an Austro-Hungarian governate:

> Three days ago, Roubles fell from 1.60 Marks to 1.30, today they went up to 1.48. Marks worth 178 Crowns yesterday today are 200. [...] It is characteristic that there was frequently a lack of small change. Now, payouts in banks in the thousands are only made with small change.[4]

Bringing monetary relations into order proved to be a difficult and lengthy process in which psychol-

Fig. 1: 50 Karbovanets banknote. Ukraine, 1918.

Fig. 2: 2 Hrywni banknote. Ukraine, 1918.

Fig. 3: 1 Leu banknote. Romania, 1919.

ogy played as great a role as economics. A quite common opinion among Belarusian and Ukrainian peasants was that the Tsarist Rouble deserved trust, not Polish or Soviet currency. Trust in the currency of a country that had already ceased to exist seemed justified at the time in the case of ore money. However,

a similar mechanism appeared even in the case of banknotes of already vanquished countries, thus, practically worthless paper. An interesting theory on this subject was developed by the American statistician, Eduard Dana Durand (1871-1960).[5] In 1920, as an envoy of the US government, he spent some time in Kiev as a witness to several changes of government. Durand was most interested in related changes of currency and, particularly, consumer behaviour. According to his observations, the Polish Mark, Tsarist Rouble, and Ukrainian Council Karbovanets, as well as Soviet Roubles, gained or lost popularity in obvious tandem with whoever ruled a city at the time. In all this chaos, hryvnia emitted by the government of Hetman Pavlo Skoropadski (1873-1945) nevertheless had the most stable position. Why? Durand speculated: 'Most likely the answer is the simple fact that peasants became accustomed to this currency, yet the thought arises that the reason could have indeed been the defeat of this government – unlike others, it was no longer capable of printing banknotes!'[6] Irrespective of whether the American's assumption is correct, it raises the most burning issue of the post-war monetary economy: the loss of consumer trust in currency.

It must be assumed that its poor state was first jointly caused by the warring powers. Romanian gold reserves to back the Lei were evacuated to Russia in the face of a German-Austro-Hungarian-Bulgarian counteroffensive, where they vanished. The Germans took charge of the remainder of the capital, thus leading the country in short time to economic ruin and rendering the Lei worthless. Neighbouring Bulgaria, although not occupied, but allied with the Reich, became an object of its ally's aggressive trade policy. Sharp debate on its trade policy continued in the Bulgarian Parliament during the war. Deputies from the left and centre recalled that opening the market to imports from Germany would destroy domestic industry, while the export of food and raw materials would impoverish the country.[7] In occupied lands of East-Central Europe, the Germans introduced their own paper currency: in *Ober Ost* this was the so-called Ostrubel (printed in Kaunas) and Polish Marks in the Polish Kingdom convertible into Reichsmarks at the rate of 1:1. Each brand of Berlin's policy in the region was based on the Reich currency, thus each each was doomed to inflation as swift as the loss in value of the Reich currency.[8]

Such an economic policy led to high prices. So long as relatively strong state structures controlled price movements, authorities mandated prices lower than dictated by the market by setting maximum prices for the most important products and countering "speculators." Although goods were relatively inexpensive, they disappeared from the market because they were not worth selling. During the course of the war the iron grip of the state nevertheless loosened and the black market reared its head by generally dictating prices much higher than official ones. The more legal this unofficial trade became, the faster did the wartime currencies lose their value. The dam burst with the defeat of Germany and Austro-Hungary. Galloping inflation became a scourge of the initial post-war years.

A challenge facing the governments of young East-Central European countries was a drastic reduction in the quantity of paper money in circulation and the attraction of capital to cover the remaining sum. This task was difficult to the extent that creating the structures of a new state required expenditure, while tax collection fell drastically. To add to this, the struggle to regain economic equilibrium also was to some extent dictated by how the country was perceived. The actions of local governments and even certain ministers were scrutinised by global markets. Certain countries and certain politicians grew in the eyes of foreign observers to inhabit the role of transformation leaders, but there was also no shortage of losers and tragic heroes: those whose ambitious plans to end chaos and restore public finances were dashed by various obstacles.

Property tax was a frequent means by which governments in the region sought material security for their actions. Most frequently this entailed a single duty on financial savings or other assets, such as land. Exemptions meant that the most affluent indeed incurred the effective cost of this tax. Czechoslovakia, Austria and Hungary decided to take this step. Results in each case nevertheless proved to be completely different. First, a look at undoubtedly the most successful of these experiments.

Successes can have many fathers and in the case of the economic transformation in the Czech lands the issue of paternity was never in doubt. Alois Rašín (1867-1923), the first Minister of Finance of the Republic, had already begun to prepare for the trans-

Fig. 4: Nicolae Titulescu (1882-1941), Romanian Minister of Finance from 1917 to 1927.

formation in the last months of the Habsburg monarchy. He had no doubt over its ultimate fall and focused his entire attention on preventing unnecessary disruptions. This right-wing politician had stated to his friend in a conversation in the spring of 1918: 'We have to know what to do in the first minute, five minutes, first half hour, hour, we have to know what to do on the first day, second [...] we have to be ready.'[9] Preparations included a plan to take over a part of the liabilities of the Austro-Hungarian Bank, withdrawal of some banknotes and stamping of those remaining in circulation, registration of citizen assets and a halt to capital flight. The stamping of Austro-Hungarian Crowns took place at the turn of February and March 1919. State borders were closed during this time and any outflow of capital was prevented. On this occasion, the Czechoslovak state seized one half of bank notes as a mandatory loan with interest of 1%. One half of deposits in banks throughout the country was also frozen. Through

Fig. 5: Alois Rašín, Czechoslovak Minister of Finance from 1922 to 1923. Memorial postcard printed after his assassination 1923.

the country as in relation to the Dollar.[11] The achievements of the transformation were marred, however, by the social cost: the higher cost of export dampened domestic production and increased unemployment. Rašín ultimately became a victim of the transformation. The reform was, from the start, was a thorn in the flesh of the Communist Party, which considered the Minister of Finance to be its primary enemy. In January 1923, he was assassinated, shot by a young Czech anarcho-communist who worked as an insurance company lawyer. Rašín's final intervention in the state of the Czechoslovak was posthumous, when his image appeared on 20 Crown banknotes.

The example of Czechoslovakia proved to be attractive, but nowhere else produced comparable effects. Further experiments with property tax undertaken by Austria and Hungary were late in relation to Prague. The unstable political situation, particularly in Hungary, and uncertainty over the terms that the victors would dictate to the losers of the First World War in Paris meant that a lengthy public discussion preceded the financial operation. As a result, holders of the largest deposits in Austrian and Hungarian banks had sufficient time to seek a safer haven for their money. However, this was not the end of the list of errors committed by the Austrians and Hungarians. Austrian terms of repayment proved to be very liberal, which encouraged bribery and undermined trust in the government's actions. Collection was also extended in time, which in conditions of high inflation immediately minimised the value of state revenues. Revenues did not serve any long-term purpose and completely drowned in the current budget deficit. Ultimately, in 1922 the idea of a single property tax was discarded in favour of a lower fixed fee. However, this was no longer a sovereign decision of the Austrian Finance Minister, but was forced upon the government by the League of Nations, which had to intervene in order to save the young republic from bankruptcy.[12]

In Hungary, taxation of greater wealth encountered somewhat different problems. First, two revolutions followed by a bloody counter-revolution slowed any sensible actions. Politicians in possession of printing presses used them without any restrictions, as a result of which Hungary became the last user of un-stamped Austro-Hungarian currency. Because of the "white terror", anything that recalled a

this action, the state was able to know the quantity of money on the market, while forestalling the outflow of capital. This knowledge served to plan and swiftly introduce two new progressive taxes: on assets exceeding 25,000 Crowns and on war profits. In seeking to gain the trust of taxpayers, Rašín secured statutory assurance that funds secured in this manner would not be used to cover the current budget deficit, but only to buy out Austro-Hungarian bonds and for certain state investments.[10] The Crown swiftly became a stable currency free of sudden fluctuations. That which distinguished Czechoslovakia from other countries in the region (with the exception of Finland) was equivalence between the value of money on the domestic and international markets. In contrast to the currencies of Bulgaria, Romania or Poland, the Crown cost the same in terms of goods acquired in

Fig. 6: 100 crowns banknote. Czechoslovakia, 1920, using a design by the Czech artist Alfons Mucha.

policy of nationalisation exposed its proponents to the charge of Bolshevik sympathies. Lóránt Hegedűs (1872-1943), Minister of Finance in 1920-1921, therefore preferred to speak of a fee to the state in exchange for profits that such tax assets produced during a time of war. Technically, the government took all assets as a "pledge," and returned them after paying a set fee (not only in cash, but also in kind). The secured funds were to repay Hungarian liabilities. Unfortunately, Hungary did not follow the path of Czechoslovakia and did not combine the introduction of a tax with the strangling of inflation. Extended repayments significantly reduced the value of revenues. However, the final blow to the Hegedűs plan came from large and small landowners, who jointly boycotted the tax. Lack of revenues from this single tax had a fatal effect on other actions aimed at rescuing the Hungarian economy. The remedial program was also hampered by uncertainty over the level of reparations that Hungary had to pay. The Minister of Finance attempted to stabilise the currency with classic economic methods, namely the cutting of expenses. His ambitious plan even envisioned an appreciation of the Crown. Despite the dedication and determination of Hegedűs, the Crown nevertheless once again started to lose value. The minister ultimately resigned

and, similarly as somewhat earlier in Austria, inflation chaos took hold in the country.[13]

Differences in the state of the economies in the three heirs of the Habsburg monarchy are best shown in statistical data. At the end of 1924, the sum of banknotes in circulation in Czechoslovakia was 78% of the equivalent sum in December 1920. In Hungary during this time, it was an astounding 1,300% and in Austria, 1,270%. The exchange rate of the Czechoslovak Crown on the US market grew between 1921 and 1924 from 1.24 cents to 3.02 cents, whereas the Hungarian Crown fell from 0.15 cents to 0.0013 cents and the Austrian from 0.038 to 0.0014.[14]

The poor effects of independent efforts at economic reconstruction in Austria and Hungary forced an intervention by the League of Nations. Financial aid and low-interest loans, however, entailed consent to interference by the powers in the internal policies of both these countries. Donors began by forcing their new subordinates to put aside the antidote they had hitherto used for all economic ailments and to halt the printing of banknotes. In Hungary, this effect was achieved through the creation of an independent emission bank, which at least in theory was to be secured against government interference. Although this decision forced upon Budapest by foreign coun-

Fig. 7: 500 mark banknote. Poland, January 1919.

tries was felt as a humiliation, real shame was yet to come. The League of Nations rendered its assistance dependent not only on a remedy of public finances, but also on the settlement of relations between Hungary and its neighbours. Premier István Bethlen was forced to take part in a series of meetings with representatives of countries against which Hungary had conducted a vigorous revisionist campaign (and which it had just fought). Talks with Edvard Beneš (1884-1948) could not take place in either Budapest or Prague. Not wanting to risk criticism and, perhaps, disturbances, both politicians preferred to meet on neutral ground in Geneva.

The experiences of Czechoslovakia, Hungary and Austria show the vital role of consumer and market trust in economic policy. It could have been earned by acting decisively, yet honestly, essentially as in the case of Alois Rašín. What mattered in unstable postwar conditions was the speed of change in order prevent the rapid flight of capital, as did certainty that public dues are not mere theft, but actually serve to re-

pay long-term war debts of countries. Ultimately, however, nearly all countries in East-Central Europe stabilised their currencies. Czechoslovakia and Finland did this best and Latvia, Estonia and Lithuania somewhat less spectacularly. Interventions by the League of Nations helped the Hungarians and the Austrians. During this time inflation was tamed in Yugoslavia, Romania and Bulgaria. Last in the region was Poland, a country where hyperinflation reigned in 1923.

The reasons for this delay at first glance appear to be obvious. Of all successor countries, Poland had the most problems to solve in seeking to unify its inheritance from the incompatible financial, transport and legal systems of three powers. The country was moreover fighting a war on nearly every border. The longest of these, with Soviet Russia, formally ended only in 1921; by this time soldiers in Czechoslovakia were only shooting when on manoeuvres. Inextricably bound to these campaigns was a general breakdown of custom, rampant banditry, and an overall disregard for law and order. Economic chaos was augmented by the late return of hundreds of thousands of forced wartime migrants. Attentive observers of Polish economic policy, however, saw many more fascinating problems. Durand, cited above, fully appreciated the exceptional nature of this inflation:

> Unlike Austria, whose curtailed resources are scarcely adequate to support its huge capital [...]; unlike Germany, Hungary and Bulgaria, which lie under the overhanging cloud of reparations; unlike Greece, which has just emerged from a war defeated, Poland has well-balanced and sufficient resources, is subject to no extraordinary financial burdens, and has been for fully three years at peace. The extraordinary expenses entailed by the war with Soviet Russia explain, even if they do not justify, the inflation of the first two years of Poland's independence. Since then, however, there has been little excuse for continuing vast paper money issues – perhaps the only excuse lies in the difficulty of gaining any foothold on the steep and glassy slope when once the sliding process had begun.[15]

In fact, the Polish case was specific. Minister Jerzy Michalski attempted to stabilise the Polish Mark on the basis of the country's own resources and higher taxes. The mere announcement of these steps produced effects: at the turn of 1921 and 1922 prices finally began to fall, even though the state was still printing Polish Marks at full steam. A stable exchange rate was maintained for several months, but immediately crashed when printing presses were reactivated (actually according to plan). A minor increase in the quantity of money in circulation, even if planned in advance, refuelled inflation; goods and services again began to swiftly increase in price. In taking part in this inflation game, Polish consumers showed a lack of trust in the intentions and competence of their own government.

The specific nature of the Polish transformation becomes even more evident when the classic question of its winners and losers is posed. The answer would not be difficult during a time of war: the costs of a war economy are primarily borne by hungry workers, those working and, ever more frequently, the unemployed. The beneficiaries are primarily more affluent peasants possessing the most sought after commodity, food. It was soon clear that this was not the case in Independent Poland. The growing political power of workers forced a series of concessions by employers and, above all, the state. Other social groups did not have such a strong bargaining posi-

Fig. 8: 1,000,000 mark banknote. Poland, August 1923.

tion, as reflected in a very original structure of prices and payroll regulations. Inflation connotes dwindling pay that desperate people seek to spend as quickly as possible, because tomorrow it could be worth less than the paper on which banknotes are printed. In Poland, meanwhile, payroll movement in many cases not only kept up with inflation, but even preceded it. Employment contracts frequently stipulated automatic pay hikes at the estimated cost of living index, which on the one hand secured employees against a loss in value of their remuneration, while on the other hand effectively hindering a limitation to the supply of money. Workers also benefited from a rent freeze. Inflation in a short period of time reduced the cost of renting living quarters from one-fifth to one-one hundredth of average worker family income. In combination with new social legislation (8-hour workday) and the announcement of a nationalisation programme, at least a part of industry seemed to offer reasonable perspectives for the poorer population. Naturally, property and landowners bore the brunt of decisions that improved living conditions for workers and peasants.

Polish exceptionalism did not rest on very high inflation, because most countries in the region suffered from it in post-war markets. The attention of observers, most frequently West European economists, rather focused on the adaptation of society to this abnormal situation. This was perhaps the most radical of the regional variants in dealing with consequences of the war. At the same time, the loose monetary policy of the Polish government most closely recalled the actions of neighbouring Germany, which, in response to demands for reparations, engaged in a mass printing of money without coverage. Poles learned how to live this way. For more than a dozen months of 1922 and 1923, it even appeared that an economy fuelled by inflation could attain great speed. Credit, mainly state credit, was difficult to obtain, but was nearly free. It was repaid in a depreciating currency. Prices rose, so that manufactured goods became more expensive. Moreover, the value of the Polish Mark abroad fell more quickly than at home, which made exports more profitable.[16] The problem, however, was that investment in East-Central Europe from the standpoint of Western finance was only feasible after local economies became more similar to common models. In returning to the histor-ical parallels with which we began our description of this first 20th century economic transformation in East-Central Europe, the message flowing from west to east could be summed up with the phrase "there is no alternative." Indeed, with regard to this issue even the chief opponent of "hard" liberalism, John Maynard Keynes (1883-1946), had a different opinion: a weakening currency destroys a capitalist economy.

By a continuing process of inflation, governments can confiscate, secretly and unobserved, an important part of the wealth of their citizens. By this method, they not only confiscate, but they confiscate arbitrarily; and, while the process impoverishes many, it actually enriches some. The sight of this arbitrary rearrangement of riches strikes not only at security, but at confidence in the equity of the existing distribution of wealth. [...] There is no subtler, no surer means of overturning the existing basis of society.[17]

Taking into account local conditions, the requirements imposed by international financial institutions were equivalent to a withdrawal of the state from certain unwritten compromises with the public.

Each analogy nevertheless has limits and a comparison of changes after 1918 and after 1989 is not an exception to this rule. As noted by György Ránki (1930-1988), at the time of the First World War, it still seemed that the economies of the region would move towards closer integration. However, together with the slow demise of armed conflict, the economic evolution of East-Central Europe first stood still and then completely changed direction.[18] Young countries arising from the rubble of empires were not at all interested in re-creating pre-war trade channels. On the contrary, they saw high customs duties, direct market intervention and rationing as a remedy for the difficulties of their own producers. At the same time, protectionism and barriers erected against foreign trade were treated as another step toward the consolidation of new countries. The extension of a single customs area to freshly acquired territories, clearly separated from hostile neighbours, became somewhat of an act of patriotism. Where local industry was in its infancy, for example, in Romania, the aim was its revitalisation and modernisation removed from murderous foreign competition.

Therefore, although the effect of the transformation after 1989 was an opening of former East Bloc country markets to foreign capital and goods, the transformation after 1918 did not have impressive effects in this regard. The monetarism of governments ready to fight inflation, even at the price of greater unemployment, taxes and a decrease in income, was tied to their protectionism of their own industry and isolationism. The post-war economic policy of East-Central Europe and the Balkans in a certain sense remained in a state of war, when common sense primarily dictates that a country should protect its own production potential against hostile competition. The price for protecting its own capital was paid by its workers and peasants, namely social groups that immediately after the First World War were considered to be the greatest beneficiaries of a transformation.

Endnotes

1. One of the last cross-sectional analyses of the systemic and economic transformation process in East Central Europe is an excellent book by Philippe Ther, *Europe since 1989: A History* (Princeton: Princeton University Press, 2016). Characteristic for this subject is also the active participation of the main architects of changes presenting their own frequently completely divergent interpretations of policies from that time. See, for example, Leszek Balcerowicz, *800 dni. Szok kontrolowany* (Warszawa: BGW, 1992); Grzegorz W. Kołodko, *Transformacja polskiej gospodarki: sukces czy porażka?* (Warszawa: BGW, 1992); Václav Klaus, *Dismantling Socialism: A Road to Market Economy* II. (Praha: Top Agency, 1992); idem, *Ekonomická věda a ekonomická reforma* (Praha: Top Agency, Gennex, 1991).

2. This was the nature, for example, of references to the economic transformation of Central Europe after 1918 in discussions on theories of rational expectations. See Thomas J. Sargent, 'The Ends of Four Big Inflations,' in *Inflation: Causes and Effects*, ed. Robert Hall (Chicago: University of Chicago Press, 1983), 41-97; Elmus Wicker, 'Terminating Hyperinflation in the Dismembered Habsburg Monarchy,' *The American Economic Review* 76, 3 (1986), 350-364.

3. Florian Kührer-Wielach, Sarah Lemmen, 'Transformation in East Central Europe: 1918 and 1989. A Comparative Approach,' *European Review of History* 23, no. 4 (2016), 573-59. At the same time a comparative analysis of GDP indices of East-Central European countries during the interwar period and after 1989 was presented by Zenonas Norkus, 'Two Periods of the Peripheric Capitalist Development: Pre-Communist and Post-Communist Eastern Europe in Comparison,' *Polish Sociological Review* 190 (2015), 131-151.

4. Juliusz Zdanowski, *Dziennik Juliusza Zdanowskiego*, vol. II: 15 X 1918 – 23 VI 1919, eds. Janusz Faryś, Tomasz Sikorski, Henryka Walczak and Adam Wątor, (Szczecin: Wydawnictwo Naukowe Wydziału Humanistycznego Uniwersytetu Szczecińskiego "Minerwa", 2014), 92.

5. Eduard Dana Durand, 'Currency Inflation in Eastern Europe with Special Reference to Poland,' *The American Economic Review* 13, no. 4 (1923), 593-608, here 594-595.

6. Ibid, 594-595.

7. George Clenton Logio, *Bulgaria: Problems & Politics* (London: William Heinemann, 1919), 221-222.

8. Wojciech Morawski, 'Inflacje podczas pierwszej wojny światowej – próba systematyzacji,' in *100 rocznica wybuchu pierwszej wojny światowej. Materiały pokonferencyjne, Nidzica 2014*, eds. Ewelina Solarek, Hubert Domański and Hubert Wajs (Warszawa: Archiwum Główne Akt Dawnych, 2015), 25-44.

9. Jana Čechurová, 'Alois Rašín – temperamentní revolucionář ve službách continuity,' in *Muži října 1918. Osudy aktéru vzniku Republiky československé*, ed. Rudolf Kučera (Praha: Masarykův Ústav a Archiv, 2011), 9-15, here 11.

10. Laszlo Rostas, 'Capital Levies in Central Europe,' *The Review of Economic Studies* 8, no. 1 (1940), 20-32.

11. Durand, 'Currency Inflation,' 601.

12. Rostos, 'Capital Levies,' 25-26.

13. Arthur Salter, 'The Reconstruction of Hungary,' *Foreign Affairs* 5, no. 1 (1926), 91-102.

14. Rostos, 'Capital Levies,' 29.

15. Durand, 'Currency Inflation', 593-594.

16. Marian Marek Drozdowski, 'Życie gospodarcze Polski w latach 1918-1939,' in *Z dziejów Drugiej Rzeczypospolitej*, ed. Andrzej Garlicki (Warszawa: Wydawnictwa Szkolne i Pedagogiczne, 1986), 146-175, here 148-150.

17. Quoted in: Niall Ferguson, 'Keynes and the German Inflation,' *The English Historical Review* 110, no. 436 (1995), 368-391, here 389.

18. György Ránki, 'The Great Powers and the Economic Reorganization of the Danube Valley after World War I,' *Acta Historica Academiae Scientiarum Hungaricae* 27, no. 1-2 (1981), 63-97.

Between Social and Economic Crisis, Between Revisionism and Political Radicalisation: Bulgaria After the First World War 1918/19-1923

Oliver Schulz

In spite of its strategic importance and its role as an ally of the central powers, Bulgaria has always received somewhat sketchy treatment in western historiography. And notwithstanding improved access to the state archives in Bulgaria since the end of the communist regime, not much has changed.[1] Until 1989, Bulgarian historiography itself remained fixated on specific highly contentious political and ideo-

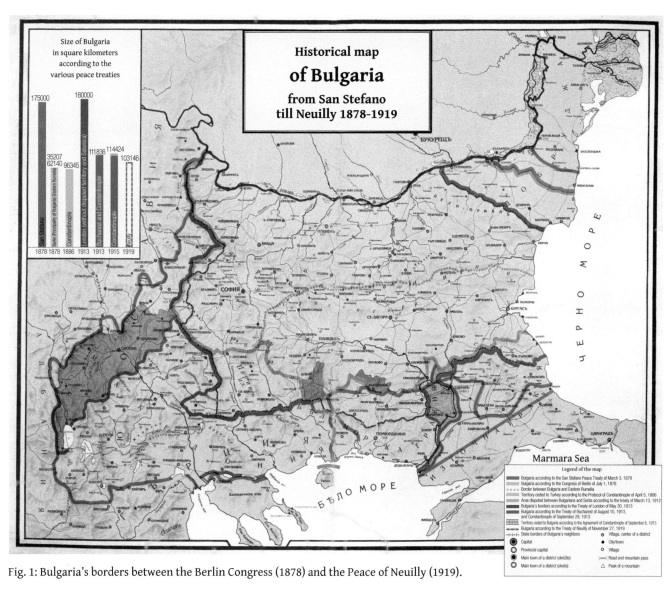

Fig. 1: Bulgaria's borders between the Berlin Congress (1878) and the Peace of Neuilly (1919).

Fig. 2: Prime Minister Aleksandǎr Stambolijski, 1919-1923.

logical topics, such as the uprising in September 1923, and even after 1989 Bulgarian historians failed to engage with any of the theoretical and methodological debates scholars elsewhere were conducting.[2] Their work remained dominated by national interpretive models that in some cases resorted to a regressive nationalistic discourse. With at least half an eye on the contemporary political situation, historiographical articles of the post-communist years have tended to exaggerate the democratic potential of the interwar years in order to offer exemplars for change and democratisation, and also to portray Bulgaria as an 'oasis of democracy'.[3] This article offers an overview of developments between 1918/19 and 1923, taking particular note of the First World War's effects on the port of Varna. It draws not only on documents from Varna's regional archives but also on materials in the regional Penčo Slavejkov library in the city of Varna. This approach has made it possible to focus very specifically on local perceptions of developments in international politics following the First World War.[4]

The Treaty of Neuilly (1919)

The treaty signed in Neuilly on 27 November 1919 must be the first point considered in any reflections

on the immediate post-war years in Bulgaria. It set in stone the effects of the second 'national catastrophe' for Bulgaria and established the new state boundaries. This second point is particularly important, since the significant number of lost territories (Western Thrace, South Dobruja and western border areas such as Caribrod and Bosilegrad, returned to Macedonia after occupation during the war) gave rise to countless problems, such as the need to take in Bulgarian refugees from these areas; this, in conjunction with other issues – not only the demobilisation of the army, now limited to 20,000 men, but also the high levels of reparations due – added fuel to the nationalist/revisionist discourse.[5]

The years between 1919 and 1923 were dominated by the military elite's and the irredentist Internal Macedonian Revolutionary Organisation's (VMRO) strong opposition to the government of Aleksandǎr Stambolijski's (1879-1923) Agrarian People's Union, which they accused of conducting a policy of surrender.

On 9 June 1923, this resulted in a military coup in which members of the VMRO murdered Prime Minister Stambolijski.[6] The Agrarian People's Union government fell and Aleksandǎr Cankov (1879-1959) established a new government that included some military personnel as ministers. Cankov's rule is chiefly remembered as the 'White Terror' exercised against real and suspected members of the Agrarian Union, communists and other opponents of the regime. The revisionist and irredentist discourse during this time was a long way from the framework established for Bulgaria in the peace Treaty of Neuilly. Neuilly had prohibited revisionism in Bulgaria's foreign policy towards its neighbours, and it is telling that an agreement was signed on a population exchange between Greece and Bulgaria that, in effect, signified that Bulgaria was abandoning any claim to Western Thrace and the Greek part of Macedonia.[7]

Due to lack of space, this article will include no further expansion on political developments in Bulgaria after 1923. The important point here is that, because of Bulgaria's political fragmentation and radicalisation, certain groups developed an interest – and not only in terms of foreign policy – in Italy and Italian fascism. Key personalities in the military coup on 9 June 1923, such as Kimon Georgiev (1882-1969) and Damjan Velčev (1883-1954) – who were also to play a

Fig. 3: Calendar sheet 'Svobodna Dobrudža' (Free Dobruja), 1919.

Fig. 4: Monument to the fallen soldiers of the 8th Infantry Regiment 'Primorski' in Varna, with the inscription 'Eternal glory to those who died defending their home country 1912-1913 and 1915-1918'. The inauguration took place in November 1936.

leading role on 19 May 1934 and 9 September 1944 – began to align their own thinking and that of their political group 'Zveno' with authoritarian, elitist notions and the idea of a corporative state. These developments were much encouraged by the world economic crisis of 1929 and its consequences. Alongside the rivalry between the various extreme-right organisations there were also forces supportive to the monarchy and the court. The military coup on 19 May 1934, in which Zveno and the Military League sought to implement their own authoritarian social policies and foster fascist developments in Bulgaria, opened up the way for the royal dictatorship under Boris III (1894-1943). The final twist emerged during the late 1930s and the Second World War, when some of those who had prepared and carried out the two revolutions in 1923 and 1934 joined forces with the communists and seized power as the 'Fatherland Front' on 9 September 1944.[8]

The Economic Effects of the First World War

The territorial losses Bulgaria sustained as a result of the treaty coincided with an already pressurised economic situation and had a significant effect on the Bulgarian economy.[9] The city of Varna, and importantly its port, was robbed of its hinterland by the loss of Southern Dobruja.[10] It was only after 1940 and under pressure from Germany that the region, a significant producer of grain crops, was returned from Romanian to Bulgarian sovereignty. The port of Varna had lost out after the First World War when the grain trade was diverted to the Bulgarian ports on the Danube; following 1940, grain was once again shipped out through Varna. Trade in metal processing and local wine production also expanded.

In the 1920s, the first shipyard opened in Varna. Even with the decline in Varna's economic signifi-

Fig. 5: The port of Varna in the interwar period.

cance and the drop in the grain trade, some entrepreneurs took on leading roles in the city's commercial life; one such was Kostadin Genov, who traded in textiles among other goods, and from 1920 to 1931 chaired the city's Chamber of Industry and Commerce.[11] Large numbers of desperate refugees were also arriving in Varna at this time, adding significantly to poverty and unemployment, and thus also to the city's economic and social challenges. In spite of entrepreneurial innovation by Kostadin Genov and Asen Nikolov, who set up a stock company trading in textiles in 1918, the situation therefore remained very tense.[12] We can thus safely say that the loss of Southern Dobruja after the First World War imposed a heavier economic loss and represented a greater sacrifice for Bulgaria than its annexation in 1940 was a gain for Romania.[13] Speaking to the Varna Chamber of Industry and Commerce, Dimităr Vlahov (1878-1953) emphasised the importance of Dobruja exports to Bulgarian external trade. The loss of South Dobruja represented a loss of about eight per cent of Bul-

garia's pre-war territory and over six per cent of the population.[14]

Absorbing Refugees After the First World War

The loss of regions previously belonging to Bulgaria, and of territories with Bulgarian populations occupied by Bulgaria during the First World War (such as Macedonia[15]), caused a large influx throughout the country of refugees from these areas. Street names in cities and villages across Bulgaria still bear witness to this population movement by evoking places and personalities from these regions (Dobruja, Ohrid and so on). In theory, these refugees had a valid claim to return to their home regions,[16] and countries neighbouring Bulgaria were committed by the Treaty of Neuilly to the protection of minorities,[17] but the reality was often very different. Moreover, the country still had some refugees in need of food and shelter from the time of the Balkan War. These included Bul-

Fig. 6: Propaganda painting of the Battle of Tutrakan, 2-6 September 1916.

garians from Turkish Eastern Thrace, who had suffered a particularly hard fate during the interwar period since, unlike Greece, Eastern Thrace had not concluded a population exchange treaty, so no agreements had been made on property rights.[18] Given these mostly very difficult living conditions, it is unsurprising that the Bulgarian Communist Party became popular among the refugee population – a point made strongly in communist historiography prior to 1989.[19]

Both towns and villages were affected by the influx of refugees and the need to provide living space and allocate land.[20] Varna's regional archives hold a number of documents that, as well as offering genealogical interest, illustrate the practical measures taken to allocate land and settlement areas for the refugees.[21] A dedicated office was set up, for example, to manage the settlement of refugees from Dobruja.[22] The settlement changed forever the appearance of the city of Varna. New residential areas were established, such as the Asparuhovo quarter, and the dis-

trict of Primorski near the port, where there was already a quarter occupied by Bulgarians from Dobruja.[23] Between 1920 and 1923, somewhere between 550 and 650 new homes were built for refugees in Varna.[24] Longer term, however, the local authorities began to resist having further refugees allocated to them, as a housing crisis was developing and this was exacerbating social problems.[25]

The Bulgarian refugees involved themselves in various organisations.[26] Since 1919, Varna had been the seat of the Dobruja National Assembly, which had moved from the Romanian town of Babadag in northern Dobruja.[27] The association of Thracian Bulgarians in the town took part in current political affairs and, for example, argued for an internationally guaranteed right for Thracian refugees to return to their homeland, and for the League of Nations to facilitate a settlement of the Thracian question. The fact that such associations existed and the nature of their activities clearly show how the revisionist and irredentist narrative that would become a defining fea-

Fig. 7: View of the beach and the promenade in Varna at the beginning of the 1920s.

ture of interwar Bulgaria was fostered at a local level.[28]

Memory Culture in Bulgaria Between the World Wars

In some cases, irredentist tendencies found expression in Bulgarian memory culture during the interwar period, for example in recollections of Macedonia and of other regions lost to Bulgaria. Following defeat in war, these groups were undoubtedly also coming to terms with wartime sufferings and the apparent pointlessness of Bulgarian losses, and giving a focus to their feelings of grief. War memorials to the fallen of the First World War were set up across the country, and in some cases the names of First World War casualties were added to memorials to those lost in the Balkan War.[29]

Memories of the First World War – the 'second national catastrophe' – were and indeed still are traumatic in Bulgaria, and have undergone numerous political reversals. The project to erect a 'memorial to an unknown soldier' in Sofia provides a telling example of this. The plan was drawn up under the Agrarian People's Union government of Aleksandăr Stambolijski and, following a somewhat turbulent history, was realised during the royal dictatorship of Boris III; following 9 September 1944, it was once again subjected to a paradigm shift in the policy governing history and memory culture. During the communist era, a memorial in a park in Sofia was burnt down and not restored until 1981 under Todor Živkov (1911-1998). The fact that the 1300th anniversary of the founding of the Bulgarian state, the activities of Ludmila Živkova (1942-1981) as Chair of the Culture Commission and the country's growing nationalist tendencies all came at the same time may be more than a coincidence.[30]

One final aspect of memory culture after 1918, and one which was to have heightened significance for Varna and the surrounding region in the light of the revised borders, is the way memories of war were expressed in neighbouring Dobruja. On the one hand, memory culture in Southern Dobruja changed somewhat under Romanian sovereignty: Bulgarian *lieux de memoire* were either destroyed or rededicated with a different focus; on the Bulgarian side, meanwhile, war memorials were given special emphasis, and many new ones were erected. The key Bulgarian *lieu de memoire* at Tutrakan was once again inaccessible, so that even after the return of South Dobruja to Bulgaria, memories of the Battle of Tutrakan remained complicated.

Following 9 September 1944, Bulgaria and Romania rather problematically became 'brother nations', and as a result were expected to overlook their past conflicts and antagonisms. Here, the South Dobruja town of Dobrich, known by its Ottoman name of 'Bazargic' under Romanian rule, served to focus conflicts of memory. A postcard in the regional archive shows a Romanian memorial to war heroes erected in 1927 that was destroyed in 1940 following the restoration of Southern Dobruja to Bulgaria by the Treaty of Craiova. The fact that Bulgaria had been an opponent of Russia's during the First World War furthermore contributed in no small measure to the difficulties encountered during the communist era by the Bulgarian project to honour General Ivan Kolev (1863-1917), who had played an important part in the First World War on the Dobruja front. The First-World-War encounter between Russian and Bulgarian troops in Dobruja was barely addressed, and it was not until after 1989, in the post-communist era, that it was possible to conduct some interesting studies of specific episodes, such as the battles near Balčik, and to carry out plans to erect various memorials.[31]

Looking to the Future

In spite of the various crises described above that dominated the years following the First World War, Bulgaria was able to find a way through the challenging conditions and to establish successful new ways forward. I have already cited entrepreneurial business activities in Varna.[12] The port lost much of its significance as an export hub, but after 1918 it was able to develop an international reputation as a seaside resort. This transformation was helped by Varna's fine geographical location, its beautiful beaches and its existing reputation as Bulgaria's 'gateway to the sea'. The development of tourism infrastructure led to important changes. Modern hotels were built that met European standards, and both the shoreline and the promenade (Morska gradina) were developed.[13] These energetic measures, taken at a challenging time, bore valuable fruit for Varna in the communist era, and in the post-communist years the tourism industry has continued to make an important contribution to the economic life of the entire region.

Taking the long view of political radicalisation in Bulgaria and of the question of refugees, it remains clear that Bulgaria still faced many political challenges after 9 September 1944, and that it has had to confront these anew after 1989. Not only have significant economic shocks followed the transformations, but extremist nationalist and revisionist voices have also returned to prominence and reinvigorated the interwar debates. Significant numbers among the population are conscious of the refugees from Macedonia, Thrace and Dobruja among their ancestry, and this issue has been loudly and deliberately conflated with issues around territorial claims. Even historians aiming to present a neutral and cautiously argued position find that conventional historiography focusing on the concepts of 'state' and 'nation' gains very little traction beyond the academic fraternity, while versions of history not only more populist in nature but also lacking academic foundation are disseminated by those who claim to be unrecognised experts on Bulgarian history and politics. The lamentable paucity of research – as in the fields of social history, the history of everyday life (Alltagsgeschichte) and of local and regional history – is now a more serious issue than it was before, even in the context of the severe general lack of research funding in Bulgaria.[34]

Endnotes

1. Cf. here Oliver Schulz, 'Neue Quellen und Zugänge zum Ersten Weltkrieg auf dem Balkan am Beispiel Bulgariens,' in *Gedenken und (k)ein Ende? Das Weltkriegs-Gedenken 1914/2014: Debatten, Zugänge, Ausblicke*, eds. Bernhard Bachinger et al. (Wien: Verlag der Österreichischen Akademie der Wissenschaften, 2017), 139-152; idem, 'Commémorer une guerre oubliée? La commémoration de la Première Guerre en Bulgarie,' *Matériaux pour l'histoire de notre temps* 113/114 (2014), 42-51.

2. Cf. for example Jono Mitev, *Fašistkijat prevrat na deveti juni 1923 godina i junskoto antifašistkoto vŭstanie* (Sofija: Izd. na Bŭlgarskata komunist. Partija, 1956). For an overview of the development of Bulgarian historiography cf. Maria Todorova, 'Bulgaria,' *The American Historical Review* 97, no. 4 (1992), 1105-1117; Daniela Koleva and Ivan Elenkov, 'Did "the Change" Happen? Post-socialist Historiography in Bulgaria,' in *(Re)Writing History – Historiography in Southeast Europe after Socialism*, ed. Ulf Brunnbauer (Münster: LIT, 2004), 94-127; Thomas Meininger, 'A Troubled Transition: Bulgarian Historiography, 1989-1994,' *Contemporary European History* 5, no. 1 (1996), 103-118.

3. Cf. for example the in many places revisionist portrayal of Nikola Altŭnkov, *Narekocha gi fašisti. Legioneri, otecpaisievci, ratnici, brannici, rodnozaštnici, kubratisti* (Sofija: TANGRA TanNakRa IK, 2004).

4. Cf. Wolfgang Höpken, 'Strukturkrise oder verpasste Chance? Zum Demokratiepotential der südosteuropäischen Zwischenkriegsstaaten Bulgarien, Jugoslawien und Rumänien,' in *Ostmitteleuropa zwischen den beiden Weltkriegen (1918-1939). Stärke und Schwäche der neuen Staaten, nationale Minderheiten*, ed. Hans Lemberg (Marburg: Herder-Institut, 1997), 73-127. Nikolaj Poppetrov is one of the most vocal critics of the very black-and-white nature of Bulgarian historiography, and even before 1989 was arguing for a clear definition to distinguish fascism from non-fascism. Cf. Nikolaj Poppetrov, 'Die bulgarische Geschichtswissenschaft über die Probleme des bulgarischen Faschismus,' *Bulgarian Historical Review* 14, no. 3 (1986), 78-93; idem, 'Faschismus in Bulgarien,' *Südost-Forschungen* 41 (1982), 199-218.

5. The text of the treaty is available online at *Digithèque de matériaux juridiques et politiques*, ed. Jean-Pierre Maury, <http://mjp.univ-perp.fr/traites/1919neuilly.htm> (accessed 25 September 2019).

6. On the part played by the armed forces in Bulgarian domestic policy, see Georgi Markov, *Parola 'sabja'. Zagovorite i prevratite na Voennija sŭjuz 1919-1936* (Sofija: Voennoizdat. Kompleks Sv. Georgi Pobedonosec et al. 1992). On interwar political developments, see Nikolaj Poppetrov, 'Flucht aus der Demokratie: Autoritarismus und autoritäres Regime in Bulgarien 1919-1944,' in *Autoritäre Regime in Ostmittel- und Südosteuropa 1919-1944*, ed. Erwin Oberländer (Paderborn et al.: Schöningh, 2001), 379-401. On A. Cankov's fascist movement, see Dimitrina Petrova, 'Sŭzdavane na narodno socialno dviženie,' *Istoričeski Pregled* 50/51 (1994/95), 33-61.

7. On the 'Thracian question' in Bulgarian foreign policy between 1919 and 1923 cf. Todor Kosatev, *Trakijskijat văpros văv vănšnata politika na Bălgarija (1919-1923)* (Sofija: Akademično Izdatelstvo 'Prof. Marin Drinov', 1996). On Cankov's foreign policy, see Milen Kumanov, 'La politique balkanique du premier gouvernement de l'Entente démocratique en Bulgarie (1923-1926),' *Bulgarian Historical Review* 2, no. 4 (1974), 3-25.

8. Cf. Poppetrov, Flucht.

9. On the economy of Bulgaria and its challenges cf. Holm Sundhaussen, 'Die verpasste Agrarrevolution. Aspekte der Entwicklungsblockade in den Balkanländern vor 1945,' in *Industrialisierung und gesellschaftlicher Wandel in Südosteuropa*, ed. Roland Schönfeld (München: Südosteuropa-Gesellschaft, 1989), 45-60; idem, 'Strukturelle Engpassfaktoren der wirtschaftlichen Entwicklung Bulgariens von der Staatsgründung bis zum Beginn des Zweiten Weltkrieges,' in *110 Jahre Wiedererrichtung des bulgarischen Staates 1878-1988*, ed. Klaus-Detlev Grothusen (München: Südosteuropa-Gesellschaft, 1990), 155-165. On the Bulgarian economy in the 20th century also see John R. Lampe, *The Bulgarian economy in the twentieth century* (New York: St Martin's Press, 1986). On the consequences of the world economic crisis in South-Eastern Europe, see Hans Raupach, 'Strukturelle und institutionelle Auswirkungen der Weltwirtschaftskrise in Ost-Mitteleuropa,' *Vierteljahreshefte für Zeitgeschichte* 24 (1976), 38-57; Roland Schönfeld, 'Die Balkanländer in der Weltwirtschaftskrise,' *Vierteljahrsschrift für Sozial- und Wirtschaftsgeschichte* 62 (1975), 179-213.

10. Georgi Pecov, *Varna 1920-1944* (Varna: Kolor Print, 2016), 7-8.

11. Ibidem, 7-10.

12. Petăr Stojanov, *Varna meždu dvete svetovni vojni (1919-1939 g.)* (Varna: Izdat. Kăšta Steno, 2003), 29.

13. Ivan St. Pénakof, *Le problème de la Dobroudja du Sud (un aspect économique et social du problème)* (Sofia: Tchipeff, 1940), 4.

14. Dimităr Vlahov, *Ikonomičeskoto i finansovo položenie na Bălgarija* (Varna: Varn.tărg.-industr. Kamara, 1920), 17, 19.

15. On Bulgarian policy in occupied territories, using Macedonia as an example, cf. Björn Opfer, *Im Schatten des Krieges: Besatzung oder Anschluss, Befreiung oder Unterdrückung? Eine komparative Untersuchung über die bulgarische Herrschaft in Vardar-Makedonien: 1915-1918 und 1941-1944* (Münster: LIT, 2005).

16. Cf. the article 'Bežancite,' *Dobrudža*, No. 222, 26 March 1919.

17. See also n. 3 above.

18. On the particularly difficult case of the East Thracian Bulgarians cf. draft newspaper article in the Varna regional archives: DA Varna, f. 798K, op. 1, a.e. 5, l. 6.

19. Georgi V. Dimitrov, *Nastanjavane i ozemljavane na bălgarskite bežanci (1919-1939)* (Blagoevgrad: BPI, 1985).

20. Cf. the case of the district of Burga: G. Popov, 'Kăm văprosa za bežancite v Burgaskija okrăg prez 1920-1923 g.,' *Izvestija na dăržavnite arhivi* 21 (1971), 137-153.

21. Cf. the case of the village of Galata in the district of Varna: DA Varna, f. 58K, op. 1, a.e. 7.

22. Cf. the article 'Bjuroto za nastanjavane dobrudžanskite bežanci,' *Dobrudžansko slovo*, no. 133, 5 December 1919.

23. Stojanov, Varna, 118.

24. Ibidem, 119.

25. 'Bežancite i žilištnata kriza,' *Varnenski obštinski vestnik* 30, no. 38 (29 January 1921).

26. Cf. a study of Bulgarians from Macedonia: Aleksandăr Grebenarov, *Legalni i tajni organizacii na makedonskite bežanci v Bălgarija (1918-1947)* (Sofia: Makedonski naučen institut, 2006).

27. For political reasons, access to this very interesting source in the Varna regional archives was limited until 1989: DA Varna f. 80K.

28. DA Varna, f. 250K, op. 1, a.e. 10, l. 41.

29. Claudia Weber, *Auf der Suche nach der Nation. Erinnerungskultur in Bulgarien von 1878-1944* (Berlin-Münster: LIT, 2006), 205-245.

30. On the early history of this project, see ibidem, 238-240.

31. Cf. for example, Darin Kanavrov, *Morskijat boj pri Balčik dekemvri 1916 g.: neizvestnoto săbitija v istorijata na bălgarskija voennomorski flot* (Sofia: Voenno Izd., 2009).

32. See also endnotes 11 and 12 above.

33. Pecov, *Varna*, 12.

34. Rumjana Prešlenova, 'Freiheit als Verantwortung. Die Historiographie in Bulgarien nach dem Umbruch,' in *Klio ohne Fesseln? Historiographie im östlichen Europa nach dem Zusammenbruch des Kommunismus*, eds. Alojz Ivanišević et al. (Wien et al.: Lang, 2002), 473-486, here 479, 483-484.

'Peasants Wait for Them with Hope': The Civil War in Belarus 1918-1922

Andrei Zamoiski

In May 1921, Officer Eliya Kopshits[1] of the Belarusian department of the Jewish Public Committee reported to the head office in Moscow about a crucial situation that had happened in Jewish communities in Southern Belarus as a result of anti-Jewish pogroms and the banditry and activities of anti-Soviet rebels. In many places, the Jews appeared defenceless, their only hope of support lying in the bigger cities with their strong Red Army garrisons. In the meantime, the local peasantry looked towards the forestry areas, where guerrilla units operated actively against the Bolsheviks. Reporting on the pogrom in the shtetl of Lyuban, he admitted that local peasants, angered by the social and economic policy of the Bolsheviks, greeted the rebels as their saviours. Relations between Christians and Jews had undergone drastic changes in the previous few years. Before the First World War, the Christians had managed to get along with their Jewish neighbours. In the years of disturbances, however, Belarusian peasants witnessed crimes committed by rebels and bandits against Jews, or even participated in them themselves.

Eliya Kopshits listed several reasons for this change: first and foremost, the campaign of grain confiscation (the so-called *prodrazvyorstka*, in Russian), conducted violently by the Soviet authorities, and crimes against. Kopshits blames the tactless speeches and actions of some Jews who served in the Soviet bodies and the Red Army, and who depicted all peasants collectively as 'counter-revolutionary agents'. From the other side, enemies of the Soviet regime engaged in anti-Jewish propaganda that successfully persuaded peasants that only the Jews were guilty in all tax deployments. Taken together, this aggravated the inter-ethnic disputes and conflicts in the region. Kopshits argues that the main destructive influence on Jewish-Christian relations in that part of Belarus

were the pogroms committed by troops led by general Stanisłaŭ Bułak-Bałachovič (1883-1940) in the autumn of 1920.[2]

Paramilitary violence spread across Eastern Europe at the end of the First World War. Saboteurs, deserters, and various armed groups that did not

Fig. 1: Stanisłaŭ Bułak-Bałachovič, cavalry officer of the Tsarist army in 1915-1918, major general of the White Army in Belarus in 1919-1920, commander of voluntary units fighting in the Polish army of the Second Polish Republic in 1920 and 1939.

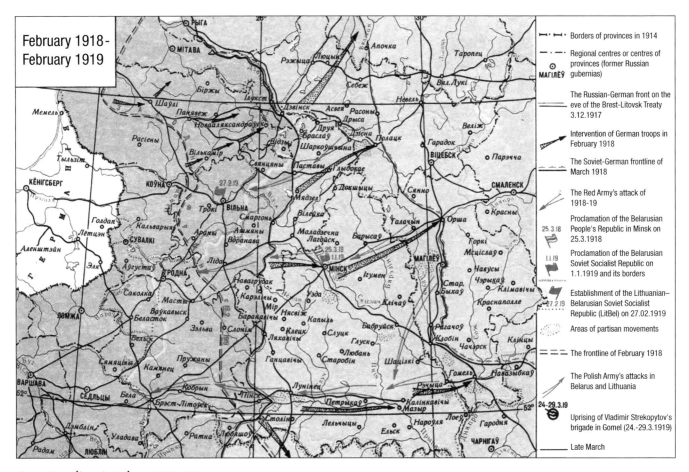

Fig. 2: Frontlines in Belarus 1918-1919.

qualify as regular army units operated in the grey zones.[3] The activities of various anti-Soviet paramilitary groups intensified local conflicts in the former Russian Empire. In Belarus, the activity of gangs consisting of enemies of the Bolsheviks, deserters, and local peasants practically paralysed life in the province.

This civil war on the periphery of the former Russian Empire has attracted and continues to attract the interest of scholars. Existing literature on the problem of establishing the Soviet regime in the region and the fighting against the Bolsheviks' enemies is rich enough. Soviet historians described the activity of anti-Bolshevik rebels only as acts of 'political gangsterism' directed against the young Soviet state. They claimed that the proximity of 'bourgeois' Poland, Latvia, and Lithuania was a decisive factor for the way the civil war developed in the region; that anti-Soviet gangs, spies, and saboteurs were thrown into the Soviet republics from the west; and that they

stayed in contact with the local anti-Soviet underground and banditry.[4] The authors did not take into account that many factors could stir up anti-Soviet sentiments among the local population, such as social and ethnic disparity on the periphery and especially in the rural areas. Some modern Belarusian and Polish authors focus mainly on the activities of the rebels, portraying them as representatives of the Belarusian national resistance opposed to the Bolsheviks.[5] However, the problems presented by the transition from the First World War to civil peace in this region are more complicated.

This chapter focuses on some episodes of the so-called 'wars after the War' on the territory of Soviet Belarus, mainly the specificity of the civil war(s) in this region. It discusses the role of Soviet policy in developments such as the escalation of violence, problems of desertion, and warlordism and interethnic conflicts under the severe conditions of the civil war.

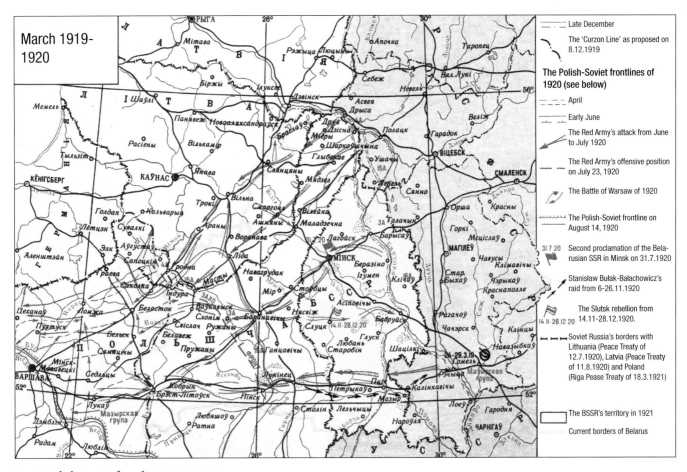

Fig. 3: Polish-Soviet frontlines, 1919-1920

The First World War had significantly affected the Belarusian lands. The Western Russian Front had cut through Belarus in the autumn of 1915, and about 1.4 million Belarusians, mainly from the western provinces, left their homeland.[6] In 1917, the February Revolution catalysed the collapse of the Russian Empire. Under the German occupation of 1918, a group of Belarusian intellectuals in Minsk attempted to establish their state, the so-called 'Belarusian People's Republic' (BNR). In January 1919, the Bolsheviks set up the Belarusian Soviet Socialist Republic, merged the following month with the Lithuanian SSR into the so-called 'LitBel'. This was later abolished by the Polish troops who occupied the region. The eastern Belarusian provinces (Gomel and Vitebsk) were included in the Russian Socialist Federative Socialist Republic (RSFSR) and were not reincorporated back into the Belarusian SSR until 1924 to 1926. On the unoccupied territories, the new Soviet regime actively introduced a variety of reforms. In the Soviet and post-Soviet literature, this period and the Bolsheviks' policy is known as 'war communism'.[7]

The new authorities brutally transformed the economy using such methods as the nationalisation of banks, companies, and factories; the requisitions of goods; the confiscation of private property; a ban on private trade, etc. Many peasants, mainly former leaseholders, were attracted by the Bolshevik agrarian programme and became active defenders of the new Soviet order. Some joined the ranks of the so-called 'Red partisans' struggling against the German and Polish forces that occupied the region. In Belarus, poor peasants and newly established 'communes' obtained plots of landlords' estates (mostly of Polish origin) and their rich neighbours. The Bolsheviks treated a smaller group of rich peasants as so-called *kulaks* or 'class enemies of the poorer peasantry'. The majority of the peasantry suffered from the requisitions and revolutionary taxes imposed by the Red Army, revolutionary committees, and other

Fig. 4: The Russian writer and revolutionary Boris Savinkov in the early 1920s.

Soviet bodies.[8] Many peasants were angry about the policies of the Bolsheviks, and the tactless behaviour of Soviet employees who participated in collecting the surplus food tax and requisitions in the rural areas. Within the *prodrazvyorstka* campaign, they demanded more than the peasant households could provide.[9] The period of so-called 'political gangsterism' coincided with the anti-Bolshevik rebel activities of the peasants, which rolled through all Soviet republics.

During the Polish-Soviet War in the summer of 1920, the Polish military command abandoned Belarus, widely employing a scorched-earth policy against the Red Army. The Belarusian SSR was restored in the summer of 1920. The re-establishment of the Soviet regime in the rural areas of Belarus spanned the period of the rebels and the anti-Jewish pogroms. After Poland and Soviet Russia had agreed a ceasefire in the autumn of 1920, the Stanisłaŭ Bułak-Bałachovič detachments attacked in Southern Belarus ('the campaign of Polesia'). Bałachovič is rightfully considered one of the most interesting and controversial characters of Belarusian history during the civil war period.[10] Like many rebel leaders, he switched sides from serving as an Imperial Russian officer to joining first the Red and then the White Army. Bułak-Bałachovič then later joined the Polish side and led the troops he called the Belarusian army. Bałachovič was supported by the Poles and by the anti-Bolshevik Russian émigré Boris Savinkov (1879-1925), the head of the Russian Political Committee in Poland.[11]

During the autumn campaign of 1920, the Red Army was unable to stop Bałachovič's troops, mainly soldiers of Russian and other nationalities who had fought against the Bolsheviks during the Russian civil war and the Polish-Soviet War. They captured several towns in the region.[12] Because of his ambition to rule, Bałachovič proclaimed the re-establishment of the power of the Belarusian People's Republic's (BNR) in Mozyr. Being a 'military minister' of the provisional government and acting in the name of the BNR, he established his own government in the Belarusian woods.[13] At the end of the autumn of 1920, during the Red Army attacks, his soldiers returned to the territory controlled by the Poles, where they were interned.[14] Simultaneously, the Red troops defeated the so-called 'Slutsk uprising', an attempt by the Belarusian regional congress of the Slutsk region to restore the authority of the BNR. In the meantime, a split in the BNR government-in-exile and its weak financial position hindered coordination between supporters of Belarusian statehood. Slutsk rebels had little time to unite their forces with Bałachovič and were disarmed in Poland. Bałachovič's 'Polesian raid' considerably worsened the situation in the whole region. Bałachovič's soldiers committed mass rapes and other crimes against civilians, mainly Jews and Soviet employees.[15] The Soviet and Jewish press abroad paid attention to his activities.[16] *Balakhoŭcy* (Bałachovič's men) became a collective name for all gangsters who operated in the region from the autumn of 1920 onwards.

The Russian Eastern Front destabilised life in the region from 1917, especially during the mass desertions. The large number of military deserters were one factor that led to the spread of so-called political gangsterism in Belarus. It is difficult to estimate the exact number of deserters in the region. During the First World War, thousands of deserters from the old Russian Imperial army and the Red Army hid in the local countryside. Numerous deserters (former peasants and workers from different regions of the former Russian Empire) remained in the woods after the collapse of the Western Front and the Red Army's defeat in Poland in the summer of 1920.[17]

Fig. 5: 'Coat of arms: Long live the Belarusian People's Republic'.

Fig. 6: Visit by the highest command of the Estonian Army to Pskov in May 1919. Stanisłaŭ Bułak-Bałachovič' (left) talks with the commander of the Estonian Army Johan Laidoner (1884-1953).

Anti-Soviet guerrillas actively recruited such deserters into their ranks. Desertions were caused by different factors. Deserters escaped from various labour duties and unresolved everyday problems, such as the lack of quarters for soldiers and the food crisis in the Soviet republics.[18] The Red Army command took severe measures to prevent desertion from its ranks. In August 1920, the Politburo of the Communist party allowed military tribunals to use the death penalty for desertion when it would be associated with active gang violence.[19] Treating it seriously, they established special bodies to combat it and utilised varying methods, ranging from amnesty to severe punishment.[20] The Soviet authorities of course attempted to inform the population about the consequences of desertion and collaboration with deserters. Nonetheless, many former soldiers in Belarus in 1920-1921 decided to stay in the forests, some of them merging with bigger gangs.[21]

Different anti-Soviet insurgent groups and gangs operated in Belarus, headed by warlords, so-called *atamans* (leaders of various 'armies' during the Russian civil war) and *batskas* (from Belarusian 'father', heads of gangs).[22] Anti-Soviet resistance in Belarus was not politically and ideologically homogeneous. The majority of insurgent leaders had only vague political ideas and acted according to their tactical considerations. As mentioned above, some of them switched sides in 1918-1920. Having initially joined the ranks of the revolutionary Bolshevik forces, they later based their ideology on anti-Communism. They led so-called 'peasant armies' and their propaganda targeted the peasantry, which constituted the majority of the population. Their ideas were a part of the ideology of peasant uprisings that swept the entire former Russian Empire from Belarus to Siberia. Among them there were strong anti-urban and anti-Semitic sentiments.[23] The agrarian ideas of the

Socialist Revolutionary Party (the SR) were very influential among the peasantry and rebels in the region. Belarusian rebel groups led by *ataman* Vyačaslaŭ Adamovič (1890-1939?) (*'ataman* Dergač') closely collaborated with the 'Belarusian Peasant Party of Green Oak'. Members of 'Green Oak' (Zyalyëny Dub) promoted the struggle for an independent Belarus, with no Russian or Polish rule on Belarusian territories.[24] *Ataman* Yurka Monič (1890-1924) enjoyed strong support among local Belarusian peasants, and is nowadays portrayed as a 'Belarusian Robin Hood'.[25] Regarding the post-war national or local order, many groups delegated political powers to their commanders abroad. The Belarusian insurgent groups that operated in Soviet Belarus from 1921 onwards subordinated themselves directly to Bałachovič's staff in Poland.[26]

Many warlords were experienced military officers of the Russian Imperial army, who just continued their 'war after the wars'. Captain Methodius (Mefodii) Karatkevič (1890?-1921), born in an aristocratic family, was an officer of the former Imperial Russian Army. His desire to take vengeance could be explained by the fact that the Bolsheviks deprived him of a large estate. Karatkevič led a gang consisting of about 1400 infantrymen and cavalrymen, which was officially subordinated to Bułak-Bałachovič in Poland. In the spring of 1921, his detachment, known for its bestial cruelty, operated in the territory of the Bobruisk district in Central Belarus.[27] During a raid in July 1921, his squad was defeated by the Red Army and Cheka units. Karatkevič and his inferiors were killed.[28] The warlord Ivan Vasilčikov (1890-1921) (*'ataman* Galak') was a former Red Army commander who led a gang that operated in the Gomel and Chernigov governorates in 1921. Former Red Army soldiers actively joined this gang, which in January 1921 consisted of 200 soldiers. This number increased three-fold several months later due to the rise of peasant anti-Soviet rebels and desertion in the region. In July 1921, the gang together with its leader was eliminated by the Gomel Cheka battalion, which consisted of Chinese soldiers.[29]

Some military leaders, such as Ilya Struk (1896-1969), who operated both in Ukraine and the southern part of Belarus, were involved in the so-called Ukrainian revolution. Struk was an *ataman* of an Ukrainian insurgent group, also known for its bestial

Fig: 7: Ukrainian *ataman* Ilya Struk.

brutality and crimes against the Jewish population. Born into a family of peasants, he had worked as a teacher before the First World War. He initially served as a Baltic Fleet Navy officer and later in 1916 became an infantry lieutenant. In 1919, he joined the Bolsheviks, then the White Army of Anton Denikin (1872-1942), and later Semyon Petljura`s (1879-1926) Ukrainian forces.[30] By 1921, his detachment included about 100 cavalrymen. The *ataman* successfully escaped abroad that same year.[31]

Soviet secret services managed to discover the close cooperation between Bałachovič's staff and the Second Department of Polish General Staff responsible for military intelligence, etc.[32] The Soviet government accused the Polish authorities of huge material losses caused by the banditry supported from abroad in the Soviet borderlands.[33] Meanwhile, the Soviet secret services actively supported anti-Polish rebels and terrorist groups in the eastern regions of the Second Polish Republic, mainly Belarusians and Ukrainians.[34]

Fig. 8: Jewish children in an orphanage in Kovchitsky in Belarus, 1920s.

Violence and political terror were put to vigorous use against political opponents and civilians. In the years of the Russian civil wars, various political forces actively promoted anti-Semitic agitation. Attacks on Jews were closely linked to a high level of aggression in the post-revolutionary society.[35] In many rural areas in Belarus, gangs brutally attacked Soviet activists and Jews, viewing them as supporters of a new Soviet order.[36] Enemies of the Bolsheviks managed to find fertile soil for anti-Semitic propaganda in villages. Deserters from the Red Army, criminal elements, and the peasantry (Belarusians, Russians, Ukrainians and Poles) participated in pogroms. The peasants often sympathised with anti-Soviet troops and bandits.[37] With the participation of some local peasants, those conducting the pogroms destroyed the property of Jews, murdered the Jews themselves, and looted and burned their possessions. However, these attacks, which were both ideological and criminal in character, targeted principally the rural Jewish population, which was widely spread across the Belarusian territory.[38]

Violence was evidently important for maintaining a certain local way of life. Along with the Red terror widely used by the Bolsheviks, the White terror was carried out actively by their enemies in the local areas. Some military leaders advocated violence as a tool of political struggle against the new order. By attacking Soviet employees and Jews, the gangsters aimed to overawe local peasants. Some gangs encouraged peasants to take part in their robberies and looting during and after the attacks and pogroms, making them culpable participants. Under the collapse of the local economies, such robberies accompanied with terror seemed to be a kind of 'redistribution' of property and goods. This chain of confiscations, requisitions, and other violent measures started with the First World War, the Russian Revolution, and the civil war.

Beginning in 1918, the Red Army, Cheka, and Soviet paramilitary troops suppressed the revolts and the banditry in the region.[39] The administration was aiming to prevent all efforts to overthrow the Soviet regime.[40] Militia brigades were set up to maintain

Fig. 9: 'Red Guards Don't Want Blood, But They Are Ready'. Propaganda poster on the 'good and strong' Russian Socialist Federative Soviet Republic and their 'troublesome' neighboring states and regions on the Western border, painted by Dmitriĭ Stakhievich Moor, 1921.

order in the countryside. These bodies mainly included local residents who participated in guerrilla groups, and former Red Army soldiers. Komsomol members (Communist youth organisation) were recruited into the militia to promote discipline among militiamen. The Soviet authorities actively recruited Belarusian, Russian, and Jewish workers to the ranks of various military detachments, such as 'communist squads', 'military-party detachments' or 'Komsomol military units'. As Belarus had a considerable proportion of Jews in cities and small towns, it was natural enough that they would serve in such units, fighting against the counter-revolutionaries and suppressing rebels in their region.[41]

In 1921-1922, the Soviet regime managed to suppress most of the anti-Soviet guerrilla detachments – not only at the point of the bayonet, but also through the implementation of the new social and economic policy known as the New Economic Policy (NEP). Anti-Bolshevik groups that infiltrated the region from Poland attacked Soviet Belarus until the mid-1920s. At the end of the decade, some peasants rebelled against the massive collectivisation and the establishment of *kolkhozes*, yet Stalin's secret services and the Red Army managed to put down such riots quite quickly.[42]

At the centenary of the end of First World War and the establishment of the Belarusian Peoples' Republic in 1918, the names of those people who struggled against the Bolsheviks are being brought back into the discourse. The crimes committed by the 'green' armies and rebels in Belarus were widely used by Soviet propaganda to demonise Belarusian nationalism. In present-day Belarus, political opponents of the authoritarian Belarusian regime of Lukashenko actively discuss the role of Stanisłaŭ Bułak-Bałachovič. For example, Belarusian internet media portrays Bułak-Bałachovič's 1920 raid in Polesia as an attempt to restore Belarusian statehood, suppressed by the Bolshevik Russia.[43] The official Belarusian side (including the government, state institutions responsible for public memory and 'official' historiography) uses previous Soviet evaluations or keeps silence on these events. In the meantime, some historians, mainly Russian-oriented, ascribe the blame to all 'Belarusian nationalists' for crimes committed by Bałachovič's troops. This tendency could be explained by the fear of a potential so-called 'colour revolution' in Belarus,

as has already materialised in Ukraine. Certain circles in Belarus and Russia aim to struggle with 'an anti-Soviet as well as an anti-Russian vision of the historical past', where Bułak-Bałachovič and other warlords managed to occupy an important place. Meanwhile, in Belarusian pop culture Bułak-Bałachovič, ataman Monič, and other rebel leaders are winning more and more popularity among Belarusian youth.[45]

Conclusion

The First World War, the collapse of the Russian Empire, the establishment of new states and borders on its ruins, the all-embracing political changes that occurred in the wake of the Russian revolution, the 1918 Brest-Litovsk Treaty, and the 1921 Riga Treaty, all greatly affected life in Belarus. The progress of the conflicts after the First World War in the region, and its brutalisation, were the result of many factors, such as the geographical location of Belarus and its legacy as a battlefield zone in the global conflicts, the dynamics of political and economic transformations in the region, and a dilemma of tangled social and ethnic relations. Desertion became a broad phenomenon in Belarus during the collapse of the Russian Imperial army. Many gangs also consisted of former Red Army soldiers. The events of the First World War and the 'wars after the War' reinforced anti-Semitism in the region, where many Jewish communities suffered from pogroms and attacks. In the period of unrest, Soviet activists and loyalists were actively attacked by gangsters and ordinary criminals. Between 1918 and 1921, peasant uprisings took place in the former Russian Empire. Angered by the Bolsheviks' policy of war communism, and by the unpopular economic and social policies and repressive measures that became an inescapable attribute of political life under the Soviet regime, local peasants clashed with the new authorities. Such activity in Belarus was characterised by numerous anti-Soviet riots committed by deserters, criminals, former members of Bułak-Bałachovič's groups and others. It happened where the Bolsheviks' positions were not strong enough, while their political enemies enjoyed certain public support in the rural areas. Under unfavourable political and military circumstances, some military leaders supported by the local peasantry struggled for an independent Belarus, which came into being only 70 years later. In Belarus, the remembrance and evaluation of this page of history remains contested to this day.

Endnotes

1. The 'Jewish Public Committee to Aid Victims of War, Pogroms and Natural Disasters,' known as 'Evobshchestkom' in Russian, was established in the summer of 1920 to assist the Jewish population suffering greatly during the wars and pogroms.

2. Report of the authorised representative of the Belarusian Commission of the Evobeshchestvo Eliya Kopshits in Evobeschestkom of the attack on the town of Lyuban in the Bobruisk district on 26 May 1921; National Archives of the Republic of Belarus (NARB), fond 782, opis 1, delo 5, list 12; printed in Lidiya Milyakova, ed., *Kniga pogromov: pogromy na Ukraine, v Belorussii i evropeĭskoĭ chasti Rossii v period Grazhdanskoĭ voĭny, 1918-1922 gg.: sbornik dokumento* (Moskva: ROSSPEN, 2007), 525-526.

3. Jochen Böhler, 'Generals and Warlords, Revolutionaries and Nation State Builders. The First World War and its Aftermath in Central and Eastern Europe,' in *Legacies of Violence: Eastern Europe's First World War*, eds. Jochen Böhler, Włodzimierz Borodziej and Joachim von Puttkamer (München: Oldenbourg Verlag, 2014), 51-66, here 58.

4. Aleksey Khokhlov, *Krakh antisovetskogo banditizma v Belorussii v 1918-1925 godakh* (Minsk: Belarus, 1981), 19.

5. On these topics see: Oleg Łatyszonek, *Białoruskie formacje wojskowe: 1917-1923* (Białystok: Białoruskie Towarzystwo Historyczne, 1995); Ihar Puškin, *Uzbroenyy supratsiŭ va Uskhodnyay Belarusi (20-30-ia gady XX st.): Dakumenty i matéryyaly* (Magilieŭ: Medysont, 2003); Nina Stuzins'ka, *Bilorus' buntivna. Z istoriï zbroynogo antyradyans'kogo sprotyvu v 20-ti rr. XX stolittya* (Minsk: Varaskin, 2012).

6. Per Anders Rudling, *The Rise and Fall of Belarusian Nationalism, 1906-1931* (Pittsburgh: University of Pittsburgh Press, 2015), 70.

7. See: Efim Gimpelson, *Voennyj kommunizm: politika, praktika, ideologiya* (Moskva: Mysl', 1973).

8. 'An Instruction to a Grain Confiscation Brigade (prodotryad), 20 August 1918', Russian State Military Archives, fond 42, opis 1, delo 278, list 23.

9. Marya Byaspalaya, *Belaruskaya vyëska u pershyia gady NEPa* (Minsk: Belaruski universitét kul'tury, 1999), 32.

10. See: Marek Cabanowski, *Generał Stanisław Bułak-Bałachowicz: zapomniany bohater* (Warsaw: PW Mikromax, 1993); Maksim Vasil'ev, 'Ataman S.N. Bulak-Balakhovich v istoricheskoy pamyati naroda,' in *Grazhdanskaya voyna v Rossii (1917-1922): istoricheskaya pamyat' i problemy memorializatsii «krasnogo» i «belogo» dvizheniya*, eds. Dmitriy Alisov and Juriy Zakunov (Moscow: Izdatel'stvo RNIIKiPN, 2016), 188-193; Jonathan Smele, *The 'Russian' Civil Wars, 1916-1926: Ten Years that Shook the World* (New York: Oxford University Press, 2017), 127.

11. Nicholas Vakar, *Belorussia, the Making of a Nation* (Cambridge MA: Harvard University Press, 1956), 115.

12. Some authors have mistakenly supposed that the 'army' managed to capture Gomel, a big industrial city and a centre of Gomel Province, which at that time belonged to Russia. Per Anders Rudling, *The Rise and Fall of Belarusian Nationalism, 1906-1931* (Pittsburgh: University of Pittsburgh Press, 2015), 115; Andrew Wilson, *Belarus: The Last European Dictatorship* (New Haven: Yale University Press, 2011), 95.

13. Later in the 1920s, the contacts between the BNR and Bałachovič were cut off, and the BNR leaders viewed him as an 'enemy of the Belarusian people' (Kastus Jesawitau, *Vospominaniya* [Memoirs], Nëman, 19939, 132-162, here 160.

14. Stanislaŭ Lis-Błoński, *Balakhoŭtsy. Svedchanni, dakumenty, dasledavanni* (Smolensk: Inbelkul't, 2014), 159-162.

15. Andrei Zamoiski, 'Military Pogroms, Jewish Self-Defense Units and the New Order in the Belarusian Lands, 1918-1921,' in *Akteure der Neuordnung. Ostmitteleuropa und das Erbe der Imperien, 1917-1924*, eds. Tim Buchen and Frank Grelka, Interdisciplinary Polish Studies, vol. 4, (Berlin: epublim, 2016), 113-130, here 122.

16. The media reported on acts of terror and vandalism in the borderlands of Soviet Belarus 'Po Sovetskoy Rosii', Izvestia, 8 March 1921, 3.

17. Khokhlov, *Krakh antisovetskogo banditizma*, 19.

18. Erik Landis, *Bandits and Partisans: The Antonov Movement in the Russian Civil War* (Pittsburg: University of Pittsburgh Press, 2008), 33.

19. Protocol of Politburo no. 34 on August 6, 1920. Russian State Archive of Socio-Political History (RGASPI), fond 17, opis 3, delo 100, list 1.

20. Khokhlov, *Krakh antisovetskogo banditizma*, 19.

21. The protocol 'The Struggle Against the Bandits' of the meeting of the Central Committee of the Communist Party of Belarus on 28 April 1921, NARB, fond 4p, opis 1, delo 425, list 54.

22. About 85 gangs in the second half of 1921 with app. 5000 rebels; Pavel Muraško, *Osobogo naznacheniya (Iz istorii ChON Belorussii. 1918-1924)* (Minsk: Izdatelstvo BGU, 1979), 91.

23. Viktor Kondrashin, *Krestyanstvo Rossii v Grazhdanskoĭ voĭne: k voprosu ob istokakh stalinizma* (Moscow: ROSSPEN, 2009), 255, 276.

24. Stuzins'ka, *Bilorus' buntivna*, 156-160, here 157.

25. A documentary on Monic'c anti-Bolsheviks struggle was filmed by the Belarusian TV channel ONT <https://www.youtube.com/watch?v=3qXYwaq87TU> (accessed 10 December 2017).

26. Stuzins'ka, *Bilorus' buntivna*, 163.

27. Panteleymon Selivanov, Pyëtr Akulov, eds., *V ogne grazhdanskoy voyny: Vspominayut veterany* (Minsk: Belarus, 1987), 137.

28. Khokhlov, *Krakh antisovetskogo banditizma*, 83.

29. Milyakova, *Kniga pogromov*, 898.

30. Joseph Schechtman, Elias Tcherikover, eds., *The Pogroms in the Ukraine under the Ukrainian Governments (1917-1920): Historical Survey with Documents and Photographs* (London: J. Bale & Danielsson, 1927), 118.

31. Milyakova, *Kniga pogromov*, 847.

32. Valeriy Nadtachaev, *Voennaya kontrazvedka Belarusi: Sud'by, tragedii, pobedy* (Minsk: Kavaler, 2008), 96.

33. Protocol of Politburo no. 34 on 6 August 1920, 'On Real Action Against the Poles for Losses Incurred by the Russian SSFR,' RGASPI, fond 17, opis 3, delo 249, list 8.

34. Wojciech Śleszyński, *Walka instytucji państwowych z białoruską działalnością dywersyjną 1920-1925* (Białystok: Prymat, 2005), 173.

35. Vladimir Buldakov, 'Freedom, Shortages, Violence: The Origins of the "Revolutionary Anti-Jewish Pogrom" in Russia, 1917–1918,' in *Anti-Jewish Violence: Rethinking the Pogrom in East European History*, ed. Jonathan Dekel-Chen (Bloomington: Indiana University Press, 2010), 74-94, here 76.

36. Muraško, Osobogo naznacheniya, 45; Ostrovskiy, '*Evreyskie pogromy*,' 70.

37. Report of Dr. Raisky at the United Meeting of Public Organizations in Gomel, 20 February 1921, YIVO Archives, Tcherikover papers, 81, folder 106, P. 8584.

38. Zamoiski, 'Military Pogroms,' 127-128.

39. Muraško, *Osobogo naznacheniya*, 79.

40. Some 'preventive' measures against the so-called 'counter-revolutionaries' were also carried out. On 6 August 1920, the entire Political Bureau under the Mozyr militia ordered all local revolutionary committees to register everyone of Polish nationality (!) who could be potentially hostile towards the Soviet regime (The State Zonal Archives in Mozyr, fond 30, opis 1, delo 2, list 4).

41. Puškin, *Uzbroenyy supratsiŭ*, 47.

42. See: Viola Lynne, *Peasant Rebels Under Stalin: Collectivization and the Culture of Peasant Resistance* (Oxford: Oxford University Press, 1996), 100.

43. On this day, the troops of general Stanislav Bulak-Balakhovich liberated Mozyr (in Russian), <https://charter97.org/ru/news/2017/11/10/268786/> (accessed 14 December 2017).

44. Vseslav Zin'kevič, *Nesvyadomaya istoriya Beloy Rusi* (Moskva: Knižnyy mir, 2017), 250.

45. The image of General Bułak-Bałachovič in mass culture (in Belarusian) <https://www.racyja.com/kultura/vobraz-generala-bulak-balakhovicha-u-mas/> (accessed 15 December 2017).

The Years of 1918-1923 as a Transformative Period of Jewish Politics

Alexis Hofmeister

Years of Comets – Years of Kaddish[1]

To many, the crumbling of imperial sovereignty in Eastern Europe after four years of war did not come as a surprise. Many places heralded it through the quiet toppling of ancient symbols, clearly showing how worn the traditional loyalties already were.[2] Signs that old certainties had been shattered abounded, and the long-established elites had finally lost all credibility during the war.[3] Tamara Deutscher (1913-1990) later retold a story about the events of 1918 often reported by her to-be husband Isaac Deutscher (1907-1967). Looking back at the events of November 1918 in the small Polish town of Chrzanów, he characterised this historical change of guards with the following anecdote:

> At the market place of Chrzanów, not far from the house of the Deutschers, stood the most impressive municipal building in the district. It was Town Hall and Police Station all in one. Over its heavy entrance door, on the big shield, was blazoned the emblem of the Habsburg Empire: a large eagle with wings spread and two heads, both crowned, looking left and right. One November day in 1918 a crowd of people gathered outside the Town Hall to talk about the latest proclamation of the last of the Habsburgs. A young boy, a hunchback, one of the least impressive characters of the town, was climbing a long flimsy ladder placed against the roof of the municipal building. The whole crowd watched his swift movements with bated breath. He reached the flagpole and then the double-headed eagle. With two or three strokes of a hammer he loosened the shield from its base; then he looked down and shouted to the people below: 'Hey, there, step aside, take care!' The crowd

Fig. 1: Market place in Chrzanów about 1910.

moved back a little. The hunchback threw the Austrian eagle straight on the cobblestones of the square. The shield and eagle smashed into a hundred pieces. Next day a new flag, the Polish flag, was flying over Chrzanów. The symbolism of the scene engraved itself on the memory of the future historian. When the moment comes, 'the least remarkable' hunchback of the little town can smash to bits the most awe-inspiring and revered imperial eagle.[4]

The historical first days of November 1918 demonstrated how fast political authority can disappear into the quicksand of uncertainty if those in power can no longer take the tacit approval of their subjects for granted.[5] In Tsarist Russia, where the Tsar had granted a parliament, the Russian Duma, in 1906 that could not, however, conceal the essentially autocratic nature of the regime, the Romanov dynasty had already fallen in 1917. The dynasties of the Hohenzollerns and Habsburgs, which had ruled their empires much more according to the rule of law, sur-

Juden!

Erscheinet vollzählig bei den

Massenkundgebungen

gegen die

Pogrome in Galizien

die am Mittwoch, den 27. November 1918, halb 7 Uhr abends, in folgenden Sälen stattfinden:

1. Bezirk: „Reichshallen", Dorotheergasse 6-8
   Hotel „Post", Fleischmarkt 24

2. Bezirk: „König Dawid", Unt. Augartenstrasse 8

20. Bezirk: Brigittasaal, Wintergasse 27.

Unter Anderem werden sprechen:

Se. Ehrw. Oberrabbiner Dr. Chajes, Abgeordneter Straucher, Adolf Stand, Staatsbahnrat Ing. Stricker, Dr. Schipper (Krakau), Abgeordneter Reitzes, Abgeordneter Breiter, Frau Anitta Müller.

Freier Zutritt.   Jüdischer Nationalrat.

Fig. 2: Poster of the Jewish National Council of Austria to come out against anti-Jewish pogroms in Galicia, November 1918.

Fig. 3: Jewish soldiers detained in the camp in Jabłonna in August 1920 during the Battle of Warsaw, one of the decisive battles of the Polish-Soviet War (1919-1920). Several thousand Jewish soldiers were suspected of collaboration with the Bolsheviks, despite their very substantial commitment for Polish independence, for instance in the Polish Legions.

vived only a year longer.[6] At the moment of crisis and of power vacuum, however, it became obvious that the different post-war societies could not agree on a common denominator. Rather, the political consensus often amounted to little more than the rejection of the old order. In Chrzanów, there were anti-Semitic riots even before the declaration of the new Polish state on 11 November 1918.[7] After the Jewish self-defence groups, composed of former soldiers, were disarmed at the behest of the Polish military, their attackers were afforded free rein. Two Jews died as a result of the violence, a large number of the roughly 14,000 Jewish inhabitants of Chrzanów lost their property and many sought refuge in Cracow.[8] In Kielce, anti-Jewish riots that broke out on the 11th and 12th of November left over 500 wounded. In Lvov, which was already experiencing a bitter conflict between Poles and Ukrainians over the control of the

city, horrific acts of violence against Jews were committed between the 22nd and 24th of November 1918.[9]

In 1919, the Polish–Soviet War gave rise to court-martial shootings in Pińsk and Vilnius, where there were 90 Jews among the victims.[10] In most of these incidents, it has been reported, conventions of honourable and gentlemanly conduct were purposely infringed. Humiliating treatment was not reserved only for the men: women, children and the elderly were included among the victims. The disarming of Jewish self-defence units as well as the exclusion of former comrades-in-arms in the Polish–Soviet War can be interpreted as a symbolic degrading and denial of comradeship, indeed as exclusion from the national community.[11]

Given the very different ways in which Jews experienced the Great War, and the crisis of long-cherished certainties during the 'dreamland'[12] of the cease-fire period, the question arises as to whether there really is just one way in which Jewish people experienced the historical moment of 1918/19. Ezra Mendelsohn (1940-2015), the North American historian of the Jewish labour movement and of Zionism, subsequently wrote of 'great expectations and an unpleasant awakening'.[13] It is scarcely surprising that the shadow cast by the later Holocaust was darkening the decades before Hitler's seizure of power and his attack on Europe as well. To this day, the historiography of the years following the end of the First World War resonates with the question of whether the extremism of the 20th century was already discernible at the end of the 'long 19th century', and whether the violence that immediately followed the end of the war was already kindling a genocidal frenzy that foreshadowed the later degeneration of the territories between the Baltic and the Black Sea into *Bloodlands*.[14] The brief period between the formal end of the First World War and the consolidation of the new post-imperial states in East-Central and South-Eastern Europe was unquestionably a time of crisis and transition. But for the Jews, it was particularly a time of worrying threats on the one hand and of pioneering departures and advancements on the other.[15] This essay will look not only at the complex historical changes but also at long-term developments.[16] It will examine a selection of individual life stories, offered here as keys to understanding the five-year period between 1918 and 1923. The lives sketched out here in brief biographies, and the autobiographical reflections of the individuals presented, open up a world of political experiences and correspondingly of political expectations.[17] Later interpretations had to try to make sense of the critical transitional phase from imperial to nation-state in the light of the fracture in civilisation represented by Auschwitz.[18]

Political Affiliations During Conflict

In 1927, the Jewish historian Simon Dubnow (1860-1941), born in the Russian Empire but living in seclusion since 1922 in Berlin-Dahlem, interrupted his work on his magnum opus, the *World History* of the *Jewish People*,[19] in order to take part in a conference in Zurich on the situation of Jewish populations in Europe, of the Yishuv[20] in Palestine and in America. Dubnow was no longer active in frontline politics

after 1918. Then as now he was considered one of the most significant historians of Eastern European Jewry. The political echo of his many writings on the theory and practice of self-government for Jewish communities and on autonomy in the diaspora resonated throughout the different Jewish minority groups in the new nation states after the First World War.[21] Calls for minority protection and internal autonomy – different from the independence of a territorial state – rang out across Eastern Europe after 1918. This was due not only to Simon Dubnow, but also to federative plans of the Austro-Marxist Karl Renner (1870-1950) and Zionist demands.[22] In Zurich, Dubnow claimed that ten years after the end of the First World War there were few grounds for hope arising from the situation in the Soviet Union. The Russian Revolution's gains in terms of individual autonomy had been lost through a rapid diminishing of economic freedom and cultural – especially religious – self-determination.[23] Dubnow was more optimistic about those Jews who, following the breakup of the multi-ethnic empires, found themselves in newly created nation states, the borders of which had been secured by the new post-war order established in the treaties drawn up in the suburbs of Paris.[24] Dubnow presumed that these Jews outside the Soviet Union would preserve and revive the heritage of East-European Jewry. The individual and collective social and cultural rights granted to the East and Central European Jews constituted, in spite of many setbacks, an undeniable success in emancipation. Statues of Jewish Autonomy, such as the one achieved in independent Lithuania, were a source of hope to Dubnow. It seemed to him as if young Jewish men and women in Eastern Europe were increasingly thinking in terms of the Jewish nation. Dubnow explained: 'I am convinced in the final bankruptcy of the whole assimilationist policy and in the victory of the national idea. [...] I believe in the future of the League of Nations and I also believe in the necessity of centralizing the political work for the protection of Jewish rights.'[25]

In 1927 in Zurich, all attempts at founding a single forum representing the interests of Jews worldwide were frustrated by conflicts within the Jewish community, at the root of which lay different understandings of the very nature of Jewishness. Did Jewry constituted a community of faith and shared destiny,

Fig. 4: Postcard (before 1918) showing the Jewish historians Simon Bernfeld (1860-1940), left, and Simon Dubnow (1860-1941), right.

resting on orthodox practice and a shared vision among the faithful, or was it a modern nation arisen from common roots and therefore rightfully striving for the satisfaction of its claims to a shared territory under international law? As early as 1919, the battle at the Paris Peace Conference to achieve minority rights for Jews had demonstrated that not all Jewish delegates shared the sense of an ethnically based identity held mostly by Jewish representatives from Eastern Europe. The American Jewish delegation saw Jewry principally as a community of faith. While a common understanding of Jewish politics was still under debate, guaranteed 'Jewish rights' already featured on the agenda of the Paris Peace Conference. They were discussed in talks and negotiations on East-European minority protection in international law.[26] Leon Reich (1879-1929), a Zionist from Eastern Galicia and a member of the Committee of Jewish delegations at the Paris Peace Conference (*Comité des*

délégations juives), once told the following anecdote to describe the situation:

'Are you hoping to find rights for Jews in Paris?' I was asked, half in jest and half in derision, by a prominent industrial magnate from Geneva. I met him on the train to Paris; ground down by the monotony of factory life, he was travelling to the French capital to lift his spirits by visiting the colourful world of reviews and variety shows [...] We were hoping to find rights for Jews. And we can say it straight: we found them. Admittedly not as plentiful as we wanted, or as would have been our fair due if we were to be satisfied as a nation; but sufficient nevertheless to avoid being absorbed into the variety of other cultures, and to see these rights as a foundation for building up our own national life.[27]

For Jewish politicians, the fundamental foreign policy problem was the fact that the major powers supported their claims as a stateless minority to be a

Originalaufnahme vom Kriegsschauplatz 1915
Jüdischer Einwohner vor den Ruinen
seines Hauses in Kutno

Fig. 5: Jewish inhabitant standing close to the ruins of his former home; part of a series of war postcards, printed by the German Jewish publisher Louis Lamm (1871-1943), 'Original Footage from the Theatre of War', 1915.

subject of international law only to a certain extent. The acknowledgement of Jewish rights in principle resulting from the Paris peace agreements and the possibility to petition to the League of Nations could not substitute for the fact that Jews had no form of an identifiable state. Lord Arthur James Balfour's (1848-1930) undertaking in respect of Jewish claims to parts of Palestine – undoubtedly a significant success on the part of the Zionist movement – was only one of a number of competing factors influencing British foreign policy. [28]

Since the late 19th century, the internal conflicts of the Jewish populations in Eastern Europe had focused on questions of affiliation, social, political and economic. After the end of the empires, however, the rules of the game had changed dramatically. Prior to the establishment of the State of Israel in Palestine in 1948, a graded cultural and political autonomy for the transnational and highly heterogeneous Jewish population in Eastern Europe, undoubtedly provided the most advanced agenda for an autonomous Jewish political life. There had already been attempts at creating a system of Jewish politics, with modern left-wing, liberal, national and religious parties in various forms, within the imperial states that collapsed in 1917/18. Now, the generation of Jewish men and women of politics born in the later 19th century had to prove themselves under the system of nation states established in the post-imperial political order for East-Central Europe. In interpreting the radical collapse brought about by the First World War and the subsequent post-war and transition periods, they referred in principle to the same fundamental ideological beliefs that were shared by their non-Jewish neighbours. [29] Apart from concerns of particular individuals, Jewish politicians tended to be guided by political priorities which were already developed during imperial times. [30] The currents of (religious)

Fig. 6: Jewish preschool class with a portrait of Vladimir Medem (1879-1923), the famous leader of the *Algemeyner Yidisher Arbeter Bund*.

traditionalist, nationalist, liberal and socialist positions must be particularly mentioned. Their proponents disagreed bitterly at times, but were prepared to build strategic alliances at other times. One could find examples of internecine conflict at various political levels, for instance on the boards of Jewish communities, in which socialists, Zionists and Agudists[31] argued vigorously over the financial equipment of various types of Jewish schools.[32] Remarkably, however, and regardless of any newly created territorial borders, the political conflicts among the Jewish populations of East-Central and South-Eastern Europe in 1918 were structurally similar and presented comparable challenges.

This was true in many ways. First, the war as well as the new social and territorial order after 1918 affected the Jews on an existential level; they were an ethno-religious diaspora population without any territory of their own, living in many of the new states as migrants without ever having crossed their borders. In 1922, more than 70% of the worldwide Jewish population – about 8.25 million people – lived in states that had not existed in their current form eight years before. About half of the 5.2 million Jews who had entered the war as subjects of the Tsar now became Soviet citizens. The other half lived in the Baltic states, Poland and the much-expanded state of Romania, where the Jewish population had tripled. The c. 2.1 million Jews of the Habsburg monarchy now lived in Romania, Hungary, the Republic of German-Austria and the new states of Poland, Yugoslavia and Czechoslovakia. Roughly 400,000 Ottoman Jews lived in

287

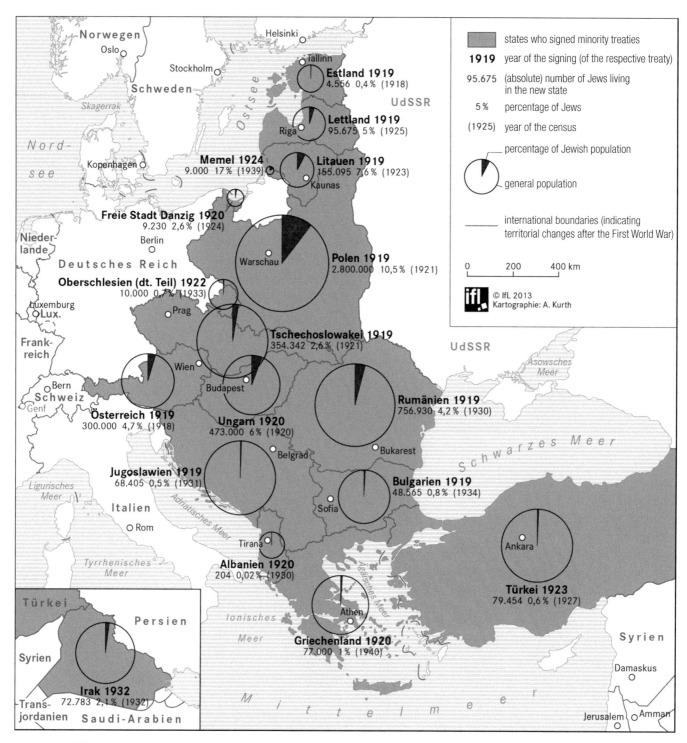

Fig. 7: Map of the minority treaties after the Paris Peace Conference of 1919, indicating the borders of the new states in Eastern Europe as well as the percentage of the respective Jewish populations of these states.

the Turkish Republic, Iraq, Syria, the Lebanon and Palestine.

The particular Jewish communities were secondly divided by economic, cultural, political and even religious characteristics.[33] Outside the Soviet Union, which is not the focus here, lived several million Jews, concentrated in part in the larger cities such as Riga (40,000), Kaunas (25,000), Vilnius (49,000), Warsaw (349,000), Lvov (77,000), Prague (32,000), Budapest (212,000), Belgrade (5,000), Iaşi (39,000), Czernowitz (75,000), Chişinău (100,000) and Bucarest (41,000), but also in rural areas such as Carpatho-Ukraine (93,000), Bukovina (176,000) and the eastern provinces of Poland, where about 10% of the population was Jewish.[34] The differences between urban and rural populations were due to some extent to cultural differences but principally to the sharp social differentiation within Jewish communities. There were also inter-generational, gender and linguistic differences within Jewish society.[35] Some were native Yiddish speakers, whose knowledge of Hebrew was limited to the minimum that they needed in order to take part in religious life. Some Jews only used the dominant language of the newly erected nation-states in which they used to live and did not want to teach their children any 'Jewish languages'. Some Zionists refused to speak Yiddish on ideological grounds. Observant and secular Jews rarely met in daily life; they read the newspapers of their own community and sent their children to different schools. The observant group was divided into opponents and supporters of settling in Palestine, while the secular community split along political lines ranging from socialists (such as Bundists[36]) and communists to various branches of proletarian Zionists. The fracturing of Jewish politics was manifest in the different institutions that claimed to speak for the majority of East European Jews, or at least for nationally minded Jews after 1918. The competing visions of who should speak for the Jewish community and what Jewish politics should aim at were struggling with each other at different levels: the local Jewish communities, the national parliaments as well as international institutions. There were, for example, various clubs and factions of parliamentarians in the Polish parliament after 1918 as well as several Jewish groups of delegates representing Jewish interests at the Paris Peace Conference.[37]

And finally – and this is the third point of similarity between the claims of all Jewish politicians following 1918 – the question of the non-Jewish allies recurred. The inherited pattern of Jewish politics rested on cooperation between Jewish and non-Jewish elites, and had been closely linked to the political framework of the *ancien régime*.[38] In the last few decades of imperial sovereignty, this pattern had come under some strain, and in 1918 it seemed as if the times had finally come to an end in which Jewish politics could be viewed as hierarchic from within and as patriarchic from without. Democratization was the keyword of the time, and there is good reason to date the origin of modern Jewish politics to the years between the turn of the century in 1900 and the final demise of the imperial era in 1918.[38]

The system of minorities protection treaties the First World War allies established for the post-war order throughout Eastern Europe and in Iraq (a successor state of the Ottoman Empire) was designed to correspond to the relevant peace treaties. The newly established post-imperial states in East-Central and South-Eastern Europe declared themselves as national states but were in fact multi-ethnic states. Germans and Jews lived as minority groups in nearly all of these states, which were either newly created – such as the Czechoslovakian Republic – or had been re-created from previously existing entities, such as Hungary and Romania. For various reasons, Jews and Germans were not regarded as an integral part of the respective nation. Individual Jewish and German politicians from these minority groups were aware of the position of minority groups from a transnational perspective, and they set up the European Nationalities Congress together in 1925. They attempted, by means of submissions to the League of Nations, to influence the situation of various minority groups in Eastern and Southeastern Europe. The German Empire could advocate for German minorities, an option Jewish people did not have at their disposal. The Jews were a historical minority group, but some of the German populations were experiencing life as a minority group for the first time in Eastern Europe after 1918: this was the case for the German groups in Bohemia, Moravia and Silesia, who were collectively designated as the 'Sudeten Germans' from 1919 onwards. Historical minorities such as Baltic Germans had a different perspective on minority protection, one that was not unfamiliar to representatives of Jewish minority groups.

Are there any ways in which Jewish politics after 1918 still exert an influence today? According to some historians, political influences born out of experiences in East-Central Europe and South-Eastern Europe continue to shape the political discourse in Israeli society today, even though the founding generation born in Eastern Europe between 1918 and 1938 has now left active political life.[40] We shall now look at some examples of Jewish political representatives in Eastern Europe, and at the scope available to them in their activities in the decisive years between 1918 and 1923.

LYON LEA

Drama in 4 Akten
von
Alexander Bródy.

Monopolfilm der Firma
Anna Christensen
Wien, VI.
Mariahilferstrasse 53.

Fig. 8: *Lea Lyon* – Poster of a popular stage play written by Sándor Bródy (1863-1924) and adapted for film in 1915, directed by Alexander (Sándor) Korda (1893-1956). It helped to popularize one of the Central Powers' major war propaganda claims by showing the relation of the Habsburg officers vis-a-vis the local Jewish population in 'liberated' Galicia in a rosy light.

Wilhelm Filderman and Mayer Ebner

Wilhelm Filderman (1882-1963) is considered one of the most significant representatives of Romanian Jewry in the 20th century.[41] He began his studies in his home city of Bucarest and gained his doctorate in law at the Sorbonne in 1909. Having fought in the First World War as a Romanian officer, he then took part in the Paris Peace Conference, where he contributed to formulating the Romanian minorities protection treaty. He advocated in the press and lobbied among the political representatives for equal treatment of the different Jewish populations in Romania. He held a leading position in the Romanian Jewish Union (Uniunea Evreilor Români, UER), an organisation he played a major part in shaping, and led the Federation of Jewish communities in Romania. Filderman promoted a policy of integration for Jews in the expanded national state of Romania after 1918. In spite of disagreeing with them strongly on some issues, he worked with Zionist organizations such as the Jewish Agency and the Jewish National Fund (JNF), and in 1926 he visited Palestine. Filderman combated Romanian anti-Semitism and promoted a programme to enable Jews living in Romania to become assimilated into an idealised civic normality, including linguistic assimilation. He was elected to the Romanian house of deputies as a member of the National Liberal Party (Partidul Naţional Liberal, PNL) and opposed the need for specifically Jewish representation of Romanian Jews in parliament. His posthumously published memoirs and diaries include little in the way of personal reflections. Rather, they extensively document his many speeches and initiatives both within and beyond Parliament.[42] As a politician, he continued to work in the way he had done in the pre-war era. He saw no need to re-arrange his political guidelines. His decision to rely on Romanian liberalism and his reference to the West European model of the national state made him an ideal point of contact for Romanian politicians and for the Entente victor nations backing the post-war European order.[43] Given the majority of Romania's educated classes' pronounced cultural interest in Paris and French models of culture, Filderman's French cultural imprint fit in very well.

Mayer Ebner (1872-1955), meanwhile, represents another variant of post-imperial politics in post-War

Romania.[44] His cultural focus was Vienna, where he had studied law at the Franz-Joseph University. An effect of his disillusionment with the bourgeois anti-Semitism in the Habsburg monarchy was his founding of the Hasmonäa fraternity in Czernowitz in 1891. Ebner, an adherent of Theodor Herzl, had taken part in the First Zionist Congress in Basel (1897), and was one of Romania's most prominent Zionists. He achieved significant success in local and district elections. He was a long-time member of the Czernowitz city council and, after his return from banishment to Siberia in 1914 by the Russian occupation forces, he represented the Zionists in the Jewish National Council of Bukovina. He campaigned for the revival of Hebrew as a national language, but at the same time edited the successful German-language *Ostjüdische Zeitung* (Eastern Jewish Newspaper) from 1919 to 1938. Although Ebner and the party he had helped to found, the Jewish Party of Romania (Partidul Evreiesc din România, PER), entered into an alliance with Filderman's Union of Romanian Jews (UER) in 1937 in order to stand up to the increasing anti-Semitism, Ebner remained one of the most outspoken opponents of the 'Romanianisation' of Jews in Greater Romania.

The biographies of Filderman and Ebner illustrate a political dichotomy that existed both within and outside Judaism.[45] The Jews in the newly incorporated border regions of Greater Romania – in the eastern (or Romanian) Banat, in the historical provinces of the Bukovina and Transsylvania – had been socially and politically integrated into the Habsburg monarchy and, after the First World War, found themselves in a state that was both linguistically and culturally alien to them. To some extent, this was true for Jews from Bessarabia, which had been part of the Russian Empire. Filderman experienced Judaism principally as a religion, and thus followed the Western European model, but Ebner saw his Jewishness as an ethnic fact, thereby representing a mindset more popular in Eastern Europe. Ebner explained his way of thinking in a speech before the Romanian senate, the upper chamber of the parliament:

If we as Jews were not seen as an ethnic minority, then it would be impossible to gain either a historical or a factual understanding. If it were true that we belong ethnically to the population among

Fig. 9: The wooden synagogue of Grodno 1926.

which we live and whose language we speak, then the Jews of the Regat[46] would be Romanians, but the Jews in Transsylvania would be Hungarian, the Jews in Bessarabia would be Russian and those living in Bukovina would have to be seen as German. I want to remark, however, that the broad majority of Jews living in these four areas besides speaking the vernacular generally speak Yiddish. The concept of a Romanian Jewry with fourfold ethnicity, however, is but nonsense.[47]

Ebner emigrated to Palestine in 1940, where he campaigned for a dualistic solution to the conflict between the Jewish and Arab inhabitants of Palestine. His biographers have suggested that this echoes the policies of federalisation and compromise of the later Habsburg monarchy.[48]

Shimshon Rosenboim and Paul Mincs

Shimshon Rosenboim (1860-1934), also known as Simon Rosenbaum, was a former member of the Russian Duma, a lawyer and an early Zionist from Lithuania; his rich political experience qualified him in various respects to represent the new state of Lithuania on the international stage. The elaboration of the Jewish autonomy statute in interwar Lithuania and the respective showcasing at the Paris Peace Conference were connected with his name.

Rosenboim was at this point Lithuania's acting foreign minister; in January 1920, at their first conference, the representatives of the Jewish communities in Lithuania had elected him as chairman of the Jewish National Council. On 15 May 1920, Rosenboim had joined the founding Seimas, the Lithuanian Parliament, as a member for the United Jewish People's List; from 1923, he sat as member for the United List of Zionists in the second Seimas. Both within the Lithuanian Parliament and outside it, he promoted the interests of the Jewish population of Lithuania. Rosenboim's political career had already begun in the Russian Empire. He joined the first Russian parliament, the State Duma, in 1906, representing the con-

Fig. 10: Shimshon Rosenboim about 1920 as depicted in 'Lietuvos Albomas' – a volume portraying the new Lithuanian elites after 1918.

stituency of Minsk as a member of the Constitutional Democrats (K-D). As a signatory of the Vyborg Manifesto, which called for resistance to Tsar Nicholas II's dissolution of the State Duma, he was prosecuted and sentenced to three months' imprisonment. At the instigation of the German occupation forces, the Lithuanian National Council, the Taryba, promoted the inclusion of Jewish politicians from Lithuania.[49] In December 1918, at a conference of Lithuanian Zionists, Rosenboim had articulated the conditions for his entry into the Taryba and the postulate for independent Jewish politics in Lithuania. With the expected Lithuanian constitution which would guarantee Jews rights, Jews should be able to achieve a position in which they could take part themselves in the legislative process and politically control the executive.[50] Rosenboim himself and two other Jewish politicians not affiliated to any party were co-opted into the Taryba.[51] Jewish politicians had to make their presence felt, given Lithuania's and Poland's competing claims to Vilnius and its surrounding region, designated as 'Mid-Lithuania' during the period between its occupation in 1920 by General Lucjan Żeligowski's (1865-1947) troops and its final incorporation into the Polish state. Rosenboim stayed in Kaunas while Jakob Wygodzki (1856-1941), who first had been Lithuanian Minister for Jewish Affairs, became chair of the Jewish community in Vilnius and subsequently joined the Polish national parliament, the Sejm. Both Rosenboim and Wygodzki, preferred the option of a Lithuanian national state in which the Jewish population would have autonomous status, and were critical of Polish imperial ambitions.[52] In 1920, the Polish occupation administration in Vilnius had drawn up policy guidelines on Jews and Lithuanians inspired by Russian models. Moreover, a part of the legal system applying to the Jewish population survived from Tsarist into Polish times and remained in force until 1931. This background must be kept in mind when looking at Rosenboim's activities at the Paris Peace Conference. Whether within Jewish circles or before a wider public, he emphasised that a strong Lithuania, incorporating both Jews and White Russians in a territory of significant size, would be the best guarantee against any Bolshevik or Polish expansionism. In its guarantee of Jewish rights, Lithuania consequently included elements of cultural and territorial autonomy and thus went further than other post-imperial states in East-Central and South-Eastern Europe.

Rosenboim observed the prohibition on contact with Polish diplomats, a loyalty that he had to defend against Jewish critics, some from Poland. He made but one further attempt to mediate in the conflict between Poland and Lithuania. In the autumn of 1921, he received the Lithuanian foreign minister Juozas Purickis's (1883-1934) permission to travel to Berlin and Warsaw to gauge the possibility of a compromise between Lithuania and Poland on the issue of the Vilna territory. When this attempted negotiation was made public, Rosenboim was suspected of betraying Lithuanian interests. Both the Lithuanian foreign minister and Rosenbaum as his deputy resigned in the wake of this affair. Lithuania increasingly lost interest in establishing a proper autonomy for its Jewish population as it became obvious that Poland would retain Vilnius and its significant Jewish population. Rosenboim served as Minister for Jewish Affairs (1923-1924) for about one more year and became increasingly aware of Lithuanian politicians' unwillingness to respect any kind of solidarity between Lithuanians and Jews. In 1925, Rosenboim emigrated to Palestine and worked as a lawyer in Tel Aviv and acted as Lithuanian consul from 1927 onwards. In 1926, Atanas Smetonas (1874-1944) established an authoritian presidential regime and Lithuanian politics veered towards authoritarianism. In 1932, Rosenboim preserved the legacy of the struggle for the rights of the Jewish minority by publishing an account of his exploration of the concept of sovereignty.[53] On the problem of protecting a minority lacking an advocate to defend it from state power, Rosenboim writes:

When one examines cases in which oppressed peoples have no one to defend them, such as the Jews, serfs and so on, it always emerges that they had no 'relatives' so that there is no one with a subjective right or a subjective duty to offer them protection. It is a regrettable fact and a testimonium paupertatis of our culture that so much injustice goes unpunished simply because there is no judge. It was therefore a major benefit that humanity in its attempt to set up an organised system for the mutual protection of rights between and among states,

Fig. 11: Portrait of Paul Mincs, 1925.

with the League of Nations, was not only considering protecting statist actors, but also included the safeguarding of citizens within their own countries.

Pauls Mincs (1868-1941), the son of a businessman from Daugavpils, studied in Saint Petersburg and Tartu, and taught law from 1918.[54] He had already campaigned on social and political issues for Jews in Russia during the Tsarist period, as both co-founder and board member of the Riga branch, set up in 1889, of the Society for the Advancement of the Enlightenment Among the Jews of Russia (*Obshchestvo dlya razprostnaneniya prosveshcheniya mezhdu evreyami, OPE*). From 1918, he was a member of the Latvian Senate and between 1919 and 1921 he acted as auditor for the Latvian government.[55] In 1920, he was promoted to Deputy Minister for Employment. He made a considerable contribution to drafting the constitution of the new Latvian state. His political activities in inde-

Fig. 12: Róża Pomeranz-Melzer (center) with Leon Reich (1879-1929), with walking cane, the leader of the Galician Zionists from Lvov at the 12th Zionist Congress in Carlsbad, 1st to 14th September 1921.

pendent Latvia embraced a wide spectrum: he chaired the association of Jewish lawyers and led the Jewish National Democratic Party. He was a member of the Jewish Agency.[56] His allegiance towards the Latvian state was not affected, even after the government declared, in 1921, that it no longer needed any representatives from the ranks of the minorities.[57] As a lawyer, he represented Latvia on the international stage, for example in the International Penal and Penitentiary Commission (Commission Internationale Pénale et Pénitentiaire) in Bern in 1934, and from 1935 in Paris at the International Bureau for the Unification of Penal Law (Bureau International pour l'Unification du Droit Pénal). Following the Soviet annexation of Latvia, he was captured and deported to a work camp in Siberia, where he died in 1941.[57]

Róża Pomeranz-Melzer and Jakub Lejb Mincberg

Róża Pomeranz-Melzer (1880-1934) was one of the few Jewish women whose social and political activities in independent Poland were publicly acknowledged. She had studied in Vienna and Paris and spent several years training in a Leipzig conservatory of music. She spoke several European languages as well as Hebrew and Yiddish. Booklets she published, such as *Der Zionismus und die Frauen* (*Zionism and Women*, 1910) and *An die jüdischen Frauen: Ein Appell zur Umkehr* (*To Jewish Women: A Call to Turn Back*, 1898), brought her recognition and identified her as both a Zionist and a defender of women's rights.[59] She founded Judiyta, one of the first women's organisations in

Fig. 13: A local group of Bundists from Mszczonów, Poland, with a portrait of Karl Marx.

Poland, and from 1909 she chaired the Organisation of Jewish Women (WIZO) in eastern Lesser Poland. She represented the Jewish women of Interwar Poland at several international conferences. In order to offer help to refugees, war orphans and pogrom victims in Western Ukraine, after the end of the First World War she undertook a fund-raising tour through Western Europe. She opened an orphanage in Lwów and established a school for deaf-blind Jewish children. Pomeranz was elected to the Polish Sejm on the list of National Jewish Parties, and from 1922 to 1927 she represented the region of Stanisławów in Eastern Galicia. She was unsuccessful when she stood in subsequent elections to the Sejm (1928) and the Senate (1930). She remained the only Jewish woman parliamentarian in the history of the Sejm during the Second Polish Republic.[60]

Róża Pomeranz-Melzer's public commitment to Zionism and to women's rights were of equal importance to her in her political life. However, it appears that her focus shifted somewhat after the turning point of 1918, when she involved herself mainly in women's politics, although Zionism was still very important to her. In 1923, she attended the First World Congress of Jewish Women in Vienna. Following the devastation of the war, she became involved in a variety of issues: social care for the many war orphans and widows; equal rights for Jewish women in post-war society; overseas emigration as a social problem; and the difficulties faced specifically by Jewish women who had no legal Jewish bill of divorce (get) and were searching everywhere for their 'disappeared' husbands.[61] The *Wiener Morgenzeitung* carried a brief interview with Róża Pomeranz-Melzer, which did not focus on the reason for her visit to Vienna. Mrs Pomeranz used the interview to give information about the situation of Jews in Poland and her parliamentary work in the 'Jewish club' in the Sejm.[62] She was cautiously optimistic about the prospects for the coexistence of Jews and Poles. The congress brought

Fig. 14: Portrait of Zsigmond Kunfi (1897-1929) from a volume of his selected essays, edited posthumously in 1930.

together Zionist and non-Zionist women, which made it impossible to reach conclusions on various controversies, including the question of Palestine. However, the women who favoured Zionism did gather together in their own groups, or were invited by their Viennese hostesses to do so. The World Congress of Jewish Women offered the first opportunity since the end of the war for Jewish women to come together in solidarity and to show their strength to the worldwide women's movement. Contacts were established and views were exchanged between Eastern and Western European women, and women from America. The World Congress of Jewish Women offered Rosa Pomeranz a wider platform for political campaigning and public appearances.

Pomeranz's life-story might reinforce the idea that few women took part in Jewish politics or made their views public after 1918. The context, however, was important: first, Eastern European countries had taken the radical step of introducing women's suffrage; second, one should not underestimate the ex-

tent to which Jewish women were socially and politically engaged across the political spectrum.[63] As examples, one could cite Sophia Dubnov-Erlikh (1885-1986), born in in Belarus and active in the Polish Bund, and Sarah Schenirer (1883-1935), who set up a school movement for Jewish Orthodox girls (*Beys Yankev*[64]) that had an influence well beyond the borders of Poland.[65]

One of the most successful anti-Zionist orthodox politicians was the industrialist Leib Mincberg (1887-1943),[66] who sat on the Industry and Trade Committee of the Polish Sejm for the orthodox Aguda Party, and chaired the Jewish community in Łódź.[67] Mincberg had had a traditional upbringing as the son of a Hasidic family. Besides Polish, Hebrew and Yiddish, he also spoke various West European languages. He was a member of the Łódź city council and worked with the Sejm and with Polish politicians for the victims of anti-Jewish discrimination, which earned him the respect of the secular Jewish members of the council. Mincberg sided with the legendary founder of reborn Poland, Marshall József Piłsudski (1867-1935), whom Mincberg assured of the loyalty of the Jewish population. Historical scholarship nowadays tends to assume that Jewish politics after 1918 moved away from the model of personal appeal to the relevant non-Jewish persons in power (*shtadlanut*). The example of Mincberg and several other influential and charismatic Aguda politicians, such as Mordekhai Dubin (1889-1956) in Latvia, nevertheless shows that even under democratic auspices the political relationship between Jews and non-Jews was not one of equals: another legacy from imperial times.

Zsigmond Kunfi

The Hungarian Social Democrat Zsigmond (or Siegmund) Kunfi (1897-1929) claimed neither religious nor ethnic Jewish affiliation. He formally converted to the Calvinism of his Transylvanian homeland. Yet as his friend and brother-in-law Zoltán Rónai (1880-1940) wrote in a biographical tribute after Kunfi's death, he always laboured 'under the burden of an invisible yellow star'.[68] Before moving to Budapest, Kunfi worked as a teacher of German and Hungarian in a grammar school in Timişoara. In 1907, his public support for a Social Democrat cost him job and his income. Kunfi edited the social democratic magazine *Szocializmus* and became a lead editor of *Népszava* (*People's Voice*). He earned little, so he supplemented his income by doing translations and writing booklets. As a Marxist, he turned to literature and joined the Sociological Society of Vienna. His many articles appeared in various places, including the liberal journals *Nyugat* and *Huszadik század* (*The Twentieth Century*) as well as in Die Neue Zeit – the theoretical journal of the Social Democratic Party of Germany (SPD), published in Stuttgart. The social democratic milieu in Hungary was probably the only place in which his career was not hindered by his humble origins, his Jewish parentage and the fact that he had distanced himself from church and religion.

As an adherent of Karl Kautsky (1854-1938), Kunfi did not share the general enthusiasm for the war, and he represented Hungary in the 1917 Stockholm peace conference for socialist parties.[69] The Hungarian delegation campaigned for a peace without annexations or contributions. In spite of his opposition to the monarchy, Kunfi supported the continuing coherence of Hungarian territories on economic grounds. He thought that disrupting the existing well-developed economic arena by creating new borders would harm the population's interests. The Hungarian delegation supported keeping Transsylvania with Hungary and preserving Hungarian access to the sea at Fiume. They saw democratisation of international and interethnic relationships as a condition for peace between the Hungarian and South Slav area as an essential requirement.[70] However, they released no statement on the Jewish population of Hungary or Eastern Europe.

Kunfi became a member of the first republican government of Count Mihály Károlyi (1875-1955), which proclaimed the republic of Hungary on 16 November 1918.[71] Following the liquidation of the Croatian Ministry, Kunfi was Minister of Employment and Public Health, and from January 1919 he was responsible for the Ministry of Education, where he advocated a strict separation of church and state. As a centrist, Kunfi 'fought externally against a peace treaty imposed by force and for self-determination of the nations, and internally against the Bolshevik ideology of force'.[72] Initially, Kunfi retained his responsibilities after 20 March 1919. He was a member of the committee of the United Workers' Party and worked as the People's Commissar for Education in the Revolutionary Council of the Hungarian Soviet Socialist government. As such, he appointed Sándor Ferenczi (1873-1933) as psychoanalyst to a professorial chair in the medical faculty of the University of Budapest. It was the first time that psychoanalysis was recognised as a medical discipline at a university. As a mark of protest, Kunfi resigned his post on 24 June 1919 and he also subsequently became dissatisfied with his role in the Soviet government of Béla Kun (1886-1938).[73] He stayed in Hungary and was therefore able to support other members of the revolutionary government fleeing the White Terror. Kunfi himself emigrated to Vienna and made a living working as a foreign editor on the social democratic *Worker's Paper* and the Hungarian paper Világosság (Clarity). He became director of the Viennese Workers' evening classes and the party school of the Social Democratic Party of Austria (SPÖ).[74] In Vienna, Kunfi became involved in Hungarian emigrant circles that were critical of the political course of the Social Democratic Party of Hungary. In 1929, he died of an overdose of the barbiturate Veronal.

Zsigmond Kunfi's activities as a politician were not, in a narrow sense, politics on behalf of a specific ethno-religious group such as the Jews. He therefore cannot be labelled a Jewish politician. His biography is given here for those 'non-Jewish' Jews who partially found a home in the Social Democratic and Communist parties of Eastern and South-Eastern Europe.

David Albala

The surgeon David Albala (1886-1942) was born in Belgrade; he had fought for his country in the two Balkan Wars of 1912-1913 and had been promoted first to captain and then to lieutenant-colonel. He was born into a Sephardic family, and after returning from his medical studies in Vienna he established and directed a group of Zionists. Even before the official founding of the Kingdom of the Serbs, Croats and Slovenes (SHS), Albala was on a diplomatic mission to America when Lord Balfour declared that his government was sympathetic to the establishment of a 'Jewish homeland in Palestine'. Albala managed to secure a diplomatic note from Serbia endorsing the Balfour Declaration. Milenko Radomar Vesnić (1863-1921), Prime Minister of the SHS-kingdom as well as foreign

Fig. 15: David Albala from Belgrade, about 1940, wearing the army uniform of the Kingdom of Yugoslavia.

minister to be, in an official letter sent to Albala stated that Serbia endorsed the Balfour Declaration.[75] Serbia was thus the first state after the United Kingdom to recognise the justification of Jewish claims to Palestine and to express sympathy with the Zionist cause. In achieving this diplomatic coup, Albala was hoping to gain the acknowledgment and support of American Jews and a wider public. There was no contradiction in his mind between Serbian nationalism, Yugoslav patriotism or Zionism.

Albala travelled to the Paris Peace Conference as a member of the delegation of the Kingdom of the Serbs, Croats and Slovenes. He defended the newly created Yugoslav state from both Jewish and non-Jewish criticism, and repeatedly highlighted how sympathetic the Serbian nation, and in particular the royal family, were towards the Jewish cause. Emphasising the historical experience of victimisation shared by Jews and Serbs helped Albala and other Yugoslav Jews to validate their assertions. Albala be-

came chairman of the Federation of Jewish Congregations in Yugoslavia and led the Zionist association Bar Giora, in which he encountered fellow combatants who had served as soldiers of the Austro-Hungarian forces in the fight against Serbia, such as the famous Croatian Zionist Aleksandar Licht (1884-1948).[76]

After his return from the Paris Peace Conference Albala launched a period of political activity that lasted nearly twenty years: he published widely, worked for a number of Jewish organisations, led the Sephardic community of Belgrade and was involved in political, educational and cultural work among Jews in the Kingdom of the Serbs, Croats and Slovenes. He also maintained many international connections. He founded the Association of Yugoslavian Jews in the United States, where he had fled before the German invasion of Yugoslavia and where he died unexpectedly in 1942.

Conclusion

There is a rich variety among the Jewish men and women active in politics who took on positions of responsibility and, in some cases, power after 1918; they include a highly heterogeneous range of individuals engaged across a wide range of interests. Yet, in spite of their differences, there are common traits to the life stories presented here, in that they share similar attitudes towards political responsibility, which led to comparable reactions vis-a-vis historical conflicts. The war years left clear traces on all these men and women. They were perhaps most deeply affected by their war service, and by the need to flee from violence and from the insecurity of uncertain civil status after the end of the imperial era. Sarah Schenirer (1883-1935), for example, moved during the First World War from her birthplace, Cracow, to Vienna, where she experienced a form of revelation. It happened in Vienna that the preaching of a Rabbi made such an impression on her that she decided to tackle the lack of education for Jewish women in orthodox households.

In 1918, the threat of vital significance to many was the expulsion of Jewish citizens declared to be foreigners, often carried out overnight. One famous person affected was Salo W. Baron (1895-1989), arguably the most significant Jewish historian of the 20th century. He was born in Tarnów in West Galicia,

Fig. 16: Jewish population in front of destroyed buildings in Sokolniki (near Lvov), 1919.

and like Sarah Schenirer he had moved to Vienna in 1914, fleeing with his parents from the advancing front. Baron gained his first doctorate in 1920 by publishing a study of the Jewish question at the Vienna Congress.[77] There were obvious parallels to the 'Jewish question' at the Paris Peace Conference, but Baron did not address them in his work. He did, however, discover from his own experience that international protection was needed for minorities such as the Jews. The threat of expulsion applied to Galician refugees to Vienna. They were, it was alleged, citizens of the new state of Poland and thus not entitled to be in Vienna, where provisions were in short supply. In order not to stay illegally in Vienna, Baron applied for a Polish passport. It was issued on 16 August 1919, but only gave him permission to travel from Austria to Poland via Czechoslovakia[78] and had to be extended every six months. The young refugee also had

to report regularly to the Vienna police to avoid an expulsion notification. It was not until 1924 that Baron was granted the permanent right to remain in Vienna and in 1926, shortly before his emigration to America, he was issued with an Austrian passport. Baron experienced a leniency that was not granted to many other Galicians in Vienna. In 1921, the council of the League of Nations ruled that the planned expulsions of stateless people and aliens was legal and that citizens of the former Habsburg monarchy had no naturalisation rights in Austria.

Against this background, it is surely no coincidence that following 1918, and later after 1945, Jewish politics were marked by the question of the protection of the rights of individuals from the power of national states. Baron, for example, was convinced that heterogeneous and multi-ethnic empires, although they may have seemed an old-fashioned con-

Fig. 17: Jewish youth group „Tsukunft" (yidd.: future) from Przemyśl, 1925. The text on the board says: 'With united effort we will build the future!'

cept, provided better protection to Jews than monolithic nation states. Only a strong international peacekeeping power with authority over a nation state could overtly guarantee that the weak would be protected by the rule of law. This explains the significance of international congresses such as the Paris Peace Conference, which came to be seen as an important and existentially significant forum for Jewish politics. The politically active personalities examined here also engaged in negotiation and communication in places such as schools, local communities and national parliaments, as well as in transnational arenas such as courts of appeal.

Remarkably, there were various attempts after 1918 at establishing competing political and ideological systems within Jewish politics. The most eloquent example of this was in Poland, where Bundists, Zionists and Agudists were engaged in parallel education and media systems, publishing newspapers and books, arguing over party and memory politics and carrying out rituals of remembrance at various and sometimes competing *lieux de mémoire*. In the Jewish

world, the events of November 1918 in Chrzanów continue to be commented from different angles and perspectives to this day. While Isaac Deutscher underlined that 'the least remarkable hunchback of the little town can smash to bits the most awe-inspiring and revered imperial eagle', the memorial book of the town of Chrzanów, published to commemorate the annihilation of the Jewish community as well as its Jewish heritage, states that Chrzanów was the site of the first pogrom anywhere in liberated Poland.[79] It draws our attention to the bloody pogroms that erupted in the aftermath of the Great War in Eastern and, to a lesser extent, Southeastern Europe.

Zionists, for their part, remember the place of Chrzanów as the birthplace of Ignacy Schwarzbard (1888-1961), a member of the Jewish faction in the Cracow city council who in 1938 was elected to the Polish Sejm and after the German occupation of Poland became a member of the Polish government in exile in France and England. He transmitted news about the holocaust to the West and promoted rescue activities for Polish Jews.

Endnotes

1. The Kaddish (Quaddiš), a traditional prayer to sanctify God, or rather his name. It is recited as a mourning prayer for the dead at the end of Sabbath liturgy in the synagogue. Johann Maier, *Judentum-Reader* (Göttingen: Vandenhoeck & Ruprecht, 2007), 92-93, 199.

2. Manes Sperber, *Sieben Fragen zur Gewalt. Leben in dieser Zeit* (München: dtv, 1978), 9-26, here 9-10. On the fading of loyalties among war-weary soldiers, which Habsburg military leaders later included in their version of the stab-in-the-back myth, *see Innere Front. Militärassistenz, Widerstand und Umsturz in der Donaumonarchie 1918*, eds. Richard Georg Plaschka, Horst Haselsteiner and Arnold Suppan, 2 vols. (München: Oldenbourg, 1974); Robert Gerwarth, *The Vanquished. Why the First World War Failed to End, 1917-1923* (London: Allan Lane, 2016), 107-112; Patrick J. Houlihan, 'Was there an Austrian Stab-in-the-Back Myth? Interwar Military Interpretations of Defeat,' in *From Empire to Republic. Post-World War I Austria*, eds. Günter Bischoff, Fritz Plasser and Peter Berger (Innsbruck: Innsbruck UP, 2010), 67-89.

3. Jörn Leonhard, *Der überforderte Frieden. Versailles und die Welt 1918-1923* (München: C.H. Beck, 2018), 11-29.

4. Tamara Deutscher, 'Introduction. The Education of a Jewish Child,' in: Isaac Deutscher, *The Non-Jewish Jew and Other Essays*, ed. Tamara Deutscher (London-New York-Toronto: Oxford UP, 1968), 1-24, here 11. Based on autobiographical texts: Daniel Schönfeld, *Kometenjahre. 1918: Die Welt im Aufbruch* (Frankfurt/Main: Fischer, 2017); A world on Edge: The End of the Great War and the Dawn of a New Age; translated by Jefferson Chase, London: Macmillan 2018.

5. Alf Lüdtke, 'Herrschaft als soziale Praxis,' in *Herrschaft als soziale Praxis. Historische und sozialanthropologische Studien* (Göttingen: Vandenhoeck & Ruprecht, 2007), 9-63.

6. Diaries as well as memoirs, were used by: Leonhard, *Frieden*, 11, 15-17 (on Franz Kafka); H[ans] G[ünther] Adler, 'Es gäbe viel Merkwürdiges zu berichten,' interview with Hans Christoph Knebusch, in *Der Wahrheit verpflichtet. Interviews, Gedichte, Essays*, ed. Jeremy Adler (Gerlingen: Bleicher, 1998), 32-60, 32-34; Miroslav Krleža, Dnevnik 1918-1922: Davni Dani II (Sarajevo: Oslobođenje, 1977), 146. Concerning childhood recollections from the Habsburg monarchy: Katarzyna Jaśtal, *Erzählte Zeiträume. Kindheitserinnerungen aus den Randgebieten der Habsburgermonarchie von Manès Sperber, Elias Canetti und Gregor Rezzori* (Kraków: Aureus, 1998), 207-209.

7. *Sefer Khzshanov. leben un umkum fun a yidish stetl - Chrzanow. The Life and Destruction of a Jewish Shtetl*, ed. Mordekhai Bokhner (Regensburg: Published under EUCOM Civil Affairs Division, 1949), 6-8, <https://digitalcollections.nypl.org/items/a9966260-653e-0133-5bc0-00505686d14e> (accessed 17 September 2019).

8. Leon Chasanowitsch, *Die polnischen Judenpogrome im November und Dezember 1918. Tatsachen und Dokumente* (Stockholm: Judaea, 1919), 36-37; Martyrium. Ein jüdisches Jahrbuch, ed. Jakob Krausz (Wien: Selbstverlag, 1922), 29.

9. Carole Fink, *Defending the Right of Others. The Great Powers, the Jews, and International Minority Protection, 1878-1939* (Cambridge: Cambridge UP, 2004), 101-130; Josef Bendow [pseud. Joseph Tenenbaum], *Der Lemberger Judenpogrom (November 1918-Jänner 1919)* (Wien-Brünn: M. Hickl, 1919); Chasanowitsch, *Judenpogrome*, 43-71.

10. William Hagen, *Anti-Jewish Violence in Poland 1914-1920* (Cambridge: Cambridge UP, 2018), 305-362; Piotr Wróbel, 'The Kaddish Years. Anti-Jewish Violence in East Central Europe, 1918-1921,' *Jahrbuch des Simon-Dubnow-Instituts* 4 (2005), 211-236.

11. In this context, scholars have on the one hand desired to acknowledge the consequences of the brutalisation resulting from the four years of the war and its de facto extension, while on the other hand wanted to interpret the post-war violence as a protest against the conventions of masculine behaviour and honour imposed during wartime. Emily Gioielli, 'Abnormal Times. Intersectionality and Anti-Jewish Violence in Hungary and Poland, 1918-1922,' in *Poland and Hungary. Jewish Realities Compared*, eds. François Guesnet, Howard Lupovitch and Antony Polonsky, Polin. Studies in Polish Jewry 31 (London-Liverpool: The Littman Library of Jewish Civilization, 2019), 313-328.

12. Ernst Troeltsch used the concept of 'dreamland' for the period between the cease-fire in November 1918 and the Paris Peace Treaty in the summer of 1919. Ernst Troeltsch, 'Nach der Entscheidung (26.6.1919),' in *Die Fehlgeburt einer Republik. Spektator in Berlin 1918 bis 1922*, ed. Johann Hinrich Claussen (Frankfurt/Main: Eichborn, 1994), 56-62, here 60-62.

13. Ezra Mendelsohn, 'Zwischen großen Erwartungen und bösem Erwachen: Das Ende der multinationalen Reiche in Ostmittel- und Südosteuropa aus jüdischer Perspektive,' in *Zwischen großen Erwartungen und bösem Erwachen. Juden, Politik und Antisemitismus in Ost- und Südosteuropa 1918-1945*, eds. Dittmar Dahlmann and Anke Hilbrenner (Paderborn et al.: Schöningh, 2007), 13-30. The ambivalence is also emphasized by Michael Brenner, 'Von Czernowitz nach Cernăuți: Politische Krise und kulturelle Blüte zwischen den Kriegen,' in *Kleine jüdische Geschichte* (München: Beck, 2012), 256-285.

14. Ezra Mendelsohn, 'Jewish Historiography on Polish Jewry in the Interwar Period,' in *Jews in Independent Poland, 1918-1939*, eds. Antony Polonsky, Ezra Mendelsohn and Jerzy Tomaszewski, Polin. Studies in Polish Jewry 8 (London: Littman Library of Jewish Civilization, 1994), 3-13; Rogers Brubaker, 'Aftermath of Empire and the Unmixing of Peoples,' in *Nationalism Reframed. Nationhood and the National Question in the New Europe*, ed. Rogers Brubaker (Cambridge: Cambridge UP, 1996), 148-178; Robert Gerwarth and John Horne, 'The Great War and Paramilitarism in Europe, 1917-1923,' *Contemporary European History* 19, no. 3 (2010), 267-273; Mark Mazower, 'Timothy Snyder's Bloodlands,' *Contemporary European History* 21, no. 2 (2012), 117-124; Piotr J. Wróbel, 'Foreshadowing the Holocaust: The Wars of 1914-1921 and Anti-Jewish Violence in Central and Eastern Europe,' in *Legacies of Violence. Eastern Europe's First World War*, eds. Jochen Böhler, Włodzimierz Borodziej and Joachim v. Puttkamer (München: Oldenbourg, 2014), 169-208.

15. Contemporaries compared the anti-Jewish riots in Poland in 1918 and 1919 to the pogroms in Tsarist Russia (Kishinev 1903, Odessa 1906) and interpreted them as the last convulsion of a finished era. The description of the epoch as 'interwar', however, suggests a kind of breathing space between the wars and is assuming knowledge of the coming cataclysms in civilisation and genocide. Leonhard, *Frieden*, 11-29; Dan Diner, *Das Jahrhundert verstehen. Eine universalhistorische Deutung* (München: Luchterhand, 1999), 21-78. Unduly optimistic about future prospects in 1918: William O. McCagg, 'On Habsburg Jewry and its Disappearance,' *Studies in Contemporary Jewry* 4 (1988), 84-95.

16. Marsha L. Rozenblit, 'The European Jewish World 1914-1919: What Changed?,' in *World War I and the Jews. Conflict and Transformation in Europe, the Middle East, and America*, eds. Marsha L. Rozenblit and Jonathan Karp (New York-Oxford: Berghahn, 2017), 32-55.

17. Reinhart Koselleck, *Vergangene Zeiten. Zur Semantik geschichtlicher Zeiten* (Frankfurt/Main: Suhrkamp, 1979), 349-375.

18. Celia Heller, *On the Edge of Destruction. Jews of Poland between the Two World Wars* (New York: Columbia UP, 1977); Jakob Lestschinsky, 'The Anti-Jewish Program: Tsarist Russia, The Third Reich and Independent Poland,' *Jewish Social Studies* 3 (1941), 141-158, here 152-158. Remarkably, the *Shoa* plays almost no role in: Szyja Bronsztejn, 'Polish-Jewish Relations as Reflected in Memoirs of the Interwar Period,' *Polin. Studies in Polish Jewry* 8 (1994), 66-88.

19. Simon Dubnow, *Weltgeschichte des jüdischen Volkes*, 10 vols. (Berlin: Jüdischer Verlag, 1927-1929). On this, see: Olaf Terpitz, 'An Enclave in Time? Russian-Jewish Berlin Revisited,' in *The Russian Jewish Diaspora and European Culture, 1917-1937*, ed. Jörg Schulte (Leiden: Brill, 2012), 179-200; Karl Schlögel, 'Simon Dubnows Berliner Tagebuch,' in *Das russische Berlin: Ostbahnhof Europas* (München: Hanser, 2007), 287-308.

20. Yishuv is the Hebrew designation of the Jewish population in Palestine. The efforts to achieve a settlement under Zionist auspices are sometimes described as the 'new Yishuv'. Following the end of the First World War, the League of Nations incorporated the southern parts of Ottoman Syria into a mandate, entrusted to the British in 1922. David Fromkin, *A Peace to End All Peace. Creating the Modern Middle East, 1914-1922* (London: Deutsch 1989).

21. Verena Dohrn, 'State and Minorities: The First Lithuanian Republic and S. M. Dubnow's Concept of Cultural Autonomy,' in *The Vanished World of Lithuanian Jews*, eds. Alvydas Nikžentaitis, Stefan Schreiner and Darius Staliūnas (Amsterdam-New York: Rodopi, 2004), 155-173.

22. Karl Renner, *Das Selbstbestimmungsrecht der Nationen in besonderer Anwendung auf Österreich*, vol. 1: Nation und Staat (Leipzig-Wien: Deuticke, 1918); James Loeffler, 'The Famous Trinity of 1917: Zionist Internationalism in Historical Perspective,' *Simon Dubnow Institute Yearbook* 15 (2016), 211-238.

23. Sophie Dubnov-Erlich, *The Life and Work of S. M. Dubnov. Diaspora Nationalism and Jewish History* (Bloomington/Indianapolis: Indiana UP, 1991), 201-203.

24. The Paris Peace Conference drew up five peace treaties between the warring nations and their successor states. These were the Treaties of Versailles (28 June 1919 – the German Empire), Saint-Germain-en-Laye (10 September 1919 – Austria), Neuilly (27 November 1919 – Bulgaria), Trianon (4 Juni 1920 – Hungary) and Sèvres (10 August 1920 – the Ottoman Empire). Other agreements were also fundamental to the new order of post-war Eastern Europe and Asia Minor: the separate peace of Brest Litowsk (3 March 1918, annulled 11 November 1918); the Treaty of Riga (18 March 1921) between Poland and the Soviet Union; the Treaty of Lausanne (24 July 1923) between the Allies and the newly established Turkish Republic.

25. 'Opponents Scored at Zurich Conference on Jewish Rights (Jewish Telegraphic Agency),' *Jewish Daily Bulletin* (New York) 19 August 1927, 1.

26. Leon Reich, 'Das Komitee der jüdischen Delegationen in Paris,' *Der Jude. Eine Monatsschrift* 8/9, no. 5 (1920/21), 439-448.

27. Leon Reich, 'Die jüdische Friedensdelegation in Paris,' in *Jüdischer Nationalkalender* 5 (1919/20 = 5680), eds. Otto Abeles and Ludwig Bato (Wien: Verlag Jüdische Zeitung), 33-45, here 33.

28. The promise to support the establishment of a 'Jewish homeland' in Palestine came very close to President Wilson's demand that the Slavic nations should enjoy the 'greatest possible autonomy' within a reformed Habsburg Federation. Wilson was not in any way envisaging an independent national state, such as he was suggesting to the Poles. As early as 1915 Sir Henry McMahon, British High Commissioner in Egypt, had given a written undertaking to Arab leaders promising 'the independence of the Arabs'. Gerwarth, *The Vanquished*, 182-184.

29. On the difference between, on the one hand, non-Jews' understanding of Jewish political commitment as mainly leftwing during the interwar years, and on the other, rightwing politicians' readiness to accept Jewish patrons and politicians, see: Bela Vago, 'The Attitude Toward the Jews as a Criterion of the Left-Right Concept,' in *Jews and Non-Jews in Eastern Europe 1918-1945*, eds. Béla Vago and Georges L. Mosse (New York-Toronto-Jerusalem: John Wiley & Sons, Israel UP, 1974), 21-49.

30. Angelique Leszczawski-Schwerk, 'Dynamics of Democratization and Nationalization. The Significance of Women's Suffrage and Women's Political Participation in the Parliament of the Second Polish Republic,' Nationalities Papers 46 (2018), 809-822; Frank Grelka, 'Gegen altes Unrecht in neuen Staaten. Nationaljüdische Akteure in Polen und Litauen nach dem Großen Krieg,' *Jahrbuch des Bundesinstituts für Kultur und Geschichte der Deutschen im östlichen Europa* 25 (2017), 65-85.

31. Members of the political movement of orthodox Jews (faithful to the Torah) founded in 1912 in Katowice. See: Gershon Bacon, 'Agudas Yisroel,' in *YIVO Encyclopedia of Jews in Eastern Europe* (19 August 2010), <https://yivoencyclopedia.org/article.aspx/Agudas_Yisroel> (accessed 17 September 2019).

32. The linked acquisition of both language and education was of crucial importance to the survival of the various models of Jewish life (secular, religious, national). On the various types of schools that were important even beyond Polish

borders, see: Shimon Frost, 'The Jewish School Systems in Interwar Poland. Ideological Underpinnings,' in Jews in Poland, ed. Andrzej K. Paluch (Kraków: Uniwersytet Jagielloński, 1992), 235-244.

33. An account of the considerable heterogeneity of Jewish life-worlds can be found in: Jonas Kreppel, *Juden und Judentum von heute übersichtlich dargestellt. Ein Handbuch* (Zürich: Amalthea, 1925), which also provides a realistic set of basic sociocultural data.

34. The numbers for Bucarest and Jassy date from 1914, while the rest of these approximate rounded numbers are valid for the early 1920s. Various criteria have been used to collect them. The principal difference is the one between confession and nationality. In Warsaw, this difference amounts to nearly 100,000 people. The number of Jews by confession was 33%, by nationality 26.9%. In 1924, 31,324 Jews lived in Prague; of these, 16,264 described themselves as Czechs, 7,421 as Germans and 5,800 as Jews. Another 466 Jews were of a different nationality and 1,800 were not citizens of the Czecho-Slovak Republic. The figures come from: Kreppel, *Juden* (1925), 315-359.

35. For the principal differentiations presented here, I am grateful to: Gershon Bacon, 'One Jewish Street? Reflections on Unity and Disunity in Interwar Polish Jewry,' in *New Directions in the History of the Jews in the Polish Lands*, eds. Antony Polonsky, Hanna Węgrzynek and Andrzej Żbikowski (Boston: Academic Studies Press, 2018), 324-337.

36. From 'Allgemeiner Jüdischer Arbeiter-Bund (Bund)'. See: Gertrud Pickhan, *'Gegen den Strom' - Der Allgemeine Jüdische Arbeiterbund 'Bund' in Polen 1918-1939* (Stuttgart: Deutsche Verlagsanstalt, 2001).

37. On Poland: Joseph Marcus, *Social and Political History of the Jews in Poland, 1919-1939* (Berlin-New York: Mouton, 1983), 261-291; on the peace conference: Oscar I. Janowsky, *The Jews and the Minority Rights (1898-1919)* (New York: Columbia UP, 1933), 264-319; Carole Fink, 'Jewish Diplomacy and the Politics of War and Peace,' in *World War I and the Jews. Conflict and Transformation in Europe, the Middle East, and America*, eds. Marsha L. Rozenblit and Jonathan Karp (New York-Oxford: Berghahn, 2017), 56-81.

38. David Biale, *Power and Powerlessness in Jewish History* (New York: Schocken Books, 1986), 118-144; Yosef Hayim Yerushalmi, *'Diener von Königen und nicht Diener von Dienern'. Einige Aspekte der politischen Geschichte der Juden* (München: Carl Friedrich von Siemens Stiftung, 1995).

39. Zvi Y. Gitelman, 'A Century of Jewish Politics in Eastern Europe. The Legacy of the Bund and the Zionist Movement,' in *The Emergence of Modern Jewish Politics. Bundism and Zionism in Eastern Europe*, ed. Zvi Y. Gitelman (Pittsburgh/Pa.: Univ. of Pittsburgh Press, 2003), 3-18.

40. The last significant Israeli politician born in Interwar Eastern Europe was probably President Shimon Peres (Szymon Perski), born on 2 August 1923 in the then-Polish Voivodeship of Nowogródek. Shlomo Avineri refers to the identity politics involved in ethnicising democratic decisions. The small majority in the Knesset in favour of ratifying the Oslo II Accord was criticised by the assassin of Yitzchak Rabin (1922-1995) for lacking a 'Jewish' majority. A similar argument was used by the murderer of Gabriel Narutowicz (1865-1922), the first Polish president, who declared that the votes of the Jewish deputies to the Sejm could not be counted among the 'Polish' votes. Shlomo Avinery, 'The Presence of Eastern and Central Europe in the Culture and Politics of Contemporary Israel,' *East European Politics and Societies and Cultures* 10, no. 2 (1996), 163-172.

41. Jean Ancel, 'Wilhelm Filderman' in *YIVO Encyclopedia of Jews in Eastern Europe* (6 August 2010), <https://yivoencyclopedia.org/article.aspx/Filderman_Wilhelm> (accessed 17 September 2019).

42. Wilhelm Fildermann, *Memoirs and Diaries*, ed. Jean Ancel, vol. 1: 1900-1940 (Tel Aviv and Jerusalem: Yad Vashem, 2004).

43. Since their shared schooldays, Filderman had apparently been good friends with Ion Antonescu (1882-1946), later the 'Conducator' of Greater Romania.

44. David Schaary, 'The Realpolitik of the Jewish National Leadership of Bukovina: From the Jewish National Council to the Jewish National Party,' in *Between the Two World Wars*, eds. Liviu Rotman and Raphael Vago, The History of the Jews in Romania 3 (Tel Aviv: Tel Aviv Univ., 2005), 267-315.

45. Hildrun Glass, 'Varianten jüdischer Identitäten und Loyalitäten im rumänischen Staat der Zwischenkriegszeit,' in *Staat, Loyalität und Minderheiten in Ostmittel- und Südosteuropa 1918-1941*, eds. Peter Haslinger and Joachim v. Puttkamer (München: Oldenbourg, 2007), 143-158.

46. The 'Regat' or 'Romanian Old Kingdom' designates the Romanian state within the borders up to 1918. It included the former principalities of Wallachia and Moldavia – also called the Danube principalities – as well as Dobruja.

47. Manfred Reifer, *Dr. Mayer Ebner - Ein jüdisches Leben* (Tel Aviv: Edition Olympia, 1947), 163.

48. Andrei Corbea-Hoisie, 'Mayer Ebner', in *YIVO Encyclopedia of Jews in Eastern Europe* (5 August 2010), <https://yivoencyclopedia.org/article.aspx/Ebner_Mayer> (accessed 17 September 2019).

49. Here and below, from Grelka, *Gegen altes Unrecht*, and Eglė Bendikaite, 'Zwischen Anspruch und Wirklichkeit: Die Politik gegenüber den Juden in Litauen in der Zwischenkriegszeit,' in *Zwischen großen Erwartungen und bösem Erwachen. Juden, Politik und Antisemitismus in Ost- und Südosteuropa 1918-1945*, eds. Dittmar Dahlmann and Anke Hilbrenner (Paderborn et al.: Schöningh, 2007), 101-120.

50. Eglė Bendikaite, 'One Man's Struggle. The Politics of Shimshon Rosenbaum (1859-1934),' *Jahrbuch des Simon-Dubnow-Instituts* 13 (2014), 87-109, here 101. Eglė Bendikaite, 'Mittler zwischen den Welten. Shimshon Rosenbaum: Jurist, Zionist, Politiker,' *Osteuropa* 58, no. 8-10 (2008), 295-302, here 299.

51. Tomas Balkelis, *War, Revolution, and Nation-Making in Lithuania 1914-1923* (Oxford: Oxford UP, 2018), 64.

52. Eglė Bendikaitė, 'Expressions of Litvak Pro-Lithuanian Political Orientation c. 1906-c. 1921,' in *The Vanished World of Lithuanian Jews*, eds. Alvydas Nikžentaitis, Stefan Schreiner and Darius Staliūnas (Amsterdam-New York: Rodopi, 2004), 89-107.

53. Samuel Rosenbaum, *Der Souveränitätsbegriff. Ein Versuch seiner Revision* (Zürich: Gutzwiller, 1932). The author empha-

sises repeatedly that the work reflects the state of the negotiations in the year 1920.

54. Paul Mintz, *Die Lehre von der Beihilfe* (Riga: Müllersche Buchdruckerei, 1892), <https://dspace.ut.ee/handle/10062/5863> (accessed 17 September 2019).

55. *1918-1920: Latvijas Republikas Pagaidu valdības sēžu protokolos, notikums, atmiņas* [1918-1920: The Republic of Latvia Provisional Government. Meeting Minutes, Events, and Memoirs] (Riga: Valsts kanceleja, Latvijas Vēstnesis, 2013), 90. The Riga museum 'Jews in Latvia' presented Mincs's life and works (13 March to 10 September 2019): Muzejs 'Ebreji Latvijā', Exhibition '*For My People and For My Country: Paul Mintz, Latvia's Statesman*' (4 March 2019), <http://www.jew-ishmuseum.lv/en/item/320-exhibition_for_my_people_and_for_my_country_paul_mintz_latvia_s_statesman_.html> (accessed 17 September 2019).

56. Verena Dohrn, *Baltische Reise. Vielvölkerlandschaft des alten Europa* (Frankfurt/Main: Fischer, 1994), 119. Mincs published works on penal law in Russian, Latvian and German. He also gave many lectures, for example: Paul Mintz, 'Das Einkammersystem in der lettländischen Verfassung,' *Rigaische Zeitschrift für Rechtswissenschaft* 1, no. 1 (1926/27), 9-18.

57. The sudden political volte-face against minorities in Latvian politics happened under the government of Zigfrīd Anna Meierovics (1887-1925), whose father was – as was widely known – of Jewish origin.

58. The surgeon Wladimir Mincs (1872-1945), Paul Mincs's brother, had successfully operated on Lenin after the attempted assassination by Fanny E. Kaplan (1890-1918). Following the German occupation of Latvia, he was interned in the Riga ghetto, where he directed the hospital. In 1944, he was transported to Buchenwald, and died there. Šarūnas Liekis, Pauls Mincs, in *YIVO Encyclopedia of Jews in Eastern Europe* (2 September 2010), <https://yivoencyclopedia.org/article.aspx/Mincs_Pauls> (accessed 17 September 2019); Šarūnas Liekis, Vladimirs Mincs, in YIVO Encyclopedia of Jews in Eastern Europe (2 September 2010), <https://yivoencyclopedia.org/article.aspx/Mincs_Pauls> (accessed 17 September 2019).

59. Rosa Pomeranz, *An die jüdischen Frauen! Ein Appell zur Umkehr* (Tarnopol: Verlag des Vereines 'Ahawath Zion', 1898); Rosa Pomeranz, 'Die Bedeutung der zionistischen Idee im Leben der Jüdin,' Die Stimme der Wahrheit. Jahrbuch für wissenschaftlichen Zionismus 1 (1905), 329-333.

60. *Pamięci Róży Melcerowej* ed. Koło Kobiet Żydowskich (Lwów: Drukarnia Przemysłowa, 1936); *Parlament Rzeczypospolitej Polskiej 1919-1927* eds. Włodzimierz Dzwonkowski and Henryk Mościcki (Warszawa: Lucjan Złotnicki, 1928), 307, 312; Dietlind Hüchtker, *Geschichte als Performance. Politische Bewegungen in Galizien um 1900* (Frankfurt/Main - New York: Campus, 2014), 118-146; Szymon Rudnicki, Żydzi w parlamencie II Rzeczypospolitej 2. rev. edn. (Warszawa: Wydawnictwo Sejmowe, 2015), 164, 498.

61. Dieter Hecht, 'Die Weltkongresse jüdischer Frauen in der Zwischenkriegszeit: Wien 1923, Hamburg 1929,' in *Geschlecht, Religion und Engagement. Die jüdischen Frauenbewegungen im deutschsprachigen Raum. 19. und frühes 20. Jahrhundert*, eds. Margarete Grandner and Edith Saurer, L'Homme Schriften 9 (Wien-Köln-Weimar: Böhlau, 2005), 123-156.

62. 'Eine Unterredung mit Frau Rosa Melzer Pomeranz – Mitglied des polnischen Sejm,' in: *Wiener Morgenzeitung* 1524 (11 May 1923), 9-10.

63. Birte Förster, *1919: Ein Kontinent erfindet sich neu* (Ditzingen: Reclam, 2018). In many places, women were also able to vote in Jewish community elections.

64. *Beys Yankev* (Yidd. for The House of Jakob), also described in Hebrew as *Beth Ya'akov*. Tobias Grill, 'Wesen, Entwicklung und Bewertung der Bet Jakob Bewegung,' in *Der Westen im Osten: Deutsches Judentum und jüdische Bildungsreform in Osteuropa (1783-1939)* (Göttingen: Vandenhoeck & Ruprecht, 2013), 295-301; Naomi Seidman, 'Legitimizing the Revolution: Sarah Schenirer and the Rhetoric of Torah Study for Girls,' in *New Directions in the History of the Jews in the Polish Lands*, eds. Antony Polonsky, Hanna Węgrzynek and Andrzej Żbikowski (Boston: Academic Studies Press, 2018), 356-365.

65. Sophia Dubnov Erlich gives an account in her autobiography of her time in Warsaw and of the political work of her husband Henryk Erlich (1882-1942), as well as her own involvement: Sophie Dubnova-Erlich, *Bread and Matzoth* (Tenafly/NY: Hermitage, 2005). On this, see: Pickhan, '*Gegen den Strom*', 293-294.

66. Sometimes also written as: Jakub Leib Müntzberg; on his biography, see: Gershon Bacon, 'Leib Mincberg,' in *YIVO Encyclopedia of Jews in Eastern Europe* (2 September 2010), <https://yivoencyclopedia.org/article.aspx/Mincberg_Leib> (accessed 17 September 2019).

67. *Agudas Yisroel* – an influential political party that affirmed the traditions of orthodox Judaism and was represented in Jewish local councils and in the state parliaments of the states of East-Central Europe.

68. Zoltán Rónai, 'Siegmund Kunfi (1879-1929),' in *Ausgewählte Aufsätze von Siegmund Kunfi*, vol. 1: *Die Neugestaltung der Welt*, ed. Julius Braunthal (Wien: Verlag der Wiener Volksbuchhandlung, 1930), 5-12, here 5.

69. On Kunfi's respect for Kautsky: *Karl Kautsky und die Sozialdemokratie Südosteuropas. Korrespondenz 1883-1938*, eds. Georges Haupt, János Jemnitz and Leo van Rossum (Frankfurt/Main - New York: Campus, 1986), 521-523.

70. The 1917 Stockholm peace conference, 'Pressekommuniqué zu den Sitzungen mit der ungarischen Delegation am 29.-30 Mai 1917 (31 May 1917),' Social History Portal, <https://socialhistoryportal.org/stockholm1917/documents/111571> (accessed 17 September 2019).

71. Balázs Trencsényi et al., *A History of Modern Political Thought in East Central Europe*, vol. 2: *Negotiating Modernity in the 'Short Twentieth Century' and Beyond*, part I: 1918-1968 (Oxford: Oxford UP, 2018), 13.

72. Rónai, *Siegmund Kunfi*, 9.

73. Trencsényi, *A History*, 108.

74. Sozialdemokratische Arbeiterpartei (Socialist Democratic Workers' Party).

75. The American War Congress and Zionism. Statements by Members of the American War Congress on the Jewish National Movement, New York: Zionist Organization of America 1919, p. 10; Pauline Albala, 'Dr. Albala as a Jewish National Worker' (Manuscript, Center for Jewish History, New York), 7-9.

76. Licht had fought in the First World War on the side of the Central Powers.

77. Salo Baron, *Die Judenfrage auf dem Wiener Kongress. Auf Grund von zum Teil ungedruckten Quellen dargestellt* (Wien-Berlin: R. Löwit, 1920), <http://sammlungen.ub.uni-frankfurt.de/freimann/content/titleinfo/102361> (accessed 17 September 2019).

78. David Engel, 'Crisis and Lachrymosity: On Salo Baron, Neo-baronianism, and the Study of Modern European Jewish History,' *Jewish History* 20, no. 3/4 (2006), 243-264.

79. *Sefer Khzshanov. leben un umkum fun a yidish stetl - Chrzanow. The Life and Destruction of a Jewish Shtetl*, ed. Mordekhai Bokhner (Regensburg: Published under EUCOM Civil Affairs Division, 1949). <https://digitalcollections.nypl.org/items/a9966260-653e-0133-5bc0-00505686d14e> (accessed 17 September 2019). *Chrzanów: The Life and Destruction of a Jewish Shtetl, New York 1992.*
<https://www.jewishgen.org/yizkor/Chrazanow/Chrzanow.html> (accessed 17 February 2020); Frank Golczewski, *Polnisch-jüdische Beziehungen 1881-1922. Eine Studie zur Geschichte des Antisemitismus in Osteuropa* (Wiesbaden: Franz Steiner, 1981), 205-208; Israel Cohen, 'My Mission to Poland (1918–1919),' *Jewish Social Studies* 13 (1951), 149-172, here 157-158.

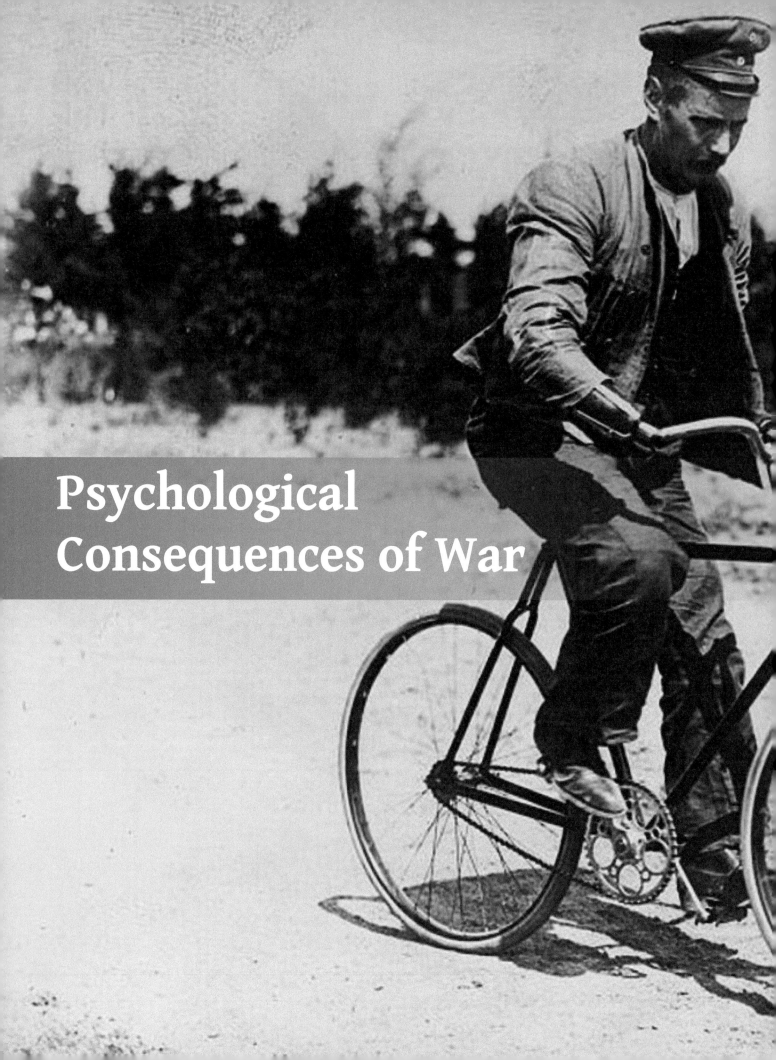

Psychological
Consequences of War

Crippled German Soldier on his bicycle, 1920s.

Slovak Politics and Society on the Brink of 1918-1919

Marek Syrný

Slovaks in pre-war Hungary

At the beginning of the 20th century, the current territory of Slovakia was a part of Austria-Hungary. Until the formation of Czechoslovakia, or rather until the exact definition of its borders by the Treaty of Trianon, Slovakia was not strictly defined. While its northern and western borders, and part of its eastern border, were clear and stable (such as Hungary's border with the Austrian dominions of the Czech lands, Poland and Galicia), the southern borders of Slovakia could not be clearly identified. In earlier documents of the Slovak National Movement, which tried to define Slovakia to achieve its autonomy, Slovakia's southern borders were generally described as an ethnic border between Slovaks and Hungarians in Upper Hungary. Some of the Upper Hungarian counties (the northernmost) appeared to be predominantly Slovak in nature; in the rest, however, Slovaks were considerably mixed with Hungarians. The varied ethnic

Fig. 1: View of Bratislava on the Danube. Postcard from 1923.

composition and intermingling of different ethnic groups in Slovakia, as well as in the entirety of Greater Hungary, had been the result of several hundred years of natural and Hungarian or Austrian state-influenced development, Turkish invasions, numerous external and internal colonisations, economic migration, and national and religious persecutions. In addition to the large and dominant Hungarian community in southern Slovakia and in some northern towns, the country also had a considerable German minority, which was located mainly in three areas (Bratislava and the surrounding area, Upper Nitra and the surroundings of Kremnica – or Hauerland, and Spiš). Larger cities contained numerous Jewish communities and, in the north-eastern part of Slovakia, Ruthenians as well. In 1905, approximately 2.85 million inhabitants lived in the territory of present-day Slovakia. According to their mother tongue, up to 1.7 million were Slovaks (60%), more than 800,000 Hungarians, almost 200,000 Germans, up to 100,000 Ruthenians and other smaller ethnic groups (Croatians, Romanians, Bulgarians, Serbs...).[1]

The Jews had not yet been reported statistically, but they were most often identified in censuses, according to the language used in their family, as Germans or Hungarians. Slovaks thus formed less than 60% of this area's population. Hungary had about 18 million inhabitants, of which approximately 1.9 million Slovaks used a Slovak language (including Slovaks on the so-called Lower Land, i.e. Hungarian, Romanian, and Vojvodina enclaves). Yet the real number of the Slovaks was a little higher than claimed by official statistics, which were affected by their survey methods and the significant illiteracy or ignorance of common people. By means of a deliberate Magyarisation policy, the proportion of Hungarians in Hungary's population changed from 47% in 1880 to 55% in 1910.[2]

The Slovaks formed about 12% of Hungary's population (excluding self-administered Croatia). They were part of Austria-Hungary, ruled by the Hungarian nobility and exposed to assimilation tendencies by the modern Kingdom of Hungary. On the one hand, after the Austro-Hungarian Compromise in 1867, economic (and partly also social) modernisation and development proceeded, but on the other hand, non-Hungarian nationalities suffered national persecution aimed at establishing a homogeneous

Hungarian state. The Hungarian state policymakers were not satisfied with merely enforcing the idea of a Hungarian political nation, but they also tried to change the national identity of its non–Hungarian population on a practical level. They did so by marginalising the national political efforts and the activities of its nationalities (in Slovakia, for example, the abolition of the Matica slovenská,[3] the minimal representation of Slovaks in the Parliament), and especially through education (the liquidation of Slovak grammar schools, the Apponyi Education Acts of 1907 enforcing Hungarian into the lower types of schools). In addition, various cultural and other pro-Hungarian associations were formed in the Upland (Upper Hungary, Slovakia) in order to promote pro-Hungarian sentiment among the common Slovak people. The Upper Hungary Magyar Educational Society (FEMKE) is a good example: this association, based in Nitra, raised Slovak orphans and children from lower class families into passionate Hungarian patriots. The Hungariancountry Slovak Educational Society (Uhorsko-krajinský slovenský vzdelávací spolok), based in Budapest, focused on the Magyarisation of Slovaks by publishing periodicals and books in Slovak (from the base of Matica slovenská's confiscated property). Moreover, Slovaks did not even have support in terms of church autonomy as did Orthodox Romanians or Serbs; both the Catholic and the Evangelical Church were affected by the Magyarisation enforced by the government.

The official political pressure pushed the nationally oriented Slovak elite towards believing in a radical change of statehood. Because their political position and socio-economic situation were not strong enough to create an independent Slovak state, which would have been too weak, national Slovak politicians finally decided to join the Slovak future with the stronger Czech statehood movement, which was also trying to liberate the Czechs from the Austro-Hungary monarchy. This crucial decision was not easy and the path towards creating a new, unique state was still very difficult and long.

Slovak Politics Before the First World War

A brief glance at the Slovak national reality before the First World War does not reveal a very nice picture. A small group of nationally conscious intellectuals was able to encourage just a small part of influential Slovak society. From 1875 to 1892, there were no Slovaks among more than 400 members of the lower house of the Diet of Hungary. And later, because of the Hungarian administration's precautions against the Slovak candidates, the situation continued to look bleak:[4] in their most successful year, 1906, Slovaks were represented by only seven Diet members; otherwise, the number remained at two or four,[5] not enough to change anything via constitutional reforms. The situation outside the nationally conscious group of intellectuals was even worse. The small town of Martin was the only centre with any real economic or social significance. Bratislava was more German and Hungarian than Slovak and so had weak relations with the rest of Slovakia. A conscious Slovak identity was present only within a smaller part of the nation, mostly among the intellectuals or emerging bourgeoisie and minor nobility, such as the lords of Turiec county. Large parts of Slovakia, at that time Upper Hungary, although inhabited by Slovaks, were not significantly aware of themselves as a nation.[6] Numerous inhabitants living in cross-border territories with Poland considered themselves Gorals, and the regions of Zemplín, Abov and Šariš, separate from the bigger towns of Košice or Prešov, were completely untouched by the Slovak national enlightenment.

Before the First World War, there had been no obvious clashes between the Slovak national movement and the Hungarian ruling power, but the apparent peace was illusory.[7] Even before the war began, the government had on a number of occasions used force, imprisonment or live firing against people at public political meetings. Two of the later most important Slovak political figures, a Catholic priest and a doctor from Ružomberok – Andrej Hlinka (1864-1938) and Vavro Šrobár (1867-1950) – both paid for their pro-Slovak activities. Sixteen Slovaks, including Hlinka and Šrobár, were accused of inciting voters at the Ružomberok polling station and went on trial.[8] Shortly after, in 1906, the so-called 'tragedy of Černová' occurred. It became synonymous with Slovak oppression not only in the Kingdom of Hungary, but in other European countries. During the consecration of a church in Černová, policemen fired at the crowd, which preferred the consecration to be celebrated by the Slovak Hlinka and refused the official

Fig. 2: Front page of the newspaper *Národnie noviny* of 30 July 1914, edited in Turčiansky Svätý Martin, showing the Slovak language version of Emperor Franz Joseph's declaration 'To My Peoples!'

representative, a non-Slovak priest. Fifteen people were shot dead and twelve severely wounded.[9]

In 1907, the government imposed the aforementioned 'Lex Apponyi' (Apponyi Education Law) on the non-Hungarian nations of the Kingdom of Hungary.[10] This law commanded all state-run schools to only use the Hungarian language (Magyar). The teachers were obliged to promote to their students loyalty and patriotism towards the Kingdom of Hungary, and any possible patriotism towards other nations was strictly prohibited.[11]

Unexpectedly, this Magyarisation effort[12] finally influenced Slovak pro-national politics in a positive way. It mobilised Slovak leaders to act and think about ways of combating this negative political development.[13] They designed similar educational activities aimed at ordinary people, the uneducated (illiterate) mass of Slovak peasants and workers, that aimed to influence and turn them into a politically committed and economically active Slovak population by means of changes that would slow yield long-lasting effects.

To support this effort, the Slovak Youth Committee in Budapest began issuing a journal, *Prúdy* (Streams), in line with the older generation of Slovak politics, which had been represented by the *Hlas* (Voice) magazine issued at the turn of the century inspired by Tomáš G. Masaryk's (1850-1937) idea of 'everyday small steps' in national work. The committee also stressed the importance of Czech and Slovak reciprocity and criticised the leadership of the Slovak National Party (Slovenská národná strana) in Martin for their conservatism and traditionalism. Bohdan Pavlů (1883-1938) and Ivan Markovič (1888-1944), later a Social Democratic deputy leader, became the journal's editors. Vavro Šrobár also influenced it with his ideas.

To sum up the situation until the neutralisation of political activities during the First World War: although the Magyarisation politics applied towards the Slovaks were a relatively mild form of oppression when compared to national repression in the Ottoman Empire or the Russian Empire, up to the end of 1914 the government persecuted hundreds of Slovaks for their nationalism, anti-militarism or so-called 'Pan-Slavism'.

These persecutions, together with other forms of political, economical, and cultural suppression, motivated and forced Slovak politicians and politics to consider and think about their options and possible courses of action to shape the future of the nation to be something other than a future under the 'yoke' of Austria-Hungary.

Czecho-Slovak Connections

Unlike the Slovak nation's very weak position in Hungary, the Czechs, who were under the administration of Vienna, were in a much better situation. As a result of negative tendencies in Austrian and, especially, Hungarian governmental policies towards Czechs and Slovaks, these two Slavic, linguistically closest nations of the Monarchy had found their way to each other. Even before the beginning of the century, the Czech political scene was obviously interested in defending and helping the Slovaks fight Hungarian oppression. The association Czechoslovak Unity (Československá jednota) – and a Slovak students' university club in Prague, Detvan – played a great role in bringing the two nations together nationally and politically. Both nations sought their famous history in the previous, romantic phase of national revival. While searching, they could not miss their common roots in the Great Moravian Empire. Even later, they had occasionally influenced one another, especially culturally. The Slovak Lutherans were still using the Czech language of the 1564 *Kralice Bible* during services. Since the beginning of the 20th century, the mutual interest in knowing each other and in cooperation had grown significantly. Czech culture and business capital found their way into Slovakia, where they were welcomed as they also strengthened Slovak social and economic life.

In Bohemia, the number of scientists professionally interested in Slovakia, especially in terms of literature, ethnography and folklore, had been increasing. In the nearby Moravian town of Hodonín, Czechoslovak Unity organised an ethnographic and economic exhibition about Slovakia, where important contacts were made between Czech and Slovak politicians as well. Czechoslovak Unity also helped to publish many Slovaks' professional and artistic publications, which would otherwise have had no chance of appearing in Hungary, or would have had to be published in Hungarian. The manifestations of cultural and social rapprochement were gradually transferred to the political level, and the Czech members of the Austrian Parliament frequently mentioned the Magyarisation of the Slovaks in Hungary.[14]

The idea of co-operation between Slovaks and Czechs was supercharged by the First World War, which crucially weakened the Austro-Hungarian Monarchy. With the help of the Entente, the ware enabled representatives of the non-governmental national movements to consider leaving the Monarchy. First, in 1915, there was the idea that the leading personality of the Czech exile political scene, Tomáš G. Masaryk, might restore the independent Czech kingdom. Later, the ambition was modified to the creation of a republic, and expanded to include the Slovaks and Ruthenians in this free state, ethnicities

Fig. 3: Poster issued by the Czechoslovak Recruiting Office in New York in 1918 and designed by the Czech artist Vojtěch Preissig (1873-1944), using a verse of the 1844 poem *Dobrovoľnícka* by Janko Matúška (1821-1877), *Už Slovensko vstává, putá si strháva* (Slovakia is rising, tearing off her handcuffs).

Fig. 4: Commemorative plaque in Pittsburgh, Pennsylvania (USA), in honour of the Pittsburgh Agreement signed on 31 May 1918, by representatives of the Czech and Slovak political exiles in the USA.

fight for the Monarchy and its war goals, grew for both national and social reasons. They did not return to the front from their vacations and convalescences, but rather escaped into the local mountains where they created the armed force that would serve the oncoming national and social revolution.[16] Some units still on the front even erupted into rebellion, and were violently suppressed (44 Slovak soldiers from Trenčín who revolted in Kragujevac, Serbia, for example, were executed).[17]

From the summer of 1918, a gradual but unstoppable dissolution of government power had begun, linked to the deteriorating fortunes of the Monarchy in the war. The domestic Slovak political scene gradually awakened under the influence of foreign actions. At first, at the 1 May Labour Day celebration in Liptovský Svätý Mikuláš, Vavro Šrobár publicly declared the effort of the Slovak nation to create a joint state with the Czechs.[18] Then, in the autumn of 1918, the Slovak political factions under the Slovak National Council officially declared the same in the name of all Slovak political bodies.[19] After the Austro-Hungarian Empire's surrender, the new liberal Hungarian government failed to retain its hold on Hungary's Slovak political scene, even though Mihály Károlyi's (1875-1955) government enforced the Act on the Autonomy of Slovakia.[20]

Slovakia in the New Czechoslovak State

Slovak politicians, disappointed by Budapest's reluctance to grant the Slovaks even a modicum of national freedom in the previous decades, definitively decided on 30 October 1918 (only two days after the factual declaration of the Czechoslovak state in Prague) to unite their fate with the Czechs in a joint state. All this happened despite the fact that Slovaks and Hungarians had lived alongside each other in Hungary, not happily, but without any outbreaks of violence (as had happened between Poles and Ukrainians, or even between Hungarians and Austrians). In the economic sphere, moreover, Slovakia had become more industrialised during the previous decades thanks to the Hungarian modernisation laws. But none of this could offer the Slovaks such opportunities as a co-government in a new state with a very close Slavic nation that was significantly more economically and socially advanced than backwards

whose country leaders in the US had expressed an interest in creating a new common state on the ruins of the Monarchy, which they predicted would fall during the war. From mid-1918, when the Entente was openly speculating about the post-war disintegration of the Monarchy, the exile headquarters of the Czechoslovak National Council gradually established itself as the future new government of the emerging Czechoslovak state. On 18 October 1918, a declaration on the independence of Czechoslovakia, the Washington Declaration, was published in American daily papers, followed by the official overthrow of the Monarchy in Prague on 28 October and the declaration of the Czechoslovak state on its home territory.

In 1918, the politically relatively 'sleepy' Slovakia's situation changed radically.[15] The numbers of Slovak soldiers deserting, because they refused to

Fig. 5: Signatories of the Declaration of Martin on 30 October 1918. Bottom row (from left to right): Karol A. Medvecký, Ján Vojtaššák, Karol Kmeťko, Juraj Janoška, Samuel Zoch, Ján Slávik, Vladimír Makovický; middle row: Emil Stodola, Ferdinand Juriga, [unknown], Ivan Dérer, Vladimír Pavel Čobrda; upper row: Jaroslav Ruppeldt, Štefan Krčméry, Emil Beňo.

Hungary, with its semi-medieval socio-political system.[21]

The transition from Hungarian to new Czechoslovak power and order was not easy. The Hungarian government received no support from either the internal security point of view, or in terms of gaining and managing a designated territory. As soon as it was clear that Austria-Hungary had lost the war and the old administration apparatus would be replaced by a new one, the authority and competences of the Hungarian bodies were impeached. Yet new Czechoslovak administrative bodies and offices had not yet formed and they had no authority or power at their disposal to compel the authority.[22] Following several months of uncertainty, chaos, and confusion, a 'people's' revolution began. In some places, the remaining elements of police forces, and pro-Hungarian officials, were able to maintain public order, but elsewhere massive attacks broke out targeting prop-

erty and people that symbolised the old era, social or national inequality, and so on.[23]

The ordinary people who had borne the brunt of fighting the war (mobilisation, requisition, short supplies, losing loved ones) for four years poured their frustration into 'raids' on richer settlements, farmsteads, manors, shops and homes of wealthier people, former elites and bureaucratic apparatus, and so on. The most common target of these attacks was Jewish property,[24] which was easily distinguishable socially and especially culturally. The Jews had been economically and socially prominent, especially during the last decades of the monarchy. They were associated with the rise of dynamic industrialisation, and the rise of trade, banking, and so on, and thus with getting richer. In addition, they were religiously, or more importantly culturally, distinct from the Christian rural working majority. In addition, because of the desire to remain in the decisive Hungarian social

Fig. 6: Celebration meeting of the newly established Czechoslovak Republic, in front of the Jan Hus Monument on Old Town Square in Prague, 1918.

elite and to merge as much as possible with the prevailing government regime so that they were not pushed away by the old establishment, the Jewish community were keen to conform to the fashion for Magyarisation or Germanisation. While this mainly concerned the use of the spoken language, Jewish entrepreneurs, self-employed individuals, businessmen and others who worked for decades to become full-fledged recognised members of the official Hungarian political nation[25] were naturally very far from the national-emancipatory ideas of the nationally oriented Slovak intelligentsia and the part of the Slovak peasantry/countryside influenced by it. When the old regime collapsed and a new but not yet established Czechoslovak regime was forming, the brunt of social and national anger thus focused on the Jews[26] and their possessions. Masses of people, 'drunk' on the absence of controlling and punishing state power and often led by armed individuals in the front, or rather by experienced former soldiers, deserters and so on, began to pillage everything they felt represented social or national inequality and exploitation.[27]

In addition to Jewish property, they often plundered the nobility's residences, taking not only food, agricultural equipment and livestock, but everything considered of value from the castles and manor houses. They destroyed, burned or otherwise discarded a great number of cultural valuables, such as larger furniture that they could not take and remove or which they considered impractical and worthless. This wave of violent popular social revolt and revolutionary 'wrath', and the plundering of private and public property, so deterred the incoming representatives of the new Czechoslovak state establishment that decades later, when plans for a coup against the collaborative regime were formed during the Second World War, the participants focused on the need to maintain public order during the coup.[28]

However, in the first months of 1919, the people's rioting and attacks on the property and offices of the former era gradually stopped and new Czechoslovak bodies and offices began to administrate the country. They also created the armed forces (army, gendarmerie) to secure the protection of general human rights, including the security of private property.[29]

Fig. 7: Czechoslovak patrol on the Danube Bridge at Komárno, 1919, during the fights against the Hungarian troops.

Ensuring the integrity of the state territory, and establishing the authority of new state bodies and the social systems was much more difficult (in terms of time, material and people).[30] The previous social structures, constructed over several hundred years, with clearly demarcated social, economic, cultural, national and political positions for particular social and national groups and populations, had suddenly been overturned. Constructing the new order began during the revolutionary break.

Previous Austro-Hungarian and German-Hungarian elites in Slovakia were suddenly members of a rejected class. The high social status they had previously enjoyed in the monarchy was now a disgrace. Pro-Hungarian and pro-Viennese officials, teachers, public officials and so on were replaced by representatives of the new Czechoslovak power, individuals who had expressed opposition, even resistance, towards the Austro-Hungarian regime during the previous era. They differed not only nationally and politically, but socially as well. The Austrian/German and Hungarian representatives of the nobility or richer senior officials who had been devoted to the monarchy were replaced by Czech, Slovak or Ruthenian/Ukrainian intelligentsia, small entrepreneurs and others who were Republicans and Democrats. It

was only natural that smaller and larger opposition groups should arise from many directions against the newly created Slavic republic, which was literally 'popular'. A huge resistance wave arose, mainly within the territory of Slovakia , the arrival of the so-called Slovak government (delegated in Prague) in Bratislava was accompanied by a great strike and demonstrations by the town's Hungarian and German inhabitants.[31] Czech, Slovak or Ruthenian-Ukrainian populations each claimed a natural right to their own state, similarly, amid the frenzy of this social and national revolutionary period, the Germans and the Hungarians also demanded their own national-political rights in the new Czechoslovak territory. Overall, they formed almost a third of the population in the Czech lands, Slovakia and Ruthenia. Like the pro-Czechoslovak forces, they also began to form so-called national committees, which represented a transitional revolutionary power with local influence. And, as the Czech, Slovak and Ruthenian-Ukrainian national committee recognised Czechoslovakia, the Germans on the Czech border recognised the notion of a so-called Republic of German Austria,[32] the Hungarians directly declared their wish to annex the territory they controlled to Hungary.

Fig. 8 and 9: Bratislava from 26-28 October 1921, the monument to Queen Maria Theresia, accompanied by the statues of a Hungarian nobleman and a Hungarian soldier, created in 1897 by the Hungarian sculptor Jan Fadrusz, was destroyed. These photographs by Marcell Jankovics from 1910 and 1921 show the monument and its destruction.

While in the Czech-German case this national dispute was resolved relatively smoothly, because, in fact, no Republic of German Austria was created and the Czech army, the police and the state authorities asserted their authority in this area relatively easily,[33] the situation in Slovakia and Ruthenia was significantly worse. It was caused by the serious instability within Hungary, triggered by the fall of the liberal pro-Entente governments. And consequently, because of the general resistance to the war's political results and the suggested territorial order for the Carpathian basin area, the Hungarian Bolsheviks came to power. Instrumentalising the attractive idea of Greater Hungary restoration or, at least, the unification/liberation of all Hungarians in the Carpathian basin from the supremacy of different nations, they promoted a socialist revolution in Hungary. Béla Kun's (1886-1938) Hungarian Red Army invaded Slovakia in May and June 1919, and conquered a considerable part of south and eastern Slovakia. A satellite Slovak Soviet Republic, which proclaimed close cooperation with Budapest and the administration of the country by Soviets,[34] was even declared for a short time in the occupied territory of eastern Slovakia in Prešov.[35] The threat of losing a big part of Slovakia, or its Bolshevisation, was clearly reversed by the threat of intervention by the Entente Powers against the Hungarian Soviet Republic followed by the withdrawal of the Hungarian Bolsheviks.

It was only after this period of turbulent change, and the fight for the inclusion of post-war Slovakia in Czechoslovakia, that the official social and national revolution, headed by Czechoslovak bodies in Prague, slowly began.[36] In contrast with the conservative Hungarian election law, all adults in the Czechoslovak Republic now had the right to vote, including women. An equally important 'revolutionary' law about land reform was adopted, which redistributed large land properties belonging mainly to the Hungarian nobility to smallholders, mid-ranking peasants and farmers. The extent of this land reform was radical in comparison with what was happening in Hungary and the Balkans. Apart from its social-political aspect, it was aimed at reducing the property held by the principal opponents of the Czechoslovak Republic. The state also gradually adopted progressive school and social reforms/laws (for example, an extended national education system was created, which had been impossible in the Hungarian era). New kinds of employment insurance companies and unemployment benefits were created as well. The relationship between state and church became more liberal. The Czech parts of the Republic in the West gradually implemented a new form of public life. The general modernisation of social life and strongly increased involvement of the masses in cultural and public life were accompanied by the creation of a wide-ranging civic society, which gradually became (with its democratic standards) a 'sad' exception in Central Europe.

Slovakia's transition from Austro-Hungarian to Czechoslovak statehood was not without problems and numerous mistakes by the new Czech and Slovak elites, yet it undoubtedly represented a significant qualitative change from which the country and its Slovak inhabitants were able to profit during the whole 20th century.

Endnotes

1. *Magyar Statisztikai Közlemények*, volume 42, (Budapest 1912), 17.
2. Roman Holec, 'Úvahy k fenoménu maďarizácie pred rokom 1918,' in *Kľúčové problémy moderných slovenských dejín 1848-1992*, eds. Valerián Bystrický, Dušan Kováč and Jan Pešek (Bratislava: Veda, 2012), 88.
3. Matica slovenská is a Slovak cultural and scientific institution founded in 1863.
4. Štátny archív Bratislava, f. Krajský súd v Bratislave I (1872-1954), box 5, National incitement.
5. Jozef Lettrich, *History of Modern Slovakia* (New York: Praeger, 1955), 34-35.
6. Ľubomír Lipták, *Slovensko v 20. storočí* (Bratislava: Kalligram, 1998), 25-31.
7. Scotus Viator, *Racial problems in Hungary* (London: A. Constable & Co., 1908), 456-460.
8. Milan Podrimavský, 'Vavro Šrobár a slovenská otázka na prelome 19. a 20. Storočia,' in *Dr. Vavro Šrobár: politik, publicista a národnoosvetový pracovník*, ed. Miroslav Pekník (Bratislava: Veda, 2012), 193.
9. Lettrich, *History of Modern Slovakia*, 37-38.
10. Milan Podrimavský, 'Slováci v podmienkach uhorského štátu na začiatku 20. Storočia,' *Česko - slovenské vzťahy - Slovensko - české vzťahy* (Bratislava: 1994), 17-26, here 22-23.
11. Ladislav Deák, 'Slovaks in the Hungarian statistics', *History and politics*, ed. Dušan Kováč (Bratislava: 1993), 93-104, here 93-95.
12. Štátny archív Bratislava, f. Podžupan (1868-1922), file 1810/1914.
13. István Bibó, *Bieda východoeurópskych malých štátov* (Bratislava: Kalligram, 1996), 162.
14. Marek Syrný, *Slovenské dejiny. 20. storočie. I. diel.* (Banská Bystrica: Fakulta politických vied a medzinárodných vzťahov, 2016), 23-24.
15. See more: Dušan Kováč et al., *Prvá svetová vojna. Slovensko v 20. storočí II.* (Bratislava: Veda, 2008), 252-265.
16. Peter Chorvát, 'Slováci v rakúsko-uhorskej armáde počas prvej svetovej vojny,' *Vojenská osveta*, no. 2 (2014), 54.
17. Marián Hronský, 'Štyridsaťštyri,' *Historická revue*, no. 4 (1994), 15-16.
18. Vojtech Dangl, 'Prvomájové zhromaždenie v Liptovskom Mikuláši v roku 1918', in *Dr. Vavro Šrobár: politik, publicista a národnoosvetový pracovník*, ed. Miroslav Pekník (Bratislava: Veda, 2012), 269-270.
19. Zdeněk Veselý, *Dějiny české zahraniční politiky* (Praha: Oeconomica, 2013),172-182.
20. Natália Krajčovičová, *Slovensko na ceste k demokracii* (Bratislava: Historický ústav SAV, 2009) 22.
21. Compare: *Dokumenty slovenskej národnej identity a štátnosti. II. diel.* (Bratislava 1998) 21-22, 44-48.
22. Krajčovičová, *Slovensko na ceste k demokracii*, 26-27.
23. *Dokumenty slovenskej národnej identity a štátnosti*, 40-41.
24. Zdeněk Kárník, *České země v éře první republiky (1918-1938). Díl první (1918-1929)* (Praha: Libri, 2000), 46-47.
25. Slovenský národný archív, f. Archiv Kanceláře prezidenta republiky Praha, k. 9. *Správa Dr. Lederera o poměrech Židů na Slovensku.*
26. Slovenský národný archív, f. Československá dočasná vláda na Slovensku, k. 1. *Leták 'Slovenskí vojaci!'.*
27. Andrej Jeshajahu Jelínek, *Dávidova hviezda pod Tatrami. Žida na Slovensku v 20. Storočí* (Praha: Vydavateľstvo Jána Mlynárika, 2009), 123-131.
28. Jozef Jablonický, *Z ilegality do povstania* (Bratislava: Múzeum Slovenského národného povstania, 2009), 154.
29. *Dokumenty slovenskej národnej identity a štátnosti*, 42-43.
30. Slovenský národný archív, f. Slovenské oddelenie Národního výboru Československého 1918, k. 1. *Správa československého komisaře Maďariče*; Ibidem. *Hospodářska správa ze západního Slovenska.*
31. Marián Hronský, *Trianon. Vznik hraníc Slovenska a problémy jeho bezpečnosti* (Bratislava: Veda, 2011), 197-198.
32. Kárník, *České země v éře první republiky*, 37-42.
33. Veselý, *Dějiny české zahraniční politiky*, 206.
34. *Dokumenty slovenskej národnej identity a štátnosti*, 96-97.
35. Hronský, *Trianon*, 225-230.
36. Josef Bartoš and Miloš Trapl, *Československo 1918-1938: Fakta, materiály, reálie* (Olomouc: Univerzita Palackého, 1994), 15-24.

Unprocessed Trauma. Polish Medicine in the Face of Psychiatric Injury in the Era of the Great War

Joanna Urbanek

As Judith Lewis Herman has stated, 'The study of psychological trauma has a curious history – one of episodic amnesia'.[1] Medical advances with regard to recognition and treatment of this type of disturbance are closely tied to the history of armed conflict. It is commonly known that the period after the Vietnam War at the start of the 1970s, when doctors began to describe and treat post-traumatic stress syndrome among former US soldiers, was revolutionary for the development of modern diagnostics in this regard. Its symptoms are also diagnosed among victims, participants, and witnesses of not only war, but also accidents, cataclysms, and individual acts of violence. However, the history of psychology and psychiatry frequently overlooks much earlier significant achievements in this field, in the first half of the 20th century. In observing the experiences of First World War participants, erstwhile researchers correctly described disorders among them characterised by fear, whereas William Halse Rivers (1864-1922) and Pierre Janet (1859-1947) effectively formulated methods for their therapy. Nevertheless, the doctors' interest was closely tied to social reality. The 1920s and 1930s, characterised by a high level of conflict and the growth of nationalisms, were not favourable to systematic attention to the suffering of traumatised soldiers. The atmosphere at the time tended to mobilise society around national symbols, including scenes of heroic battle. An image of brazen heroes obscured the stories of real people, bearing deep psychological scars. On the other hand, the multiplicity of various types of afflictions of a neurotic and dissociative (psychotic) nature led to observations and conclusions. Only after many years, in the second half of the 20th century, did medical researchers follow them up, when study of the human psyche matured to reflection on the alarming consequences of the Second World War.

Fig. 1: William Halse Rivers, English anthropologist and psychiatrist, known for his work treating First World War soldiers who were suffering from shell shock.

First Studies of the Psychiatric Effects of Wartime Experiences in the USA and Europe

An American military physician, Jacob Mendes Da Costa (1833-1900), who at the time of the Civil War termed symptoms such as shortness of breath, perspiration, diarrhoea and chest pains as 'irritable heart', is considered to be the first to draw attention

Fig. 2: American physician Jacob Mendes Da Costa.

to the impact of wartime experiences on a soldier's nervous state.[2] His observations describe that which contemporary psychologists call combat stress.[3] Da Costa ordered the immediate withdrawal of these soldiers from the frontline and their convalescence. It is worth mentioning that his studies were known to Polish military doctors, who referred to them immediately after the First World War when they found numerous examples in their own practice. Symptoms were interpreted as a type of 'general neurosis' involving factors of a psychiatric nature. Indeed, their experiences led to conclusions on the beneficial effects of physical activity and staying at health resorts, which would significantly improve the health of patients within several months.[4]

The history of subsequent studies of wartime trauma is tied to the search for the aetiology of hysteria. This disorder was at first solely diagnosed in women. However, in 1882, Jean-Martin Charcot (1825-1893), the author of initial findings on this subject (from whom Freud drew inspiration), stated that a certain percentage of illnesses also applied to men. He thereby launched a fierce dispute among physicians that can be deemed ideological, since it concerned the axiom of inequality of the sexes from the standpoint of shape and resistance of the nervous system. It is not surprising that nervous disorders among men began to be ascribed to their particular predispositions, intellectual inferiority, or even moral depravity. Charcot's opponents included the particularly prominent German neurologist Hermann Oppenheim (1857-1919), who believed that nervous disorders were caused by damage to the nervous system. This thesis became the basis for modern studies of the brain as well as some fundamentally daunting interpretations by doctors who were seeking damage to the central nervous system in all instances of more or less significant 'nervous disorders'. Advocates of this tendency included Friedrich Schultze (1848-1934), who argued that neurosis and neuro-psychosis can be caused by even minor injuries if the illness encounters fertile ground in the form of a weak organism.[5] Clinical patients at the time were not soldiers, but workers and victims of work accidents. Their problems immediately raised scepticism and charges of simulation, which also endangered the reputation of researchers announcing the results of their studies.[6]

Researchers developed great interest in railway disasters. They were particularly spectacular in a world in which speed of movement increased many fold over the course of several decades. The complex of symptoms afflicting people suffering injuries in such accidents was termed railway-spine and subsequently railway-brain by the English surgeon John Eric Erichsen (1818-1896). He was essentially the first to describe post-traumatic stress syndrome, which was not yet formally diagnosed. However, he considered it to originate from spinal damage, and not psychological suffering from traumatic experiences.[7] This same line of research was continued by Ernst von Leyden (1832-1910), who searched for progressive inflammation of the spinal cord and meningitis among the psychiatrically ill. In his 1979 study, the German doctor declared that the symptoms described by Erichsen only applied to patients experiencing a rail collision while seated backwards to the direction of travel.[8] Only another German psychiatrist, Carl Moeli (1849-1919), concluded that the

Fig. 3: An Australian Advanced Dressing Station near Ypres, Belgium, in 1917. The wounded soldier in the lower left of the photograph has the 'thousand-yard stare' indicative of shell-shock.

symptoms described by Erichsen were unrelated to changes of an organic nature, but rather arose from psychological trauma. The above neurologists' findings repeatedly made reference to analogous disorders observed among soldiers.

There was further progress in the study of neurosis during the Russian-Japanese War. At that time, Emil Kraepelin (1856-1926) described his diagnosed so-called injury neurosis (injury hysteria) by declar-

ing that it stemmed solely from psychiatric reasons. Another Russian physician, Grigori Shumkov, described his observed symptoms of this illness in a work called 'Aerial contusion from experiences of the war of 1904-1905'. They entailed paralysis of sensation and motor skills in one half of the body, as well as strong negative reactions to cold or heat and changes to atmospheric pressure. In contrast to Kraepelin, however, he stated that this illness was caused by

Fig. 4: The Russian physiologist Ivan Pavlov.

Fig. 5: The English physician and psychologist Charles Samuel Myers.

bullets passing in close range of a soldier's head. Studies in this direction were conducted by Ivan Pavlov (1849-1936), who experimented on sheep. He stated emphatically, however, that the claim of higher air density along the flight path of a bullet allegedly causing this illness was wrong, as no such phenomenon could be observed among animals. Working in Paris alongside the Polish psychologist Adam Cygielstrejch (1886-1935), he declared in his 1912 doctoral thesis, *Les conséquences mentales des émotions de la guerre*, that the central nervous system of a patient becomes 'poisoned' by negative psychological experiences, thus leading to psychological disorders.

The First World War marked a milestone in the history of studies on injury stress among soldiers. Numerous instances of anxiety and permanent reactions persisting after withdrawal from the frontline, various disorders, and a rapid rise in military hospitalisation produced a multitude of publications. Renowned psychiatric authorities, starting with Sigmund Freud (1856-1939), revised their positions on previously diagnosed nervous disorders.

Authors of important studies during this time included the British physician Charles Samuel Myers (1873-1946), who published an article on so-called 'shell shock' in the renowned periodical *The Lancet* in 1915.[9] He thereby made famous a term that also provided a strictly physiological clarification of psychological problems soldiers were already facing at the start of the war. His thesis was elaborated upon by Frederick Walker Mott (1853-1926).[10] Mott believed that patients' disorders arose from the rupture of blood vessels in their brains, caused by a sudden change of atmospheric pressure during artillery explosions. This was a loud voice in the dispute with advocates of the psychological aetiology of nervous disorders, which led to numerous disagreements. From that point on, doctors elaborating on Mott's claims in their work focused on a study of neurological responses. Yet they were helpless in the face of patients' psychological suffering. From the standpoint of present-day medicine, this reasoning led to the wilderness of impersonal treatment of the mentally ill. It produced a true mania of measurement and the development of hermetic, yet wildly imprecise, terminology. Literature from that time is now an interesting historical source showing how the advancement of military technology, including the growing importance of artillery, overwhelmed doctors unable to comprehend the impact of this machinery of death on the human organism.

There were exceptions among psychiatrists. In Britain, William Halse Rivers (1864-1922) has particular merit for rendering true assistance to patients suffering from nervous disorders. He credited his findings to a meeting with the poet Siegfried Sassoon, a war hero whose harsh experiences on the front guided him toward pacifism. Sassoon, surely suffering from the yet undiagnosed post-traumatic stress syndrome (manifested by mood swings, persistent flashbacks to the frontline and nightmares), entered a clinic run by Dr Rivers, who applied treatment based on regular conversation sessions in an atmosphere of respect and confidentiality. Rivers discovered that one of the mechanisms of war neurosis is an attempt to mentally cut off from looming stimuli associated with armed conflict.[11] In psychiatry, an analogous phenomenon of detachment by a victim of violence or accident is called disassociation. Rivers used the term 'repression', drawn from psychoanalysis. An American student of Freud, Abram Kardiner (1891-1981), sought to introduce similar methods in his practice in observing that symptoms of war neurosis essentially do not differ from hysteria diagnosed among women.[12] His studies nevertheless did not produce any broader echo in a society already focused on new peacetime problems. The subject only reappeared with another global conflict: in 1941, Kardiner published a fundamental study, *The Traumatic Neuroses of War*, providing a clinical description of what was later called post-traumatic stress syndrome, and essentially did not differ much from present-day diagnostic criteria.[13]

Observation of traumatised soldiers returning from the First World War front greatly influenced the views of Sigmund Freud himself. Initially, he thought that the source of their problems was a conflict between the peacetime attitude of a soldier and the fighting instinct. On the other hand, however, he swiftly began to observe other possible causes by noting an excessive number of stimuli to which soldiers were exposed. In his 1920 book *Beyond the Pleasure Principle*, he formulated his own theory of psycho-

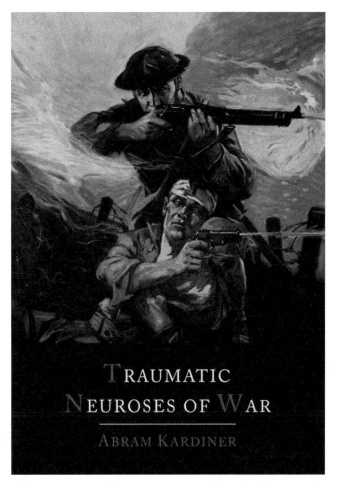

Fig. 6: Book cover of *Traumatic Neuroses of War* by Abram Kardiner, 2012 edition.

logical illnesses as a disruption of the natural protection barrier of the ego that in normal circumstances controlled the death instinct (tanatos), as opposed to the life instinct (libido). He continued his reflections on war trauma in his 1926 book *Inhibition, Symptoms and Anxiety*, in which he expounded his hypothesis of fear as a basis for traumatic reactions. Perhaps commitment to his own previous findings and a desire to maintain consistency induced him to define traumatic situations in categories that he compared to the threat of castration or the loss of one's mother.[14] Freud's reflections lacked a direct link between fear and objective threat in situations facing soldiers during combat. The founder of psychoanalysis included wartime trauma in a broader context of typical psychological challenges, which, in his opinion, generally confronted mankind. As Ruth Leys notes, Freud's writing at that time was characterised by uncertainty and ambivalence. After all, this was a difficult period in the personal life of the renowned psychiatrist.[15]

Other Austrian researchers of psychological wartime trauma also included Erwin Stransky (1877-1962), an opponent of Freud, who in 1918 wrote about his convictions that were supported by the already fashionable race ideology. Stransky, gaining experience in the army as a physician, described numerous individual cases in his work. They ranged from apathy to outbursts of unprecedented aggression among soldiers or collective psychotic states (hallucinations) observed in certain units, usually associated with defeat in battle.[16] Fledgling psychiatry in the first half of the 20th century did not lack an evaluative approach to patients. Causes of disorders were almost always attributed in full or in part to a patient's personality, and not to external factors. The greatest thinkers of that time succumbed to this temptation of this explanation, and 'hysteria' gained its name from the theory of its source in the womb. Such an approach left the social system intact and eliminated or 're-educated' individuals who could threaten it by speaking about abuses. The repressive side of science was primarily exposed in relation to persons lacking full legal status: women and children.

However, social transformation expanded the spectrum of doctors' interests, as well as the potential of abuses. Thus, the development of social insurance systems in Europe in the 19th and early 20th century required expertise on the state of health of compensation seekers. Patients frequently arrived with injuries to the head or spine from work accidents that caused paralysis, tremors, slurred speech or perception, or symptoms of a psychiatric nature. Many of them were diagnosed (or treated in advance) as malingerers. At times, however, the authenticity of suffering left no doubt. In order to reconcile disbelief in employer guilt with empirical observation, the term *Rentenneurose* (pension neurosis) appeared (far more bluntly coined by Polish authors as 'concupiscence neurosis'). Proponents of this approach included the German psychiatrist Adolf von Strümpell (1853-1925).

In the field of military psychiatry, analysts of disorders among soldiers were subjected to particular pressure. There was no shortage of commentary that psychological illnesses originate from moral degradation. The Canadian psychiatrist Lewis Yealland (1884-1954), during his practice in England promoted 're-education' by force: embarrassment of patients, threats, and even electrical shock as punishment. Experiences of the First World War nevertheless led to the conviction among researchers that it is possible for psychological trauma to occur without physical harm to the nervous system (fright neurosis – *Schreckneurose*). A concept prevailed that assumed both an external and internal aetiology of nervous disorders. Still under the influence of psychoanalysis, the Jewish-German academic Alexander Herzberg (1887-1944) found conflict to be the source of neurosis, which could be caused by external factors or a patient's personality.[17]

The above findings and disputes unfolded in a rapidly developing international environment of researchers, who were usually well acquainted with the findings of professional colleagues in other countries. This is evidenced by common reference to foreign medical literature. German, Austrian, French, British and Polish doctors also completed foreign internships by selecting mentors interested in a similar subject matter and centres for testing new treatment methods. Nevertheless, the arbitrary application of certain procedures, terms, and diagnoses must be emphasised. Communities of physicians supporting given interpretations and methods of treatment were akin to feuding sects – completely ignoring their competitors' contradictory results. This was possible because there was no internationally recognised register of illnesses (presently the ICD – International Statistical Classification of Diseases and Related Health Problems and DSM – the Diagnostic and Statistical Manual of Mental Disorders). Work on it lasted from the second half of the 19th century and accelerated at the end of the 1920s due to efforts of the League of Nations, although primarily causes of death were initially registered, and published statistics were incomplete. Available medical handbooks provided their authors' independent classifications and thus diverged depending on individual experiences and approaches.

Wartime Injuries and Polish Science – Research

The research interests of Polish psychologists and doctors, as well as the challenges they faced, did not essentially deviate from global trends. Their perspective was shaped by access to foreign medical literature and training, which frequently took place in Vienna, Berlin, as well as at Russian, Swiss, or French institutions.[18] Polish doctors studied and earned their titles in the framework of systems prevailing in three countries: Austria-Hungary, Germany, and Russia. Naturally, in addition to Polish, they also employed the language of the country where they practised, usually in conjunction with French as the prevailing *lingua franca* among the educated and, more rarely, English. These factors positively affected the degree of education and medical knowledge, as did contacts between Polish doctors and the international scientific community. Together with the emergence of the Second Republic of Poland, a gradual integration of researchers ensued within a common country. Yet, they still represented various directions, knowledge, and experience, but they now published and taught in Polish while also holding regular meetings.

The First World War contributed to the development of interest in the psychiatric condition of soldiers. However, most reviewed post-war Polish publications on military psychology and psychiatry focused on the subject area of leadership and discipline. A relatively new, but very popular, area of interest in interwar Poland was psycho-technique – tools to measure the features of candidates for the military profession, particularly pilots.[19] In 1920, researchers inaugurated experimental studies at the newly founded Soldier Individualisation Department on the cognitive development of officer candidates. With time, Section IV for anthropological-psycho-technique studies was formed at the Supplementation Department.[20] Its task, above all, was control over a future leadership cadre.

During this time, the Psychological Section at the Military Knowledge Association expanded with the aim of a broader reflection on military psychology issues, including the application of psychological knowledge in times of armed conflict. The Sanitary Training Centre in Jazdów had a psychology laboratory headed by Janina Ostaszewska. Works by Stefan Baley (1885-1952), Władysław Witwicki (1878-1948), Tadeusz Kotarbiński (1886-1981), and Józef Maria Bocheński (1902-1995) were published by the Main Military Bookstore. Publications of foreign authors like Charlotte Bühler (1893-1974) and William Mc-

Fig. 7: The Baltic German psychiatrist Adolf von Strümpell.

Dougall (1871-1938) that were propagated in Poland also gained broader attention.[21]

The above institutions, however, had fundamental flaws. Researchers used extremely expensive equipment measuring such indices as muscle tension or heart rhythm for studies based on dubious theoretical grounds and without observing the basic methodological principles of a psychological experiment. Excitement over new reaction measurement techniques, serving to give the researcher access to the secrets of the human personality and thought, was – as mentioned above – quite typical for this period of European science. It can be called exploratory. As we know, its bitter fruit also included German experience and pseudo-medical studies tasked with confirming racial theories.

A multitude of definitions abounded in Polish academic literature, arising from the vagueness and arbitrary use of certain terms, as noted above. Doctors themselves were aware of these limitations and inadequacies in prevailing science. Stefan Borowiecki

Fig. 8: The Polish psychologist Władysław Witwicki.

(1881-1937), in describing his experiences in military neurology and psychiatry during the First World War, decided to use the most voluminous and general terminology in his writings about reactive disorders.[22] He underscored the gravity of psychological shock itself in the aetiology of disorders, but also drew attention to a fact vital from the standpoint of present-day medicine, namely, that symptoms of an illness may develop with time and sometimes only manifest their entire spectrum long after the causal event. On the other hand, however, he was unable to clearly distinguish between specific features. Among states of anxiety he included psychotic (dissociative) symptoms, which, although related, belong in a different category according to present-day medicine. Therefore, his important observations, essentially leading toward the currently recognised diagnosis of post-traumatic stress, lacked clarity.

The interwar editions of the periodical *Lekarz Wojskowy* (Military Physician), from 1920 onwards, show clearly the huge amount of material that doctors contributed from their experiences with patients affected by war. The most frequently addressed issue was venereal diseases: syphilis was a plague among soldiers, and it threatened also to spread in peacetime. Another subject treated in many articles was wounds, their dressing, their complications, and prosthetics. A third significant consequence of armed conflict that emerged in Polish lands in 1920-1923 was malaria, called 'dab' in Polish literature. It peaked in 1921, when nearly 53,000 cases were registered, mainly in Polesie. Authors of texts in *Military Physician* devoted much attention to this subject. Disorders of a psychiatric and neurological nature (often classified arbitrarily) were in fourth, albeit prominent, place. Reactive neurosis (also called traumatic, reactive traumatic, etc.) was the main subject. As for arbitrary use by doctors of a complex and often empty terminology, Babiński's reference can be cited to the story of Don Quixote, who knocked on the door of an inn one night. When the keeper asked who he was hosting, so many titles were presented that the frightened innkeeper replied that he was unable to host so many outstanding guests in his humble abode.

Adam Chełmoński (1861-1924), a doctor specialising in internal medicine, head of the Infant Jesus Hospital in Warsaw, had the opportunity as a court expert to observe numerous psychologically ill patients ascribing their affliction to accidents. In a 1922 publication employing German terminology, he postulated a change of the term *Neurosis traumatica* in favour of *Schreckneurose* by arguing: 'only negative emotions are necessary to evoke any type of neurosis [...] traumatic neurosis frequently appears in such circumstances in which there is absolutely no physical injury'.[23] Chełmoński argued that bodily injuries actually protect against problems of a physical nature. Here, he cited instances of attention being drawn from pain of a psychological or existential nature by the feeling of physical ailment (flagellants). In his view, only a minuscule number of accident victims actually experienced neurosis. He also cited the prevailing opinion, especially in German and British psychiatry, that a significant role in the appearance of traumatic neurosis was played by the desire for compensation (*Rentenneurose*). It is noteworthy that in his work, which was written after the end of hostilities, he did not recall war invalids when recounting his findings in the pre-war period based on a study of

Fig. 9: Cover of the periodical *Lekarz Wojskowy* (Military Physician), April 1920.

civilian invalids, namely persons seeking a pension from the German social insurance system.

Bronisław Karbowski (1884-1940), chief physician of the 44th Kresy Riflemen Regiment, also gained his experiences with patients suffering from neurosis as a result of war. In his work, he, in turn, cited studies of the French psychiatrist André Léri (1875-1930) dating from 1918. Patients experiencing shock from explosions at close range were observed to have dilated pupils and a reduced heart rate, at times deafness/hearing hallucinations, and headaches, whereas symptoms of a psychological nature included: a slowdown in cognitive processes and muted emotions together with amnesia from the moment of explosion to the regaining of consciousness. In most cases, patients returned to full health after several days or weeks. However, in certain cases the illness became chronic by assuming forms of hysteria.[24] Typical manifestations in this regard were psychogenic paralysis of the muscles that were in a permanent state of tension, causing trembling or unnatural body curvature (victims could not walk or walked with protrusion of the upper part of the body, thus affecting posture and balance). Other symptoms, also lacking organic basis, included loss of hearing, sight, or the ability to speak. Another symptom diagnosed as hysterical was a sudden fear reaction during exposure to specific stimuli – objects or situations, at times broadening to an increasingly broader spectrum of everyday situations, so that the patient was prevented from functioning normally in society, and was certainly unable to return to military service.

This symptom, in the context of its origin (front-line combat), would now be unambiguously interpreted as evidence of the hitherto still unknown post-traumatic stress syndrome.

The psychiatrist and neurologist from Poznań University, Stefan Borowiecki, in recounting Willy Hellpach's (1877-1955) findings, attributed nervous illness to disruptions caused by the need to become independent and assume responsibility. He claimed that a so-called *neurasthenia reaction* was more frequently observed in wartime among officers than rank-and-file soldiers.[25] Yet, he failed to perceive that awareness of one's own psychological state remained at a lower level among those statistically less educated. Medical care in villages from which most recruits originated certainly affected the outcome of studies. After demobilisation, they returned to their families who preferred to avoid disclosure of their state to the local populace, and they were thereby expunged from medical records.

Polish psychiatrists quite rarely perceived symptoms among their patients that are typical for a present-day diagnosis of post-traumatic stress syndrome and depression. It can be assumed that such a state of

Fig. 10: The Polish physician Bronisław Karbowski, major in the health service reserve of the Polish Army.

knowledge stemmed from a lack of awareness among patients themselves that their suffering and downturn in mood over the course of months can be classified and treated as a psychological disorder. If their state was not clearly observable, they were generally not hospitalised and continued their service. In extreme instances, they adopted a passive stance during battle and perished or deserted. Individuals displaying extremely atypical behaviour or constituting a threat to their environment came under the care of psychiatrists.

There were exceptions among researchers, those attuned to more subtle signals from patients. While practising in Austria-Hungary (Kingdom of Galicia and Lodomeria), Jan Nelken (1878-1940) stated that general apathy was at times observed among former soldiers as a result of 'traumatic experiences', which he explained as limited sensitivity for the purpose of psychological self-defence. Moreover, 'inability to rid memory of various traumatic events, usually marked by cruelty (memory hallucinations, dark states, vivid war dreams)'[26] was frequently observed. Nelken was describing the phenomenon of intrusion known in present day PTSD diagnosis. In a text published as early as August 1915, Aleksander Pański (1862-1918) (associated with Łódz and Warsaw, in the Russian Empire until 1915) also made reference to a prevailing feeling among his patients of depression caused by a series of psychological shocks on the battlefront. He wrote that 'their pessimistic mood gives rise to a weariness with life and a contempt for it, bordering on suicidal tendencies', stipulating previously, however, that new types of weaponry and the new nature of war proved to be pernicious in their effects, even to those with a strong psychological constitution.[27]

During the First World War, Polish military physicians observed a mass outbreak of certain disorders such as an epidemiological spread of so-called reactive psychoses in Austro-Hungarian partition areas in 1917 and 1918, especially in Lwów in the spring of 1917. They disappeared entirely with the collapse of the Austro-Hungarian monarchy and disintegration of military service. Symptoms of the illness usually appeared among soldiers immediately after vacation leave or several days before returning to a unit. Fits of rage, prompted by a clear loss of orientation, appeared suddenly and frequently in public places. Victims lost their sense of reality. Unease over the situation facing loved ones at home could nevertheless be discerned in uncontrolled screams ('where are my brothers – give it back – let me go – you are guilty – my dog, my dog – give me a gun – I don't want to live, don't want to live',[28] shouted a man whose two brothers were killed in action). Others fell into a stupor. Their bodies' positions recalled that adopted during hysterical outbursts, as described by Charcot. The men's behaviour was characterised by a high degree of fear. Some were also aggressive, particularly toward any officers they encountered. In Lwów, 10% of all psychiatric cases during that time manifested such symptoms.

This phenomenon began to be called 'street' or 'holiday' psychosis and it was treated with utmost suspicion. However, upon extensive analysis only 4% of patients were deemed imposters. The researcher Jan Nelken immediately drew attention to the mechanism (known among present-day psychiatrists) of 'escape into illness' – the reaction of an organism to stimuli with which the psyche is unable to cope, whereby symptoms serve to draw an individual from the true source of problems. He underscored that the afflicted who were sent to the front without assistance swiftly returned to hospital with symptoms of even greater nervous breakdown, whereas transfer to a civilian environment instilled calm.[29] In interpreting the behaviour of soldiers on leave, Nelken noted the *antizipierte Nostalgie* – 'anticipated nostalgia' described by the Austrian psychiatrist Erwin Stransky (1877-1926), a vision of return to the front from a family environment that produced such drastic resistance from the organism.[30] He noted that soldiers from the Małopolska region reacted especially strongly when sent to distant reaches, to Italy.[31] Interestingly, their psychotic thoughts did not address combat at the front itself. Usually, their subject matter revolved around a vision of death in the family, betrayal by a loved one or loss of home.

Nelken also recalled instances of mass sensual illusions that affected entire units during combat. Exhausted troops experienced collective hallucinations of a religious nature, whereby visions of divine and saintly intervention appeared in the context of waiting for help and rescue from oppression. Less spectacular, but also more frequently observed, were auditory and visual delusions of an encroaching enemy. They usually occurred at night when visibility was

Fig. 11: Medical orderlies tend to the wounded in a trench during the Battle of Flers-Courcelette, France, in mid-September 1916. The man on the left is suffering from shell shock.

limited and fear was exacerbated.[32] Such types of occurrences ended in court rooms, as soldiers were accused of simulating madness and of cowardice.

Although most researchers focused on the study of neurological responses – the discovery of disorders of a hysterical nature – or searched for genetic or inbred sources of symptoms, the clear influence of the behavioural psychology flourishing in Europe could nevertheless be observed in certain articles. Doctors therefore interpreted symptoms as a learned reaction to a stimulant. Henryk Higier (1866-1942) recalled the case of an officer who reacted with vomiting to each hostile attack, because in his first battle he had to hide at the bottom of a latrine. This trauma immedi-

ately produced a conditioned response and rendered him unfit for further military service.[33]

Attention should be given to a form of case description and treatment, which, perhaps in addition to the publications of Nelken and Pański, was characterised by a large degree of objectification of patients. Illustrations included photographs of men stripped naked for 'image' purposes or photographed during examinations or rehabilitation without respect for their dignity. Even their faces were not covered. Naked invalids were photographed when attempting to walk (independently or with attendants or equipment such as rods or crutches). To the extent that photographs in movement can be explained by the

Fig. 12: The Austrian psychiatrist Erwin Stransky.

desire to show typical body position in given disorders (muscle flexion), this was completely unfounded in the case of photographs made en face in a standing position.[34] Photographs of patients were used in medical publications as engravings, similarly to illustrations and medical books or anatomic atlases. Their interpretation can be provided by Foucauld's theory of knowledge as a form of exercised power through the use of science (together with its complex terminology and authority) to regulate the life of individuals.[35] In the face of war, the health and ailments of millions of men became a public affair and a subject of great interest by state authorities. In this case, it can be argued that the humiliation of patients, including sexually, was an inseparable element of and price for medical care, as an indirect and harsh penalty for interrupting their service at the front.

Statistics and Care of Patients

Academic works from that time are devoid of any statistics that might yield an estimate of the number of patients suffering from war neurosis. Available

data is very general or scant, even in the case of those hospitalised, as it concerned specific facilities in a limited time perspective. It also cannot be summarised, because researchers employed quite arbitrary terminology in their calculations. Although I have not found statistics on the period of the First World War, we nevertheless know the overall number of patients admitted to military hospitals (not civilian, where most war combatants were surely brought) on account of neurosis in years following the end of armed conflict. In 1922, this was 1,828 persons (namely, 6 per 1,000 serving in the military). This number slowly and systematically decreased with time after the end of armed conflict.[36] This data nevertheless does not reveal much about the actual prevailing psychological state of soldiers (including combatants treated in military institutions). First of all, it only covers those who were hospitalised, namely recognised cases. Secondly, we do not know what

Fig. 13: The publication *Krieg und Geistesstörung* (War and mental disorder) by the Austrian psychiatrist Erwin Stransky, published in 1918.

percentage of those treated suffered from disorders caused by wartime experiences and how many were new illnesses.

How were those suffering from psychological illnesses induced by warfare cared for in practice? We can only respond to this question in relation to former soldiers. Civilian victims of war were beyond the realm of reflection in medical literature and most likely received far less professional care. Sending them to a mental institution depended on their family's awareness and will. Meanwhile, soldiers were under the constant observation of colleagues and superiors, which is why atypical behaviour was more swiftly noted.

A soldier manifesting symptoms of psychiatric disorder was usually sent to a garrison hospital. If it lacked psychiatric care, he was then dispatched to one of several civilian institutions in Poland specialising in the treatment of psychological illnesses. During observation, psychiatrists also decided on the future fate of patients: ongoing hospitalisation or invalid pension. The extent to which earning capabilities were lost was specified. If it exceeded 15%, patients were given a war invalid pension. Of note here was the problematic issue of adjudication based on percentage terms. Although the state of patients, according to data from the Care Section Branch of the Ministry of Military Affairs, swiftly improved after their transfer from service to hospital conditions, it also frequently worsened after they left.[37] Soon afterwards, however, financial issues and the desire to regulate adjudication led to a stiffening of regulations. In 1923, the principle was introduced that 'the mentally ill who are not dangerous to their surroundings and whose freedom of movement in public life is minimally or not limited at all cannot be deemed completely unfit for work'. In such cases, evaluation was set at a maximum of 50% of their lost earnings capabilities. Instances of 'nervous weakening' (neurasthenia – depression) and hysteria (psychological injuries based on wartime trauma) were to be 'assessed thoroughly and re-studied' in grave instances in the belief that the patient would rapidly return to health.[38]

From 1917, Poles serving in the Austro-Hungarian Army were sent to Polish institutions, which thus possess certain data on the frequency of psychiatric trauma or of the onset of psychological illnesses

Fig. 14: Illustration from *Przegląd Lekarski* (Medical Survey, no. 48, 1917). Soldier learning how to walk again at the neuropsychiatric clinic at Jagiellonian University in Cracow. The man is naked from the waist down to show readers the position of the patient's limbs.

among soldiers during that time. In the same year, 20 to 50 new patients arrived daily at only one neurological-psychiatric clinic at the Jagiellonian University in Cracow. This should be considered a sizable number given that it only served Poles from Galicia (the northern part of Austria-Hungary).[39]

Not all soldiers released due to psychiatric trauma found a place at medical facilities. If their state was deemed stable and further military service or independent functioning was no longer possible, the role of caregiver obviously rested with the family. Efforts were made to at least fundamentally regulate these actions. After the war, sections for war invalid affairs were established at County Supplementation Departments (responsible on a daily basis for the registration of further annual military service recruits) to maintain appropriate records. Their authority also included control over 'conscientious care of mentally ill invalids taken in by families'. Unfortunately, families, inadequately informed of the rights accorded to invalids (above all, financial support) in practice frequently remained without assistance. For example, a certain Bazyli Kuryłowicz from the district of Sokółka was drafted into the Russian army in 1915. He was soon taken prisoner and returned mentally ill in 1918. Until 1922, he stayed at the expense of his family at a civilian psychiatric clinic in Tworki near Warsaw. He was then deemed completely unfit for work. Unfortunately, Kuryłowicz was deprived of a pension, because when his brother applied for it in his name – once he had been approved as the legal guardian of the invalid – it was outside the one-year deadline set for those released from the army to apply to the state for financial assistance as an invalid. This negative decision was overturned following an Administrative Court judgment, yet the family still had to fight for a fair judgment (which required financial outlays and determination), while supporting their relative with their own means. Anyone so ill that they were incapable of independent existence, especially in the settlement of complicated administrative matters, was left to themselves if they received no care from those closest to them. The Polish state made no initiative to handle their cases.[40]

The treatment of patients diagnosed with neurosis did not achieve standardisation during the 20-year interwar period. References were made to various methods aimed at 'eliminating neurotic automatisms and introducing normal cognitive mechanisms'. In serious cases, patient isolation in closed institutions was recommended together with Charcot's 'education therapy', Déjérine's persuasion method, Dubois' dialectic or corrective method, Janet's gymnastics of the will, Oppenheim's cognitive exercises, Bernheim's waking suggestions, Forel's hypnotic state, autosuggestion (Coué), reaction methods (Breuer) and shock (Liébault), characterology (Klage), Adler's psychotherapy, and Freud's psychoanalysis. The above terms conceal a quite archaic technique, as the contemporary reader may only be familiar with the latter two. Nevertheless, closer attention should be given to methods developed by the French neurologist and psychologist Pierre Janet. Like Freud, Janet felt that work with recollections was imperative to treat patients, frequently with the aid of hypnosis. He sought to rework and redefine them, thus reducing fear. A

revolutionary aspect of his approach was the treatment of memory as a collection of stories whose form an individual can alter through a change of approach and training of a strong will. A similar approach can be found in the early 21st century in investigative-behavioural therapy.[41] Although Polish doctors were familiar with new psychotherapy methods, regular psychoanalysis sessions were obviously a luxury reserved only for wealthy eccentrics. I have not found any description in Polish medical literature of a case involving a war invalid subjected to such treatment, even though it cannot be excluded that such attempts were made. An analysis of Polish medical literature nevertheless reveals great interest among certain Polish psychiatrists in psychotherapy methods then practised in Europe, as opposed to antiquated yet still unfortunately adopted 're-education' methods (such as isolation and discipline). They included the strongly present psychoanalytical trend (including wildly popular hypnosis) and less invasive actions, certainly not harmful, to provide patients with a peaceful and stable environment in which they could rest and, in milder cases, gradually return to health.

In practice, the mentally ill who are capable of independent functioning at a basic level were sent to spas and baths, as warm baths were considered to calm the nervous system. Henryk Higier pointed out the effectiveness of several week-long stays in sanatoriums. He underscored that their mineral waters helped treat neurotic patients better than those to whom specific facilities were initially dedicated (e.g. Ciechocinek or Krynica were established to ease the suffering of heart patients). Thus, Higier seemingly failed to perceive the role of a change of surroundings and rest among the limited number of stimuli for treating milder cases of neurosis. He believed that this state could be improved through 'mineral salts, carbonic acid gas, radium substances[42] present in sanatorium air and water. Other Polish researchers, in accordance with observations of their foreign professional colleagues, declared the salutary role of staying at a peaceful abode, far from the dreadfulness of the front. These not very revolutionary conclusions regarding the ability of the human psyche to regenerate in accommodating conditions nevertheless led to more humane and personal relations with patients. Above all, in accordance with the golden rule of Hippocrates, they did not cause even greater harm.

Fig. 15: Scene in the tent for patients suffering from war neurosis. The American Red Cross had established a hospital for these men in the forest of Chateau Chambord, near Blois, France, 1918.

A review of methods applied toward patients admitted to specialist hospitals includes a work by Jan Piltz (1870-1930) on the subject of the neurological-psychiatric clinic at Jagiellonian University. Piltz treated patients as immature people, gently or 'harshly', in other words, from a position of authority and superiority. Hysterical outbursts (because hysteria itself was considered to be inborn and a rather indelible mental defect) were also 'treated' in Cracow through psychological violence. For example, symptoms were to quickly subside, particularly when blackmail was employed against patients by denying correspondence from families. Patients were isolated from external stimuli through denied contact with family, walks, or any correspondence. Treatments took place irrespective of patient protests, with dec-larations that they would continue until cured. They constituted torture in the name of misunderstood proper therapy. To the extent that professional curiosity guided the approach to exceptionally drastic methods known from abroad (intimidation, setting beds on fire to force the patients lying in them to flee), there is no indication of such brutality taking place at Polish institutions.[43]

Piltz considered that the most effective psychotherapy aimed at motivating a patient, exercising his 'strong will' and explaining reasons for his state. Like Freud, doctors considered mere understanding of the nature of topological symptoms to lead to recovery. However, in contrast to psychoanalysis (which, actually, in its classic form is still not considered in the early 21st century an effective form of help in over-

Fig. 16: The Polish neurologist and psychiatrist Jan Piltz.

coming trauma), Polish doctors took an active role in the therapeutic process without limiting themselves to merely listening, but also by offering 'suggestions' – seeking to guide a patient towards a 'correct' interpretation of an illness and attempting to strengthen the internal desire for treatment. This was not at all obvious, as they noted, in the case of neurasthenic patients (suffering from depression) and men fearing return to the front. Doctors appeared to completely misunderstand the sources of these fears. I have not found many pronouncements demonstrating an understanding of the terrifying reality of frontline service. The already repeatedly noted *Rentenneurose* was also cited in the context of no patient improvement, despite the application of all available medical treatment. Hopes of obtaining war invalid privileges connected with their condition (for example pension or a state concession for a small kiosk selling tobacco) were to effectively block patients and prevent progress in treatment[44]

Piltz also considered the use of a low-voltage electrical current (so-called Faradisation) a very effective method of eliminating symptoms diagnosed as hysterical – unnatural spasms or twisting of limbs. An electrode was applied to a twisted limb, thus forcing movement of a blocked muscle. Therefore, a patient, in unintentionally performing this movement, 'recalled' how to actively perform it himself.[45] This method should not be associated with electroshock therapy (ECT).

So-called hysterics found themselves in dedicated sections at certain large institutions. An effort was made to isolate them from neurological patients (with disorders stemming from damage to the nervous system). Nevertheless, deliberate placement in general psychiatric wards, thus stimulating the desire of pensioners for a cure, served to foster arousal of the will. From today's perspective, this method must be viewed as another example of the oppressiveness of the healthcare system at that time. The scene of almost permanently institutionalised untreated schizophrenics or those afflicted with severe alcoholism, who were merely isolated from society and suppressed with psychoactive means, had to be another psychological shock repeatedly traumatising war invalids.

The problem of wartime psychiatric trauma was rarely a subject raised by state authorities. Yet, it should be noted that in Poland the problem was treated on equal terms with other health complications arising from military service. Victims were therefore eligible for a military pension, which, according to binding regulations, was dependent on the degree (percentage) of loss of earning capabilities in a civilian profession. Psychiatric illness nevertheless eluded such a simple classification, which is why more 'objective' factors were sought, more measurable than the degree of human suffering. Doctors were recommended to declare a maximum of 45% lost earning capability if a patient posed no threat to himself or his environment, and 100% if such threat was found. Usual procedures required a military commission to examine an invalid pension applicant. In the case of mentally ill patients, an opinion issued by a treatment facility sufficed. This was a convenience for applicants, but resulted in certain arbitrary treatment of patients by psychiatrists not necessarily well informed of adjudication.

Fig. 17: Jan Piltz with his staff at the neuropsychiatric clinic at Jagiellonian University in Cracow, Poland.

Conclusion

Despite the atrocities and exhausting conditions to which soldiers were subjected on front during the First World War, doctors still showed a tendency to seek weakness in the character of their patients. This approach led to stigmatisation. From the start of the 20th century, some of them more frequently turned their attention to the situational basis of psychiatric illnesses. The First World War experiences of doctors, particularly when they observed injured young and until recently fit men, contributed to a more empathetic change of approach toward psychiatric patients. Unfortunately, such an approach did not take root in Polish society during the 20-year interwar period, when the young Polish state needed a heroic

vision of its most recent history. In light of serious internal problems, an unfavourable international situation, and the active promotion of militarism in the 1930s, there was a shortage of funds, interest, and time for proper care of war victims. I have focused on soldiers in this article for a reason. The experiences of millions of civilians, many among whom also surely bore psychological scars as a result of war, did not arouse the interest of Polish or foreign academics at the time. This can perhaps be explained by their utilitarian approach to these issues, which was principally an effort to maintain soldiers fit for combat and to prevent desertion.

To the extent that their real-life medical practice inspired and actually forced doctors to deal with the subject of an organism's reaction to the stress of war during the wartime period and thereafter, subsequent researchers focused on studies of recruits and on officer training, while forgetting about the psychological consequences of war and their psychologically ill victims. The Norwegian psychiatrist Leo Eitinger (1912-1996), dealing with the psychological trauma of those rescued from the Holocaust, underscores the defensive nature of losing interest in extensive study of the psychological state of victims:

War and victims are something the community wants to forget; a veil of oblivion is drawn over everything painful and unpleasant. We find the two sides face to face; on one side the victims who perhaps wish to forget but cannot, and the other all those strong, often unconscious motives who very intensely both wish to forget and succeed in doing so.[46]

Mechanisms blocking public sensitivity can therefore have a defensive and adaptive nature.

Finally, focus on the traumatic side of war has been undermined by a heroic narration of the dedication of thousands of frequently anonymous people, 'unknown soldiers' serving the homeland. Jay Winter, in his fundamental work on memory in the First World War, outlines the course taken by societies in Western Europe from grief (usually demonstrated individually) to the inclusion of war victims in a brave tale – heroisation. This process helped soldiers deal with nightmares, as it provided them with context and meaning. Frequently unspeakable states – fear, desperation, physical and psychological pain – were hidden from social consciousness with pride and hope of proper compensation, which frequently took the form of purely declaratory gratitude to believers. For financial and ideological reasons, Poland exceptionally lacked eagerness to commemorate the suffering of war victims. The myth of brave soldiers in Polish voluntary units (particularly Legionnaires) was rapidly conceived, while overlooking, in the collective consciousness, the hundreds of thousands mobilised in occupation armies. Their experiences were solely reduced to the real or imagined drama of fighting alongside their countrymen, but dressed in the enemy's uniforms.

Endnotes

1. Judith Lewis Herman, *Trauma and recovery. The Aftermath of Violence - from Domestic Abuse to political Terror* (New York: Basic Books, 1997), 7.
2. Jacob Mendez Da Costa, 'On irritable heart: A clinical study of a form of functional cardiac disorder and its consequences,' *American Journal of the Medical Sciences*, 61 (1987), 17-52.
3. Bret A. Moore, Greg M. Reger, 'Combat stress and team to control combat stress from a historical and contemporary perspective,' *in Combat Stress. Theories, Research and Management*, eds. Charles R. Figley and William Nash (London: Routledge, 2007), Polish volume editor: Stanisław Ilnicki (Warszawa: PWN, WIM, 2010).
4. Adam Huszcza, W. Gordon, O t. z. sercu żołnierskim (Wyjątek z pracy). Praktyczne zdobycze klinicznej kardiologii – w okresie od r. 1900-go (The Brit. Med. Journal no. 3/31 1/I. 1921), *Lekarz Wojskowy*, no. 51 (1921), 1639.
5. Friedrich Schultze, 'Über Neurosen und Neuropsychosen nach Trauma,' in *Sammlung Klinischer Vorträge*, ed. Richard von Volkmann (Leipzig: Breitkopf & Härtel, 1891), 135-154.
6. Ibid.
7. John Eric Erichsen, *On Railway and Other Injuries of the Nervous System* (Philadelphia: Colllins, 1867), PA: Henry C. Lea.
8. Bronisław Karbowski, 'O dominujących poglądach w sprawie tak zwanej nerwicy kontuzyjnej,' *Lekarz Wojskowy*, 14 (1920), 5-20.
9. Charles S. Myers, 'A contribution to the study of shell shock,' *The Lancet*, 1 (1915), 316-320.
10. 'The Effects of High Explosives upon the Central Nervous System,' *The Lancet* 1 (1916), 331-338.
11. William Halse Rivers, 'The repression of war experience,' *The Lancet*, 194 (1918), 173-177.
12. Judith Lewis Herman, *Trauma and recovery. The Aftermath of Violence - from Domestic Abuse to political Terror* (New York: Basic Books, 1997), 23-35.
13. The American Psychiatric Association did not enter post-traumatic stress syndrome into the diagnostic handbook until 1980.
14. Ruth Leys, 'Freud i trauma,' in *Antologia studiów nad traumą*, ed. Tomasz Łysek (Kraków: Universitas, 2015), 109-137.
15. Ibid.
16. Erwin Stransky, *Krieg und Geistesstörung: Feststellungen und Erwägungen zu diesem Thema vom Standpunkte angewandter Psychiatrie* (Wiesbaden: Verlag von J.F. Bergmann, 1918).
17. Alexander Herzberg, 'Der Erregungshemmungskonflikt in der Ätiologie der Neurosen,' *Allgemeine ärztliche Zeitschrift für Psychotherapie und psychische Hygiene*, vol 1, no. 7 (July) 1928. Einschliesslich der klinischen und sozialen Grenzgebiete. Organ der allgemeinen ärztlichen Gesellschaft für Psychotherapie.
18. An example is Jan Nelken, who as a young doctor worked in Zurich for Eugen Bleuler, founder of the term schizophrenia, in conducting studies together with Carl Gustav Jung (then senior assistant at the same institution). He gained his position upon recommendation of his Kraków superior, Jan

Piltz, who more than a decade earlier helped found this clinic after studying in Bern.

19. Janusz Gąsiorowski, *Bibliographie de Psychologie Militaire/Bibliografia Psychologii Wojskowej*, (Warszawa: Główna Księgarnia Wojskowa, 1938).

20. Andrzej Felchner, Marek Komasiński, 'Początki psychologii i psychotechniki w Wojsku Polskim,' in *Psychologia a żołnierska służba* (zbiór materiałów z dyskusji zorganizowanej przez Wojskową Akademię Medyczną i redakcję miesięcznika 'Wojsko i Wychowanie'), eds. Franciszek Seweryn and Janusz Tomiło (Warszawa: Wydawnictwo Czasopisma Wosjkowe, 1995), 7-8.

21. Andrzej Felchner, Marek Komasiński, 'Początki psychologii i psychotechniki w Wojsku Polskim,' in *Psychologia a żołnierska służba* (zbiór materiałów z dyskusji zorganizowanej przez Wojskową Akademię Medyczną i redakcję miesięcznika "Wojsko i Wychowanie"), eds. Franciszek Seweryn and Janusz Tomiło (Warszawa: Wydawnictwo Czasopisma Wosjkowe, 1995), 8.

22. Stefan Borowiecki, 'Klasyfikacja zaburzeń psychicznych reaktywnych i ich stosunek do tak zwanych nerwic,' *Rocznik Psychiatryczny*, vol. XXII, (Warszawa: 1934), 9-27.

23. Adam Chełmoński, *Rola uszkodzeń cielesnych w powstawaniu nerwicy urazowej?* (Warszawa: 1922), 1.

24. Bronisław Karbowski, *O dominujących poglądach w sprawie tak zwanej nerwicy kontuzyjnej*, 5-20.

25. Stefan Borowiecki, 'Klasyfikacja zaburzeń psychicznych reaktywnych i ich stosunek do tak zwanych nerwic,' (Warszawa: Wydawnictwo 'Rocznika Psychiatrycznego,' 1934), 7.

26. Jan Nelken, *Psychozy reaktywne w oświetleniu wojny światowej i służby wojskowej*, 78.

27. Aleksander Pański, 'W sprawie nerwicy wskutek kontuzji i wstrząsów wojennych,' *Medycyna i Kronika Lekarska*, no. 34 (1915).

28. Jan Nelken, 'Psychozy reaktywne na wojnie,' *Lekarz wojskowy*, no. 30 (1921), 945.

29. Jan Nelken, 'Psychozy reaktywne w oświetleniu wojny światowej i służby wojskowej,' *Rocznik Psychiatryczny* (1934), 72-90.

30. Erwin Stransky, *Krieg und Geistesstörung: Feststellungen und Erwägungen zu diesem Thema vom Standpunkte angewandter Psychiatrie* (Wiesbaden: Verlag von J.P. Bergmann, 1918).

31. Jan Nelken, 'Psychozy reaktywne na wojnie,' 941-950.

32. Jan Nelken, *Psychozy reaktywne w oświetleniu wojny światowej i służby wojskowej...*, 78-79.

33. Henryk Higier, 'Nerwice ogólne, psychonerwice i nerwice narządowe we współczesnej medycynie wewnętrznej a racjonalne ich leczenie (odczyt wygłoszony w Tow. Medyc. Społeczn. 10 maja 1929),' in *Warszawskie Czasopismo Lekarskie*, no. 24-25 (1929), 20.

34. Jan Piltz, 'Przyczynek do nauki o t. zw. nerwicach wojennych i ich leczeniu,' *Przegląd Lekarski*, no. 48 (1917), 395.

35. Michel Foucault, *Society must be defended. Lectures at the Collège de France*, ed. Małgorzata Kowalska, (Warszawa: Wydawnictwo KR, 1998).

36. Central Military Archive, I 302.4.2153.

37. Kraków National Archive, General Care Section Branch at the Ministry of Military Affairs, 29.276.2.

38. New Files Archive in Warsaw, Presidium of the Council of Ministers, Rect. 63 t. 1c. Instruction of the Ministry of Military Affairs, Ministry of Labour and Social Welfare and Ministry of Justice for a military-medical commission to examine war invalids.

39. Jan Piltz, 'Przyczynek do nauki o t. zw. nerwicach wojennych i ich leczeniu,' *Przegląd Lekarski*, no. 48 (1917), 395.

40. Kraków National Archive, General Care Section Branch at the Ministry of Military Affairs in Kraków, 29.276.1.

41. Bessel A. van der Kolk, Onno van der Hart, 'Onno van der Hart, Natrętna przeszłość: elastyczność pamięci i piętno traumy, in *Antologia studiów nad traumą*, ed. Tomasz Łysek (Kraków: Universitas, 2015), 139-174.

42. Henryk Higier, 'Nerwice ogólne, psychonerwice i nerwice narządowe we współczesnej medycynie wewnętrznej a racjonalne ich leczenie (odczyt wygłoszony w Tow. Medyc. Społeczn. 10 maja 1929),' *Warszawskie Czasopismo Lekarskie*, no. 24-25 (1929), 20.

43. Jan Piltz, 'Przyczynek do nauki o t. zw. nerwicach wojennych i ich leczeniu,' *Przegląd Lekarski*, no. 48 (1917), 400.

44. Jan Piltz, 'Przyczynek do nauki o t. zw. nerwicach wojennych i ich leczeniu,' *Przegląd Lekarski*, no. 48 (1917), 401.

45. Jan Piltz, 'Przyczynek do nauki o t. zw. nerwicach wojennych i ich leczeniu,' *Przegląd Lekarski*, no. 48 (1917), 398.

46. Leo Eitinger, 'The concentration camp syndrome, and its late sequealae,' in *Survivors, Victims and Perpetrators*, ed. Joel E. Dimsdale (New York: Hemisphere, 1980), 141.

Women's Fight for Civil, Social and Political Rights in Czechoslovakia, Hungary and Poland

Karolina Łabowicz-Dymanus

The years 1918-1923 were significant for equality movements. During this short period, nineteen European countries granted women civil and political rights. In 1918, Austria, Estonia, Georgia, Germany, Hungary (where rights were nevertheless restricted until 1945), the United Kingdom and Ireland (restricted until 1928), Latvia, Lithuania, Poland and Russia offered political rights to women; in 1919, Belarus, Belgium (restricted until 1948) and the Netherlands followed; in 1920, so did Albania and Czechoslovakia; and in 1921, Armenia, Azerbaijan and Sweden did as well. Women citizens willingly exercised their passive and active electoral rights in the first national elections open to them, in which a significant number of women not only voted but also stood as candidates. The first women candidates were elected to take seats in national parliaments or were nominated to represent their states as ambassadors. Furthermore, international organisations fought to improve the situation and equality of women. For example, the United Nations secured social rights for women workers, including maternity protection. Unfortunately, this does not mean that all rights were fully implemented: few women were actually elected or nominated for official state positions.

Several different galvanising forces had driven this shift towards equal rights. The general impetus for democratisation and the popularisation of Liberalism[1] – two integral elements of the origins of the modern state and modern citizenship – both played a vital role. The democratic system was also seen as a model of stability. The region was a hotbed of potential conflict and instability caused by the collapse of the empires of Austria-Hungary, Russia and Germany. Their former territories had been devastated by savage conflicts, originating in disputes over frontiers and the national status of minorities, and fuelled

Fig. 1: Poster 'Votes for Women – Wanted Everywhere' from 1909, drawn by the British suffragette Hilda Dallas (1878-1958).

by territorial claims or contradictions between social groups and their political ambitions. Tension had been increasing between radicalised right-wing extremists and traditional conservatives, and between the socialist labour movement and the workers' councils that were taking root thanks to the impact of the Russian Revolution. Under such circumstances, many women's rights supporters considered women and their female virtues as 'helpers' in constructing stable nation-states. They were acting as modern citizens but were still underprivileged and in fact deprived of rights, although women contributed to the national revival movement, actively participated in the First World War, took positions as professionals and factory workers, paid taxes, etc. This changed rapidly after 1918, when women become a symbol of modernity. They were modern *par excellence*[2] – they took new roles in society, the family and the professional field. In the very brief period after 1918, before Central and Eastern European societies turned to conservatism, the modern image of women had been used as a powerful weapon to both modernise the living environment and to 'cure' psychological, social and cultural backwardness.

Towards Equality

In no country did women gain political and civil rights without a struggle. However, the traditions of women's activism and the suffragette movements were different in Western and Eastern European countries. Feminist movements in Central and Eastern Europe operated on a much smaller scale than their American and British counterparts.[3] At the turn of the century, the Western suffragettes claimed that women's rights had to be equal to men's rights.[4] At the same time, the subjects under the imperial rule of Russia, Germany and Austria-Hungary had rather limited rights, although Austria-Hungary granted certain political rights for particular groups of Czech, Slovak, Hungarian and Polish men and women. Hence, the struggles for independence in these countries appear to have been a general galvanising force[5] in the universal suffrage movement and to have promoted the broader development of civil society.[6]

Women's enfranchisement was fought for not as a separate cause, but rather as a 'joint track' in the campaign for sovereign states and nations.[7] Nationalism was accompanied by other factors, such as: general social changes within societies; historical conditions that forced women to take social positions of their men were no longer able to fill because they had died in the war; and economic transformation in the

process of modernisation in which the shift of labour from agriculture to other domains took place rapidly and more intensively for women than for men, mainly in industry, trade and public services.[8] As a consequence, feminists argued that those citizens who had legal responsibilities and paid taxes also deserved rights in making decisions. However, most political parties, nationalist and socialist alike, had seen women rights as a secondary issue.

The left-wing forces were prone to defend universal suffrage on grounds of principle, whereas right-wing forces defended women rights on strategic grounds – both shared an easy predisposition to sacrifice justice for women for 'more important, urgent or compelling' causes.[9] They argued that the emancipation of women should follow the liberation of the state/or of the proletariat/or both – the opinions varied between parties and individual politicians.[10]

Mothers of the Nation

The other triggering factor in electoral reforms was the recognition of women's commitment to the national movements and emphasising the idea of equality for modern nation-building. It partly originated from the belief that the path towards national self-consciousness begins in the family and that the mother plays a significant role in this process.[11] The idea of 'Mothers of the Nation' became stronger from the mid-19th century onwards, drawing on the development in women's education, which was believed to contribute to the improvement of national culture and the mother tongue.[12]

The strength of the National Revival Movement helped women formulate their demands for equality in education, as they made use of the fact that a nation in need of liberation from its oppressors is also in need of educated mothers for its sons and daughters.[13] Later in the debate, those who supported women's rights based their argument on a concept of 'social motherhood'. It was emphasised that women's feminine qualities would benefit both women and society once they had been admitted to public and political life. 'Mothers of the Nation' represented female virtues such as morality, dedication and above all motherliness. These 'motherly' values not only made women fit for politics, they were also thought to help achieve a peaceful and united state and a better, more just society. In Central and Eastern Europe, therefore, the relationship between feminism and nationalism was very strong.

The First World War and the Women's Suffrage Movement

For women in the West, as well as those in countries struggling for independence such as Poland, Czechoslovakia, Hungary, Estonia, Latvia and Lithuania, the contribution of women in the First World War played an important role in gaining universal suffrage. However, suffragists were divided by their different approaches towards the war. The International Women's Alliance called for pacifism and worked for peace, while other feminist groups urged service in the war effort or even direct military involvement – but all women saw the war as an opportunity to claim political and civil rights for themselves.[14] Many suffrage supporters saw women's war contributions as a trigger in a possible shift from women's assigned social role as passive citizens, who could not request any active participation in state affairs, to citizens with full rights.[15] As noted above, the idea of modern citizenship included the concept of the citizen soldier who, as a defender of the nation, was endowed with full rights, especially political ones. As the Austrian historian Brigitta Bader-Zaar has pointed out:

> Suffragists were thus one of many groups who recognized the opportunity to claim citizenship and to emphasize women's service to the nation during the war. They expanded the idea of citizenship to include themselves as active, not passive members of the nation and argued that women were 'citizens with duties towards the general public'. Their relief work was proof of their 'patriotism and their fitness for citizenship'; they were the 'soldiers on the home front'.[16]

However, many scholars stress that the 'illusionary nature of wartime change', as Higonnets has phrased it, lasted 'only for the duration', after which came backswings.[17] Although the situation of women did change after the First World War, the old relationships of domination and subordination were retained. There was also a discrepancy between the situation of Western and Eastern European women.

Fig. 2: 'Patriotic emancipation' – Waleria Frąckowiak wearing the uniform of an ensign in the Army of Greater Poland, Poznań 1919.

In Western Europe, the wartime struggle created opportunities for many women to go to work and take on the roles of their absent men; in the nations struggling for sovereignty, meanwhile, women had already been attempting to take on male roles for decades. In most cases, active women were still forced to seek political influence by gaining access to male decision-makers in private spheres (salons), which were traditionally associated with femininity.[18]

One example of the combined factors of 'soft power', diplomatic forces and active service during the First World War is provided by the devoted Polish feminist Aleksandra Piłsudska (1882-1963) née Szczerbińska, Marshall Józef Piłsudski's (1867-1935) life partner. Piłsudska had been involved in the main

Fig. 3: Aleksandra Piłsudska, Polish feminist and life partner of Józef Piłsudski.

The First Women Deputies in National Parliaments

On January 1919, in the first general parliamentary election to the Polish Legislative Sejm (Diet), women's participation was noticeable (66.9% of the female electorate voted, along with 71.5% of the male electorate). However, only six women were elected as Deputies (1.38% of all Diet members), and none were chosen as Senators. In years to follow, the number of women representatives to Parliaments remained extremely low (2-4% overall). Public opinion was male dominated, and although the socialist, peasant and nationalist parties all made intensive efforts to win women's votes, women candidates to the Parliaments were openly discriminated against, as their names were placed on lists of candidates in the positions doomed to fail.[20]

In 1918, Hungarian women also attained suffrage, although in a limited form. According to the law accepted by the Autumn (Democratic) Revolution, literate women above the age of 24 were granted electoral rights. In the spring of 1919, a new political turn swept away these regulations and the Hungarian Soviet Republic introduced universal rights to vote. However, electoral rights were linked with trade union membership, and 'non-proletarians' were thus excluded from the elections.[21] After the brief era of the Soviet commune, ending in autumn 1919, the new right-wing rule that defined the following decades overturned these regulations, restricting electoral rights and linking them to the census (according to age, literacy, property or family status). Universal suffrage rights were introduced in Hungary only after the Second World War in 1945.[22]

Hungarian women first participated in elections in 1922, and the first woman member of Parliament, Margit Slachta, was elected that year. Hungary was also the very first state in the world represented by a woman ambassador – Rózsika Schwimmer (1877-1948). Mihály Károlyi's (1875-1955) government named this Hungarian-American feminist, suffragette, journalist and politician the ambassador to Switzerland in 1918.

In its first constitution, the independent Czechoslovak state granted men and women equal suffrage rights in 1920, and women actively participated in the Parliamentary elections that same year. Thirteen women were elected to the Chamber of Deputies (300

revolutionary movement of the Polish Socialist Party since 1904, and she actively participated in the partisan, subversive actions of an illegal guerrilla unit, the Combat Organisation of the Polish Socialist Party (Organizacja Bojowa Polskiej Partii Socjalistycznej) led by Józef Piłsudski. The most famous action was the so-called Bezdany raid in 1908, when Piłsudski and twenty others, including Aleksandra Piłsudska and three future Polish Prime Ministers Tomasz Arciszewski (1877-1955), Aleksander Prystor (1874-1941) and Walery Sławek (1879-1939), assaulted a Russian train carrying tax revenues near Vilnius. Piłsudska was also a leader of the Women's League – a women's military group with 20,000 members during the First World War.[19] Thus, we can speculate that it was Aleksandra Piłsudska who helped her hesitating husband to make a final decision on the issue of electoral reform. On 28 November, Polish women finally obtained full political rights. However, the law excluded minority women and those from the autonomous province of the Silesian Voivodeship.

Fig. 4: The feminist, journalist, and politician Rózsika Schwimmer.

elementary schools. Women members of Parliament also originated from different social backgrounds, with the majority coming from the upper and middle class. It was women from the intelligentsia elite that had previous experience of activity in public institutions, had benefited from the female education movement, were involved in the phenomenon of women's publishing works and had actively participated in paramilitary organisations during the First World War. In consequence, women deputies were better prepared to play an active role in politics than the majority of elected men.[24]

The Rights of Working Women

There was no unity in the feminist movements, and working-class and middle-class women generally fought for different goals. Access to higher education, professional training and electoral rights was a key struggle for middle-class women, who saw civil and political rights as a prerequisite of an active citi-

Fig. 5: The American feminist Charlotte Garrigue, wife of Tomáš Garrigue Masaryk.

seats) and three to the Senate (150 seats). 54% of the voters were women, as opposed to 46% men. In years to follow, the number of women representatives to Parliaments rose gradually.[23] Czechoslovak women found supporters in President Tomáš Garrigue Masaryk (1850-1937) and First Lady and American feminist Charlotte Garrigue (1850-1923) (whose maiden name Masaryk adopted). They supported higher education for all women, involvement in the labour market and society in general as well as political rights; thus, Czechoslovak suffragettes did not need to fight as hard for equal rights as women in other countries.

In all these countries, the group of women deputies was distinguished by its educational background. Two-thirds of the women representatives were university graduates, with the remaining third having graduated from secondary schools. In contrast, a quarter of the men had only graduated from zenship and social equality. This group also benefited the most from the intense changes in social hierarchy as new occupations emerged, mainly in the arts, science and the civil service.[25] Female labour rapidly expanded in those sectors. However, women were not readily accepted as professionals and were encouraged to leave their positions, especially white-collar work, on marriage.

Proletarian women in general fought for social rights for working women, in particular the extensive protection of maternity rights, employment protection, absent representation by unions, night work for women and a minimum age in industry. All groups fought for equal pay for equal work and against discrimination in promotion procedures to

higher professional ranks.[26] In 1919, women achieved an international standard-setting declaration for working conditions and the Maternity Protection Convention passed by the International Labour Organization (ILO) Convention at the ILO Conference held in Washington. The ILO, a United Nations agency, had decided upon the adoption of certain proposals with regard to 'women's employment, before and after childbirth, including the question of maternity benefits'.[27] In addition, the same organization regulated a maximum number of working hours per day and week, protection of children and young persons, worker protection against sickness and injuries, and recognition of freedom of association. The areas of improvement listed remain relevant today.

Fig. 6: Women activists on the way to a rally in Warsaw, 1930. At the head Stanisława Woszczyńska (1879-1967; front row, 2nd from the left) and Justyna Budzińska-Tylicka (1867-1936; with a tie and white shirt).

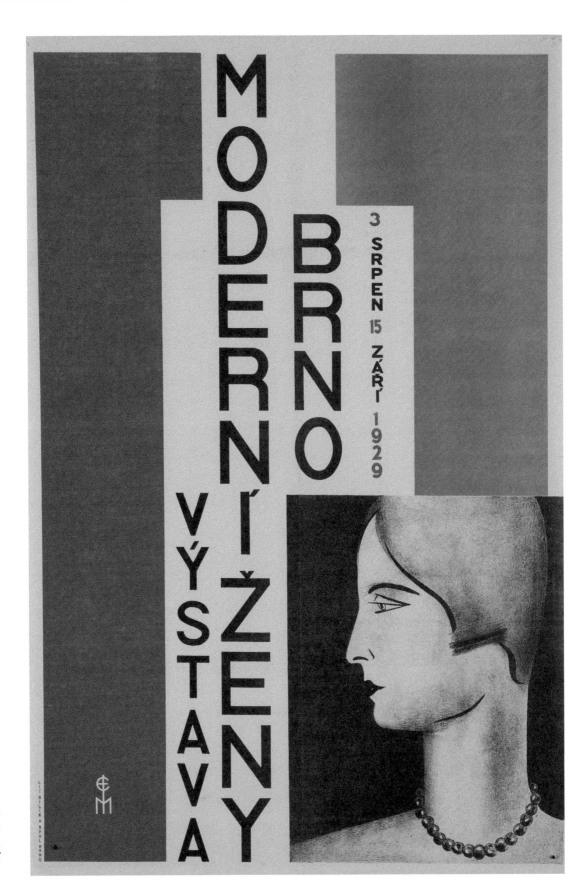

Fig. 7: Poster of the Exhibition of the Modern Woman (*Výstava moderní ženy*), Brno 1929.

The years 1918-1923 – just after women attained political rights and for the first time exercised them in national elections – were a period of optimism and belief in the radical improvement of women's situation and in equality, but they were shortly followed by a more sobering period. Although women attained full electoral rights and entered the public sphere, they were successfully kept from political power in legislative bodies, for example by putting women's names last in candidate lists. Thus, women were disappointed with the limits of their political influence. Many feminists, especially those of a younger generation, now more strongly emphasised equal rights and stressed full equality with men as the only way for women to gain agency and finally achieve full citizenship.[28]

While the constitutions of many newly founded states offered equality for both men and women, the debate was really only just starting on women's citizenship and their new role in society. Equality rights were not fully implemented and women were discriminated against in all fields. Even as women were very slowly becoming accepted as professional colleagues, their promotion to higher positions was limited. Similarly, women were admitted to universities and academies, including higher education in law and medicine, but they had little opportunity to work as academics after graduation.

It wasn't until the late 1920s that the new or modern woman and 'femininity' were promoted by publications such as the Czechoslovak magazine *Moderni divka* (The Modern Girl) or *Civilizovaná žena* (The Civilized Woman), exhibitions such as *Výstava moderní ženy* (The Exhibition of the Modern Woman, Brno 1929) or the Polish book and film *Prokurator Alicja Horn* (Prosecuting Attorney Alicja Horn, 1933). The story of Horn was a fiction, as there was no woman attorney in Poland until 1937, and the first woman judge was nominated only in 1929. Women trained themselves as professionals, but women's rights were put on the back burner.

Endnotes

1. Jo Vellacott, 'Feminist Consciousness and the First World War,' *History Workshop* 23 (1987), 81-101.
2. Anne Higonnet, 'Women, Images, and Representation,' in *A History of Women in the West, vol. V: Toward a Cultural Identity in the Twentieth Century, Françoise Thébaud* (Cambridge, MA: Belknap Press: An Imprint of Harvard University Press, 1996), 345-401.
3. Birgitta Bader-Zaar, 'Women in Austrian Politics, 1890-1934. Goals and Visions,' in *Austrian Women in the Nineteenth and Twentieth Century. Cross-disciplinary Perspectives*, eds. David F. Good, Margarete Grandner and Mary Jo Maynes (Providence: Berghahn Books, 1996), 59-90, here 62.
4. Judit Acsády, 'The Debate on Parliamentary Reforms in Women's Suffrage in Hungary, 1908-1918,' in *Suffrage, Gender and Citizenship. International Perspectives on Parliamentary Reforms*, eds. Irma Sulkunen, Seija-Leena Nevala-Nurmi and Pirjo Markkola (Newcastle: Cambridge Scholars, 2009), 242-258, here 255-256.
5. Ruth Rubio-Marin, 'The Achievement of Female Suffrage in Europe. On Women's Citizenship', *International Journal of Constitutional Law* 1, vol. 12 (2014), 4-34, here 21.
6. Gary B. Cohen, 'Nationalist Politics and the Dynamics of the State and Civil Society in the Habsburg Monarchy 1867-1914,' *Central European History* 2, vol. 40 (2007), 241-278, here 244.
7. Rubio-Marin, 'The Achievement of Female Suffrage in Europe. On Women's Citizenship,' 23; Maria Dulębianka, *Polityczne stanowisko kobiety* (Warszawa: Ster, 1908), 3.
8. Anna Żarnowska, 'Women's Political Participation in Inter-War Poland: Opportunities and Limitations,' *Women's History Review* 1, vol. 13 (2004), 57-67, here 63; Amalia Ribi Forclaz, 'A New Target for International Social Reform: The International Labour Organization and Working and Living Conditions in Agriculture in the Inter-War Years Source,' *Contemporary European History. Special Issue: Transnational Cooperation in Food, Agriculture, Environment and Health in Historical Perspective* 3, vol. 20 (2011), 307-329, here 307-329.
9. Rubio-Marin, 'The Achievement of Female Suffrage in Europe. On Women's Citizenship,' 9.
10. Robert M. Ponichtera, 'Feminists, Nationalists, Soldiers. Women in the Fight for Polish Independence,' *The International History Review* 1, vol. 19 (1997), 16-31, here 18; Dulębianka, 'Polityczne stanowisko kobiety,' 7.
11. Lindovská, Nadežda. 'Feminism is an Insult in Slovakia', *Theatre Journal* 3, vol. 47 (1995), 381-392, here 382.
12. Acsády, 'The Debate on Parliamentary Reforms in Women's Suffrage in Hungary, 1908-1918,' 242-258.
13. See: Anna Żarnowska, 'Prywatna sfera życia rodzinnego i zewnętrzny świat życia publicznego – bariery i przenikanie (przełom XIX i XX wieku),' in *Kobiety i świat polityki. Polska na tle porównawczym w XIX i w początkach XX wieku*, eds. Anna Żarnowska and Andrzej Szwarc (Warszawa: Instytut Historyczny UW, 1994), 5-28.
14. Birgitta Bader-Zaar, 'Controversy. War-Related Changes in Gender Relations. The Issue of Women's Citizenship,' in *1914-1918-online. International Encyclopedia of the First World*

War, eds. Ute Daniel, Peter Gatrell, Oliver Janz, Heather Jones, Jennifer Keene, Alan Kramer and Bill Nasson (Berlin: Freie Universität Berlin, 2014), <https://doi.org/10.15463/ie1418.10036> (accessed 19 January 2018); Vellacott, 'Feminist Consciousness and the First World War,' 86.

15. Andreas Fahrmeir, *Citizenship. The Rise and Fall of a Modern Concept* (New Haven: Yale University Press, 2007), 119.

16. Bader-Zaar, 'Controversy. War-Related Changes in Gender Relations. The Issue of Women's Citizenship'.

17. Margaret R. Higonnet and Patrice L.R. Higonnet, 'The Double Helix,' in *Behind the Lines. Gender and the Two World Wars*, eds. Margaret Randolph Higonnet, Jane Jenson, Sonya Michel and Margaret Collins Weitz (Yale University Press, 1987), 31-48.

18. Żarnowska, 'Women's Political Participation in Inter-War Poland: Opportunities and Limitations,' 62.

19. Andrzej Garlicki, 'Aleksandra Piłsudska', in *Polski Słownik Biograficzny* 26, vol. 2 (Wrocław: Zakład Narodowy im. Ossolińskich – Wydawnictwo Polskiej Akademii Nauk, 1981), 303-304.

20. Żarnowska, 'Women's Political Participation in Inter-War Poland: Opportunities and Limitations,' 58-59.

21. Acsády, 'The Debate on Parliamentary Reforms in Women's Suffrage in Hungary, 1908-1918,' 242.

22. Andrea Petö, 'Hungarian Women in Politics,' in *Transitions, Environments, Translations. Feminisms in International Politics*, eds. Joan W. Scott, Cora Kaplan and Debra Keates (New York, London: Routledge, 1997), 153-161, here 54.

23. Dana Musilova, 'Mothers of the Nation: Women's Vote in the Czech Republic,' in *The Struggle for Female Suffrage in Europe. Voting to Become Citizens*, eds. Blanca Rodríguez-Ruiz and Ruth Rubio-Marín (Leiden–Boston: Brill, 2012), 207-223, here 209-222.

24. Żarnowska 'Women's Political Participation in Inter-War Poland: Opportunities and Limitations,' 58-59.

25. Forclaz, 'A New Target for International Social Reform: The International Labour Organization and Working and Living Conditions in Agriculture in the Inter-War Years Source: Contemporary European History,' 307-329.

26. Rubio-Marin, 'The Achievement of Female Suffrage in Europe. On Women's Citizenship,' 15; Vellacott, 'Feminist Consciousness and the First World War,' 81-101.

27. 'Maternity Protection Convention', *Convention concerning the Employment of Women before and after Childbirth (Entry into force: 13 June 1921) Adoption: Washington, 1st ILC session (29 November 1919) - Status: Instrument with interim status (Technical Convention)*; <http://www.ilo.org/dyn/normlex/en/f?p=NORMLEXPUB:12100:0::NO::P12100_INSTRUMENT_ID:312148> (accessed 19 January 2018).

28. Bader-Zaar, 'Controversy. War-related Changes in Gender Relations. The Issue of Women's Citizenship'.

History of Memory

'The Table of Silence' by Constantin Brâncuși at Târgu Jiu, Romania.

The Creation of New Politics of Memory as a Consequence of a State's Rebirth:
A Case Study of Poland in the First Postwar Years

Bartosz Dziewanowski-Stefańczyk

On 10 November 1918, Józef Piłsudski (1867-1935) arrived in Poland from Magdeburg Fortress, where he had been imprisoned in July 1917 after refusing to swear an oath to the German emperor. His arrival is often illustrated with a photograph depicting him surrounded by a crowd. This is, however, inaccurate – only a few people greeted Piłsudski on that autumn morning, and none of them was a photographer. Adam Koc recalled the event as follows: 'On the night of 10 November I received a message that the commandant would arrive at Warsaw at 5 o'clock in the morning. [...] There were few people to welcome him, because the commandant's arrival was unexpected.'[1]

The photograph was taken in December 1916 and was first used in 1926 as part of creating the image of Piłsudski and a founding myth of the Second Polish Republic shortly after the May coup d'état of that year.[2] Although the discourse on the Second Republic of Poland's politics of memory became formalised after 1926, as Mieczysław Biskupski put it,[3] we can

Fig. 1: Józef Piłsudski on Warsaw railway station after his arrival, seemingly on 10th of November 1918 (released from German prison in Magdeburg), however the photo was shot two years earlier.

trace the beginnings of these politics conducted by institutions of the emerging state back to the period of the war itself.

In 1919, Polish historians were still intensely involved in the Paris Peace Conference, yet it seemed that their future role would not be as vital for the existence of the nation as it was during the partitions. The distinguished historian of early modernity Władysław Smoleński (1851-1926) therefore stated the following during his inaugural lecture at the University of Warsaw that year:

[T]he conditions of independent existence destroy the main reason why history was considered one of the means of rescue [...] future scholars of the Polish past, free from the temptation to provide the nation with rescue instructions, will be protected from one of the most important difficulties hindering our predecessors in finding the truth. Their search will be aided by the best skills guide, one alien to those of the past – selflessness.[4]

I believe, however, that although the role of history has changed since the 19th century, it was still important for politics in 1919.

The examples of official politics of memory, i.e. those conducted by the state, chosen for this paper will be based on Edgar Wolfrum's classical understanding of the politics of memory:

The politics of memory is a field of action and politics in which different actors load their specific interests onto history and attempt to put it to political use. It is targeted at the public and seeks to create legitimising, mobilising, politicising, scandalising, defaming and other effects within the political struggle.[5]

The above-mentioned state institutions are the actors of these politics and use the politics of memory to achieve different political goals. According to Lech Nijakowski, therefore, '[t]he politics of remembrance consists of all of the intentional actions of politicians and officials with formal legitimacy aimed at the consolidation, removal, or redefinition of specific contents of social memory'.[6] As Peter Steinbach has put it, the politics of memory are not so much about the past as they are about power over the public's mentality and influencing the future.[7] This paper's aim is thus to present how history served, or was used by, the emerging state and its politics during the Great War and in the first years of the Second Republic of Poland. It will investigate the old and new realms of memory that were celebrated then, how the new official memory influenced the public sphere and how the new state presented its image abroad.

History and Diplomacy During the Great War

The most important goal of the emerging state's politics of memory was to secure Poland's border lines and legitimise its rights – not so much to new areas as, above all, to its status as an independent state. Historians working for various organisations, including some abroad, were therefore to prove that Poland should gain independence and that it was strictly connected with Western Europe. The first works in this field began within the Supreme National Committee, established on 16 August 1914 in Cracow. More than 30 historians cooperated with the Committee, which published over 25 books and many articles, including ones published in foreign journals. Their aim was to create a national consciousness in society and convince foreign opinion not only that Poles were able to create an independent state, but that this was in Europe's own interest.

One of the most important Polish scholars who published abroad and directed his texts in support of Polish independence mainly to the West European elites was Szymon Askenazy (1866-1935). He initially blamed England and France for the partitions, but in 1917, when the international situation changed and Poland began to seek good relations with the Entente states, Askenazy emphasised the strong ties between Poland and the United Kingdom. In London, August Zaleski (1883-1972), sent there by Józef Piłsudski, issued among other texts his brochure *Landmarks of Polish History*. He compared the Polish political system to the English one and argued that these were the only two European countries to have created democratic institutions in the early modern period, and that the reconstruction of Poland was an indispensable element of peace on the continent. Wilhelm Feldman (1868-1919), living in Berlin, wrote in support of the reconstruction of the Polish state. And the

Fig. 2: Congress of the Supreme National Committee in Cracow, Collegium Maius, 1916.

cultural historian and Slavist Aleksander Brückner (1856-1939) presented Polish statehood in opposition to the myth of the so-called *'polnische Wirtschaft'* – an alleged organisational and governmental ineptitude. In his writings, he strongly opposed Russia and supported the relationship of the Lithuanian, Belarusian, and Ukrainian lands with Poland.[8]

In addition, the Polish National Committee in Paris had a large group of historians who wrote texts justifying the Polish demands. One of the crucial issues in the talks with the British prime minister was that of granting Gdańsk to Poland. Władysław Konopczyński (1880-1952) and Wincenty Lutosławski (1863-1954) argued that this city must remain in Poland, using abundant historical arguments.[9] Maps also served as an important tool for Poland's unofficial diplomacy. The most famous was the atlas published in 1916 by the Polish professor of geography Eugeniusz Romer (1871-1954).[10]

Of course, the Polish delegation was not the only one to use historical arguments in order to create new borders. We can only speculate how this kind of diplomacy actually influenced the decisions made during the conference. The arguments for Poles' rights to their own sovereign state were not unreasonable, as the Paris Conference revealed. At that time, the British Prime Minister David Lloyd George (1863-1945), who held a negative view of Poland, argued against the Polish territorial demands, claiming that the Polish nation 'did not manage to demonstrate the ability to maintain constant independence throughout the whole history'.[11]

Old and New Celebrations

New traditions and myths crucial for the emerging country started to be created at the end of the war. At first, however, the focus lay on celebrating old anniversaries, such as the Constitution of 3 May 1791 and the November (1831) and January Insurrections (1863). Very early on – in April 1919 – the Polish Sejm decided that the Constitution of 3 May should be celebrated as a national holiday.[12] These celebrations also served current political needs. In 1921, they were supposed to underline the political stability by comparing the 1791 constitution with the one passed on 21 March that year. Moreover, by renaming – on 3 May 1921 – Warsaw's Warecki Square (plac Warecki) to 'Napoleon Square' (plac Napoleona) on the centenary of the French emperor's death, Polish authorities wanted to highlight the Polish-French alliance. It was part of a campaign aimed at strengthening Polish–French relations, which was important due to the Polish struggles to join Silesia to Poland.[13]

At last, historians could also study those topics that had been banned during the partitions. One such issue was the January Uprising.[14] The new legal regulations for the status of veterans confirmed the vital importance of the uprising to the new authorities'

politics. As early as January 1919, Józef Piłsudski commanded the January insurgents to join the Polish Army, for financial reasons, and on 2 August 1919, a fixed salary for the November 1831 and January 1863 insurgents was passed. Although almost none of the November insurgents was alive at that point, it was meant to show the continuity of the Polish fights for independence. Military units were often given the names of January insurgents.[15]

It is also worth mentioning that on 1 August 1919, the Parliament restored the highest Polish military distinction, the Virtuti Militari Cross, and the first decoration with a silver cross took place during the anniversary of the January Uprising – on 22 January 1920. The theme of the uprising was so important that it became the canvas for one of the first Polish feature films – *The Year 1863*, directed by Edward Puchalski (1874-1942) in 1922.[16] The key figures in the celebration of the uprising were veterans, the so-called living monuments of heroism.[17] The uprising was also combined with celebrations of other an-

Fig. 3: Napoleon Square in Warsaw, 1920s.

Celebrating Polish Independence

The first national holiday established by law in 1919 commemorated the opening of the Polish Parliament on 10 February. Later that year, much of Poland celebrated 5 November – which was related to the proclamation by Germany and Austria-Hungary of the Kingdom of Poland in 1916. Independence Day was officially celebrated on 9 November 1919. The Right (Narodowa Demokracja) stressed, among other things, the signing of the Versailles Treaty in June 1919, since their leader, Roman Dmowski (1864-1939), was also the leader of the Polish delegation to the Paris Peace Conference. The Right emphasised their role in asserting Polish interests against the Germans in the uprisings in Silesia and in Greater Poland, which Piłsudski could not claim as his successes; later, they tried to diminish Piłsudski's role in defeating the Soviet Army in the Battle of Warsaw in 1920 by creating a legend of the so-called 'Miracle at the Vistula River'.[20]

Moreover, according to Marcin Jarząbek, Dmowski perceived Poland's participation in the war as more

Fig. 4: Marshal Józef Piłsudski rewarding French Marshal Ferdinand Foch with the Virtuti Militari Cross, 1921.

niversaries associated with the army – e.g., the insurgents were often invited to the legion ceremonies.

From the very beginning, recent history had been celebrated in Poland. In 1919, the country celebrated the march of the First Brigade on 6 August as the Day of the Army. In 1923, however, this holiday was moved to 15 August, to commemorate the 1920 Battle of Warsaw.[18]

The most important discussion, which started on the eve of Poland's re-establishment, was the question of when Polish independence began and who deserved credit as its main architect. New symbols and realms of memory were created and introduced in a process of discussions and internal political fights. Over time, anniversaries related to recent history began to emerge, and we can thus observe a growing discussion between politicians and historians on the starting date of Poland's independence, the main factors leading to it and the persons who played the most important role.[19]

Fig. 5: Insurgents of the January 1863 uprising laying wreath on 3 May 1926 at the newly erected Tomb of the Unknown Soldier in Warsaw.

of a great tragedy than a heroic fight. This might be the reason for the Polish Right's failure to implement clear politics of memory before the 1926 coup.[21] The Left, on the other hand, associated the symbolic day of Polish independence with the creation of the socialist government, led by Ignacy Daszyński (1866-1936), in Lublin on 7 November 1918. In addition, persons most closely connected with the establishment of Poland's new statehood – Ignacy Paderewski (1860-1941) and Wincenty Witos (1874-1945) – did not acknowledge the importance of the Armistice date, i.e., 11 November 1918.[22]

Although the group created around Józef Piłsudski could not agree on a date of independence, Piłsudski's role was well acknowledged. It should be stressed that the creation of the Piłsudski myth began very early on – during the war itself – and was strictly connected with the Polish legions. A substantial percentage (around 40%) of the legionaries belonged to the intelligentsia, and so they themselves produced songs, poems and other texts, in which they praised Józef Piłsudski – the commander of the first brigade. The brigade's distinctiveness was underlined by his behaviour and looks, aimed at creating the Polish Army. Already in 1915, Juliusz Kaden-Bandrowski (1885-1944), a member of the First Brigade, published a book entitled *Piłsudczycy* – Piłsudskites. Polish legions were unique but not united, as there were numerous tensions between their officers regarding the role of the legions role in gaining Polish independence or in creating a trialistic Austro-Hungarian-Polish monarchy. This conflicting memory sparked various tensions in the reborn Polish state.

Despite his critics, by the end of the war the myth of Piłsudski was already established and connected with the legend of the Polish legions. Regardless of their indisputable merits, even more important was what the legions symbolised - a founding myth for

Fig. 6: Polish 2 Złoty banknote from 1919 with the image of Tadeusz Kościuszko (1746-1817).

Fig. 7: Józef Piłsudski during a parade celebrating the independence day in front of the Tomb of Unknown Soldier in Warsaw, 11 November 1926.

the young state. The legendary status of both the legions and Piłsudski were also linked with the memory of the Kościuszko and the January 1863 uprisings. It is worth underlining that Piłsudski himself also influenced the memory of the legions and thus also his own legend by his writings on recent history.[23] This was, however, a selective memory, as the official memory included mainly Poland's struggle for independence and not its alliance with the Central Powers.[24]

One of the moments when the official date celebrating independence could be recognised was the year 1920. On 22 October, the Bureau of Internal Propaganda of the Presidium of the Council of Ministers in Warsaw selected 11 November as a temporary date for celebrating Poland's emancipation or rebirth.[25] However, the main festivities were organised for 14 November (on a Sunday) and were connected with awarding Józef Piłsudski the rank of Marshal of Poland.[26]

The rightist governments tried to diminish Piłsudski's role,[27] so support among the veterans helped provide the strong political base he needed. The first celebrations of the First Cadre Company's 1914 march from Cracow were organised for 5 August 1922 in the form of the Congress of Legionaries combined with a historical reenactment of their march.[28] This Congress was one of the first occasions institutionalising a cult around Piłsudski.[29] The Right gained more votes in the November elections and Piłsudski soon afterwards withdrew from active political engagement. From that point, the importance of the independence day celebrations dwindled. Still, the date of Independence Day was not yet settled. In a 1924 lecture, Piłsudski himself stated that the most important dates were either the 22 November (when he was appointed Provisional Chief of State) or 28 November 1918 (when he announced the date of the parliamentary elections).[30] Even though he had withdrawn from politics in 1923, his legend was further cultivated in order to integrate his proponents. This was one of the aims of Piłsudski's book devoted to the Battle of Warsaw, in which he not only presented himself as a successful leader, but also criticised his opponents, who at that time were ruling Poland.[31] His legend was strengthened through the works of the Institute for the Study of Contemporary National History in Poland (Instytut Badań Najnowszej Historii Polski), established in 1923 and renamed the Piłsudski Institute (Instytut Józefa Piłsudskiego Poświęcony Badaniu Najnowszej Historii Polski) in the late 1930s.[32] Piłsudski's cult flourished after the 1926 coup and served as means of legitimising the new regime, emphasising the links between the people and the new Piłsudski government, even though it was criticised by the opposition. The Piłsudski cult served especially as an important means of integrating Silesia with Poland, as the memory of the Silesian uprisings was neatly mixed with the memory of Piłsudski.[33]

In 1926, i.e. after the May coup, Prime Minister Józef Piłsudski issued a circular in which he stated that 11 November should be celebrated as Independence Day. Although this circular dealt only with the year 1926, it in effect introduced this day as the official date of celebrations. From that point on, more vivid discussions between different political options concerning this date and the role of particular politicians in achieving independence thus began to politicise the memory. Irrespective of the official celebrations, left- and right-wing parties conducted their own celebrations during the 10th anniversary of independence in 1928, underlining the different visions of the recent Polish past.[34] Eventually, however, a single official memory emerged from this polyphony of narratives, and it was Piłsudski's version that prevailed, with 11 November crowned as Independence Day.[35]

Memory Politics and the State

In the first years after 1918, the issue of the nation dominated the school programmes. Moreover, in the first decade of Polish independence, the history textbooks presented a number of personalities whose actions enabled Poland to gain independence. Later, however, the role of Piłsudski was highlighted and after 1926, there is clearly a discourse of integrating the society and country around statehood.[36] Due to the inherited differences of the Polish lands after the partitions, the idea of the state was the most general common denominator.

The Ministry of Art and Culture was speaking of the key importance of culture for state cohesion and security as early as January 1920:

> The Polish state has grown, it must merge the Poles, it took the Belarusian, Ruthenian provinces, it is about to take Masuria, Silesia, and Spisz. Keeping these provinces with bayonets and butts is impossible in the 20th century. Our country cannot be united by force: we must seek a different path, and this is our culture. [...]. A state institution of propaganda for Polish culture should therefore be created.[37]

The symbolic sphere was directly related to the politics of memory. It was previously one of the important fields of conflict over identity between the Polish population and the partitioning authorities. Therefore, the issues of caring for monuments, statues, (re)naming streets etc. were of crucial importance. Probably for this reason, one of the first actions of the new Polish authorities – even before the end of the war – was to pass a resolution on art conservation and restoration care, issued by the Regency Council in October 1918.[38] The Ministry of Culture and Art emphasised:

> In creating this statehood, we must care for its autonomous independence, political, military, economic, as well as its autonomy and cultural separateness. [...] Without chauvinism, but with a proper understanding that it is the only weapon against Germanisation or Russification, one should strive with all the consciousness [...], to have [among others] our architecture, separate art.[39]

This notion was also shared by those artists who, like Władysław Skoczylas (1883-1934), promoted a so-called 'Polish national style' in arts.[40] Therefore, efforts were made to re-Polonise space. In December 1920, the Ministry of the former Prussian District issued a ban on building in Dutch, Swiss, or Prussian styles. Newly built villas were to take inspiration from the Polish court style or the Kashubian style.[41]

Fig. 8: Józef Piłsudski protects the Poles from the 'red danger' in the graphic by Władysław Skoczylas, around 1920.

Fig. 9: Staszic Palace in Warsaw in the Byzantine style.

From 1924, a major reconstruction of the Staszic palace in Warsaw began, which the Russian authorities had rebuilt in the Byzantine style in the late 19th century.[42] At the same time, the Orthodox Church of Saint Alexander Nevsky in Warsaw's Saxonian Square (plac Saski) was pulled down.

Poland's new culture of memory was also created in the public sphere by referring to the Great War, subsequent conflicts, and the nation's newly won independence. Łódź's New Market Square (Nowy Rynek) was renamed 'Freedom Square' (Plac Wolności) early as 1919.[43] The symbolic sphere was changed by the establishment of war cemeteries and the identification of all the separate graves of those killed during the war. A little later, the authorities began commemorating the memory of the so-called Lvov Eagles, the young defenders of Lvov in the fights against the West-Ukrainian People's Republic. As a symbol of the new memory politics, they also awarded the city the

Virtuti Militari Cross.[44] Lvov is moreover connected with the Warsaw Tomb of the Unknown Soldier built in 1925, in which the remains of one of the defenders of Lvov were buried.[45] This tomb is an example of transferring foreign means of commemoration to Poland. At the same time, however, it was nationalised by referring to names of battles fought in the 'local' border conflicts.[46] It later became one of the most important places where Poland celebrated gaining her independence.

Foreign Memory Politics

Polish historians' activities during the Paris Peace Conference were supported by exhibitions. From January to March 1919, an exhibition was organised in Paris devoted to the Polish-French relationship, pointing to its centuries-long history.[47] The use of history also supported Polish diplomacy after the

Fig. 10: Staszic Palace after the restauration in 1924.

Peace Conference. The exhibition organised by the Office of Foreign Propaganda of the Presidium of the Council of Ministers in Paris from April to June 1921 was strictly connected with Polish foreign policy. It opened shortly after the February conclusion of the political and military agreement between Poland and France and after Poland and Russia signed the Riga Peace treaty in March 1921, but before the Allied Powers' final decision on the affiliation of Silesia. The exhibition showed, among other things, Jan Matejko's (1838-1893) work *Batory at Pskov*, significant in the context of defeating Soviet Russia, as well as a bust of Józef Piłsudski. The exhibition was praised in Paris, for example by this newspaper journalist who had recognised the true meaning of the project: '[A]n exhibition of Polish artists currently open in Paris would have no reason if it were not a better presentation of our past and current allies, our Polish allies [...]. The exhibition seems to be a very successful diplomatic event.'[48]

Reborn Poland was able to present its image to the world during the World's Fair in Paris in 1925 – the first such exhibition after the war. In order to show its strength, its centuries-old traditions, and its affiliation with Western European culture, and in an attempt to acquire France as an ally, Poland exhibited its folklore and Western classical art. However, the exhibition did not specifically refer to the traditions of the country's nobility, as Western Europe often perceived this as one of the reasons for Poland's downfall and identified it with bad organisation.[49]

Summary

The beginnings of the Second Republic of Poland's politics of memory date back to the actions undertaken by various institutions striving for Polish sovereignty during the First World War. Poland was forced to prove its right to independence both during the war and after 1918, often using historical argumentation. Shortly after gaining independence, discussions on its beginnings began. Thus history not only united the nation, but also divided the different political groups who were supposed to legitimise it. The topics neglected so far – such as the cult of the January insurgents – were also incorporated in the new politics of memory. It seems that although historians did not have to provide the means of rescue, contrary to the above-quoted professor Władysław Smoleński, history after 1918 was still involved in Polish politics.

Endnotes

1. *Rok 1918 we wspomnieniach mężów stanu, polityków i wojskowych*, ed. Jan Borkowski (Warszawa: PIW, 1987), 209.

2. Marcin Krzanicki, *Fotografia i propaganda. Polski fotoreportaż prasowy w dwudziestoleciu międzywojennym* (Kraków: Universitas, 2013), 50-51, 160.

3. Mieczysław B. Biskupski, *Independence Day. Myth, Symbol, and the Creation of Modern Poland* (Oxford: Oxford University Press, 2012), 46.

4. Quote from Andrzej F. Grabski, *Zarys historii historiografii polskiej* (Poznań: Wydawnictwo Poznańskie, 2000), 166-167.

5. Edgar Wolfrum, *Geschichtspolitik in der Bundesrepublik Deutschland. Der Weg zur bundesrepublikanischen Erinnerung 1948-1990* (Darmstadt: Wissenschaftliche Buchgesellschaft, 1999), 25.

6. Lech M. Nijakowski, *Polska polityka pamięci. Esej socjologiczny* (Warszawa: Wydawnictwo Akademickie i Profesjonalne, 2008), 44-45.

7. Joanna Andrychowicz-Skrzeba, *Polityka historyczna w Polsce i Niemczech po roku 1989 w wystąpieniach publicznych oraz publikacjach polityków polskich i niemieckich* (Gdańsk: Wydawnictwo Naukowe Katedra, 2014), 27-28.

8. Jerzy Maternicki, *Idee i postawy. Historia i historycy polscy 1914-1918. Studium historiograficzne* (Warszawa: PWN, 1975), 116, 126, 151-179; Janusz Sibora, *Dyplomacja polska w I wojnie światowej* (Warszawa: PISM, 2013), Jolanta Kolbuszewska, 'Historia w służbie propagandy? Współpraca polskich historyków z Naczelnym Komitetem Narodowym w latach 1914-1917,' in *Pamięć i polityka historyczna. Doświadczenia Polski i jej sąsiadów*, eds. Sławomir Nowinowski, Jan Pomorski and Rafał Stobiecki (Łódź: Wydawnictwo Naukowe Ibidem, Instytut Pamięci Narodowej - Komisja Ścigania Zbrodni przeciwko Narodowi Polskiemu, 2008), 274-275.

9. Władysław Konopczyński, *Dziennik 1918-1921*, part 1, eds. Piotr Biliński, Paweł Plichta (Warszawa: Muzeum Historii Polski; Kraków: Ośrodek Myśli Politycznej, 2016), a. o. 319, 349; Wincenty Lutosławski, *Gdańsk and East Prussia* (Paris: Imprimerie Levé, 1919).

10. Maciej Górny, *Kreślarze ojczyzn. Geografowie i granice międzywojennej Europy* (Warszawa: Instytut Historii PAN, 2017), 67-70, 171.

11. *Sprawy polskie na konferencji pokojowej w Paryżu w 1919 r.: dokumenty i materiały*, vol I, (Warszawa: PWN, 1965), 133.

12. Kazimierz Badziak, 'Od święta narodowego do państwowego. Tradycja Konstytucji 3 maja w II Rzeczypospolitej,' in *Konstytucja 3 maja w tradycji i kulturze polskiej*, ed. Alina Barszczewska-Krupa (Łódź: Wydaw. Łódzkie, 1991), 195, 198.

13. Marian M. Drozdowski, 'Obchody święta 3 maja w Warszawie – stolicy II Rzeczypospolitej,' in: Konstytucja 3 maja w tradycji..., 474; A. Zahorski, *Z dziejów legendy napoleońskiej w Polsce* (Warszawa: PZWS, 1971), 145; *11.11.1918. Niepodległość i pamięć w Europie Środkowej*, eds. Włodzimierz Borodziej, Maciej Górny and Piotr Tadeusz Kwiatkowski (Kraków: MCK, 2018), 93f.

14. *Ministerstwo kultury i sztuki w dokumentach 1918-1998*, ed. Andrzej Siciński, Adam G. Dąbrowski, Jerzy Gmurek (Warszawa: IK, 1998), 149f.

15. Anna E. Markert, *Gloria Victis. Tradycje Powstania Styczniowego w Drugiej Rzeczypospolitej* (Pruszków: Ajaks, 2004), 18, 34-40, 71-84; Marcin Jarząbek, *Legioniści i inni. Pamięć zbiorowa weteranów I wojny światowej w Polsce i Czechosłowacji okresu międzywojennego* (Kraków: Universitas, 2017), 86; Julia Eichenberg, *Kämpfen für Frieden und Fürsorge. Polnische Veteranen des Ersten Weltkriegs und ihre internationalen Kontakte, 1918-1939* (München: Oldenbourg Verlag, 2011), 128f.

16. Adam Redzik, 'Powstanie styczniowe i X muza w okresie II Rzeczypospolitej', in: *Powstanie styczniowe w pamięci zbiorowej*, eds. Agnieszka Kawalec, Jerzy Kuzicki (Rzeszów: Wydawnictwo Uniwersytetu Rzeszowskiego, 2017), 442.

17. Jolanta Załęczny, *Tradycje patriotyczne elementem kształtowania zbiorowej świadomości historycznej w II Rzeczypospolitej* (Warszawa: Muzeum Niepodległości, 2017), 151-166.

18. Załęczny, *Tradycje...*, 205.

19. Andrzej Garlicki, 'Spory o niepodległość,' in *Rok 1918. Tradycje i oczekiwania*, ed. Andrzej Garlicki (Warszawa: 'Czytelnik', 1978), 7-8; Przemysław Waingertner, 'Argumentacja historyczna w wielkich sporach politycznych II Rzeczypospolitej,' in *Pamięć i polityka historyczna....* See a list of the various dates suggested in Piotr T. Kwiatkowski, *Odzyskanie niepodległości w polskiej pamięci zbiorowej* (Warszawa: NCK, 2018), 241.

20. Adam Dobroński, 'Obchody Święta Niepodległości w II Rzeczypospolitej,' in *Święto Niepodległości – tradycja a współczesność*, ed. Andrzej Stawarz (Warszawa: MN: Fundacja 'Polonia Restituta', 2003), 12.

21. Biskupski, *Independence Day*, 36, 41; Jarząbek, *Legioniści i inni*, 146.

22. Biskupski, *Independence Day*, 22; Heidi Hein-Kircher, *Kult Piłsudskiego i jego znaczenie dla państwa polskiego 1926-1939* (Warszawa: Wydawictwo Neriton, 2008), 290-291.

23. Elżbieta Kaszuba, *System propagandy państwowej obozu rządzącego w Polsce w latach 1926-1939* (Toruń: Adam Marszałek, 2004), 128-129; Biskupski, *Independence Day*, 10-15, 20; Jarząbek, *Legioniści i inni...*, 71-74; Andrzej Chwalba, *Legiony polskie 1914-1918* (Kraków: Wydawnictwo Literackie, 2018), 252-260, 354; Hein-Kircher, *Kult*, 267.

24. Eichenberg, *Kämpfen für Frieden*, 55.

25. Biskupski, *Independence Day*, 38.

26. Załęczny, *Tradycje*, 185.
27. Bartosz Korzeniewski, '11 listopada 1918,' in *Polskie miejsca pamięci. Dzieje toposu wolności*, eds. Stefan Bednarek, Bartosz Korzeniewski (Warszawa: NCK, 2014), 345.
28. Andrzej Garlicki, *Józef Piłsudski 1867-1935* (Kraków: Znak, 2012), 363-368.
29. Hein-Kircher, *Kult*, 268.
30. Biskupski, *Independence Day*, 44.
31. Garlicki, *Józef Piłsudski*, 431.
32. Waingertner, *Argumentacja historyczna*, 296; Hein-Kircher, *Kult*, 95.
33. Hein-Kircher, *Kult*, 274-279, 289-295.
34. Barbara Wachowska, 'Od 11 listopada do 11 listopada, czyli spory o symboliczne święto niepodległości Polski,' *Acta Universitatis Lodziensis, Folia Historica* 54 (1995), 15-17; Maria Nartonowicz-Kot, 'Spór o tradycje. Łódzkie obchody święta niepodległości w pierwszym dziesięcioleciu Polski odrodzonej,' *Rocznik Łódzki*, 62 (2014), 67-68; Kwiatkowski, *Odzyskanie niepodległości*, 240-246.
35. Jarząbek, *Legioniści i inni*, 163-165.
36. Mariusz Menz, 'Szkolna edukacja historyczna w Polsce w latach 1918-1939. Koncepcje – dyskusje – realizacje,' in *Współczesna edukacja historyczna. Doświadczenia, oczekiwania*, ed. Justyna Budzińska, Justyna Strykowska (Poznań: IH UAM, 2015), 103-108; Kwiatkowski, *Odzyskanie niepodległości*, 253.
37. *Ministerstwo kultury i sztuki w dokumentach 1918-1998*, 48.
38. *Dekret Rady Regencyjnej z 1918 r. o opiece nad zabytkami sztuki i kultury z komentarzem czyli eseje o prawie ochrony dziedzictwa kultury*, eds. Kamil Zeidler, Magdalena Marcinkowska (Gdańsk: Wydawnictwo UG, 2017).
39. *Ministerstwo kultury i sztuki w dokumentach 1918-1998*, 49.
40. Agnieszka Chmielewska, 'Styl narodowy w Drugiej Rzeczypospolitej: artyści a wizerunek odrodzonego państwa' in: *Naród, styl, modernizm*, ed. Jacek Purchla, Wolf Tegethoff, coop. Christian Fuhrmeister, Łukasz Galusek (Kraków: Międzynarodowe Centrum Kultury; Monachium: Zentralinstitut für Kunstgeschichte, 2006), 190f.
41. Małgorzata Omilanowska, 'Polen an der Ostsee. Die Konstruktion einer visuellen Staatsidentität,' in *Aufbruch und Krise. Das östliche Europa und die Deutschen nach dem Ersten Weltkrieg*, eds. Beate Störtkuhl, Jens Stüben, Tobias Weger (München: Oldenbourg, 2010), 52-53.
42. Piotr Paszkiewicz, *Pod berłem Romanowów. Sztuka rosyjska w Warszawie 1815-1915* (Warszawa: IS PAN, 1991); Tadeusz Jaroszewski, *Księga pałaców Warszawy* (Warszawa: Interpress, 1985).
43. Nartonowicz-Kot, *Spór o tradycje*, 72.
44. Dobroński, *Obchody Święta*, 8.
45. Iwona Luba, *Duch romantyzmu i modernizacja. Sztuka oficjalna Drugiej Rzeczypospolitej* (Warszawa: Wydawictwo Neriton, 2012), 129-130.
46. Eichenberg, *Kämpfen für Frieden*, 60.
47. *Świadectwa obecności. Polskie życie artystyczne we Francji w latach 1900-1939. Diariusz wydarzeń z wyborem tekstów*, part 1, Lata 1900-1921, ed. Anna Wierzbicka (Warszawa: Wydawnictwo Neriton, 2012), 389-391.
48. *Świadectwa obecności*, 465.
49. Luba, *Duch romantyzmu*, 253-260; Agnieszka Chmielewska, 'Czym jesteśmy, czym być możemy i chcemy w rodzinie narodów?' in *Wystawa paryska 1925. Materiały z sesji naukowej Instytutu Sztuki PAN. Warszawa, 16-17 listopada 2005 roku*, ed. Joanna M. Sosnowska (Warszawa: IS PAN, 2007), 65; Bartosz Dziewanowski-Stefańczyk, 'World fairs as tools of the Polish diplomacy in the interwar period,' in *World Fairs and International Exhibitions: National Self-Profiling in an International Context, 1851-1940*, eds. Joep Leerssen and Eric Storm, (forthcoming).

The Non-Overshadowed Experiences of the Great War and Their Manifestations in Lithuania, 1914-1926

Vasilijus Safronovas

Although the First World War was caused by tensions in Eastern Europe, quite a few historians, as if reaffirming the words of Winston Churchill (1874-1965), have until recently portrayed Europe's Eastern Front as an 'unknown war'.[1] The remembrance of that war in the region remains particularly under-examined and little investigated. For a long time, researchers knew next to nothing about how the Great War was remembered in the countries of East-Central Europe in particular, Lithuania included, and many historians have argued that this remembrance simply did not exist. In a presentation given as early as 1998, Darius Staliūnas stated that in inter-war Lithuania 'the focus was on those who perished in the fights for Independence, but not in the First World War'.[2] Ten years later, Vejas Gabriel Liulevicius claimed essentially the same thing: Lithuanians, he wrote, perceived the period of the Great War as a 'passive experience', which 'was followed by the active engagement of the Wars of Liberation from 1918-1920'.[3] Rasa Antanavičiūtė argued in a similar vein that Lithuanian 'memories of the Great War were totally eclipsed by memories of the Wars of Independence' and that Lithuania 'represents a radical example of the almost complete oblivion of the Great War in public memory and commemoration'.[4] Meanwhile, Tomas Balkelis pointed out several years ago that the oblivion surrounding the Great War was due not to the Wars of Independence, but to the conflict between Lithuania and Poland over Vilnius in the 1920s and 1930s, which became a major impediment to, or a competitor of, the remembrance of the Great War.[5] There is little question that the conscious emphasis placed on the Wars of Independence (1919-1920) in Lithuania overshadowed the importance of the Great War, at least for a part of Lithuanian society. This assessment, however, is based on the entire 22-year

period of Lithuanian independence. I argue in the present paper that in the first decade, and especially before the coup of 1926, there was more room for manifestations of Great War experiences that were completely unrelated to the Wars of Independence.

The Role of the 1926 Coup

The 17 December 1926 military coup in Kaunas, the 'temporary capital' of Lithuania, replaced the democratically formed Socialist cabinet with a rightist

Fig. 1: Antanas Smetona, President of Lithuania 1919-1920 and 1926-1940.

Fig. 2: A vignette representing the Lithuanian detached battalion in Vitebsk 1917-1918, one of the Lithuanian national units created in the Russian army.

government led by Augustinas Voldemaras (1883-1942). Antanas Smetona (1874-1944), who in the years of the Great War had led a faction representing the political interests of the Lithuanians in the *Ober Ost* area and, in 1919, became the first President of the Republic of Lithuania, 'returned' to the presidency.

How did the 1926 coup influence Lithuanians' dominant attitudes towards the Great War? It brought about several changes. First, it is true that the wars after the Great War, that is the armed defence organised by the Lithuanian government for the territory it claimed from the Red Army, Poland and the Pavel Bermondt-Avalov (1877-1974) troops,

began to be called 'the Wars of Independence' already in the mid-1920s, several years before the coup. Their importance, however, grew considerably after the coup as the Nationalists (Tautininkai), especially under Augustinas Voldemaras's cabinet (1926-1929), were increasingly concerned with fostering good relations with the army that had brought them to power. To be specific, the role of principal coup organisers and implementers was played by the so-called Slaptoji karininkų sąjunga [Secret Union of Officers], mainly those of the younger generation who counted their contributions to the fights for Lithuania from 1918. Their active role in organising the coup was virtually predetermined through the policies pursued in Lithuania by the left-wing government established in June 1926. The political decisions of the Socialists, which caused the army a lot of anxiety, pushed the participants of the Wars of Independence to rally rapidly and organise a lobbying association, the Lietuvos kariuomenės savanorių sąjunga [Association of Lithuanian Army Volunteers], in 1926-1927.[7] Having come to power unconstitutionally, the Nationalists tried to retain the favour of both the army and the largest veterans' association. The ruling elites therefore paid a great deal of attention to the commemoration of the Wars of Independence and of those who had perished in them. Particularly favourable occasions to demonstrate this concern were the tenth anniversaries of independence and the founding of the Lithuanian Armed Forces, both commemorated in 1928 by honouring the soldiers who perished in the Wars of Independence throughout the country.

Second, between 1920 and 1926/27, under the conditions of parliamentary democracy, there was no consensus over who deserved the most credit for establishing the country's freedom. Several conceptions of how different individuals and groups contributed to national independence existed simultaneously. One of them highlighted the role of fighters for Lithuanian freedom in the Wars of Independence. Another gave the credit to the protagonists of the Lithuanian national movement. A third version emphasised the attempts of various Lithuanian political actors to articulate political ideas and to act on behalf of all Lithuanians during the years of the Great War. This mix of views changed only after the coup, when the newly established Lietuvos kariuomenės savanorių sąjunga and the government led by Augustinas Voldemaras began to demonstrate their support for one another. Former volunteers of the Wars of Independence received pensions and benefits, including priority in the assignment of parcels during the Lithuanian land reform. When the state began distributing volunteer medals in 1928, the volunteers of the Wars of Independence were lauded as having proven exceptional merit to their homeland.

At the same time, many veterans of the Great War had not been very supportive of the idea of an independent Lithuania during the Wars of Independence.

Officers and veterans who had already been working in the civil service in late 1918 were the most common examples. In January 1919, the Lithuanian government mobilised many of them to become the first commanders and trainers of volunteers who joined the army in the early years of the republic. Moreover, at least 70 to 80% of Lithuanian parliamentarians spent the years of the Great War either as civil displaced persons in the depths of Russia, or as soldiers of the Russian Army on the front lines and in the garrisons. Their experiences of the Great War differed from those of the majority of Lithuanians, who spent the war under German occupation. These soldiers and displaced people returned to Lithuania after the war, but their repatriation continued intensively until 1921 and, in some cases, even until the late 1920s. Most of them returned home during or after, not before, the Wars of Independence. As a consequence, they were not able to join the struggles for independence as volunteers, were instead in some cases mobilised into the ranks of the Lithuanian Army, and therefore enjoyed no public status or the resulting social guarantees and privileges. This meant that a great number of publicly active figures, even among the high-ranking officers in the Lithuanian Army, had no reason to emphasise their experiences in the Wars of Independence, while their Great War experiences were not overshadowed by similar concerns.

All this explains why, under conditions of democratic pluralism preceding the 1926 coup, before the Wars of Independence became more important, Lithuanians should have had more opportunities to manifest their different experiences in the Great War.

War-time Losses and Their Role in Recalling War Experiences

In the early 1920s, the events of the Great War still preoccupied the minds of many Lithuanians, predominantly because of issues related to war losses. Virtually from the first weeks of the Great War onwards the front line kept moving forth and back within the future Lithuania's territory, and did not stabilise on the present western border of Belarus in October 1915. From 1914 to 1915 much of the territory's population was voluntarily or forcibly displaced, and the region suffered enormous economic losses before it was occupied by the German Army. For the next several years, most Lithuanians experienced a full range of 'colonial practices' in the land ruled by General Erich Ludendorff (1865-1937), the *Ober Ost* or Supreme Commander of All German Forces in the East, the General's 'personal kingdom'.[8]

After the war, the Lithuanians recalled the German occupation as anything but a positive experience. For three and a half years, the Germans acted as colonial subjugators and were inclined to see the Land *Ober Ost* as no more than a stockpile of resources (including human ones) that could be used to meet the needs of the German army. Conditions were so harsh that this experience presumably shaped many Lithuanians' essential understanding of the concept of occupation. Moreover, the German occupation did not end with the armistice of Compiègne but continued until 1919. In 1923, the amount of war losses in Lithuania was estimated at 258 million US dollars,[9] equal to approximately nine annual national budgets.

Providing relief to those who suffered material damage during the war became a salient part of the Lithuanian political agenda for several years after 1918. The enumeration of war losses throughout the country together with Lithuania's economic recovery after the war were two of the government's most vital tasks. The Russian government and public activists encouraged people to record their material losses from the beginning of the war up to the years 1918-1919, when the Lithuanian government set up a new encompassing record of war damages. The issue of compensation was nonetheless linked to the outcome of negotiations with Soviet Russia and Germany, so the Lithuanian government was, for the time being, only able to offer minimal support to a population that had lost its homes, livestock and property.

When negotiations with Soviet Russia finally began, the compensation for war-time losses became one of the most important issues on the table. The paragraphs describing Russian commitments to return documents, works of art, movable cultural property, property of public associations and state institutions, private deposits of Lithuanian citizens and their personal goods that had been shifted from the future Lithuanian territory to the depths of Russia constituted a significant portion of the text of the Moscow Peace Treaty signed on 12 July 1920. In addition, Soviet Russia recognised Lithuania's right to

claim compensation for war damages incurred after 1 August 1914 from a third party.[10] All of these commitments triggered considerable expectations in Lithuanian society. Further negotiations over the return of specific property and compensations continued for several years, during which citizens were writing letters to the authorities, laying claim to lost property and deposits. Regardless, Russia was ultimately only able to carry out a rather inconsiderable part of the commitments it had assumed under the Moscow Treaty.

The outcome of the German negotiations was equally disappointing. The Lithuanian government had high expectations of the meetings that began in 1922. However, the German government clearly stated from the outset that 1) no one would force it to pay more than what the German state, already impeded by war reparations to France, was able to raise, and 2) Germany itself had financial counter-claims against Lithuania for German investments in regional infrastructure during the period of occupation and German post-war military and financial aid to Lithuania.[11] In effect, these opposing points of departure stalemated the negotiations from the outset. In the mutual agreement signed on 31 May 1923 in Berlin, both parties refused to agree to any of the other's compensation claims.[12]

Despite the fact that the calculation of war damages consumed much energy and aroused many expectations among Lithuanian citizens in the first post-war years, neither Soviet Russia nor Germany was fundamentally willing to reimburse the Lithuanian government's claims – and the government itself had rather limited possibilities of providing support for war victims, restricted as it was to funds from its slender national budget.

A case in point is the way Lithuania dealt with the issue of social welfare for those disabled in the war. During the period of parliamentary democracy, veterans of the Great War could send a kind of tribune to defend their interests in the parliament, arguing that they had essentially fought in the first battle on the road towards Lithuania's freedom. On this basis, the legalisation of concessions or social welfare for disabled First World War veterans met with no legislative obstacles. According to the new Law on Soldiers' Pensions issued by the Lithuanian parliament in August 1925, the pensions of those who became

Tauroggen nach unserer Einnahme

Fig. 3: The town Tauragė/Tauroggen on the border between Germany and Russia in the future territory of Lithuania, destroyed during the war hostilities, German postcard 1915.

disabled in the First World War while serving in the Russian Imperial Army were to be equal to the Lithuanian army's war disability pensions.

But Legislators could hardly have imagined the scope of those who would be affected by the new law. The law gave disabled veterans hopes of becoming state-sponsored pensioners instead of recipients of lump sums and public relief, and they flooded the government with thousands of requests. The number of applications quickly exceeded the anticipated quota several times over. The government soon realised that it lacked sufficient funds: It was forced to suspend the law's implementation, dashing the hopes of disabled veterans, and postponed finding a solution to the issue of social welfare for disabled veterans until 1930[13] (1932 in the Territory of Memel, which formerly belonged to Germany and was annexed by Lithuania in 1923).

These various issues related to the material and physical war losses alone testify that Lithuanians actively debated the social and economic problems caused by the Great War during the country's first decade of independence and, in many cases, even made them the centre of their attention. These problems made memories of the Great War relevant, even if no rituals or ceremonies of political commemoration of First World War losses emerged in Lithuania during this period (the Territory of Memel proving the only exception[14]). Not to mention that war memories were triggered by traumatic personal losses. A decade after the war, the Lithuanian press could still write: '[I]n our village [...] an old man [...] is complaining about his grief, as his sons were killed in Russia during the Great War. Three sons.'[15]

Representation of War Experiences

How did Lithuanians represent the Great War, and what moods were created in Lithuanian society when communities with different experiences of the war

Fig. 4: Cover of Jaroslavas Rimkus' (pseudonym Šilietis) album of drawings showing various scenes from popular memories about the German occupation in Lithuania 1915-1919.

„KULTŪRTRĖGERIAI.“

Vokiečiai išnaikino Lietuvoje daug knygy-
nų. Lygiai naikindavo jie mokyklų butus,
mokslo priemones ir baldus. Taip buvo valo-
mas kelias vokiečių kultūrai. Lietuvių mokyk-
los vokiečių globoj vėliau virto vokietinimo
lizdais.

"KULTURTRAEGERS."

The Germans destroyed not only many
libraries in Lithuania, but also school supplies
and buildings, even the furniture. In this way,
the road for German culture was being prepared. Lithuanian schools, under German direction later became Germanization centers.

Fig. 5: Drawing by Jaroslavas Rimkus (pseudonym Šilietis) about German 'Kulturträger', 1915.

still cherished hopes that problems caused by the war
would be overcome rapidly and effectively? The
Lithuanian media depicted a variety of experiences,
and no single narrative had as yet been imposed
through a homogenisation of public interpretation of
the war's significance – although the thrust of the
future narrative stating that Lithuanian independence was a result of the Great War was already circulating. Nevertheless, communities with different war
experiences were still manifesting 'their own' versions.

In the early 1920s, the Lithuanian intelligentsia
began to publish egodocuments written during the
war and conveying the daily routine of German occu-

Fig. 6: General Leonas Radus-Zenkavičius.

pation. These texts were primarily diaries and notes made during various stages of the war. In 1921-1922, the Mūsų Senovė [Our Antiquity] magazine printed fragments of diaries by Liudas Gira (1884-1946) and Aleksandras Dambrauskas (1860-1938), as well as notes by Petras Klimas (1891-1969);[16] all of them were still active public figures. Notes by Pranciškus Žadeikis (1869-1933), a priest in the Lithuanian-Latvian border town of Skuodas, were issued in a separate book in 1921 (the second part was published in 1925).[17]

In 1925, Mikas Gudaitis (1880 to post-1941) published another work of this genre.[18] The same year saw the publication of the first part of the talented writer Gabrielė Petkevičaitė's (1861-1943) diary.[19] All of these works captured a glimpse into the daily routine of German occupation most Lithuanians had experienced. They sought to portray, as the priest

Žadeikis wrote, the 'terrible times'.[20] However, the Lithuanian intelligentsia were not the only ones to share their memories of the German occupation. Upon returning to Lithuania from Russia, Jaroslavas Rimkus (1888-1976), with the pseudonym Jaroslavas Šilietis, decided to convey the German occupation in drawings, without having experienced it himself. He apparently gathered recollections and conducted interviews, as evidenced by the lines in the preface of his drawing album issued in 1922: 'It was a very easy matter to collect material for this book because every Lithuanian who lived under the German occupation seemed an unending source of information about German cruelty and misdeeds.'[21] Rimkus drew and gathered together several hundred cartoons depicting the daily life of Lithuanians under the essentially colonial regime of *Ober Ost*. The book's preface, which was distributed throughout Lithuania in the 1920s, stated the following: 'Among the ruined countries of Europe, Lithuania is one of those which have suffered the most.'[22]

The representation of Lithuanian war experiences was of course not limited to accounts of the trauma of German occupation. The year 1924 saw the début of the magazine *Keturi vėjai* [Four Winds], named after the avant-garde literary trend. The first issue included the publication of Saliamonas Šmerauskas's [ps. Salys Šemerys] (1898-1981) play script *The Death of the Death*.[23] That same year, the *Keturi vėjai* also published a book of Šemerys's poetry, *The Grenade in the Breast*, followed by *A Heart Burning Flame-Thrower* two years later.[24] The young poet's works were full of references to the First World War and clearly expressed an anti-militaristic attitude. Admittedly, Šemerys was not the first Lithuanian author to communicate such an attitude to the Great War. Juozas Tumas [ps. Vaižgantas] (1869-1933) had already conveyed something similar in his short stories at the war's start. What do the Catholic priest Vaižgantas and the avant-garde poet Šemerys, 30 years his junior, have in common? Both spent the Great War outside the future territory of Lithuania, in the depths of Russia. Thus they did not experience the German occupation and were guided by other stimuli and other personal experiences.

The veterans of the Great War, in turn, had yet another perspective. In 1921, an early version of *Who's Who in Lithuania* – the representative *Album of Lithuania* –

was published. It included photos and biographical notes of several Lithuanian officers, and some of them highlighted the experience of service in the Russian Army during the Great War. The biographical notes of Col. Vincas Grigaliūnas-Glovackis (1885-1964) gave a rather detailed account of what he was doing and where he served during the Great War.[25] The biographical notes of Pranas Klimaitis (1885-1940) revealed his activities in the organisation of national units in Russia and later in the battles against the Bolsheviks in Siberia.[26] As indicated in the biographical notes of Lt. Col. Kazys Ladiga (1893-1941), 'he received all the military awards that were presented to senior officers of the Russian Army with the exception of St. George's Sword'; in reference to the Great War, the text added 'He made efforts to serve well so as not to defame the name of a Lithuanian.'(sic!)[27] The descriptions of other officer-veterans of the Great War paid more attention to post-war experiences and the contribution of the Lithuanian state's army. At least in the 1921 *Album of Lithuania*, however, they were not in the majority.

Some senior officers perceived the experience of the Great War as a foundation for military learning and believed that Lithuanian military doctrine should be formed on its basis. Such a task was clearly formulated by Gen. Leonas Radus-Zenkavičius (1874-1946), former senior Russian Imperial Army officer, a division commander who also worked at the General Staff of the Red Army for several years before his return to Lithuania. He wrote several reviews of the memoirs of Ludendorff, Erich von Falkenhayn (1861-1922) and Paul von Hindenburg (1847-1934) for Lithuanian magazines.[28] But he also authored some original works on the tactics and strategy of the Great War, including his *Sketch of the Great War*, an outline of nearly 300 pages.[29]

A considerable number of officers were concerned with yet another aspect of their military experience. They collected documents and wrote memoirs about the national movement among the ranks of Lithuanian soldiers who served in Russia from 1917 to 1919. This activity let other soldiers comprehend their merits for Lithuanian independence and the creation of the Lithuanian Army. The first memoirs of this kind were published as early as 1919 to 1922, and their publication continued throughout the entire period of Lithuania's independence.

Conclusion

So far, researchers discussing the memory and representation of the Great War in Lithuania have tended to treat Lithuanian society as a monolith. This picture may change, however, by expanding the approach and focusing on different social actors for whom the war was a significant part of their experience, and on what they later did with those experiences. I argue that different meanings assigned to both the Great War experiences and the problems they caused were circulating in inter-war Lithuania. Lithuanians remembered, discussed and wrote about the Great War; until at least 1926, it was not yet overshadowed by the Wars of Independence, and it never completely disappeared from the Lithuanian public space. This was not so much an outcome of parliamentary democracy, as martial law and censorship functioned throughout the inter-war period in Lithuania, but rather a result of a 'warm' post-war situation in which debates over compensation for war losses still triggered the memories of war experiences and no single narrative about the 'Lithuanian experience' in the Great War had yet been forged. In the early 1920s, the prevalent trend was to portray and remember the Great War as a misery that was largely brought about by the German occupation. However, since Lithuanian war experiences were much more diverse, the treatments of this war also varied, and the memoirs of the period display a range of approaches.

Endnotes

1. Cf. Winston S. Churchill, *The World Crisis*, vol. 5: *The Unknown War. The Eastern Front* (New York: Charles Scribner's Sons, 1931).
2. Darius Staliūnas, 'Der Kult des Unbekannten Soldaten in Litauen,' in *Über den Weltkrieg hinaus. Kriegserfahrungen in Ostmitteleuropa 1914-1921*, ed. Joachim Tauber, vol. XVII/2008, *Nordost-Archiv* (Lüneburg: Nordost-Institut, 2009), 248-266, here 248.
3. Vejas Gabriel Liulevicius, 'Building Nationalism: Monuments, Museums, and the Politics of War Memory in Inter-War Lithuania,' in *Über den Weltkrieg hinaus. Kriegserfahrungen in Ostmitteleuropa 1914-1921*, ed. Joachim Tauber, vol. XVII/2008, *Nordost-Archiv* (Lüneburg: Nordost-Institut, 2009), 230-247, here 232.

4. Rasa Antanavičiūtė, 'The Memory and Representation of World War I in Lithuania,' in *The Art of Identity and Memory. Toward a Cultural History of the Two World Wars in Lithuania*, eds. Giedrė Jankevičiūtė and Rasutė Žukienė (Boston: Academic Studies Press, 2016), 175-202, here 191, 176.

5. Tomas Balkelis, 'Memories of the Great War and the Polish-Lithuanian Conflict in Lithuania,' in *The Empire and Nationalism at War*, eds. Eric Lohr, Vera Tolz, Alexander Semyonov and Mark von Hagen (Bloomington: Slavica Publishers, 2014), 241-256, here 242, 244, 246.

6. This article is largely based on the results of comparative research into the Great War's role in Lithuanian and East Prussian societies and cultures during the interwar period: Vasilijus Safronovas, Vytautas Jokubauskas, Vygantas Vareikis, Hektoras Vitkus, *Didysis karas visuomenėje ir kultūroje: Lietuva ir Rytų Prūsija* (Klaipėda: Klaipėdos universiteto leidykla, 2018). For more on the Lithuanian case, see also the collected papers in *The Great War in Lithuania and Lithuanians in the Great War: Experiences and Memories*, ed. Vasilijus Safronovas, vol. XXXIV of *Acta Historica Universitatis Klaipedensis* (Klaipėda: Klaipėda University Press, 2017).

7. Cf. Aušra Jurevičiūtė, *Buvusių karių organizacijos ir jų vaidmuo Lietuvos vidaus politikoje 1923-1940 m.* Daktaro disertacija (Kaunas: Vytauto Didžiojo Universitetas, 2009); Aušra Jurevičiūtė, 'Savanorių kūrėjų vienijimosi idėjos įgyvendinimas 1926 metų rudenį,' *Parlamento studijos* 8 (2009), 87-106.

8. Werner Conze, *Polnische Nation und deutsche Politik im Ersten Weltkrieg*, vol. 4 of *Ostmitteleuropa in Vergangenheit und Gegenwart* (Köln-Graz: Böhlau, 1958), 87.

9. Albinas Rimka, 'Lietuvos karo nuostoliai,' *Mūsų žinynas* 14 (1923), 314-319.

10. 'Lietuvos Taikos Sutartis su Rusija,' *Vyriausybės žinios*, 30 Nov. 1920, no. 53.

11. *Lietuvos centrinis valstybės archyvas* [*Lithuanian Central State Archives*], f. 383, ap. 7, b. 280, l. 243-248, here l. 247.

12. 'Lietuvos ir Vokietijos karo nuostolių ir ob-Osto pinigų likvidavimo sutartis,' *Vyriausybės žinios*, 22 Oct. 1924, no. 173.

13. For detailed information on different solutions to the problem of compensation for wartime losses, see the following articles: Vytautas Jokubauskas, '"The Tsar would not have Taken away our Pensions": Compensation for Russian Army First World War Invalids in Interwar Lithuania,' *Lithuanian Historical Studies* 21 (2017), 79-106; Vasilijus Safronovas, 'Didžiojo karo sureikšminimo Rytų Prūsijoje ir Klaipėdos krašte prielaidos: nuostolių kompensavimo klausimas,' *Lietuvos istorijos metraštis* 1 (2017), 127-168.

14. During the war, the Territory of Memel (Klaipėda region) belonged to East Prussia, its population served in the German Army and cultural relations continued to exist between the region and Germany throughout the interwar period. Therefore, the remembrance of the Great War in that part of Lithuania was similar to that in Germany and East Prussia.

15. 'Pranašas su vyžomis,' *Diena*, 6 October 1929, no. 61.

16. Liūdas Gira, 'Vilniaus gyvenimas po Vokiečiais. 1916 m.,' *Mūsų senovė* 2 (1921), 21-38; 'Vilniaus gyvenimas po Vokiečiais. 1917 m.,' *Mūsų senovė* 3 (1922), 410-424; A[leksandras] Dambrauskas, 'Mano užrašai', *Mūsų senovė* 3 (1922), 398-409 and 4-5 (1922), 796-807; P[etras] Klimas, 'Mano kelionė po Lietuvą 1915 metais,' *Mūsų senovė* 4-5 (1922), 545-556.

17. Pr[anciškus] Žadeikis, *Didžiojo karo užrašai*, part I (Klaipėda: Lituania, 1921); part II (Klaipėda: Rytas, 1925).

18. Mikas Gudaitis, *Lietuva 1917 metais. Kelionės po Lietuvą vokiečių okupacijos metu* (Klaipėda: Rytas, 1925).

19. G[abrielė] Petkevičaitė, *Karo meto dienoraštis*, parts I-II (Kaunas: Varpas, 1925 and 1931).

20. Žadeikis, *Didžiojo karo užrašai*, I, 4.

21. [Jaroslavas Rimkus] Jaroslavas Šilietis, *Vokiečių okupacija Lietuvoje 1915-1919 m. paveiksėliuose ir trumpuose jų aprašymuose = The German Occupation in Lithuania 1915-1919 Related in Pictures and Short Descriptions* (Kaunas: Varpas, 1922), iv.

22. Ibid., iv.

23. [Saliamonas Šmerauskas] Salys Šemerys, 'Mirties mirtis,' *Keturi vėjai* 1 (1924), 34-39.

24. [Saliamonas Šmerauskas] Salys Šemerys, *Granata krūtinėj* (Kaunas: Keturių vėjų leidinys, 1924); [Saliamonas Šmerauskas] Salys Šemerys, *Liepsnosvaidis širdims deginti* (1919-1926) (Kaunas: Pr. Stiklius, 1926).

25. *Lietuvos albumas*, eds. J. Markevičaitė and L. Gira (Kaunas: n.p., 1921), 319-320.

26. Ibid., 338-340.

27. Ibid., 349.

28. See *Mūsų žinynas* 2 (1921), 157-166; *Mūsų žinynas* 4 (1922), 142-143.

29. [Leonas] Radus-Zenkavičius, *Trumpas Didžiojo karo eskizas* (Kaunas: Vyr. Štabo Karo mokslo skyrius, 1924).

Did the Great War End? Memory and Memorialisation of the First World War in Romania

Florin Abraham

Introduction

In the Romanian collective mentality, the First World War is perceived not only as an event generating enormous suffering and loss of life, but also as a necessary and unavoidable sacrifice for the creation of Greater Romania. According to Romanian mythology, nothing sustainable can be achieved without sacrifice. The legend of Manole the Builder, which refers to the 16th-century construction of the Curtea de Argeş Monastery, claims that the walls kept crumbling until Manole buried his pregnant wife Ana between the walls of the cathedral.[1] It is no coincidence that the Curtea de Argeş Monastery afterwards became a sanctuary for Romania's kings, being considered a symbolic place of Romanian spirituality.

In Romania, the First World War is known not so much as the 'Great War' or as a regular military confrontation, but as the 'War of National Unification',[2] a new military *Risorgimento*, after the 1877-1878 war of independence against the Ottoman Empire. The approximately 335,000 people who died just among the military (from a total of 900,000) are not considered 'victims', but 'necessary heroes' for the country's unification. In the popular perception, Romania emerged from the First World War as a winner, even if historically the situation is much more complex.[3]

The official interpretation of the First World War has undergone several metamorphoses during the last hundred years, on both the national[4] and the international level.[5] In the case of Romania, during the interwar period, the First World War was considered the most important political and military event and the final point of a *Risorgimento* that began in the mid-19th century. Romania entered the Second World War precisely in order to defend what it had made so many sacrifices to conquer in the Great War.

During the first two decades of the communist regime, the official interpretation was the Soviet one: the First World War was a consequence of imperialist rivalries, a 'conflict of bourgeoisies'. The regime censored references to the union of Bessarabia with the motherland, but this changed after 1960; the First World War was reintegrated in the nation's history as an essential moment, even if the communists had played no role in it. After the fall of communism, the Romanian Revolution of December 1989 became the new central event of an official, though not hegemonic, narrative. This narrative no longer emphasised the nation's heroism through the dead soldiers from the two world wars, but through the 'anti-communist resistance' which, according to the predominant narrative, had included almost the entire nation. The issues of the First World War and of the Great Union were rediscovered after Romania's accession to the European Union and used as a tool to strengthen national identity which, it was considered, had been eroded by globalisation and European integration.

The Interwar Period and the Second World War: The Burden of the Recent Past

Most ethnic Romanians integrated the First World War into their memory as the continuation, on a much wider and more violent scale, of 19th-century history. Some minorities, mainly Hungarians, perceived the war as a great tragedy. The idea of achieving a great state to encompass the majority of Romanians had just been realised and was considered a miracle paid for with the lives and blood of many countrymen. The idea of a 'Great Romania' therefore became dominant in the interwar period, in political and cultural life alike.[6] Participation in the war was

Fig. 1: General Alexandru Averescu, painted by Valentin Tănase, 2015.

battles of 1917 (Mărăşti, Mărăşeşti, Oituz). These mausoleums contain the remains not only of soldiers from the Romanian Army, but also of those from the Central Powers army. The government also set up several cemeteries, in which the remains were to be laid according to the army from which they originated (Entente or Central Powers), but there are numerous cemeteries in which these remains were laid regardless of the religion of the deceased (for example, in Mangalia).[8]

Numerous veteran associations have kept the memory of the war alive. Political parties have included specific provisions for their war veterans' programmes.[9] The main beneficiaries of the agrarian reform (1921) were the war veterans and the survivors of those who died in the First World War. War veterans, orphans, and widows suffered during the Great Depression when the state reduced its aid. In spite of public and often violent protests against the government, in the 1930s state benefits remained below the level necessary for a decent life. Although it would have been strategic for the veterans to join together to defend their interests, they did not succeed in doing so.

The war and the Great Union served as dominant themes in literature and the visual arts, treated by artists such as Liviu Rebreanu (1885-1944), Camil

an important source of political legitimacy. King Ferdinand (1865-1927) was called the 'unifier', which meant that the German dynasty of Hohenzollern-Sigmaringen was fully accepted as a 'Romanian/national dynasty'. One of the war's heroes, General Alexandru Averescu (1859-1938), became Prime Minister of Romania (1920) and his People's Party enjoyed broad popularity during the general elections of May 1920.

In 1921, the Romanian government established a 'Heroes' Day', to be celebrated at Pentecost. Under the Monarchy's patronage, steps were undertaken to create memorial places for the victims of the First World War. Various monuments such as statues and triptychs were created for war heroes all over Romania. The heroes' names were also given to various settlements or streets.[7] The Arch of Triumph in Bucharest and the Cross from the Caraiman Mountain (2291 m) are only two of the most visible monuments dedicated to Romania's victory in the First World War. The most important mausoleums are those dedicated to dead and missing people from the

Fig. 2: The Arch of Triumph in Bucharest was built 1935/36, drawing, 2017.

Petrescu (1894-1957), Cezar Petrescu (1892-1961) and Gheorghe Brătianu (1898-1953).

The territorial losses of the summer of 1940 (Bessarabia and Bukovina to the Soviet Union, part of Transylvania to Hungary) shocked Romanians. The sacrifices of the First World War now seemed pointless, a sense of futility that triggered the collapse of King Carol II's (1893-1953) regime and his banishment from the country. Seemingly paradoxically, Romanian society therefore at first viewed General Ion Antonescu's (1882-1946) establishment of a military dictatorship, with its implicit promise of recovering a part of the lost territories, with great hope. Yet Romania's entry into the war alongside the Axis powers meant the emergence of a new generation of widows, orphans and victims on the front, and hope turned into despair. After the end of the Second World War, the issue of the legacy of the Great War was eclipsed by new geopolitical and social realities.

The Totalitarian Era:
From *Damnatio Memoriae* to Selective Past

The issue of Romania's involvement in the First World War presented multiple ideological challenges to the Communist Party of Romania, which had recently come to power thanks to Soviet support. The first resulted from Lenin's taking Russia out of the war by signing the Treaty of Brest-Litovsk (3 March 1918), in order to ensure the final success of the Bolsheviks in the struggle for power. This decision was legitimised by the theory that the First World War was a confrontation of imperialist forces, while the working class was advocating pacifism. Romania's Sovietisation implicitly meant an ideologisation of historical interpretation. Secondly, Romania's position towards Bessarabia had to be clarified, as the province had been occupied by the USSR in 1940 and remained within the Soviet Union. Lies and mystifications were the communists' only solutions. In the schoolbook *Romania's History*, issued in 1947 and intended for secondary schools, coordinator Mihai Roller conveyed the communists' position: Bessarabia's union was illegitimate because the 'reactionary Romanian government' had hindered the revolutionary Soviets.[10]

In the 1948 issue of the same schoolbook, the authors extended this approach towards Transylvania.

The Bolshevik interpretation was that Transylvania 'joined' (and not 'united with') the Old Kingdom, and that this had happened under 'armed pressure' and not as a result of the openly expressed will of the majority ethnic group, the Romanians. Such mystification is also obvious in the book's description of the military intervention against Hungary in 1919, which omits the attack on the Romanian troops and condemns the 'military intervention against the revolution in Hungary'. Third, what was called the 'labour movement in Romania' did not play a major role in the Great Union, unlike the paramount role of the monarchy and the 'historical parties', which were banned in the early stages of the country's communisation. Recognising the exceptional dimension of the Great Union from the perspective of the Romanian state would implicitly have meant confirming the legitimacy of the monarchy and the bourgeois parties, an unacceptable hypothesis for the totalitarian party-state. Finally, but no less importantly for the government, the most difficult problem concerned the veterans, invalids, widows, and orphans of the Second World War, who had to be provided with the resources necessary for survival. The heroes of the First World War thus entered into a true and ideologically motivated *damnatio memoriae*, and the communist regime did not completely abandon war invalids; it helped them materially, while keeping them anonymous.

The *damnatio memoriae* operation was multidimensional. The regime not only falsified history in schoolbooks and university curricula, including the removal from libraries and burning of books discussing the First World War, but also took other actions.[11] It changed the names of places or streets memorialising the First World War and altered monuments dedicated to war heroes by eliminating any reference to King Ferdinand and Queen Marie (1875-1938).

The exit from the Soviet paradigm of the First World War was made with difficulty and incompletely. The essential reason was Bessarabia and Bukovina, as communist leaders tried to avoid disputes with the Soviet Union around this issue. The communist regime acquired a national tinge at the end of the Gheorghiu-Dej (1901-1965) regime and, then, during Ceausescu's time, a part of the historical truth began to be officially recognised.[12] The Great

Fig. 3: King Ferdinand of Romania 1914-1927, painted by Valentin Tănase, 2015.

Union began to be mentioned in official documents of the Romanian Communist Party (PCR), schoolbooks, and university curricula, by referring only to Transylvania and obliterating the issue of Bessarabia and Bukovina. In 1968, Romania officially celebrated the half-centenary of the union of Transylvania with Romania. On the other hand, from the 1970s onwards, the issue of national unity became the subject of a new nationalist mythology, its roots being sought in the pre-Roman Antiquity, the so-called 'centralised and independent Dacian state'. This orientation in historiography and literature has been called 'protochronism'.[13]

The spectacular recurrence of the First World War theme in the official memory accepted by the communist regime was achieved by bringing back into cultural circulation the literary and historiographical works related to the first world conflagration (but with elements of censorship).[14] Film production easily conveyed to the public the message designed by political factors. There were subsidies for movies

such as *Ecaterina Teodoroiu* (1978), which tells the story of a young woman who enrols in the army as a volunteer, is wounded while fighting on the first line of the front, and then dies in the 1917 military confrontation with the Central Powers army. In 1964, the public was presented the movie *Pădurea spânzuraților (Forest of the Hanged)*, after the novel (inspired by true events) written by Liviu Rebreanu in 1922. The main hero of the film is a young officer from Transylvania who is forced to fight against his fellow Romanian countrymen and decides to desert, but is caught and sentenced to death by hanging. Another movie is the screen adaptation of the novel *Ultima noapte de dragoste, întâia noapte de război (Last Night of Love, First Night of War*, 1930) written by Romanian writer Camil Petrescu, undertaken by director Sergiu Nicolaescu (1930-2013) in 1979-1980. The movie relates both the love story of a young officer of the Romanian army and the drama of war.[15]

During the period of the communist regime, no great memorial places were built for the heroes of the First World War; the existing ones were only maintained to avoid decay. They even entered the educational circuit, becoming places of memory meant to instil patriotism in young generations.

The Post-Communist Period: Between Oblivion and New Recall of Memory

Over eight decades after the First World War, in a society heading towards the unknown, searching for a rebirth of democracy and transition to the market economy, the issue of the first world conflagration has become a preoccupation of historians and a chapter in schoolbooks, but not an important public subject. Veterans of the First World War have almost entirely vanished, much like the participants in the creation of Greater Romania. The memory of the First World War seems to have lost its active force for the present, in the absence of the characters who animated it.

In the mid-1990s, Romania's major preoccupation became NATO and acceptance in the European Union, which also had consequences for public policies of First World War memorialisation.

In 1990, Romania's national day became 1 December, when the 1918 union of Transylvania with the Kingdom of Romania is celebrated. The official public

Fig. 4: Image from the film 'Pădurea spânzuraților' (Forest of the Hanged), 1964.

discourse does not emphasise the causal relationship between the Great War and the Great Union and avoids references to the war – implicitly, to the war against the Central Powers[16] – so as not to bring back painful memories to the nation's new NATO and EU allies (Germany, Austria, Hungary). This strategic approach to historical events makes it seem as though the Great War were over, the heroes commemorated for their individual and collective sacrifice (as an act of civil compassion), not as part of a (geo)political discourse with any meaning for the future. During the interwar period, references to the heroes from the War for National Unification were correlated first with the danger of Hungarian revisionism and then with the rise of Nazism. In contrast, after 1990 the victims – either from the Entente or from the Central Powers camp – were commemorated as examples of the possible consequences of war.

The Romanian government did not invest significant sums in new great memorial places dedicated to those who died during the First World War, but instead restricted itself to maintaining existing ones. City halls or various military units created new memorial places, of smaller and local interest, some-

times for victims of all wars waged by Romania (1877-1878, WWI, WWII).

After the 2008-2010 economic crisis and the renewed nationalisation of policies in Europe, countries became increasingly preoccupied by their national identity. The commemoration of the centenary of the outbreak of the First World War became the object of competing narratives in Europe.[17] Transnational history offered the following narrative: nationalism and rivalries between great powers led to the First World War; Leninism-Stalinism and Fascism/Nazism were born from the First World War, which generated a new world conflagration; the solution to the issue of war in Europe was European integration (European Union); the best guarantee against new conflict in Europe is a deepening of European integration.

Another type of narrative looks at the First World War as a great geopolitical catastrophe that toppled the German and the Austro-Hungarian empires, creating a European power vacuum that would then become one of the main causes of the Second World War.[18] According to political reinterpretation of this historiographical interpretation, the situation of ethno-cultural minorities that was created by the

Fig. 5: Monument to the Heroes of the Engineer Arm, built 1929, drawing, 2017.

Versailles treaties remains unsolved until the present day, thus legitimising interference in the sovereignty of other countries in order to 'offer protection to the nation beyond state borders'. The explanatory model is the following: military defeat in the First World War was followed by an 'unjust peace' imposed by victorious great powers; because the 'Versailles system' was unjust, demands to revise borders or change the political organisation of countries emerging or expanding after the end of the First World War were legitimate.

Another kind of historical narrative was created in Romania, in the context of the return of discussions about First World War drama and its consequences.[19] In the absence of a significant Eurosceptic political concept or of illiberal theories of democracy, Romanian society broadly accepted the historiographical narrative produced in the transnational paradigm and rejected theses challenging the legitimacy of the Versailles treaties. Romanian historians often stress that the Versailles system was confirmed – in its essential lines – both at the end of the Second World War and by the Helsinki Final Act; border changes in Europe (with the exception of the 'velvet divorce' between the Czech Republic and Slovakia) were achieved only through war (see the implosion of former Yugoslavia).

Romania is one of many countries – including Austria, Poland, the Czech Republic, Slovakia, Baltic States, and Serbia – with a state policy of celebrating the 100-year anniversary of the creation of the modern state or its territorial extension. In July 2016, for the celebration of 100 years from the entrance into war on the side of the Entente, the Centenary Department was established, subordinated to the Prime Minister. A year later, in 2017, the structure was integrated into the Ministry of Culture. That same year, the government adopted the 'Law Concerning the Centenary of the War for National Unification (1916-1919) and the Centenary of the Great Union'. This is a significant act for historical narrative, as it legally formalises a historical reality, mainly concerning the causal relation between the First World War and the creation of Greater Romania. The interwar title returns and the war's purpose is teleologically fixed: 'for national unification'. Significantly, the First World War period was also extended past 11 November 1918, in order to commemorate the victims of

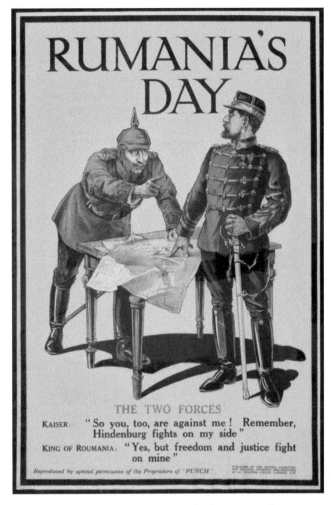

Fig. 6: British propaganda poster with the Romania´s entrance into war on the side of the Entente in 1916, designed for the Central Committee for National Patriotic Organisations, London.

the 1919 military confrontations (the Romanian army's campaign against the Hungarian Soviet Republic .

The celebration of the Centenary has become a space of political consensus between Romanian political parties, for multiple reasons. Political and intellectual elites considered that, as after Romania's NATO and EU accessions there was no other national project around which society could rally, a new symbolic moment such as the memory of the First World War and the Great Union could be a useful tool for social mobilisation. In a general context in which mass media mainly offers negative and conflicting news, the Great Union's symbolism can have a positive effect, helping to reduce Romania's social anomy. The manner in which the Great War has been commemorated, with a special emphasis on memorialising all victims, is also an implicit assumption of the European Union's liberal democratic values.

Romania celebrated the end of the First World War and the Great Union in several different ways: local authorities organise public events within the main memorial places, in memory of those who died in the war,[20] and a vast programme of publications about the First World War and political and diplomatic events related to the Great Union has been published. The Romanian Academy took on the coordination of scientific publications, but several universities and research centres are also working towards this objective; the government awards several types of distinctions and medals for people, civilian and military institutions or administrative-territorial units (towns, villages). The Romanian Orthodox Church, claiming an essential role in national identity, inaugurated at 25 November 2018 the National Cathedral of Redemption, a few days before the centenary of the Great Union. According to the Romanian Patriarchate's official discourse, the gigantic building serves as the 'national cathedral', thus expressing the thesis of unity between the Romanian ethnic group and the Christian-Orthodox confession. This approach to the main ecclesiastical institution of Romania is very influential in the public discourse. Although Romanian society does not fully accept this hegemonically ambitious narrative of the Orthodox Church, especially in the intellectual segments defined as 'European', it is tacitly supported by most political parties, for electoral purposes.[21]

Concluding Observation

Over the last century, the memorialisation of the First World War has witnessed various contents, forms, and motivations, related to the specificity of the political regime and the influence of geopolitical factors. The massive losses Romania suffered during the three years of military conflict imposed a heavy burden on the Kingdom of Romania and instilled the need to keep alive the memory of deceased soldiers. This has meant the creation of memorial places in settlements in which the main military confrontations took place. The war also figured strongly in interwar literature and visual arts. During the Second World War, the heroism of soldiers from the preced-

ing world conflagration was offered as a model of military bravery, the more so as some of them, including General Ion Antonescu, had participated in both wars.

Soviet ideological correctness expelled the 1917-1918 period from Romanian history, only for it to be gradually reintroduced after 1960 in official memorialisation. Artistic productions financed by the communist state were the most important political message of the Communist Party in taking on and becoming reconciled with its own past. Afterwards, in the context of celebrating the Centenary of the Great Union, the memory of the Great War was revitalised, with an emphasis both on the war's drama – including all victims, from both the Entente and the Central Powers – and on the patriotism of Romanian soldiers. Romania's current narrative emphasises both the drama produced by the war (the humanist message) and the need to keep awake the nation's conscience in case the country's unity is threatened (the patriotic message).

Officially, the Great War ended a century ago, but its legacy was too strong, since Germany's National Socialist totalitarian regime wanted to rewrite its end through a new world conflagration. The fourth and fifth generation after the First World War hope that the demons of populist extremism will remain locked in the past – yet historians know that humanity only rarely learns from its errors.

Endnotes

1. Catalina Florina Florescu and Ma Sheng-mei, *Transnational Narratives in Englishes of Exile* (Lanham: Lexington Books, 2018), 38.
2. Constantin Kirițescu, *Istoria Războiului pentru Întregirea României 1916-1919*, 2nd edn (Bucharest: Editura Casei Școalelor, 1925), passim.
3. Glenn E.Torrey, *The Romanian Battlefront in World War I.* (Lawrence: University Press of Kansas, 2014), 293-313.
4. Lucian Boia, *Primul Război Mondial. Controverse, paradoxuri, reinterpretări* (Bucharest: Humanitas, 2014), passim.
5. Jay Winter and Antoine Prost, *The Great War in History. Debates and Controversies, 1914 to the Present* (Cambridge–New York: Cambridge University Press, 2005), 192-212.
6. Irina Livezeanu, *Cultural Politics in Greater Romania: Regionalism, Nation Building and Ethnic Struggle, 1918-1930* (Ithaca: Cornell University Press, 2000), 5-6.
7. Silviu Hariton, 'War Commemorations in Inter-War Romania: Cultural Politics and Social Context', in *The Great War and Memory in Central and South-Eastern Europe*, ed. Oto Luthar (Leiden: Brill, 2016), 137-161.

8. Maria Bucur-Deckard, *Heroes and Victims. Remembering War in Twentieth-Century Romania* (Bloomington–Indianapolis: Indiana University Press, 2010), 49-72.

9. Constantin Iordachi and Blasco Sciarrino, 'War Veterans, Demobilization and Political Activism: Greater Romania in Comparison,' *Fascism. Journal of Comparative Fascist Studies* 6, no.1 (2017), 75-115, here 93.

10. Mihail Roller (ed.), *Istoria României. Manual unic pentru clasa a VIII-a secundară* (Bucharest: Editura de Stat, 1947), 627.

11. Ionuţ Costea, István Kiraly, and Doru Radosav. *Fond Secret. Fond 'S' Special. Contribuţii la istoria fondurilor secrete de bibliotecă din România – Studiu de caz. Biblioteca Central Universitară 'Lucian Blaga'* (Cluj-Napoca: Editura Dacia, 1995), passim.

12. Nicolae Ceauşescu, *Expunere prezentată la Sesiunea comună solemnă a C.C. al P.C.R., M.A.N. şi activul central de partid şi de stat consacrată Centenarului proclamării independenţei de stat a României, 9 mai 1977* (Bucharest: Editura Politică, 1977), passim.

13. Katherine Verdery, *National Ideology under Socialism. Identity and Cultural Politics in Ceauşescu's Romania* (Berkeley: University of California Press, 1991), 167-188.

14. Augustin Deac, *Caracterul participării României la Primul Război Mondial* (Bucharest: Editura Politică, 1973); Gheorghe Stoean (ed.), *România în Primul Război Mondial: contribuţii bibliografice* (Bucharest: Editura Militară, 1975).

15. Călin Căliman, *Istoria filmului românesc (1897-2017)* (Bucharest: EuroPress, 2017), passim; Cristian Tudor Popescu, *Filmul surd în România mută: politică şi propagandă în filmul românesc de ficţiune (1912-1989)* (Iaşi: Polirom, 2011), passim.

16. Claudiu-Lucian Topor, *Germania şi neutralitatea României (1914-1916). Studii istorice* (Iaşi: Editura Universităţii 'Alexandru Ioan Cuza', 2017), passim.

17. Jay Winter (ed.), *The Legacy of the Great War: Ninety Years on* (Columbia: University of Missouri Press, 2009), passim.

18. Norman A. Graebner and Edward M. Bennett, *The Versailles Treaty and its Legacy. The Failure of the Wilsonian Vision* (Cambridge: Cambridge University Press, 2011), 38-66.

19. Mihail E. Ionescu (ed.), *Românii în Marele Război. Anul 1915. Documente, impresii, mărturii* (Bucharest: Editura Militară, 2015); Mihail E. Ionescu (ed.), *Românii în Marele Război. Anul 1916. Documente, impresii, mărturii* (Bucharest: Editura Militară, 2017); Babriel Leancă, *L'entrée de la Roumanie dans La Grande Guerre. Documents diplomatiques français (1er janvier – 9 septembre 1916)* (Paris: L'Harmattan, 2016); Alin Ciupală, *Bătălia lor. Femeile din România în Primul Război Mondial* (Iaşi: Polirom, 2017).

20. Monumentele Marelui Război, Oficiul Naţional pentru Cultul Eroilor, <https://once.mapn.ro/pages/view/121> (accessed 21 March 2018).

21. Lavinia Stan and Lucian Turcescu, *Church, State, and Democracy in Expanding Europe* (Oxford: Oxford University Press, 2011), 134-149.

Appendices

Timeline of military and diplomatic events in Europe, 1914–1924

1914

Jun 28
Archduke Franz Ferdinand of Austria (1863-1914) and his wife, Duchess Sophie, are assassinated at Sarajevo by Gavrilo Princip, student and member of the 'Black Hand' Bosnian-Serbian secret organization

Jul 5–6
Austria-Hungary seeks German support in the case of a war against Serbia ('Mission Hoyos')

14 Jul
The Council of Austro-Hungarian Ministers is determined on war action against Serbia

19 Jul
The Council of Austro-Hungarian Ministers approve the text of the ultimatum against Serbia

Jul 20–23
Visit of a French government delegation to St Petersburg

Jul 23
Austro-Hungarian ultimatum to Serbia

Jul 24
The Russian Crown Council declares its support to Serbia

The German government submits a note to the Entente governments approving the Austrian ultimatum to Serbia

Jul 25
The Serbian government orders mobilization; Austria-Hungary severs diplomatic relations with Serbia; the Serbian government is translocated from Belgrade to Nish

Jul 28
Austria-Hungary declares war on Serbia

1914

Jul 29
Communication between German Emperor Wilhelm II (1859-1941) and Russian Tsar Nicholas II (1868-1918)

Jul 30
German ultimatum to Russia

General mobilization of Russian troops

Jul 31
In a message, German Emperor Wilhelm II tries to convince Romanian King Carol (1839-1914) I to enter the war on the side of the Central Powers

Aug 1
Germany declares war on Russia

French troops mobilise

Italy declares neutrality

Alliance treaty between Germany and the Ottoman Empire

Aug 2
Józef Piłsudski (1867-1935) becomes commander of the Riflemen's Federation (Związek Strzelecki) at Cracow

German troops enter Kalisz, Częstochowa and Będzin

Aug 3
Germany declares war on France

Romania declares its neutrality

Aug 4
Britain declares war on Germany in reaction to the invasion of neutral Belgium

Aug 4–10
Military confrontation between the British Navy and the German Imperial Navy with their cruisers Goeben und Breslau in the Mediterranean Sea

Aug 5
The Ottoman Empire closes the Dardanelles

1914

Montenegro declares war on Austria-Hungary

Aug 6

Austria-Hungary declares war on Russia

Serbia declares war on Germany

Aug 8

Montenegro declares war on Germany

Aug 10

Austria-Hungary invades Russia

Aug 11

France declares war on Austria-Hungary

Aug 12

Britain declares war on Austria-Hungary

Aug 14

In the Russian Duma, Polish deputy Wiktor Jaroński (1870-1931) declares the Polish Circle's (Koło Polskie) support for Russia

Aug 16–24

Austro-Hungarian defeat against Serbia in the Battle of Cer

Aug 17

Two Russian armies, counting 650,000 men, enter East Prussia; Battle of Stallupönen

Aug 23–30

The Russian troops undergo a defeat in the Battle of Tannenberg, against a German army commanded by Paul von Hindenburg (1847-1934)

Aug 23–Nov 11

Russian troops enter Galicia; Battle of Lemberg/Lviv: Russian troops capture Lemberg

Aug 23

Austrian victory over Russian troops in the Battle of Kraśnik

Aug 24

Józef Piłsudski forms the Polish Legions (Legiony Polskie)

Aug 31

The Russian capital is renamed from St Petersburg to Petrograd by order of Tsar Nicholas II

1914

Sept 2–Nov 11

Austrian troops defeated by Russians at Rava-Rus'ka

Sep 6–Oct 4

The Battle of the Drina River between Austro-Hungarian and Serbian troops ends with heavy losses on both sides and is followed by a trench war

Sep 7–14

Defeat of the Russian Narev Army in the First Battle of the Masurian Lakes; the German army takes 45,000 Russian prisoners of war

Sep 14

The Slovak League (Slovenská liga) in the USA proclaims the Slovak nation's right to self-determination

Sep 15

Czernowitz/Chernivci, the capital of Bucovina, is occupied by Russian troops

Sep 24

Russian troops enter Hungarian territory

Sep 24–Mar 22 (1915)

Siege of the fortress of Przemyśl, which is captured by Russian troops

Sep 29–Oct 31

Battle of Warsaw between German and Russian troops

Oct 1

A secret Romanian-Russian agreement about the neutrality of Romania

Oct 4

The 'Manifest of the 93' is published in Germany, signed by intellectuals supporting German warfare

Oct 9–Nov 1

Occupation of Belgrade by the Central Powers

Oct 10

Death of King Carol I of Romania, succeeded by his nephew Ferdinand I (1865-1927)

Oct 16

The 'Declaration of the University Professors of the German Empire' in favor of duty and loyalty is published, signed by 3,000 German scholars

1914

Oct 22
Austro-Hungarian troops re-conquer Czernowitz/Chernivci, the capital of the Bucovina

Oct 29
The Ottoman fleet bombards Russian Black Sea ports

Nov 1
Russia declares war on the Ottoman Empire

Nov 2
Serbia declares war on the Ottoman Empire

Nov 4–5
France and Britain declare war on the Ottoman Empire

Nov 11
Sultan Mehmed V (1844-1918) declares Jihad (Holy War) on the Entente states

Nov 11–Dec 5
Battle of Łódź between German and Russian troops

Nov 16–Dec 15
The Battle on the Kolubara River ends with a Serbian victory over an Austro-Hungarian army

Nov 25
Declaration of the Polish National Committee (Komitet Narodowy Polski) by Roman Dmowski (1864-1939) at Warsaw

Nov 27
Austro-Hungarian troops quit Czernowitz/Chernivci

Dec 1–13
Austro-Hungarian troops prevent Russian troops from entering Hungary in the Battle of Limanowa

Dec 22–Jan 2 (1915)
Ottoman defeat against Russian troops in the Battle of Sarikamish, Caucasia

Dec 28
Italian troops occupy Vlora, Albania

1915

Jan 2–Apr 12
Russian offensive in the Carpathian Mountains

Jan 22
German-Austrian Carpathian offensive begins

Jan 25
Beginning of food rationing in Germany

Jan 31
German troops use combat gas (Xylylbromide) in the Battle of Bolimów against Russian soldiers

Feb 7–22
Russian defeat in the Second Battle of the Masurian Lakes and retreat from East Prussia; the German army takes 100,000 Russian prisoners of war

Feb 19
Allied offensive against the Dardanelles (Gallipoli campaign) begins

Mar 18
Russian troops occupy Memel/Klaipėda

Mar 22
Russian troops capture the fortress of Przemyśl

Apr 24
Beginning of the Armenian Genocide within the Ottoman Empire: deportation of Armenian intellectuals from Constantinople

Apr 25
Allied forces land on Gallipoli Peninsula

Apr 28
Beginning of the German offensive in Lithuania and Courland

May 2
Beginning of the Eastern offensive of the IX German Army and the IV Austrian Army (Gorlice-Tarnów offensive)

Apr 4
Italy leaves the alliance with Germany and Austria-Hungary

May 15–Jun 23
The Polish Legions win the Battle of Konary against Russian troops, with heavy losses on both sides

1915

Jun 3
Austro-Hungarian troops re-conquer the fortress of Przemyśl

Jun 11
Serbian troops occupy Albania

Jun 23
Italy declares war on Austria-Hungary

First Battle of the Isonzo confronting Austro-Hungarian and Italian troops

Creation of the military government for 'Ober Ost' (German-occupied territories in Courland, Lithuania and Belarus)

Jun 27
Austro-Hungarian troops re-enter Lemberg

Jul 6
At Geneva, in a speech dedicated to the 500th anniversary of the martyrdom of Jan Hus (1369-1415), Tomáš Garrigue Masaryk (1850-1937) outlines his idea of a Czechoslovak state without the Habsburg Empire

Jul 18–Aug 3
Second Battle of the Isonzo confronting Austro-Hungarian and Italian troops

Aug 5
German troops enter Warsaw

Aug 15
Italy declares war on the Ottoman Empire

Sep 5
Tsar Nicholas II appoints himself Commander-in-Chief of the Russian Army

Sep 19
German troops enter Vilnius

Oct 7–Dec 4
Invasion of Serbia by German, Austro-Hungarian and Bulgarian troops

Oct 14
Bulgaria declares war on Serbia and enters World War I

Oct 15
Britain and Montenegro declare war on Bulgaria

Oct 16
France declares war on Bulgaria

1915

Oct 18–Nov 4
Third Battle of the Isonzo confronting Austro-Hungarian and Italian troops

Oct 19
Italy and Russia declare war on Bulgaria

Nov 10–Dec 2
Fourth Battle of the Isonzo confronting Austro-Hungarian and Italian troops

Nov 10–Dec 4
Kosovo offensive of German, Austro-Hungarian and Bulgarian troops against the remnants of the Serbian army

Oct 15
Czech and Slovak exile organisations in the USA sign the Cleveland Agreement

Nov 15
The Czech Foreign Committee (Český komitét zahraniční) is formed

Dec 6–12
Defeat of French and British troops by Bulgarian units in the Battle of Kosturino

1916

Jan 5–17
Austro-Hungarian victory over Montenegro

Jan 9
End of the Gallipoli campaign, Ottoman victory

Feb 5–Apr 15
Russian victory over the Ottoman Empire in the Trebizond campaign

Mar 1–15
Fifth Battle of the Isonzo confronting Austro-Hungarian and Italian troops

Mar 17
In a Russian-French agreement, the 'Polish case' is declared a matter of interior Russian politics

Jun 4–Sep 20
Russian Brusilov offensive in Galicia against the Central Powers

Apr 4–Jun 6
Victory of the Polish Legions over Russian troops near Kostiuchnówka/ Kostyukhnivka, Volhynia

Aug 4
Romania and the Entente sign the Treaty of Bucharest, promising territorial gains in Austria-Hungary

Jun 6–Aug 17
The Sixth Battle of the Isonzo ends with the Italian occupation of Gorizia

Aug 17
Treaty of Bucharest between Romania and the Entente

Aug 27
Romania declares war on Austria-Hungary, and its troops enter Transylvania, occupying Kronstadt/Braşov

Aug 28
Italy declares war on Germany; Germany declares war on Romania

Aug 29
Paul von Hindenburg and Erich Ludendorff (1865-1937) become commanders of the German Highest Army Command (Oberste Heeresleitung, OHL)

Aug 30
The Ottoman Empire declares war on Romania and starts military operations in Dobruja

1916

Sep 1
Bulgaria declares war on Romania, and its troops – together with German units – enter the Dobruja, occupying the Fortress of Tutrakan/Turtucaia on September 6

Sep 5–7
Battle of Dobrich/Bazargic between forces of the Central Powers and Russo-Romanian troops

Sep 14–17
Seventh Battle of the Isonzo confronting Austro-Hungarian and Italian troops

Sep 17–19
First Battle of Cobadin in Dobruja

Sep 29–Oct 5
During the Flămânda offensive, Romanian troops attempt to invade Bulgaria

Sep 9–Oct 12
Eighth Battle of the Isonzo confronting Austro-Hungarian and Italian troops

Oct 19–25
Second Battle of Cobadin in Dobruja

Nov 1–4
Ninth Battle of the Isonzo confronting Austro-Hungarian and Italian troops

Nov 9
Formation of Polish Armed Forces (Polska Sila Zbrojna, 'Polnische Wehrmacht')

Nov 15
The Romanian War Council decides to suspend the Transylvanian campaign after heavy losses

Nov 21
The Austrian Emperor Franz Joseph I (1830-1916) dies and is succeeded by his great-nephew Karl I (1887-1922)

Nov 29–Dec 6
The Battle of Bucharest ends with the occupation of Romania without Moldava by troops of the Central Powers

Dec 6
Formation of the Provisional Polish State Council (Tymczasowa Rada

1916

Stanu) by the German and Austrian occupational forces

Dec 30
Assassination of Grigori Rasputin (1869-1916) in Russia

1917

Jan 7
Formation of the National Committee of Romanian Emigrants from Austria-Hungary Comitetul Naţional al Românilor Emigranţi din Austro-Ungariaat Iaşi

Mar 8–15
The February Revolution in Russia overthrows the monarchy

Mar 16
Vladimir I. Lenin (1870-1924) arrives at Petrograd from his Swiss exile

Mar 28
The Council of Workers' and Soldiers' Delegates at Petrograd proclaims the legitimacy of Poland's strive for independence

Apr 6
The United States of America declares war on Germany

May 3–4
Mass protests of workers in Petrograd

May 12–Jun 17
Tenth Battle of the Isonzo confronting Austro-Hungarian and Italian troops

Jun 30
Greece declares war on the Central Powers

Jul 1–19
Russian failure in the Kerensky offensive against the Central Powers

Jul 16–17
Petrograd July Days (public unrest)

Jul 21
Alexander Kerensky (1881-1970) Prime Minister of the Russian Provisional Government

Jul 22
Józef Piłsudski arrested by German forces and imprisoned at Magdeburg, after he renounced the Polish Legions' oath of fidelity towards Germany

1917

Jul 22–Aug 1
Offensive of the Romanian Army and Battle of Mărşăşti

Aug 6–Sep 3
Battle of Mărăşeşti between German and Romanian troops

Aug 8–22
In the Battle of Oituz, German and Austro-Hungarian troops defend the Oituz Gap against a Romanian offensive

Aug 18–28
Eleventh Battle of the Isonzo confronting Austro-Hungarian and Italian troops

Sep 1–5
German troops take Riga

Oct 5
Promised creation of the Kingdom of Poland, declaration by Emperor Wilhelm II of Germany and Franz Joseph of Austria

Oct 12–20
Operation 'Albion': German invasion of the Estonian islands

Oct 24–27
Twelfth Battle (Battle of Caporetto) of the Isonzo confronting Austro-Hungarian and Italian troops

Nov 7
October Revolution in Russia; the Petrograd Soviet seizes the Winter Palace

Dec 7
The United States of America declares war on Austria-Hungary

Dec 9
Cease-fire of Focşani between Romania and the Central Powers

Dec 15
Armistice between Russia and the Central Powers

1918

Jan 29
Battle of Kruty (Ukrainian-Soviet Russian War)

Jan 30
More than one million German workers participate in the 'January Strikes' for peace, democracy and better working conditions

Feb 1
Mutiny of the sailors at the Austro-Hungarian navy base of Cattaro

Feb 18–Mar 8
As a consequence of the unsuccessful peace negotiations with the Russian government, the Central Powers start 'Operation Faustschlag' in the southern sector of the front

Feb 21
German troops capture Minsk, Belarus

Feb 24
German troops capture Zhytomyr, Ukraine

Feb 25
German troops capture Tallinn, Estonia

Feb 28
German troops capture Pskov and Narva

Mar 2
German troops capture Kiev, Ukraine

Mar 3
Soviet Russia signs the Peace Treaty of Brest-Litovsk with the Central Powers, surrendering its claims to Ukraine, to the Polish and Baltic territories and to Finland

Mar 5
Provisional peace of Buftea between Romania and the Central Powers

Mar 13
Austro-Hungarian troops conquer Odessa

Mar 25
The Penza Agreement guarantees the free passage of the Czechoslovak Legion to Vladivostok

Apr 30
Czech and Slovak exile organisations in the USA conclude the Pittsburgh Agreement

1918

May 7
Peace Treaty of Bucharest between Romania and the Central Powers (which was never ratified)

May 21
Ottoman troops invade Armenia

Jun 5
Versailles Declaration of the Prime Ministers of France, Britain and Italy for the creation of an independent Polish state

Jun 8
German intervention in the Caucasus

Aug 1
British troops enter Vladivostok

Aug 3
Allied troops land at Archangel

Aug 5
The Czechoslovak People's Army of Komuch takes Kazan from the Red Army

Aug 16
US troops overrun by Bolshevik troops at Archangelsk

Aug 17
Turkish troops overthrow Caucasus

Sep 1
US troops land in Vladivostok, Siberia (until 1920)

Sep 4
US troops land in Archangel

Sep 8–23
Formation of the Provisional All-Russian Government at the Ufa Conference, with the help of the Czechoslovak Legion

Sep 14–29
Vardar offensive of joint Serbian, French and Greek forces against Bulgarian trenches

Sep 15
Victory of the Entente on the Balkan front

Sep 27
Capitulation of Bulgaria

Sep 30
Armistice between Bulgaria and the Entente states

Oct 21
Outbreak of revolutionary unrest in Austria

1918

Oct 27
Austria offers to the Allies an armistice and a separate peace

Oct 30
Bulgaria declares cease-fire

The Ottoman Empire signs an armistice with the Allies at Mudros

Oct 31
Liberation of Cracow Russian from Habsburg rule after the long-lasting partitions of Poland

Nov 1
Proclamation of the Western Ukrainian People's Republic; Ukrainian troops take over the power at Lwów, which stimulate the Polish-Ukrainian military conflict

Nov 3
Revolt of the German sailors and troops at Kiel, Hamburg, Rostock, Bremen and Berlin

The armistice of the Allies with Austria-Hungary is signed at Padova, Italy

Nov 7
Armistice signed in Compiegne, France

Nov 10
Romania renews the war against the Central Powers

Nov 11
Matthias Erzberger (1875-1921) and leader of the German Armistice Commission, signs the cease-fire in the Compiègne Wood on Germany's behalf, end of fighting at 11 a.m.

Nov 13
Soviet Russia cancels the Treaty of Brest-Litovsk

French and British troops occupy the area around Constantinople

Nov 18
Alexander Kolchak (1874-1920) becomes commander of the All-Russian Government

1919

Jan 18
Opening of the Paris Peace Conference

Jan 27
The Czechoslovak Legion seizes control of the Trans-Siberian Railway

Feb 3
The Red Army is defeated in a series of clashes with the White Russians

Feb 14–
Gradually beginning of the Polish-Soviet War

Mar 26
League of Nations Convenant adopted at the Paris Peace Conference

Apr 20
Polish Army captures Wilno/Vilnius from Red Army

Apr 28
Constitution of the League of Nations accepted by the Paris Peace Conference

May 2
Munich, Germany, occupied by regular Reichswehr and Freikorps troops

May 19–
Turkish War of Independence

May 22–July
First Battlle of Riga between the Latvian Army, German Freikorps, Baltic Landeswehr against the Red Army

Jun 6
Finland declares war against Bolsheviks (Finnish Civil War)

Jun 28
The German delegation signs the Peace Treaty of Versailles

Aug 4
Hungarian Soviet Republic overthrown by the Romanian Army, Béla Kun flees to Vienna, later to Soviet Russia

Sep 10
The Austrian delegation signs the Peace Treaty of Saint-Germain-en-Laye

Nov 3–11
Second Battle of Riga, Latvian Army supported by Estonians and the British Royal Navy against the German Frei-

1919

korps, Baltic Landeswehr and the West Russian Volunteer Army

Nov 14
The Red Army takes Omsk

Nov 16
Admiral Miklós Horthy (1868-1957), head of the Hungarian Army, seizes Budapest

Nov 19
US Senate rejects the Treaty of Versailles

Nov 27
The Bulgarian delegation signs the Peace Treaty of Neuilly

1920

Jan 10
League of Nations founded

Jan 20
The Red Army takes Irkutsk

Jan 21
End of the Paris Peace Conference

Feb 7
Armistice between the Red Army and the Czechoslovak Legion Admirad Alexander V. Kolchak (1874-1920) surrenders to the Bolshevik troops and is executed

Apr 20
Polish Army captures Wilno/Vilnius from Red Army

Apr 28
Soviet Russian troops occupy Baku

May 5
German-Latvian Peace Treaty signed

Polish and Ukrainian troops seize Kiev, following the Red Army's counter-offensive a month later

Jun 4
Peace Treaty of Trianon between Hungary and the Allies

Jun 6
Baron Pjotr Nikolaevich Wrangel (1878-1928) opens White Russian offensive against Red Army

Jun 25
League of Nations places International Court of Justice in The Hague (Den Haag), Netherlands

Jul 12
Peace Treaty between Lithuania and RSFSR

Aug 10
Peace Treaty of Sèvres between Turkey and the Allies

Ratification of the Treaty of Versailles

Aug 11
Peace of Riga, ackowledged independence of Latvia by RSFSR

1920

Aug 12–15
'Battle of Warsaw' between Poland and troops of the Red Army after the campaign of Red Army in Eastern Poland

Aug 14
Treaty between the Czechoslovak Republic and the Kingdom of Serbs, Croats and Slovenes (first step towards the Little Entente)

Nov 1
Headquarters of the League of Nations move to Geneva, Switzerland

Nov 12
Treaty of Rapallo between Italy and the Kingdom of Serbs, Croats and Slovenes: Italy annexes Zadar and establishes the Free State of Fiume

Nov 15
First general assembly of the League of Nations

Dec 16
Bulgaria admitted to League of Nations

1921

Jan 3
Turkey makes peace with Armenia

Jan 24
Paris Conference on reparations held

Feb 12–25
Soviet Russian troops invade Georgia

Mar 18
Peace Treaty of Riga signed, Poland enlarged

Apr 23
Treaty between the Czechoslovak Republic and the Kingdom of Romania

Jun 7
Treaty between the Kingdom of Romania and the Kingdom of Serbs, Croats and Slovenes

Aug 23
USA signs Peace Treaty with Austria

Aug 25
USA signs Peace Treaty with Germany

Aug 29
USA signs Peace Treaty with Hungary

Oct 13
Treaty of Kars between Soviet Russia and Turkey

1922

Jan 6–13
Conference of Cannes concerning German retribution payments

Apr 10–May 19
Genoa Conference: unsuccessful attempt to coordinate the reconstruction of Europe and Western relations with Germany and Soviet Russia

Apr 16
Treaty of Rapallo between Soviet Russia and Germany

Aug 31
Treaty between the Kingdom of Serbs, Croats and Slovenes and the Czechoslovak Republic

Sep 9
Turkish troops conquer Smyrna and murder Greek civilians

Sep 18
Hungary admitted to League of Nations

Oct 11
Turkey and Greece sign cease-fire

1923

Jul 24
Treaty of Lausanne between Turkey and the Allies

Dec 17
The League of Nations nominates the Davis Commission in order to establish an agreement over the Memelland

1924

Jan 27
Treaty of Rome between Italy and the Kingdom of Serbs, Croats and Slovenes

Timeline of political events in Central and Eastern Europe, 1917–1923

1917

Feb 18
First major strike of the Russian February Revolution starts at Putilov Factory in Petrograd, Russia

Mar 8
International Women's Day and riots in Sankt Petersburg, Russia

Mar 15
Last Russian Tsar Nicholas II (1868-1918) abdicates and nominates his brother Grand Duke Michail (1878-1918) to succeed him

Sep 18–22
Wilna Conference: Lithuanian politicians demand an independent, democratic state of Lithuania

Nov 7
Vladimir I. Lenin (1870-1924) and the Bolsheviks seize power and overthrow the provisional government in Russia

Dec 6
The Finnish Parliament declares the independence of Finland

Dec 25
Declaration of the Ukrainian People's Republic of the Soviets in Kharkiv, Ukraine

1918

Jan 8
US President Woodrow Wilson outlines his 'Fourteen Points' for peace after the Great War before Congress

Jan 16
Strikes in Austria and Germany

Jan 22
Historian and politician Mychajlo Hrushevskyj (1866-1934) proclaims Ukraine a free republic, giving birth to the Ukrainian People's Republic (Ukrajinska Narodnja Respublika, UNR)

Jan 25
Russia declared a Republic of Soviets

Feb 9
The Central Powers and the Ukrainian People's Republic sign the so-called 'Bread Peace' in Brest-Litovsk

Feb 1
Russia adopts the Gregorian calendar

In Finland, General Carl Gustav von Mannerheim (1867-1951) gathers the 'White Guard' to mount a counter revolution against the Bolsheviks

Feb 16
Lithuania declares independence from Russia and Germany

Feb 24
Estonia declares independence from Russia

Mar 4
First recorded case of Spanish flu (at Funston Army Camp, Kansas)

Mar 7
Finnish-German alliance

Mar 9
Russian Bolshevik Party becomes the Communist Party

1918

Mar 11
Moscow capital of Soviet Russia

Mar 13
Trotsky gains control of the Red Army

Mar 25
The Belarussian People's Republic is established

Mar 27
Bessarabia joins Romania

Apr 9
Latvia proclaims independence

Apr 29
Pavlo Skoropadsky (1873-1945) becomes Hetman of Ukraine

May 26
Georgian Social Democratic Republic declares independence from Russia

Armenia defeats the Ottoman Army at Sardarapat

May 28
Azerbaijan gains independence and declares itself a Democratic Republic

Armenia declares independence from Russia

Jun 29
Provisional government opposed to the Bolsheviks established at Vladivostok

Jul 4
Ottoman Sultan Mehmed VI (1861-1926) ascends the throne

Jul 10
Russian Soviet Federal Socialist Republic (RSFSR) was formed

Jul 17
Execution of the Romanov family in Yekaterinburg, Siberia

Sep 1
US troops land in Vladivostok, Siberia (until 1920)

Oct 3
Boris III (1894-1943) becomes king of Bulgaria, abdication of Tsar Ferdinand I (1861-1948)

Max von Baden (1867-1929) becomes chancellor of the German Empire and

1918

supports an armistice with the Entente powers

Oct 16
Declaration 'To my faithful Austrian peoples!' (Völkermanifest) by Emperor Karl I of Austria-Hungary offering equal rights to all nations of the Habsburg Empire, in a federal state state

Oct 17
German Emperor Wilhelm II (1859-1941) flees to the headquarters at Spa in occupied Belgium

Oct 18
Czechoslovakia declares independence from Austria-Hungary

Oct 19
Declaration of the State of Slovenes, Croats and Serbs in Zagreb

Formation of the Ukrainian National Council

Formation of the National Council of the Teschen Silesia

Oct 26
Resignation of Germany's supreme commander Erich Ludendorff (1865-1937)

Oct 28
Czechoslovakia gains independence

Oct 29
The Croatian Parliament at Zagreb declares itself independent from Austria-Hungary; foundation of the Republic of the Serbs, Croats and Slovenes

Oct 30
Slovak National Council asks for creation of a Czechoslovak state

Oct 31
Proclamation of independence of Hungary from the Habsburg Monarchy; victory of the Aster revolution in Budapest, formation of Mihály Károlyi's (1875-1955) national government

Nov 3
Austro-Hungarian Empire dissolves

Poland proclaims independence from Russia after World War I

1918

Revolt of German sailors and marines at Kiel

Nov 6
Republic of Poland proclaimed

Nov 7
Formation of a revolutionary government at Munich; the independent socialist politician Kurt Eisner (1867-1919) proclaims the Free State of Bavaria

Nov 8
Proclamation of the 'People's State of Bavaria' in Munich, Germany

Nov 9
German Prime Minister Max von Baden (1867-1929) announces the abdication of Emperor Wilhelm II of Germany and transfers the governmental responsibilities to Friedrich Ebert (1871-1925)

Parallel proclamation of the German Republic at Berlin by the social democrat Philipp Scheidemann (1865-1939) and the Socialist Republic of Germany by Karl Liebknecht (1871-1919)

Nov 10
Formation of a German Council of the People's Deputies by Friedrich Ebert (1871-1925, social democrat) and Hugo Haase (1863-1919, independent social democrat)

Nov 11
Austrian Emperor Karl I of Habsburg (1887-1922) de facto abdicates

Proclamation of the Polish Republic at Warsaw

Romania announces that it had unilaterally abrogated the Treaty of Bucharest and re-entered the war

Nov 12
Proclamation of the German-Austrian Republic at Vienna

Nov 13
King Friedrich August III of Saxony (1865-1932) abdicates

Stahlhelm forms as an anti-communist, anti-French and anti-Polish paramilitary unit in Magdeburg

1918

Nov 14
Proclamation of the Czechoslovak Republic

Nov 16
Hungarian People's Republic proclaimed

Nov 18
Latvia declares independence from Soviet Russia with Prime Minister Kārlis Ulmanis (1877-1942)

Nov 22
Józef Piłsudski becomes chief of state in Poland

Polish forces attack the Jewish community of Lviv/Lvóv/Lemberg

Nov 24
Béla Kun (1886-1938) forms Hungarian Communist Party

Nov 26
The Podgorica Assembly votes for the 'union of the people', declaring assimilation with the Kingdom of Serbia

Nov 28
The General Congress of Bucovina votes for the union with Romania

Nov 29
Serbia annexes Montenegro

King Wilhelm II of Württemberg (1848-1921) abdicates as the last German sovereign

Dec 1
Serbian-Croatian-Slovene Kingdom ('SHS State') proclaimed at Belgrade

At Alba Iulia/Karlsburg/Gyulafehérvár, the Romanians living in the Kingdom of Hungary declare the adhesion of Transylvania, the Banat and other former Hungarian regions to Greater Romania

Dec 14
Pavlo Skoropadsky abdicates as Hetman of Ukraine

Dec 16
German troops evacuate Finland

Dec 17
Power in Germany seized by the First German Congress of Workers' and Soldiers' Councils

1918

Dec 20
Landing of Allied troops in Crimea and in Latvia

Dec 27
Greater Poland Uprising in Grand Duchy of Posen against the German rule

1919

Jan 1
Belorussian Soviet Republic established

Pressburg/Bratislava annexed by Czechoslovak troops

Jan 5–12
Uprising of German Spartacus organisation in Berlin brutally suppressed by German troops

Jan 11
Romania annexes Transylvania

Hungary's National Council recognized Mihály Károlyi (1875-1955) as Prime Minister

Jan 15
Socialist politicians Rosa Luxemburg (1871-1919) and Karl Liebknecht tortured and murdered by Freikorps members in Berlin

Jan 18
Ignacy Jan Paderewski (1860-1941) becomes Polish Prime Minister

Jan 19
National elections in Germany to form a National Constituent Assembly

Jan 23-30
Czechoslovak-Polish border conflict over Teschen Silesia

Jan 25
Founding of the League of Nations

Feb 6
Opening of the German Constituent Assembly at Weimar

Feb 11
Friedrich Ebert (SPD) elected President of Germany by the German Constituent Assembly

Feb 21
German National Assembly accepts incorporation of Austria

Bavarian prime minister Kurt Eisner (1867-1919) assassinated in Munich, Germany

Feb 23
Foundation of the Fascist Party in Italy by Benito Mussolini (1883-1945)

1919

Mar 2
First Congress of Communist International opens at Moscow

Mar 3–11
General strike in Germany, organised by Communist Party (KPD)

Mar 4
Foundation of the Comintern at Moscow as a federation of all communist parties

Elections for the Austrian National Assembly

Demonstrations of members of the German minority in Czechoslovakia violently dissolved

Mar 12
Austrian National Assembly affirms incorporation into Germany

Mar 19
US Senate rejects the League of Nations

Mar 21
Foundation of the Hungarian Soviet Republic at Budapest, President Mihály Károlyi abdicates

Mar 23
8th Congress of the Russian Communist Party re-establishes a five-member Politburo (Vladimir I. Lenin, Leon Trotsky, Josef Stalin, Lev Kamenev, Nikolai Krestinskij)

Apr 3
Austria expels all Habsburgs

Apr 7
Kurt Eisner and his revolutionary government Bavaria proclaimed as a Soviet Republic, while the legitimate government of Prime Minister Johannes Hofmann (1867-1930) flees from Munich to Bamberg

Apr 20
King Nikola of Montenegro (1841-1921) abdicates

May 19-
Turkish War of Independence

Jun 20
Philipp Scheidemann resigns as chancellor of the German Republic

1919

Jul 17
Finland adopts constitution

Jul 31
Weimar Constitution adopted, establishing the German Republic

Aug 11
The German Constituent Assembly at Weimar votes a democratic-parliamentarian constitution

Aug 17
First Silesian Uprising in Upper Silesia against Germany

Sep 12
Italian poet and right-wing agitator Gabriele D'Annunzio takes Fiume/Rijeka for Italy

Adolf Hitler (1889-1945) joins the Deutsche Arbeiterpartei (DAP) as its seventh member

Oct 6
Aleksandar Stamboliyski (1879-1923) becomes Prime Minister of Bulgaria

Nov 27
Ignacy Jan Paderewski resigns as Polish Prime Minister

Dec 10
Nobel Peace Price awarded to US President Woodrow Wilson

Dec 15
Fiume/Rijeka declares its independence

1920

Jan 16
Georgia declares independence

Feb 2
Estonia declares its independence, recognised by the RSFSR (Dorpat Peace)

Feb 10
General Józef Haller (1873-1960) performs symbolic 'wedding of Poland to the sea'

The Kingdom of Serbia-Croatia-Slovenia admitted to League of Nations

Plebiscite in Schleswig: North Schleswig ceded from Germany to Denmark

Feb 24
Formation of the NSDAP at Munich

Mar 1
Miklós Horthy elected Regent of Hungary by the Hungarian National Assembly at Budapest

Mar 13–17
Unsuccessful military group plot in Germany lead by the state officer Wolfgang Kapp (1858-1922); in response, Red Ruhr Army activities in the Ruhr Industrial Area

Mar 28
Tomás Garrigue Masaryk elected President of Czechoslovakia

Apr 20
Balfour Declaration makes Palestine a British Mandate

Apr 23
The Turkish Grand National Assembly at Ankara denounces the government of Sultan Mehmed VI and announces a temporary constitution

Apr 27
Ukraine declares independence

May 7
RSFSR recognises Georgian independence

Jun 6
First parliamentary elections in Germany; losses for the 'Weimar coalition'

1920

Jul 28
Duchy of Teschen divided between Czechoslovakia and Poland along the Olza River

Aug 20
Beginning of the Second Uprising in Upper Silesia

Sep 8
Gabriele d'Annunzio (1863-1938) proclaims the Italian Regency of Carnaro at Fiume

Oct 10
Plebiscite in Carinthia: South Carinthia in favour of Austria

Oct 17
First parliamentary elections in Austria: victory of the Christian Social Party

Carinthian plebiscite, most of Carinthia remains part of the Austrian Republic

Nov 15
Danzig/Gdańsk declared 'Free Town' under mandate of the League of Nations

1921

Jan 20
Daghestan Republic formed inside the RSFSR

Republic of Turkey declared

Mar 1–17
Sailors' revolt at Kronstadt, Russia, bloodily repressed by Bolshevik troops

Mar 17
Vladimir I. Lenin proclaims New Economic Politics (NEP)

The Second Republic of Poland adopts the March Constitution

Mar 17–Apr 1
'March fights' in Germany under influence of Comintern

Mar 20
Plebiscite in Upper Silesia under the auspices of the League of Nations

Mar 23
Germany declares it will be unable to meet its reparation payments

Mar 26–Apr 6
First restoration crisis in Hungary after Karl von Habsburg crosses the Hungarian border

Apr 11
Turkestan ASSR forms in RSFSR

May 2
Third Silesian Uprising against Germany

May 23
Battle of Annaberg in Upper Silesia, German Freikorps and Selbstschutz troops against Polish insurgents and troops with an armistice under Allied supervision on July 5

Jun 28
New constitution for the Kingdom of Serbs, Croats and Slovenes ('Vidovdan Constitution')

Aug 16
King Petar I of SHS (1844-1921) dies, Aleksandar I (1888-1934) becomes new king

1921

Aug 14–20
Declaration of the 'Serb Hungarian Republic of Baranja-Baja' from Hungary fails due to lacking support from Belgrade

Aug 26
Former German minister of finances Mathias Erzberger (1875-1921) assassinated

Oct 20–Nov 6
Second restoration crisis in Hungary with Karl von Habsburg attempting again to seize power in Budapest; the Hungarian parliament bans the Habsburg from Hungarian territory

Dec 14–16
Plebiscite at Sopron/Ödenburg and in the Burgenland, Sopron remains to Hungary

403

1922

Jan 2
Crimea declares independence

Jan 8
Elections in the Wilna area with a strong majority for the pro-Polish forces

Mar 3
Italian fascists occupy Fiume/Rijeka

Apr 3
Josef Stalin (1878-1953) is appointed General Secretary of the Russian Communist Party

Apr 7
Constitution for the Burgenland, the former West Hungarian territories in Austria

Apr 22
South Ossetian Autonomous Region forms in Georgian SSR

May 15
Germany turns over East Upper Silesia to Poland

May 28–June 2
Parliamentary elections in Hungary

June 24
German foreign minister Walther Rathenau (1867-1922) assassinated

July 5
Introduction of the Nansen passport for stateless refugees, on the initiative of the Norwegian polar expert and diplomat Fridtjof Nansen (1861-1930)

Sep 16
Turkish troops chase Greeks out of Asia

Oct 4
Protocols of Geneva between Austria, Great Britain, France, Italy and Czechoslovakia

Oct 6
The Great Powers withdraw from Istanbul

Oct 10–11
Elections to the first Sejm in Lithuania: the Christian Conservatives and the Agrarians gain a majority

Oct 28
Italian fascists conduct the March on Rome

1922

Nov 1
Mustafa Kemal Atatürk (1881-1938) takes Constantinople from the last Ottoman sultan, Mehmed VI, and proclaims the Republic of Turkey

Dec 1
Polish state chief Marshal Józef Piłsudski resigns

Dec 9
Polish-Swiss hydroelectric engineer and politician Gabriel Narutowicz (1865-1922) elected President of the Republic of Poland

Dec 10
Fridtjof Nansen granted the Nobel Peace Price

Dec 16
Polish President Gabriel Narutowicz assassinated by a nationalist

Dec 20
Polish parliament elects socialist politician Stanisław Wojciechowski (1869-1953) as President

Dec 30
Creation of the USSR as a federation of RSFSR, Ukrainian SSR, Belorussian SSR and Transcaucasian SSR

1923

Jan 9–16
Lithuania seizes and annexes the Memelland, accepted by the Allies on February 16

Jan 11
Occupation of the German Ruhr Industrial Area by French and Belgian troops

Feb 18
Czechoslovak finance minister Alois Rašín (1867-1923) assassinated by an anarchist

Apr 18
Poland annexes Central Lithuania

May 12–13
Elections to the Second Sejm in Lithuania: Christian Democrats gain a majority

Jun 9
Bulgarian Prime Minister Aleksandar Stamboliyski (1879-1923) and King Boris III overthrown by soldiers under the command of general Ivan Valkov (1875-1962)

Jun 14
Bulgarian Prime Minister Aleksandar Stamboliyski assassinated

Aug 6
Gustav Stresemann (1878-1929) named chancellor and foreign minister of Germany

Sep 26
End of the passive resistance in the Ruhr industrial area proclaimed

Oct 24
General Otto von Lossow (1868-1938) calls Reichswehr to Berlin to form a dictatorship

Oct 29
Republic of Turkey declares independence

Nov 2–27
Street fights in Aachen, Germany, lead to establishment of the Rhenish Republic, with its seat at Koblenz, Germany

1923

Nov 8–9
Adolf Hitler and Erich von Ludendorff stage the 'Beer Hall Putsch' in Munich

Nov 12
Adolf Hitler arrested for attempt to seize power

Nov 23
German army commander General Hans von Seeckt (1866-1936) with special mandate bans NSDAP and KPD

Nov 30
Wilhelm Marx (1863-1946) becomes German chancellor

Image credits

Introduction

1. Wikimedia Commons
2. Narodowe Archiwum Cyfrowe, 3/1/0/9/1304
3. *Frontul Mărăşeşti*, year 3, no. 15, October 1933, 1 (Biblioteca Digitală, Cluj-Napoca)
4. *The New York Tribune*, 9 November 1919
5. Narodowe Archiwum Cyfrowe, 3/22/0/-/379/7
6. *Schweizer Illustrierte Zeitung*, 21 May 1921
7. *Muskete*, 16 January 1919
8. Wikimedia Commons
9. Europeana, Österreichische Nationalbibliothek, k.u.k. Kriegspressequartier, WK1/ALB034/09350
10. Österreichische Nationalbibliothek, k.u.k. Kriegspressequartier, WK1/ALB102/30976
11. Wikimedia Commons
12. Wikimedia Commons, Dr. Franc Sušnik's central library of Carinthia, in Ravne na Koroškem, Slovenia
13. Emil Horn, *Mihály Biró*, (Hannover: PlakatKonzepte, 1996)
14. Wikimedia Commons, Muzeum Narodowe Warszawa
15. Arhivele Naţionale ale României
16. Wikimedia Commons
17. Österreichische Nationalbibliothek, k.u.k. Kriegspressequartier, WK1/ALB088/25693
18. Borys Stepanovych Butnik-Siverskii, *Sovetskii plakat epokhi grazhdanskoi voiny, 1918-1921* (Moskva: Izd-vo Vses. knizhnoĭ palaty,1960), poster number 486
19. Narodowe Archiwum Cyfrowe, 3/22/0/-/242/1
20. Bundesarchiv, Bild 183-S36074
21. Wikimedia Commons, Centralne Archiwum Wojskowe
22. Wikimedia Commons
23. Wikimedia Commons
24. Wikimedia Commons
25. Imperial War Museum, London
26. Wikimedia Commons
27. Wikimedia Commons
28. Wikimedia Commons
29. Wikimedia Commons
30. Wikimedia Commons
31. Wikimedia Commons
32. *Der wahre Jakob*, 1921
33. Wikimedia Commons
34. *Illustrierte Kronen Zeitung*, 2 December 1918
35. Národní knihovna v Praze
36. *Der wahre Jacob*, no. 902, 1921
37. Wikimedia Commons, Magyar Elektronikus Könyvtár, Budapest
38. *Le Petit Journal*, September 1920
39. Wikimedia Commons, *Videňské noviny* vol. 16, 20 (1921)
40. Biblioteka Uniwersytecka w Toruniu
41. Wikimedia Commons
42. *Vorwärts*, 9 November 1917
43. *l'Humanité*, 9 November 1917
44. Wikimedia Commons
45. Book cover, 1922
46. Wikimedia Commons
47. Wikimedia Commons
48. Wikimedia Commons
49. Bundesarchiv, Bild Y 1-488-10112
50. Image from the film 'J'accuse', France 1919
51. Staatsbibliothek zu Berlin
52. Gróf Esterházy Károly Múzeum Pápa, Hungary
53. Image of 'National Trust', Wallington, Northumberland, UK
54. Wikimedia Commons
55. Russian State Library, Moscow
56. Biblioteka Uniwersytecka w Poznaniu
57. Wikimedia Commons, Bundesarchiv, Bild 146-1987-028-03
58. World Digital Library
59. Forward Association, YIVO encyclopedia

60. Wikimedia Commons

61. From the documentary 'Moskau an der Spree', fluter, Nikita Zibisow

Jay Winter

1. Wikimedia Commons

2. Leopold Haimson with Giulio Sapell (eds.), *Strikes, Social Conflict and the First World War. An International Perspective* (Milano: Feltrinelli, 1992)

   Table 1. Konrad Roesler, *Die Finanzpolitik des Deutschen Reiches im Ersten Weltkrieg* (Berlin: Duncker & Humblot, 1967), Appendix Table 13

   Table 2. Theo Balderston, 'War Finance and Inflation in Britain and Germany, 1914-1918,' *Economic History Review* vol. 42, 2 (1989), Table 8, 237

3. Urban Media Archive of the Center for Urban History of East Central Europe, collection of Ihor Kotlobulatov, Lviv

4. Wikimedia Commons

History of Conflicts

Image: *Bericht über den Zustand der Kunstdenkmäler auf den verschiedenen Kriegsschauplätzen und über die deutschen und österreichischen Maßnahmen zu ihrer Erhaltung, Rettung, Erforschung.* Ed. Paul Clemen with assistance of Gerhard Bersu, vol. 2 (Leipzig: E.A. Seemann, 1919), 111

Jochen Böhler

1. Wikimedia Commons, Russian State Library, Alexander Apsit

2. Getty Images

3. Copy right of the map: Peter Palm

4. Narodowe Archiwum Cyfrowe, 1-H-356-10

5. Hoover Institution Archives, James A. Stader Papers, Stanford

6. Narodowe Archiwum Cyfrowe, 1-H-476

Ibolya Murber

1. Österreichische Nationalbibliothek, Otto Croy, NB 502811-B

2. Österreichische Nationalbibliothek, Bruno Frei, Pk 3306, 17

3. Österreichische Nationalbibliothek, Richard Hauffe, S 646/15

4. Wikimedia Commons

5. Wikimedia Commons

6. Österreichische Nationalbibliothek, Pf 27.556 D (1)

7. Universität Pécs, Bibliothek für Sozialwissenschaften, Plakatsammlung (Magyar-szovjet plakátok 1917-1977)

8. Österreichische Nationalbibliothek, PLA16341478

9. Österreichische Nationalbibliothek, Albert Hilscher, H 680/1

Rastko Lompar

1. Wikimedia Commons

2. Petar Požar, *Jugoslaveni-žrtve staljinskih čistki: dokumentarna kronika* (Zagreb: Nova knj., 1989)

3. National Library of Serbia

4. *Četrdeset godina: zbornik sećanja aktivista jugoslovenskog revolucionarnog radničkog pokreta.* Knj. 1, 1917-1929 (Beograd: Kultura, 1960), 42

5. National Library of Serbia, postcard

6. *Zbornik sećanja aktivista jugoslovenskog radničkog* vol. 1, (Beograd: Kultura, 1960)

7. Wikimedia Commons

Attila Simon

1. Fórum Kisebbségkutató Intézet (Forum Minority Research Institute)

2. Fórum Kisebbségkutató Intézet (Forum Minority Research Institute)

3. Fórum Kisebbségkutató Intézet (Forum Minority Research Institute)

4. Fórum Kisebbségkutató Intézet (Forum Minority Research Institute)

5. Title page of *Kassai Munkás* (The Worker of Košice), 25 January 1919

6. Fórum Kisebbségkutató Intézet (Forum Minority Research Institute)

7. Fórum Kisebbségkutató Intézet (Forum Minority Research Institute)

8. Fórum Kisebbségkutató Intézet (Forum Minority Research Institute)

9. Fórum Kisebbségkutató Intézet (Forum Minority Research Institute)

Wolfgang Templin

1. Library of Congress

2. Library of Congress

3. Wikimedia Commons

4. Provisorial map of the Ukrainian People's Republic, 1919. *The People's Atlas*. London Geographical Institute (ed.), (London: 1920), 50

5. Diplomatic notes of the Ukrainian delegation to the Paris Peace Conference from February to April 1919. Library of the University of Toronto

6. Österreichische Nationalbibliothek, Pf 27.556 D (1)

History of Ideas

Image: Wikimedia Commons

Burkhard Olschowsky

1. Wikimedia Commons

2. Deutsche Fotothek, reproduction of a image of the Uljanov family for a book at the Lenin Museum in Moscow; Photographer: Richard Peter sen. (1965)

3. Wikimedia Commons

4. Wikimedia Commons, New York Evening Mail

5. Österreichische Nationalbibliothek, k.u.k. Kriegspressequartier, WK1/ ALB099/29907

6. Wikimedia Commons, Istituto Centrale per il Catalogo Unico, Roma

7. Wikimedia Commons, Bundesarchiv, Bild 183-R92623 / CC-BY-SA 3.0

8. Encyclopedia of Virginia, https://web3.encyclopediavirginia.org

9. Book cover

10. Wikimedia Commons, Library of Congress

11. Cartoon by Clifford Berryman, https://fineartamerica.com

12. Penobscot Marine Museum in Searsport, Maine

13. Wikimedia Commons

14. Wikimedia Commons, Bundesarchiv, Bild 102-12859A

15. Library of Congress

16. Wikimedia Commons

17. Cartoon of Walt Munson, *American Economist* 64 (1919)

18. Wikimedia Commons

19. Wikimedia Commons

Marco Bresciani

1. Wikimedia Commons, www.trevisotoday.it

2. Wikimedia Commons

3. Wikimedia Commons

4. L'archivio fotografico dell'Istituto Luce, Roma

5. Book cover

6. Fototeca Civici Musei di Storia e Arte, Trieste

7. Book cover

8. Book cover

9. Museo Nazionale, Roma, poster painted by Carlo Vittorio, 1932

Piotr Juszkiewicz

1. Deutsches Historisches Museum, Berlin/A. Psille

2. Wikimedia Commons

3. Wikimedia Commons

4. Muzeum Sztuki, Łódź

5. Wikimedia Commons, Pushkin Museum of Fine Arts, Moscow

6. Public Domian, https://www.wikiart.org

7. Wikimedia Commons

8. Wikimedia Commons

9. Wienbibliothek im Rathaus, Plakatsammlung, P-441

10. Wikimedia Commons, Bwag

11. Wikimedia Commons

12. Wikimedia Commons

13. N. A. Miljutin, *Sozgorod. Probleme des Planens sozialistischer Städte. Grundlegende Prinzipen bei der Planung und beim Bau von Siedlungen in der UdSSR* (Berlin: DOM, 2008)

Territorial History

Image: Wikimedia Commons

Arnold Suppan

1. *Washington Evening Sun*, 18 February 1919

2. Woodrow Wilson Presidential Library

3. Digital Commonwealth, Massachussetts Collection Online

4. Postage stamp of 'Deutschösterreich', 1920

6. Cover of the magazine *La Domenica del Corriere*, 10-17 November 1918

7. Book title by František Cajthaml, *Sláva a pad provincie Deutschböhmen* (Ústí nad Labem: 1919)

8. Postcard emitted in Vienna by the 'Hilfsverein für Deutschböhmen und das Sudetenland', 1919

László Szarka

1. Wikimedia Commons
2. Map designed by the Research Institute of Ethnic and National Minorities, Budapest
3. Wikimedia Commons
4. Wikimedia Commons
5. Wikimedia Commons
6. Map designed by the Research Institute of Ethnic and National Minorities, Budapest
7. Wikimedia Commons
8. Contemporary postcard, private

Andreea Dăncilă

1. From The Historical Atlas by William R. Shepherd, University of Texas at Austin, 1911
2. http://www.vaidavoevod.ro
3. Wikimedia Commons
4. Wikimedia Commons, contemporary postcard
5. University Library of Szeged
6. Wikimedia Commons, https://transilvaniareporter.ro

Marcela Sălăgean

1. Wikimedia Commons
2. Wikimedia Commons
3. Wikimedia Commons
4. Wikimedia Commons, Bundesarchiv, Bild 183-2000-0518-507
5. Wikimedia Commons
6. Wikimedia Commons
7. Wikimedia Commons
8. Wikimedia Commons

Beka Kobakidze

1. Imperial War Museum, London
2. Design of the map: Andrew Andersen and George Partskhaladze
3. Georgian National Archives
4. Georgian National Archives
5. Design of the map: Andrew Andersen and George Partskhaladze
6. Design of the map: Andrew Andersen and George Partskhaladze

7. Georgian National Archives
8. Georgian National Archives

Economic and Social History

Image: Wikimedia Commons

Maciej Górny, Włodzimierz Borodziej

1. Wikimedia Commons
2. Wikimedia Commons
3. Wikimedia Commons
4. Wikimedia Commons
5. Wikimedia Commons
6. Wikimedia Commons
7. Wikimedia Commons
8. Wikimedia Commons

Oliver Schulz

1. National Library 'Kiril i Metodi', Sofia
2. Wikimedia Commons
3. Regional Library, Varna
4. Regional Library, Varna
5. Regional Library, Varna
6. Contemporary postcard, http://denstorekrig1914-1918.dk
7. Regional Library, Varna

Andrei Zamoiski

1. Estonian Archives EAA
2. Atlas gistoryi Belarusi, eds. Larisa Yazykovitch et al. (Minsk: Belen, 2004)
3. Atlas gistoryi Belarusi, eds. Larisa Yazykovitch et al. (Minsk: Belen, 2004)
4. Wikimedia Commons
5. Wikimedia Commons
6. Estonian Archives EAA
7. Z.S. Ostrovskiy, Evreyskie pogromy v 1918-1921 gg. (Moskva: Izdatel'stvo shkola i kniga, 1926)
8. Z.S. Ostrovskiy, Evreyskie pogromy v 1918-1921 gg. (Moskva: Izdatel'stvo shkola i kniga, 1926)
9. New York Public Library, Manuscripts and Archives Division

Alex Hofmeister

1. Wikimedia Commons

2. Österreichische Nationalbibliothek, Jüdischer Nationalrat für Deutsch-Österreich, PLA16304026

3. Institute for Jewish Research YIVO

4. Museum of the History of Polish Jews (POLIN), Postcard

5. Österreichische Nationalbibliothek, Louis Lamm, KS 16322101

6. Jewish Historical Institute (ZIH), Warszawa

7. Leibniz Institut für Länderkunde (IfL), Leipzig; Source: Sächsische Akademie der Wissenschaften und Dan Diner (ed.), *Enzyklopädie jüdischer Geschichte und Kultur*, vol. 4 (Stuttgart et al.: J. B. Metzler, 2013), 191

8. Österreichische Nationalbibliothek, Imre Földes, PLA16300086

9. Narodowe Archiwum Cyfrowe, 3/1/0/9/1431/1

10. Wikimedia Commons, Lietuvas Albomas (Berlin: Elsner, 1921), 47

11. Jewish Museum of Latvia, Private collection of Shaul Cohen-Mintz and Daphna Cohen-Mintz

12. The David B. Keidan Collection of Digital Images from the Central Zionist Archives: Photographs on the History of Zionism and Israel/Judaica Division, Widener Library, Harvard University

13. Jewish Historical Institute (ZIH), Warszawa

14. Wikimedia Commons, Zsigmond Kunfi, *Die Neugestaltung der Welt* (Wien: Wiener Volksbuchhandlung ,1930)

15. The David B. Keidan Collection of Digital Images from the Central Zionist Archives: Photographs on the History of Zionism and Israel/Judaica Division, Widener Library, Harvard University

16. Narodowe Archiwum Cyfrowe, 3/22/0/-/379/5

17. Centralna Biblioteka Judaistyczna

Psychological Consequences of War

Image: Wikimedia Commons

Marek Syrný

1. Österreichische Nationalbibliothek, AKON, AK082_413

2. Slovenský Národný Archív, Bratislava

3. Library of Congress

4. Photo: Tobias Weger, 7 November 2019

5. Múzeum Slovenského Národného Povstania, Banská Bystrica

6. Múzeum Slovenského Národného Povstania, Banská Bystrica

7. Wikimedia Commons

8. Wikimedia Commons, Private Archive Ákos Neidenbach, Csabánko, Hungary

9. Wikimedia Commons, Private Archive Ákos Neidenbach, Csabánko, Hungary

Joanna Urbanek

1. Wikimedia Commons, Henry Maull

2. Wikimedia Commons, National Library of Medicine

3. Wikimedia Commons

4. Wikimedia Commons

5. Wikimedia Commons

6. Book cover, 2012 edition

7. Wikimedia Commons

8. Wikimedia Commons, Narodowe Archiwum Cyfrowe, Władysław Miernicki, 20-114

9. Cover of the journal, Biblioteka Narodowa, Warszawa

10. Wikimedia Commons, Instytut Pamięci Narodowej

11. Reddit Inc

12. Austria-Forum, Christian Brandstätter Verlag, Wien

13. University Library of Tübingen

14. Journal *Przegląd Lekarski* nr 48 (1917), Jagiellonian Library, Kraków

15. Wikimedia Commons, American Red Cross

16. Wikimedia Commons, *Rocznik Psychjatryczny Zeszyt* 16 (1931)

17. Wikimedia Commons

Karolina Łabowicz-Dymanus

1. Wikimedia Commons

2. Magazine Polityka

3. Wikimedia Commons

4. Wikimedia Commons

5. Wikimedia Commons

6. Narodowe Archiwum Cyfrowe, Edward Dulewicz, 1-P-32-9

7. Moravská galerie, Brno

History of Memory

Image: Wikimedia Commons

Bartosz Dziewanowski-Stefańczyk

1. Narodowe Archiwum Cyfrowe, 1-H-223-1
2. Wikimedia Commons
3. Contemporary postcard, private
4. Wikimedia Commons
5. Narodowe Archiwum Cyfrowe, 1-P-2864-3
6. Wikimedia Commons
7. Narodowe Archiwum Cyfrowe, 1-P-2943-3
8. Wikimedia Commons, Cyfrowa Biblioteka Narodowa Polona
9. Wikimedia Commons
10. Wikimedia Commons

Vasilius Safronovas

1. Wikimedia Commons
2. Lithuanian Central State Archives
3. Lithuanian Central State Archives, postcard
4. Book cover of J. Shilietis, *Vokiečių okupacija Lietuvoje 1915-1919 m. paveiksléliuose ir trumpuose jų aprašymuose /The German Occupation in Lithuania 1915-1919*. Related in Pictures and Short Descriptions (Kaunas: Varpas, 1922)
5. Pages of Jaroslavas Šilietis' drawings album showing various scenes from popular memories about the German occupation in Lithuania 1915-1919
6. Lithuanian Central State Archives

Florin Abraham

1. Valentin Tănase
2. Muzeul Național al Literaturii Române, Bucarest
3. Valentin Tănase
4. Screenshot from the film 'Pădurea spânzuraților'
5. Muzeul Național al Literaturii Române, Bucarest
6. Central Committee for National Patriotic Organisations, London

Contributors

Abraham, Florin

PD Dr. habil., Associate Professor in Political Science at the Faculty of Communication of the National University of Political Science and Public Administration in Bucharest and senior researcher within the National Institute for the Study of Totalitarianism. Research priorities: Central European history in the 20th century, democratisation of European post-communist societies, history of international relations and of the European Union.

Böhler, Jochen

PD Dr. habil., substitute for the chair of East European History at the Friedrich Schiller University in Jena since 2019. Research priorities: Eastern European history (regional and transnational); war, violence and occupation research; nationalism studies.

Borodziej, Włodzimierz †

Professor at the History Department of Warsaw University. Latest research priorities: international relations during the 'short' 20th century; the Great War, its aftermath and remembrance in Eastern and Central Europe; the first three decades of the III. Republic of Poland (1989-2019).

Bresciani, Marco

Ph.D., Researcher in Contemporary History at the Department of Political and Social Sciences at the University of Florence. Research priorities: intellectual and political history of antifascism and antitotalitarianism, fascism in Italy and Europe, post-war transitions and crises.

Dăncilă, Andreea Ineoan

Ph.D. in History, Custodian at the David Prodan Memorial Museum, Cluj-Napoca, Romania. Research priorities: post-war revolutions (1918-1919); cultural, political and ecclesiastical Transylvanian elite (1900-1919), diplomatic relations between Romanian Kingdom and Austria-Hungary (1900-1919).

Dziewanowski-Stefańczyk, Bartosz

Ph.D. in History, Deputy Head of the academic department at the European Network Remembrance and Solidarity (ENRS). Research priorities: Polish-German relations, Polish cultural diplomacy and memory politics, monetary history.

Górny, Maciej

Professor at the Tadeusz Manteuffel Institute of History at the Polish Academy of Sciences. Research priorities: history of East Central Europe in the 19th and 20th centuries, history of science, history of historiography and First World War studies.

Hofmeister, Alexis

Ph.D., Lecturer at the chair of East European History at Basel University. Research priorities: comparative imperial history of Russia, Jews and other minorities in Eastern Europe, autobiographical texts as historical sources.

Juszkiewicz, Piotr

Professor at the Institute of Art History at Adam Mickiewicz University in Poznań. Research priorities: history of art, history in Central and Eastern Europe, Polish Modernism from the 1890's to 1960's, Polish and European art criticism from 18th century to 20th century.

Kobakhidze, Beka

Ph.D., Associate Professor at Ilia State University in Tbilisi, and lecturer at the Georgian Institute of Public Affairs (GIPA). Research priorities: Democratic Republic of Georgia (1918-1921); contested regional history, narratives and memories of modern Caucasus; historic geopolitical intersections of Russia and the political West in the Caucasus.

Łabowicz-Dymanus, Karolina

Ph.D., Lecturer at the Institute of Art at the Polish Academy of Sciences. where she now works as a faculty member. Research priorities: writing of art history in Poland in the 1950s, cultural dimensions of the global Cold War, theory and aesthetics of art from the socialist to the contemporary era, artistic and institutional responses to the post-1989 transformation.

Lompar, Rastko

Ph.D., candidate in History at the University of Belgrade and Research Associate at the Institute for Balkan Studies of the Serbian Academy for Sciences and Arts. Research priorities: fascism and anticommunism in the Kingdom of Yugoslavia, religion and nationalism in the Kingdom of Yugoslavia, history of the Communist Party of Yugoslavia.

Murber, Ibolya

PD Dr. habil., Associate Professor at the Eötvös Loránd University in Budapest/Szombathely. Research priorities: Austro-Hungarian relations in the 20th century, interwar paramilitarism in Central Europe, crisis management in post-war Austria and Hungary.

Olschowsky, Burkhard

Ph.D., Research Associate at the Federal Institute for Culture and History of the Germans in Eastern Europe, Oldenburg. Research priorities: German and Polish history in the 20th century, biographical studies, comparative social history.

Rydel, Jan

Professor at the Institute for Political Science at the Pedagogical University in Kraków, Poland. Research priorities: German-Polish and Austrian-Polish relations in the 19th and 20th centuries, politics of memory, military history.

Safronovas, Vasilijus

Ph.D., Research Professor at the Institute of Baltic Region History and Archaeology of Klaipėda University. Research priorities: Baltic history in the 19th and 20th centuries, memory studies, conceptual history and mental geography, First World War impact on the Lithuanian and East Prussian cultures and societies.

Sălăgean, Marcela

Professor at the Department of International Studies and Contemporary History at the Babeş-Bolyai University in Cluj-Napoca, Romania. Research priorities: contemporary history of Romania, political regimes and international relations in the 20th and 21st centuries.

Schulz, Oliver

Ph.D., historian, Lecturer at the Unit of Formation and Research (UFR) Languages, Cultures, Communication, Department for German Studies at the Université Clermont Auvergne, France. Research priorities: nationalism and anti-Semitism, international and global history, war in historiography and memory.

Simon, Attila

PD Dr. habil., historian, Director of the Forum Minority Research Institute in Samorin and Associate Professor of the Selye János University in Komárno. Research priorities: history of Slovakia between the two world wars, history of Hungarians in Slovakia between the two world wars, history of Jews in Southern Slovakia.

Suppan, Arnold

Emeritus Professor of East European History at the University of Vienna and full member of the Austrian Academy of Sciences. Research priorities: East-Central Europe in the 'short' 20th century, the Habsburg monarchy and its aftermath, history of the Austrian Academy of Sciences.

Syrný, Marek

PD Dr. habil., Assistant Professor at the Faculty of Political Science and International Relations at University of Matej Bel and historian in the Museum of the Slovak National Uprising, both in Banská Bystrica. Research priorities: Slovak history in the years 1938-1948, European and Slovak history in the 20th century, anticommunist exile after WW II.

Szarka, László

PD Dr. habil., Associate Professor and Senior Researcher at the Institute of History of the Centre of Human Sciences in Budapest and at the Department of History at the Selye University in Komárno. Research priorities: history of national policy in Austria-Hungary in the 19th century, history of minority policy during the interwar period in Central Europe, history of the multi-ethnic nation-states in East Central Europe.

Templin, Wolfgang

M.A., philosopher, publicist, protagonist of the democratic opposition movement in the GDR. Research priorities: Polish and Ukrainian history of the 20th century, history and politics in Eastern Europe, reappraisal of the history of the German Democratic Republic.

Urbanek, Joanna

Ph.D., historian and psychologist, curator at the House of European History in Brussels. Research priorities: social history of Europe in the 20th century, history of medicine, European contemporary history in exhibitions.

Winter, Jay

Charles J. Stille Emeritus Professor of History at Yale University. Research priorities: First World War, history and memory, cultural history.

Zamoiski, Andrei

Ph.D., historian, German-Russian Museum in Berlin-Karlshorst. Research priorities: history of Jews in Eastern Europe, history of the Soviet Union, digital humanities.

Index of places

Index of persons